The Complete Guide to

Fishing

The Complete Guide to

Fishing

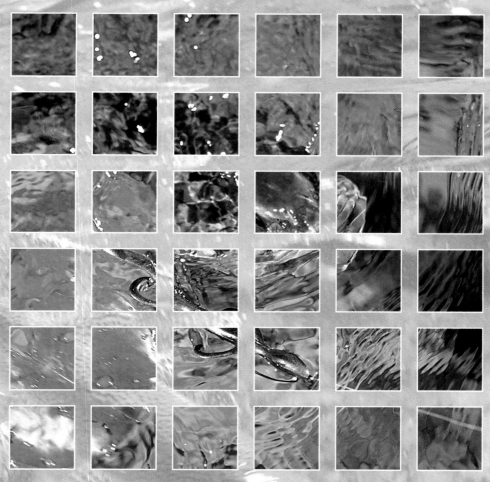

• The History of Fishing • The Fish and its Habitat
• Spinning and Baitcasting • Angling • Flyfishing
• Trolling • Ice Fishing • Building your own Rod
• The Fisherman's Cook Book

CHARTWELL BOOKS, INC.

Authors

Jens Ploug Hansen, Per Ola Johannesson,
Lefty Kreh, Christian Lundberg, Arthur Oglesby,
Jan Olsson, Steen Ulnitz, Anders Walberg,
Bo Wessman, Bengt Öste

Photography

Johnny Albertsson, Niclas Andersson
(www.flyfishphoto.com), Erwin Bauer,
Håkan Berg, Bill Browning,
Richard F. Calogiovanni, Göran Cederberg,
Mikael Engström, Martin Falklind,
Mikael Frödin, M.L. Giovannetti, Peter Grahn,
Herman J. Gruhl, Jens Ploug Hansen,
Tom Huggler, Heinz Jagusch,
Per Ola Johannesson, Christer Johansson,
Jan Johansson, Johnny Johansson, Peter Kirby,
Steen Larsen, Per Lindberg, Munir Lotia,
Christian Lundberg, Christer Mattson,
Dick Mermon, Leif Milling, Mike Modrzynski,
Karin Mönefors, Kristian Nilsson, Tony Osvald,
Elsbeth Pfenninger (copyright: Dr Hans F.
Pfenninger), Erkki Salmela, Doug Stamm,
Dick Swan, Björn Thomsen, Steen Ulnitz,
Henry F. Zeman.

Illustrations

Gunnar Johnson, Tommy Gustavsson,
Lennart Molin , Ulf Söderqvist,
Peter Grahn, Munir Lotia.

THE COMPLETE GUIDE TO FISHING has been originated,
produced and designed by AB Nordbok, Gothenburg, Sweden.

Publisher
Gunnar Stenmar

Editorial chief
Anders Walberg

Design, setting & photowork:
Reproman AB, Gothenburg, Sweden

Illustrations:
Ulf Söderqvist, Thommy Gustavsson, Peter Grahn,
Lennart Molin.

Translator:
Jon van Leuven

Nordbok would like to express sincere thanks to all
persons and companies who have contributed in
different ways to the production of this book.

World copyright © 2002
Nordbok International,
P.O.Box 7095, SE-402 32 Gothenburg, Sweden.

Published in the USA 2002 by
CHARTWELL BOOKS, INC.
A Division of Book Sales, Inc.
114 Northfield Avenue, Edison, New Jersey 08837

ISBN 0-7858-1521-X

Printed and bound in Portugal 2002

Contents

Preface

Whatever their language and nationality, sportfishermen around the world are united by one thing – the passion for fishing with a rod, line and hook. Perhaps the sources of this enjoyment should be sought in our ancient, inherited instincts. When all is said and done, not many generations separate us from our primeval ancestors.

For even if our clothes and customs mean culture, we are still wild enough in genetic terms. As such "civilized savages", we experience deep satisfaction in feeling a fish gobble our deceptive baits, and the same excitement makes us fight the fish

with everything our age has to offer by way of rods, reels, line and bait.

These are the result of thousands of years of practical fishing, not to mention the latest in industrial high technology. A profound genuine sense of nature and its diversity is often essential for what we call fishing luck. This depends in fact, more on knowledge of the prey's life and environment than on the harvest of chance.

We must take advantage of every trick if fish are to be duped by our clever baits, well-laid hooks and imaginative fly-patterns. In other words, sportfishing takes place entirely on the fish's conditions – we always have to try and lure the fish somehow into biting. The greater our knowledge, the better we succeed. Yet much

of the challenge surely lies in this very uncertainty: can we imitate the fish's natural prey so well that it mistakes our lies for the truth? Here is a question at the heart of the joy of sportfishing.

The Complete Guide to Fishing provides an extensive compilation of detailed information about sportfshing. A clear knowledgeable introduction for beginners to all forms of fishing, it also serves as an entertaining and inspiring reference book for the experienced fisherman. A myriad of topics are covered, from the anatomy of the fish to flyfishing, angling and the history of sportfishing around the world.

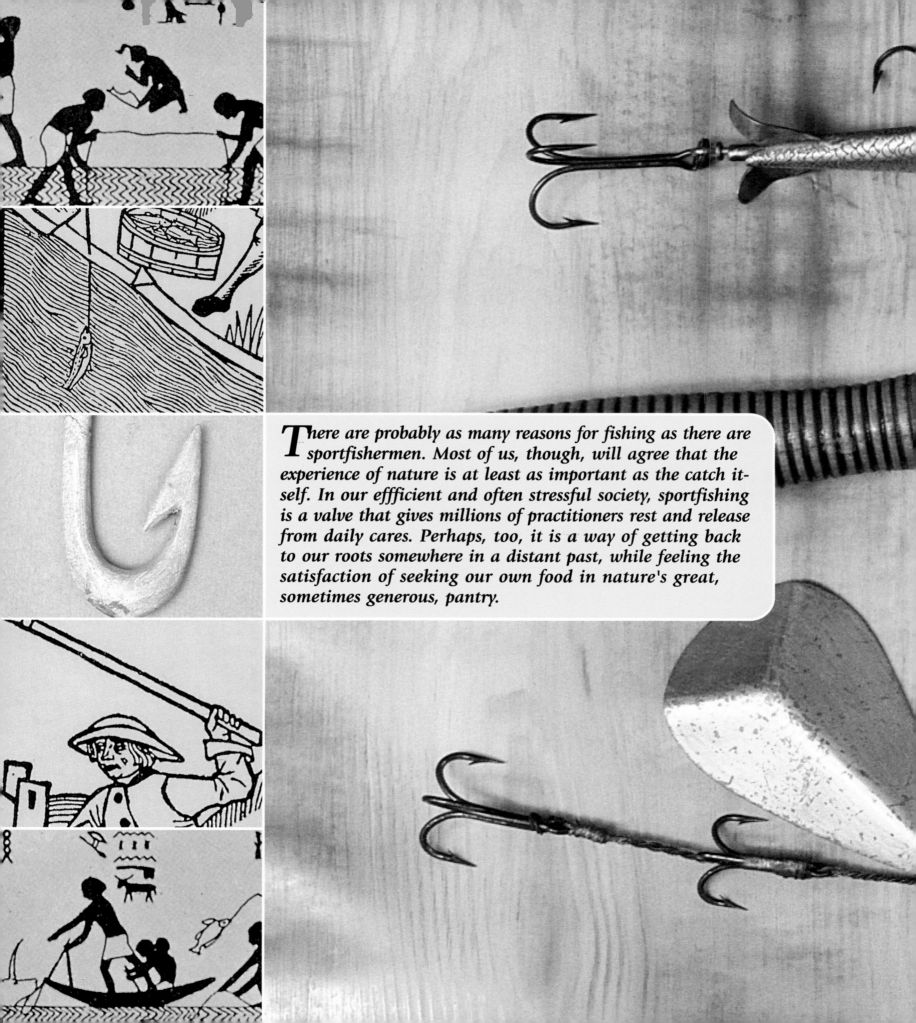

There are probably as many reasons for fishing as there are sportfishermen. Most of us, though, will agree that the experience of nature is at least as important as the catch itself. In our effficient and often stressful society, sportfishing is a valve that gives millions of practitioners rest and release from daily cares. Perhaps, too, it is a way of getting back to our roots somewhere in a distant past, while feeling the satisfaction of seeking our own food in nature's great, sometimes generous, pantry.

Through newspapers, radio, TV and other mass media, ideas spread faster today than ever before in history. Methods which have long been tested, and found effective under certain conditions, tend to be diffused at an ever quicker pace around the world. Experience from the United States is applied in Europe, and typical European methods such as angling have begun to catch on in the States during recent years. In southern and central Europe, ever more eyes are directed toward Scandinavia for new and more profitable methods of fly-fishing. And when it comes to trolling in lakes or the sea, America has shown the way for fishing in other parts of the world.

How sportfishing will look in the future is hard to predict exactly. But in order to understand the national variations in equipment and technique at present, it can be useful to take a deep dive into human history and see how fishing started long ago.

The first hooks

Man has taken his food from nature for hundreds of thousands of years—hunting, fishing, and gathering plants to supply his daily meals. The strongest and most inventive people lived longest, and this constant fight for survival inevitably also shaped their relationship to the surroundings. Creativity was not only a sign of ingenuity, but rather a necessity under difficult circumstances of existence.

We know very little about how the first human beings fished, but they must have soon discovered the enormous food resources in lakes, seas, and running waterways. These consisted of shellfish, mussels, and seals, as well as fish. No doubt people began to catch fish by using their bare hands, then gradually learned that sharp pins and other primitive fishing equipment were far more effective. Scientists are not at all sure which equipment was used before around 30 000 - 40 000 BC, but archaeological finds indicate that three main kinds were employed later.

Spears served primarily for fishing in shallow lakes and rivers, and in the sea to catch, for example, seals. Woven nets and various sorts of traps were placed in the richest fishing areas. The third type, which is also most interesting for sportfishermen, was the hook. Exactly when and where hooks were adopted is unknown, but it was probably in southern Europe about 30,000 BC. These barbed hooks were made chiefly of

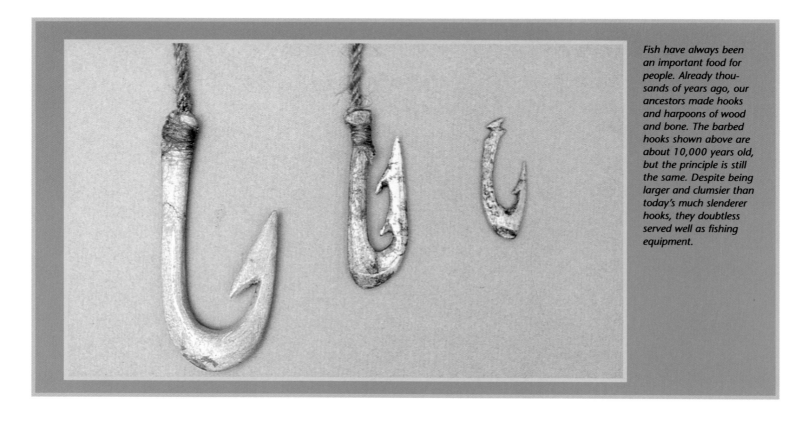

Fish have always been an important food for people. Already thousands of years ago, our ancestors made hooks and harpoons of wood and bone. The barbed hooks shown above are about 10,000 years old, but the principle is still the same. Despite being larger and clumsier than today's much slenderer hooks, they doubtless served well as fishing equipment.

bone, but presumably also of wood. The hooks were fastened on a line made of animal sinews or thin, tough plant materials such as roots, vines and certain grasses. They were baited with worms, mussels, small fish, or whatever else might attract the big ones to strike.

As the millennia passed, hunting peoples turned into more or less settled farmers. Thus, they became less dependent on wild animals, and domestic beasts provided new economic security. Yet peasants never managed to tame fish, and it was natural that fishing continued to be very important as a food supplement.

The development of angling

Archaeology proves that the art of angling was relatively refined as early as 7 000 years ago. Among the finds are floats which were cut from bark and used in fishing with hooks. Three thousand .years later on, Egyptian paintings showed how to fish with a rod, top-knotted line, and hook. This is the first evidence that people actually practiced a kind of fishing which, at least superficially, was quite similar to the angling of today.

From fishing with natural bait, it is not a big step to using artificial bait, and we can safely assume that long ago there were, for instance, model fish whittled out of wood. Another likelihood is that people soon realized how closely the natural prey of fish can be imitated by hairs and feathers.

"Already the old Greeks. . ." as the saying goes—and what would sportfishing be without them? It was Theocritus who, about 300 BC, wrote the first literary description of fishing with hook and rod. He spoke of using a "bait deceitfully dangling from the rod", and there is good reason to believe that fishing for enjoyment was first done in ancient Greece. Theocritus and his social class certainly had no need to fish for food.

By around 200 BC the Chinese had developed sportfishing so far that silk lines and metal hooks were being employed. At the same time, the Macedonians fished with artificial baits made of hair and feathers. Such down-hooks, more like jigs than flies, were doubtless just as effective as the ones we now use. How far advanced these people were, and not only in terms of culture or education, is clear from the fact that iron hooks began to be manufactured in Europe only three centuries later, in the middle of the Iron Age.

This Egyptian painting, some 4,000 years old, includes pictures of different kinds of fish. Among the subjects in the lower section is some sort of angling. No older representations of fishing with a rod, line and hook are yet known.

The Treatyse of Fysshynge wyth an Angle was written as early as 1425, but its publication delayed until 1496. This illustration shows the treatise's first page as it looked in the original edition.

The complete angler

Even if mankind ha derived great pleasure from fishing throughout its long history, regular sportfishing belongs to the past 450 years. This is the art of fishing with hook, line and rod for pure enjoyment and leisure. A milestone in its own evolution was *The Treatise of Fyshynge Wyth an Angle*, published in England in 1496. Probably written by a nun, Dame Juliana Berners, this work was part of the *Book of St. Albans*, which told the nobility and other "gentlemen" about hunting, fishing, and other elite pastimes of the age.

The "treatise" dealt, however, not only with techniques and methods, but also with the fisherman's relationship to nature. It had an enormous influence on the development of sportfishing for more than two centuries afterward, and became a source of inspiration for later writers of better known works on the subject. According to its viewpoint, the sportfisherman should also

be a nature-worshipper, philosopher and idealist. The sport was to be developed to perfection and a real fisherman ought to make his own rods, lines and artificial bait, as well as being able to collect and use different kinds of natural bait correctly. The harder a fish was to catch, the greater was the sport of fishing.

Just 150 years later, in 1653, appeared Izaak Walton's *The Compleat Angler*, subtitled "The Contemplative Man's Recreation", which is a classic known all over the world today. Together with Charles Cotton's chapter on fly-fishing from 1676, the book has been published in more than 300 editions until now.

Walton's work aroused interest with its presentation of methods for fishing with rod, line and hook. It also established sportfishing as a tradition for the first time. Fishing solely for enjoyment, and thereby valuing the experience of nature at least as highly as the fishing itself, became a popular idea along with the term "sportfisherman". Development of equipment and methods for sportfishing was one objective, but nearness to nature and "the great adventure" was another important ingredient in fishing. The farther away—and harder to fish—a body of water was, the more sporting the activity became. A true sportfisherman was, to a large extent, a "hardship romantic".

Equipment and its long evolution

Fishing gear and techniques developed rather slowly from the mid-seventeenth century until the early nineteenth century. The main reason was, of course, that sportfishing still had only a few practitioners and these stuck to old traditions. Top-knotted lines made of horsehair, long clumsy rods of jointed wood, and relatively simple tied flies were their customary armament.

Even if one could occasionally buy reels of multiplicator type during the early nineteenth century, fishing continued until the heyday of industrialism to resemble Izaak Walton´s approach in the 1600s – priority was given to the experience of nature. The only pioneering change in equipment concerned the hooks. Around 1650, their durability began to be improved by hardening. They were still fashioned by village smiths, but gradually the needlemakers took them over, turning the old handicraft into a large-scale industry. As a result, hooks also became lighter and suppler, although they remained pretty crude by today´s standards.

With the industrial revolution in the mid-nineteenth century, equipment saw an ever more rapid development. Technical innovations and mass production offered wholly new opportunities for sportfishing by people other than "nobles and gentlemen". The winds of change also brought new techniques and methods of fishing. It was now that people began to seriously question Izaak Walton's ideas of 200 years before.

Thus sportfishing, a pleasure of the privileged until around 1850, began to attract an ever wider public in both Europe and the United States who were interested in fishing with rod and hook. New types of fishing waters were "discovered" and eyes were opened to nontraditional kinds of sportfishing, especially in the sea. The old lyrical ideals of nature were regarded by many as snobbish, and different groups of sportfishermen took shape.

The fly-fishermen, who had almost exclusively fished with dry flies and "classical" wet-fly patterns during the nineteenth century, were those who held most firmly to Waltonism. They considered a correctly prepared imitation of a natural insect to be, from the sporting standpoint, far superior to fishing with live or dead bait – an opinion which survived long into our own century.

Yet it was also the fly-fisherman who mainly advanced the development of new and more purposeful equipment, not least in regard to rods. These went through several stages of improvement in the early 1800s. For example, experiments were conducted with

The complete angler himself, Izaak Walton, is shown here with his fishing equipment. This drawing was on the title page of the jubileum edition exactly 200 years after his first edition of 1653

different kinds of wood, such as hazel, hickory, lancewood and greenheart, in order to find the perfect rod material. The first split-cane rod was created by an American violinmaker in 1846. This gave bamboo a breakthrough as rod material, and revealed a method of construction that outdid all earlier ones. Split-cane rods were not only comparatively light and easy to handle, but also gave a longer cast. Despite their many advantages, the method took another quarter-century to become effective enough for profitable mass production.

Developments proceeded in other areas as well. Multiplicator reels had to wait for some time into the nineteenth century before they began to be used by a larger group of sportfishermen, and then primarily in America where they proved popular in seafishing, for striped bass among others. These early bait-casting reels were both clumsy and sluggish, giving a relatively short cast. Nor were they helped by being used together with thick, unpliant lines of cotton and linen. Some attention was therefore paid to developing new and better lines. The success in manufacturing oil-impregnated silk lines in the 1870s was regarded as a big step forward, since the casting length could thus be tripled.

Towards modern fishing

Although adequate techniques of making rods and lines were invented during the nineteenth century, reels (and principally bait-casting reels) were still a serious problem. Heavy casting-weights were needed to reach out to the fishing grounds. So it was good news when the first spinning-reels came onto the market in the early 1900s. The prototype of today's spinning-reel was created at Bradford, England, in 1905. Things went fast after that, in view of its obvious advantages. Most important was the longer cast, but it also made the troublesome back-lash—common with the multiplicator type—easier to avoid.

Coming to the years before World War II, we find two innovations that have been perhaps the most decisive promoters of sportfishing around the world during the past three decades: synthetic lines and the glass-fibre rod. These thin, flexible lines offered even the novice a chance of learning rather quickly how to cast, with no real problems. The glass-fibre rod's durability and low cost meant that one did not have to suffer a hole in the pocket to try fishing.

Popularity has stayved with the glass-fibre rod, no doubt mainly because it is easy to mass-produce and therefore cheap, but also due to its continual improvement. However, with the rapid development of artificial-fibre materials at present, we can expect that glass-fibre rods will be replaced by even better tvpes in the future. This was first indicated in the mid-1970s, when the first carbon-fibre rods appeared. These were lighter than glass-fibre, and indeed reminiscent of the split-cane rod's superb casting properties, but their initial prices were terrifying. It took a while before they could compete, yet they then caught on strongly, first among fly-fishermen and next with spin- and spool-fishermen.

New materials will always influence the rod market. A declining group of sportfishermen still considers the split-cane rod to be unbeatable in casting ability and drilling feel. Others have high hopes that the new materials will yield revolutionary rods with amazingly light weight, fine balance and optimal casting power. The rods now being produced from carbon-fibre, boron, glass-fibre, and various mixtures of these, have at any rate brought us a good way along the path to perfection.

A further field of development is that of artificial baits. Perhaps the main link between the fish and fisherman, baits have also become more effective and suitable. Not the least successful have been rubber and plastic imitations, which now occupy a firm place in the equipment of most sportfish-ermen. Jigs are another much-adopted type and, in many cases, they have replaced both spoons and spinners. The general trend is an increasing preference for rubber, plastic, and feathers, since these have proved very catch-yielding.

Using hair and feathers to imitate the natural prey of fish is a tradition two thousand years old, so it is no accident that those materials have retained their popularity. But the fly-patterns have naturally diversified and evolved during this long span of time. The constant effort to improve catching ability has given flyfishermen a deep interest in entomology. Flies must be as similar as possible to the fish's natural prey, and "classical" patterns have consequently lost importance in favour of many new designs— not least the nymphs, streamers, and so-called lure animals.

We cannot speak of sportfishing's development without recognizing the crucial role of boats, which enable us to reach new fishing grounds and raise our effectiveness. During the past twenty years, boat-fishing has become ever more common on both lakes and seas. New methods of fishing have emerged, particularly in the surface and middle lavers, while new species have a caught the sportfisherman's interest. Many boats are also specially equipped for trolling and big-game fishing; even special types of boats are manufactured for sportfishing. Moreover, the echosounder, once used almost exclusively by professional fishermen, has come to be an important tool of the sport for locating fish.

Environmental conservation

The industrial revolution, which made it possible to manufacture better and more effective fishing equipment at relatively low prices, has also led to destruction of the natural environment at a an ever-increasing rate. Pollution of water and air, in many places around the world, has killed off sensitive fish species such as the sea trout.

With the spread of "civilization", conflicts between nature and culture have become ever more tangible. Our enormous energy needs, for instance, are satisfied by the expansion of hydroelectric power plants. Cities grow continually with houses and roads built in areas which once held waters rich in fish. Agricultural overfertilization has given us dead bottoms in lakes and the sea. Water diversion, dredging, dams, and other direct interference with natural waterways have changed the living conditions for fish. Finally, changes in the chemical content and temperature of water have done much harm to

Salmon fishing has had an exclusive aura even in our century. Depicted here in the lovely landscape of Scotland is a fisherman landing a fine day´s catch, attended by his gillies.

sportfishing. To find fairly undisturbed water, the sportfisherman must go ever farther out into the "wilderness".

Fortunately, one can also hear rising voices against uncontrolled pollution in both Europe and the United States. In addition, many of the deteriorated fishing grounds are being "restored". This and the implantation of fish have created far better conditions for sportfishing. In some places, especially in America, an effort has been made to create completely new fishing areas in the sea with artificial reefs. Thanks to the erection of huge amounts of concrete, macadam and rubber tires in especially favourable spots, a bottom environment has resulted where fish thrive and a very high class of fishing can be enjoyed.

Why sportfishing?

The thought of competitive fishing would probably make Isaac Walton spin in his grave. This says quite a lot about the transformed relationship between fish and fisherman which has emerged during the past three centuries. Prize and specimen fish are now an important part of sportfishing all over the world, not least for anglers. Most fishing magazines publish lists of record fish caught, and results of different kinds of competitions. Even many manufacturers of equipment proudly display pictures of "dream fish" caught with their gear. The great upsurge of seafishing in our century also led to the foundation of a special organization in the United States in 1939, the International Game Fish Association (I.G.F.A), chiefly for collecting information about record fish caught at sea, as well as in fresh waters during recent years.

But sportfishing means not only catching fish—it involves a closeness t~ nature which few other sports can match. For some people, it is the joy of catching many and big fish; for others, it provides a good time together with friends. Certain practitioners appreciate the solitude of quiet waters far from the daily ratrace, while a lot of us want to taste the great adventure at sea far from land. The competitive element in hunting large or specimen fish can be attractive, or the calm and contemplation may be enough without caring about the catch.

Which type of fish is preferred, and what kind of water the line is to get wet in, are matters of individual choice. The important thing is not what distinguishes us, but a common interest that unites us. Whoever has become an avid sportfisherman possesses a hobby that lasts for life and can be varied almost indefinitely—whether by actively fishing, by sitting at the fireside with an exciting book about fishing, by making one's own equipment, or by dreaming oneself away to a favourite stretch of water during the dark winter evenings.

*F*ishing with success owes a great deal to knowledge about the fish, their surroundings and prey, not only about your own methods and equipment. How fish will react to baits, how their environment determines factors such as the choice of bait and fishing technique, and how their prey indicate the right bait as well as its presentation, are keys to winning on the water.

Many of us think that the sciences of fish and water are needless for making a good catch, but nothing can be more wrong. Such lessons give us a much better grasp of the fish's situation, and lay the basis for finer enjoyment, not to mention rewards, when fishing. They may even prove to be essential for having any chance to hook the fish under difficult conditions. So they deserve a place in our baggage as much as do our equipment, tackle and baits.

To keep things simple enough, however, the next pages will take up only what is relevant for sportfishing in general, and for spinning and baitcasting in particular. Around the world we encounter a huge number of fish species, each adapted to its surroundings – and the variations in types of fishing water are so wide that we have to concentrate on their fundamental patterns.

It is certainly true that one can spend a lifetime at the same fishing water without entirely figuring out what makes the fish take a special bait in given circumstances. But here lies much of the mystery and excitement in fishing. Being constantly sure about the fish's location and appetite would indeed lead to boredom, if not to overfishing. Nature's apparent capriciousness may, in fact, be the driving force behind our enthusiasm at the sport.

The fish

Virtually all fish are cold-blooded creatures with fins and a spine, living in water and breathing through gills. Few other similarities between them exist, though. Nearly 20,000 species of fish occur on Earth, and their adaptation to varying environments has resulted in amazing diversity. Body structure, colouring, surrounding water temperature and depth and salinity, possibilities of spawning – these and further factors combine in maximizing every species' ability to feed, protect, and multiply itself.

Their cold-bloodedness (poikilothermy) means that, unlike mammals, fish have a metabolism and other body functions adjusted to the water temperature. When it gets cold, they become sluggish and lower their food intake. The colder

Most of the fish species in lakes follow a seasonal migration pattern. In spring, the fish move from bottoms to warmer shallow water (above). When the surface water in summer becomes too warm, they descend 5-10 metres to the thermocline (middle). In autumn as the water cools, the fish can be found in both deep and shallow areas, but go ever deeper with the fall in temperature.

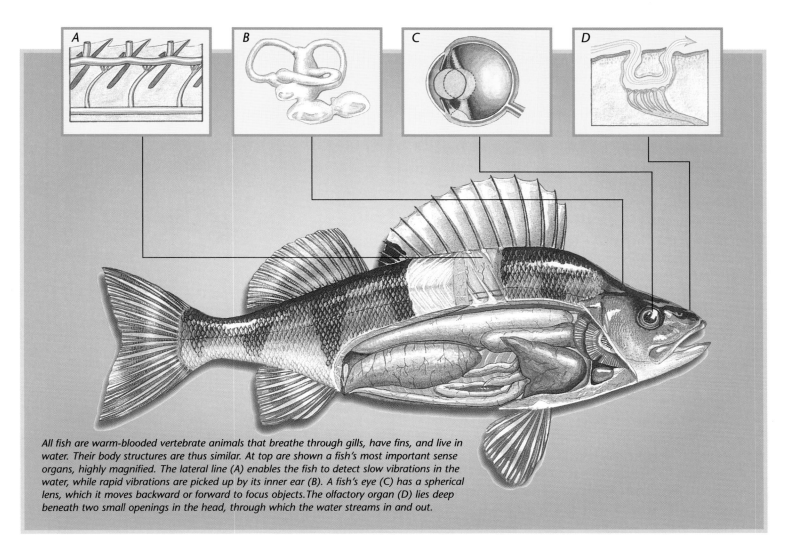

All fish are warm-blooded vertebrate animals that breathe through gills, have fins, and live in water. Their body structures are thus similar. At top are shown a fish's most important sense organs, highly magnified. The lateral line (A) enables the fish to detect slow vibrations in the water, while rapid vibrations are picked up by its inner ear (B). A fish's eye (C) has a spherical lens, which it moves backward or forward to focus objects. The olfactory organ (D) lies deep beneath two small openings in the head, through which the water streams in and out.

it is, the less they eat – even if food is abundant nearby. This is the main reason why, in ever colder waters, the fish are increasingly hard to tempt with bait.

Every fish has its optimum temperature: it is most active within a narrow range, such as 10-15° C (50-59° F). With extreme activity, its metabolism and appetite are vigorous, also making it eager to take bait. If the water becomes colder, the opposite happens, depressing both the fish's activity and its urge to satisfy either hunger or fishermen. In a word, negative impact on the fishing arises when the water is colder or warmer than the optimum temperature.

The fish tries to find areas or layers or water where the temperature feels more comfortable. For example, in autumn or winter, the colder water forces it to seek the warmest places – usually near the bottom. During the spring, when the water

warms up fast in the surface and in shallow coves, the fish prefers to circulate there. But in summertime, the surface water is so warm that the fish descends to a suitably cool level. Consequently, our chances of catching it are improved by fishing in the areas or levels with temperatures as close as possible to the optimum temperature of that fish species.

A fish's senses

To orient itself in the surroundings, a fish uses its senses just as we do. It can see, hear, smell and taste – but it also has a lateral line, comparable to a hearing organ, extending from the head to the tail. This allows the fish to feel pressure waves in the water, and to determine their direction. It can thus locate objects in either light or darkness. Here is a valuable aid to its search for food during the night, at great depths, or in murky water.

Yet most of the fish species that interest us, when spinning and baitcasting, hunt primarily by sight. A fish's eyes are "designed" with the power of seeing in two directions at the same time. It can focus on an object with both eyes, too, when judging exact distances. This field of vision, or "window", lies straight in front of it and is rather narrow, however, being adapted only to relatively short distances.

The eyes of predatory fish are, as a rule, most suited to feeding in daylight. Still, there are exceptional species with a highly developed ability to see in the dark. Among the best examples is the pikeperch (zander and walleye) – a distinctive night and dusk hunter. Its habit is to sneak up on prey under cover of darkness and attack them quickly. This strategy, of course, requires it to see better in the dark than its prey do.

Considering a fish's limited talent for seeing far away, your bait must be moved – or otherwise made attractive – if the fish is to notice it at all. The bait should send out pressure waves that can be detected by the fish's lateral line, but strong reflections of light or trails of scent also draw attention. A typical instance of lures that generate pressure waves is the spinner, whose rotating spoon produces waves a fish can hear at long distances. Similarly, a plug may contain rattles whose sounds attract fish. This enables you to search a larger area, or entice a less gullible fish onto the hook. However, there is scarcely any artificial bait which can perfectly imitate its natural model. For the same reason, fish that are difficult to trick can seldom resist a correctly presented natural bait, whose smell and taste are genuine.

The fish's senses of smell and taste contribute much to its capacity for orientation and finding food. Some species, like eels, have superb smelling powers, and most fish can detect smells from far away. This has led to increasing experiments with combinations of artificial bait and fragrant substances – as well as to the fact that natural baits are often superior when the fish inhabit a relatively limited area.

Besides locating food, the fish's smell organ – which lies around its nose – helps it to recognize an approaching danger. For example, the smell of a seal can make fish dissolve their school instantly and flee in panic toward all directions. Even during long migrations, smell plays a great role. Thus salmon show phenomenal precision in finding their way back to the river where, much earlier, they were spawned and spent their first years.

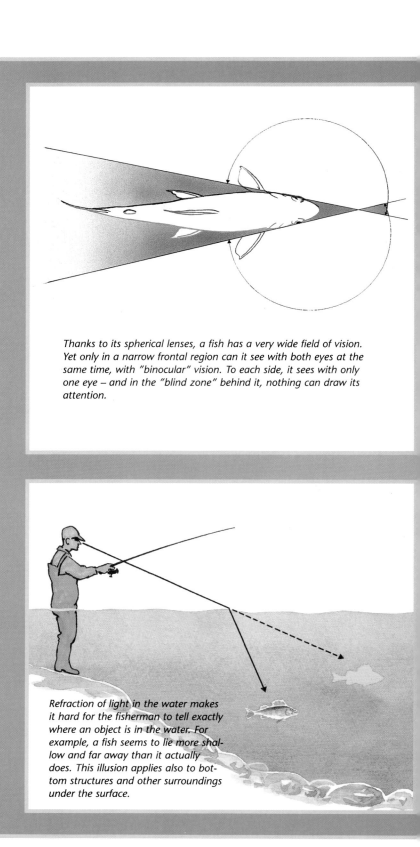

Thanks to its spherical lenses, a fish has a very wide field of vision. Yet only in a narrow frontal region can it see with both eyes at the same time, with "binocular" vision. To each side, it sees with only one eye – and in the "blind zone" behind it, nothing can draw its attention.

Refraction of light in the water makes it hard for the fisherman to tell exactly where an object is in the water. For example, a fish seems to lie more shallow and far away than it actually does. This illusion applies also to bottom structures and other surroundings under the surface.

A fish can see out of the water through its "window", shaped like an upside-down cone with an angle of about 97.5°. This is formed by the directions in which refraction allows light to reach the fish from above the water surface. As a result, the closer a fish is to the surface, the smaller its field of vision upward.

Unlike humans, a fish can move its eyes independently of each other. As shown here, it is thus able to look down (or forward) with one eye and up (or backward) with the other. Still, it can focus on objects with both eyes only inside its binocular field – directly ahead, up or down.

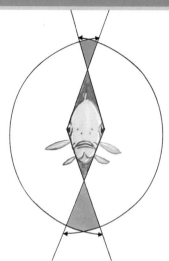

The eyes' way of working also gives the fish an extensive vertical range of vision. Despite seeing with only one eye to each side, it has binocular focusing power in the upward and downward directions as well as in front.

The fish's "window" angle expands above the water surface, so a fisherman has great difficulty in avoiding detection. Shaded parts of this illustration show how much the fish can see of the fisherman in clear, sunny weather. It is therefore important to keep a low profile when near the water. By sitting in a boat, or crouching on the shore, self-exposure is minimized.

Instinctive behaviour

But the biggest difference between us and fish is that they cannot think rationally. A fish does not choose when it bites, nor does it think before it takes or rejects a given bait. Whether fish think at all is doubtful, though we may like to say they do. Their actions are best termed instinctive: special stimuli, or signals, make them respond automatically in some way. A question that has continually intrigued sportfishermen throughout the world is why fish prefer one particular bait and seem completely uninterested in another. Equally baffling is why a fish repeatedly swims after a bait without taking it, and then may suddenly gobble it with violent force.

The short answer is that a certain stimulus, in a certain situation, can release a certain pattern of action. Usually the bait's colour and shape are what trigger the fish's response, but additional factors may influence the "decision" to bite. The more "key stimuli", or main bite-triggering features, are built into a bait, the greater are its chances of being taken. Also typical of an attractive bait is its exaggeration of some key stimuli. These may be its shape, colour, manner of moving, or generation of sound waves. Again, a good example is the spinner, with a rotating spoon that sends out strong pressure waves able to release the fish's strike-reflex.

Hunger and territory

The commonest cause of a bite, obviously, is that the fish feels hungry. A famished fish hunts food, and can therefore be tempted rather easily to take bait. The bait's characteristics somehow signal "food", and thus release the bite. It is a matter of stimuli that activate the fish's instinctive reflex when anything edible appears nearby.

As mentioned, there are situations when the fish shows a clear interest in the bait but still does not take it. Such passiveness is explained chiefly by a low level of activity, due for instance to the water temperature, the air pressure, or the fish

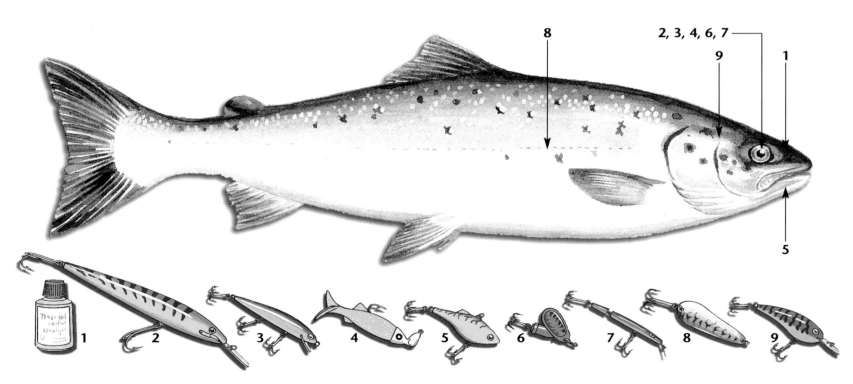

Different types of lure affect the fish in diverse ways – and the more of the fish's sense organs are stimulated, the greater the chances of catching it. Properties that mainly release the fish's instinctive striking reflex are (1) smell, (2-3) shape, (4) size, (5) consistency, (6) action, (7) colour, (8) vibrations and (9) sound. Most lures, of course, are made "irresistible" by exaggerating these typical stimuli.

Rainbow trout have many of the traits that characterize a good sportfish. They are usually eager to bite, and thus relatively easy to catch, besides being pugnacious – and excellent to eat. Here is a well-fed specimen entering the net to be landed.

having just eaten something else. In any case, a hungry fish eats best – and an actively hunting predator needs fewer stimuli to be tempted than does a recently fed, sluggish one.

Another reason why the fish bites may be territorial behaviour. This involves, not an active hunt for food, but aggressive acts to defend, for example, a spawning or holding place. Perhaps most typical are salmon, which stop eating before they migrate up a river, yet continue to take baits – preferably in strong colours – that cross their path. Food has nothing to do with their reflex, which is a lingering urge to bite and/or a defence against invaders of their territory. Frequently the fish become a little more aggressive when the bait's colour agrees with the species' spawning hues, such as red. A key stimulus is then the bait's red colour.

The water

Water environments are almost as diverse as fishing waters. But they share many characteristics too, and can be divided into categories that occur in every part of the world. The roughest distinction is between fresh, marine and brackish waters, followed by that between still and flowing waters. What makes such types of water different, and how does it influence the fish? This is extremely important for the choice of fishing method, technique and tactics.

All water on Earth comes from the sea. The sun's heat produces steam and clouds, which the winds blow over land. There the clouds drop water in the form of rain or snow, to collect in brooks that merge into streams and then rivers. These empty into the sea, where the same hydrological cycle begins anew. But the water carries other substances, in amounts that are not the same throughout the cycle. They give rise to several properties which determine the various living conditions of fish. Examples are the salt content, oxygen content, and acidity or pH value.

Salt, oxygen, and acidity

Almost any fish is able to change its environment from fresh to salty water and vice versa. This is because a saltwater species has a lower salt content than the surrounding water, while a fish in fresh water has a higher salt content than that water. In other words, the two kinds of fish differ less in salinity than the water types do. This necessary balance is regulated largely by the fish's urine quantity and gill functions. Although regu-

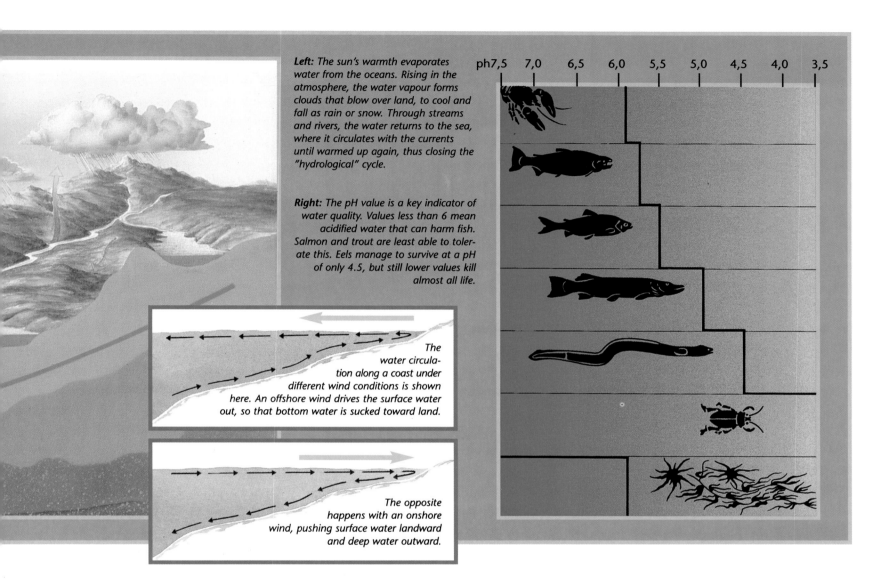

Left: The sun's warmth evaporates water from the oceans. Rising in the atmosphere, the water vapour forms clouds that blow over land, to cool and fall as rain or snow. Through streams and rivers, the water returns to the sea, where it circulates with the currents until warmed up again, thus closing the "hydrological" cycle.

Right: The pH value is a key indicator of water quality. Values less than 6 mean acidified water that can harm fish. Salmon and trout are least able to tolerate this. Eels manage to survive at a pH of only 4.5, but still lower values kill almost all life.

The water circulation along a coast under different wind conditions is shown here. An offshore wind drives the surface water out, so that bottom water is sucked toward land.

The opposite happens with an onshore wind, pushing surface water landward and deep water outward.

ph7,5   7,0   6,5   6,0   5,5   5,0   4,5   4,0   3,5

lation of salt is vital for fish – as for human beings – there are only a few species which can maintain the regulation in both fresh and salty waters. Familiar instances are salmon, sea trout and eels, but it can also be done to some extent by pike, pikeperch, perch and cod. Hence, these species occur rather commonly in brackish waters.

Living organisms need oxygen as well. The water receives oxygen mainly from the air – due to rain, currents, waves, and storms that stir up the surface. Likewise, the rapids and falls in a river add oxygen to it, a primary reason why the areas just below them are often good fishing places, since the fish there have a better supply of oxygen. Yet the leading source of oxygen in water is photosynthesis: submerged algae and green plants use energy from sunlight to generate oxygen.

Another crucial aspect of the water's quality is its pH value. Water with a value of 7 is called neutral. A lower pH value makes the water acidic, whereas a higher one makes it alkaline. Elements such as calcium are alkaline, so waterways through areas with plenty of these (for example in limestone) are naturally alkaline. But when the pH value is below 6, the water is said to be acidified – and at values below 4.5, nearly all life in the water is extinguished. Today, acidification of waters in the industrialized parts of the world is increasing constantly, because ever more nitrogen and sulphur are being released in the air to fall upon land and water with precipitation. To "restore" (neutralize) acidified waters inland, large quantities of calcium must be added continually.

To hunt effectively, the majority of fish species depend on light. Pike, for instance, live mainly in rather shallow waters at 1-12 metres. Hence they see poorly in darkness, and need good illumination to make use of abilities such as distinguishing colours.

The perch is a typical night hunter. It lives in deeper water that is comparatively dark, where an ability to notice different colours is not important. Not only good at seeing in very murky conditions, this fish has also evolved a special strategy for hunting food in darkness.

Light and sound

The conditions for light and sound in water are quite different from those in air. Sound actually travels much faster in water, at about 1,500 metres per second, compared to 330-340 in air. Thus, water is by no means a silent realm, something we sportfishermen are rarely aware of. The sharp acoustics in water are a good reason for us to be as quiet as possible when fishing. This applies especially to fishing from a boat, but even on land it is advisable to "sneak" toward the shore and avoid scaring the fish.

Fish do have ears – internal and filled with fluid, allowing them to register high-frequency vibrations in the environment. However, the principal organ enabling them to "listen" is the lateral line. This fluid-filled channel can detect low-frequency sound waves, and is so sensitive that the faintest pressure waves are felt. Since water is an excellent conductor of sound and the fish have such well-developed hearing organs, our fishing must be adapted accordingly. As noted above, the best rule for oneself is to move noiselessly at the water – although one may benefit by using "noisy" baits, which draw the fish's attention and hopefully trigger a strike-reflex.

As for illumination, we find the opposite relationship: light waves are absorbed far more quickly in water than in air. Even in very clear water, only about 1% of the sunlight is left at a depth of 150 metres. The conditions for light in murky water are still worse, and this may be important when fishing, as the fish's ability to notice the bait with its sight is seriously impaired.

The role of colour

In the spectrum of visible light, blue colours have the most energy, and red colours the least. The practical result is that blue – and next green – are the colours which penetrate deepest in water, while red is absorbed first. When spinning in deep water, the fisherman should thus select baits of blue and green, which are most visible, and avoid the red ones. But silver is the "colour" that best reflects light in deep water, so this is the obvious choice for fishing at depth and/or in murky water with poor visibility.

Some fish species can see colours better than others do. Among the leaders in this respect are pelagic fish – those which live in the middle layer or the surface water, and hunt chiefly in daylight. Species that live at the bottom in deep water, where the light is so weak that colours hardly exist, are endowed by nature with much worse colour vision, doubtless since it would be wasted on them. In recent years, lures with fluorescent colours have become increasingly common. These hues are strengthened if hit by the ultraviolet rays in sunlight, and can then be seen at long distances. As the UV rays are relatively intense in weak light, fluorescent baits work best under bad light conditions.

Currents and temperature

A continuous circulation process goes on in lakes, the sea and, not least, waterways. It greatly influences not only the supply of nutrients and oxygen, but also the variations in water temperature. Currents in turn are affected by the winds, changes in the air's pressure and temperature, and phases of the moon. Tidal currents are due mainly to the moon's and, in some degree, the sun's pull on sea water. These enormous swings of the world's water masses appear most clearly in the ebb and flow of tides, which can alter the water level by up to 15 metres at, for example, the coasts of northwestern France and of Newfoundland.

The interval between ebb and flow is about 12 hours and 25 minutes, or half a "lunar day". Since a solar day is only 24 hours, the time of every ebb or flow is therefore advanced by 50 minutes every day – a shift that will persist as long as the oceans do. Moreover, when the earth, moon and sun are in line with each other, at the new and full moons, a "spring tide" occurs. The difference in water level is then largest, as the ebb water is lowest and the flow highest.

Fish in coastal marine waters tend to move in search of food with the same rhythm as the tides, so the periods before and after an ebb or flow are comparatively good for fishing. Thus, many sportfishermen around the world rely on "bite tables" which are derived from the moon's movements and their tidal effects. Such tables, of course, are more relevant to fishing in the sea than in lakes and other inland waters.

Water circulation

Primarily in the world's temperate zones of climate, the temperature differences in lakes influence the water's density and weight. This creates a regular circulation, with horizontal layers of water, which are most distinct in deep lakes. During summer, the warm water is lighter than cold water, and forms

Color

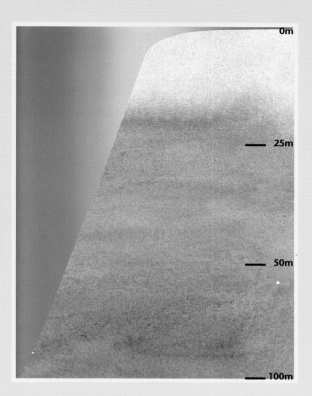

Light is absorbed much more strongly in water than in air. Its different wavelengths are absorbed at varying rates as it penetrates water. First the red component disappears, next the yellow, then the green and finally the blue. Thus, what illuminate deepest are the blue-green parts of the spectrum. But at depths of 100 metres, the light is too weak even for plant photosynthesis, giving life little chance.

0m
25m
50m
100m

Temperature

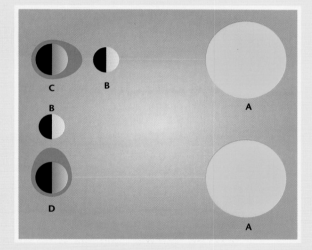

The fishing along coasts is often greatly influenced by tides, which sweep marine food – and therefore also preyfish – toward the land. Tides and their effects on the water level are caused by the pull of the sun and moon on the seas. Spring tides (C), the strongest kind, occur at the time of a new or full moon, when the sun and moon are in a straight line with the earth. Neap tides (D) are much weaker and occur at the half-moon, when the three bodies form a right angle.

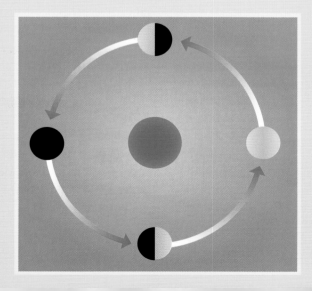

For coastal fishermen, it is essential in many parts of the world to know when the tides will occur. Strike tables are calculated on the basis of the tidal cycle and the moon's position relative to the sun and earth. Here the moon's phases are shown throughout a month. A neap tide occurs at each half-moon; the spring tide is highest and lowest at the new and full moons respectively. But a "moon day" is 24 hours and 50 minutes long, so the tides shift in time by 50 minutes every day.

There is much truth in the saying that 90% of the fish are in 10% of the lake. Since fish migrate regularly according to factors such as the wind, temperature and food supply, they are sometimes very hard to find – a particular surprise to the beginner. But some places are fairly sure bets for fishing: inflows and outflows, underwater banks, deep edges, coves, headlands, isles, straits, and overgrown shores.

During winter, the water masses are relatively stable. As water is heaviest at +4°C, this is the bottom temperature. When the spring sun warms up the surface, the masses begin to move and mix...

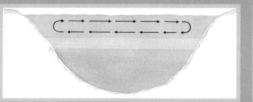

until the temperature in the surface is so high that the water separates into layers. These often result in a thermocline, between warm, oxygen-rich surface water and cold bottom water. Across it, the temperature may fall by up to a degree per metre...

but when the water cools in autumn, and all the water approaches the same temperature, the layers mix again. This restratification goes on until the heaviest water is once more at the bottom.

the surface layer. But since water is most dense at 4° C (39° F), the opposite relationship can occur in winter, with the warmest water at the bottom. Consequently, during spring and autumn when the water warms up or cools down, these layers exchange places, the temperature at one time being equal throughout the water mass. It is mainly in summer that the movements of layers produce great contrasts in temperature.

Between the surface layer (epilimnion) and the bottom layer (hypolimnion) lies the thermocline (metalimnion). This zone may be only a few metres deep, yet within it the temperature difference is largest, varying by as much as 10°C (18° F) from its upper to its lower boundary. Often we find species such as pikeperch, pike, bass and perch in the surface layer, and others like trout and salmon in or just above the thermocline, because the former have a higher optimum temperature than the latter.

In lakes, too, the wind may influence the water temperature and the currents. A gale can drive water toward one part of the lake, so that powerful undercurrents return this water when the wind dies or changes direction. Both the gale and the following circulation increase the supply of oxygen in the water, which can stimulate the willingness of fish to take bait.

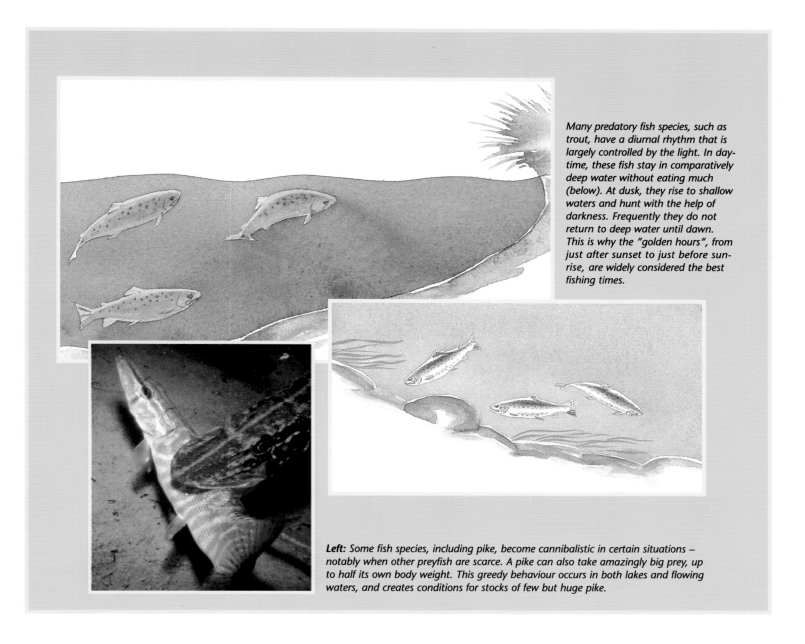

Many predatory fish species, such as trout, have a diurnal rhythm that is largely controlled by the light. In daytime, these fish stay in comparatively deep water without eating much (below). At dusk, they rise to shallow waters and hunt with the help of darkness. Frequently they do not return to deep water until dawn. This is why the "golden hours", from just after sunset to just before sunrise, are widely considered the best fishing times.

Left: *Some fish species, including pike, become cannibalistic in certain situations – notably when other preyfish are scarce. A pike can also take amazingly big prey, up to half its own body weight. This greedy behaviour occurs in both lakes and flowing waters, and creates conditions for stocks of few but huge pike.*

Hunters and their prey

Where the predatory fish are located in different seasons and types of water is determined by several factors. In addition to the water temperature, currents, depth, salinity and bottom structure, we have to know where the fish can most easily feed.

The shore zone of a lake is normally richest in species of fish. Hence, the competition for food is also greatest there. Species that are highest in the "food chain", namely predators, often need – at least temporarily – to enter the shallow waters in search of food. A predator that commonly occurs very near shores is the trout. So, at times, do other species such as pike, bass and perch.

While pike enjoy somewhat cooler water, and approach the land chiefly during spring and autumn, bass and perch love warm water and are frequently quite active in shallow coves when these have warmed up well. Perch always strive toward the warmest water and are thus found both at the surface layer during summer, and in the least cold bottom layer during winter.

Flowing waters are an environment to which some species are better suited than others. The streamlined body shapes of,

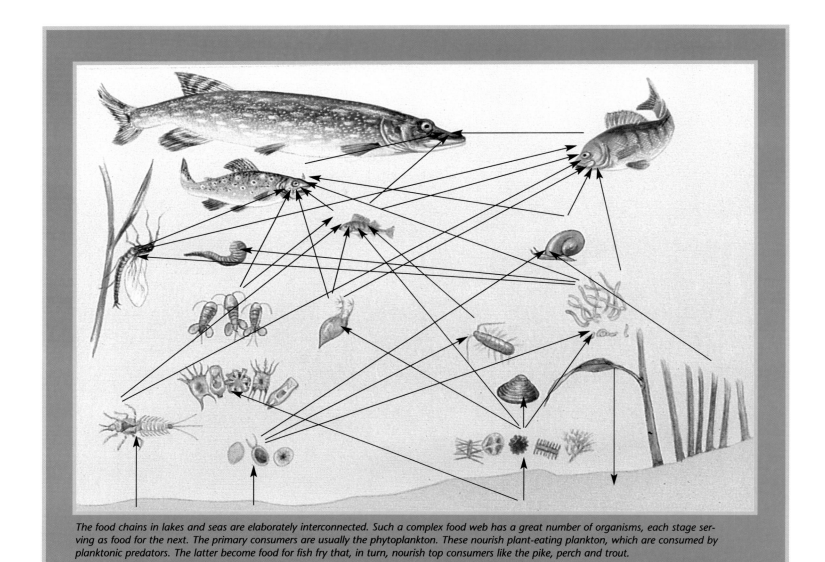

The food chains in lakes and seas are elaborately interconnected. Such a complex food web has a great number of organisms, each stage serving as food for the next. The primary consumers are usually the phytoplankton. These nourish plant-eating plankton, which are consumed by planktonic predators. The latter become food for fish fry that, in turn, nourish top consumers like the pike, perch and trout.

for instance, trout and grayling enable them to live even in strong currents. Bottom-dwelling species, such as catfish, can also endure fast currents in spite of their less smooth forms, because they are very good at taking shelter behind stones and in holes on the bottom. However, pike are among the species that do not thrive in strong currents, and therefore inhabit deep holes or backwaters, as well as the calmly flowing parts of streams.

In the sea, for obvious reasons, spinning and baitcasting is usually confined to the shallows and to areas near land. Here the supply of food, and the locations of predatory fish, depend mainly on the bottom's depth and character, and on

the water's salinity, currents and tides. Spool-shaped species such as mackerel and pollack live in the middle layer, but can easily rush from one level to another during their tireless quest for prey. Distinctive bottom-dwellers like flatfish stay as far down as possible – and between these extremes are many more species with their own ways of adapting to local marine conditions.

Fish and nutrients

Food chains of diverse kinds exist in all water environments. These sequences of hunter, prey, prey's prey, and so on, differ primarily between fresh and salty waters, but also within each

Above: As a rule, large predatory fish try to maximize their food intake with a minimum of effort. This means gaining as much as energy as possible while losing as little as possible. One result of the energy-saving principle is that a fish prefers a single big mouthful over several small ones.

Right: A largemouth bass heads for the surface to take a well-presented lure. In an instant, it's on the hook...

of the two realms. Rather than surveying how such chains are built up, we need only note that the fish of interest in spinning and baitcasting – predatory species – are almost always at the top of their chains. Perhaps the best example is the pike, a so-called top predator which heads the chain everywhere it lives.

Predators eat other fish, or insects, that are lower down in the chain. Where, when, and how they do so is important for us to know, since we try to catch predators by presenting natural or artificial bait as though it were edible. In general, a predator hunts more or less actively by pursuing schools of small fish, such as vendace, smelt and herring. If you come upon a school, its predators are likely to be close behind.

Small fish also have their optimum temperatures, seasonal migrations, and places that provide food or shelter – and their predators must follow in order to eat them. With this in mind, one can usually find relatively good fishing spots. Preyfish often linger in shallows, on underwater ridges, and at deep edges. Equally rewarding may be deep holes, fast-flowing parts of the water, and areas with submerged springs. Worth searching, too, are inflows and outflows, whose oxygen supplies and temperature variations are appreciated by numerous species of fish.

Migrations and meals

Apart from certain fish that migrate far in the sea, predators in lakes and other still waters frequently undertake regular journeys to follow their prey. These travels may depend on the time of day or the season, and are most influenced by the food supply, water temperature, and spawning period.

Such migrations also occur in streams, rivers and other waterways, but to a lesser extent. The predators in flowing waters have a much stronger habit of waiting for the food to arrive, rather than actively seeking it. Lying in a current lee to "ambush" passing prey is characteristic of species ranging from trout to pike.

In conclusion, old hands at spinning and baitcasting commonly catch fish where a newcomer fails, and not just due to luck or chance. The basic reason is knowledge and experience, gathered during a long time of practical fishing. Despite adverse odds, a clever fisherman can get a big one on the hook precisely through awareness of where the fish is holding, when it is hungry, and how – with which methods and baits – it can best be tricked into taking. There are no shortcuts into the record book: you have to keep fishing and go on learning from whatever you catch, as well as from whatever gets away.

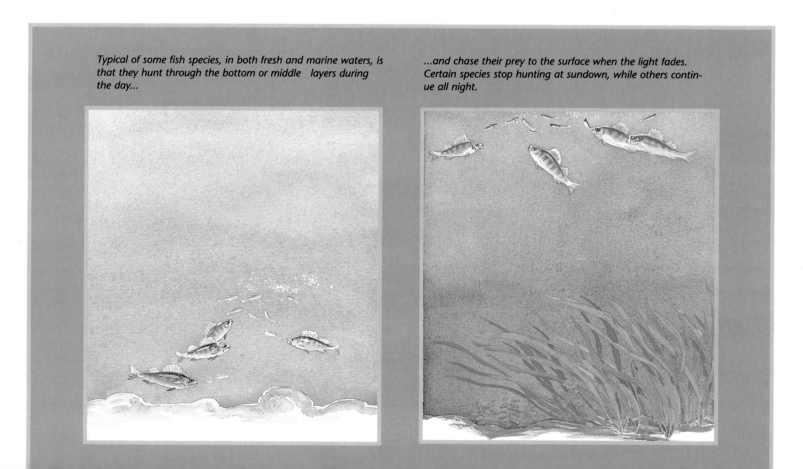

Typical of some fish species, in both fresh and marine waters, is that they hunt through the bottom or middle layers during the day...

...and chase their prey to the surface when the light fades. Certain species stop hunting at sundown, while others continue all night.

In temperate regions, flowing waters characteristically originate in high mountains, where their sources are cold and well-oxygenated. The strong, fast current is ideal for fish such as trout.

The upper parts of a river's middle section are comparatively deep, with a slower current. The water's oxygen content is still quite high, and there is a greater diversity of species.

Farther downstream, the current is still slower and the river becomes shallower and wider. Typical here are eel, perch, and possibly anadromous (seagoing) species.

In the lowest section, the water tends to be sluggish and murky. The bottom is often muddy, with abundant reeds and other rooted plants. Prominent species are pike and various whitefish.

*E*very day millions of sportfishermen all over the world devote themselves to spinning and baitcasting. This enormous popularity owes, of course, to the extraordinary diversity of this way of fishing and its ability to challenge the majority of well-known fish species.

Spinning & Baitcasting

Equipment

No equipment is so all-round that it suffices for everything from trout and salmon to pike and bass – or for fishing in both big and small waters. One can, though, require that the gear be adapted to as many forms of spinning and baitcasting as possible. If different kinds of fishing are envisaged, several setups are therefore necessary: for example, a light one-handed rod for small waters, a light two-handed rod for larger fish and waters, and a stronger two-handed rod for heavy spinning.

Lacking the right rod and a suitable reel with correct line strength, casts that are far and exact enough cannot be made. In addition, the rod and reel must be able to guide the bait's movements while retrieving it, and to register the faintest take.

Hardly a year goes by without the tackle manufacturers announcing new refinements and clever details on rods and reels that are to render them indispensable. The really essential point is thus to evaluate one's needs, not just rely on printed advice. Indeed, those with most experience in spinning and baitcasting have learned to limit their equipment.

Rods

The development of rods has gone forward much faster than that of reels. Fibreglass rods predominated during the 1960s, and carbon-fibre rods arrived in the early 1970s. The latter were at first considered too expensive for widespread acceptance, but some years later came cheap composite rods – with a blend of fibreglass and graphite, which is now most common.

Graphite and composite rods have many advantages over the earlier fibreglass rods. They are lighter, relax faster after the cast, are more obedient when retrieving, and can better register cautious takes as well as the movements of artificial lures.

Action and length

A rod's action, or how it responds when casting and playing out a fish, is determined partly by the thickness of the rod and partly by how the material is used.

Slow action describes a rod that bends along its entire length. It casts accurately, has the backbone to wear out a fish and the resilience to withstand dives. Unfortunately, they are often not strong enough to set the hook well and they require an experienced angler.

A medium-action rod has more power for setting the hook as well as the backbone and stiffness necessary for high casting precision. Only the tip half of the rod bends when playing the fish.

Fast-action rods bend in the upper third section. They have good casting qualities, set the hook fast and hard and have backbone, but do not cast accurately. Because the action is in the tip one-third of the rod, these rods are less sensitive during retrieval.

Extra fast action means that only the top one-quarter of the rod bends. This type of rod has fantastic casting abilities and is often used for competition casting and surf casting, but this means that little action is transferred down the rod to the hand grip. For surf casting using natural bait, a slow-action rod is often used instead.

It should be remembered that the rod action does not indicate what casting weight the rod is suited for.

The rod's strength and its ability to cast various weights are determined by the tapering of the tip and the diameter of the rod as well as the mixture and use of the component materials. Throughout the years manufacturers have used several simple but effective systems to choose the right rod. Some designate the casting weight, such as 14-28 grams (1/2-1 oz) which means that the rod is strong enough to cast lures of that weight. As a rule, lures weighing 8-10 grams (1/4-3/8 oz) and as much as 35 grams .(11/4 oz) can be cast on such a rod. But the casting weight limits cannot be stretched too far. Other manufacturers use a number system, often dividing rods into fourweight classes. For example, class 1 would include ultra-light rods with casting weights of 2-10 grams (1/16-3/8 oz). Class 2 weights are 10-20 grams (3/8-3/4 oz), class 3 are 20-30 grams (3/4-11/8 oz), and class 4 includes casting weights of 40-100 grams (1 1/2-3 1/2 oz). The classes give no information about the length of a rod.

Some fishing situations call for particular rod lengths and for that reason it is a good idea to follow a few general rules when choosing a rod. Boat fishing often needs a shorter rod

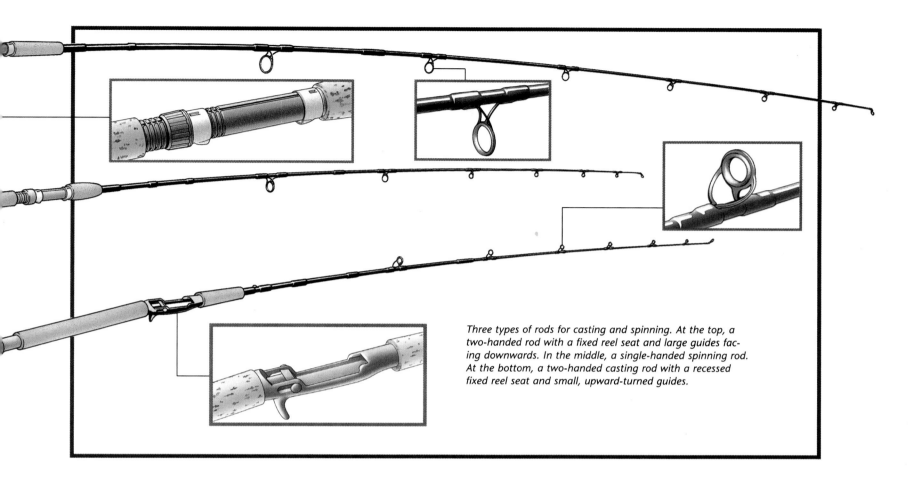

Three types of rods for casting and spinning. At the top, a two-handed rod with a fixed reel seat and large guides facing downwards. In the middle, a single-handed spinning rod. At the bottom, a two-handed casting rod with a recessed fixed reel seat and small, upward-turned guides.

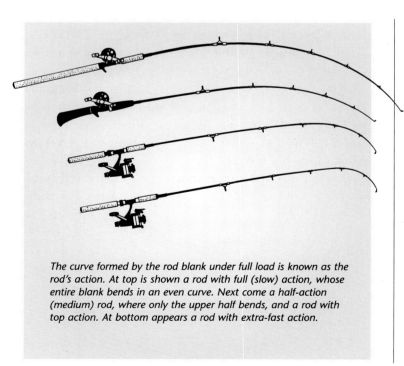

The curve formed by the rod blank under full load is known as the rod's action. At top is shown a rod with full (slow) action, whose entire blank bends in an even curve. Next come a half-action (medium) rod, where only the upper half bends, and a rod with top action. At bottom appears a rod with extra-fast action.

for light lures and slightly longer rods for heavier lures. Fishing in a small river or stream is often best with a longer rod so the lure can be kept free of trees, bushes and grass along the shore, and to provide better control of the lure in the current.

Large open water areas require a longer cast and with it a longer rod. In general, a long rod casts better than a short one, even if both are designed for the same casting weight. Long rods are more sensitive to sudden movements of a fish when being landed, but when fishing under low hanging branches a long rod will only get in the way.

Casting weight

Most rods are built for a particular casting weight. To make the rod as useful and easily sold as possible, the casting weight is often stated with a wide margin. For instance, 10-40 grams are frequently recommended on a 9-foot rod. In truth, such a rod is commonly best suited to a casting weight of 15-25 grams. It can, of course, cast with weights of both 10 and 40 grams, but then does not yield a pleasing cast, and neither does it react naturally during the cast. In order to cast artificial lures of 10 or 35-40 grams, one should instead choose a rod with a casting weight of 5-20 or 30-80 grams.

Ferrules

Most rods consist of two parts, but there are some longer two-handed rods of 11 feet that have three parts. Each joint is called a ferrule, and may be designed in different ways. A topover ferrule is most common: the rod's upper half projects down over the lower half. A spigot ferrule is among the most secure: the rod blank, built in a single piece, is cut in the middle and a short, massive graphite tube is glued into the lower part. The upper part is slid down over this spigot. On many cheap rods, the top part is simply stuck into the bottom part.

Rod guides

Ceramic guides are now standard on nearly all rods. Some years ago, ceramic guides were high-quality products from makers like Fuji and Seymo – but today many rods have guides of much worse quality. Good ceramic guides cause minimal friction and last long, but "unknown" brands can be weak and break easily. Often the latter's insert falls out or cracks form in the guide.

Ceramic guides are one-legged on light rods and two-legged on strong rods. They are also frequently bigger on spinning rods than on rods intended for multiplier reels.

Rod handles and reel seats

The rod handle consists of cork or foam rubber (EVA = evaporin). Both types are excellent and give a good grip. Most older fishermen doubtless prefer cork as a natural material, which insulates at least as well as EVA. Since many rods are standardized products, one often finds that an 8-foot rod, for example, has been provided with the same length of handle

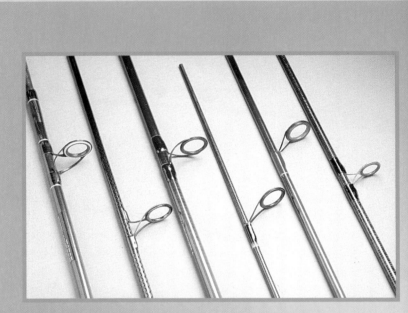

Most rods have ceramic guides. From the left are shown a standard Fuji guide, Fuji SIC guide, Seymo Supaglide, one- legged ceramic guide, one-legged guide of worse quality and (at far right) a gold-coloured rod guide of the brand Hardloy.

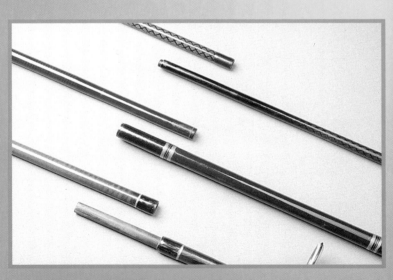

There are different ways of designing the joints between rod parts. Above is a top-over ferrule, the commonest joint type, with the top part slid down over the lower part. In the middle is a type of ferrule often seen on cheaper rods, with the top part slid into the lower part. Below these is a spigot ferrule, regarded as the strongest and most secure type of rod ferrule.

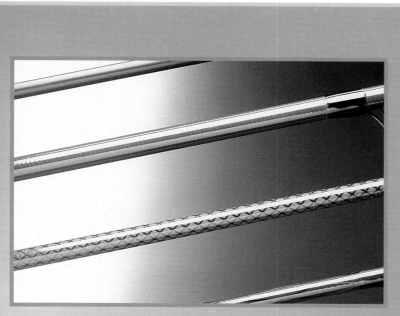

Today the majority of rods are made from graphite, but differ in the appearance and finish of their blanks. At top is a matt-polished blank of High Modulus graphite. Next come an unpolished blank and a Whisker High Modulus graphite blank. At bottom is a blank of kevlar-reinforced IM6 graphite.

Rod handles are now made almost exclusively of cork and foam (EVA-grip or a kind of foam rubber), and the reel seats primarily of composite and/or metal. In this photo are seven two-handed rods with different types of handles and reel seats. Except for multiplier rods with finger-hooks, most reel seats can be combined with both open-face spinning reels and multiplier reels.

as a 9-footer. On quality rods, however, the rod handle's bottom part is better proportioned.

The reel seat is made of metal and/or composite material, and has two locking rings. Nowadays most rods use a screw-down reel seat: the front part of the handle has a built-in threading, which locks the reel foot. It tends to be thicker than a standard handle.

On rods for multiplier reels, the seat is designed differently, even though such a reel can easily be used in ordinary seats on rods made for spinning reels. Many rods constructed for baitcasting reels have a depressed seat that allows an improved finger-grip, and commonly also a finger-hook or a pistol-grip.

Telescopic rods

For spinning and baitcasting, telescopic rods have never been a success, apart from their great popularity in some countries like Germany. One of their disadvantages is that this construction does not give a very pleasing action. Due to the separate parts of the rod, the guides are also often too far apart, causing a lot of friction on the line – especially when playing large fish. Moreover, these rods are comparatively heavy. A telescopic rod is ideal for journeys, but the guides should always be protected by a holster during transportation.

Reels

Spinning reels and baitcasting reels are superb within their respective fields of use. A spinning reel is easiest for a beginner to operate, and it is best suited to light casting weights of 2-10 grams. A baitcasting reel, however, casts farthest with weights from 10 grams upward. This reel's structure also better conveys the feel of a fight and the contact with a fish, as the line is in direct touch with the spool during the fight. Besides, a multi-reel has very good power transmission and, therefore, makes it easier to fight big fish with a small reel.

On the other hand, in a headwind where the lures are readily blown sideways, problems can arise with a baitcasting reel: the accelerating force does not stop when the lure has been cast, and a backlash may well result. But while retrieving, the contact with the lure is better with a baitcasting reel.

Spinning reels

Anyone can learn to cast with a modern spinning reel after just a few hours' training. Sizes range from the smallest UL types, through fairly large reels that suit almost all fish species, to big reels for salmon and sea fishing. Nearly all

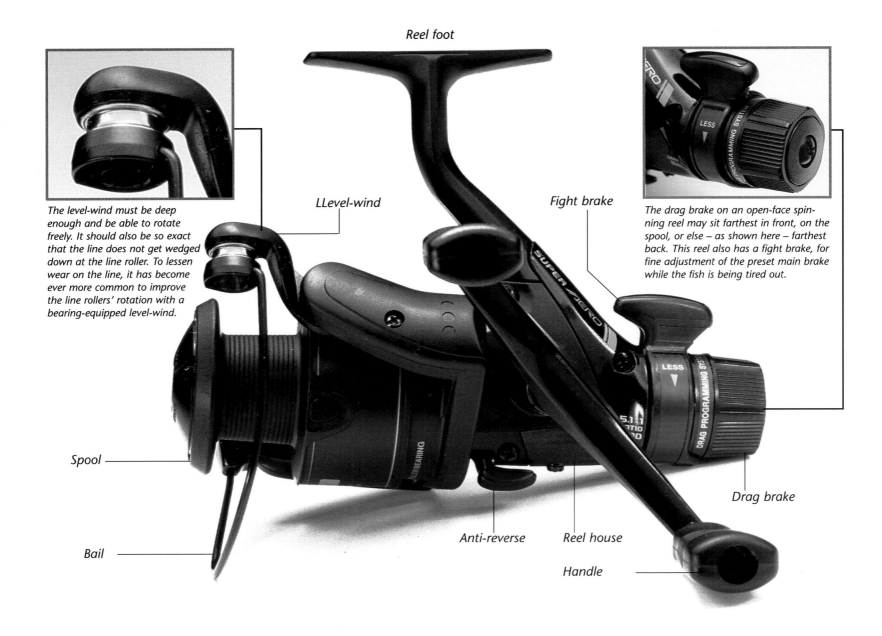

Reel foot

LLevel-wind

Fight brake

The level-wind must be deep enough and be able to rotate freely. It should also be so exact that the line does not get wedged down at the line roller. To lessen wear on the line, it has become ever more common to improve the line rollers' rotation with a bearing-equipped level-wind.

The drag brake on an open-face spinning reel may sit farthest in front, on the spool, or else – as shown here – farthest back. This reel also has a fight brake, for fine adjustment of the preset main brake while the fish is being tired out.

Spool

Drag brake

Anti-reverse

Reel house

Bail

Handle

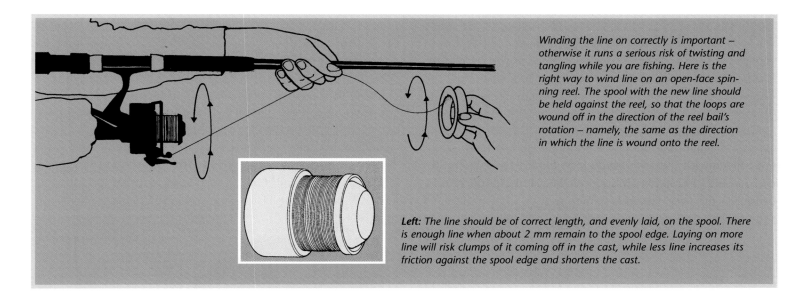

Winding the line on correctly is important – otherwise it runs a serious risk of twisting and tangling while you are fishing. Here is the right way to wind line on an open-face spinning reel. The spool with the new line should be held against the reel, so that the loops are wound off in the direction of the reel bail's rotation – namely, the same as the direction in which the line is wound onto the reel.

Left: *The line should be of correct length, and evenly laid, on the spool. There is enough line when about 2 mm remain to the spool edge. Laying on more line will risk clumps of it coming off in the cast, while less line increases its friction against the spool edge and shortens the cast.*

spinning reels are made according to the same principle, although the drag may be placed differently and the brake discs manufactured of different materials. The spool's form and the handle's way of folding may also vary.

The design of the reel handle makes it possible to retrieve the lure with either your left or right hand. The reel may also have a few, or many, ball bearings. The number of ball bearings is often a sellers' argument, but in fact there are many examples of reels with 3-4 bearings that last longer than others with 5-6 bearings.

The material of which the reel itself is made has varied in recent decades. Most reels were once made of aluminium, followed by graphite reels during the 1970s. These, however, were not very durable and the trend is now back toward aluminium reels, although graphite reels will continue in the low-price category.

Gearing

Today the majority of reels have a helical pinion, but some – mainly German ones – still have a worm pinion. This is a simple and practical design, which at first goes a little more sluggishly than a helical pinion but soon becomes "run in". To put it briefly, the worm pinion is a quite reliable gear that can last for years, and not a few have worked for 30 years.

The open-faced spinning reel is probably the world's most widespread type of reel. It is simple to handle – not least for beginners – and gives long, safe casts. Light lures from 2 to 10-15 grams also suit it very well. No matter whether the drag sits at its front or rear, this is an effective tool for tiring out even big fish.

Baitcasting reels

In contrast to spinning reels, the baitcasting reel has a rotating horizontal spool. The handle drives the spool by means of toothed wheels, whose gear ratio depends on the kind of fishing intended. Normally the ratio is around 5:1.

Granted that many of the modern small baitcasting reels are technical wonders, the basic principle of a baitcasting reel is elementary. But a certain amount of training is needed to cast with this reel. Despite its frequently well-planned brake system, beginners in particular are bound to suffer a backlash when the spool overwinds in the cast.

Prices are often much higher for baitcasting reels than for spinning reels. Like the latter, baitcasting reels of graphite were made during the 1980s, but time has shown that aluminium reel houses are best. In terms of design, there are two types of baitcasting reel: the classic cylindrical reel with round side-gables, and the more low-profiled variety. Both types have excellent mechanics and satisfy all the requirements of spinning and baitcasting.

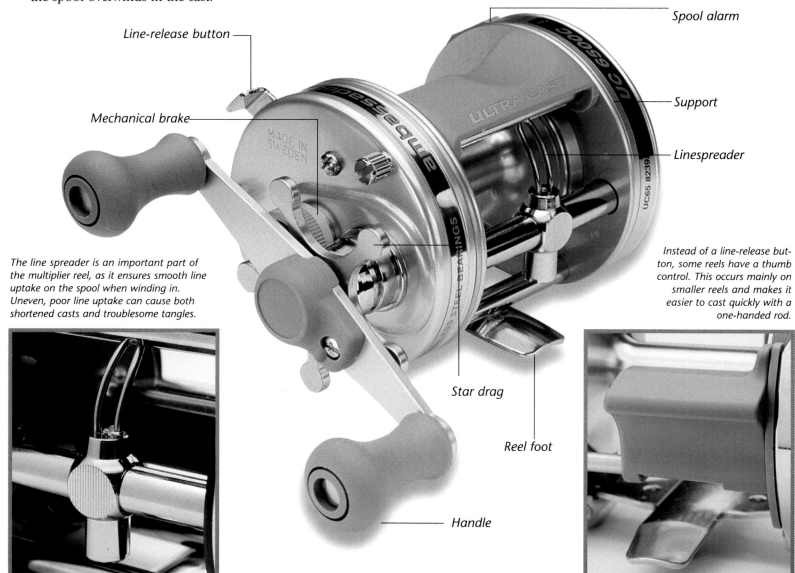

Line-release button

Spool alarm

Mechanical brake

Support

Linespreader

The line spreader is an important part of the multiplier reel, as it ensures smooth line uptake on the spool when winding in. Uneven, poor line uptake can cause both shortened casts and troublesome tangles.

Instead of a line-release button, some reels have a thumb control. This occurs mainly on smaller reels and makes it easier to cast quickly with a one-handed rod.

Star drag

Reel foot

Handle

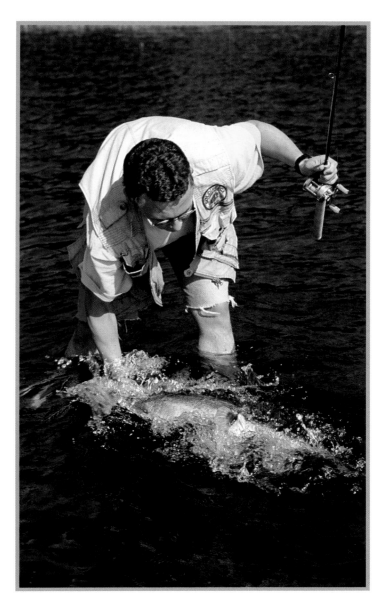

Most multiplier reels today have effective cast-braking systems, both centrifugal and mechanical, to lessen the risk of running the spool too fast when casting.

When laying line onto a multiplier reel, the line's spool should be held so as to rotate in the same direction as the reel's spool. Stick a pencil into the line spool's mid-hole for smooth turning, and keep the line stretched between your fingers while laying on. The reel is full when 1-2 mm are left to its spool's upper edge.

Care and maintenance

Reels can be damaged by salt water and dirty fresh water. Hence they should always be rinsed after a fishing trip, then dried and sprayed with silicon. Simultaneously the brakes should be loosened, as the discs may otherwise deform, making the reel's brake uneven and jerky. The handle knob and the bail springs should be given a couple of drops of oil, which will also benefit the line roller. With a baitcasting reel, you do yourself a service by putting a drop of oil on the screw. If the reel is used regularly, it should undergo a thorough service each year as well.

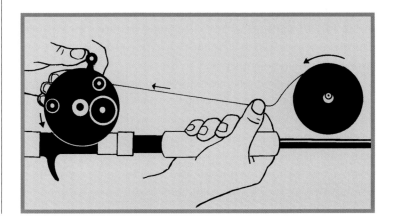

Lines

Nylon and monofilament lines are manufactured from a nylon raw material, consisting of tiny balls that are heated and pressed through holes of different sizes. The threads are then cooled over rollers that also stretch them, so that they become soft and elastic. Lines of good quality (and high price) are usually impregnated with waterproof substances, which settle between the nylon molecules and prevent the line from absorbing water – thus increasing the breaking strain. Lines can also be surface-treated with, for example, teflon. In sum, making a fishing line is not as simple as it may sound.

Knot strength and elasticity

Lines are often classified, meaning that you have a guarantee of the line breaking only at a certain load. But this raises the price, and such lines should not be bought unless you need to fish with them.

The best knots can provide a knot strength of 90-100 percent, while bad knots – or weaknesses in the knot itself – reach a knot strength of only 50-60 percent. Wear resistance also varies: some lines crack after a single snag on the bottom, or tear to pieces in the line guides after a few hours of fishing. Others, however, will last for many fishing days without a sign of weakness.

When you hook and fight a wild fish on a short line, elasticity is essential. But on a long line, lack of resilience is best. Some lines, in any case, stretch by at least 15-30 percent if they are wet. Generally, soft lines are more elastic than stiff ones.

It is always difficult to give good advice on which type of line to use, but the broad rule should be to choose soft lines for small reels. A stiff line does not lie so well on such a spool, and can easily lift off during the cast – perhaps resulting in a tangle. During cold and frost, it is best to fish with soft lines, since a stiff line then has a greater tendency to break.

Lines age at different rates. Sunlight, continual dampness, and chemicals can destroy a line. Neither should it come in contact with oil, mosquito spray, petrol and the like. Preferably store it in a dark place, and check it at regular intervals even while fishing. Especially the outermost metres of line are loaded hard during the cast, and by snags on the bottom, so they should be discarded before each new fishing trip.

Braided lines

The new braided multifilament lines are characterized by a very high breaking strain in relation to their diameter. They consist of many fibres, and were introduced by a German company that called its line Corastrong. The fibres, termed coramid, probably contain kevlar. Other, competing line manufacturers use fibres designated as spectra. Both of these line types, which are comparatively expensive, often come in blends with different fibre materials, to improve their knot strength and applicability.

These lines have rapidly won popularity, and will undoubtedly become even more widespread as their prices sink. Regarding cost, a common practice is to fill the reel partly with cheap nylon line, before winding on the expensive multifilament line.

The weak points of multifilament lines are the knots. One can recommend the Trilene knot, but a Uni-knot should be used for the nylon back-line. These lines also have certain weaknesses during frost, mainly due to ice formation.

Knots

No part of the spinning fisherman's "chain" of equipment is stronger than its weakest link – the knot. Incorrect or poorly tied knots can decrease the breaking strain by up to half. Still, there are dozens of knots that have survived for decades despite their weaknesses. The best approach is to learn three or four durable knots well, and thus be able to tie few but secure knots.

The spool, or arbor, knot comes in handy when the line is to be tied on the spool of a multireel or spinning reel. It is really just a simple three-turn clinch knot. The traditional clinch knot itself can be improved by giving the line an extra pass through the eye. This results in a so-called Trilene knot, with a breaking strain of 95-100 percent.

The right equipment

Water, species and fishing method, along with personal preference, determine an angler's fishing tackle.

Ultra-light fishing for small species calls for a short light rod, from 150-180 centimeters (4.5-6 feet) long, a small reel carrying a line capacity of 100-125 meters (108-135 yds), and a line diameter of 0.10-0.23 mm test strength. Choose a rod with a casting weight from 2 to 10 grams. This tackle is best

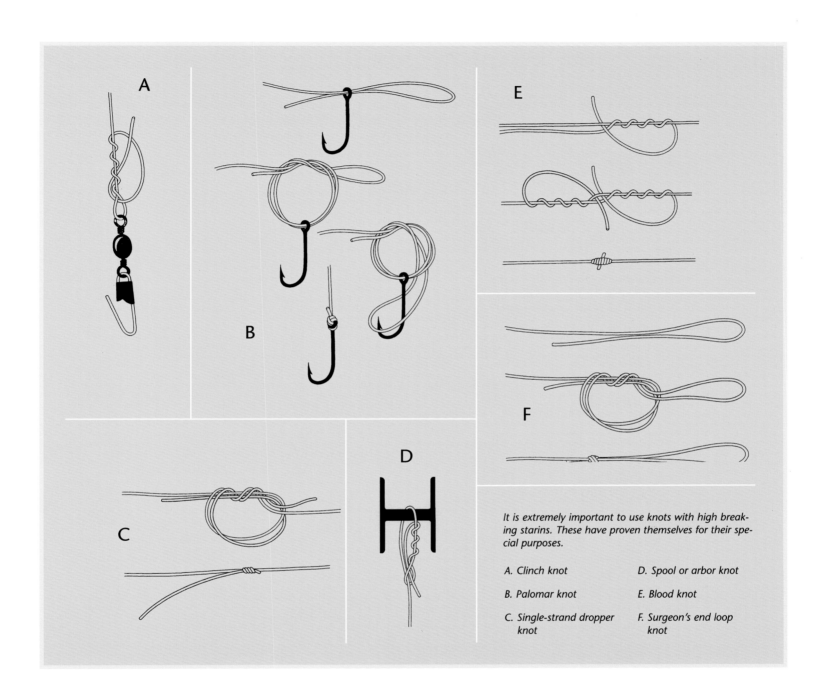

It is extremely important to use knots with high breaking starins. These have proven themselves for their special purposes.

A. Clinch knot

B. Palomar knot

C. Single-strand dropper knot

D. Spool or arbor knot

E. Blood knot

F. Surgeon's end loop knot

for fighting small trouts, bass and pikes. It is particularly suitable for boat fishing, for smaller ponds, rivers and streams.

Light spinning tackle is a supple rod about 6.5-7.5 feet long with a casting weight of 10-20 grams, a small reel and 0.23-0.30 mm diameter line. This is agood basic tackle combination that provides enormously satisfying fishing, but it is also

reliable when fishing for trout, bass, small pike or salmon. A lightweight rod with an extra long handle for two-handed casts gives extra strength and control.

A classic, all-round tackle consists of a rod of 7-9.5 feet with a casting weight of 12-28 grams (1/2-1 oz), a medium-sized reel and 150-180 meters of 0.25-0.35 mm diameter line.

Parts of the hook

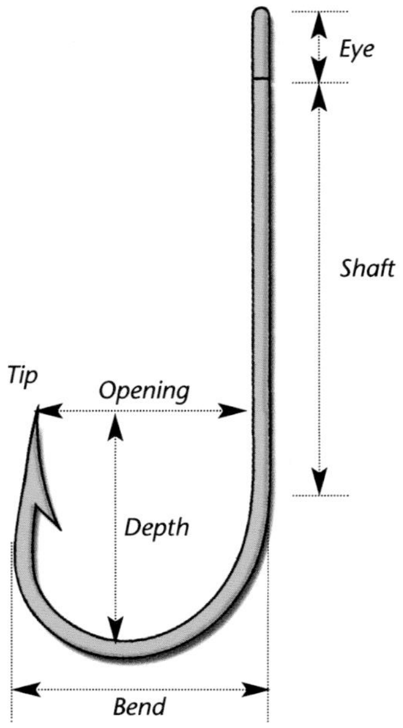

Eye

Shaft

Tip

Opening

Depth

Bend

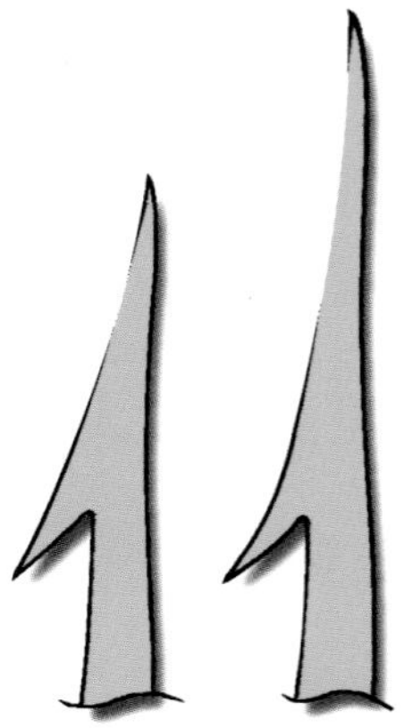

A rule of thumb is that a short hook tip penetrates more easily in hard-mouthed fish, while a long hook tip gives a better grip in soft-mouthed fish.

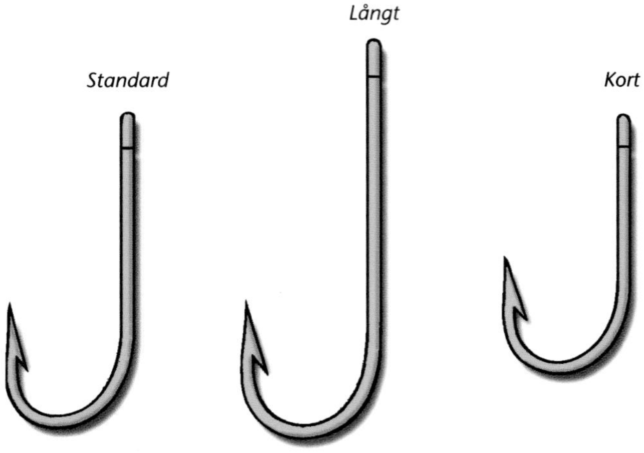

Standard

Långt

Kort

The same hook can have different shaft lengths. Those shown here have a normal – standard – shaft length (at left), a long shaft (middle) and a short shaft (right).

Hooks, swivels, rings and leaders

The hook is the light-tackle fisherman's most important detail, but it is often the piece of equipment given the least attention. What good are a rod, a reel, a line and lure that function as a perfect "casting machine" if the hook is weak, the point is not sharp enough, the connecting rings are weak—or if the fish can cut the line!

Hooks are available in more than 50,000 different shapes and sizes. They can be basically grouped as single, double or treble hooks. A single hook is commonly used with spoons, pirks and jigs, while double hooks are used sometimes with plugs. Treble hooks are the preferred hooks for artificial lures, even though they do not work as well as single hooks. When the force of a strike or of setting the hook is distributed over three points, none of them penetrate as well as when that same energy is concentrated in just one point. Experience has shown that treble hooks get more bites but lose more fish, while a single hook gets fewer bites but lands more fish.

Certain artificial lures are designed for fishing with either single or treble hooks, some even for double hooks. A jig is a traditional single hook lure, while plugs are traditionally treble hook lures.

The parts of a hook

The parts of a hook are the eye, the shank, the bend, the point, the gap and the barb. These parts can vary in shape and description, bearing names such as Hollow Point, Needle Eye, Kirbed Shank, and Reversed Point. In general, the names stick to the point—a round eye exactly that, a tapered eye has a tapered wire for an eye, and so on. Hooks with points curving inwards are usually [or natural bait and hooks with straight points are for spinning with artificials.

Hooks vary from size 28, only a few millimetres long, to size 18/0, which is a rugged shark hook. As the scale stretches from 28 down to 0, the hooks become large and larger, and as the scale progresses from 1/0 to 18/0 they continue to increase in size.

Hooks are made of wire of carbon, steel, or stainless steel. The wire is tempered in various ways so that some hooks are soft and some are hard. Some hooks are tin/nickel-plated for salt water, others are bronzed for use mainly in fresh water. Hooks can be coloured blue or red or gold. Blue or brown hooks provide camouflage; red hooks are used for red lures that look like boiled shrimp or the larvae of the mosquito *Ghironomidae*; gold hooks are used to make artificials extra attractive.

Most fresh factory hooks seem sharp and pointed at first glance, but the criterion for a sharp hook is if it can dig into a fingernail. If it cannot, it needs to be sharpened with either a whetstone or a file. Big hooks are sharpened with a file, smaller ones with a whetstone. After each strike or bottom snag the hook point should be checked and sharpened if necessary.

Split rings, swivels and snaps

Split rings, round or oval-shaped, are mounted either on the hook or the swivel. Oval connectors give the hook the most flexibility. This piece of equipment is usually the first bit of tackle to rust, so it is wise to keep a good supply in your tackle box.

A swivel is a thrust bearing used to connect the line and the lure. They were designed to eliminate the line twist that is commonly caused by rotating artificial lures. They come in many shapes and forms for different types of fishing. One special kind of swivel that is used with artificial lures has built-in ball-bearings to make it even more effective when trolling.

Snap swivels are used to make changing lures easier and faster. Once the snap is attached to the line, the lure can be changed by opening and closing the snap rather than tying a new knot. A snap, however, makes the lures more visible and even slightly heavier. The size of a snap should be kept to a minimum, especially when using small lures. A large snap can immobilize lightweight lures and perhaps make the fish skittish

and suspicious. Snaps come in many shapes and sizes. Some are almost selflocking and are reliable when put under pressure, but others are weak. No-knot fast snaps are the very smallest snaps, designed for the quick changing of fliers or suspended lures.

Leaders

Leaders are not only for fishing predators with mouths full of sharp teeth. They are also useful when the last few meters of line are constantly being worn and abraded, when being dragged over rocks, boulders, branches and roots, i.e. when trolling. Casting is also hard on a line. Using a leader with a smaller diameter than the line makes the lure move more naturally. When fishing with a fluorescent line an effective technique is to use ordinary line which has less visibility on the one or two meters of line that are closest to the lure.

A leader is made either of strong monofilament or of several strands of wire that are covered with nylon. Pike, muskellunge and other fish with sharp teeth can fight and bite hard enough to damage the line or even to break it off. By tying a strong piece of line (25-40 cm with a breaking strain of 20-30 kg) at the end of the line, the fish has something to sink its teeth into.

Wire leaders are probably the most durable, but they are much more visible than nylon leaders. Both leaders can easilybe made yourself. A nylon leader requires a snap, a swivel and a suitable piece of line. A wire leader is made from sleeves, a swivel and a snap. A simple method of forming a loop in the end of a coated wire is to twist the tag end around the standing part of the coated wire 5-6 times and then heat itwith a match. Pre-tied leaders are available at all bait-and-tackle shops.

Swivels and snaps. (Left, from top:) Standard snap, Rosco snap, Berkley CrossLok. (Right, from top:) Standard swivel, Sampo ball-bearing swivel, three-way swivel. (Bottom:) A bait lock of the Not-a-knot type.

Casting Techniques

The ways of casting in practice are about as numerous as the fishermen who perform them. All of us develop our own casting style according to body build and equipment. But the rod's action and length are primary determinants of the casting method. Even competition casters have a special style of casting.

A cast involves a rapid acceleration of the rod – no matter whether you use a rod with one or two handles, and cast underhand or sideways. The technique cannot be taught as a theory: it must be learned by training. A bad cast is usually due to an unrhythmical or jerky casting movement. Thus a comfortable posture before the cast is important, and other circumstances play a role too. The leading types of cast are the overhead (overhand) and the side-cast.

The overhead cast

This precise technique begins by sighting at the target with the rod, from whose tip the bait hangs down 20-50 centimetres. The rod is brought behind your back, normally over the right shoulder, although some prefer to raise it over the left shoulder. Then the rod is accelerated forward over the same shoulder, aiming toward the target. A rod with top action needs slightly greater "sting" in the cast than a rod with whole action, which is little more than pushed upward during the forward movement.

The line is released when the rod is most flexed and points somewhat over the target. If the rod is well enough tensed in the cast, and if you have aimed exactly and let the line go at the right moment, you will hit the target. But if you release the line too soon, the bait will fly up in a high arc and fall in front of you. If released too late, the bait will strike the water before you like a projectile.

The overhead cast is not very easy to learn for a beginner, who often lets the line go too early or late. Neither is this cast safe when fishing from a boat, where you have difficulty in controlling a bait that hangs behind you. Nor does an overhead cast reach as far as a side-cast, which flexes the rod more and makes it travel farther.

An overhead cast can be performed with both a one-handed and a two-handed rod. In the latter case, the greatest transfer of energy is produced with the right hand, which controls the line release at the moment of casting and, simultaneously, pushes the rod forward. The longer and more powerful a rod is, however, the more pressure is given by the left hand, which is stretched backward. In really strong surf-casting rods, the left hand pushes most, while the right hand serves mainly for guidance.

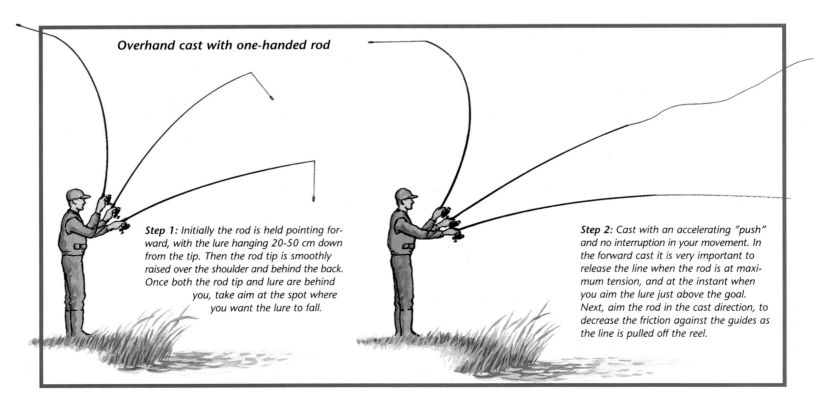

Overhand cast with one-handed rod

Step 1: Initially the rod is held pointing forward, with the lure hanging 20-50 cm down from the tip. Then the rod tip is smoothly raised over the shoulder and behind the back. Once both the rod tip and lure are behind you, take aim at the spot where you want the lure to fall.

Step 2: Cast with an accelerating "push" and no interruption in your movement. In the forward cast it is very important to release the line when the rod is at maximum tension, and at the instant when you aim the lure just above the goal. Next, aim the rod in the cast direction, to decrease the friction against the guides as the line is pulled off the reel.

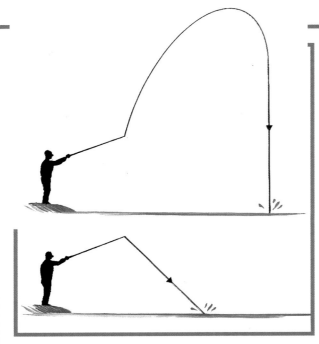

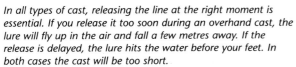

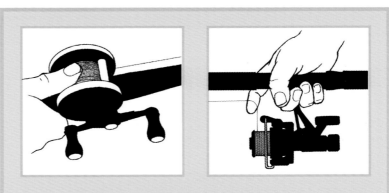

During the actual cast, the line must be able to shoot off the reel as easily and friction-free as possible. On a multiplier reel, the spool is released before starting the cast, and then your thumb is held against the spool until the line is to be let go. On a spinning reel, the bail arm is lowered with one hand while you lock the line with the other hand's forefinger or middle finger.

In all types of cast, releasing the line at the right moment is essential. If you release it too soon during an overhand cast, the lure will fly up in the air and fall a few metres away. If the release is delayed, the lure hits the water before your feet. In both cases the cast will be too short.

Overhand cast with two-handed rod

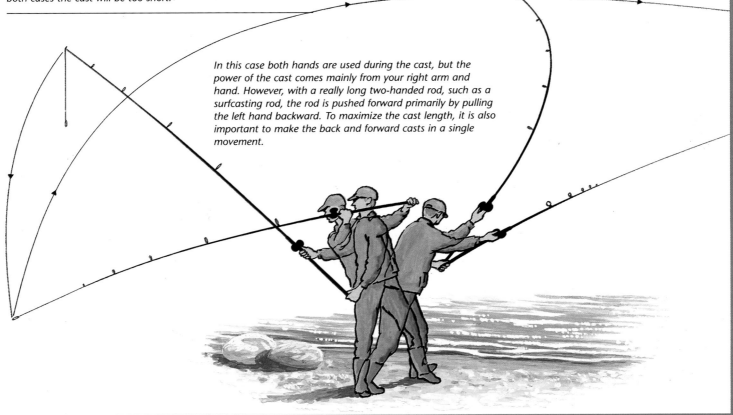

In this case both hands are used during the cast, but the power of the cast comes mainly from your right arm and hand. However, with a really long two-handed rod, such as a surfcasting rod, the rod is pushed forward primarily by pulling the left hand backward. To maximize the cast length, it is also important to make the back and forward casts in a single movement.

The side-cast

A side-cast is begun by bringing the rod horizontally backward. Depending on the rod's action, a forward acceleration is then made – still horizontally – and the rod is brought slightly upward, at which point the line is let out. Too early or late a release will send the bait flying to the right or left, respectively. You cannot aim with a side-cast, so it lacks precision, but it does yield greater force and a longer cast. In addition, the casting arc is longer than in an overhead cast, which means that the rod is flexed better. Even more flexing can be attained in the back cast, which continues in the forward cast, with a continuous movement that feels natural. This cast is excellent in a headwind, and the casting distance may be increased – if the rod's length and action permit – by having a little more line between the rod tip and the bait.

Side-casts are ideal for light spinning, where exact casting is not required. This cast is also often used from a boat, while sitting in the prow or stern to lay the casting arc outside the boat, without any danger for others aboard. Either a one-handed or a two-handed rod can be used to side-cast.

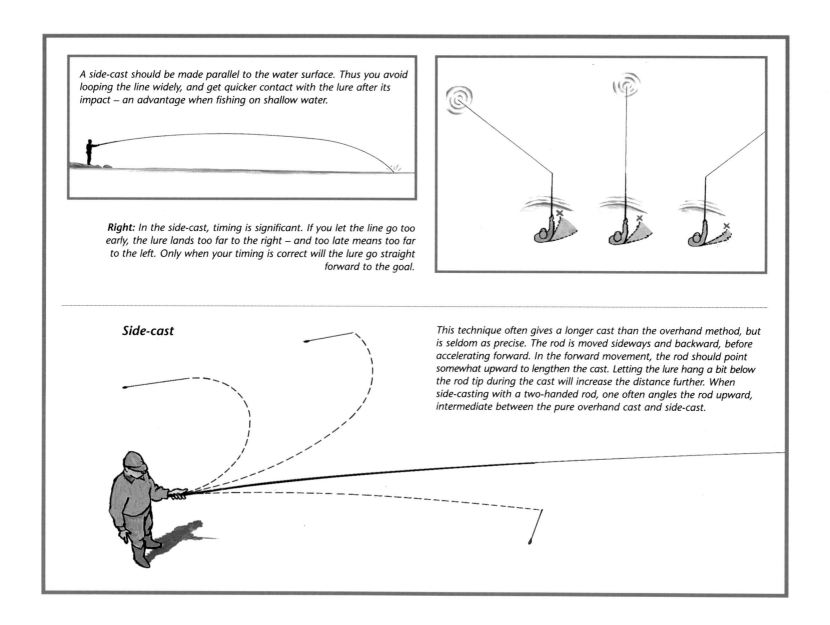

A side-cast should be made parallel to the water surface. Thus you avoid looping the line widely, and get quicker contact with the lure after its impact – an advantage when fishing on shallow water.

Right: *In the side-cast, timing is significant. If you let the line go too early, the lure lands too far to the right – and too late means too far to the left. Only when your timing is correct will the lure go straight forward to the goal.*

Side-cast

This technique often gives a longer cast than the overhand method, but is seldom as precise. The rod is moved sideways and backward, before accelerating forward. In the forward movement, the rod should point somewhat upward to lengthen the cast. Letting the lure hang a bit below the rod tip during the cast will increase the distance further. When side-casting with a two-handed rod, one often angles the rod upward, intermediate between the pure overhand cast and side-cast.

The pendulum cast

This is a short precision cast, and is best done with a spinning reel. The bait is started in a swinging movement with the free line, whose length may be from 30-50 centimetres to nearly the whole rod length. Once a fair swinging speed is reached, you aim at the target and release the line. Such a cast is used chiefly on confined waters surrounded by brushwood and branches, or wherever a cast of only a few metres is needed.

Left: The pendulum cast is very useful on minor waters with a high demand for precision. This photograph shows a typical situation: in the small deep holes are salmon, which have to get the lure presented properly with short but exact casts. Here the pendulum cast has the best chance of fishing the lure just where the fish are.

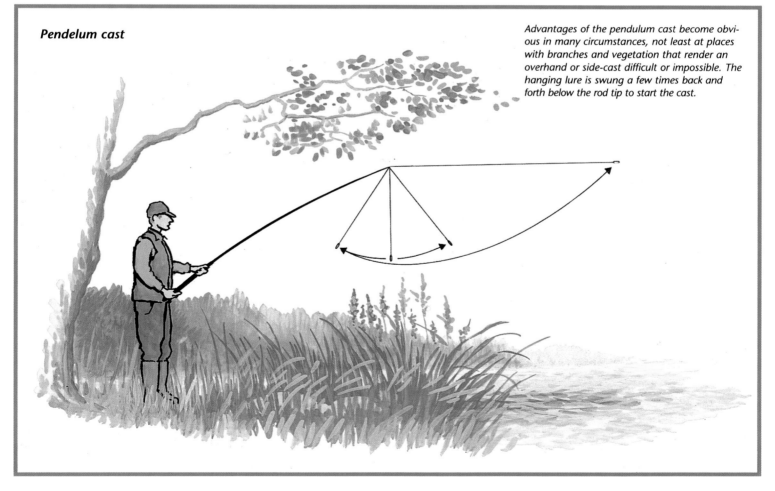

Pendelum cast

Advantages of the pendulum cast become obvious in many circumstances, not least at places with branches and vegetation that render an overhand or side-cast difficult or impossible. The hanging lure is swung a few times back and forth below the rod tip to start the cast.

Baits

Artificial lures can be divided into spoons, pirks, spinners, wobblers, jigs, and combinations of these, as well as plastic animals and flies. Each group includes thousands of variants. The types also differ in form, size, colour, weight and material. Spoons, pirks, spinners, and most jigs are sinking lures, but there are both sinking wobblers and floating ones. Within each group of lures, however, we can recognize the following main characteristics.

Spoons

Nearly all forms are found among spoons, but the majority have a real spoon- or S-shape. Their name is due to the fact that many of the first classic examples were spoon-like. Initially they were even fashioned from spoons – and few sportfishermen have avoided making a spoon out of just that utensil.

Both the spoon- and the S-shape hold these lures on course in the water. They should neither stray out to the sides, nor glide up to the surface when being retrieved. Their movement, besides the light, is also what enables the lures to send out reflections. Yet in principle only two types of spoon exist: broad, round and oval spoons – such as standard pike spoons – and long, thin spoons.

Broad spoons

A broad spoon moves slowly when it is retrieved at a normal rate. If the retrieval speed increases, the spoon begins to rotate and fishes ineffectively – a behaviour which is ever less pronounced for more slender spoons. The round and oval spoons imitate small fish, such as roach and crucian carp, while elongated spoons are imitations of smelt, bleak, sand lance, and small herring.

Generally, broad spoons are employed in still waters – for pike, perch and pikeperch – and have a calmly wobbling movement. Slender, elongated spoons are used in flowing waters and for coastal fishing. These do not wobble as much, and can be retrieved at high speed, or can stand quite motionless in the current and work. There are also spoons of thick sheet metal, which gives a longer cast, or of thin sheet that is more suitable for trolling.

Broad spoons. (From top, left to right:) Hammer, Ruggen, Pikko and Storauren, Crocodile Stubby, Atom, Moss Boss, Lillauren, Utö and Jurmo.

Weedguarded spoons. (From top:) Hobo, Atom Giller, Favorit Vass.

Weedless spoons

These spoons, usually of the broad type, are equipped with thin, stiff, single-strand wire that protects the hook. It is springy and thus exposes the hook to the fish when they bite. The hook shield prevents the hook from catching on weeds or other plants. Such spoons, therefore, are used only in areas with plenty of vegetation.

Their hooking abilities are, however, not the best, and this type of spoon involves a greater risk of losing the fish than do spoons without weedguards. Moreover, the hook is often fixed solidly to the spoon and cannot be replaced. Weedless spoons are designed mainly for pike fishing, and are to be retrieved in the same way as a broad spoon.

Certain large spoons in the class of 18-35 grams (1/2-1 ounce) are provided with two or three treble hooks, on the theory that they hook the fish better since it bites the lure crosswise. Practice has shown, however, that the line often hangs itself in the first hook or the middle hook, and that the fish is hooked better with only one treble hook.

Broad, round and oval spoons perform best, as a rule, at depths of 1-1.5 metres if they weigh 5-10 grams, at 1.5-2.5 metres if 10-20 grams, and at 2.5-5 metres if 20-35 grams. Only in clear water with vigorously hunting fish can you expect to succeed with spoons when the depth exceeds 5 metres.

Elongated spoons

Slender, thin and long spoons, with or without an S-bend, are imitations of fast-swimming fish. They are retrieved more rapidly than oval and round spoons, since a quick retrieval is just what they are intended for. Their primary use is in flowing waters, where retrieval is relatively slow and the current makes the spoon look alive. They are also used in coastal fishing for marine fish such as sea trout, cod and mackerel. The marine species that take elongated spoons are often fast swimmers with a slender body form.

This type of spoon was originally moulded in lead. But lead

Fishing with broad spoons

A broad spoon is ideal for any kind of spinning in lakes and in the calmer parts of waterways – for perch, pike, musky and pikeperch. Use the countdown method, and let the spoon sink almost to the bottom before starting to retrieve. The spinning speed is correct when you notice the lure's movements in the rod tip. Vary the speed with spin-stops and a slow or rapid retrieval. Bear in mind that a predatory fish normally takes the lure during a spin-stop, and often when the line is slack.

As long as the spoon moves in deep water, it is retrieved with the rod tip lowered. When it enters shallow water, the rod tip should be lifted. Thus you keep closer contact with the spoon and can control its deep movements better. Some spoons have a built-in pattern of uneven movement: during retrieval, they lurch through the water but stray to one side at regular intervals. This unpredictable gait can make the spoon a true "killer".

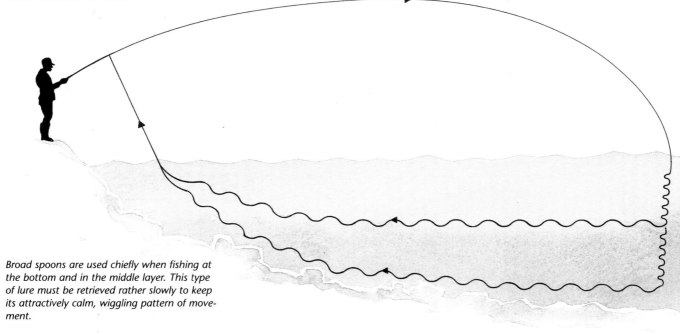

Broad spoons are used chiefly when fishing at the bottom and in the middle layer. This type of lure must be retrieved rather slowly to keep its attractively calm, wiggling pattern of movement.

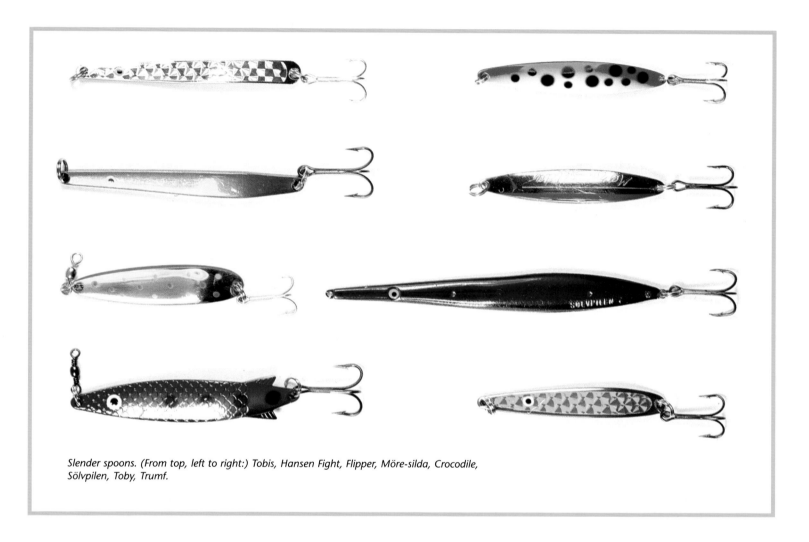

Slender spoons. (From top, left to right:) Tobis, Hansen Fight, Flipper, Möre-silda, Crocodile, Sölvpilen, Toby, Trumf.

is a soft material, so the finish is not very durable on these spoons, or on pirks, whose painting and lacquer flake off when they hit rocks. Some lead-moulded pirks do have hard lacquer, yet it easily cracks if they hit rocks or snag on the bottom.

The drawback of lead-moulded pirks is that they are compact and heavy in comparison with their size. They cast well, but must be retrieved rapidly to avoid settling firmly on the bottom. The lead-moulded spoons and pirks that are produced today, though, have a larger bearing surface and less elongation than previously. For environmental reasons, lead-moulded lures will probably disappear from the market in time.

During recent decades, such small lead-moulded spoons and pirks have been gradually replaced by spoons made of iron or brass sheet. Some of these are straight and have a linear gait in the water. Others have a slight S-bend and are retrieved more slowly. This type of spoon combines the best properties of the earlier lead-moulded pirks with a more lively, attractive movement. Its elongated form also allows a fine cast. The spoon's rear part is often a little wider or heavier than its front part.

Elongated spoons do not twist the line as readily as the oval and round spoons. Their hooking abilities are excellent, too. Spoons of 5-15 grams are used at depths of 1-1.5 metres, 10-20 grams at 1.5-3 metres, and 20-35 grams at 3-5 metres.

Fishing with elongated spoons

Elongated spoons are meant to catch fast-swimming fish in waters with wide surfaces – such as sea trout, cod, garfish and mackerel along coasts, or trout in lakes. Just as with broad spoons, the countdown method is employed when retrieving, if the predatory fish are holding on the bottom. Usually, however, they circulate in the middle layer or at the surface.

Its design makes this type of spoon best for rapid retrieval, when it imitates species like smelt, sand lance, and bleak that swim intermittently through the water. Repeated spin-stops and a varied speed of retrieval are also important when fishing with such lures. During spin-stops, a well-balanced spoon will sink horizontally and rotate around its own axle.

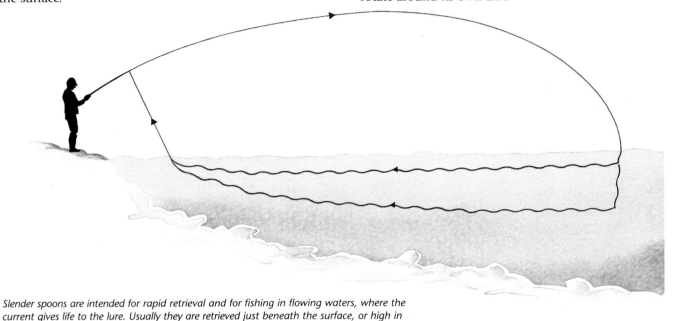

Slender spoons are intended for rapid retrieval and for fishing in flowing waters, where the current gives life to the lure. Usually they are retrieved just beneath the surface, or high in the middle layer, and ideally at a varying tempo with irregular spin-stops.

Pirks

A pirk (alternatively called a pilk, metal casting jig, diamond jig, or jigging spoon) may weigh from 40-50 up to 500 grams, when used in marine fishing for cod, pollack, cusk, mackerel and other predators. Pirks were originally a Scandinavian lure, employed by professional fishermen to catch cod. This group is very big, including hundreds of types and sizes, but generally they can be divided into light pirks for casting in shallow water (5-20 metres) and heavy pirks for casting in deeper water.

Some pirks are still made of lead and, being heavy and compact, serve very well in deep water, where the current is strong and the boat drifts fast. Other pirks, with a larger surface, are manufactured of brass or iron. These are livelier, for calm and less demanding conditions such as still or shallow water. The line thickness also influences the choice of pirk. So-called braided lines, based on spectra or kevlar, with a small diameter relative to their strength, enable one to use a lighter pirk.

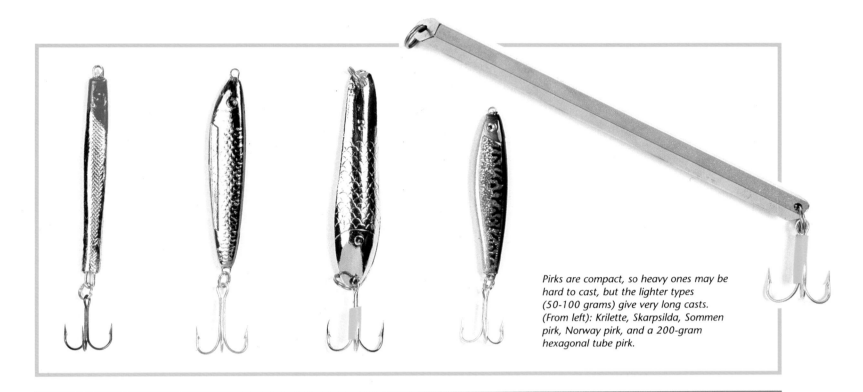

Pirks are compact, so heavy ones may be hard to cast, but the lighter types (50-100 grams) give very long casts. (From left): Krilette, Skarpsilda, Sommen pirk, Norway pirk, and a 200-gram hexagonal tube pirk.

Fishing with pirks

The lighter pirks are intended for casting on deeper water, often from a boat. They are retrieved in a jerky, varied manner – either on the bottom, where cod and cusk are found, or in the middle layer with its pollack and mackerel. During retrieval, one must also take account of the depth and the boat's drift, normally casting in the direction of drift.

Heavy pirks come into play for pirk fishing, or vertical fishing. Here the pirk is sunk to the bottom, and then the reel is coupled in. The rod's up-and-down movements give vitality to the otherwise compact pirk. In deep water and strong currents, pirk fishing requires you to have constant contact with the bottom, so that the pirk does not lift off it.

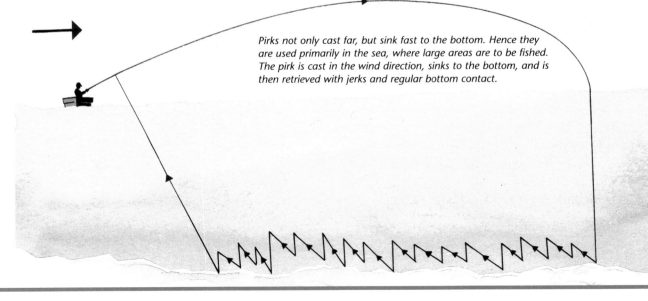

Pirks not only cast far, but sink fast to the bottom. Hence they are used primarily in the sea, where large areas are to be fished. The pirk is cast in the wind direction, sinks to the bottom, and is then retrieved with jerks and regular bottom contact.

Spinners

A spinner has the simple structure of a spoon that rotates around a wire or body, and moves straight in the water. It is actually amazing that so many predatory fish are tempted by spinners, which do not resemble any fish – as spoons and wobblers do. The spinner's body stays still while the spoon turns and gives it life. Moreover, the spinner continually sends out reflections, and the vibrations from the spoon attract fish. Numerous fish species that never take spoons or wobblers can be drawn to a spinner, such as various whitefish species.

Standard spinners

A standard spinner is made from a stiff, single-strand wire with a loop at each end, one for the hook and one to tie the line on. All spinners have a body, except some that are intended for very shallow water. In front of the body are a bead and a bend in which the spoon is mounted. The bead, made of plastic of metal, provides a light gait and minimizes friction between the body and the rotating spoon.

It is essentially the spinner body's size and weight that, together with the spoon's form, determine which waters and depths the spinner is suitable for. A heavy body is able to spin in deep water and strong currents. A light body, for example on the classic Mepps spinner, gives a superficial gait that is most effective in shallow and slow waters.

The spoon's construction reveals how the spinner moves in the water. A short, broad spoon rotates slowly, so the spinner travels high, which is good for fishing in shallows. Such a spoon rotates more vertically in relation to the body, too. If you want to fish deeper with this type of spinner, it cannot be done with a bigger and heavier spinner of the same type, since the spoon creates a correspondingly greater lifting force and keeps the spinner at the same depth. Instead, you must choose a spinner with a relatively heavier body, or with a thinner and longer spoon, which will not only go deeper but can be retrieved faster.

A spinner works superbly on most predatory fish, but is less effective in cold water. For it must go at a certain speed if the spoon is to rotate, and thus often runs too high for fish in cold water.

A further variation is seen in spinners with a feather hackle

Standard spinners.
(From above): Lindy Big Fish, Musky Killer.

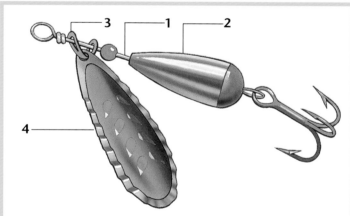

Regardless of the spoon's shape and the spinner body's design, the basic construction is the same: a rotating spoon that emits sound waves, which predatory fish interpret as small fish fleeing. A spinner's parts are the wire axle (1), spinner body (2), wire bail (3) and spinner spoon (4).

around the treble hook. Large "bucktail" spinners, with a dense skirt of deer hair there, are used for musky fishing. Alternatively, an octopus skirt on the treble hook can obtain the same effect. This yields a long, billowy, enticing spinner with a total length of about 20 centimetres (8 inches). Standard spinners are meant for fishing in shallow or medium-depth waters, down to 3 metres.

Fishing with standard spinners

The majority of standard spinners are relatively light lures that sink slowly and do not cast very far. If you start the retrieval with a jerk on the rod tip, you can be sure that the spinner rotates, but you often feel it through the weight or resistance on the rod tip.

A standard spinner is fine for flowing waters, where it can even be made to stay at the same spot in the current, and to rotate and work at different tempos. If the current is too strong, though, the spinner will lift toward the surface. These spinners are most attractive if you avoid spin-stops but vary the retrieval speed and keep the spoon rotating.

Again, the spinner is excellent for retrieving near the bottom – in both still and flowing waters. But as soon as its resistance to the rod tip disappears, the spoon's rotation will have collapsed. By lifting the rod tip or retrieving a little faster, you can restart the rotation. Thus, the spinner's resistance on the rod allows you to check that it is working properly, and make it go just as slowly or as near the bottom as you want.

In flowing water, a spinner is usually considered best for fishing downstream. However, spinning upstream is a quite effective method, as the spinner approaches the fish like a natural prey.

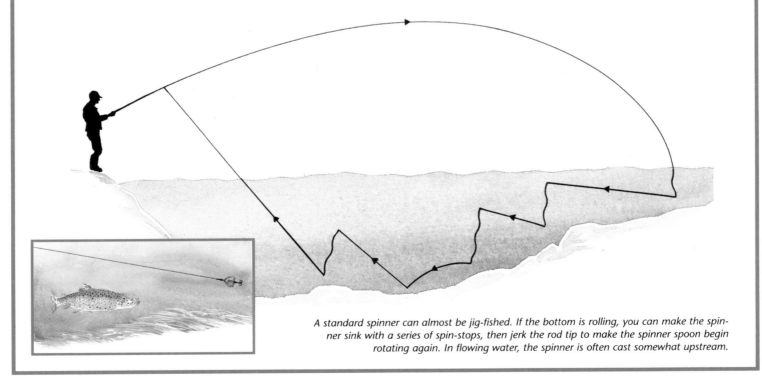

A standard spinner can almost be jig-fished. If the bottom is rolling, you can make the spinner sink with a series of spin-stops, then jerk the rod tip to make the spinner spoon begin rotating again. In flowing water, the spinner is often cast somewhat upstream.

Wobblers (plugs)

In contrast to spoons and spinners, which look like small fish only from particular angles, a wobbler is three-dimensional. Most plugs today are made of plastic, but balsa wood was once common. Plugs of balsa are still used to some extent, and many sportfishermen consider these more lively.

If you compare a balsa and a plastic plug with the same appearance and form, the balsa plug displays a lot more vitality. However, it is less durable and often suffers damage from fish teeth and impacts. Plugs are fantastic lures for pike, trout, salmon, musky, perch, and a long list of salt-water species. There are innumerable plugs which can float, sink, deep-dive, "hover" or serve for trolling. Some are also made for fishing right in the surface.

Floating plugs

Most plugs float, which means that they have a lower specific weight than water does. Thus, a plug floats because it is filled with air chambers or bubbles. The majority of wooden plugs, too, can float. A plug is provided with a "bill" or lip (or jaw-spoon) of metal or plastic, which makes it dive or cut down through the water when being retrieved. This bill is fixed on most plugs, but on a few it is adjustable so that the plug can descend to different depths. Some plugs are two-part constructions, and have a more lively slithering gait.

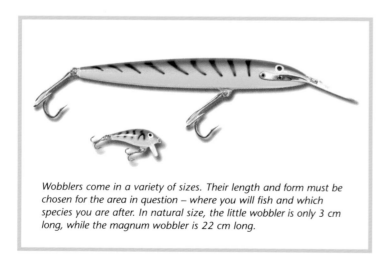

Wobblers come in a variety of sizes. Their length and form must be chosen for the area in question – where you will fish and which species you are after. In natural size, the little wobbler is only 3 cm long, while the magnum wobbler is 22 cm long.

Wobbterm

Floating wobblers.
From top left to right: Down Deep Rattlin Rap, Ukko Tipsy, Invincible, Tobimarv.

From top: Clown, Crawdad, Firetige.

Suspending wobblers: Husky Jerk and Suspending Rattlin' Rouge.

Suspending wobblers

These wobblers have the same density as water, and thus neither sink nor float, so one can make them "hover" freely at any desired level. They maintain this depth even during long spin-stops and extremely slow retrieval. Fishing with such wobblers may be very effective when the fish are sluggish and hard to catch.

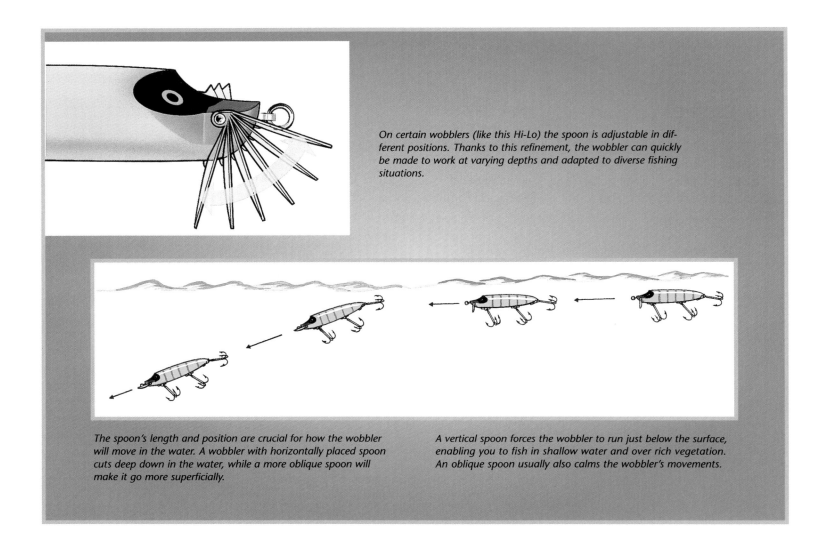

On certain wobblers (like this Hi-Lo) the spoon is adjustable in different positions. Thanks to this refinement, the wobbler can quickly be made to work at varying depths and adapted to diverse fishing situations.

The spoon's length and position are crucial for how the wobbler will move in the water. A wobbler with horizontally placed spoon cuts deep down in the water, while a more oblique spoon will make it go more superficially.

A vertical spoon forces the wobbler to run just below the surface, enabling you to fish in shallow water and over rich vegetation. An oblique spoon usually also calms the wobbler's movements.

The plug's bill, in combination with the retrieval speed, determines how deeply it can dive and whether it wobbles little or much in the water. If the bill is small, the plug moves relatively little, but a large bill makes the plug livelier. If the bill lies almost horizontally, the plug will cut deep into the water, while a more transverse bill gives the plug a calmer gait. With a nearly vertical bill, the plug goes slowly and almost in the surface. In addition, some plugs have an adjustable metal bill that can be bent up or down to change the degree of diving.

Other forms of adjustment exist to influence the movement of a floating plug. For example, some plugs have two knot eyes, the upper one producing a deep gait and the lower one a more superficial gait. The plug may also be weighted with lead, a bit up on the line, so that it can go deeper. The Rapala or Duncan knot is common on small, finely balanced plugs. A fixed knot, tied high in the plug's eye, deepens its dive somewhat. If the fixed knot is slid down as far as possible in the eye, the plug will go more superficially. However, floating plugs are always limited as regards their fishing depths, due of course to their specific weight in comparison with water.

Many plugs are equipped with two or three treble hooks. By removing one or two of these – or substituting, for instance, thinner hooks – the plug acquires a lighter and livelier gait.

Fishing with floating plugs

The faster a plug is retrieved, the deeper it goes. But the rod tip must be kept low. In the last part the retrieval, the plug will wander up toward the surface, and then it is especially important to hold the rod tip down at the water.

Most floating plugs are intended to fish at depths of 1-6 metres. Since they float, numerous spin-stops will let them ascend toward the surface and – as the retrieval continues – dive again. This is a very effective technique

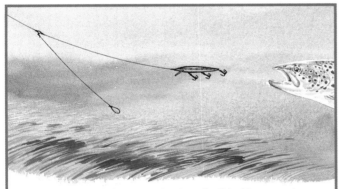

A floating wobbler that is weighted can be fished just over the bottom, even in strong current and at relatively great depth. Too short a line between the three-way swivel and the lure, though, can worsen the wobbler's lively gait.

for retrieving them. In cold water, though, floating plugs are not so effective, since they demand a reasonable speed of movement in order to work at the bottom – and this speed is often too high, so a sinking plug or a lead-weighted floating plug is more effective.

In flowing waters, a floating plug has two advantages. It can be allowed to drift with the current down to an assumed holding place, and then be retrieved. Moreover, you can stop during the retrieval so that the plug soars over submerged obstacles such as plants and stones.

Floating, deep-diving plugs are recognizable by their frequently compact body, but also by the extra-long bill which makes the plug cut down to depths of 3-8 metres. On the other hand, a plug requires a certain retrieval speed if it is to reach maximum depth. Too slow a retrieval leads the plug to work inefficiently; and if you retrieve too fast, it will cut out in the water.

This type of plug is quite good at depths of 3-6 metres – and extremely effective for searching slopes at 3-7 metres, where it often hits the bottom and creates sounds that attract pikeperch, walleye and perch. The large versions of these plugs are mainly devoted to trolling for pike, musky and saltwater species.

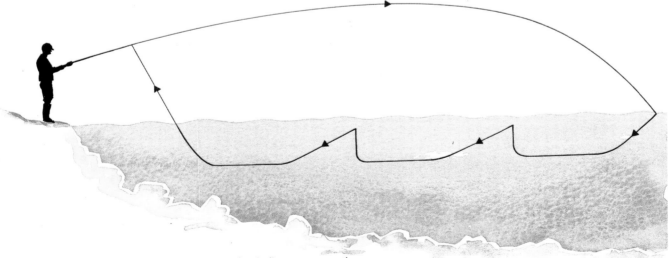

The wobbler floats on the water after being cast out, but it dives as soon as the retrieval begins. During spin-stops, it will rise toward the surface, working down again when the retrieval resumes.

Fishing with sinking plugs

The speed of descent varies among sinking plugs. Small sizes are intended for depths of 2-3 metres, and the larger plugs can be used down to 8-10 metres, but it often takes at least half a minute for the plug to reach the bottom. You should thus use the countdown method for this type of plug.

When the retrieval is begun, the plug will slowly lift from the bottom. Hence, numerous spin-stops are important to make it stay at the bottom, where most predatory fish linger. You may then need to release a little line regularly, by switching over the bail on a spinning reel or disengaging the spool on a multiplier reel.

Sinking plugs are better than floating ones for fishing in cold water, since they can be retrieved slowly.

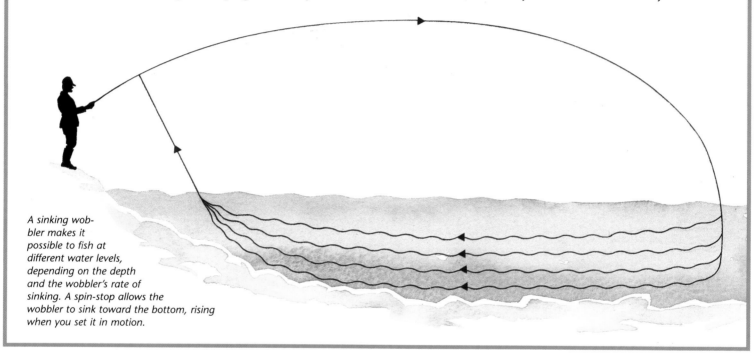

A sinking wobbler makes it possible to fish at different water levels, depending on the depth and the wobbler's rate of sinking. A spin-stop allows the wobbler to sink toward the bottom, rising when you set it in motion.

Sinking plugs

A floating plug cannot, unless it is weighted, be used with the countdown method at great depths. Here the sinking plug is better suited. Such a plug is normally made of plastic, having no air chambers or bubbles. The plastic may either be denser than water or contain weighting. Wooden plugs also exist in sinking versions.

Usually the package shows whether the plug is sinking (S) or floating (F), but you can often tell the difference by feeling its weight in your hand. As with most floating plugs, the depth-going of a sinking plug depends on the bill's size, placement, and cleavage of the water, besides the location of the knot eyes. The plug can be adjusted, too, by changing the bill or replacing the hooks. A few deep-going plugs with a long bill can work down to 7 metres.

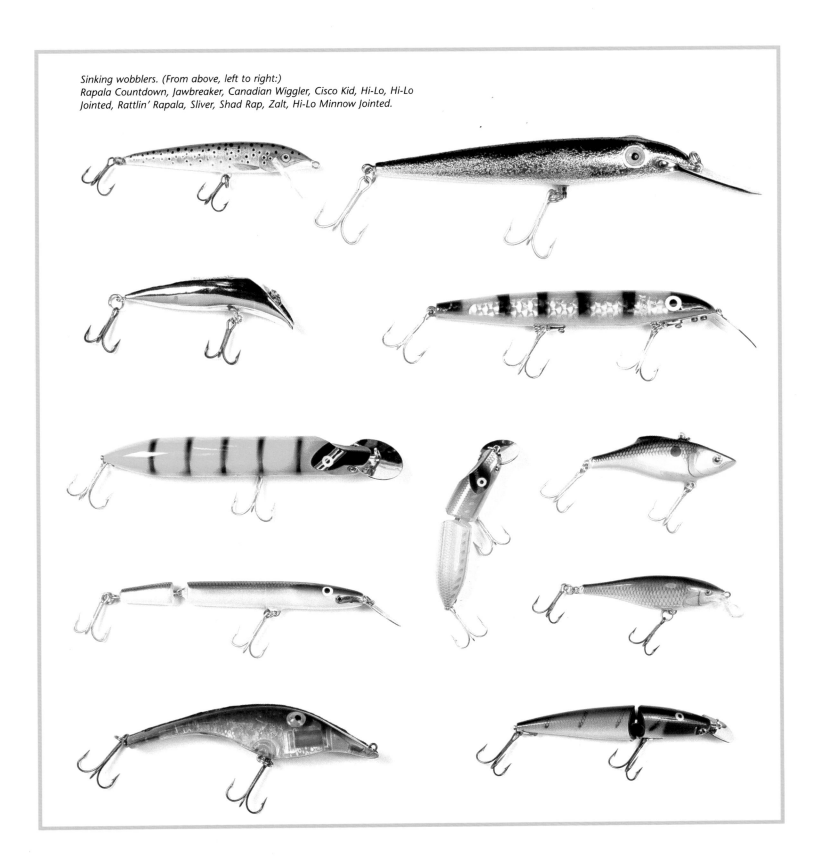

Sinking wobblers. (From above, left to right:)
Rapala Countdown, Jawbreaker, Canadian Wiggler, Cisco Kid, Hi-Lo, Hi-Lo
Jointed, Rattlin' Rapala, Sliver, Shad Rap, Zalt, Hi-Lo Minnow Jointed.

Jigs

The jig belongs to the classic artificial baits in American bass fishing. Although occasional jigs appeared on the European fishing scene during the 1960s, only in the 1970s did they really enjoy a breakthrough for pike and pikeperch fishing. Then they became an increasingly common option to other lures in, for example, trout fishing at rivers and lakes – and next for fishing in shallow marine waters. This is strange, as there can hardly be any cheaper or better artificial bait than a jig, which long ago was included in the survival gear of various fleets together with hooks, lines and other emergency accessories.

Normal lures, such as spoons and plugs, have built-in patterns of movement. The jig is different. At first sight, it looks most like a lump of lead with a tuft of feathers or plastic and an upturned single hook. In spite of that, there are diverse designs of American jigs – and some forms go back to the 1920s and 1930s. The keel and projectile types are intended for flowing waters, where the jig's shape makes it cut downward. The ball types are meant for spinning in still waters, while the banana and mushroom types apply to light jig fishing from a boat and to fishing in deep water.

Some jigs also carry a long bill. In this respect they resemble a plug, but the jig lacks the plug's ability to cut down into the water. Other jigs are provided with propellers or small rotor blades. The knot eye – which is the hook eye as well – may have a forward orientation to keep plants off the hook. But most jigs have the eye on top of the lead head, which is moulded around the hook. The latter is nearly always of Aberdeen type and browned, gilded or nickel-plated.

Jigs with a rubber body are cheap to work with, since you can buy replaceable bodies for them. However, some toothed predatory fish can destroy a rubber body in no time. If you get a bad bite or the fish is difficult to hook, it may be because the jig body is too long – but a body made of hair, feathers or rubber can be shortened with a knife or scissors to facilitate hooking. Rubber jigs are best stored in tackle boxes marked "Wormproof", which prevent certain chemicals in the rubber bodies from smearing off, or melting both the bodies and the box's plastic. Bodies of each colour should be kept in a separate plastic bag. This will also keep them from drying out.

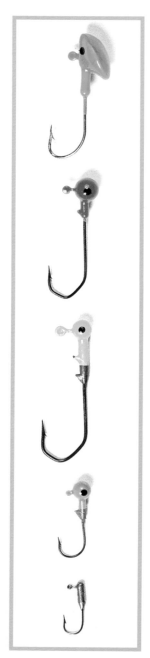

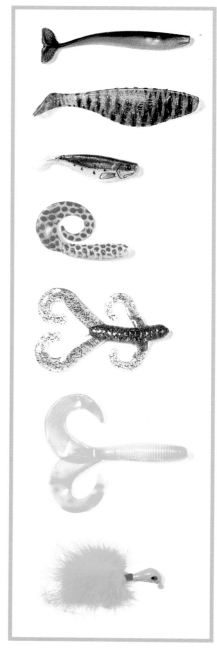

Above left: Jig heads come in a range of colours, forms, sizes and weights. Some common variants of jig heads are round, oval, tubular, banana-shaped, keel-shaped and conical. The hook's appearance may also differ according to the area, and to the type of jig body it is intended for.

Above right: The jig was originally the typical bass lure, but many people now consider jigs effective for diverse species in both fresh and marine waters. A jig's lively plastic tail enables it to be fished in very slowly without losing its attractiveness. Despite its simple design, it works fine in most fishing situations.

Fishing with jigs

All of the lures discussed previously are retrieved. But a jig has to be both "worked" and retrieved. The jig itself is dead, and the fisherman must bring it alive with rod and wrist movements during the retrieval. Vigorous jerks along the bottom are needed – whether long tempting jerks, or short chopping jerks, depending on the kind of fish you are after. Correct use of a jig is certainly a craft, but it can yield great satisfaction in the right hands.

Maintain continuous contact with the jig, but do not stretch the line so much as to affect the jig's gait. Make a strike at the least suggestion of a take. In contrast to spoons, plugs and other lures, it is quite common that a jig's construction attracts cautious nibbles without hook-ing the fish. Apart from flies, almost no other type of artificial bait is in such close touch with the fish at the taking stage. Many people believe that a jig is suited only to fishing on hard bottoms without vegetation; but if there is any vegetation, you should use an ultra-light jig that bounces off the plants. The hook does not snag, since it is turned upward.

Jigs have many practical advantages. Their aerodynamic shape gives long casts even in a headwind, and the compact head allows exact casts as well as good bottom contact. Moreover, a jig cuts down into the current better, so it is easier to keep in contact with the bottom than are other types of lure.

Jigs are primarily used for fishing along the bottom. Retrieval should be varied, and the jig fished in with alternately short and long jerks of the rod, so that it "hops" across the bottom. When fishing in flowing waters, the jig is cast across them or obliquely downstream, and retrieved with small tugs. A good presentation technique is essential if the jig is to behave irresistibly.

Casting floats

There are occasions in spinning when a spoon, plug or spinner is too large a lure for the predatory fish and, for example, a fly is much more suitable. Especially salmon in many waters can be so shy and cautious that big lures do not work. The diminished appetite for large bait may be due to the water temperature or level, insect hatchings, the season, spawning or other conditions.

An alternative is then to spin with flies in the surface, aided by a casting float. This device comes in two basic versions. One, the Bonnand type, is shaped like a cigar, with a red top, and contains lead as a weight. It is filled with air and can also be used as an ordinary float. At each end is a hole to tie the main line or the leader in.

The other version is the classic plastic "bubble", or Buldo. A transparent or colourful ball with two knot eyes, it can be opened via two small rubber valves and filled with water – the casting weight – so that it floats exactly in the surface. Also available are oval variants to be filled with water.

The fly should be on the end of a leader 1.0-4.5 metres long. Many sportfishermen use a permanently fixed leader, which is tied to a casting bubble. There are two kinds of sliding leader. The first is a 50-cm length of 0.40-mm line, inserted through the bubble and provided with a swivel at each end for the leader or main line. When the fish takes the fly during retrieval, you thus have 50 cm of "loose line" which the fish can pull out together with the fly. The second kind, used when you want to give more "loose line", is made by ending the leader with a swivel, to which the main line is tied after being inserted through the casting bubble. This swivel serves as a stopper.

Casting floats essentially function as casting weights. In recent years, however, different sorts of casting weights have been introduced. These are normally made of plastic or wood, with casting weights built or moulded into them. They are used in the same way as casting floats – with both a fixed and a sliding leader.

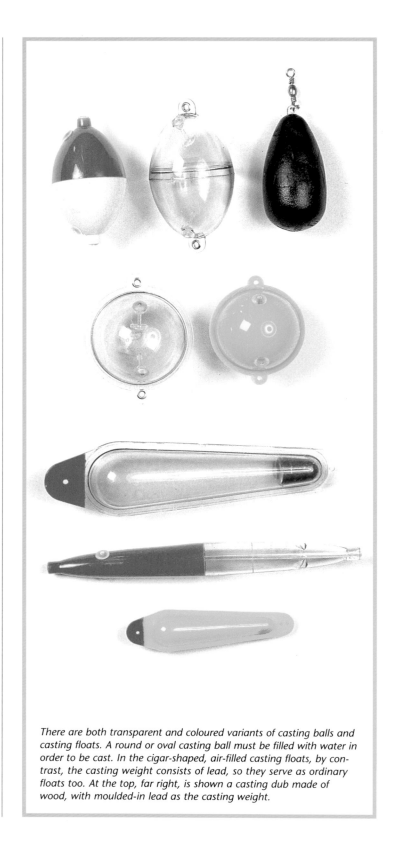

There are both transparent and coloured variants of casting balls and casting floats. A round or oval casting ball must be filled with water in order to be cast. In the cigar-shaped, air-filled casting floats, by contrast, the casting weight consists of lead, so they serve as ordinary floats too. At the top, far right, is shown a casting dub made of wood, with moulded-in lead as the casting weight.

Fishing with casting floats

To fish with a long leader and an often heavy casting weight, you need a relatively long, strong rod and a line of 0.25-0.35 mm. The cast is carried out when the leader lies in front of the fisherman in the water – never behind. Retrieval should be slow with many pauses, depending on which species of fish you are after. A lot of sportfishermen dislike this method, since the fishing is monotonous and may even be boring. But there is no doubt of its effectiveness.

Plastic bubbles can be weighted so much that they sink. In some put-and-take fishing, weighted "neutral" and "sinking" bubbles are frequently used at depths as great as 5-8 metres.

If you want to fish deep with a fly, you can weight the leader with lead shot, or perhaps tie a piece of fast-sinking flyline into the leader.

The strike should be delivered with a smooth, controlled movement, because the plastic bubble gives quite a resistance in the water. Beginners have a habit of making too hard a strike, which results in the line breaking at the bubble.

Casting floats are useful in both still waters and rivers, where they enable a fly to fish just as well as the flyfisherman's floating line with a fly.

Fishing with a sliding leader means that the fish is given a little loose line when it takes. The two swivels function as stops, both when retrieving (left) and when the fish has taken the lure (right). Many think that a permanently mounted leader gives better hooking, but that the contact with lure and fish is improved by a sliding leader.

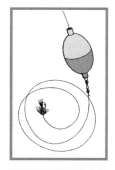
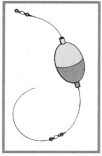

***Right:** Shown here are three methods of mounting a casting float on the line. Above is a permanent mounting, and below it are two variants with a sliding line.*

***Below:** In Scandinavia, fishing with long-casting balls has become a frequent – and rewarding – way to present traditional flies for coastal sea trout.*

Spinning with flies

Spinning does not by any means rule out the possibility of using flies in deep water. If the fly is weighted slightly up on the line, it can be fished at depth in both still and flowing water. In Scandinavia the so-called "spinning-fly" method is thus applied to trout, salmon and seagoing trout in streams and rivers. However, this has angered flyfishermen and been forbidden in many places due to its effectiveness.

The leader is 1-1.5 metres long, of 0.20-0.40 mm line, depending on whether trout in small rivers or salmon and sea trout in large rivers are fished. It is tied in a three-way swivel, the distance to the sinker being 20-30 cm long. The choice of fly is not very difficult. Ordinary trout flies serve for all forms of trout fishing, while double-hooked flies or tube flies are used for salmon and sea trout.

Lagging flies

It often happens that a predatory fish pursues a plug, spoon or spinner without biting – no matter what type of bait or retrieval technique is used. In this case, a "lagging" fly offers both an alternative and a surprising arrangement that can trick the fish. You simply knot a fly in a short or long leader on a spoon, plug or spinner, after removing the hook(s).

Char is a typical fish species that gladly takes a lagging fly. Perch, pike, trout, and garfish in salt water, too, respond positively to it. But the fly tends to get hung up in the main line when casting against the wind, so a lagging – or perhaps "persistent" – fly should be used only in calm weather or with the wind at your back.

Droppers

Droppers are flies, plastic animals, or micro-jigs that are tied to the line above the lure. They markedly increase the chances of catching fish, since many predators are curious and often become "envious" when they see a little fish being chased by a bigger one. Perch, trout and bass, as well as marine species like sea trout, mackerel and cod, readily take droppers. The droppers are tied in a leader 30-50 cm over the main lure, and it is frequently only to them that the fish reacts.

Spinning with a fly can yield fine catches in rivers with salmon and sea trout. This salmon could not resist a weighted tube fly, fished at the bottom.

Fishing with spinning flies

Spinning with a fly in flowing water can be done exactly as with a spoon. All the fishing is oriented directly or obliquely downstream, so that the fly swings in toward your own bank. By paying out line or lifting the rod, you can make the fly work deeper or higher. During this process, you regularly raise and lower the rod to "pump" the fly in: it more or less zigzags against the current as it approaches your bank.

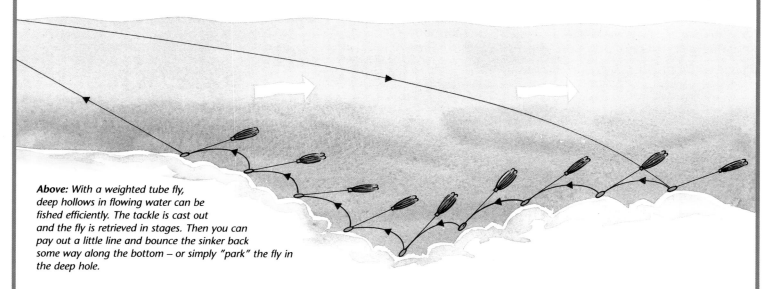

Above: With a weighted tube fly, deep hollows in flowing water can be fished efficiently. The tackle is cast out and the fly is retrieved in stages. Then you can pay out a little line and bounce the sinker back some way along the bottom – or simply "park" the fly in the deep hole.

The spinning fly can be weighted by attaching the sinker to the main line, either directly or via a leader. The leader, which should be thinner than the main line, is then fastened in a swivel or three-way snap. But the line between the swivel and fly must have the same breaking strength as the main line.

It is not unusual for predatory fish to become "envious" when they see a smaller fish hunted by bigger ones, and this reaction is what makes the dropper an effective attractor. A dropper is normally attached to a leader 30-50 cm above the lure. Likewise, a fly dragged after the lure can attract a bite, but the leader should then be only about 10 cm long.

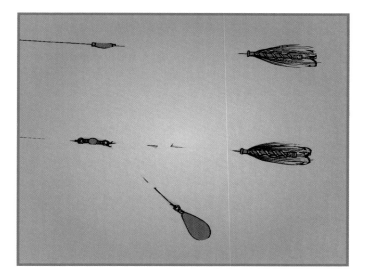

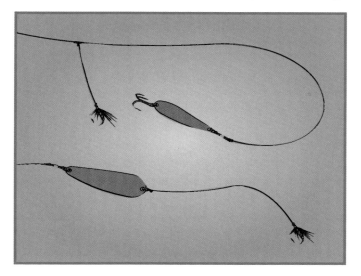

Jerkbait

No other spinning technique is as demanding as jerkbait-fishing. When mastered, it also gives the greatest rewards in terms of spectacular takes and, under certain conditions, efficient catches.

Jerkbait-fishing has long been an established technique for pike and musky in North America. Since the early 1990s, its fame has also spread across most of pike-crazy Europe. The name comes, of course, from jerking the bait. Unlike a plug, whose nose-bill gives it a gait, a jerkbait has no bill and is dependent on the "life" that the fisherman gives it.

Technique

The fisherman stands up, casts out, points the rod straight toward the bait, and brings it home by jerking downward with the rod. After each jerk, the arc of line that has been created is wound in, and the rod is moved back to the starting position, until the line is stretched again and the fisherman makes a new jerk. Short and sharp jerks, or slow and spaced jerks, give the bait different kinds of behavior. Preferably the fisherman should maintain a certain rhythm. A jerkbait is designed so that, with a good rhythm, it swims in a zigzag, gliding to one side at each jerk and to the other side at the next jerk.

Since the technique relies on the fisherman's ability to jerk the rod toward the water surface without hitting it, jerk rods are short. They are also stiff, for casting weights up to 150 grams, so that the jerks will be transferred to the bait. As a friend said of somebody else's jerk rod, it's "soft as a broomstick". In order to hook the fish with such a short rod and not lose anything from the movement, the fishing is done with inelastic braided lines of at least 30 lbs weight. Between the line and the bait is a leader about 30 centimetres long, which must be stiff for the jerks to make the bait shoot out toward the sides, and to lessen the risk of the bait getting caught up in the cast.

Baits

The baits fall into two general types: stickbaits and tailbaits. The latter have a spoon at the rear, which steers the bait downward during a jerk. The angle of the spoon can be changed for diving to different depths. Stickbaits are, in somewhat simplified terms, a stick with treble hooks and the most common jerkbait. In standard form, these baits go down to at most a metre below the water surface, since they can float. Hence, the technique is best in shallow waters, down to four

Jerkbait-fishing is one of the most reliable methods for big pike.

or five metres if the water is clear. This, in turn, means that jerkfishing is superb during early springtime, when the fish wander into shallow spawning areas, and during late autumn when they come in toward the shallow edges again.

If a standard jerkbait is weighted – by boring a hole in front of the midpoint, pushing in a fair amount of lead and gluing it shut – the bait can be made to run deeper. With a weight that keeps it suspended, neither sinking nor floating, it can be fished home very slowly, which is extremely effective when the water is really cold.

Opposite top: The baits are meant to imitate large, injured preyfish. This group of lures is represented here by a Fatso.
Opposite bottom: Jerkbait-fishing gives the greatest rewards in terms of spectacular takes and afficient catches.

Choosing the bait's colour

Many factors determine the effect of colour in artificial baits, so the rules for selecting colours cannot be strict. Besides, when the fish are on the take, colour often has no importance at all. But you should base a colour on the fish's natural prey. Some fresh waters are dominated by prey-fish such as crucian carp and rudd, which are imitated with gold and copper colours – while roach, bleak and smelt can be imitated with silvery colours. In clear flowing waters with trout and salmon, natural colours commonly do best.

Even the water's colour can influence the choice of colour. Frequently good in brownish waters are silver, copper and nickel, or strong and fluorescent colours. In dark, murky water, silvery and fluorescent colours are notably effective, and this applies equally to the cold months when the fish are much less active. Provocation is another key ingredient in selecting colours: you can choose one that provokes the fish to bite, such as a fluorescent colour.

The significance of colours is best understood by knowing which colours of light are absorbed in the water. In clear water, nearly all colours penetrate to a depth of 5 metres; below this, the red colours are absorbed while yellow, green and blue prevail. Spinning, however, is done mainly in shallower waters where all colours are visible.

Predatory fish in shallow waters often have bright colours. For example, a perch in clear shallow water has red fins and a yellowish body, whereas in murky deep water it has yellow or grey-white fins and light-grey scales. Thus, in shallow waters the choice of colour is important, but in deep water the challenge is rather to use lures that the fish can see and to present them in the right way.

Size and gait

Many fishermen are insecure when spinning, and arm themselves with numerous types of lures, until they find good ones. Then they gradually limit themselves to a handful of lures, whose gait and catching qualities they have confidence in. They know how their "favourites" fish at different depths, and the retrieval speeds and techniques – as well as colours – which are best in the water at hand.

Some general rules, though, exist for choosing the correct lure. First, a lure's weight should make it possible to fish effectively in the given water. If the fish are far out, the lure must

Left: The value of lure colours is often exaggerated, but in many waters the colour can be as influential as the lure's shape, size and movements. As a rule, in brownish and murky water (upper photo) strong colours should be used – such as silver, copper, gold, flash and fluorescents. In clear water (lower photo) natural and dark colours are recommended instead, such as silver – alone or combined with blue or black – and zebra or "nature colours". One must also, of course, take account of which preyfish occur in the given water, at what depth the lure will work, and whether the sky is bright or dark.

be heavy enough for casting to them. If they are standing deep, the weight of the lure should enable it to fish along the bottom, throughout the retrieval distance.

Big fish are normally attracted by large lures, since they prefer taking a single mouthful to many small bites. Likewise, if the water becomes murky or disturbed by wind and weather, you should choose a larger lure with more flash or colour. The worse the water gets, the less shy the predatory fish are.

The movements of artificial baits point to a further rule. Salmon and trout, as well as bass and perch, are most tempted by lures that have a quick, enticing gait. On the other hand, relatively slow movements draw predators such as pike, pikeperch and musky.

Finally, one should keep in mind all the external factors that affect the choice of lure: the wind, weather, season, air pressure, the water's level and colour, its temperature and clarity, and the type of bottom – sandy or muddy, vegetated or bare, flat or rolling. Lakes or waterways, and the times of day you fish at – such as morning, evening, or in bright sunshine – are further variables. In addition, of course, the choice will depend on the fish's spawning, migrations, feeding habits, and the preyfish in your water. These are factors you cannot do much about, but must adapt to.

When spinning, however, a fisherman has full control over certain essentials: how the lure is presented – at what depth and retrieval speed – and its colour, gait and size. In sum, adeptness at spinning does call for a fair share of experience.

The right lure in the right situation

Experienced fishermen know that faith in a particular lure can be more important than the lure itself. This is undoubtedly because a believer in the lure's superiority fishes with greater self-confidence and presents it more attractively. Greater experience also brings a better ability to choose baits that attract fish in given situations, and to present them in a manner realistic for the fish. However, this depends on the fish being willing to bite. Presenting the right bait correctly is thus not enough: one has to fish at the right place and time as well. Coaxing a scared, sluggish or sated fish onto the hook is much harder than tricking an active and hungry one...

Fishing in fresh waters
Pike

The pike (*Esox lucius*) is one of the biggest predators in fresh water, and a more popular quarry today than ever before. It inhabits lakes, pools, rivers and streams, ranging from northern Norway to Italy and far into Asia, as well as in much of the eastern and northeastern United States, Canada and Alaska. However, pike are not happy in Arctic, deep, cold lakes or high mountain waters. Like numerous other freshwater species, they tolerate a certain salt content. They can live in seas with salinity up to 0.7% and are therefore also common in, for example, large parts of the Baltic.

Pike have all the hallmarks of a good sportfish. Their way of life, appearance, and ability to grow heavy are fascinating to many sportfishermen. In Europe their weights exceed those in America. Pike of around 20 kilograms (44 pounds) are landed every year by Europeans, while the limits are 15-18 kg (33-40 lbs) in North America, although most places yield pike of up to 6-7 kg (13-15 lbs). This species also has some close relatives. The chain pickerel, weighing up to 1.5 kg (3.3 lbs), and two even smaller species, occur only in North America. Another instance is the muskellunge, and Asia boasts the Amur pike.

Spinning for pike

A hungry pike is not hard to get on the hook, but as a rule the fishing calls for an awareness of spinning methods and baits, and of the pike's holding places. In early spring, late autumn and winter, the water is cold and you have to retrieve slowly. Artificial lures should be worked across the bottom with many spin-stops, alternating slow and rapid retrieval. Between late spring and early autumn, the warmer water increases the fish's activity, so the retrieval must be livelier and still more varied.

Spinning for pike can be categorized by the depth of water involved. In shallow water, light spoons of thin sheet metal

Pike are a popular species of sportfish in numerous countries, mainly because this gluttonous predator can grow very large and is common in many waters. It can also offer exciting and spectacular fishing.

Vital facts

When the water warms up in spring, the pike prepare to spawn. A female pike grows larger than males, and is followed by one or more of them during the mating. Her eggs hatch after 10-15 days and the fry live on food such as small insects and larvae. Once a few centimetres long, the young pike begins to eat fish fry. It grows fastest in water with plenty of preyfish whose sizes suit its successive years of growth. The pike has a vigorous appetite and prefers preyfish weighing 10-15% as much as it does. If the preyfish are abundant, it usually eats a big meal 1-2 times weekly, instead of constantly chasing little fish. This manner of hunting characterizes stocks of large pike, while small pike are in a continuous state of growth and therefore feed more often. Probably as a result, the pike is famous for rising to bite in particular periods. It is also cannibalistic, and it eats a great deal besides fish – including frogs, water voles, and young birds.

Pike hunt chiefly by using their sight, but have well-developed senses of taste and smell – as is shown by the ease of catching them with dead baitfish. They are most active in daylight, and studies have revealed that they become almost totally inactive in darkness.

Though normally staying at the bottom, pike are sometimes found much higher up. Thus, it is not quite true that pike are typical bottom-fish dwelling among reeds and tree roots. They are especially active in autumn and just after spawning. During these periods, too, they often occur in the shallows. Summer brings them into deeper water, for example at submerged edges and shoals. But in cold climates, as in Scandinavia and Canada, you can fish for big pike in shallow water throughout the summer.

are used. Small spinners of 7-12 grams are classic lures for pike, but light spinners with large spoons and a high gait are also very effective. Floating plugs are superb when spinning in shallow water. As soon as the water temperature rises, surface plugs start to pay off among reeds, water-lilies and other vegetation. Even the biggest surface plugs, such as the Suick, do excellently in shallows.

In wider lakes, pike move to deep water during the late spring. Once they go below 3-4 metres, however, heavier equipment is needed. Before the retrieval begins, the lures should be given time to sink to the bottom, since that is where the pike are lurking.

Heavy drags of 25-35 and sinking plugs are fine in deep water. As you retrieve, many pauses should be made, enabling the lure to stay at the bottom all the time. Fishing with weighted, floating plugs may also be effective. The line or leader is weighted according to the depth, the retrieval speed, and the plug's size and weight. Small plugs, of course, require less weighting than big ones.

Weight-forward spinners are the only type of spinner that works well for pike in deep water. This type is used down to 8-10 metres.

A pike's jaws are endowed with hundreds of teeth that can quickly shred the line, so it is always essential to use a steel leader when spinning. A leader 20-35 cm (8-14 in) long is perfect, but you can tie your own leaders with, for example, nylon line of 0.65-0.75 mm.

Pike fishing with natural bait

The practice of fishing with dead or live baitfish is widespread primarily in Great Britain and Central Europe, where this tradition has existed for ages. It is most effective in coloured and hard-fished waters, especially during the cold months and when the holding places of pike tend to be well-defined and

---

Left: When a pike is on the take, it seldom proves hard to tempt with a spinner, spoon or wobbler. Often, though, one must know where the pike are holding, and adapt one's spinning method accordingly.

Right: Among the most effective lures when spinning for pike is a wobbler (plug), whose movements and shape imitate the fish's natural prey quite well. A wobbler can also be fished at nearly all depths, and is thus able to trick deeply dwelling big pike onto the hook.

familiar. Compared to the mobility of spinning, every form of fishing with natural bait has a limited degree of water coverage – yet experience shows that large pike are often caught with baitfish.

The majority of live baitfish with lengths of 10-20 cm (4-8 in) can be used, such as roach, bleak and other whitefish. However, it is forbidden to use live baitfish in several countries, including Norway, Holland and Germany. Fishing with dead baitfish is usually done with roach and herring, but pieces of eel have also proved their worth.

There are two main ways of fishing with baitfish. One is float-fishing, with a fixed or sliding float, depending on the water depth. The baits can be presented either at the bottom or in free water. The other method is bottom-fishing with a fixed or sliding tackle, possibly combined with a sliding float.

Both live and dead baitfish are mounted with a treble hook in the tail. Many pike fishermen use two treble hooks for dead bait – one in the tail and one in the side. The hooks are placed with their tips pointing backward, since the pike normally take the prey crosswise and turn it in their jaws, then swallow it with the head forward. This fishing employs a steel leader 35-40 cm (14-16 in) long. In the case of dead baitfish, one often uses a bite indicator, and usually fishes with two rods at the same time. Treble hooks of sizes 4-10, depending on how big the preyfish are, serve ideally here. The best size for baitfish is 15-20 cm (6-8 in).

Spinning with dead baitfish is also enjoyed in some countries. Most simply, the baitfish is mounted with a treble hook in the upper and lower jaws, and another in the side. Then the baitfish is weighted with lead on the leader, and retrieved slowly or in jerks. Floats may also be used for simple spinning.

Ready-made tackle for spinning with baitfish is available as

Natural baits can be extremely rewarding in some types of water. But this fishing requires much greater knowledge of the fish's locations than does spinning with artificial lures. Perch and roach are common baitfish, and other small fish can also appeal to pike.

well. Such a tackle consists of two or three small treble hooks, a leaded head, and a loop which is run into the baitfish. In recent years an East European tackle, the Drakovitch, has won notable popularity for spinning with dead baitfish. It simplifies a type of tackle that has existed for decades in Central Europe. The retrieval is done in jerks near the bottom with repeated spin-stops.

Fighting and landing the fish

During the fight, an even and strong pressure is kept on the pike, and in shallow waters it does its best to leap. In many countries, fish are traditionally released to the water. For this purpose, a pike can be either beached or else landed with a large hand-net. But a net is unsuitable when you fish with big plugs, since the hooks easily catch in its meshes. A gaff is also commonly used in some countries, being carefully drawn into the lower jaw corner. Alternatively, the pike can be gripped beneath the gill with a leather or working glove. Small pike may be landed by taking a firm grip over the neck.

Small pike can be landed easily with a steady grip over the neck, but for larger ones a net or gaff should be used. An important point is to tire the pike out thoroughly before landing it, since otherwise it may shake itself off the hook. Once it is weary, it can be led into the net – which should then be in the water – and lifted.

Muskellunge

The musky (*Esox masquinongy*) is a relative of the pike that occurs in the northeastern United States and in southeastern Canada from Lake Abitibi down to Lake of the Woods. Farther south, it lives in the upper Mississippi and Ohio Rivers, in New York, Pennsylvania and Tennessee, North Carolina and Georgia, as well as in the St. Lawrence River and the Great Lakes. It can grow larger than pike – up to 25 kg (55 lbs). Excessive sportfishing for decades has decimated its stocks, and examples over 10 kg (22 lbs) are now rare. Yet specimens of 10-15 kg (22-33 lbs) are still caught every year in, for example, the St. Lawrence and its tributaries. While even so-called professional sportfishermen must devote several days to hooking a musky, it is considered by many to be the ultimate "pikefish".

Vital facts

The musky spawns in shallow water, preferably on a smooth bottom with tree roots and branches, at about the same temperature as for pike – but the spawning occurs at night. Afterward, the musky stays in shallow clear water, around vegetation banks, seldom at depths of more than 4-5 metres.

Occasionally these fish wander out to deeper water, where they are nearly impossible to catch. In rivers, they prefer the deep calm parts, and their most typical holding places are at inflows. They stay in the same areas during most of the summer, although the warmth in rivers often makes them migrate higher up.

Musky grow fast, and eat like gluttons in springtime. Late summer and especially autumn are regarded as best for musky fishing. The females become larger than the males, and the growth is most rapid in the northern latitudes of distribution. One musky of 69.7 lbs (31.6 kg) has been age-determined to 30 years. The fish's menu is identical to the pike's, as is its way of hunting.

Left: The musky, a close relative of the pike, occurs only in North America. It normally weighs 11-22 lbs (5-10 kg) and is caught chiefly in autumn, with artificial or natural baits.

Among other terms for this fish are muskalonge, lunge, blue pike and muskallunge. It is long and slender, somewhat paler than a pike, and has distinct wide vertical stripes. There are three subspecies within the musky's region of distribution. It is thought to have originally lived in salt water and migrated up the Mississippi – where the stocks were isolated due to the Ice Age, and from where it later spread out. Fossils show that it also existed in southern Europe during the Tertiary period.

Spinning for musky

Musky can be caught both by spinning and with natural bait on tackle, but spinning is the usual method. In general, rapid retrieval gives the best results. Large "bucktail" spinners, spinnerbaits and buzzbaits are designed for musky. This was originally also true of many of the surface plugs which are now used for pike.

Most big muskellunge are females, and are normally caught in September and October – often during the afternoon. Musky fishing demands a lot of patience. The fish is a loner and frequently needs a great number of casts to be tempted into taking. Pike may follow the bait once or twice before taking, but this behaviour is more typical of musky.

Right: A "freshwater crocodile" has taken the bait and tries desperately to get free of it during the fight's last phase.

Zander

The European pikeperch, or zander (*Stizostedion lucioperca*), is naturally distributed across Eastern Europe, Russia and southern Siberia. From there it has spread to western Europe and occurs from southern Scandinavia down to the northern parts of Italy and Spain. It has even been implanted in Great Britain, though not appreciated by English anglers. Zander also live in brackish water, and can be found throughout the Baltic.

A close relative is the Volga zander, in southeastern Europe as well as much of Russia and Siberia. In the United States and Canada are two others – the walleye and sauger.

This fish enjoys murky water, where it faces no competition from pike. It hunts smaller fish such as roach, bleak and perch. Wide waters are its preferred habitat, to depths of at least 4-5 metres.

Spinning for zander

Sight, smell and hearing are all used by zander when they hunt. But the spinning technique used for pike has no impact on these fish, since they cannot swim as fast or see as well. The key to zander fishing is slow retrieval with good bottom contact and, ideally, bait that "jabs" the bottom – thus relying on the fish's hearing and sight.

Probably one of the best types of artificial lures for zander is the jig. Its special body and upturned hook also make it easy to fish just over the bottom.

A jerky retrieval creates sounds that attract pikeperch. Jigs with silicone bodies are extremely effective. The combination of a jig with fish strips is arousing, too, as it activates the zander's sense of smell. Many scent-impregnated rubber bodies work superbly on zander. In all seasons and water temperatures, you should retrieve slowly and jerkily, though a bit faster during the hot months. A jig performs as spectacularly in still waters as in flowing waters, where the zander prefer deep channels with stones and considerable current.

Weight-forward spinners are well suited to spinning for zander. They not only give better bottom contact, but can be

Pikeperch are active in darkness, and spend most of their time at the bottom in deep water. They should be fished by retrieving slowly and trying to keep in contact with the bottom.

retrieved in jerks and continue to rotate as they sink. Moreover, the spinner head generates clear sounds when it hits the bottom.

Spinning with a plug – which may be a "deep-going" type with a rattle and a long bill – is unbeatable for zander. The rattle makes sounds that attract the fish while the deep-diving plug's spoon jabs the bottom. It was once commonly believed that zander are partial to small preyfish, and thus also small

baits, but with experience they are found to gobble even big plugs of up to 20 cm (8 in).

No matter what type of artificial bait you use, false bites are frequent, and time alone can teach you to distinguish "bottom contact" from a zander's cautious nibble. Hence it is important to use needle-sharp hooks and, if possible, replace the treble hook with a thinner one – especially in water with lots of little zander.

Vital facts

Zander spawn from late March until the beginning or middle of April, at a higher temperature than for pike. The sticky eggs are laid on branches and stones in shallow water. River mouths, too, are favourite spawning places. After a few weeks the spawning ends, when the temperature reaches 15-16° C (59-61° F). But windy weather can quickly silt up the eggs and the spawning bottoms. This is one reason why zander stocks are classified according to good and bad years.

Soon after hatching, young zander eat water-fleas and plankton. Next they adopt a menu of fish fry and small fish. Similarly to pike, they are also cannibalistic.

The zander has a special way of hunting, which is shown by its shape and body structure. Being less slender than the pike, it cannot swim fast. Yet its night vision is excellent, and it has large eyes that shine like reflectors in a lamp's light. It is built to live on the bottom, where it can follow prey for long distances. The prey is attacked from behind. Zander in general are active fish in cloudy weather and at night.

During the summer, zander move out to the shoals and edges in deep water. At evening and night, they return to hunt in shallow water or higher levels. Towards morning when it gets light, they swim back to the depths. These daily migrations also occur in autumn. During that season and in winter, they often run up rivers and streams. Zander always prefer hard bottoms – stone, sand, cliffs and banks. Small ones are quite sociable and frequently form little schools to stay in limited areas. Large zander are usually solitary.

It is typical for a stock of zander that the fishing is good for some years but then deteriorates. Such variations are presumably due to the supply of prey-fish. Many waters contain zander of 1-3 kg (2.2-6.6 lbs) and bigger ones only exceptionally. In other waters, there can be a few years of fine fishing for medium or large zander, whereupon the fish die out – to revive a few years later. Examples of 1-2.5 kg are the rule, while weights of 5-8 kg (11-18 lbs) are rare and the maximum is 12-14 kg (26-31 lbs).

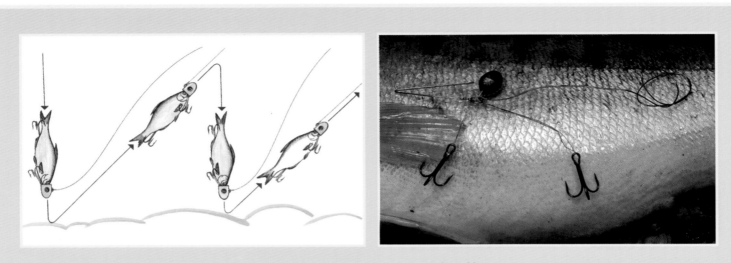

When fishing with natural bait, the weighted baitfish is fished in with repeated spin-stops and good bottom contact. The upper picture shows a so-called Drakovitch rig, with a shackle that is run into the baitfish's belly.

Keep in mind that zander are most active by dark – whether in the morning, evening, night, or during cloudy and windy days. On the whole, low-pressure weather is best. On bright days the fish must be sought in deep water. Particularly during winter and just before it ices up, shallow water can yield zander. What the species may lack in fighting spirit – compared for example to pike and trout – it definitely outweighs with its unpredictable behaviour, which has thrilled sportfishermen down the centuries. Besides, it is a marvelous food fish.

Zander fishing with natural bait

The zander's manner of using its senses make it a true challenge to catch with natural baitfish. It bites somewhat hesitantly and may be shy. A sliding tackle is therefore best used. This allows the fish to swim away with the bait and feel no resistance from the sinker. You can also combine sliding tackle with a sliding float.

An electronic bite indicator is employed when you have fish strips, fillets, or dead baitfish on the hook. A steel leader is not necessary, but this or some other strong leader material is worth using, since the fishing often takes place in waters that also contain pike. A nylon leader of 0.35-0.40 mm is quite adequate, unless you fish in areas with roots, stones and other obstacles that the fish can exploit.

When fishing with live baitfish, the treble hook is inserted in the back or tail, or between the dorsal and tail fins. With dead baitfish or fish strips, though, it is stuck in the tail root or the thin part of the strip. Use hooks of size 6-10 according to the bait's size. Baitfish of 12-16 cm (4.5-6.5 in) are fine for zander.

All fishing with natural bait is done on, or just over, the bottom. During the night, zander move upward in the water, so at a lake's shoals and edges it is occasionally best to fish a couple of metres above the bottom.

Opposite left: The pikeperch is not famous for being a great fighter, but it is an excellent foodfish. Since it can be difficult to hook, sharp and slender hooks are often necessary.

Opposite right: Being relatively shy, a pikeperch frequently takes the bait with careful hesitation. Gliding tackle is thus usually best for catching it, either at the bottom or some metres up.

Perch

The perch (*Perca fluviatilis*) occurs all over Europe, Asia and North America, except in the Arctic regions and in clear, cold mountain lakes. It also enjoys brackish water and is common along the Baltic coasts. There are perch in the smallest meres as well as the biggest lakes and rivers. This fish is easily recognized by the black stripes over its back, and its red or yellow fins. Its colours tend to be strongest in clear water. It weighs from a few tenths of a kilogram up to 2-3 kg (4.4-6.6 lbs).

Spinning for perch

Because of their capricious inclination to take bait, perch provide exciting experiences for sportfishermen. One day they may attack whatever moves, and the next day you may try everything in the bait-box with no results. If a perch follows a spoon, spinner, jig or plug without biting, this is a sign of unwillingness. A varied retrieval with many spin-stops and tugs is then important. Impulsive and unusual methods of

Vital facts

Perch spawn in shallow water during early spring, and then move to deeper water. While the perch in shallow lakes and rivers pursue a vagabond life, big lakes contain both pelagic perch that hunt in deep water, and typical shallow-water perch that occur near the shores almost all year round.

Being a distinctively predatory fish, the perch prefers clear water – but in murky water its spawning opportunities are often better, and neither its eggs nor young are as easily noticed by other fish. Thus coloured waters tend to have abundant stocks of small perch.

This is a sociable fish and usually lives in schools of varying size. They gather at deep edges, shoals, in deep parts of streams, at boat piers or bridge pillars. A school also gives good protection against higher predators.

retrieval are frequently essential to attract such perch. Even a particular movement may be what triggers their reflex – or a certain colour of bait, since perch have excellent colour vision. Once the first perch has taken bait, it commonly starts a chain reaction and others do so as well.

Perch are not confined to the bottom: often they occur 2-3 metres up. During the summer, they may hunt small fish in the surface, and their presence in big lakes is often revealed by diving gulls. It is therefore wise to search a body of water in different ways, for example at the bottom, just above it, in the middle layer and at the surface.

However wild and greedy the perch is when biting, it can be sly and unreachable when, for instance, the weather makes it unwilling. There are many indications that its mood is influenced by the air pressure. A stable low or high pressure is normally good for the fishing, yet a rapidly falling or rising pressure may lead perch virtually to stop hunting. Still, some sportfishermen have quite the opposite impression about how air pressure affects the fishing.

Spinning for perch can be pursued with almost all types of artificial lures, but certain types do work better than others. Spinners and small spoons are traditionally used in shallow waters, although fishing with a jig is usually best. In deep waters, great success is often achieved with a heavier jig, a lead-headed spinner, or deep-going sinking plugs.

Using a dropper, a little fly or micro-jig, above the lure is a fine trick to play on perch. Their innate curiosity, together with envy of the little prize, can provoke a bite. Slow, jerky retrieval is especially worthwhile with dropper flies, which can also be baited with worms, larvae, or a piece of fish skin. Moreover, perch love strong or contrasting colours such as red/black, orange/yellow and white/red. Marked "eyes" on a jig may yield further attraction.

Opposite: Characteristic of a perch are its black transverse stripes from the back down toward the abdomen, and red or orange-yellow fins. The clearer the water is, the stronger the colours tend to be.

Bass

The American bass may well be the most popular sportfish in the world. There are six species and four subspecies of American black bass, but in practice they are divided into smallmouth bass (*Micropterus dolomieu*), weighing up to 4 kg (8.8 lbs), and largemouth bass (*Micropterus salmoides*) which can weigh nearly 10 kg (22 lbs). These have different distributions. Smallmouth bass originally lived in the northeastern United States and southeastern Canada, and have not spread as far as largemouth bass. The latter first inhabited the eastern USA, from the Great Lakes to Florida and the prairies, but has spread by implantation and now occurs in all the western states. It has also been quite successfully implanted in Mexico and Central America, as in Guatemala and Costa Rica. The same was done in Cuba as early as 1915, and it exists in Hawaii. Largemouth bass even reached Brazil in 1926, and can be found in 16 African countries such as Morocco and South Africa.

In 1879 an English biologist brought the bass to Europe, and it was implanted in many countries – including Hungary, Austria, Switzerland and Russia – but died out. Today there are small stocks in the southern parts of Germany and France, although it is more widespread in Italy and Spain. At most places in Europe it weighs hardly over 2 kg (4.4 lbs), but Spain has the best bass waters and yields specimens up to 5 kg (11 lbs).

In the USA, bass have spread along with people, being regarded as a good "reserve fish" to keep on farms. All canals, lakes, rivers, reservoirs and small ponds now contain bass. These fish tolerate high temperature, multiply easily and grow fast. Their inability to live in many countries is due to their need of warm water at 20° C (68° F) during May and June, when they spawn. On the other hand, they survive in water up to 30° C (86° F). Yet they cannot take murky or muddy waters, and have thus done poorly in many African countries, whose rivers are often turbid.

Bass are extremely popular sportfish, notably in the USA. They occur in both deep and shallow waters, but are typical warm-water fish, so one usually finds them in the water areas with highest temperature.

Vital facts

After the spawning, which takes place in shallow water, fishermen begin to spin for bass. However, the fishing depends on the weather and improves as it gets warmer. Bass have a broad diet – from small worms and insects to fish fry, small fish, mice and frogs. They often behave sociably and may move in little schools, groups or "packs", but are also found individually.

As a rule, bass alternate between deep and shallow water but do not go very far. They presumably maintain territories and spend most of the time there at the bottom. When encountered in shallow water, they stay near vegetation – reeds, lilies, trees, and whatever else can provide shade or protection, as well as edible small fish.

Bass fishing is not difficult once you find the quarry. This is the real problem, besides deciding the right type of artificial bait. At the start of the season, the bass are in shallow water where the temperature is highest, and as it approaches 20-21° C (68-70° F) your chances improve. Later in the season, when the water gets too warm, the bass move to deeper water and must be sought at the bottom – very seldom in the middle layer. While they linger among plants and stones in shallow water, deep water finds them at reefs, edges and shoals, as preyfish gather there too. In the morning and evening, the bass return to shallow water along the shores – and notably in vegetated waters, fishing in the morning is best of all. Towards autumn and winter, the bass are again wherever the temperature is highest.

Spinning for bass

Bass fishing is not easy in deep water, and the finest experiences are obtained in shallows that help you to hook the fish. A bass can see extremely well, which makes the bait's colour important, but it is still more essential to retrieve slowly at depth along the bottom. However, even if this applies to four out of five fishing trips, the fifth may show that a rapid retrieval is better. Generally, you should retrieve near the bottom, although there are rare occasions when bass can actually be caught at the surface – for example during the morning and evening. Of course, surface fishing for bass is more common in shallow clear lakes, ponds and rivers.

Fishing with a jig is the oldest and most widespread method of spinning for bass. But it requires the fisherman to have control over the bait's movements, since the jig itself shows little life during a uniform retrieval with no variations. Proper jig fishing involves casting out, letting the jig sink, and then spinning it in with short tugs – slowly or with rapid changes of movement.

The fishing is easy over smooth bottoms, but it becomes much harder in areas that are rolling, vegetated, or full of trees and roots. Particularly for smallmouth bass, it is necessary to fish at the bottom, because this species tends to stay on bottoms with stones and cliffs. Largemouth bass are more readily caught somewhat above the bottom, as they are drawn to plants and other sources of shade.

When fishing from a boat in shallow water, you can benefit by using spinnerbait. This is retrieved in the surface at first and then allowed to sink, so as to attract the attention of bass.

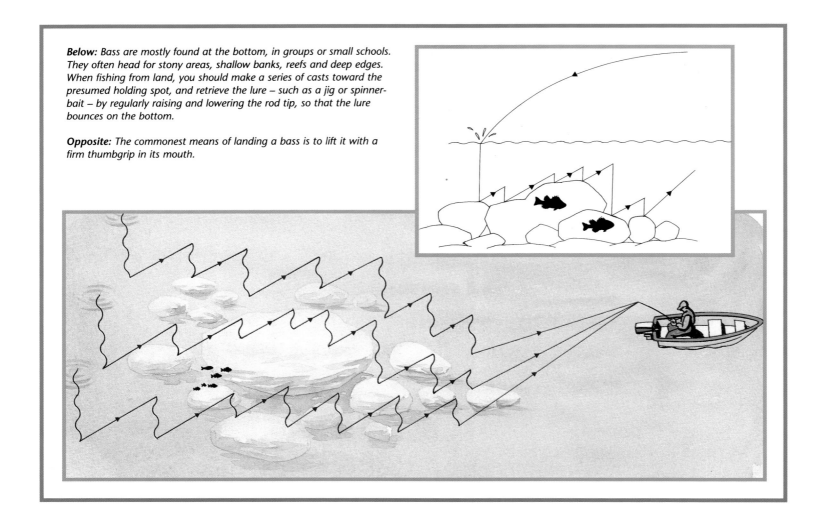

Below: *Bass are mostly found at the bottom, in groups or small schools. They often head for stony areas, shallow banks, reefs and deep edges. When fishing from land, you should make a series of casts toward the presumed holding spot, and retrieve the lure – such as a jig or spinnerbait – by regularly raising and lowering the rod tip, so that the lure bounces on the bottom.*

Opposite: *The commonest means of landing a bass is to lift it with a firm thumbgrip in its mouth.*

Spoons, spinners, and all sorts of plugs – surface types, sinking and floating – are excellent both in shallow water and out to several metres of depth. In deeper water, deep-diving plugs and weight-forward spinners are recommended. There is no doubt, however, that most sportfishermen find greater excitement in fishing the shallows with surface plugs, as well as with plastic worms. These long silicone creatures are mounted on a hook, forming a so-called Texas rig, which comes in different versions.

As in so many other kinds of sportfishing, one should fish for bass with thin lines and small baits on a bright day in clear water. Warm days and periods call for concentration on the morning hours, starting to fish before it gets light. A rippled surface is often more advantageous than mirror-smooth water. You should also keep quiet and avoid making noise in a boat or with its engine

Bass fishing with natural bait

If the fishing is slack, natural baits are frequently best – such as small live fish, lampreys, bee larvae, grasshoppers, sala-mander, crustaceans, leeches and worms. All kinds of natural bait for bass should be set on a single hook, so that they look more lively. Use as little weighting as possible – and as small a float as possible, if you prefer to fish with a float. Once the bait sinks after the cast, be sure that the bass can easily pull out line when it bites, and then make your strike.

Right: Many sportfishermen consider plastic worms to be a thrilling way of catching bass. No matter whether you use a Texas or Carolina rig, the fish can hardly resist the long silicon worm on it – as this largemouth bass learned.

Far right: Just as for many other species, the "golden hours" of morning and evening are generally best for bass.

Bluegill

The bluegill (*Lepomis macrochirus*) is a popular "public fish" in the United States. Its colours differ widely between waters, but it often has 6-8 stripes across its back and sides, which may be yellowish or dark blue. It seldom weighs more than 1 kg (2.2 lbs), although some are nearly twice as heavy. Bluegill were originally distributed from Minnesota down to the Great Lakes, southward to Georgia and westward to Arkansas. Today the species is implanted in numerous small ponds in almost every state.

Spinning for bluegill

Catching a bluegill is commonly the first fishing experience for a child, and the pleasure of it may last a lifetime. This is an entertaining, wild and bite-crazy fish, taking the tiniest of artificial lures – spinners, spoons, and primarily jigs. As a rule, one succeeds best with a slow, varied retrieval. But you may well have to try different types of bait before you find just the one that triggers the fish's reflex. At times, the very first cast attracts a bite – and next a whole school can dissolve as soon as the bait hits the water. In any case, wherever the first bluegill is caught, more of them are likely to be available. An imaginative retrieval with light equipment can yield many fine rewards.

Panfish is a collective name for bluegill, crappie, perch and "white perch". Here we see a bluegill, which not only tastes fine but is also an enjoyable sportfish, taking either artificial or natural baits.

Vital facts

Bluegill live in clear, small ponds and lakes with vegetation, overhanging and fallen trees, but can also be found in city environments such as parks. The fish spawn in May and, for a few days, the fry are protected by the male. They grow slowly, often resulting in overpopulation of the water. Their diet consists of larvae, water insects, crustaceans, and occasionally small fish or fry. Bluegill tend to occur in rather shallow water, although big ones are sometimes caught in deeper areas. They swim in dispersed schools of no great size.

Bluegill fishing with natural bait

Perhaps the most familiar way of catching bluegill today is with a float, a single leader, a couple of lead shot, and a worm on a small hook. Yet combinations of artificial and natural baits are frequently better, such as small jigs baited with mealworm, earthworm or larvae.

sides. They often weigh up to 1 kg (2.2 lbs) and the record exceeds 2 kg. Both species are just as generous and willing to bite as the bluefish.

Spinning for crappies

Crappies also resemble bluegill in being a great challenge to catch with ultra-light spinning gear. The smallest spinners, spoons and plugs are very effective, but jigs are probably the best choice, since the fish often circulate in overgrown waters and in places with vegetation, branches and rough bottoms. The fish stay at the bottom regardless of whether it is in a sunny, shallow cove or in deep water.

Crappie fishing with natural bait

These fish eagerly take natural bait. A single float with a leader, and a hook baited with a worm or a small fish, are convenient and profitable. As in fishing for bluegill, you can also use artificial lures – chiefly jigs that are baited with a fish strip, a whole little fish, worms, larvae or some other accessible bait. Normally baited jigs are used, but the fish then needs a bit more time to swallow the bait before you strike. Crappies have a large mouth and are tired out by keeping an even pressure on the line with no jerks.

Vital facts

Crappies thrive in lakes, ponds, and slow-flowing rivers or streams throughout the USA. Black crappie is most common in the northern states, while the white species occurs in the south. They enjoy clear water with vegetation and overhanging trees – mainly willows – where shade and protection are provided by rich plant life. Enthusiastic crappie fishermen thus often build shelters in the water, for example with mats made of reeds or branches.

The fish can be caught by either day or night, from some time after spawning until the autumn. Dusk, however, is regarded as the best hour. This is a popular quarry for ice-fishing, too. Like bluegill, crappies can overpopulate the water. They live on insects, worms, crustaceans, fry and small fish.

Crappie

Here is another extremely popular fish, which – along with bluegill, perch and "white perch" – is known as panfish, since all of them are wonderful to eat. The two species are black crappie (*Pomoxis nigromaculatus*), which has black patches spread over its sides, and white crappie (*Pomoxis annularis*) whose patches are merged into stripes across its back and

Catfish

A catfish is easily recognized by its flat head, which comprises 20% of the body – and by its "beard" of barbels, or feelers, which are a tenth as long as the body. Catfish occur on every continent, and there are hundreds of species in the world. Apart from the sturgeon, and carp species in the Amazon and eastern Asia, catfish are among the biggest of all fish in fresh waters. The European wels (*Siluris glanis*) grows largest, to over 200 kg (440 lbs), followed by other species in the Amazon and Mekong Rivers, while the smallest catfish in the group Silurodei are only a few centimetres long.

A further example is the electric catfish, *Malapterus electricus*, which can generate up to 350 volts. In the United States are several species, such as the flathead and the blue catfish, weighing as much as 25-50 kg (55-110 lbs). Channel catfish are also common, but they seldom weigh more than 8-9 kg (18-20 lbs).

The wels originally lived in Central and Eastern Europe as well as in Asia. It has spread to, and been implanted in, many countries – and today it inhabits a number of rivers in France, Italy, Spain and Germany. The northern limit of its distribution runs through southern Sweden and Finland and the Baltic.

Spinning for catfish

One can scarcely believe that catfish, with their relatively poor eyesight and dependence on dusk or murky water for much activity, will take a plug or spoon – but the fact is that they do. They are intrigued by preyfish that appear sick or move oddly, and this is a basic feature of spinning. Artificial baits should be brought in with jerks and, at the same time, hit the bottom. Two types of lure are most suited to such retrieval, plugs and large jigs, even though spoons and spinners can also trick catfish.

The colours are not very important when spinning, but strongly coloured or fluorescent plugs have proved effective. The plugs should be retrieved with regular impacts on the bottom. Large jigs, perhaps combined with fish strips, or whole

Catfish can be very big and are then eager for large prey, so they are usually caught with natural baits – especially fish weighing up to about 3.5 lbs (1.5 kg).

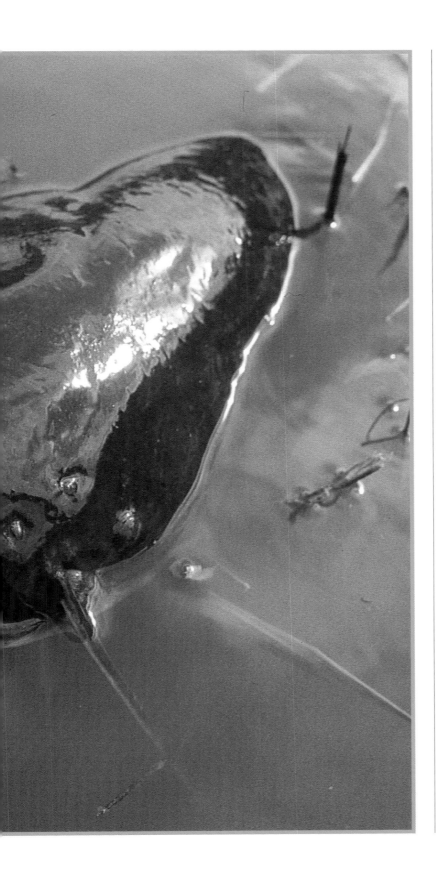

Vital facts

These fish are typically adapted to warm water and become most active in summertime. They spawn in shallow water when the temperature is at least 20° C (68° F). Their eggs are laid on branches, roots and plant remains. The fry grow rather fast, are 30-40 cm (12-16 in) long after two years, and measure 50-80 cm (20-32 in) after 3-4 years.

To begin with, the young eat mostly larvae, worms and fish fry. Soon they are big enough to consume water voles, frogs and the like. Catfish are also cannibalistic, but their greediness is debatable. They eat less in comparison to their weight than, for example, pike do – for catfish are not as active. It is known from fish farms that a catfish must eat 6-7 kg (13-15 lbs) of fish for every kilogram of weight it gains.

When the catfish attains a certain size, it occupies a territory and forms a stock there. Catfish are found in lakes, but rarely in very deep water. They occupy the calm parts of rivers and streams, although seldom the deepest holes. Avoiding currents, they are drawn to areas with fallen or overhanging trees that offer shade and shelter. Tributaries from other rivers are also attractive holding places.

While catfish can be caught by day, they are quite active at night. Traditionally good times for fishing are the evening, night and dawn. Their activity is notably dependent on the temperature, and increases primarily when it gets warmer, whereas less warmth can make them almost completely stop biting. Thunderstorms with rain and a rising level of unclear water, too, can heighten their activity. Then they enter shallow waters to feed – but with a sinking level of clearer water, they lapse into inactivity. Catfish are preferably caught with live or naturally dead bait, and spinning for them has become more frequent in recent years.

fish on jig bodies, are superb as well. Moreover, whole fish on a tackle like the Drakovitch have become popular in spinning.

Catfish do not have "dangerous" teeth, so a leader of 0.50-0.70 mm is sufficient for spinning – as resistance to bottom stones and other obstacles, rather than to the fish's teeth. Often a catfish follows the lure and misses a few bites before it is hooked. You should cast repeatedly over a place where catfish are thought to be, since they are attracted by the lure's impact on the surface and its gait along the bottom. This fishing, of course, calls for strong spinning equipment and a reel that holds lots of thick line, such as 0.40-0.60 mm.

Catching catfish with natural bait

Natural baits are demonstrably effective on a night-hunter like the catfish, and are used by almost everyone who fishes for it. The bait may be dead or live fish, fillets or halves of fish, liver, earthworm snippets, leeches, and meat from mammals – even live or dead frogs, in countries where this bait is permitted. Among the classic types of bait are hen intestines and innards. Baitfish can weigh 100-500 grams, according to the size of fish you are after.

Bottom fishing with a sliding float and sliding tackle is the commonest method. At night, a bite indicator is used. When fishing from a boat, paternoster tackle is a standard accessory.

Many holding places of catfish are overgrown with vegetation, branches, roots and diverse hindrances. One fishes with a sliding float and fixed tackle, possibly of the paternoster type, and ideally somewhat above the bottom in order to avoid obstacles. Small catfish, in particular, often go higher over the bottom to take baitfish, and can thus be caught in the surface as well.

Observations show that catfish move away from their holding places twice each day – just before sunrise, and just before sunset – to hunt for food. Therefore, many fishermen concentrate on these times, unless they are familiar with a holding place and can serve the bait exactly on or near it.

The equipment must be strong, especially at places with plenty of obstacles. Frequent use is made of line up to 0.65 mm, on multiplier or spinning reels. A very strong, metre-long leader of nylon, steel wire, or kevlar may be needed to resist branches, roots and stones.

There is also a Hungarian attractor, the "kuttjer". It consists of a short cane with a handle and a little flat head, as big as a large coin. Used chiefly when fishing from a boat, it is swung down into the water with a regular rhythm, every 1.5-2 seconds. Its sound resembles the pop of a champagne cork, and brings up catfish to bite. This device has become common in many countries, on both drifting and anchored boats.

Striking, fighting and landing the fish

When spinning, you must give a strike as soon as you feel a catfish taking, or spitting out, an artificial lure. But if fishing with natural bait, you should delay the strike a few seconds. Since the catfish's mouth is hard, the strike must be stiff – and it may have to be repeated, so that you know the hook is driven in. Catfish are in the habit of immediately, after the strike, heading back to their shelter among fallen trees or branches.

The fish should be held strongly, as it is very tough and persistent. During the fight, it often stays at the same place and can be difficult to get moving. You may succeed in making it swim by throwing stones at the place or otherwise frightening it with sounds.

An inexperienced fisherman can land a catfish with a large net, or a gaff in the middle of its lower jaw. The expert frequently uses a working glove to grip its lower jaw, with the thumb in its mouth. But a big fish requires extra manpower, for two hands are often necessary – one around the jaw and one in the gill.

Above: A hefty catfish has been landed after a long, tough struggle. Specimens of this size can scarcely be landed by oneself, and at least two men are needed here.

Left: A "kuttjer" in action. This attractor is slammed repeatedly on the water, and its sounds apparently stimulate catfish to bite.

Trout

The trout (*Salmo trutta*) has demonstrated great adaptability as a species. It occurs in clear, oxygen-rich waters, streams, mountain brooks and lakes, where several forms of it have evolved. In biological terms, the brown trout (*Salmo trutta fario*), the lake-run trout (*S. t. lacustris*), and the sea trout (*S. t. trutta*) belong to the same species. In many waters, all three of these develop from the same fish – depending on whether the offspring stay in flowing water, move into lakes, or migrate to the sea. They acquire different behaviour and colouring, but only a test of their scales can prove which is which.

Brown trout and lake-run trout were originally distributed in Europe – from the Mediterranean to northern Norway and Iceland, westward to the British Isles, and eastward far into Siberia. Trout were introduced to the eastern United States in 1883, then to New Zealand and other continents, such as South America, Africa and parts of Asia. However, these trout are not as tolerant of water temperatures as rainbow trout are. The ones implanted around the world derive from Loch Leven in Scotland, a lake north of Edinburgh that was once famous for its healthy, fast-growing stock of trout.

The size of brown trout varies widely according to their food supply. In European waterways, specimens of 2-3 kg (4.4-6.6 lbs) are unusual, while such weights are common in, for example, New Zealand. The maximum in flowing waters is 10 kg (22 lbs), but anything around 0.5-1 kg (1.1-2.2 lbs) is considered a fine brown trout.

Spinning for trout

The brown trout's manner of life differs between mountain rivers or brooks and the lowlands, whose nutritious, clear, oxygenated streams can make the fish quite selective about food. In flowing waters, the usual method is downstream fishing with spinners, spoons or small plugs. One then searches holding places – holes, furrows, banks of vegetation and so on. In a large waterway, you cast downstream toward the opposite bank, let the bait swing into the current, and retrieve it. Thus you can carry the search metre by metre downstream.

The trout – which, in flowing waters, is a typically territorial fish – lives mainly on insects, but increasingly adopts a fish diet as it grows. Thus it becomes ever easier to fool with spoons, spinners and plugs.

Vital facts

Trout in the northern hemisphere spawn from October until December. The fry become territorial, and this trait is kept throughout their lives in flowing waters. Trout have diverse periods of activity, determined mainly by the supply of insects. Brown trout are active primarily in the morning, evening, and briefly at midday.

Trout consume insects, larvae, worms and fish fry. They usually also develop cannibalistic tendencies. In waterways, about 90% of their food comprises insects that drift with the current, and 10% of surface insects. When hunting, they use their eyesight and, as shown by numerous studies, their lateral line organ.

The holding places of trout are those that enable them to spend as little energy as possible in resisting the current, and where they can find plenty of food – at current edges, shorelines and holes. Brown trout often choose shady places, unlike rainbow trout which happily live in free water.

Trout also live in lakes of all sizes. In a small lake, they cruise about and frequently enter the shore zone. Here they live chiefly on insects, crustaceans, larvae and worms, as well as fish fry. Vegetated areas, promontories, shallows, and stream outlets attract them most. During the summer, they move out to deep water, but often approach land in the morning and evening. While the brown trout in flowing waters can be hard to catch, the fish in lakes are more willing to bite. Consequently, trout have been implanted in many lakes known as "put-and-take" waters, where the sport's quality is determined by the stock and the fishing pressure. In large lakes with inflows that allow the fish to spawn, lake-run stocks with big fish develop. Various European lakes contain lake-run trout, which are either shiny with black spots or bronze-yellow.

A spinner works very well in flowing waters, as it runs smoothly in the current and is easy to guide by moving the rod up, down or sideways.

Insert: *A hooked trout often exposes itself at the surface by leaping and splashing. This habit obviously makes the fishing more fun, since you can see the fish during most of the fight.*

The fish in flowing waters are often shy and see the fisherman at a great distance. It is therefore wise to fish cautiously and throw no shadows on the surface – in other words, make oneself "as little as possible". When fishing downstream, the bait comes from behind and the trout see it for only a moment. They probably do not aim very well at a lure and, hence, often miss the bite, or else follow it and become frightened.

Upstream fishing, which reaches beyond the fish, requires better contact with the lures. These should work in a lively fashion and are retrieved a bit faster than the current speed. The advantage is that the trout sees the lure soon, can "time" its bite, and is usually hooked securely. But upstream fishing is much harder than downstream fishing, because the current keeps the lure working.

A spinner is the best type of bait in flowing water. Its blade's rotation creates a high gait, while the spinner maintains a good "grip" in the water. If you lower the rod, or retrieve more slowly, the spinner goes deeper. When you lift the rod or slightly speed up the retrieval, the spinner will rise in the water. It can be steered in the right path at holding places by moving the rod sideways.

Spoons can also be used in flowing water, though they do not "grip" the water as well as spinners do. A spoon is therefore usually led away from the current – or up toward the surface.

Floating plugs are excellent for fishing in shallow currents. They cannot be cast so far, but you can let them follow the current to within a couple of metres from the holding place and then retrieve. A floating plug may also be weighted, a short distance up on the line. In deeper waterways with relatively strong currents, sinking plugs are used.

Jigs are less common for trout fishing in flowing waters. Yet a jig is easy to cast, sinks rapidly, and is suited especially to fishing in current furrows and deep holes.

The trout in flowing waters are both shy and fastidious. It is not unusual for flyfishing on a popular waterway to catch more trout than spinning does. However, spinning with flies is quite feasible. You weight the line 60-80 cm (24-32 in) up, for example with lead shot, and use a trout fly with a single or double hook – or a small tube fly. The fly can swing in the current, or be retrieved like a spinner.

Trout have good colour vision. The rules for bait colour exist to be broken, of course – but in general one uses silver, nickel, yellow, and fluorescent colours in murky water, high water levels, darkness, and strong winds with surface waves. In clear water, low levels, and bright weather, it is best to try subdued colours and copper, but also dark hues and black.

In lakes or put-and-take waters, the same types of bait are employed, and spoons may be equally profitable. A casting Buldo together with a fly is effective in lakes, too. The Buldo can be attached in two basic ways – sliding and fixed. In the first case, the stopper consists of a swivel, to which is tied a leader

length of 1.2-3.5 metres (4-12 feet) depending, among other things, on the depth and on how shy the trout are. When the fish takes the fly, it can pull line without feeling resistance from the bubble. In the second case, favoured by many sport-fishermen, the casting bubble and a quick strike are combined to hook the fish well.

Trout fishing with natural bait

In small flowing waters, no bait is more effective for trout than a drifting worm on an unweighted line. The worm is fished either upstream or downstream, and the current brings it down toward the trout. In wider or deeper waters, the worm tackle can be weighted with lead shot slightly up on the line.

But the simplest method is to fish with a float and a fairly long leader that is weighted according to the current and

When spinning in flowing water, it is normally best to cast the lure obliquely upstream. Once the lure has sunk, it is retrieved with a taut line along the bottom, and should more or less flutter along. If the current is weak, you may need to liven the lure by tugging with the rod tip, while retrieving slowly to make it bounce along the bottom.

Trout should be played with even pressure and relatively light force on the drag, so that the fish is not prevented from pulling line off the reel if it rushes.

depth. The hook is baited with a worm. The float then drifts with the current while you walk downstream after it or "trot" out line. A pull on the float shows that the trout is biting, but only when it disappears under the surface do you strike.

Substantial waterways are often fished with a tackle that may have a three-way swivel, but using a leader of 80-120 cm (32-48 in) and a sinker on its end. Again the hook is baited with a worm. This tackle is cast obliquely downstream and swings in toward – or over – a holding place, so that you maintain bottom contact.

In a lake, there are two means of fishing with natural bait: the simple tackle with a float – fixed or sliding, depending on the depth – or using a casting bubble and worms, which is retrieved. Both methods are extremely effective in most waters.

Although worms are the classic bait, one can very well fish with larvae, insects, crustaceans, small fish, or other natural baits. During late summer and autumn, or early in spring, waterways can also be fished – where this is allowed – with salmon eggs or the roe of trout and salmon. Eggs and roe are fished with or without a float, or else on bottom tackle which moves in the current.

Fighting the fish

The leaps of trout are well known to all sportfishermen. Yet a trout goes wild only if your drag is set too hard. So you have to follow the strike with an even pressure, letting the fish pull out line if it wants. Then it is landed with a net, or slid up on land if the shore is smooth.

Sea trout

While the sea trout (*Salmo trutta trutta*) is biologically the same species as brown trout, it is anadromous – migrating between marine and fresh waters, swimming up the river where it was born just as salmon do. Originally sea trout were distributed in northern Europe. The stocks now in other parts of the world derive from implanted brown trout, which in some places have formed anadromous stocks – as in New Zealand, Argentina and the Falklands. In eastern North America, a smaller stock of sea trout inhabits, for example, Newfoundland, Nova Scotia, Maine, New York and Connecticut. A true stock of sea trout was first introduced to North America in 1958.

In Europe, sea trout are common in the British Isles, Iceland, the Faeroes, Norway, Sweden, Denmark, Finland, the Baltic region and Poland. There is also a small stock in northern Germany and northern France. Those in the Baltic Sea are notable for rapid growth, and the Mörrum and Emån are well-known streams with large and vigorous sea trout.

Different strains of sea trout vary in their development. At most places, they seldom weigh over 2-3 kg (4.4-6.6 lbs). Large specimens occur in only a few Norwegian rivers, the Swedish Baltic rivers, Danish streams, and some rivers in Poland, the Baltic states and Finland, where they may weigh up to 10-14 kg (22-31 lbs) although the rule is 3-6 kg (6.6-13.2 lbs).

Spinning for sea trout

The methods of fishing for sea trout differ widely in northern European rivers. But the clearer and brighter the water is, the more predominant flyfishing tends to be, while spinning and baitcasting has better chances in relatively dark, murky, deep waterways.

Spinning with spoons, plugs and spinners is done primarily for silvery ascending fish and strongly coloured sea trout. The fish select the same holding places as brown trout, and sea trout are then often caught by spinning downstream. In general, small artificial lures are used in small streams with little fish, while large baits come into play for big fish in wider waters.

Opposite: Sea trout live in the ocean during most of the year, but run up rivers in the autumn to spawn. The seagoing trout seldom weigh more than 4.5-6.5 lbs (2-3 kg), but in some places – notably the Baltic – they can be much heavier.

Vital facts

Sea trout spawn in the autumn, and the fry stay for 1-3 years in the waterway. When 16-22 cm (6-9 in) long, they migrate to the sea during March-April and, the same year or the next, return up the same waterway. Trout that have spawned go to sea in early spring, and some die – mainly males. Once in the ocean, they need a few weeks to regain their condition, becoming shiny and fat. Towards autumn, when ascending the waterway, they acquire spawning colours and the males develop a hooked lower jaw.

The ascent begins early in large waterways, but during autumn in small ones. Unlike salmon, sea trout ascend under cover of darkness – and they usually choose dark, protected resting places, whereas salmon often swim freely in the current. Sea trout do not normally feed in fresh water, and when they do it is not because of hunger. Their willingness to bite is connected with the development of spawning colours, milt and roe. The shinier a fish is, and the less mature in regard to milt or roe, the better its probability of biting in fresh water. Coloured fish do not bite eagerly – except those with strong dark colours, which can become aggressive as the spawning time approaches.

Sea trout ascend waterways in the greatest numbers when the water level is rising or high, so the fishing is usually best then. Newly run, silvery trout still have their bite-instinct from the period in salt water, and take bait regularly in large waterways. In smaller ones, fortune smiles during the evening, night and morning. The biting behaviour of sea trout also varies considerably with their environment. In Great Britain and Norway, fishing at night is common – but in Denmark and Sweden, for example, the fishing is excellent on dark, windy days with a high water level.

A sea trout obeys its instinct to bite for a short time after leaving the ocean and running up in fresh water.
Flood tides and/or high water levels tend to provide the best conditions for hooking this fish.

Frequent choices of bait are spinners weighing 5-12 grams. Their substantial resistance in water makes them well suited to deep, slow retrieval, although fresh-run fish can be gluttonous and relish a spinner or other lure that is retrieved fast. Spoons are used less, but have long been reliable for sea trout in Swedish and Danish waterways. Early in the season, naturally coloured lures in silver/black or yellow/black are popular, but late in the season – when the fish are strongly coloured – fluorescent hues may have greater success.

During the winter, sea trout in the ocean do not tolerate normal salinity and low temperatures. They either move out to warmer deep water, or else migrate into fjords or up the lower parts of rivers. These fish are often small and not yet mature – in Scandinavia they are called "Greenlanders". Their appetite is diminished by the cold water, but otherwise they are in fine condition. Only small bait can catch them, such as spinners, worms or – when spinning – little flies, as mentioned above for brown trout.

In some countries like Denmark, Sweden, Poland and the Baltic states, there is also spring fishing for out-spawned sea trout. It is best in mild weather, but can deteriorate rapidly with the slightest variations in water and air temperature. The condition of spawned-out fish is acceptable in certain waters, yet in others they may be very starved and should be returned.

Sea trout fishing with natural bait

Whether in a Norwegian river, a minor brook in the Hebrides, a Danish or Polish stream, fishing with worms is one of the safest methods for sea trout – from the newly ascended and coloured fish to the Greenlanders and the spawned-out emigrants.

One can fish in small streams with a worm, float, and no weighting. In large waterways, one uses single fixed floats that can carry sinkers of 1 to 10-15 grams, depending on the depth and current. A sinker on the end of the line, and a leader with a worm hook, allow you to make the hook glide in the current before the sinker – a more delicate presentation. A leader with 1-1.5 metres (40-60 inches) to the hook, and a short leader to the sinker, is quite common in rivers with comparatively great depth and good current.

However, worms are not the only type of bait applicable to sea trout. Cooked red shrimp are a superb alternative, especially in the spring and for Greenlanders. During the cold season and in spring, trout or salmon roe is used on single or treble hooks.

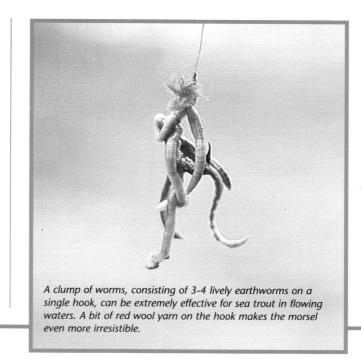

A clump of worms, consisting of 3-4 lively earthworms on a single hook, can be extremely effective for sea trout in flowing waters. A bit of red wool yarn on the hook makes the morsel even more irresistible.

When fishing with worms, cast the bait obliquely upstream and let it bounce down along the bottom, while you follow it with the rod and reel in any loose line. The tackle combines a three-way swivel with one leader to the current sinker and one to the hook carrying the clump of worms. The same tackle and technique can be used if you fish with a spinning fly: just replace the hook and worms with, for instance, a tube fly.

Rainbow trout

The rainbow trout (*Salmo gairdneri*) originally inhabited North America, in the mountains north of Mexico up to southwestern Alaska and the Aleutians. It also occurs in Kamchatka. The first examples came to Europe by way of Germany in 1880. Next the species reached Denmark, inspiring many pond farms. As a pond fish it then spread to numerous countries, some of which implanted it in waterways. This has been done on several continents, since the fish is rather robust and tolerates higher temperatures than brown trout do. Today it lives in Africa – for example Kenya, Morocco and South Africa – as well as in Japan, New Zealand, Tasmania, Australia, and in South American countries including Ecuador, Chile, Peru and Argentina.

Hallmarks of the rainbow trout are its purple or pink stripes along the side, and lots of black spots on the back and fins – mainly the tail fin. It has thirty subspecies, but its progenitor is the cutthroat trout (*Salmo clarkii*) which occurs in North America, from Prince William Sound in Alaska down to northern California and several of the Rocky Mountain states. There are also various crosses between rainbow trout and the cutthroat, which itself has at least six subspecies in western America. Moreover, we find cutthroat which are anadromous. Those inland could once weigh nearly 20 kg (44 lbs), although seagoing cutthroat seldom exceed 6-7 kg (13-15 lbs). The cutthroat is not considered as interesting a species for sportfishing as rainbow trout.

The rainbow trout lives stationary in rivers and streams, where it rarely weighs over 2-3 kg (4.4-6.6 lbs). Further, it has a lake-living form that, during most of the year, remains in lakes and only migrates up the tributaries in order to spawn or feed, chiefly eating salmon roe. Perhaps best known are the rainbow trout in Alaska's Lake Iliamna, where they grow to more than 10 kg (22 lbs). The Kamloops trout becomes even bigger.

Anadromous rainbow trout – called steelhead – migrate between rivers and the ocean. In their home waters, the Pacific rivers of the American west and northwest, they approach weights of 20 kg (44 lbs) at some places, although 4-8 kg (8.8-17.6 lbs) is commonest.

Rainbow trout are recognizable by the pink or violet stripe all along the side, and the many black spots on the back and fins. This species occurs naturally in North America, from where it has been implanted in Europe.

Vital facts

Unlike brown and sea trout, the rainbow trout spawns in flowing waters from January until early May. In waters with brown trout, the two species compete intensely. Where rainbow trout have been implanted or have escaped from farms, we often observe normal spawning behaviour – but without reproduction.

The rainbow trout does not seek the same holding places and territories as brown trout. It thrives in current edges and the main current, but in shallower waters, and it is more mobile than brown trout. In many North American rivers with ascending salmon, the stationary rainbow trout pursue the diverse salmon species (such as king, coho and sockeye), living at times on salmon roe. Also in contrast to brown trout, rainbow trout flourish in small groups or schools. They always feed on insects, larvae, leeches, crustaceans and so forth, though not as prone to eat fry and fish as brown trout are.

Appreciated as an implantation fish, the rainbow trout exists in numerous put-and-take waters, where it patrols pelagically along the shores. It often gathers at inflows and can also live in free water, even at fairly great depths.

Above: Compared with other trout, rainbow are more mobile and frequently swim in schools. They are also more attracted to shallow waters, both at current edges and in the main current. Further, they prefer smaller artificial lures with strong colours.

Left: Although rainbow trout usually eat larvae, insects and crustaceans, they can also, of course, be caught with baitfish such as sculpin. Worms, salmon eggs and roe are other natural baits that may appeal to them.

Spinning for rainbow trout

The artificial baits preferred by rainbow trout are small ones, whereas brown trout take both small and large lures. Since rainbow trout stand more freely in the current, the same methods of spinning can be used as for brown trout. This is also true in lakes and put-and-take waters. Rainbow trout have a definite taste for red colours and fluorescent, or bright red or orange, lures – ranging from little red spinners to orange flies for spinning.

Rainbow trout fishing with natural bait

The manner of catching brown trout with natural bait can just as well apply to rainbow trout. It benefits, however, by decorating the worm hook with a bead or a piece of orange or red wool thread. Fishing with salmon eggs or roe is also quite effective for rainbow trout, which eat roe during the winter regardless of whether they live in a western American or a Scandinavian river.

In put-and-take waters, these fish are often caught with diverse types of red or orange dough-balls that contain salmon-egg flavouring. Berkley's Power Bait assortment is the best-known type of dough for them. The balls are fished either stationary with bottom tackle, or with floats. In both cases, the baits become more lively if you retrieve them slowly with long pauses.

Steelhead

The seagoing form of rainbow trout inhabits rivers in western America. Also called steelhead by sportfishermen are the lake-living form in North America and the rainbow trout found in the Great Lakes. But the seagoing steelhead is silvery in the ocean and in lakes, as well as during its run upriver. At first sight, it can be recognized only by the many black spots on its tail fin, adipose fin and dorsal fin. After a short time in flowing water, its characteristic pink stripe becomes clearer. As spawning approaches, the fish grows spotty and acquires a pale purple stripe along the side.

Unlike sea trout and salmon, steelhead feed in fresh water and, moreover, they survive the spawning – in contrast to all species of Pacific salmon. Steelhead weigh 2-6 kg (4.4-13 lbs) but, notably in the rivers of British Columbia, they can reach 15 kg (33 lbs).

The rainbow trout that were brought to Europe have been genetically manipulated to yield the perfect farming fish. Yet some still have their instinct to migrate seaward. Plenty of escaped or implanted rainbow trout in northern Europe thus head for the ocean when they reach a certain size. Marine fish farms of rainbow trout have occasionally even caused accidents, with fish slipping out to wander along the coasts. At many places, they also migrate up waterways, though unable to reproduce.

Spinning for steelhead

In the rivers of western America and those flowing into the Great Lakes, steelhead run during almost the whole year. However, there are distinctive spring, summer and winter runs. As a rule, the fish ascend Pacific rivers all year round too, but with some variations depending on the latitude.

Steelhead are famous in flyfishing literature, especially with reference to small, clear rivers in the states of Washington and Oregon. But they also take different types of spinners, and roe in particular – a trait that is shared by the "steelheads" caught in Scandinavian rivers. Steelhead migrate upriver in small schools, and choose holding places in a manner that recalls salmon. Generally, they select neither dead water nor the fastest water. Current edges and middle furrows in a waterway are ideal stops for steelhead.

Here one can catch them on, for instance, small spinners which are fished across the current or retrieved slowly over the bottom. It is important to fish near the bottom, especially in northern British Columbia; and many western American rivers are fished stationary with so-called Spin-N-Glo. These light spinners are "anchored" with a leader and a lead weight on the bottom, the line is pulled taut, and the rod is placed in a Y-shaped branch. When a steelhead passes the baits or sees them from its holding place, it usually bites. The treble hook on a Spin-N-Glo can also be provided with roe before it is "parked".

Some rivers in Washington and Oregon are fished with small shrimp-like crustaceans, weighted with light sinkers. In other rivers, and around the Great Lakes, fishing with salmon eggs or roe is extremely popular. Using one to three big salmon eggs on a little single hook, perhaps weighted with a couple of lead shot, is an easy and elegant way to catch steelhead. Elsewhere, bigger roe clumps are set on a correspondingly larger single hook.

In Scandinavian rivers and streams, steelhead are often caught as a by-product of fishing for brown trout, sea trout and salmon – on spinners, spoons, plugs and flies alike. Roe, too, is used to catch them in some Danish streams and southern Swedish rivers which are renowned for abundant ascents of rainbow trout.

Opposite top: The steelhead is the seagoing form of rainbow trout. When fresh-run, it may look confusingly like a salmon, but is easy to identify by the numerous black spots on its tail, adipose and dorsal fins.

Opposite bottom: Steelhead are fished near the bottom, ideally with small spinners. These are powerful, pugnacious fish and can cause hair-raising fights if challenged with the right gear.

Arctic char

Besides having a seagoing form, the Arctic char (*Salvelinus alpinus*) lives in cold clear lakes, mountain rivers and brooks with Arctic temperatures. Its distribution, spanning the whole northern hemisphere, includes northern Canada – for instance Baffin Island – as well as Greenland, Iceland, northern Norway, Sweden, Siberia and Alaska.

Furthermore, we find Arctic char in central and southern Norway, southern Sweden, Finland, the Lake District of England and Scotland, mountain lakes in the Alpine countries, and the former Soviet Union. Yet the stocks outside the normal area of distribution often have small fish, as in the Lake District and many Alpine lakes, where even dwarf forms occur. An exception is Lake Sommen in Sweden, which has yielded char of 8-9 kg (18-20 lbs). The fish usually weighs 0.25-3.0 kg (0.55-6.6 lbs), but the seagoing form can grow remarkably large, as on Baffin Island where examples over 12 kg (26 lbs) have been caught.

Arctic char belong to the numerous salmon species that evolved from the same progenitor at the same time – when a land bridge existed between Siberia and Alaska. This bridge caused the evolution of a southerly strain of char – the Dolly Varden (*Salvelinus malma*) – and of a northerly one which spread to Canada, Europe and Siberia. The two species are very similar, and are related to the brook trout, which – along with North American lake trout – is thought to share the same progenitor.

Spinning for char

Char live on small bottom animals, and sometimes on fish fry or larger prey. Precisely because their food comprises so few animal species, they tend to be selective. During the short summer, they may swim in the surface and take insects.

Above right: Landlocked Arctic char are found primarily in areas with an Arctic climate. Typical of the species are its red-orange or red-pink abdomen, and its dark green back with green spots. These colours, already strong, are reinforced when the fish acquires its spawning appearance.

Below right: The seagoing form of Arctic char is shiny when it runs upriver. But after only a short time in fresh water, it becomes strongly coloured in the manner typical of landlocked Arctic char.

Within their region of distribution, Arctic char occur chiefly in lakes, but periodically also in rivers and tributaries. In a lake, the char patrol along the edges toward deep water. With colourful spinners and spoons, one can usually catch them during their hunting raids over the deep edges near land.

Curiosity is a trait of char, and they are easily tempted by artificial baits, but do not bite as eagerly as trout. A trout that follows the lure is immediately frightened if it sees the fisherman, whereas a char seems less timid and often keeps after the bait for several casts in a row. The char in lakes are fished in deep water and above deep edges near land. Both spinners and spoons are fine baits, and should be retrieved in a varied manner upward over the edge, with numerous spin-stops. Small lures with red colours appear to be most attractive.

Vital facts

Arctic char spawn in autumn and early winter. They grow slowly, as do many other Arctic fish. Schools are formed until the char weigh 300-500 grams, and bigger char live alone. Their diet includes insects, crustaceans, mosquito larvae, and snails. The char has a pink or red-orange abdomen, and a dark green back with yellow spots. Its colours become brighter when it spawns. It inhabits lakes, patrolling along the shores, but can also swim in the surface or enter the tributaries and wander up rivers.

The seagoing form, as fry, spends 3-7 years in a river. It emigrates between February and May, to grow briefly in the sea – often for just a few months. Still shiny, it begins to acquire colours after a short time in the river. Males acquire a hooked lower jaw, turning orange-red on the abdomen and green on the back, while females are less colourful. Unlike salmon and sea trout, all char are presumed to run upriver each summer. They eat little during their river journey.

One of the surest ways to make char bite is to replace the treble hook on a spinner or spoon with a short leader of 20-40 cm (8-16 in), to which a trout fly is tied – for example, a simple, classic fly such as Red Tag Palmer or Black Zulu. Spoons and spinners are retrieved slowly with lots of short jerks and spin-stops.

The use of a casting Buldo and a leader with fly is also effective for fishing in lakes when the char hunt insects at the surface. Retrieval must be slow but at an even tempo. Char bite cautiously, and only when their resistance is felt should you strike.

In mountain brooks and rivers, char prefer the calmest areas. The lure is retrieved as in trout fishing. Possible holding places are searched, or the cast is laid obliquely downstream to let the spinner move in the current while you retrieve it.

The American Dolly Varden behaves in exactly the same way as the char, and can be caught by identical methods.

As for seagoing char, their willingness to bite has been found to differ across the Arctic region. In Canada, Greenland, Iceland and Siberia, they gladly take spoons – but in the clear rivers of northern Norway, they quite seldom take spoons or spinners. As mentioned, they eat very little when they run up rivers, and the longer they stay in fresh water the more enthusiastically they take artificial baits.

The fish are inclined to swim in the quieter parts of rivers, where they can hold in limited schools. Small spoons, possibly with a red hackle or red spots, are excellent for seagoing char. Retrieval has to be slow and deep, the spinner ideally going just over the bottom. When you manage to catch one char, others are likely to be at the same place. The fish rise with high water, so the fishing usually depends on the tides and melting snow.

As the fish migrate up through lakes, they grow more interested in biting. Here they patrol the edges toward deep water and frequently swim in the surface. They now increasingly resemble the stationary char in behaviour and way of life.

Char are caught with natural bait as well – for instance worms, larvae and maggots. However, it is primarily in spinning and flyfishing that the species has gained such popularity.

While Arctic char mostly eat insects, spinning with spoons can be rewarding, especially if the treble hook is replaced by a 10-cm (4-inch) leader and a little fly.

Eastern brook trout

The eastern brook trout, (*Salvelinus fontinalis*), has the same progenitor as do North American lake trout and Arctic char. Its natural distribution lies in eastern North America and westward to the Rocky Mountains, but it is readily displaced by rainbow and brown trout. The richest stocks of eastern brook trout are in Labrador, where the Minipi River with its tributaries is best known for one of the largest stocks of fish weighing up to 3 kg (6.6 lbs). Also famous for this species is God's River in Manitoba.

Eastern brook trout were introduced to Europe for pond-farming in the late 1800s, but were out-competed by the rainbow trout. Still, they have always been regarded as one of the most beautiful trout species, and were thus implanted in many of Europe's clear mountain rivers and streams, where they continue to thrive. They rarely become bigger than 30 cm (12 in), while those in ponds can reach 2 kg (4.4 lbs). Today, they are cultivated to some extent and the species is crossed with rainbow trout or ordinary brown trout. It has also been implanted in Argentina.

Spinning for brook trout

All traditional lures are applicable to these fish, with the same methods that catch other trout in brooks, rivers and streams. Big specimens in the northeastern United States, though, are caught on large lures – mainly spinners and spoons. The

Vital facts

Spawning occurs in autumn and winter. The fry grow slowly, living on insects, larvae and crustaceans; once larger, they add young fish to their diet. Eastern brook trout are characteristically found in sizeable rivers with calm currents. In the Minipi and God's River, they also take mice and lemmings. Small stocks of the species have proved to be anadromous, migrating between rivers and the sea, but seldom are as big as the stationary freshwater-living ones, or as pale and shiny.

retrieval should be relatively deep and slow, since the fish does not take food in the surface as often as rainbow and brown trout do.

The fish's lovely colours and deep red, fine-tasting meat have made it a popular implantation fish in many put-and-take waters, whose temperature and clarity suit this much-liked species. Moreover, it can be caught with worms and other natural baits, in the same way as rainbow and brown trout.

The brook trout is a relative of Arctic char and lake trout. This beautiful fish is native only to North America, but has been implanted in Europe and other regions. Large spoons and spinners usually catch it, if fished deeply and slowly. Shown at right is a colourful pair of brook trout while spawning.

From the mid-19th century until some decades into the 20th, many well heeled English fishermen journeyed to Norway in quest of salmon. This painting from the same period still hangs in one of the socalled "English houses" where they lived during their visits.

H·R·H· THE PRINCE OF WALES VISIT TO SYLTEBÖ ERISFJORD AUGUST 1885.

COUGHT IN SEAPOOL BY OFFISERS OF H·M· ROYAL YACHT "ALBERT AND VICTORIA." WEIGHT 35 LBS.

Atlantic salmon

The Atlantic salmon (*Salmo salar*) has given rise to a sport-fishing culture and history that no other species of fish can approach. It existed over a century ago in most European countries, but its stocks have declined due to dams, pollution, intensive professional fishing, and diseases – so much that, in central Europe today, it inhabits only a few rivers of northern Spain and France. Yet it still visits many rivers in Great Britain and Ireland, Iceland and the Faeroes, one river in Greenland, and hundreds of rivers in Norway, Sweden and Finland, as well as in various Russian rivers.

Salmon diseases come primarily from marine farming and, despite repeated efforts to restrict them, it has to be observed that the wild salmon in northern Europe face a risk of extinction in the near future. Probably even the genes of "wild salmon" will be strongly blended with those of cultivated salmon, which has serious implications for the wild salmon's survival, especially in Scandinavia and Scotland.

Atlantic salmon are also found in North America, running up rivers in New Brunswick, Quebec, Maine and Nova Scotia. Only in this region, during recent years, has it been possible to see improvements in the stocks – thanks to the buying up of salmon quotas from professional fishing in the North Atlantic. Perhaps one of the most virgin areas with intact salmon strains is the Kola Peninsula, although the discovery of its world-class fishing in the 1990s has led to a minor decline even there.

The Atlantic salmon is often termed the "king of fish", as it is strong and full of fight, besides reaching weights over 65 lbs (30 kg). Fresh-run individuals are silvery and – unlike sea trout – tend to have only black, cross-shaped spots above their lateral lines.

Vital facts

Atlantic salmon spawn in rivers and streams during autumn and early winter. The fry stay in the waterway for 2-3 years, and the silvery young salmon migrate to the sea during March-April. After 1-2 years at sea, each salmon returns to migrate up the same river, to the spawning bed and the brook where it was born several years earlier. This is one of nature's most astonishing feats, and has fascinated people for centuries.

The salmon ascent takes place from early spring until well into autumn, depending on the latitude. After a time in the river, the salmon become coloured, and males develop a strongly hooked lower jaw. The struggle for females and spawning places is hard for males, and some of them die after spawning – as do some females. How much of the stock perishes, though, we do not know for sure.

The surviving salmon descend to the sea and, at best, come back up the river once or twice in the following years. Compared to other species, the fry have a high survival rate – but things can go wrong, both during the spawning and while the yolk-sac fry are still in the spawning pit. Rain, melting snow and high tides, for example, can destroy the spawning banks or silt them over, so that the fry die. And if the fish do grow up, they occupy territories in competition with, among others, stationary trout. In many waterways, predatory fish such as pike may consume young salmon, especially when they travel toward the sea. Hydroelectric turbines and similar obstacles also reduce the stocks.

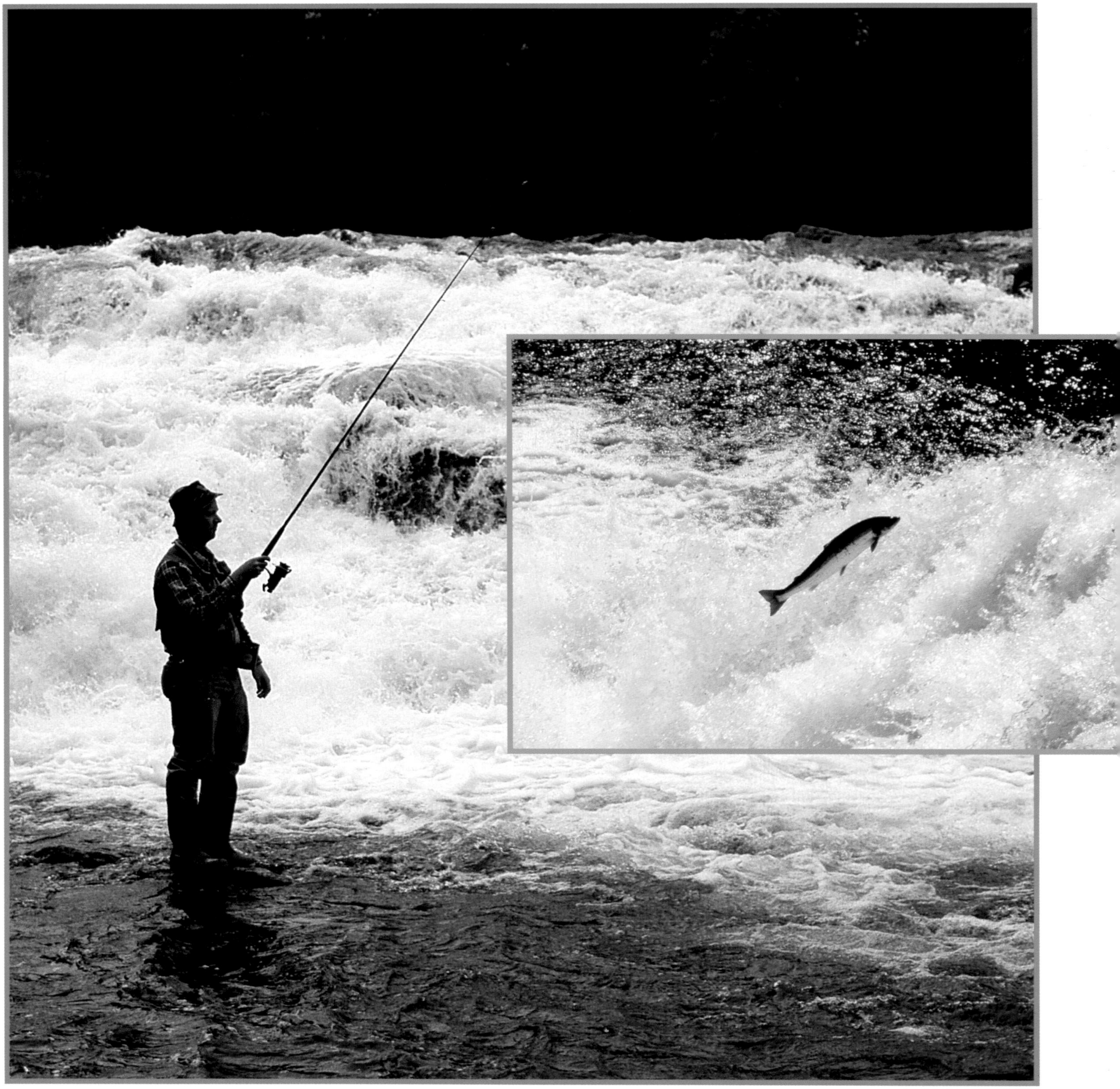

Salmon strains develop differently. Some have genes giving faster growth than others. Small salmon, or grilse, together with medium-sized salmon of 4-7 kg (8.8-15.4 lbs), predominate in all rivers, while large salmon of more than 10 kg (22 lbs) are common in few. The best-known rivers for big salmon include the Alta and Namsen in Norway, the Mörrum in Sweden, the Derwent in northwest England and the Tweed on the border between England and Scotland, besides certain rivers in the Kola Peninsula.

Spinning for Atlantic salmon

Salmon fishing involves a paradox: what is the point of serving food to a creature that eats nothing? Ever since the sport began, fishermen have wondered about this, for the fish do happen to bite. There are many theories about why they take bait. Fresh-run, silvery salmon often bite with frenzy at the start of the season. Some of us believe that this is because certain individual "springers" retain their biting instinct. Others think they are driven by a need to fight for resting and holding places in the river, chasing other fish away and, consequently, taking a fisherman's bait.

Later in the summer, the salmon accept small lures in the surface, such as a little spoon or a fly. These are presumed to revive an instinct of youth, when the fish lived on insects in the river. Once the salmon acquire their colours, the time approaches to compete over spawning places. They now become aggressive, and take bait for that reason.

Factors like the weather play, of course, a considerable role. Not the least important is the water level. When it changes, the salmon grow uneasy. Whether it rises or falls, therefore, the fisherman has a good chance – though a falling level is usually best. Both precipitation and melt-water influence the fishing in this way. The lower parts of rivers are also affected to some

Left: When the salmon migrate upriver to spawn, they are in good condition and thus a favourite quarry for sportfishermen. During their swim to the spawning areas, the salmon often have to pass serious obstacles such as wild rapids. River sections with these obstacles are normally good for fishing, since the salmon pause here before resuming their journey.

Right: Several theories exist as to why salmon bite in rivers even though they do not eat anything. Whatever the reason, it remains true that they can be coaxed to take artificial or natural baits. A time-tested method of salmon fishing is to put a piece of red wool yarn and a clump of earthworms onto the hook.

A typical river stretch, shown above, is illustrated below in cross-section. Salmon occur mainly at the inflows and outlets of pools. In relatively long and wide pools, however, the fish prefer to hold at the current's outer edges. Yet in shallow or fast-flowing areas, they take positions in the current lee near large rocks.

degree by tidal patterns in the sea, as the salmon ascend at high tide and migrate upriver in groups or small schools. Thus, one often finds that the salmon have distinct biting periods in the lower stretches.

The holding places can be very diverse. Large salmon choose the most suitable places, commonly in deep water, while those of medium and small size are banished to shallow water. Salmon often select a current edge, but the necks of rapids are excellent, and long current furrows are ideal.

Some places are more appropriate for flyfishing than for spinning. Yet if, for instance, you see only 2-3 metres of water at the opposite bank – or amid the current – and one metre at your own bank, this is a good site for spinning.

Early in the season, when the water is cold and the level high, you should fish so deeply and slowly in the river that you occasionally feel the spoon or plug hit the bottom. This can be done by casting toward the opposite bank, or obliquely downstream, and then lowering or raising the rod to keep the bait moving at the bottom. As a rule, shiny salmon at a given place will bite during the first two or three casts. To go on casting at the same place any longer is usually a waste of time.

In the middle of the season, the water has sunk and the holding places have changed. One seldom catches salmon in totally calm water, so the bait should move with the current, at the same speed or a bit faster. If the bait slows down, lift the rod or reel in a little line – and vice versa if it moves too fast, although in general it will do better if moving too fast than too slowly.

When the water level is low and the temperature exceeds 10-14° C (50-57° F), the salmon often go into faster water. While their holding places change during the season, so does the size of ascending salmon. The big salmon tend to arrive at the beginning of the season, followed by medium-size and small ones. However, large individuals sporadically run even at the end of the season in many areas. Also late in the season, the fish become coloured and more aggressive, frequently biting after several casts at the same place.

Salmon fishing in a river of average magnitude calls for strong spinning equipment: either a baitcasting reel or a spinning reel, with line of 0.40-0.45 mm, except later in the season when a line of 0.35-0.40 mm can be sufficient. But in small rivers, lighter equipment is used. Spoons, spinners and plugs are excellent bait throughout these months. Early

in the season, spoons of 20-40 grams are often used, as the salmon then stand deep and the water level is high. Many people also fish with floating or sinking plugs of 11-13 cm. Once the water has sunk, spinners of 8-15 grams may be tried too.

Experience shows that, well into the season, salmon take small bait – chiefly flies. Spinning can be done with a fly aided by a casting bubble, or some other kind of casting weight. The flies are of the same type as in flyfishing, such as small single- or double-hooked ones of size 2-10. The leader should be 3.5-4 metres (11.5-13 feet) long, and the fly should swing in the current – as if you were flyfishing. A casting bubble works best in big, lazy rivers, where you can speed up the fly as it swings toward your bank.

Spinning is also possible with a fly and no casting Buldo. Instead you fish with a leader of 1-2 metres (3.3-6.6 feet) to the fly, and a leader of about 20 cm (8 in) to a suitable sinker. This tackle is superb during the whole season, and the fly can be fished exactly like a spoon. Early in the season, and in cold water, one often uses large bushy red-yellow tube flies of 12-16 cm (4.8-6.4 in) with simple patterns. Later on, black or dark tube flies are best. The fly may "hang" in the current, but it becomes more lively if, at the same time, you "pump" it forward and backward in the current – for example by lifting and lowering the rod with some quick movements. Here is an elementary method that can reward the newcomer, too. Yet remember that spinning with a fly is prohibited in, among other countries, Norway.

Fishing for Atlantic salmon with natural bait

Salmon will also take natural bait, though fishing with shrimp is not allowed in Norway. At many rivers in Great Britain, shrimp are still fished on hook tackle. A single hook is used in some places, and one or two small treble hooks elsewhere. Even whole, dead baitfish on hook systems were previously employed in salmon fishing.

Most common, however, is fishing with worms. In certain countries such as Ireland, fishing with a float is widespread, while worms on bottom tackle are used in other lands. The hooks are normally of size 1/0-3/0, baited with a bunch of worms. Attached to the hook are a leader 1-2 metres (3.3-6.6 feet) long, and a second leader that is weighted with a fairly heavy sinker, so that the worms swing in the current at the same speed as a spoon or fly.

Striking, fighting and landing the fish

Salmon bite in many different ways. Some take the bait explosively and hook themselves. Others are more cautious and require you to strike. If fishing with natural bait, both shrimp and worms, you may feel the fish either taking violently, or "chewing" on the bait for several seconds – perhaps up to a minute – before swallowing it, which is the signal for you to strike. Inexperienced salmon fishermen have notable difficulty in judging when to strike, if fishing with worms or shrimp. After the salmon bites, it should initially be allowed to run the show. This is true of all fishing – but in the case of salmon, patience is essential. A further paradox of the sport is how many people react when they hook their first salmon: as soon as it bites, they want to get it up on land immediately, since they are afraid of losing it. Instead, let the fish set the pace, and look for a place to land it only when it shows signs of tiring out, for example by turning its belly upward.

A salmon is landed with a firm grip on the tail. It becomes paralyzed and is quite calm when lifted out of the water. On smooth, shallow shores, the fish is best slid onto land. You walk backward and, every time the salmon thrashes, pull it a little up on land, until it lies on its side and can be lifted high and dry.

Many fishermen also use large nets, although these can be hard to handle. The gaff, too, is still used in some European countries. A tailer is a gentle landing aid, but it demands adeptness. In America and in the Kola Peninsula, there are special restrictions on fishing and rules for returning the fish to water. For instance, in Kola all the fish must be returned.

Powerful rushes may enable the fish to escape from the hook, or to break the line. The closer the fish is to the rod tip, the greater the risk of losing it. By quickly lowering the rod tip, you can prevent a rushing fish from tearing itself free. But the line should always be stretched taut, and the drag should not be set too hard.

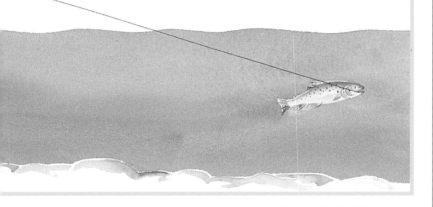

In contrast to the majority of other fish species, a salmon can be gripped securely around its tail-fin root. It then becomes immobile, and lets itself be lifted or dragged ashore in a calm manner.

Even when the fish shows an urge to leap out of the water, it is best to lower the rod tip and, if possible, keep the rod parallel with the water surface. This reduces the pressure on the line, and usually makes the fish stop its acrobatics.

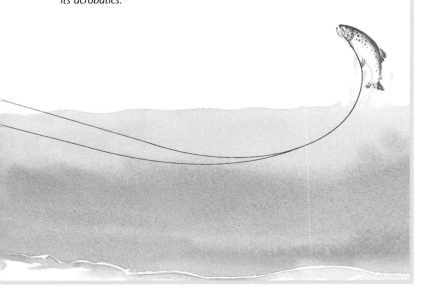

King salmon

The king salmon (*Oncorhynchus tshawytscha*) is the biggest among the six species of Pacific salmon. Five of these live on the American side of the Pacific Ocean, while the sixth – cherry salmon – exists only in Kamchatka and northern Japan. Other names for the king salmon are the chinook, quinnat, spring, and tyee. Specimens of 30 kg (66 lbs) are not uncommon, and whoppers weighing over 40 kg (88 lbs) have been caught in rivers such as the Kenai in Alaska and the Skeena in British Columbia. But the average weight is 8-12 kg (18-26 lbs).

Unlike the other salmon species, king salmon are known for their migrations far up into river systems. In the Yukon River, they swim almost 3,000 kilometres. King salmon in the sea are silvery with irregular black patches, even on the back and tail fin. Moreover, they have black pigment on the mouth and throat. This species is distributed from northern Alaska to California and, on the Asiatic side, from Kamchatka to northern China. It has also been implanted in the Great Lakes, where it thrives and grows to 12-13 kg (26-29 lbs).

Spinning for king salmon

These fish bite much more eagerly than Atlantic salmon do – from the moment they approach the river mouth to the time they begin spawning. Trolling fishermen are busy already in the sea and estuaries, and fish are pursued with artificial baits and salmon roe as they run upriver. For holding places, they choose deep holes, current edges, brinks and backwaters. But unlike Atlantic salmon, they often prefer deep, dark, calm water. Many rivers are murky and partly muddy, so the inflows from clear tributaries can be counted on as holding places – especially at the creeks in which king salmon spawn. Only young king salmon, weighing up to 2-3 kg (4.4-6.6 lbs), rise to the surface for small bait such as flies.

Atlantic salmon usually betray their presence by leaping in the river, but king salmon almost always go to the bottom and

stay there. They often stand in dense schools, whereas the medium-sized and large Atlantic salmon are territorial and gather only at difficult passages or rapids.

During the fight, king salmon are considerably heavier and tougher than Atlantic salmon – yet by no means as wild and ungovernable. Just after biting, they normally show themselves once at the surface, while an Atlantic salmon may leap repeatedly as it struggles.

This fishing needs heavy equipment, often combining line of 0.40-0.60 mm with a very strong rod. Lures for king salmon include the Pixie, Spin-N-Glo, Tee Spoon, and diverse deep-going plugs that ideally contain rattles. Virtually all types of artificial lure work well, if fished deep and slow – almost crawling over the bottom, down to the salmon or

Left: The giant of Pacific salmon is the king (chinook) salmon, which can weigh over 90 lbs (40 kg). Those that run upriver during the spring and early summer are silvery, but the ever later migrants become increasingly coloured.

Above: *Robust equipment is needed to catch king salmon, as they are tough and heavy during the fight. In addition, they gladly choose deep holding places, where the lure has to be fished just over the bottom.*

Vital facts

There are various strains of king salmon. They migrate upriver from January until late autumn, but the primary ascent in most western American rivers is made between May and early July. In contrast to coho salmon, the king salmon runs up large rivers, and it spawns from July until November. The fish that ascend during springtime often choose tributaries, whereas the autumn-running fish select the main river. A further difference is that the salmon ascending in early summer are always silvery, while the late ones are slightly coloured as they ascend. All the salmon die after spawning, as do other salmonoid species in western North America.

The fry feed on insects, crustaceans and larvae in the waterways. They migrate into the ocean during the next or the following summer. Dead salmon fertilize the basically barren waterways, so their fate is naturally beneficial. On reaching the sea, the young salmon grow rapidly, and 2-8 years later they return up the same rivers.

among them. The salmon stand close together and, to avoid hooking them badly, it is only allowed in many rivers to use single hooks.

Nobody questions the power of king salmon – they are tough until the end. Since they usually form schools, one can catch several in the same place. Evidently they are not as shy as Atlantic salmon.

In the Great Lakes, fishing is also done from the shore around river mouths. Between early summer and early autumn, there are chances of catching king salmon when they migrate up the rivers. This is a typical wading sport, and succeeds best in the morning or evening, as the fish swim into deep water to eat during the daytime. One uses strong spinning rods, line of 0.30-0.36 mm, and spoons of 20-40 grams. Piers and breakwaters, as well as sand-banks and headlands near these ascent rivers, are other good fishing sites for king salmon.

Fishing for king salmon with natural bait

As the salmon approach the estuaries, they are subjected to intensive trolling – called mooching. The fish are caught with artificial lures, but whole or half herrings on hook tackle are also popular. When the fish run upriver, it is generally safest to use salmon roe, particularly if all else fails. Salmon roe is often packed in orange nylon net with fine meshes – as big as a walnut – and set on a single hook. Then the roe clump is fished with either a float, free line, or bottom tackle, allowed to swing in the current toward the salmon. In contrast to Atlantic salmon, which frequently bite on one of the first occasions when they are presented with artificial or natural bait, the king salmon is characteristically coaxed into biting by repeated casts with roe.

Left: A king salmon does not leap as often as an Atlantic salmon. During the fight, it shows itself at the surface only on rare occasions – like this!

Right: Once the king salmon have migrated up in spawning rivers, a cluster of salmon roe serves well as bait. A fine-meshed nylon stocking can be used to make clumps of roe. These are placed on a single hook and fished swinging in the current to entice a salmon.

Coho salmon

The coho or silver salmon (*Oncorhynchus kisutch*) is, along with king salmon, the most popular sportfishing species in western North America. It occurs from California to Alaska, besides Kamchatka and down the coast to Japan. It is entirely silvery, with small black patches over the lateral line, back and fins. Its average weight is 3-6 kg (6.6-13.2 lbs), although individuals are known to reach 12-14 kg (26-31 lbs). In 1967 these salmon were successfully implanted in the Great Lakes, where – together with other trout and salmonoid species – it has contributed to the region's impressive fishing. Coho salmon migrate upriver from July until early October.

Spinning for coho

Coho are also caught at sea, as are king salmon. Trolling or mooching for them is very common. They take spoons, or herring on tackle, at river mouths and in nearby marine waters. In the Great Lakes, spinning is done at the estuaries and from adjacent banks, headlands, piers and breakwaters, just as for king salmon.

However, the coho is more eager to bite than king salmon are. It migrates up small coastal rivers, often in sizeable schools, and then chooses quiet stretches of water or current edges as holding places – but it keeps away from other salmon, such as chum. Unlike king salmon, it is content to stay in relatively shallow water. If the river flows through lakes, one frequently finds big schools of coho leaping at the outflows.

Coho are primarily a wonderful quarry for flyfishing, but they can be caught with small spinners of size 2-3, and on spoons of 5-12 grams. While king salmon are readily duped by bright red-orange spoons and spinners, in the case of coho it is better to use spoons and spinners made of silver or brass. Small baits should be retrieved slowly, as close to the bottom as possible – without losing speed. The bite is often cautious but resolute, and only when you start to put pressure on the fish does it begin to leap, approaching the surface much more frequently than a king salmon does.

Almost no fishing with roe is done for the coho, in contrast to king salmon. Thus, it is a distinctive spinning and flyfishing species.

Above: *The greedy coho (silver) salmon normally weighs under 22 lbs (10 kg) and migrates up small rivers near the west coast of North America, ranging from California to Alaska. There it tends to remain in relatively shallow water, and eagerly takes small, colourful spinners and spoons.*

Right: Coho are generally cautious biters, but become lively when they are hooked and feel the line's pressure. Frequently, they leap in the air and thrash in the surface more than they stay in the water.

Vital facts

The coho runs up large rivers as king salmon do, but more commonly it chooses small coastal rivers when migrating into fresh water. In addition, it travels a shorter distance up the rivers than do king salmon, and thus exposes itself less to the dangers and difficulties faced by that species.

Coho are silvery during their run upriver, but later in the season one can also see lightly coloured fish ascending. The spawning takes place between October and February. The fry migrate into the sea either during the next summer, or 1-2 years later. They remain there for 2-4 years, although seldom wandering as far from the home river as do king salmon. In the ocean, coho feed on shrimp, cuttle-fish and fish. The stock of silver salmon in western American waters has decreased in recent years.

Fishing in marine waters

Cod

Throughout winter, English surf-fishermen challenge the cod (*Gadus morhua*) along their country's southern coasts. In Scotland, it is caught all year round. American coastal fishermen vanquish it during autumn and winter, from Cape Cod to Nova Scotia. Much-desired by practitioners of spinning in Norway, Denmark and Sweden, it has not surprisingly given rise to many of the traditions in coastal fishing.

The cod's main distribution covers the North Sea and the coasts of Norway, Iceland and the Faeroes, but it is also common on the east coast of North America. Its colours vary, though: on mixed bottoms in shallow water it is dark brown, while cod from sandy bottoms and deep water are paler. Red, or mountain, cod is the term for cod that live in shallow water and have a strong red-brown to deep orange colour, even on the abdomen.

Coastal cod seldom weigh more than 3-4 kg (6.6-8.8 lbs), except at some places in Norway – such as powerful tidal currents – which regularly yield specimens of 8-10 kg (18-22 lbs). But cod at sea can reach striking weights. In northern Europe, 20 kg (44 lbs) is not unusual and fish exceeding 30 kg (66 lbs) have been caught, for example, at Yellow Reef off northern Jutland, in Öresund and off Lofoten. In North America, boats have brought up cod that reach 40 kg (88 lbs).

Spinning for cod

Cod are caught by spinning from harbours, piers, long shallow shores and rocky coasts. They often prefer deep water and mixed bottoms. The spinning equipment must be robust and long-casting, such as rods of 9-11 feet with strong multiplier or spinning reels, line of 0.30-0.40 mm, and spoons or pirks of 20-40 grams in silver, copper, red or fluorescent colours. Since the cod is a bottom-fish and often goes into seaweed after being hooked, you can benefit by replacing the treble hook with a single hook, which causes much fewer bottom-snags.

One of the most frequent errors, when spinning in deep water, is to start the retrieval immediately after the impact. Spoons or pirks are then retrieved high over the bottom –

In many parts of Europe and North America, cod are caught regularly by coastal spinning. These fish are so widespread in some regions, especially in northern Europe, that traditional coastal fishing is based on them.

without being seen by a single cod. Thus, the lure must be allowed to sink the whole way down, before you tighten up the line and begin to retrieve. The rod is lifted and lowered, as you reel in the spoon or pirk so that it constantly grazes the bottom. In the shallows near land, these movements should continue but the retrieval is a little faster. This technique can be refined once you have a correct feeling for the given depth and bottom conditions: a retrieval that keeps the lure just above the bottom will soon seem natural.

Bottom-snags are almost impossible to avoid, but the worst ones are prevented by choosing the right weight on the spoon or pirk, combined with the right retrieval speed. Unfortunately, cod fishing often means lost lures. If you do not get a bite, the reason may be that no cod are present because the bottom is smooth, sandy or muddy. Cod are

Vital facts

There are many strains of coastal cod, often with different habits of migration and spawning. When the spawning time approaches, they head for certain marine areas with suitable temperature and salinity. Spawning proceeds from January until March and, in some places, also during April. Subsequently, the cod disperse to shallow areas and banks in the sea, or toward the coast, where their diet includes crustaceans, crabs, sand lance and herring.

The cod's senses of smell, sight and feeling are highly developed, and it uses them all when seeking food on the bottom. It can also be found in the middle layer or the surface, hunting sand lance and herring. The best season for coastal cod is from autumn until early spring. Yet at northerly latitudes, as in Norway, the warm months and especially autumn are thought most rewarding.

nearly always found on mixed bottoms with stones, seaweed, mussels and the like.

Dropper flies occasionally give results – due not to simultaneous bites on the pirk and dropper, but since the dropper is better at stimulating cod to take. You can use droppers made of feathers, plastic worms, or single hooks with jig tails. If fishing with a dropper, you must attach strong leaders of, for example, 0.45-0.60 mm line – or even stronger line in areas with big cod.

When the cod hunt herring or sand lance along the shores, rapid retrieval is most effective, as the cod frequently bite a little above the bottom or in the middle layer. At other times, cod are selective and may only swim at the bottom to eat crabs. It is then especially important to spin with good bottom contact, and make the spoon or pirk almost crawl across the bottom to imitate a crab. Under these conditions, red-coloured spoons are superior. Generally, cod in deep water enjoy taking spoons and pirks with bright yellow and red colours.

However, in shallow water and along gentle shores with 2-4 metres of water, varied bottom vegetation, seaweed and stones, it is wrong to use the above technique of retrieval. Strong spinning equipment is still used here, such as a rod of 9-11 feet, line of 0.30-0.40 mm, and a pirk or spoon of 15-30 grams. As soon as the lure hits the water, you start to retrieve at a uniform tempo, possibly with a few spin-stops, so that the lure goes in the middle layer – neither in the surface water nor too near the seaweed.

Regardless of whether you fish in deep or shallow water, there are often more cod where you catch one. The area can be searched with casts in a fan pattern or, along shallow shores and cliffs, by walking for some metres and making parallel casts outward. In such places, the times before and after sunset are good for fishing, as the cod then move toward land.

If you fish from a boat over shallows, it is best to drift across promising current edges or areas known to have cod. This method involves two principal techniques. First, the pirk or spoon can be let down on the side that the boat drifts away from – the wind side – and the rod is continually lifted and lowered, maintaining bottom contact. Second, you can cast with the wind from the lee side and retrieve while jerking the rod up and down. The latter method demands good contact with the spoon or pirk, since you must also compensate for the boat's drift.

Spinning for cod is often done from rough coasts with breakers. The essential equipment includes long rods, strong reels, 0.30-0.40 mm line, and long-shafted nets. Shown at far right is a much quieter form of coastal spinning, from a float-ring close to the shore.

Cod fishing with natural bait

Scandinavians traditionally spin for cod with artificial bait, either from a boat or from land. In other countries such as Germany, Holland and Great Britain, natural baits are used to catch cod.

The given marine or coastal environment dictates the choice of methods and baits. Bottom fishing with natural bait at cliffs, piers and harbours can employ simple equipment. A strong rod of 9-11 feet, line of 0.35-0.45 mm, and a suitable casting weight, as well as paternoster tackle with one or two leaders, and hooks of size 1/0-3/0, are about all the items you need.

Cod are omnivorous, but some types of bait are preferred: lugworms, ragworms, herring strips, mussel meat, shrimps and cephalopods. After baiting and casting the hook, you can either hold the rod in your hand or lay it, within view, on a cliff or place it in a rod-holder. As soon as a cod bites, you make a strike.

At open coasts with sandy beaches, hard current and waves, surfcasting gear is essential. The rods are 11-13 feet long, specially designed for this rough environment. Most people prefer baitcasting reels, but spinning reels work well too. Due to the wear on the line when casting, it is necessary to have an extra-thick line tip, which must be long enough to form 5-6 turns on the reel spool before the cast. The cast itself requires a lot of training and, not least, familiarity with the equipment and how it is loaded.

Fighting the fish

When a cod bites, it heads for the bottom to hide itself among seaweed or stones. A superficially placed treble hook will thus easily catch in the weeds. You must therefore quickly put pressure on the fish, to lift it off the bottom. This is called "pumping in" the cod. With hard lifts of the rod, it is forced upward, while you reel in line each time the rod is lowered. The fish can be landed with a gaff and net, or slid up onto land where this is allowed by the coastline.

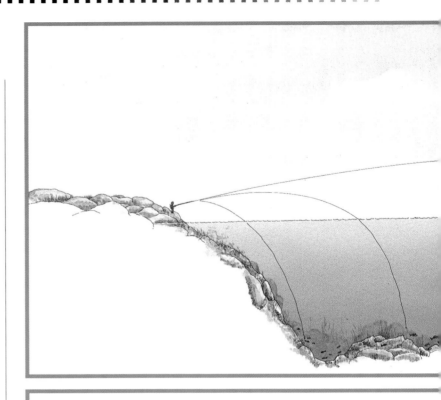

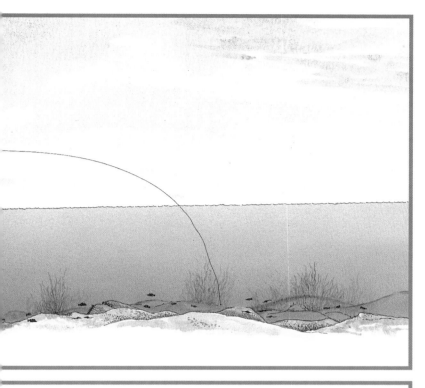

Left: Cod often occur where the water is deep even near shore and the bottom is thus not influenced by weather, wind and tides. Here they can hunt close to land, so a relatively short cast is sufficient.

Below: A cod usually weighs 1-5 kg (2-11 lbs). It is seldom a hard fighter, but appeals greatly to gourmets. By quickly "pumping" it up from the bottom after it bites, you can avoid bottom snags.

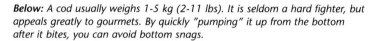

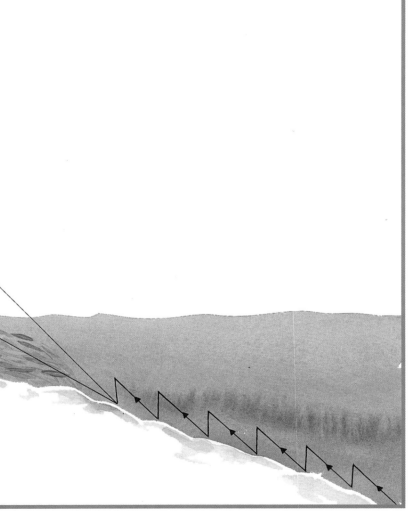

Left: Since the lure must be retrieved just over the bottom, snags may be hard to prevent. But as illustrated here, it is easier to lift the line over seaweed and other vegetation with a long rod than with a short one – especially when the lure approaches the shore.

European pollack

The European pollack (*Pollachius pollachius*) is one of the greatest challenges along rocky coasts of the Northeast Atlantic, where the chances are best of catching this beautiful fish. It is easy to recognize from its bronze-yellow, torpedo-shaped body, big brown hunter's eyes, strong underbite, and notably the dark lateral line that distinguishes it well from the coalfish. Although a type of cod, it has no barbels.

Pollack occur from the Faeroes and northern Norway to Morocco and the Mediterranean, but are chiefly distributed around the British Isles as well as southern and central Norway. They prefer rock coasts with good current and water circulation, living mainly at depths of 4-5 to 50 metres but found as far down as a hundred metres. They are drawn primarily to wrecks, sunken rocks and underwater cliffs. At the coasts, they weigh 0.5-2 kg (1.1-4.4 lbs), and examples up to 4-5 kg (8.8-11 lbs) are seen. Farther out to sea, wrecks have yielded pollack of 9-10 kg (20-22 lbs), which is the maximum.

Right: Pollack are a type of codfish but often live pelagically. They are fast and strong, and large pollack can offer exciting sport with powerful rushes toward the bottom.

Vital facts

Known spawning grounds exist off southern Norway and in the North Sea, where the spawning lasts from February until April. When the young are a few centimetres long, they wander toward the coasts, where they grow up, living on worms, crustaceans and fishfrye. Once larger, they eat small fish – mostly sand lance, herring and sprat – but sometimes also mysis shrimp and other small crustaceans. The pollack is not a bottom-fish like cod, but holds a bit over the bottom. At sundown and on dark, windy days with disturbed water, it usually moves up to the middle layer. It may even be found in the surface at dusk.

Spinning for pollack

Since they tend to hunt somewhat up from the bottom, at rocky cliffs or in surface water, pollack can be caught with relatively light spinning equipment. Exposed rocky coasts with strong currents and deep water are ideal places.

When spinning, it is most important to search all water layers with light, lively spoons or pirks, preferably in subdued colours such as copper, red/copper or green/blue. Pollack are occasionally rather fastidious, and may only take a certain bait of a special colour, size or type. Jigs are often superb for pollack. A little compact pirk with a single hook, carrying a fish strip, is also very lively and inviting.

The retrieval can be made with accelerations ending in long stops. Then the bait sinks through the water and can be reeled in again. It is during the pause, or when the bait resumes moving, that the pollack usually bites. The bite is hesitant and heavy, followed by a violent rush toward the bottom – which means your drag must be finely adjusted.

Droppers are effective, too, particularly in daytime when pollack take small lures. However, the risk is that the leader will snap if the fish dives and the pirk catches in seaweed.

Pollack fishing with natural bait

The pollack is a distinctly predatory species suitable for spinning, but it can very well be caught with natural bait that is fished with a float in breaking waves. A small float with a hook of size 1-1/0, baited with attractive fresh-cut sand lance, herring or mackerel, and swaying irresistibly in the swells, is excellent for pollack. Nor is it uncommon to catch these fish while float-angling for wrasse, which thrive in the same coastal environments.

Top: Jigs can be the right medicine for evasive pollack. Pirks baited with fish strips are also attractive when the pollack are choosy.

Bottom: Pollack are commonly found along rocky coasts where the water is kept moving by, for example, currents. In this case the pirk and droppers have crossed the path of a school of pollack.

Coalfish

The coalfish (*Pollachius virens*), widely called pollack, is another member of the cod family. Characterized by a dark-grey back, white lateral line and shiny tin-coloured abdomen, it lacks barbels and has a clear underbite. Its distribution resembles that of cod, but the southern limit goes through the Bay of Biscay, the northern boundary passing Iceland and southern Greenland. Coalfish also occur along the eastern coast of North America, from Newfoundland to New York.

Small specimens are often encountered off rocky coasts, and in deep water close to land – even just a few metres away. Large coalfish, weighing from 5-6 kg (11-13 lbs) up to the maximum of 25 kg (55 lbs), swim as far down as 400 metres.

Spinning for coalfish

These are extremely greedy creatures. Small coalfish, in particular, bite almost anything that moves. Spoons, pirks and droppers are therefore outstanding lures for them. Since the fish often hold in free water, you have to search it from top to bottom when working from a rocky coast, pier or breakwater, and remember that they may be right in the surface when evening or cloudy weather comes. Their hunting for small fish in the surface is commonly revealed by seagulls.

Vital facts

Coalfish spawn in the open sea, between January and April, at certain places with suitable temperature and salinity. The fry consume plankton but, as soon as this stage is over, the fish approach land. Weighing from a couple of hundred grams up to 1-1.5 kg (2.2-3.3 lbs), they may appear in enormous schools offshore, especially at rocks. The young coalfish feed occasionally on shrimp, otherwise on fish fry – mainly herring and sand lance – while the latter species are eaten by larger coalfish. Throughout their lives, coalfish form schools and seldom stay at the bottom, usually swimming some metres above it and nearly reaching the surface. As with European pollack, they rise at evening and night or in cloudy, windy weather.

The retrieval must be quick and varied. Keep in mind that coalfish, like pollack, may also bite when the spoon or pirk leaves the surface for a new cast. This fishing is not at all difficult, and anybody can land a fine catch of coalfish with no problems after locating them. While good places for pollack tend to be permanent, schools of small coalfish are frequently found by chance.

Large coalfish rarely swim next to land, so examples of 2-3 kg (4.4-6.6 lbs) are regarded as superb along coasts. But one area where big specimens can be caught from the coast is Saltströmmen, at Bodö in northern Norway. Local fishermen have brought up coalfish weighing over 20 kg (44 lbs) in November and December, a time when few people are out with spinning equipment at that latitude. Such prizes are taken with powerful rods, line of 0.60 mm, baitcasting reels and 200-gram pirks.

Above: The coalfish is a beautiful, gluttonous codfish that gladly takes a pirk, spoon or dropper.

Right: At rocky coasts, small coalfish often swim near land, but they may hold almost anywhere between the bottom and the surface. Varied retrieval, preferably with the countdown method, is therefore important in locating a coalfish school.

Mackerel

The mackerel (*Scomber scombrus*) is the ocean's mini-tuna. Its torpedo-like body puts it among the speed demons of the deep. A pelagic predator, a school fish, and a summer guest in the northern part of its distribution – from the top of Norway, past the Faeroes and Iceland, to Newfoundland – it occurs as far south as the Mediterranean and, in America, Cape Hatteras.

The native North Atlantic mackerel lacks a swim-bladder. An almost identical species, the Pacific mackerel (*Scomber japonicus*), lives from Alaska to Baja California, as well as on the Asiatic side of the Pacific and in the Indian Ocean. It resembles the former species, but has a swim-bladder. A third species is the Spanish mackerel (*Scomberomorus maculatus*), which ranges from Chesapeake Bay to Cuba on the American side of the Atlantic, and along the North African coast to the Canary Isles. Mackerel normally weigh up to 1 kg (2.2 lbs) and sometimes over twice as much.

Vital facts

Mackerel overwinter at depths of 400-600 metres in the Skagerrak and west of the British Isles. Those west of Ireland swim toward the Irish, English and Scottish coasts, whereas mackerel in the North Sea and Skagerrak approach the coast of Norway and enter the Skagerrak and Kattegat during springtime. Before then, they have spawned in deeper water, and spawning proceeds in free water near the coast.

The stocks of mackerel have suffered great changes, and the fishing was poor for many years in the 1960s and 1970s. Professional fishermen discovered their overwintering areas in the deeper parts of the North Sea, and could double the catches – which has irreparably harmed these stocks.

Spinning for mackerel

When the first mackerel head for the coast, between May and early July, they are hungry and tend to attack any moving object – including spoons, pirks and droppers. But later in July, having fed on sand lance and the young of herring and sprat, they become less eager to bite. It is then chiefly in the morning and evening, as they approach land to hunt, that fishing pays off. Their presence is often shown by gulls and other seabirds, which dive at the mackerel hunting small fish in the surface.

Spinning is done from cliffs, piers and breakwaters, where the water is deep and vigorous. Long-casting equipment with line of 0.30 mm, a shiny pirk of 20-50 grams, and a leader tied of 0.35-0.45 mm line, with a couple of little droppers made from feathers – in white, blue and green colours – suits the work perfectly. The water is searched from the bottom to the surface. Mackerel hunt in all water layers, but at dawn and dusk they swim in the uppermost layer and can frequently be seen in the surface.

Mackerel fishing with natural bait

Float-fishing for mackerel can be done wherever the fish exist. However, primarily in the later summer when they bite less greedily, natural baits usually yield results – even at midday as they go deeper.

Since the mackerel prefer to swim at 2-5 metres of depth, this fishing makes use of sliding floats. A float that carries 5-15 grams of lead is suitable, together with a leader having a hook of size 4-8 and a small fresh-cut strip of herring or sand lance. The fishing depth is adjusted by means of a stop-knot or a rubber stopper. For example, you can fish first at 4-5 metres and, if unlucky, try higher up in the water. When the fish bites, you are seldom left in doubt – but on some days the float only shakes a bit, and you have to strike immediately or the monster goes missing.

There are several species of mackerel. This is the North Atlantic variant, which has no swim bladder and can move easily between different depths. To find the depth at which it is hunting, one must often fish all levels according to the countdown method.

Garfish

The garfish (*Belone belone*) lives along the European coasts from the Arctic Circle, past the Faeroes, down to Morocco. It, too, is a summer fish in Scandinavian waters. The Mediterranean and the Black Sea also contain garfish. Yet its main habitats lie around the British Isles. Some closely related species inhabit tropical and subtropical seas.

Spinning for garfish

This is a marvellous sportfish, slender and beautiful, often seen more in the air than in the water when it has been hooked. One rarely meets a predatory fish which occurs so abundantly and is still so hard to catch.

Garfish frequently pursue a spoon or pirk without taking. Such "imitators" are noticed especially in the early part of the season, before their spawning has finished. After spawning, however, the biting begins and the fish can be sought at headlands or banks, from piers or breakwaters, and off coastal rocks, preferably where the current is strong.

These fish are ideal to challenge with light spinning equipment and spoons of 8-25 grams. Elongated, silvery spoons are best. Treble hooks of thin metal have proved to give superior

Vital facts

After overwintering to the south of Ireland, garfish arrive at the Scandinavian coasts in April or May. First come the big ones, often weighing about 1 kg (2.2 lbs), soon followed by the rest. Garfish spawn among seaweed and eel grass in shallow waters, once the sun has warmed these up. The spawning takes place in May and June, although it may last until August in some areas. Early during the season, garfish swim in schools, and small schools are commonly observed in the shallows. But when spawning is over, they spread out and appear both in the surface and in deep water. Here they eat fish fry, shrimp and stickleback. Late summer and early autumn find them retiring to the west.

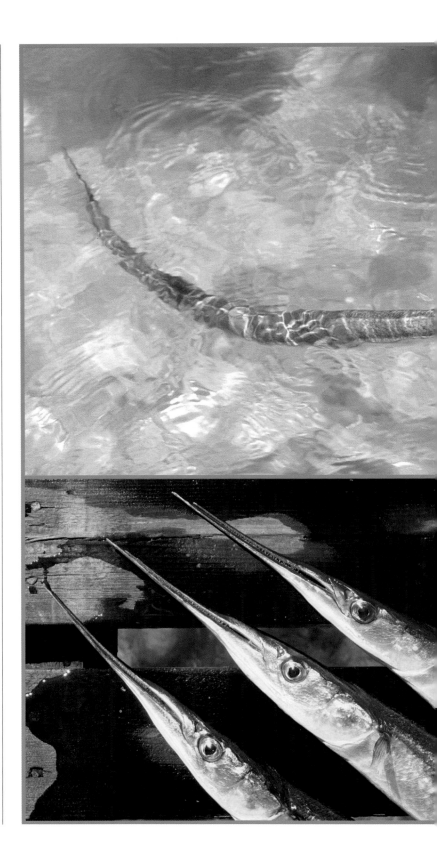

results. The garfish's mouth is small and not always easy to hook. Therefore, many of us remove the treble hook and tie it to a short nylon leader. This should not be longer than the spoon, since otherwise the hook may get caught in the main line during the cast.

The retrieval should be even and rapid. Do not be surprised if the fish follows the lure time and again. Once the fish bites, avoid delivering a strike and just tighten up the line well, to fight the fish with a softly set drag.

Catching garfish with natural bait

While the species is quite suitable for spinning, it also falls for natural bait. All you need is a fixed float with 1-1.2 metres of line to a small hook of size 4-8, carrying a small fresh-cut strip of herring or mackerel. Cast out and let the float lie still or drift with the current. The garfish swallow the bait with no trouble, and then you strike.

Left: The garfish is a slender, rapid swimmer with a long, hard "beak". It can be difficult to hook, but fights admirably and often leaps into the air.

Below: Light equipment, sharp treble hooks, and fast retrieval are the three rules of thumb for conquering garfish. They frequently travel in schools and, once found, can yield an abundant catch.

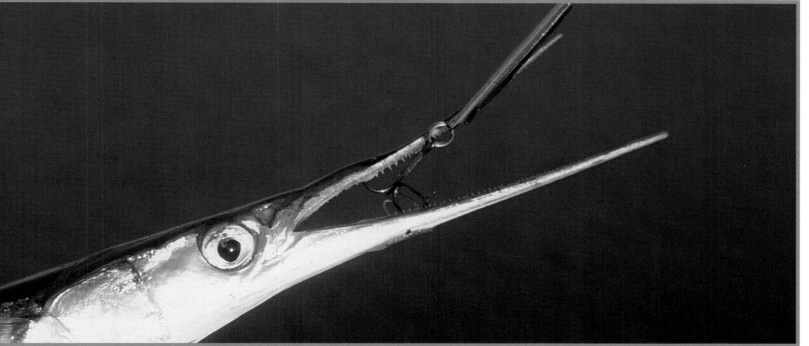

Sea trout

Equally exciting to match wits against are the ocean's silvery racers, sea trout (*Salmo trutta trutta*). Catching them in salt water is a Danish national sport – though also done with flies and Buldos at, for instance, estuaries in Orkney and the Shetlands after World War I. Coastal spinning was started by Danish sportfishermen during the inter-war period, but it developed mainly in the 1950s, at the same time as the equipment became ever better and could cast farther. In recent

Vital facts

Sea trout hunt along all shallow sections of coast that have rivers or waterways which the fish can run up to spawn in. After they spawn and return to the sea, they are emaciated and begin to eat worms, fish fry, herring and sprat. They become shiny and silvery, regaining their weight after a few weeks.

These fish stay along the coasts almost all year round, and can be caught in any month. But some periods are better than others, spring and autumn being excellent. During autumn, though, sea trout are not as willing to bite as in the spring.

The fish prefer mixed, varied bottoms with current, weeds, sand, stone and mussels. Consequently, good fishing places include banks, headlands and rocky points. From May throughout summer, the coastal water in many areas is too warm, so the sea trout move into deeper water, returning to the coast from evening until morning.

Some sea trout migrate up in streams and rivers as soon as June, while others head for fresh water during the autumn and early winter. The winter also brings many shiny non-spawning fish into coves and estuaries with lower salinity – and here they are found on soft, rather uninteresting bottoms.

decades, coastal fishing for sea trout has spread to Sweden, Norway and Germany.

Sea trout are distributed from northernmost Norway to the Dutch and French coasts, as well as around the British Isles. This fishing, however, is popular especially along the coasts of Denmark, southern Norway, and Sweden. The Baltic Sea contains notably large sea trout, and big ones also occur at the Danish coasts. Fish of 2-5 kg (4.4-11 lbs) are not uncommon. On the other hand, sea trout in Norway, Great Britain and Ireland are relatively small.

Spinning for sea trout

Since most sea trout cruise along the coasts, the fishing depends on chance. Thus, knowing what places they visit is very helpful. At the beginning of the year, they are attracted by ragworms, which gather to mate during early spring. Mussel banks and eel grass contain many kinds of animals – such as shrimp, worms, small fish and fry – that draw in sea trout, too. The more open, stony, current-combed coasts, where sand lance and small herring live, can be similarly rewarding.

Limited areas for coastal fishing are searched by casting in a fan-shaped pattern, or in various directions. The open coasts are fished with a cast every five or ten metres, according to the water's clarity.

Fishing is commonly combined with wading, which allows you to reach deeper water and cover larger areas, besides keeping closer contact with the fish itself.

The fishing can be divided into light, and somewhat heavier, spinning. In the former case, one uses spoons of 5-15 grams with light spinning or baitcasting rods and 0.15-0.23 mm line. Elsewhere, one may be forced to fight against wind and weather, requiring longer casts – so one frequently chooses stronger rods, 0.25-0.30 mm line, and elongated spoons or coastal wobblers of 15-30 grams.

Retrieval, during the spring and autumn, should be fast with repeated jerks or spin-stops, at each and every cast. In the winter, since the water is cold and the fish are less active, a calmer and slower – but still varied – retrieval is most effective. Dropper flies can also give results in certain places.

Coastal fishing for the seagoing form of trout requires equipment that is long-casting but relatively light. Good local knowledge, and lures which imitate the fish's natural prey, may be essential during the periods when sea trout are hard to trick.

It is often necessary to cover a promising stretch of coast thoroughly. Finding sea trout may also require one to move along the shore, while making a series of parallel casts or casting in a fan-shaped pattern.

Fishing with a casting bubble and flies enjoys wide popularity. The Buldo is a great aid especially in winter and early spring, when cold water prevails or when the fish are mostly focusing on a single type of food, such as ragworms. It is also worth using a casting bubble in summer until August-September, when sea trout are less eager to bite.

Fishing for sea trout with natural bait

Natural baits are often served to sea trout. Most simply, where the water is deep enough and a stony shore exists, you can fish with a fixed float and a short line to a hook with worms. But the absolutely best method is spinning with a Buldo and a leader of 1.5-3 metres with a single hook and worms.

The baits employed are earthworms, ragworms and herring strips. In some areas, small fish such as sprat and sand lance are preferred. Spinning with a casting bubble and natural baits is done all year round, with a slow retrieval and ideally some pauses so that the bait and hook can sink. If you want them to go deeper, the leader may be lengthened and weighted with a couple of lead shot, or a short piece of sinking fly-line can be tied to the line tip.

Slender spoons weighing 10-20 grams, and a dropper on a short leader of 20–30 cm (8-12 inches), are a combination that not even big sea trout are likely to resist.

Coastal spinning for sea trout should be done by presenting the lure just above the bottom. The retrieval must be varied and lively, with regular jerks and spin-stops, in order to entice sea trout.

European bass

The European bass (*Dicentrarchus labrax*) is the star species of sportfishing in Great Britain. Hardly any other fish around the British Isles has meant so much for the development of coastal fishing, surfcasting, and their equipment. Rods, reels, lines, leaders and other accessories have undergone enormous refinement in recent decades due to the fish's popularity.

These bass live chiefly around the British Isles, in the Bay of Biscay, on the Atlantic coast of the Iberian peninsula, off Morocco and in parts of the Mediterranean. They also occur

Vital facts

Open, surf-filled shorelines are the primary habit of European bass. Along beaches interrupted by rocky outcrops and breakwaters, they hunt sand lance, herring and crabs. Often they wander about at only half a metre of depth. Being attracted to river mouths and fresh water, they can also be caught from piers and barriers that give them shade on bright days in clear water.

Both on coasts with surf and in estuaries, the first hours after an ebb tide are considered good for catching bass. But no other firm rules exist for the fishing. They move to deep water in wintertime, and can be harvested almost all year round in Ireland. The spawning lasts from March until June in the British Isles, and takes place during late winter in the Mediterranean. These fish are widely prized by professional fishermen, and are universally regarded as fine food.

Fishing for European bass can be highly diverse. In some periods it is incredibly easy to get them to bite – on simple bottom tackle, a spoon or a mackerel tackle. At other times, particularly in clear water, they may become extremely shy and suspicious of any bait. Occasionally they fight like crazy, even in water just a few inches deep, or else become very lazy and virtually swim up on land by themselves without pressure from the rod.

in the Black Sea, and some are found at the coasts of southern Norway and western Sweden. The latter region has lately received ever more bass.

Weights of 5 kg (11 lbs) are seldom exceeded, and 1-2 kg (2.2-4.4 lbs) is most common. Professional fisherman, though, have landed bass weighing more than 10 kg (22 lbs). The species belongs to a family with several hundred representatives in subtropical and tropical waters.

Spinning for bass

This fish is caught mainly with natural bait. Despite being a genuine predator with well-developed eyesight, it does not attract direct efforts at spinning in most places. Such spinning is practiced, however, along the Dutch coast at many wrecks in relatively shallow water – with good results on pirks and spoons. In Great Britain, the species' homeland, spinning for it is not so common. To make it bite, the fisherman needs clear water, and thus has little success under murky conditions. The best season for spinning is from June until October. Classic spoons and pirks such as the Toby are excellent for bass. Bridge pillars, piers and breakwaters should be fished from, besides rocky headlands and underwater shoals in shallow water.

Fishing for bass with natural bait

When natural bait is used, these fish can be tempted at all sorts of places – river mouths and fjords, shore structures, open beaches and stony coasts. The fishing is easiest where the cast length does not matter much, as in estuary areas and from piers. Often, though, an acquaintance with the tides is essential, because bass are known for hunting over large shallow areas when the tide comes in. As mentioned, one does well to fish soon after the low tide.

Standard equipment for bass on open coasts is a rod 10.5-11.5 feet long, with a casting weight of 50-90 grams and line of 0.30-0.35 mm on a baitcasting or spinning reel. A thick line tip is also necessary. Bass are usually fished with a paternoster tackle – either fixed, which is most simple and effective, or sliding – and a single hook of size 1/0-3/0. Since the fish-

European bass are extremely popular in, for example, Great Britain – where they have strongly influenced the development of coastal fishing techniques and equipment. Normally they weigh 1-2 kg (2.2-4.4 lbs), but individuals over 5 kg (11 lbs) have been caught.

A number of bass have been landed at last. This voracious predator tends to prefer relatively shallow waters, taking both artificial and natural baits.

ing often occurs amid currents or waves, most people use a breakaway weight that is anchored on the bottom. The baits include lugworm, sand leeches, cuttlefish, sand lance, or small peeler crabs.

The great majority of bass fishermen need only be able to cast 40-90 metres. This is quite enough, as in many places one can wade into the surf – wearing waders. Moderate surf is best, and so is cloudy weather in general, although the fishing can be superb even in strong sunshine. A bite from a bass may show itself in various ways – ranging from a couple of tugs on the rod tip, to a slack line or a ferocious pull on the line.

Left: *Breakers and rocky coasts are favourite spots for the coastal fishermen who go after bass. The first hours after the ebb tide are usually most rewarding.*

Right: *Bass are temperamental fish – sometimes very easy to catch, but shy and wary during other periods. Here, a slender spoon has given good results.*

Striped bass

The striped bass (*Roccus saxatilis*) is a favourite of sport-fishermen along the eastern coast of America, from St. Lawrence Bay down to northern Florida, and in the Gulf of Mexico from western Florida to Louisiana. Yet the most famous stretch is from South Carolina to Massachusetts. This fish was introduced on the Pacific coast towards the end of the last century, and is thus also found from the Columbia River mouth in Washington to the Los Angeles area in California. Here the best-known place is San Francisco Bay, whose fishing is far better than on the east coast.

Striped bass resemble the European bass in many ways, but can grow much bigger. Examples approaching 50 kg (110 lbs) have been caught by professional fisherman, and up to 30 kg (66 lbs) by coastal fishermen. The commonest weights, how-

Vital facts

During the eastern winter, striped bass stay in Chesapeake and Delaware Bays. From there, a minor emigration of bass occurs in the winter. The fish spawn in river mouths from April until June, depending on the latitude. One renowned spawning area is the Roanoke River in North Carolina. They weigh scarcely half a kilogram (1 lb) when two years old, and 10 kg (22 lbs) when aged seven. The females grow bigger than the males. Striped bass are more or less omnivorous: their diet includes grey mullet, flatfish, herring, anchovy, lobster, crabs, shrimp and mussels. In spite of that, they eat selectively – when offered a certain type of food, they often concentrate on it and may therefore be unwilling to bite. Some bass stocks migrate locally, and there are two long major migrations every year: northward in springtime along the coasts of New Jersey, New York and New England, then southward in autumn. These occasions, especially the latter, provide the best coastal catches.

ever, are 3-8 kg (6.6-18 kg). On the east coast, striped bass have been fished hard by professionals for long periods, suffering serious stock reduction. Still, this spectacular fish is available if you are on the coast at the right time and place. Moreover, it has been implanted successfully in large lakes in North and South Carolina.

Fishing for striped bass

Spinning is done with very strong spinning or surfcasting gear, and large plugs or spoons. Rods of 10-11 feet, and ample spinning or multiplier reels filled with 0.35-0.45 mm line, are standard. Wind, weather, currents, migrations and, not least, the supply of preyfish are influential – and suddenly these bass may appear for a short time near land, where they can be caught. Early morning and the evening are profitable, but night fishing with natural bait is also common.

Bottom fishing with natural bait is as frequent as spinning. Among the baits used are small fish, worms, crabs, fish fillet, and sand lance. But the leaders, hooks, and other equipment must be adapted to the widely varying conditions of this fishing, from the surf on open coasts to the rocks and breakwaters where spinning is possible. It is tough work, and can prove demanding indeed.

Striped bass may be up to 2 metres (6.6 feet) long, and then weigh about 50 kg (110 lbs), but specimens of 3-8 kg (6.5-18 lbs) are most common. These are distinctive predators and call for comparatively strong gear, combined with either artificial or natural baits. In the tough fishing along wave-worn coasts, surfcasting is the usual method.

Top left: When fishing for red drum in the "Texas style", one wades out with a big lure until chest-deep. Then the lure is let down and one wades back to shore, to await the fish's bite.

Bottom left: Red drum are often fished in the dark hours. These fish live in shallow water – eating smaller fish, mussels and crabs, for instance – and thus take both natural and artificial baits.

Above: Tarpon are characterized by their many silvery scales and their bone-hard mouths. They are also, of course, famous for high leaps in the air and for being able to snap the strongest lines...

Other large sportfish

There are many other fine species of sportfish, such as the **Bluefish** (Pomatomus saltatrix) which is found in nearly all subtropical parts of the Atlantic, in the Black Sea and Mediterranean, and along the Atlantic coasts of the Iberian peninsula, northwest Africa, the Canary Islands, Azores and America. It is hard to give any general advice about choice of equipment since, for example, catching bluefish that weigh a kilogram in a Florida bay is very different from casting against wind and waves on the open coast of New Jersey. Yet under all conditions, this is a fast and wild opponent.

Weakfish (Cynoscion regalis) occur along the east coast of the United States, and can be encountered in the shallower waters of coves and river mouths. This popular sportfish is often easily caught with bottom tackle.

Red drum (Sciaenops ocellatus) are found on the American coast. A bottom fish, living chiefly on crustaceans, this species is best caught in the morning and evening with robust equipment.

Tarpon (Megalops atlanticus) live throughout the Caribbean and along the coasts of many West African countries. A tarpon weighs from a few kilograms up to hundreds, and has excellent fighting qualities. The fishing is normally done from a boat with plugs or natural baits.

For the dedicated angler, great adventures beckon from nearly all waters. Every movement on the surface becomes an attraction and we can spend days and weeks with tireless optimism trying to catch fish with our baits. The enormous time that generations of anglers have spent with varying success on fishing waters around the world provides us with knowledge embracing all the angler needs to pursue effective fishing.

Angling

The history of modern angling

Catching fish with a baited hook is a practice that has certainly existed as long as human beings, but modern angling is usually associated with the age that has given us TV and computers. However, read these quotations:

"Chop up some cat or rabbit meat... mix with bone-meal... or other meal. Add sugar or preferably honey... knead it with the hands. Form... bait balls."

"...throw a bit of the dough into the pond or river where you intend to fish. If you... throw small balls of the dough into the water now and then, a few days beforehand... if the pond is large, you can lure the fish to a particular place, and do your fishing with hopes of success..."

This is modern carp fishing in a nutshell. With a prebaiting strategy and recipes for bait which if boiled, would have been boilies, a high-tech bait for carp. Today's fishermen have only exchanged cat and rabbit meat for milk powder and the like.

The above quotations are from a book, *The Compleat Angler*, which was published in England in 1653. Thus, modern angling has much older roots than most people realize, when they follow a prebaiting strategy for large bream or buy boilies in the store. Izaak Walton, the book's author, came from England, and it is largely the developments in Great Britain that we have to thank for modern angling.

Specimen angling

During the 1950s some fisherman began to go after big carp in the waters of Reedmire, in Wales. Although it was then believed that carp were impossible to catch (Walton's work in the 1600s had been forgotten), these efforts succeeded. The pioneer, Richard Walker, landed a carp of 19.9 kg (44 lb). It was christened Clarissa and became a new English record, lasting until well into the 1970s. Walker and his colleagues established the principles that we see in modern angling directed at large fish – specimen angling. The fish must be handled with respect and released, and today there are many waters in Europe where fish that have been caught several times bear their own names.

The success with carp stimulated directed angling for other species, and soon there were 'specimen groups' all over the country, specializing in pike, bream, eel and so on. These groups experimented freely with bait. During the 1970s the idea arose that paste made of egg and various sorts of flour

could be boiled to produce a bait that was both adored by carp and ignored by smaller fish. A magic ball – the boilie – was born and the carp-fishing boom, which has by now conquered the continent, began.

Equipment

Hunters of huge fish also found that contemporary equipment was not very good, which led to the development of today's modern rods for angling with a reel. The same period also brought refinements in fishing with a rod that has no reel, the 'top knot' angling rod, in countries such as Italy and France. In the wake of the new gear, interest in fishing contests grew, and rods for light float angling have thus acquired the name of 'match rods'. In Italy, competition angling has expanded so far as to become the nation's biggest public sport after football!

Above: Modern angling is a source of enjoyment and relaxation as well as comradeship and ranges from carp fishing to catching predators

Right: In modern angling it is a basic principle that the fish should be treated respectfully and returned to the water

Equipment

Rods

Light float angling

Match rods are made for angling with light floats that carry 0.5–10 grams. (0,17-0,35 oz) In order to be able to cast the tackle of float, sinker and hook, thin lines of 0.10–0.18 mm (0,004-0,007 in) are required. The rods have many rings to prevent the lines from catching against the blade. Their length is around four meters, and the action depends on the kind of fishing. More top action is needed to fish fast for species such as bleak and roach, with rapid response to quick takes a few rod lengths out. Deeper action suits fishing with heavier floats at a greater distance, or for larger fish, since more line has to be lifted when hooking and one must minimize the risk of breaking the line if the fish lunges.

Light bottom angling

Rods for light bottom angling, of about 10–45 g (0,35-1,5 oz), come in two types. A quivertip rod reveals the take at its tip. It has exchangeable tops for different kinds of fish-ing. In strong currents or at great distances, a stiffer top is needed. Close up, and in still waters, the top should be soft-er. Such rods are around 11–12 feet (3.5 m) long. A ledger rod, which is around 10-feet (3 m) long, has a threaded top-ring, where an extra top can be screwed on. It can be fished with a screwed-on quivertip or a swingtip (see Bottom angling).

Heavier bottom and float angling

Rods for heavier bottom angling, of 45–150 g (1,5-5,2 oz), are synonymous with carp rods. However, they are also used for other heavy work such as pike angling. They are classified in pounds, usually 1–3 lbs (0.4–1.3 kg). The fishing distance determines the rod's action and power. Really long casts, over 100 m (330 ft), call for the most power and top action, but are also more risky as the fish may tear loose, especially when near the net. A softer rod with lower class, about 2 lbs (1.Kg), can be considered an all-rounder. It catches up the fish's lunges better, decreas-ing the risk of a line break or of losing the fish by tearing the hook loose.

The rod holder is a prerequisite for effective bottom angling, here with a quivertip rod.

A quivertip rod for bottom angling is up to 12-feet (3.5 m) long and has exchangeable tops with different stiffness.

In the netting phase, the risk is greatest that the fish will be lost if it makes a wild lunge. A weaker rod absorbs the lunge much better than a stiff rod.

Swingers hang by an arm attached to the rod holder or rack. The best models have movable weighs on arms so that the resistance can be adjusted. A swinger holds the line stretched and ensures that line movement (when a fish takes bait) is sensed by the electronic bite indicator so that it bleeps and blinks.

Long rods

A long rod has the line knotted at its top. There are two variants: telescopic rods of fixed lengths from 10–45 feet (3–14 m), which are fished with full line length, and the 'take-apart' rod, which can be disassembled in parts about 5 feet (1.5 m) long. The latter is fished with a short line, about a meter from the rod tip to the float. When the fish bites, the fisherman pulls the rod in until the length of line is sufficient for dividing the rod and lifting in the fish, or drawing it over the net. This rod has a length of 20–50 feet (6–16 m).

Reels

The spinning reel is the angling reel. Special models for light float and bottom angling have extra-shallow spools, so that there is no need for many hundred meters of thin line to fill them to the right depth.

For heavier angling, as in carp fishing, or on the bottom for pike, the most often-used models have a 'baitrunner function' – a button on the reel that can free the spool and enable a fish to pull line. When the button is pressed, a pre-set brake intervenes.

Bite indicators

Apart from the quivertip and swingtip, there are two types of indicators: electronic, with signaling by sound and light, and mechanical. The latter is used in combination with an electronic one, to make it react regardless of whether the fish swims toward or away from the fisherman, and to show clearly which rod the take is on.

Mechanical

With a 'monkey climber' the fisherman can have an open bail on the reel, allowing the fish to pull line without resistance. At the take, the 'monkey' climbs up on the pin, until more line is released from the reel and it slides back down. If the fish swims inward, the 'monkey' falls. A 'swinger' is adapted to fishing with baitrunner reels, and has a weighted arm that hangs on the line near the electronic indicator. A pure 'hanger' indicator is also popular with a baitrunner, but cannot be as nearly weightless on the line as a 'swinger'.

Electronic

Electronic indicators are used in all angling where a long time may pass between bites – for example by carp, sheatfish, pike and tench. They are both rod holders and bite alarms, bleeping and blinking when the line moves. The best kinds have adjustable volume and sensitivity, as well as a light diode that shines for several seconds after the line has moved, so that one can see which rod is involved. Such an aid is essential when fishing for species that bite cautiously, or in carp fishing when smaller fish dart in to pull at the hook bait, so that the fisherman can tell which bait may need to be changed.

Rod supports

Bankstick.

A bankstick is a telescopic 'stick' that serves as a rod holder, alarm and so on.

Rod holder

When fishing without a bite indicator, a rod holder is necessary. It is threaded to screw onto a bankstick. Ideally, the rod can be placed in several positions to find the best one for seeing the take.

Rod rack

For fishing with several rods at once, it is common to use a rack on legs. Both a bite indicator and bite alarm can be kept there. This is invaluable in places where a bankstick cannot be set firmly in the ground.

Nets

A net is indispensable. Smart fishermen always have their net ready and close to hand. The first take can mean a dream fish. And how many times have I myself stood trying to screw the net together with a big carp doing its best to wriggle loose? A good net has a knotless, fine mesh. It is wide and deep enough for a large fish to go in easily. For pike and carp, it must be at least a meter wide, but 60 cm (2 ft) is sufficient to hold a tench or bream, for example.

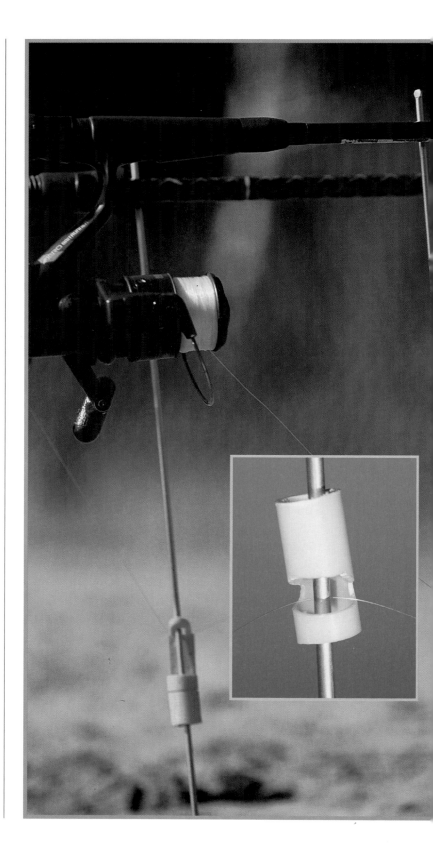

The monkey climber hangs on a pin with the line locked between itself and the pin. It climbs up when a fish bites, or falls if the fish swims inward. It is perfect for fishing with an open bail, so that the fish can pull line without resistance. Then the monkey climbs until line is released from the spool, slides down and climbs again, and so on.

Hook and line

Nylon line in dimensions from about 0.06 to 0.45 mm (0.002-0.02 in), despite the success of braided lines, is the best line for angling, with few exceptions. Hooks come in countless models with special properties. Line dimensions, hook models and sizes are given in the sections on different species.

Other accessories

Also useful in modern angling are scales, to weigh the fish before it is returned, and many other gadgets to make the fishing comfortable. These include special tents, parasols, beds and the like.

The carp fisherman sits protected from the rain under a parasol, the rods being rigged with bite alarms and indicators so that the slightest movement of line by a fish gives a clear signal in the form of a waving swinger and blinking, bleeping alarm.

Modern angling is often directed at species such as carp, sheatfish, pike and tench, whose bites may occur at long intervals. This has led to the development of electronic alarms and many other aids for the fisherman's comfort – including special tents, parasols and beds.

The net must be able to hold the biggest fish you can imagine biting. For carp and pike, it should be at least a meter wide.

Fish management

Modern angling, with few exceptions, is a matter of catching and releasing the fish. Every caught fish must therefore be treated with care and respect, to be in the same condition when it is returned to the water as before it took the bait. Photographing the fish for posterity commonly precedes the release.

Accessories and handling

Carp fishing has been developed into a kind of art, but all fish should still be handled equally well if they are to be released. What follows here is advice on how to deal with the catch from the moment it is netted until it returns to its natural element. Considerateness starts before the fishing trip. With these accessories and methods, the risk of damaging the fish is minimized.

Landing net. A net with soft, knotless mesh yarn.

Carp sack. A keep-sack that the fish can be laid in while, say, waiting for comrades to help with photography, or setting up your own camera. A carp sack is made of soft nylon cloth that lets in water. Fish that are placed inside it will normally stay still and recover.

Carp rug. A carp rug is a soft 'fish mattress'. It is wetted before laying the fish on it, to protect the fish's slime layer, and prevents damage if the fish thrashes about. The rug is used both when the hook must be removed and when photographing. Generally the fish stays calm if its eyes are covered with, for example, a carp sack. If the fish has spent time in a sack, it will usually have regained strength, so one must be ready for wriggles and leaps. Big fish are held low over the rug to avoid injury, should the fisherman lose his grip. If a large fish such as a carp begins to twist loose, it can be held with a hug, pulling it toward the body and locking your arms round it.

Really large fish, such as pike of monstrous dimensions, should not be lifted completely if the fisherman is on top. Then it is easier to lift only the pike's head and front body, letting the rest stay lying on the rug. The fish must never be held upright with a grip on the gills or head, as this can damage its internal organs.

Disgorger. A disgorger is for loosening single hooks, and forceps for treble hooks. If the hook is badly stuck in the fish's throat, it can be better to cut the line or leader than to try loos-

A carp sack, made of soft nylon cloth that lets in water, is perfect for storing fish in while waiting for a photo. There they stay still and can recover after the fight.

ening the hook and risk serious bleeding. A large pike is held firmly when laid on its back; the fisherman straddles it and lifts up its head.

Returning the fish

Lower the fish into the water and keep hold of it. Move it carefully back and forth if it seems exhausted, so that fresh water enters its mouth and streams over the gills. Grip it with one hand by the narrow part of the tail and support it with the other hand. Keep hold until it swims away by itself.

Top: A carp rug – a soft 'fish mattress' is used to lay the fish on when it is measured, the hook is removed, and while photographing.

Bottom: A big fish is held low over the carp rug to avoid injury if the fisherman should drop it.

Top: Small single hooks are best loosened with a disgorger.

Bottom: Hold the fish in the water and, if it seems exhausted, move it back and forth so that fresh water flows in through its mouth and over the gills. Do not let go until the fish swims away under its own power.

Float angling – match angling

Match angling might appear complicated, but the principles are simple. With these in your baggage, you have a solid basis for varied fishing under widely different conditions and for numerous species – roach at the quay, bream at 40 m (130 ft) from land, spring perch in the deep holes of streams, grayling in the fast stretches of rivers, or tench at the reed edge on a balmy summer morning.

The float has an obvious function. It should succeed as rapidly as possible in presenting the bait where a fish is, to get a bite – and show the bite clearly. The tackle must also operate so that you are continuously able to keep the line stretched between the rod and float. Good line control is essential for hooking the fish before it lets go of the bait.

Flowing water

Stick float. A classic technique for flowing waters is to fish with a stick float. This is a thin, sensitive, pen-shaped float for low sinking weight, with an upper fuselage made of balsa and an underbody of bamboo. It is attached with rubber rings at top and bot-

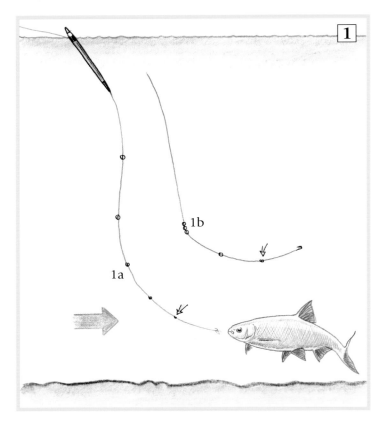

Match angling with loosefeeding near land is superb for a number of species.

tom (like the Avon float below). By putting on an extra ring when tackling up, you avoid re-tying the tackle if one ring breaks.

The sinkers are spread along the line, with the heaviest one closest to the float and the lightest, called the signal shot, nearest the hook (Ill. 1a). Its placement and size determine how rapidly and clearly the take is seen. Cast out with a side-cast, where the line is 'feathered' – braking the cast with your finger against the reel – just before the tackle lands. Then the line stretches out and you see the bait taken 'on the drop' from the surface to the bottom.

The float should travel with the current downstream, the bait going before the tackle. The bail on the reel is open. Your index finger locks the line against the reel while the rod tip follows the float downstream. Line is released when the rod tip is moved back, with your finger off the reel. If the float dives, you lock the line again with your finger, raise the rod and hook the fish. Now and then the float is restrained and the bait rises, then falls through the water when the float is released again. The bite often comes when the bait is braked.

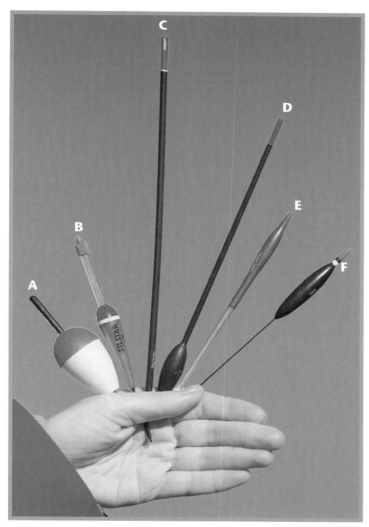

Different types of floats. From left: (A) Type previously used in Scandinavia for perch angling with baitfish – being large, chubby and insensitive, it is everything a modern float should not be. With such a float, the take cannot be seen before the fish has swallowed the bait and swum away. (B) An adequate float for perch fishing with a small baitfish. (C) Waggler for fishing in flowing waters, or still waters at close range. (D) Antenna float for medium to long distance in still waters. (E) Stick float and (F) Avon float for flowing waters

Roach is a classic match-angling species. Taken with a stick float in flowing waters, or an antenna float in still waters, combined with loosefeeding.

Combined with 'loosefeeding' (see Prebaiting) and light baits such as maggot, casters and corn grains, this method is very effective for fish that can stand anywhere between the surface and bottom – roach, rudd, chub, ide and grayling. If the fish is standing closer to the bottom, a clump of shot is placed deeper, with the others spread below them. The bait will come down fast but its falling and rising movement can still be exploited (Ill 1b)

A stick float is only useful in weak currents and one or two rod lengths out, at depths to about 10 feet (3 m), since it is easily pulled under. In strong currents, or if the fish will be standing farther out, an Avon float is more suitable.

Stick floats and Avon floats are usually fished with an overdepth – greater distance between the float and hook than the water depth, between 2–6 inches (5–15 cm). When the tackle is braked with the finger against the reel edge, the bait still wanders forward along the bottom. If the bite occurs only 'on the drop' and when you hold back strongly, the fish will stand higher and the distance between hook and float can be decreased

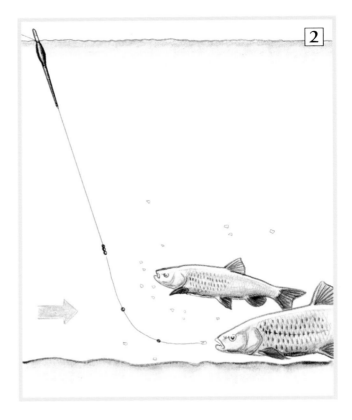

Avon float

An Avon float is also tackled at top and bottom, but has a larger and more robust fuselage than the stick float (Ill. 2). It can bear more weight and take the bait deeper through stronger currents without being pulled under. Further, it can be held back and make the bait rise without the float rising out of the water – which would make it difficult to see the takes.

Since the Avon float is normally used for fish that stand deep, the shot is mostly placed in a clump about two-thirds of the way down from the float, the rest being spread out down to the hook. (The distance between shots should decrease all the way down to the hook, to prevent tangling by their catching on each other during the cast; this rule applies to all float tackle.)

The technique resembles that for stick-float fishing. You brake the tackle lightly and let the bait travel first. The Avon

Top left: Match angling is perfect for small baits such as a corn grain or a maggot.
Bottom left: Simple corn attracted one bream after the other.
Opposite Top: Even big carp can be taken with match angling.
Opposite Bottom: Fishing with an Avon float and waggler is ideal for chub.

Grayling are readily caught with a maggot and a stick or Avon float.

__Opposite:__ Loosefeeding – casting or shooting out hooked baits – is an excellent method of prebaiting when fishing at close range, in both flowing and still waters.

float is also excellent for fishing with large bread baits, which are very buoyant and need plenty of weight to be brought down to the right depth. It is used to catch chub, ide, large rudd and roach that stand deep. Moreover, it is perfect for 'long-trotting', where the float is allowed to travel far, up to 20–30 m (65-100 ft), for instance, when fishing for grayling or perch.

Waggler

In waggler fishing, the bait goes after the tackle (Ill. 3). This is fine when the fish stands at the bottom and wants bait that moves slowly. The float is fastened at the bottom and is fished with overdepth. The signal shot and the baited hook are dragged along the bottom by the current. A waggler float does not need to be held back to be effective, and it can be fished with upstream casts.

The sinker weights are placed in a clump 1.5–3 feet (0.5–1 m) over the bottom, with a few isolated shot between them and the signal shot. The stronger the current, the larger the sinker required to stay on the bottom, so the bigger the float. While it travels with the current, the float

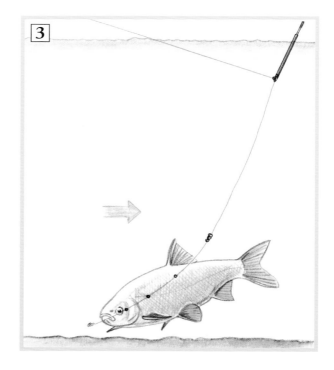

acquires a waggling gait as the sinker catches and lets go – hence the name of the method and the float.

Waggling is suitable for bream in every season, as well as for roach, perch and other species when the conditions make the fish stand at the bottom – cold weather or a hard current.

If the fish refuses to take a bait that moves at the pace of the tackle, you need to hold the float back. Try an Avon float with overdepth, which can be restrained without being pulled under. Release the tackle slowly downstream, little by little.

Still waters

At close range

Most still water float fishing is done with antenna floats – either with only one long antenna, such as a waggler float, or also with a long extra fuselage. They are fastened at the bottom through a small ring.

Fishing in middle to bottom waters

Up to seven or eight meters from land, a straight antenna float with a millimeter-thick extra top, or 'insert', is perfect. Buoyancy from a body is not needed; the float carries enough weight for casting and for bringing the bait to the desired fishing depth. With a few millimeters of insert over the water surface, the float is hypersensitive.

The shot are placed mostly around the float, as casting weight and so that it will rise directly, making the take visible. Just over halfway down, a 'semi-large' shot is placed. The next is the signal shot, 4–6 inches (10–15 cm) from the hook. This is a simple, sensitive tackle for virtually all fish that move between the bottom and a meter up. The halfway shot keeps the line stretched and quickly brings the bait to a depth where it slowly, attractively falls toward the bottom.

Depending on the takes, the sinkers are adjusted. If they delay minutes after the cast, the halfway shot is moved downward, as the fish wants the bait at the bottom. If they come lightning-fast, the fish takes the bait in the middle water, so you should move more weight up toward the float, or fish more shallowly.

Lift bite – fish at the bottom

When fishing at close range on the bottom, as for tench, a strong antenna float is needed It must carry a shot heavy enough to lie on the bottom and hold the bait in position. Sinkers that are sufficient as casting weight and to set up the

float are placed around the float, but not more than enough to sink half the antenna. A sinker at the bottom should pull down until 1–2 cm (0.4-0.8 in) of the float sticks up. If the fish takes the bait and lifts the sinker, the float rises – a classic lift bite that thrills the heart of every lover of tench fishing. When the fish takes the bait sideways along the bottom, the float wanders away and is slowly pulled under.

Wind and surface current

When there is a wind or surface current, the line needs to be sunk between the float and rod tip Then an antenna float with more weight at the float is used. The extra sinker weight stabilizes it and gives extra casting length. Otherwise, the weighting is the same as for fishing in middle to bottom waters.

The cast is made some meters too long. With the rod tip under the surface, the line is wound in until the float reaches the fishing spot. Then the line is pulled under the surface and you can fish sensitively in spite of wind and current.

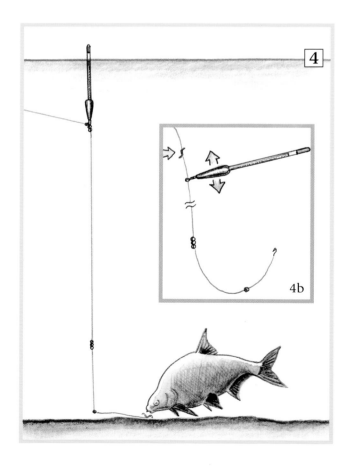

4

4b

At long distance

For fishing at distances of 50–130 feet (15–40 m), large antenna floats are needed, with a body that takes considerable weighting (Ill. 4) – both to provide a long cast and to give good line control, since the effect of current and wind on the line increases with distance.

Most of the sinker lead is placed around the float, making it shoot like an arrow through the air. Farther down are some more robust sinkers to take the bait quickly down to the fish. How the sinkers sit there depends on the fish species. For fish such as roach, which can stand some way up in the water, the tackle resembles that for fishing in middle to bottom waters. For bottom-living fish such as bream, one or two pairs of large sinkers sit between the bulk and the signal shot. When the bait is to be presented on the bottom, often a big shot must lie on the bottom so that the float will not drift away due to current and wind. A sunken line works best.

There are antenna floats for long-distance fishing with a weighted body. They are excellent if you do not want much sinker on the line, as when the fish take bait in the middle water. In addition, they are good when a gliding float is needed, for fishing at greater depth than the rod length. The tackle then looks as described above, except that the float rests against the deeper shot and is stopped higher up on the line by a stop knot (Ill. 4b).

Weighted floats with a thin insert are of limited use. Small models can be employed for fishing at close range, when the fisherman wants a little shot on the line, but at long distance they do not work because the insert cannot be seen.

Sounding

A prerequisite for effective float angling is to sound the fishing depth. Sounding gives information on where slopes exist and terminate, whether there are deep holes, and what rubbish or vegetation may be out of sight on the bottom. Which part of the fishing place do roach or bream stand in? Which float should be chosen? How should it be adjusted if they do not bite, or stop biting?

A float angler sounds the place most easily by putting an extra weight on the hook and casting around in the area, so as to set the float properly. Special sounding sinkers are available, but at short distances it is also possible to use a heavy sinker such as an SSG clamped around the hook.

Close-range fishing with a light antenna float works very well for carp.

Bottom angling

Originally, bottom angling was an alternative when float angling did not work – for fishing at a great distance or depth, in strong currents or by dark. It has since grown into a very exciting technique of its own. In many cases, it is a better choice than float angling, not least for bottom species such as eel, tench, bream and carp. But it also helps in hunting bigger fish, which are often found on the bottom and may need to be caught under special conditions, as in the darkest hours of night.

Below and right: A good deal of bottom angling for large fish such as carp, eel, and tench is done with the rod in the holder, an electronic bite alarm and a monkey-climber, since there may be a long wait.

Gliding bottom angling

In spite of its simplicity, the gliding technique of bottom angling is very effective for numerous species. Its ordinary variant can use standard spinning equipment, although a slightly longer rod of three meters (9 ft) or more is often best.

Gliding tackle for bottom angling is most easily made by threading the line through a pear sinker's swivel, knotting the hook on the line end, and stopping the sinker about 20 inches

With a light stave at the top of the quivertip, it works perfectly after darkness falls.

(50 cm) up with a clamped lead shot. This works at close range with light sinkers of 15–25 grams (0.5-0.9 oz), but if the fishing is to be done with bigger sinkers or at greater distances, the lead shot may slide on the line and damage it at the cast.

Nylon leader. Instead, tie a leader of nylon with a hook and a swivel to the main line, after threading the line through the sinker's swivel. A plastic bead between the sinker swivel and the leader protects the knot. This is a simple and good tackle for fishing with large baits such as worms or some corn grains – for eel, tench, perch, bream and other species.

If you do not want to use an electronic bite alarm when fishing with gliding bottom angle, fold a piece of aluminum foil over the line between the first and second rod rings. The foil will rise at the take and fly off at the strike, without risking any tangle.

Soft leader. A variant of gliding tackle, developed for carp fishing with soft leader material and boilies (boiled paste balls – see the chapter on baits), has the sinker attached to a plastic tube that the line is threaded through. A soft leader is used for tackle-shy fish, and the tube prevents the leader from tangling in the cast. The tube is longer than the leader to keep the hook from catching. The knot is protected by a plastic bead.

For all boilie fishing, a hair rig is outstanding, since the hook gets exposed and fastens better. An advantage with soft leader material is that it can be used to tie the hair rig – a line stump at the hook that the bait is threaded upon. This tackle also works well for tench. An adequate leader length is 16 inches (40 cm) for carp and 10 inches (25 cm) for tench. There are plenty of soft leader materials. My usual choices are 'Merlin' for carp and 'Silkworm' for tench, of the English brand Kryston. Soft leader materials are sensitive to wearing by stones and so forth, but Merlin has always endured, in contrast to other similar materials. Silkworm of 12 lbs (5.4 kg) strength, which is very thin and supple, is perfect for tench

Bottom angling is the only possible method when the fish are so far out that a cast with float tackle cannot reach them.
In addition, wading is sometimes needed to come in contact with the fish.

fishing and can take the strain from reeds, pondweed and water lilies during the wildest fish fights.

Fixed tackle – bolt rig

Carp fishing with boilies has also yielded tackle with a fixed sinker, called a bolt rig. The fish takes the bait in its mouth and the hook digs in when the leader is stretched against the sinker. The fish 'bolts' and the fisherman lifts the rod to drive in the hook. Generally the strike is lightning-fast, and the line tears off the reel so that the rod shakes in the holder!

This method was developed for tackle-shy fish in England. In certain hard-fished waters, carp have now learned to shake loose the hook if it is on a soft leader, often without the fisherman getting a single indication of a take! Hence, a return has been necessary to stiff nylon leaders, which make it harder for the fish to get rid of the hook after taking the bait in its mouth.

A bolt rig is created most easily with a stop knot just behind the sinker, if nylon leader is used – or behind the plastic tube if a soft leader is used. In both cases, a little plastic bead is required as a stop for the knot. This tackle is extremely effective when fishing with small boilies for tench. The leader must be very short, 4– 6 inches (10–15 cm). For carp, it can be longer, up to 12 inches (30 cm), but normally a short leader is better for cautious fish. My fishing comrades and I have taken big carp in late autumn on a leader as short as 7 inches (18 cm).

The technique of a fixed sinker and hair rig is also good with baits other than boilies, such as corn, bread paste and cheese. All that is demanded of the bait, to function on a bolt tackle, is that it should not be so soft that it comes loose.

Helicopter rig

A nearly tangle-free tackle for fishing with a fixed sinker and soft leader is the helicopter rig. The leader cannot get caught in the tackle, and it whirls around the line like a propeller during the cast. The technique is similar to that of the preceding tackle with short leaders. It is especially good when fishing at long distance, or where the bait has to lie in for a considerable time. For example, during long dark autumn nights, the bait lies in the same place for 10–12 hours, since it is impossible to cast again with precision. Another such situation occurs in sensitive waters where several splashing casts can frighten shy fish away. At that point, a tangle can ruin a whole fishing tour!

Quivertip (lower) and swingtip (upper).

Hook, sinkers, plastic beads – only these are needed for simple gliding bottom angling.

Quivertip and swingtip angling

In the quick fishing with bite indicators at the rod top – quivertip and swingtip – the fisherman sits with a hand on the rod handle, while the rod rests in a holder in front, ready to hook at the slightest movement. The swingtip is an extra tip that hangs from the top ring by a piece of soft rubber tubing. The take is seen when the tip rises or falls as the fish moves the sinker.

The choice between a swingtip and quivertip depends on personal taste. A swingtip is also limited by its sensitivity to wind and current, but it is superior if the fish are very cautious, or when fishing for species such as bream and tench with baits like corn or worms. Then the take may need to be 'waited out' – instead of hooking at the first indication, the fisherman waits until the swingtip has risen a little farther. With a quivertip, the take could be missed in such a situation, as the resistance to the fish increases the more the quivertip is bent.

In flowing waters and at greater distances, the quivertip is best, being easier to cast with. When fishing for species such as chub, rudd, perch, roach and bream in flowing waters – or at dark when going after roach, for instance – it is combined with a swimfeeder. To enable the fisherman to see the take in the dark, a small light stave is taped at the top.

Tackle

The most common tackle for light bottom angling is a 'paternoster', with the sinker in a leader of 8–12 inches (20–30 cm), tied to the main line 2–3 feet (70–100 cm) above the hook. The longer the sinker leader, the farther the fish can move with the bait before it feels the sinker's weight. The shorter the hook leader, the more quickly the rod tip shows when the fish takes. The lengths are varied according to how the fish are biting, so that clear indications will result in hooked fish.

Fishing with a swimfeeder is excellent for serving the prebait right at the hook bait, when bottom angling for a number of species.

***Top:** Bottom angling with boilies is extremely effective for tench.*
***Bottom:** Bream are a classic species in bottom angling with a swingtip or quivertip.*

The sinker can be exchanged for a swimfeeder to obtain a tackle for serving prebait on the bottom near the bait. This works best with a short hook leader, so that the hook bait and the prebait will not land too far from each other.

With heavier sinkers for fishing at great distance, or a swimfeeder heavy with prebait, the sinker leader may glide on the line during the cast. The solution is simple – a reversed paternoster. The sinker or swimfeeder is tied to the main line, and the hook leader is tied to it 8–12 inches (20–30 cm) farther up (This makes it easy to change to a thinner hook leader, as is sometimes necessary if the fish are cautious, without the entire tackle becoming too weak. For example, the main line can be 0.18 mm (0.007 In) and the leader 0.14 mm (0.005 In).

Sinker weights

The same principle holds for the sinker weight in bottom angling as in float angling: as light as possible, without causing a risk that the casts are too short or that the bait does not reach the bottom at the right place due to current. In flowing waters, when fishing for chub, rudd, roach and the like, the sinker's weight is particularly critical, and you may need to test several sizes before finding the perfect sinker.

The ideal is a sinker that barely manages to hold the bottom without being pulled by the current. The outward cast is made somewhat upstream, the bail is closed and, when the

Top: When the water is really cold, bottom angling is often superior to float angling, as the fish want a bait that lies still on the bottom.

Bottom: For eel, the gliding method of bottom angling is simplest and best.

A golden carp is returned after having plucked a boilie on a helicopter rig.

sinker reaches the bottom, it should preferably bounce a few times before it stops some way downstream of the fisherman. The current's force on the line makes the quivertip tense up in an arc. At the take, the sinker lightens and follows the fish downstream, giving it great difficulty in getting free of the hook. This is a kind of bolt effect, very effective for bites that can otherwise be hard to hook on.

In ordinary bolt-rig fishing, on the other hand, the sinker must not be too light, since the technique assumes that the fish will partly hook itself. With too light a sinker, there is a risk that the fish only feels the hook without letting it dig in. The weight should not be under 45 g (1.5 Oz) for carp, or 25 g (O.9 Oz) for tench.

Sounding

Simple sounding to find the right fishing depth, vegetation and so on, can be done with the help of the sinker. It does not give as good a picture of the fishing depth as sounding with a float, but is sufficient in most cases, and nothing else is possible when the fishing occurs far out.

Cast out and check the time until the sinker reaches the bottom. Bring the rod in, and feel how the sinker moves. If it slides, the bottom is probably a clean one such as clay. If it moves heavily but evenly, the bottom is soft and the sinker is plodding down in. If it catches and comes loose, the bottom may be very soft or have vegetation that brakes the sinker. Slight scraping means sand or gravel, while sharp bumps indicate stones.

Look for unusual places, where the fish stand. Clean sections amid dense vegetation are hot spots, and vice versa. If there is much soft bottom, areas with sand are perfect, and vice versa. The prebaiting should be concentrated there and the bait left lying.

The long rod

Top knot angling, with a line tied to the rod tip, gives perfect presentation of the bait. The fisherman can guide the tackle with centimeter-precision, let it wander a short distance with the current, hold back and let go again a little, thus almost 'vacuum-cleaning' the area of fish. This technique is preferred in competition fishing, unless the distance is too great or the fish that may bite are so big that they can tear off the tackle if the fisherman is unable to let out line.

Float tackle

This tackle is light, since no special casting weight is needed: the tackle is lifted out and the float need only carry the weight required to get the bait down to the right depth. Floats for still water are very slender, have low buoyancy, and can bear weights of less than a gram. Floats for flowing water are more compact and buoyant, as additional weight is necessary for the bait to reach a correct depth and maintain it, without the float rising in the water when held back and making the fish's take hard to see.

Middle and lower water layers. Tackle for roach, and other fish from the middle waters to the bottom, has a concentrated weight – an elongated 'Olivetti' sinker, somewhat down on

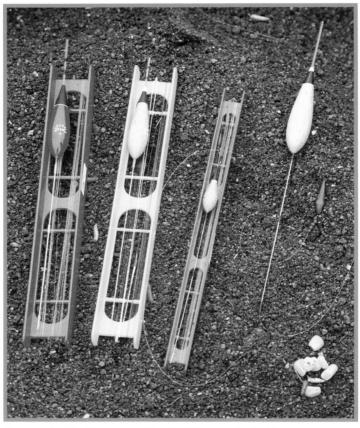

Since top knot tackle is so sensitive, the fisherman ties it at home where he/she has full control over how much weight is put on. Prepared tackles are stored in the attic and marked with weight, how the sinkers are placed, etc., so that one can change within seconds to the perfect tackle. The stronger the current, the lower the float's buoyancy sits. The floats shown here are for slowly flowing or still waters.

A long 'take-apart' rod gives the fishing great precision. When the fish are biting well, this approach is faster than both match angling and bottom angling, which makes it preferable for competition fishing.

← *Fishing with a long rod calls for a full-length line, enabling the fish to be lifted directly in. No time is wasted with this technique.*

→ *Take-apart means that the fishing can be done with the rod length that is best for the occasion. The line between the rod tip and the float is less than a meter. When fishing farther out than the fishing depth, you can pull in the rod until the position is suitable to take the rod apart and lift in the fish – or draw it over the landing net, if too big for the tackle to lift.*

the line – and below this a series of small shot, spread out in a similar way as for a stick float. The larger sinker quickly brings the tackle to the depth where the fish are, and the smaller weights keep the line stretched to the hook, which makes the tackle very sensitive to takes 'on the drop'.

At the bottom. Tackle for bream and other bottom fish have an Olivetti sinker placed closer to the hook. Below it are only one or two shot, which normally lie on the bottom. This allows the bait to lie still on the bottom until the fisherman, with a small movement of the rod, pulls it a short distance and waits again .

Flowing water. The difference in flowing waters is basically just that you need larger weights and that the Olivetti sinker is often closer to the hook. The fish usually stand deeper, and more weight is needed to get the bait rapidly down through the current, as well as to restrain the tackle.

Take-apart

With a take-apart rod, the fishing is exact to the millimeter. The line between the rod tip and the float is shorter than a meter, and the slightest movement with the rod is transferred to the tackle. A little line over the water surface makes it easier to control the tackle if the wind is strong. This technique is used primarily in competition fishing, and has been developed for the most hard-fished waters, with fish that are small or shy of tackle. Here you need lines, sinkers and floats that are as thin and light as possible in order to get any bites at all.

The combination of thin line – leader material down to 0.06 mm (0.002 in) is used – and a short line means that the tackle can easily break off. Therefore, a 'shock absorber' is often included: a rubber band about a meter long, placed in the top part of the rod, where it softens the fish's lunges and jerks. With this technique, surprisingly big fish can be caught even on very thin lines. Occasionally, the rubber is stretched several meters when a sizable fish pulls away.

Prebaiting– the foundation for success

Prebaiting brings more bites by bigger fish. It has made catchable and sought-after sportfish out of species that were regarded as too wild forty years ago.

Although prebaiting is the basis of modern angling, it does not automatically yield fish. Like other fishermen, the angler must choose the place where the chances are greatest that fish will exist or pass by, before he prebaits – apart from competition fishermen who have to make the best of their position and, nonetheless, find their chief weapon in prebaiting.

The fish's natural behavior is the key. How do wind and current influence it? Where in a lake does a certain species live, at what depth, on which bottom?

Sounding

The specimen fisherman has a good deal to learn from competition fishermen about sounding. They investigate their place in detail. Where do slopes exist and flatten out? Are there deep holes, invisible vegetation, or rubbish on the bottom? Then they decide how and where to fish and prebait.

Sounding also gives other kinds of information. Where are different species located at the fishing place? Which tackle works best? How should it be adjusted if the fish do not bite, or stop biting? (See the technical sections on sounding.) Prebaiting before sounding is like fishing blindly.

Loosefeeding

To cast a few baits out at a time, or shoot them out with a sling, is called loosefeeding. It is done regularly in order to attract and captivate the fish, but not so often – or with so many baits – that the fish become satisfied.

When to loosefeed. Loosefeeding is perfect for bottom angling and float angling at a short distance, in both still and flowing waters. The latter require the fisherman to judge where the current takes the free food. The hook bait should go the same way, at the same depth. Baits such as maggots and casters (the pupae of maggots) can drift for a long distance, and must be cast upstream of the fishing spot. Heavier baits such as corn sink quickly and are cast just over the float. Loosefeeding is often better than accompanying the hook bait with prebait bread, which satisfies the fish more – especially in winter, when it is easy to prebait too much.

Loosefeeding involves casting the baits or shooting them out with a slingshot. In still waters, the prebaiting can be done exactly over the fishing spot; when float angling, the float can be aimed at. In flowing waters, the fisherman must estimate how far the stream takes the baits before they reach the right fishing depth – where the hook will be.

Specimen anglers get valuable lessons from competition fishermen, who investigate the spot thoroughly before prebaiting. One prebait may be laid just outside reeds, for fish that cruise along the inner edge, and another prebait farther out at an interesting structure such as the next edge.

Tactics. The arrangement of float and sinker may need adjustment during the fishing. Frequently the fish stand deep at first, when the float must be set so that the bait is directly on or over the bottom. Food cast out makes the fish rise, and ever more bites can come higher up in the water. Shallower fishing is then needed, with the lead shot more dispersed so that the tackle catches in free water.

Baits may still fall past the fish and be left lying. These can attract larger fish that calmly pick up food from the bottom. Set the float deeper again after a while and make the day's biggest catch.

Bread prebaiting

Bread prebait is brown dried bread – lightly 'toasted' and white – which is untreated, mixed with additives to give taste or special qualities. These may be sticky ingredients that make

Rudd is a species that responds well to loosefeeding, for example with corn or maggots.

For carp, loosefeeding with corn near land is an excellent method.

Left: When fishing near the surface with bread, for example, one also loose-feeds the attractor baits around the hook bait with a slingshot.
Above: Bread prebait is a 'transport medium' for the attractor baits, and draws fish with a good scent and taste. Before shooting out a load, it is good to squeeze all the balls, making them easier to shoot with precision.

the bread hold together, or others that make it crack quickly. This depends, for example, on whether the fisherman wants the prebait to break up on the surface or on the bottom. Ready mixes can be bought.

The prebait has two functions. First, it carries baits such as maggots, worm, corn and other morsels to a fishing place far out, or through strong current. And secondly, it attracts the fish with its scent and taste. The fact that the prebait is eaten should be kept in mind so as not to prebait excessively.

Mixing. Bread prebait is moistened at intervals. The dry bread is put in a bowl, water is poured in, and the blend is stirred until the prebait holds together, without feeling sticky when you take a handful and squeeze. Then it is left standing for half an hour to absorb, before mixing in more water – with caution, since too much can easily be added.

Additives for taste and scent are applied before the wetting if they are in powder form, or with the water if they are in liquid form.

Once the prebait is adequately wet, the bait is mixed in. Maggots are added only when they are about to go out, because lying in wet prebait can liquefy them.

Close range – at the bottom. When fishing at close range for large bottom fish, bread prebait is ideal for getting the bait to the bottom. The bread sneaks the prebait past small fish.

But it is important for the ball to hold together until it reaches the bottom. The same is true of fishing in strong currents. If the prebait breaks up too soon, fish are lured away from the place, as they follow the cloud of prebait downstream. To make prebait that holds well, 20–40 percent of white bread can be mixed with the brown.

Close range – free water. The opposite is done when fishing in free water, as for roach in the summer, or by float angling in flowing waters for chub and rudd. They want the bait in the middle water and are attracted by a cloud of prebait. Pure brown bread, lightly squeezed, works perfectly.

Long range. Prebaiting at a greater distance for bottom species, such as bream, is more difficult. The prebait has to hold in order to be cast or slung out. The bait must get to the bottom quickly so as not to draw smaller fish. But prebait balls that crash down like cannonballs can kill the fishing.

If a few small fish are about, the best prebait balls are those that can take being slung out, but crack on the surface. Shoot them out with a low trajectory, so that they crack with a low 'puff'. Mix in 15–20 percent of white bread, and be very careful with the wetting. It is a good idea to sieve the prebait after wetting. If there are many small fish, abundant prebaiting is done at the outset with prebait that holds, and then none as long as the fish are biting well.

Left: Bread prebait is shot out with a slingshot.
Below: Tench is among the many species that are attracted by a blend of bread prebait and hook baits.

Frequency. A golden rule in all prebaiting is to do a little and do it often. Start with a couple of prebait balls and follow with a smaller ball every ten minutes. If the fish bite immediately, increase the amount. In summertime, a little can be thrown out for every bite. It requires both simultaneous action and precision to hook and play fish while also throwing food to the right place.

Flingbread. Dry bits of bread in the prebait are fatally effective for numerous species, when fishing with bread as a bait. This includes chub and rudd during summer longtrotting or swimfeeder fishing in autumn, winter and spring – as well as tench, carp and bream, caught by the lift method or by bottom angling with a swingtip.

The dry bread floats with the current, or climbs slowly toward the surface in still waters, and helps to create a real explosion of the prebait from a swimfeeder.

Swimfeeders

With a swimfeeder, prebaiting is done right at the hook bait. There are special models for maggots, closed at the ends but having holes for the larvae to crawl out through. Swimfeeders for prebait bread are open at the ends.

Winter technique. Since the prebaiting is exact, there is scant risk of overdoing it. This makes a swimfeeder good for fishing in the cold season, as when going after chub, barbel, rudd and roach. By using a swimfeeder only during the first three or four casts, then exchanging it for a sinker, the risk of excessive prebaiting is further reduced.

Distance fishing. A swimfeeder is superb at greater distances, where prebait can be hard to throw out exactly. It is also a good tactic when there are big fish at the bottom under schools of small fish.

In distance fishing with a swimfeeder, one begins by casting often during the first 10–15 minutes. The tackle should lie for only half a minute or so at a time. Once this basis is established, the tackle can lie longer and the bites determine the amounts of prebait. Many bites lead to frequent casts and much prebait, and vice versa. The prebaiting is adapted to the quantity of fish at the spot.

As the prebaiting should draw the fish to the hook bait, the casts must be exact. Aim at something on the other side of the lake or stream, and cast equally far each time. This is especially hard at great distances. Therefore, cast about a meter farther out than the fishing spot and set a wide rubber band over the spool,

A swimfeeder is superb for placing the prebait precisely at the hook bait, for prebaiting little during the colder seasons, for getting prebait through schools of small fish to bigger fish on the bottom, and for prebaiting at great distances.

before you start to prebait. With prebait in the feeder, cast so that the spool is stopped by the rubber band. When the tackle has landed, wind in a few turns and every cast will be right.

Prebait bread for a swimfeeder should be less wet than when it is thrown out. Then it explodes from the feeder when the bread absorbs water.

Opposite:
Top: Bream is a classic 'swimfeeder species'.
Bottom: During the cold season, swimfeeder fishing is one of the best methods for chub, since it spreads small portions of attractive worms exactly at the hook bait with little risk of excessive prebaiting.

Tench are among the species, including carp, which respond best to boilie prebaiting.

Prebaiting with boilies

Boilies are particularly good when prebaiting for tench, since they largely sort out undesired fish. The fish must also learn to eat then, as they are not natural like worms and maggots. Once boilies are eaten, they are amazingly effective and the fish become almost 'addicted'. The required time varies between waters. In some cases they are taken immediately; in others, it may take weeks. In certain waters they work ever better with each season.

Method. The most common tool for boilie prebaiting is with a slingshot, but a casting tube is often better if the baits are to go really far out.

Quantity. The choice of place is very important, as boilie prebaiting takes time and work. One must have an idea of how many fish may come to the spot. In waters with fish such as roach and bream, however, it is difficult to prebait too much because they eat up the boilie remains, unless carp and tench have done so after a couple of days.

If a tour is to continue for a week or two, it is good to begin with a small quantity every few days during the first week, and to prebait more on a daily basis during the second week.

Pattern. Spread out the prebait at first, so that the fish learn to recognize the bait. Cover their routes around the fishing place. Then bring the prebaiting inward and, finally, do it only where the hook baits are to lie.

Opposite:
Top left and bottom left: A casting tube is an alternative to a slingshot for getting boilies far out. It can easily be made from a plastic tube of suitable diameter. It is also good for rapidly strewing large amounts of particle bait such as corn near land.
Right: Water-soluble PVA string is a fine method of pinpoint prebaiting with boilies. It is good in cold water or where much fishing has taken place earlier with abundant boilies.

When fishing, prebait just around the hook bait. Prebait more in the summer and less in cold water, when five or six baits can be enough.

PVA. To avoid excessive prebaiting when fishing in autumn, the prebaiting can make use of a PVA string, which dissolves in water after a few minutes – if it works as it should. Try it ashore, with some baits on a stump of string.

Thread 4 to 6 baits on a piece of PVA string and tie it directly to the hook. After the cast, the string dissolves and the prebait lies some centimeters from the hook bait.

There are also small bags, and net-tubes of PVA that can be cut to a suitable bag length. They are filled with boilies, corn and so on, tied to the tackle and cast out. Thus one can prebait a whole portion precisely at the hook bait.

Combination prebaiting

Prebaiting that blends boilies and particle baits such as corn is effective for species such as carp and tench. The small baits attract and engage the fish without satisfying them, and the fish find good morsels just like the fisherman's hook bait. This tactic is common in large lakes of Southern Europe with plenty of fish, where masses of food are needed to keep the fish at the place, and the prebaiting is often done easily from a boat.

If the fisherman has no boat, a 'spod' can be used. This is a swimfeeder filled with a few deciliters of small bait. It is cast out to the fishing spot with another rod, emptied and wound in again for a new load.

Prebaiting

With prebaiting one tries to gain several advantages:

- Luring the fish to start eating at the spot. Separate baits are cast into the water and make bite-shy fish curious.
- Attracting more fish to the spot.
- Persuading the fish to eat a special bait.
- Reducing the fish's suspicions. If they swim up every time they eat corn, they will stop eating corn. If they eat 100 grains before being hooked, the corn will work longer.

Far left: *Bags of PVA can be used to lay small portions of boilies and particle bait for tasting near the hook bait.*

Above : *A 'spod' is a little swimfeeder that is loaded with small bait and cast out with an extra rod. This is an excellent way of prebaiting at a distance with particle bait.*

Bottom: *In Southern Europe, prebaiting is done with huge quantities of baits in many waters, since the water temperature is high and the fish are plentiful and gluttonous. Either a boat or a 'spod' is used.*

Baits for angling

All the baits used in angling are of natural origin. And only the angler's imagination sets the limits: everything from worms, larvae and seeds, to pastes that the angler concocts in the kitchen with flour and other ingredients can be included. Here a choice of baits is presented, with tips on tackle and a deep dive into the manufacture of angling's 'high-tech' bait – the boilie. Throughout, the basic principle is that the hook size is selected according to the bait's size.

Right: Worms, or combination, worm/caster or worm/corn are one of the best baits for bream.

1 Boilies are the super-bait for tench and carp. The bait sits on a hair rig (see the chapter on carp), locked against the little stop. The hook must be un-angled and strong enough for carp, in sizes 2–6 for baits of 16–20 mm (0.6-0.8 in). Here is the Fox Specialist Carp, series 2, size 2. Tench require a thinner hook of size 8–10 for baits of 10–14 mm (0.4-0.5 in). This is the Drennan Starpoint, size 10. The thin silicon piece behind the bait fixes it in the right position on the hook.

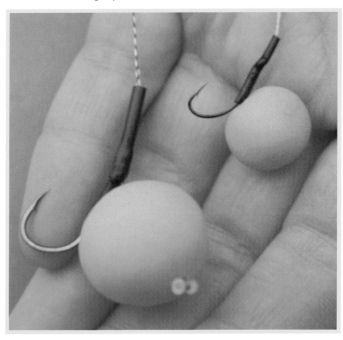

2 Corn is a universal bait for carpfish. And no bait is simpler to find than by buying a can of corn. Hooks of size 10 for several corn grains and size 14 for a single one. Use a slightly thicker hook for tench and chub, such as the Drennan Super Specialist. For bream, roach and rudd, you need a thinner hook, like the Kamazan B530.

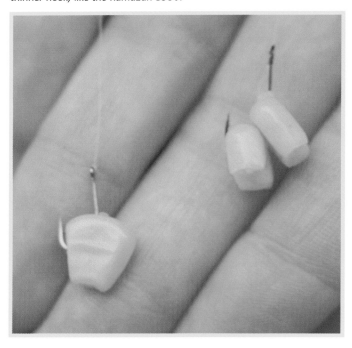

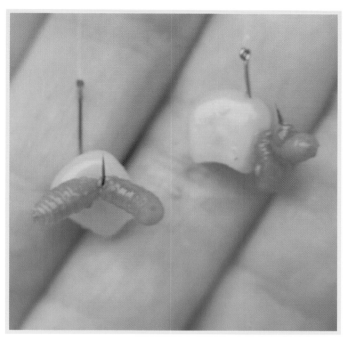

3 *Corn and maggots are among the commonest and best combination baits. Here on a thinner hook, Kamazan B530 for bream, roach and rudd, or a thicker hook such as Drennan Super Specialist for tench, chub and barbel. Size 10.*

4 *Earthworms are some of the most familiar and effective baits for big fish. A hook of size 2–4 is adequate for eel. Tench, chub, perch and carp require size 4–6. They stay fresh longer if kept cool in moistened newspaper.*

5 *Caterpillars are excellent for whitefish, perch and bream. They should be mounted through two or three segments on one end for maximum mobility. Hook size 10–14, here for bream on a Kamazan B530 size 10.*

6 *Pieces of fish are good for eel, burbot, pikeperch and pike. Here is half a smelt on a Fox Specialist Carp, series 2, size 4.*

7 Shrimp is a lethal bait for eel, chub and tench, among other species. For eel, it should sit as shown here. The hook is a Fox Specialist Carp, series 2, size 4.

9 The inner crumb from white bread, which should be fresh, is good for all carpfish and is used widely for roach, rudd and chub. A strip is folded round the hook – push it over the hook eye. It hangs fluffy around the hook without hindering the hooking. Small pieces loosen and drift attractively with the current.

8 White bread does well for all carpfish. The hook must have a wide gap so that the bait stays on. It is superb for chub and rudd in float or bottom angling, and as floating bait. Here a piece of crust is on a Drennan Wide Gape Specialist, size 6, in a morsel adequate for chub.

10 Bread paste is another classic carp-fishing bait. Wide-gap hook, size 4–10. White bread is wetted and kneaded into a non-sticky paste. Other tit-bits, such as blue cheese for chub, can be kneaded into the paste for extra appeal. The hook must have a broad gap, as does the Drennan Wide Gape Specialist, here in size 6.

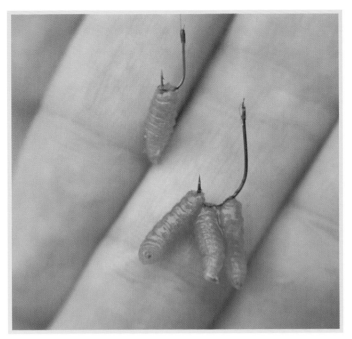

11 Cheese is a time honored chub bait. The hook is a broad-gap model such as Drennan Wide Gape Specialist, here in size 6. A piece of cheese is kneaded until soft and shaped into a ball. It hardens when dipped in water, giving good protection against attacks by small fish, or a piece can be cut directly from the cheese and attached to the hook as it is.

12 Maggots, or fly larvae, are the primary bait for roach and rudd when fishing with loosefeeding. Single ones on hook 18, or bunches for bigger fish such as bream, like three shown here on size 10 (Kamazan B 530).

13 Casters, or pupated maggots, are regarded in England as especially good for large roach. They also do well for bream. Must be fished on a thin hook such as this Kamazan B 530, size 18.

14 Worms and casters are fine for most whitefish, and outstanding for larger bream. With a caster, the worm sits better during long casts. Casters require a thin hook such as the Kamazan B 530, here in size 10.

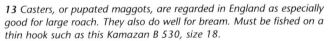

Boilies

Ready-made boiliers can be purchased, but it is much more fun to fish with your own. They often catch more fish, too, and are cheaper. In addition, they can be tailor-made for special conditions. This is not even hard. Ingredients can be found in ordinary shops or sportfishing stores.

Raw materials and equipment

Raw materials

- **Dry mix:** either ready-mixed or home-mixed (see recipe at the end). The flour it contains determines the boilie's nutrient content, hardness and density.
- **Eggs** (six, and about 1 lbs of dry mix, give around 2 lbs of baits).

Ingredients and equipment for making paste. Ready-blended dry mix, flavorings, oil, large bowl to blend in, whip, wooden ladle, and table knife to scrape the ladle with.

Blend the flavorings, oil, powder additives such as sweetener and nutrient supplements, and water. Whip thoroughly.

- **Flavoring and aromatic substances.** They attract the fish, give the bait a good taste, and enable the fisherman to create a bait with unique taste and scent.
- **Sweetener.** Sweets are adored by carp and make other tastes "richer". Can be anything from concentrated sweeteners to sugar.
- **Nutritious supplements.** Amino acids, vitamins and minerals.
- **Oil.** Gives the bait more fat content and makes it easier to roll.
- **Water.** Helps distribute the flavorings and improves the rolling.

Pour in about 3 cups of dry mix and blend well. Work in more and more powder.

Place the ready paste in a plastic bag. Let it "rest" for 10-30 minutes.

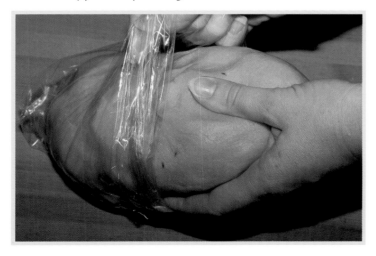

Equipment

- **Rollboard.** A tray with parallel half-tubes and matching lid. Lengths of the dough, as wide as the tubes, are laid across the board and the lid put on. Press down, and the lengths are divided and shaped into round balls when the lid is moved back and forth. Then it is swept forward to roll them off the tray. Such a board saves time and is available for baits from 8 to 28 mm (0.3-1 in) thick, as well as in different widths for 8-10 to 20-30 baits per dough length.
- **Food syringe.** Load it with half a mix per session. Different nozzles are used to vary the diameter of the dough length pressed out, so that it fits the rollboard. This tool is handy when many mixes are made at once. If a syringe is used, the mix should be softer than when hand-rolling, so that it can be pressed through. A sticky mix can be helped through with a little flour on the nozzle.
- **Cutting-board,** to roll and slice the dough lengths on.
- **Sharp knife,** for cutting the dough to the right length.
- **Baking-plate,** to lay the balls on while waiting for boiling. Flour it to prevent the baits from sticking.
- **Large pot.**
- **Colander,** for pouring out baits made from boiled paste.
- **Towel,** to lay out the baits until they dry.
- **Plastic bags** for freezing.
- **Pen** for marking the bags (mix, taste, day).

Rolling equipment. At left: large board and syringe (with nozzles for different bait sizes). At right: smaller board for hand-rolled lengths of dough, cutting-board to roll lengths on, and a sharp knife to cut the lengths with. Roll a whole mix and lay the balls on a floured baking-plate to await boiling.

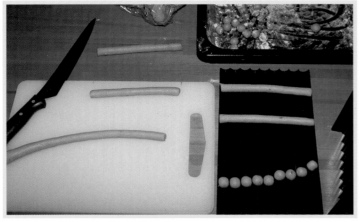

Left: *Lengths of dough are rolled and cut; two are laid across the board. The lid is put on, pressed, moved back and forth, then out over the plate at last with the ready balls.*

Below: *With the syringe, two or three lengths are pressed out across the board, the lid goes on, and after a few swipes the balls are finished.*

Bottom left: *After rolling a mix, it is tipped into a large pot of water being heated. Stir carefully so that they do not stick. In 2–3 minutes the baits are done, even if the water has not reached boiling point.*

Bottom right: *From the pot, the baits are poured into a colander.*

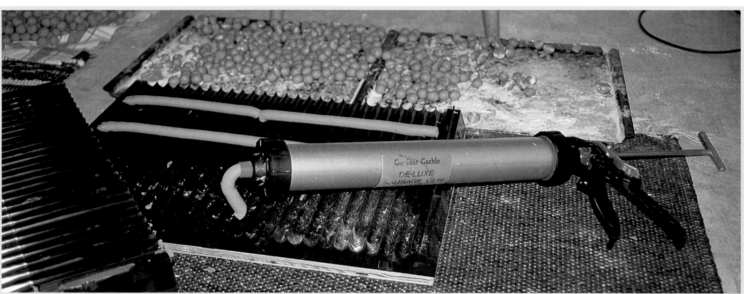

Flow plan for smooth work

1. Dry-mix ingredients to make 5-10 mixes each time, which saves effort. Between the rollings, keep the mix in a bucket with tight-fitting lid.
2. Blend the wet phase: 6 eggs, flavorings, water and cooking oil. Add sweetener and nutrient/vitamin supplement. Whip.
3. Pour in about 3 cups of dry mix and blend well. Using all the powder at once makes it hard to mix, spreads the ingre-

From the colander, tip the baits onto a towel. Roll them occasionally with your hand for all-round drying.

dients unevenly and toughens the paste. Then add more powder and work it in until the paste is semi-soft without sticking. Let the paste "rest" in a plastic bag for 10-30 minutes. The powder absorbs the fluid well, the paste stiffens and it becomes easier to roll. If it is too soft after resting, knead in more mix.

4. Roll lengths of suitable diameter on the rollboard or press them out with a syringe. Cut in lengths that fit the board's width, or press them out across the board. Make about ten lengths before rolling. Dry lengths roll badly. The number that can be made between rollings depends on how fast the paste dries, which varies with different mixes. The balls are laid on a floured baking-plate until the whole mix has been rolled.
5. Boil. Fill a large pot halfway with water and heat it. Pour in all the mix at once, and stir at regular intervals. It does not matter if the water stops boiling, as less of the flavoring and aromatics will then disappear. Pour out in a colander after a suitable time (depending on the mix and desired hardness, 2-3 minutes are usually enough) and quickly onto a towel for drying.
6. Dry thoroughly, for at least 1-2 and ideally 10-12 hours; longer time gives harder baits. Roll the baits around with your palm now and then, to dry them all over, before being packed in plastic bags and frozen. Boilies last for at least a year when frozen. One mix per half hour is about what one person can expect to manage without a syringe.

Drying - an alternative to freezing

Boilies take up much freezing volume, but an alternative is drying - mankind's oldest method of conservation.

1. Mix and boil as usual.
2. Dry the baits on a towel for 1-2 days, rolling them at times with your hand.
3. Place the baits in women's nylon stockings (it is worth buying a dozen pairs at a lingerie sale). A knee-length stocking holds about one and a half mixes.
4. Hang the stockings in a drying cupboard and run it for 1-2 hours at moderate power (too high a temperature cracks the baits). Lift the stockings a few times so that the baits shift and air reaches everywhere). At room temperature it takes longer, about a week.
5. Store the baits in a dry airy place, for instance hanging in the stockings, until they are used.

If the baits are to be preserved by drying, fill a ladies' stocking with them after 1–2 days of drying on a towel. The stockings are then hung in a dry place.

The baits become very hard, so a bag of frozen hook baits is needed when fishing. Dried baits can be soaked in a water mixture with a little taste/scent substance to acquire extra fragrance. Thus, 12-24 hours before they are to be used, pour them into a large plastic bag (1 mix), add diluted flavoring (1 part to 10-15 of water), blow up the bag, close it and shake. Keep shaking until all the liquid is absorbed. Dried baits have a lifetime of several years. Once in the water, they still emit an aroma and are loved by carp in spite of their hardness!

Recipes

HNV (High Nutritional Value)

Mix with a balanced nutrient content (protein, fat, carbohydrates), which becomes ever better as the fish learn how beneficial it is. With this mix, and accompanied by two friends, I took over 50 carp in a Swedish lake of 600 hectares with hardly a hundred carp in it, during 14 days of fishing. Two thirds of what other fishermen caught in the lake all season!

Dry phase: 1/4 cup milk albumin, 3/4 cup casein, 1/4 cup calcium caseinate (milk proteins), 1 cup milk powder, 1 2/3 cups full-fat soy flour, 1/4 cup egg albumin (protein), 1/4 cup wheat gluten, 1/4 cup semolina, 1/4 cup wheat-bran, 1/4 cup sugar, 2 tsp vitamin supplement (for dogs, from a pet shop). Liquid phase: 6 eggs, 3 Tbsp cooking oil, 2 Tbsp water, flavoring andaromatic substances (we had two combinations: 2 tsp kiwi + 3 drops eucalyptus oil, and 2 tsp hazelnut + 1 tsp peanut oil).

Base mix

"Service-store mix". To be used directly, or blended with a cup or two of fish meal or bird food (from a fishery or pet shop). It gives simple variants that are very effective due to their inherently carp-attracting tastes and scents.

Dry phase: 1 1/4 cups milk powder, 1/2 cup soy isolate, 1 2/3 cups full-fat soy flour, 1 1/4 cups semolina. Liquid phase: 6 eggs, 2 Tbsp cooking oil, 1 Tbsp water, flavoring and aromatic substances.

Both of the above recipes can be supplemented with concentrated sweeteners and so forth. For baits with different qualities, vary the proportions between ingredients. Milk proteins, egg albumin and semolina give harder baits; casein and semolina make them heavier, while egg albumin, soy isolate and caseinates make them lighter.

Opposite.
Top: *Worms, corn, bread, maggots, boilies...the list of good tench baits is long.*
Bottom: *Bread bits are a classic bait for chub.*

Carp

Cult fishing

From an obscure occupation of eccentrics, carp fishing has grown into a cult for people from all social classes. By now the dominant branch of modern angling, and of carp equipment and baits, it enjoys a turnover in the multi-millions. Many of the techniques that were originally developed for this 'queen of the river' are also increasingly used for numerous other species.

Size

The popularity of carp fishing has to do, of course, with the fact that the fish can become very big indeed. There are carp weighing over 40 kg (88 lb) in North America, perhaps over 50 kg (110 lb). Specimens over 35 kg (77 lb) have been landed in Southern Europe, and over 20 kg (44 lb) in Scandinavia. With their size goes raw strength, and whoever has hooked a wildly rushing carp of 10 (22 lb) or 15 kg (33 lb) understands the comparison to catching onto a fast-approaching freight train.

Hard to fool

But it also has to do with the difficulty of luring carp and the bad experiences they teach. A carp fisherman who wants to succeed in the long run must be thoughtful. Plan, lay up strategies, and have an idea of why he proceeds in a certain way to trick the next giant into making a mistake. At the risk of irritating some practitioners of spinning, I like to point out a difference: every spinning cast requires a second's thought – about where to cast – and the cast is fished for something like twenty seconds. Behind every carp-fishing cast lie many hours of preparation, and it can fish for twenty hours.

Curing the soul

Last, but not least important, is the contrast between laid-back immobility and explosive excitement. On the spot, after all preparations are made and the baits are cast at carefully selected locations, all you can do is wait. A wait that gives such calm and total relaxation that it is a form of cure for the soul. Like a spice, there is always the feeling that something can happen in a fraction of a second.

Choice of place

A key factor of success in fishing for carp is the choice of place.

Left: The charm of carp fishing includes the total relaxation a fisherman experiences while awaiting a bite, after the baits are cast out and the rods are in the holders.

A golden reward as a carp morning breaks.

The simplest and most general rule is that it is best to fish where the wind blows in, with the wind in your face.

Obviously, though, other factors play a role – and an ever more significant one as the fishing session becomes longer, or the campaign is extended at a given place with prebaiting. It is rather meaningless to begin three weeks of prebaiting in a southward-opening cove because the wind blows from that direction just then, but from other directions 95 percent of the time. Thus, for longer fishing, it is better to choose a place that lies right for the wind during the following days of fishing, or for most of the season if the effort continues for a month or more.

Structures

Carp mainly eat from the bottom and are attracted by bottom changes. Most of the food is there. Currents bring organic material, and a varied bottom provides space for all the small animals that live on it. The principle is about the same as the fact that dust does not collect in the middle of a flat floor, but in corners, around furniture, behind the TV and so on.

Such areas are called structures in fishing terminology. Examples are a reedy edge where a slope planes out, a shallow section of an even bottom, an area with hard bottom surrounded by soft bottom, and a pondweed belt surrounded by free water. Precipices, vegetation, and bottom contrasts can be found by casting about with a sinker, weighing 60–80 g (2.1-

Top: *A fish with a paddle of this size is understandably strong. Hooking a 10 kg (20 lb) carp can be compared with catching a hook on a passing train.*

Bottom: *Two-toned carp are a special variant, usually due to a nerve injury that has put the fish's color control out of order. It can also be seen in other carpfish such as bream and tench.*

Top: *Mountain carp are closest to wild carp, and big specimens are the carp fisherman's most coveted quarries.*

Bottom: *Carp include all possible variants of color. Such are the well-known kio carp, also an enjoyable pond and aquarium fish, as well as golden-hued 'common' carp.*

2.8 oz), and slowly pulling it in while feeling how it behaves (see the chapter on bottom angling).

One of the very best and most neglected structures is the shore zone – but more about that later.

Baits

Boilies

The leading baits for carp fishing are boilies. They sort out smaller fish that are undesirable in the context of carp. Hence it is perfect for the prebaiting campaigns that raise the chances of success.

An aspect to consider, especially when visiting waters with hard fishing pressure, is the benefit of boilies with high nutritional value. This theory was quite popular during the 1970s when boilies were a novelty, but today it tends to be forgotten. A nutritious bait, after prebaiting, will be preferred by the fish to a bait with low nutrient content.

Here a domestic devil has an advantage, since he possesses full control over what is in the bait. He can also tailor-make it in other ways and acquire a lead over other fishermen. For just as in all fishing, doing things differently pays off. The taste, size, color, and nutrient content should be varied.

Perfect taste

The desire to find the perfect bait is a key factor behind the development of boilie flavors. Fruity ones were used most at first, but now there are no limits to what is mixed in the search for unique taste and scent. Or how does octopus with whiskey sound? Personally, I prefer more natural variants, and have had greatest success with types such as raspberry, tutti-frutti, hazelnut and pistachio.

Particle baits

Preserved corn is the most universal particle bait, but there are plenty of others. Fodder corn, chickpeas, soybeans, kidney beans, tiger nuts, peanuts, and hemp are examples.

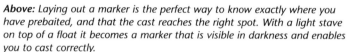

Above: *Laying out a marker is the perfect way to know exactly where you have prebaited, and that the cast reaches the right spot. With a light stave on top of a float it becomes a marker that is visible in darkness and enables you to cast correctly.*

Top right: *The carp's sucking mouth and barbels are well suited to plucking bait from the bottom, and the entire area around its mouth is full of taste and scent receptors, giving it a fine sense of smell. Carp fishermen make use of this by flavoring their bait in all possible ways.*

Right: *With the boilie on a short hair right next to the hook, the fish is hooked perfectly in the corner of the mouth.*

Canned corn is ready to use, but dry particle baits need to be prepared. They are placed in water for one or more days, and then boiled. This prevents them from injuring the fish. A fish that eats dry baits could even die when they swell in its stomach. When soaking, the baits can be given a personal touch by adding some flavoring. The duration of soaking and boiling, as well as how the baits take up tastes vary for different baits. The bigger and harder they are, the longer it can take. But a good main rule is to soak them for at least a day and night.

Top right: A waggler or antenna float, leaded overdeep, and a little corn are all that is needed for sneak fishing.

Bottom: Fishing in the magic margins offers close encounters.

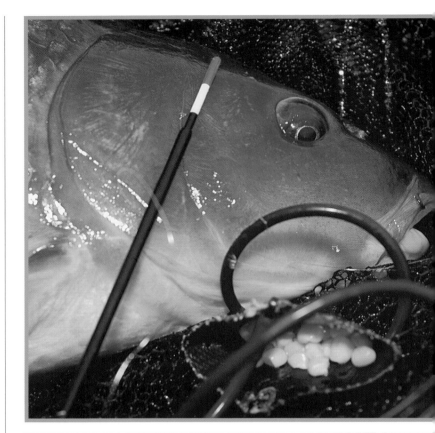

The 'hair rig'

For boilies and large particle baits to be effective, the hook must be exposed. Therefore a 'hair rig' is used: a stump of line with a ring at the end, tied to the hook in diverse lengths and variants, The bait is threaded with a boilie needle, similar to a knitting needle, and is prevented from falling off by a piece of a matchstick or a 'boilie stop'. The rig's name derives from the fact that its 'hair' was initially made by the 'inventor' from strands of his own hair.

Short hair

I use mostly short hair. To minimize the risk of the bait 'obscuring' the hook tip, a short piece of silicon tubing is placed on the leader .When the boilie has been threaded on, the tubing is pushed up over the hook eye against the boilie. The hook then lies alongside the bait, at a 90-degree angle. It catches efficiently, almost always in one of the carp's mouth corners, and sits securely – while easy to loosen without damaging the fish.

Hook

The best boilie hooks are chemically polished with a straight shaft, and have a wide gap and an inward-curved tip. They catch well with no risk of tearing up the fish's mouth. Sizes 2–6 prevail, the choice being adapted to the bait size.

Hook baits 'Pop-up'

As hook bait, ordinary boilies or particle bait can be used. Better, however, is a hook bait that distinguishes itself, so that the carp finds it faster than others. A common variant is a floating hook bait, or 'pop-up'. Normally it is weighted with a lead shot, so as to hover a few centimeters above the bottom. It is seen better and can more easily release attractive scents.

Boosted baits

Hook baits that are 'boosted' – dipped in a diluted mixture of flavorings, amino acids and the like – are deadly effective.

Since carp primarily use their superb sense of smell to find food, a bait that smells more than others will inevitably be taken first. Further versions of a 'plum in the pudding' are a larger hook bait, a different color, more on the rig, and so on.

Prebaiting

One cornerstone of the carp-fishing world is prebaiting. It teaches the fish to eat at a given place and is often necessary for making them pick 'unnatural' particle baits or boilies without suspicion.

Distance fishing

In lakes and reservoirs of Southern Europe, techniques have been developed for prebaiting that were unimaginable to the pioneers on small English fishing waters. A boat is used to row out both the prebait and the bait. The fishing can be done at distances of over 400 m (1300 ft). To find the way back to the prebaiting spot, a marker is set out, such as an empty bottle.

Marker advantages

Markers are beneficial in all waters. They show exactly how the prebaits are distributed. You then know, instead of only guessing, when the bait lies just right. In waters with much vegetation, there may be areas of half a square meter that are free and perfect for the hook bait.

By using floats with a light stave, a marker works just as well at night, when it would otherwise be impossible to cast out quite correctly.

Surface fishing

Bottom angling is the predominant method of carp fishing (see tackle and principles in the chapter on bottom angling). But under special conditions, when the fish swim high in the water, opportunities for surface fishing arise. If the fish go really near land, one can fish with only a hook on the end of the line.

'Controller'

Usually a special float called a 'controller' is needed. It is weighted so as to protrude only about a centimeter above the

Below: A broad-gap, rather thin hook, such as the Drennan Wide Gape Specialist, is a perfect bread hook.

Carp fishing offers fine close battles like bullfighting.

surface, where the line glides through its top. The controller provides both casting weight and a way of keeping the line properly stretched. The leader length depends on how shy the fish are. A good starting length is 1.5 m (5 ft)

Baits: bread

Bread is among the simplest and best surface baits. If carp stand still, or slowly cruise under the surface, it is suitable to throw out some pieces of bread. Few things can make one as nervous as when the pouting mouth of a 10 kg (20 lb) smacking carp sucks in the bread and comes ever closer to the piece with the hook. If the fish takes the bait, one must keep a cool head. The commonest cause of a missed catch, when surface fishing, is that you strike back too soon. This is almost a spinal reflex when the bait is sucked in, but you have to wait. And when you feel ready to hook, wait a little longer. Even though I know this, on several occasions I have pulled the bait out of the mouth of a big carp that took me hours to lure in for taking it.

Baits: cat and dog food

Other surface-fishing baits are floating cat and dog food. Since the pieces are small, a similar effect is achieved with them as when fishing with particle baits. The fish eat many of them and become less suspicious. With smooth, patient work it is possible to get a whole group of carp to eat them, which amplifies the effect. The more are eating, the more they compete, and the easier they are to fool. When five or six carp suck in bait after bait, cruising like mini-submarines in the surface layer, the time is right to lay out the hook bait carefully. With polarized glasses and a sharp eye, you will also have seen which fish is biggest and can focus on catching it.

Fishing in the margins

From surface fishing, there is only a short step to sneak-fishing, just below the rod tip, and out to a few rod lengths away. Here is a recollection from carp fishing somewhere. It has begun to grow light when I arrive.

I let down the gear ten metres from the shore, put together the ready-tackled rod and start to sneak forward. On my knees I approach the edge of reeds. With a metre to the water, I settle myself and lob out the tackle. The float lands with a little splash. Cautiously I lay down the rod so that it rests in the reeds and sticks out a metre. Around the float I throw a couple of handfuls of corn.

Bubbles and spatter

Suddenly some bubbles rise near the float, and my pulse goes up. What was that? A slight shake of the float top. The float shakes again and is pulled under at an angle. I hook when it disappears. Two metres out, the water explodes. I stand up and get splashed, then hold on with all my might. At first I think I have stopped the fish, but it makes only a pause under the rod tip before taking off. The reel screams as the fish madly tears out line. Only when it has taken twenty metres do I put a stop to the beast, despite holding on so hard that the rod creaks. It goes up with a powerful whirl in the midst of a thick pondweed belt. There I had lost two fish the previous morning.

I am fishing alone, and the bottom has a metre-thick layer of sediment, so I do not dare to wade after the fish. If one's feet get stuck there, one stays put. Instead I try to bring the fish in. With the rod pointing straight toward it, I back up very slowly. It follows for five metres, like a nice big dog on a leash, before it has had enough. There is a huge splash and it frees itself from the hook. After winding in the tackle, I still have water dripping from my glasses and the pondweed is swaying in the swell.

Magical shores

The fishing that season was to demonstrate what I already knew – how good the area along the shore is. In five attempts, of some hours each, I got around twenty bites, and landed seven. Despite an effort to hold the fish hard after each bite, to prevent them from rushing into the vegetation, I failed. Of the first six bites, I lost five before learning from my mistakes. None of the fish took the bait farther from land than five metres – most took it only a rod length out, and a couple less than a metre out.

The fishing took place in a lake that covered three hectares, but the magic of the shore is equally strong in larger lakes. In a lake that measures 350 hectares, all of my carp have come up less than four metres from land, even though I was fishing at the same time with at least one tackle as far out as fifty metres. Here, precision fishing at overhanging branches or along the shore's sloping rocky edges has been very effective.

The lake's larder

It is not surprising that shore fishing should be so good. Where land meets water, there is a constant inflow of fish food to the lake. Rain washes down insects and worms; bugs are continually falling into the water from branches and other plants. The shore is simply the best-filled larder in most lakes. From a fisherman's viewpoint, it cannot be better. Placing a bait perfectly under the rod tip is also easier than laying it on a shallow plateau or a deep cliff thirty metres out – whose exact position you first have to find.

Matched tackle

Adeptness with such large fish, in waters murky with vegetation, calls for equipment with the right combination of strength and softness. If the fish gains speed, it usually gets away, so the tactic is to hook and hold on for dear life. Then the line cannot be too weak – 0.30 mm (0.01 in) is a minimum – or the rod too inflexible. Otherwise there is a risk of the line snapping or the hook being torn out. A rod of 12–13 feet with full action is ideal. It works softly and has reserve strength even when bent down to the handle.

With a small bag for snacks, bait, slingshot, carp bag, and tackle items over your back, a net in one hand and the rod in the other, you are ready to sneak along the shore. Far from traditional carp fishing with a rod bag, carp bed, sleeping bag and alarm, this is fishing for close encounters and battles with creatures of 10–15 kilo (22-30 lbs), the bullfights of the carp arena.

Tench

Tench are among our most handsome and exciting candidates for angling. They vary from shimmering olive-green to flaming orange, with watchful ruby-red eyes. Strongly reminiscent of carp, they have a similar body form and another mysterious reputation.

Tench fishing extends over the whole spectrum of angling methods, but has increasingly shifted towards a scaled-down carp technique with boilies. In some waters, this has given the fishing a renaissance – when boilies are introduced, it often becomes ever better.

The minimal carp method

Small soft boilies

Carp techniques for tench are like those for their namesake, but there are crucial differences. In particular, the boilies that are used should be 10–14 mm (0.4-0.5 in) wide, instead of the carp's standard 16–22 mm (0.6-0.8 in). And a key factor is the consistency. Carp boilies can be as hard as pebbles and still catch fish. Tench boilies must be softer. If fish such as chub and roach did not also like small, soft, tasty balls, the ideal would be boilies so soft that they nearly mash when picked up.

It is troublesome to roll mini-boilies, but as long as the bait industry does not supply consumers with soft boilies, there is no option. Roll up your sleeves, bring out bowls and pots, flour blends and flasks of scent and start rolling.

Tackle

The tackle is the same as for carp. I have had most success with firm bolt rigs of the 'straight' type – with the sinker locked on the line and the leader in front. The leader must be shorter than for carp, about 15 cm (0.5 ft), and its material the softest, most flexible available.

For carp, short hair is needed to attach the boilie at the hook. For tench, I use even shorter hair. It is hard to knot hair rigs of 14–15 mm (0.5 in), but it pays off. A bolt rig with a short leader, very short hair, and mini-boilies is superb. The bites literally explode.

Float angling

The lift method. A traditional approach to tench is angling with an antenna float and the lift method (see the section on

Top: Tench vary from deep olive-green to flaming orange, with a ruby-red eye like the dot over the 'i'.

Bottom: Dawn is the primary time for tench.

float angling). The float is fished over-deep, with a sinker on the bottom so that the bites – when the fish takes up the bait and sinker – will make the float rise. The distance between the shot and the hook is varied until you find one where the bites are clear and the strike yields a hooked fish. Begin with 10 cm (4 in).

Over vegetation

In the water above vegetation, it is necessary to fish differently. The float is adjusted so that the bait hangs just over the plants, easy for fish to see and with no risk of hooking rubbish.

Traditional bottom angling

Bottom angling with paternoster tackle and swimfeeder is also effective for tench. The leader is kept quite short to get the hook bait just at the edge of the feeder's chum pile. A variant is to combine a maggot with a maggot-filled feeder closed at both ends, instead of an open one with maggots and bread chum.

With this technique, fishermen often use two hook leaders so as to fish with different baits. In my opinion, such a procedure is not beneficial. Tench fishing commonly occurs near vegetation and the risk is that a second leader will snag after a bite, resulting in a lost fish.

Choice of place and prebaiting

The place. Where to fish for tench is determined by the same factors as in carp fishing. Here too, it is a matter of finding the hot bottom structures. The difference is that tench are more partial to vegetation.

The prebait. Prebaiting with boilies is done as with carp. It can be advantageous to begin by also using breadcrumbs, which attract the fish rapidly. You may, of course, design prebaiting campaigns for traditional baits too, but these attract other fish as well. Thus, the choice is often to prebait during the fishing itself – with bread crumbs if the fishing is done far from land, or by loosefeeding if you fish near land or from a boat.

Particle boilies

A special variant is fishing with boilies and particle baits made of boilie paste. Then you use a spod (see the section on pre-

You can normally find tench in or near vegetation.

baiting) to create a sparse carpet of small baits around the hook bait, or a plastic bag filled with small baits and tied to the tackle.

Traditional baits

Worms, maggots and bread are among the best baits for tench, my favorites being earthworms. Many a tench is also taken on corn – but just like carp, tench learn rapidly from their mistakes.

The English tench guru Len Head writes, in his book Tench, that corn often works well at first, but that the fish soon become suspicious. He describes the result: "Lightning-quick bites on the float tackle, hardly leaving time to hook the fish.

Opposite:
Top: *Fishing with small boilies and scaled-down carp technique is hard to beat for catching tench.*
Bottom: *Just like carp fishermen, the tench fisherman carefully returns the fish to the water.*

Below: *Boilies for tench should be small and soft, and the leader material flexible.*

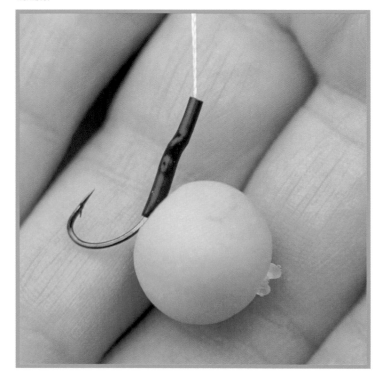

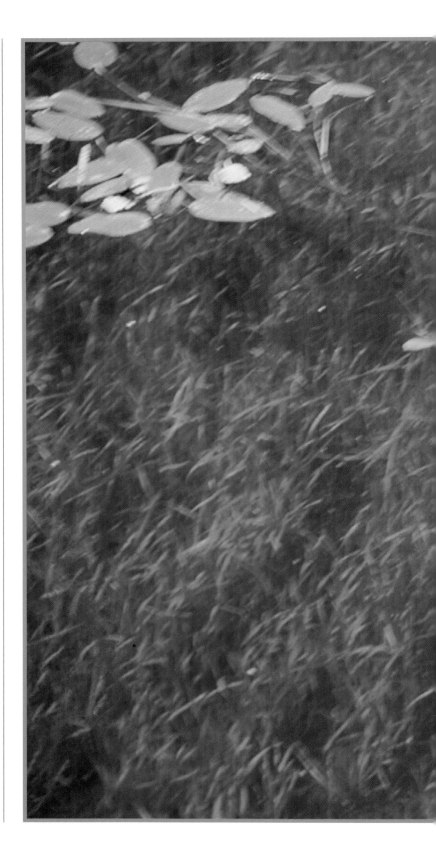

When the tench swim over dense vegetation, the solution may be float angling with the bait set to fish over the plants.

And the fisherman's experience the following morning, when he discovers that tench under cover of darkness have cleaned out the chubbing spot of every corn but one, the one with the hook in it."

Flavoring

A way to lengthen the life of corn bait is to color and flavor it. The fish will then regard it as new bait, and can temporarily be as 'easy to catch' as when the corn was fresh in the water. A fisherman can also improve his chances relative to others by adding a taste of his own. The same is true when fishing with boilies. Examples of good tastes are almond, kiwi and banana.

Equipment

Boilie fishing

Ideal tench rods for boilie fishing are of the carp model, 11 feet (3.3 m) long and half-action. On such gear, hooked tench give real fights that are pure enjoyment. Most of them take off on a first sizzling rush then change between fast sidewise attacks and bullish dives toward the bottom. The reels are the same as for carp fishing.

Float and bottom angling

For traditional bottom angling, the usual equipment of 11–12 feet (3.5 m) is used. I prefer a swingtip rod, since the bites often need to be waited out. For float angling, thicker match rods of 13–14 feet (4 m) are perfect. The line must be 0.22 - 0.25 mm (0.08-0.01 in) thick, as the fishing often takes place in vegetation.

Tips on drilling

Frequently a tench rushes away, just after biting, straight into the nearest pondweed belt or reed bed. If so, you should let enough line out to hang in an arc from the rod. Give the fish time – several minutes may pass, but it usually emerges again. When the line begins to move, you need only resume the pressure. In this way, nine out of ten hooked tench can be dealt with.

Bream

Tips on prebaiting

Prebaiting is essential for maintenance of bream fishing, and its principles are simple. Moisten some bread chum and mix it with well-known bream magnets such as maggots, corn and worms. The mixture is formed into tangerine-sized balls that are delivered with a slingshot to the fishing spot. In summer, ten to fifteen balls are a good start.

Bream love sweets. Vanilla sugar is a fine, cheap additive. Super-sweet ones in powder form are nice but costlier. Effective flavors are vanilla, cola, cream-like tastes, and the strong sweet one of molasses. Concentrated flavorings or sweeteners in liquid form can be added to the water that the bread crumb is moistened with.

Technique

The standard method for bream is bottom angling with a paternoster tackle. The hook leader should be about a meter long, and the sinker leader 40 cm (1,3ft). Instead of a sinker, a swimfeeder can be used, but this is desirable mainly when the water is relatively cold, as the fish then need much less food.

Equipment

Quivertip

A quivertip or swingtip rod of 11 feet (3.35 m) is ideal. With the quivertip a bite tends to begin with some brief tugs, then the tip is bent softly and stubbornly. Only at that point should you hook the fish strongly.

Swingtip

Unless the current or distance is against it, I use a swingtip. After casting and tensing up the line, the rod hangs obliquely downward instead of tensely. A bite is shown by a rise or fall of the tip. The resistance does not increase when the line is stretched, and there can be a longer wait before the fish feels any resistance. This last advantage can make the difference between good fishing and frustrating attempts to hook fish.

Reel, line and hook

A spinning reel with line of 0.18–0.20 mm (0.007 in) suits the rods and the fishing. Nylon line is best, since bream swim

Above: Bottom angling with a swingtip for bream is a great summer pleasure.

Top right: A large bream arches to the surface.

Bottom right: Finding a bream school and prebaiting correctly can yield true action.

in schools and a flat line produces many more false signals from fish running into it. Sinkers that weigh 15–25 g (0.7 oz) cover most situations. The hook is selected according to the bait's size, 10–12 being good for several corn grains, a bunch of maggots or a big caterpillar. Hook sizes of 12–14 are appropriate for smaller bait: a couple of maggots, one or two corn grains or a small caterpillar. Combine the baits and test them until the bites come fast.

Right: *A big bream on its way into the net.*

Opposite:
Top: *Worms, corn, maggots and casters – these are candy for bream.*
Bottom: *Hold the fish by its tail spool and lay it in the water.*

Choosing the place

It is important to choose the right place, even though fish must be attracted there by prebaiting. To prebait where no fish pass by is as silly as fishing on dry land. Often the best approach is to fish in the wind.

In most lakes the bream follow definite routes when seeking food. These are often connected with deep cliffs at the transition to flatter bottoms. Here, bottom material accumulates and creates good conditions for the favorite food of bream: water-dwelling worms (the freshwater cousins of earthworms) and fly larvae. Such cliffs are found by sounding. At or just outside the edge is where you should cast out the prebait and fish. In flowing waters, schools of bream patrol the calm sections.

Tactics

Cast out to the far side of the prebaited area. Let the bait lie for some minutes, pull it in half a meter, tighten up and wait a few more minutes, before retrieving the tackle. Often the bite comes after an inward pull. Wait till the swingtip is lifted, or the quivertip is bent considerably. Hook the fish and feel the thrill of the first solid resistance. I wonder how many times a fish weighing a kilogram has convinced me that something much bigger has taken the bait.

As long as the bites keep coming within a few minutes of the cast, it is best not to prebait any more – this frequently frightens the fish rather than attracting them. The best time to do so is when the bites have almost ceased. Then the fish are departing, or else the school has mostly been fished up, and further food will revive their interest or prepare for the next school.

If no bites come immediately, and they seldom do, it is advisable to cast out a little ball of chum every quarter or half hour, to keep a scent of food in the water above and around the chumming spot, so that fish are drawn there faster.

Chub

Surface fishing

The summer technique of floating-bread fishing is difficult to beat. With a soft rod, preferably of the match type at 12–13 feet (3.5–4 m), and a single hook on a 0.16 mm (0.006 in) line, you are ready. Somewhat longer casts are obtained by dipping the bread piece for an instant in the water. To fish at greater distances, towards the other side of a small stream, for instance, a controller is tied on (see the section about carp). The most important tip is to delay the strike until the line is stretched.

Bottom angling

For chub, the most common method is bottom angling with a quiver rod of 11–12 feet (3.5 m) and paternoster tackle. The sinker is determined by the current conditions (see the previous section on bottom angling). A swimfeeder loaded with bread chum and small bread flakes can be worth trying, if you sit a little longer at a particularly profitable holding place. Once cast out, the swimfeeder contents more or less explode, and fluffy bread bits whirl with the current, attracting fish that stand downstream to bite eagerly.

Baits

White bread is one of the best baits. It smells good and, in bottom angling, it floats a little upward to move attractively in the current. Cheese, both in pure form and as paste, is another classic. Corn has yielded many chub, as have chickpeas and other particle baits. Pieces of sausage, luncheon meat, shrimp and snails – the chub benefits from anything edible. It pays to vary the baits, since they are usually most effective at the start.

The best hook for large baits such as bread, cheese and shrimp is a broad-gapped, thin, chemically polished model of size 2–4.

Holding places

Chub are a species for flowing waters. During summer, they are found in the fastest parts of the current – behind or beneath fallen branches, under overhanging trees, and within the bottom current's channels between waving wreaths of vegetation. They are often in surprisingly shallow water, which gives them an excellent position for taking food that comes swirling along. Then they rise, suck it in, and return to shelter.

Their winter holding places are often deeper, in more calmly flowing water. They hold still behind or below branches, trees

Above: In the summer, chub keep to the strong currents and linger under branches, in channels among vegetation, and at other sheltered spots.
Top centre: *Cheese can be fished in either piece or paste form.*
Top right: *During the winter, calm backwaters are preferred by chub.*
Bottom right: *A large mouth and black-edged scales are hallmarks of chub.*

and the like. While they now seldom hold in the fastest current, it is usually not far away.

Mobility is superiority

A key to success is to vary your location. Walk along a fair stretch and fish for ten to thirty minutes, then move to the next possible holding place. Any bites will be hard and hungry, almost heart-stopping. The rod may be nearly ripped away, though generally after a few short shocks of warning. In the winter, it can be rewarding to try a little longer at a good place, since the fish there may need more time.

Night fishing

The best time for big fish is during the first hours after nightfall, regardless of whether in summer or winter. But especially during the summer, fishing all night is a smart investment.

Roach

Roach is a classic species for the angler. Most of us come into contact with it through our first attempts to fish during childhood, and it often yields the bulk of the fish in angling competitions. Before the carp boom a big roach was one of the specimen fisherman's most desirable trophies. While a roach of only 900 g (1.8 lb) is considered large, this fish is a worthy opponent. Pugnacious and tricky, it can be caught all year round, with all methods of angling.

Method

Float angling. Trotting with a stick float, combined with loosefeeding, was developed largely for catching roach. The tackle is as light a stick float as possible, with the shot spread out on the line so that bites are seen clearly 'on the drop', as the fish may be holding anywhere between the bottom and the surface.

Loosefeeding

The fisherman shoots or throws out some maggots, casters or hemp corn, and lets the tackle wander with them downstream. Now and then the tackle is held back carefully so that the bait rises. If no bites come, the tackle is adjusted so that the bait fishes closer to the bottom or surface. This is done by moving the sinker downward or upward, combined with setting the float deeper or more shallowly. Often the fish rise ever higher in the water and the float has to be fished more shallowly.

The top knot

For the top knot, the tackle builds on the same principle, with the sinker weight evenly spread from the depth where the fish are expected to be, down to the signal shot nearest the hook. With the top knot, the fisherman can follow the tackle exactly and, since it is more sensitive than reel-rod tackle, it works better on cautious fish.

Bottom angling

Closed swimfeeder. In still waters, bottom angling with a swimfeeder on a paternoster tackle is excellent for large roach. During the day, the fish often swim into deeper water, which calls for longer casts. With a swimfeeder, the prebaiting is always perfect. Frequently it is best to avoid bread chum and load only with hook baits, because bread does not attract small roach. The fishing is then done with a closed swimfeeder, which

Float angling and loosefeeding with maggots or corn is a classic method for roach.

has no openings in the ends. It is loaded with maggots and closed by a lid. The baits crawl out through small holes.

Open swimfeeder

The alternative is a little bread chum, as plugs in an open feeder. You can then use other baits than those that crawl out by themselves. Examples are corn and casters – maggot larvae. The latter are known for attracting big roaches and can float. A couple of casters on a thin hook of size 14, with a leader of thin line, lifts a little from the bottom and is seen better by the fish. Another classic big-roach bait consists of some white bread crumb squeezed around the hook. A hook size of 6–10 is then adequate.

Fishing by dark

Bottom angling with a paternoster is also best for nocturnal fishing in flowing waters. A leader length of around one meter to the hook, and 20–30 cm (0.6-0.9 ft)) to the sinker, is a good starting-point. If the fish are hard to hook, there are two solutions. Lengthen the leader until the bites are reached, or use a really short leader of 20–30 cm (0.6-0.9 ft) so that the fish hooks itself against the sinker. The latter is usually most effective in the dark.

Roach often provide the bulk of the weight in angling contests.

Equipment

A light match rod about 13 feet (4 m) long is ideal. For bottom angling, an 11-foot (3.3 m) quiver rod with a soft top is used. The line should be thin, 0.12–0.15 mm (0.005 in). Thicker line is used in water where the risk is great that the fish will get stuck, or when fishing at a long distance.

Prebaiting

If you fish with bait, it is good to mix small pieces in the prebait. Hemp, both mashed and whole, is another magnet for roach. If bread chum is used, one does well to fish with a 'lift bait' – casters or bread – over a sparse carpet of chum.

Where to fish

Flowing waters. In flowing waters roach are found at the edges between stronger and weaker currents. The stronger the current, or the colder the water, the more the fish move into calm backwaters. Also rewarding are the insides of curves, from a third of the stream's width out to the middle. In summertime, the fish may linger in strong currents of shallow water, preferably among stretches of swaying vegetation.

Still waters. Roach swim along both the upper and lower parts of submerged cliffs, and especially on the shelves if any exist. They also stand along reeds and other vegetation edges, as well as near the inlets and outlets of streams. In both still and flowing waters, the fishing is often good next to, or above, gravelly sections. Places with an onshore wind are best unless it is really cold.

When to fish

In wintertime the fishing is normally best during the lighter hours of the day. But the rest of the fishing season is different. For large roach, night fishing is preferable, notably during the first hours after dark falls and the last hours before dawn. In lakes, the fish then approach shore to eat, which makes them easier both to reach and to trick. Yet in flowing waters, too, the chances are greatest of catching big fish when it is dark.

Rudd

Bottom angling. With its underbite and close-set eyes high on the head, a rudd looks like a fish that takes food from below. In spite of this, many large rudd are caught by bottom angling. Why? One of the most effective techniques is fishing with big pieces of bread that float upward in the water. The leader length is chosen so that the bait stays near the surface, even though the sinker remains on the bottom. At a depth of just over a meter, a leader of 1.5 m (5 ft) is enough in flowing waters – for deeper water, the leader is longer. The tackle is an ordinary paternoster.

Float angling
In flowing waters

Diverse forms of float angling are also effective, such as classic Avon or stick-float fishing with loosefeeding of corn or maggots. In this case, you should fish with the float adjusted so that the bait rises a little in the water. Restrain and release the line so that the bait lifts and falls, a movement that attracts the fish in free water.

A variant is an Avon float that carries plenty of weight, combined with large bread baits. The weight is then set two-thirds of the way down on the tackle, and must be great enough to sink the bread. Fished a little down in the water, the bait covers considerably wider areas than if it were bottom-angled.

In still waters

A technique appropriate to still waters is a light stick float tackled 'top-bottom', with the sinkers collected directly under the float to provide casting weight. With baits that float or fall very slowly, this tackle suits fish that want their bait high in the water. At longer distances, a light controller and long leader are used.

Tackle

Rudd are fighters and make determined rushes, but are not giants. Quivertip rods of 11 feet (3.3 m), for casting weights around 20 g (0.7 oz) and a line of 0.15–0.16 mm (0.005 in), or lighter match rods with line of 0.14–0.16 mm (0.005 in), are perfect.

Prebaiting

Besides loosefeeding in float angling, a swimfeeder is an established aid to catching rudd. When bread is the bait, the feeder is fished in the same way as for chub. It is loaded with bread chum and small bread bits that drift with the current.

Baits
Bread

The rudd's miniature mouth makes it easy to underestimate the size of the bait, but rudd that weigh over a kilogram take bigger bait – up to half the size of a matchbox. This may be because they use their sight to find food, and a larger bait is easier to see. For such big bait, you need hooks of sizes 4–6 with a wide gap and thin metal, sharp as a needle. Desirable, too, is a little barb to penetrate better, as on Drennan's 'Wide Gape Specialist', my favorite for bread baits.

Floating alternatives

It can pay off to try other floating baits, obeying the same principles as for bread. Small floating boilies on a hair rig, or pieces that keep a couple of corn grains floating, are examples. Their aroma is also attractive, and can be varied if the fish lose interest. One variant is to lay maggots in the water. These begin to float after a while, and a bunch on a thin-shafted hook will stand up in the water like a piece of bread.

Bottom baits

Despite their appearance, rudd are caught on the bottom as well. Other good baits are worms, corn and maggots when fished traditionally.

Place

Rudd are found in the richly vegetated coves of lakes, and in calmly flowing backwaters of streams. They prefer to linger alongside or inside the plant stands. In the evening, they enter very shallow water.

Time

It is possible to catch rudd at all times of year when the water is open, but the biggest ones are usually caught early in springtime. Night fishing is extremely productive, and my comrades and I have frequently fished along stretches that seemed totally lifeless until the arrival of dark set the bites going.

*Opposite. **Top left:** With float angling and baits such as bread, maggot and corn, the quieter parts of streams can be effectively fished out.*
***Top right:** Blood-red fins are characteristic of rudd.*
***Bottom:** The goldfish of the lake, caught on bottom-angled bread.*

Pike angling
Ordinary float angling

Modern angling is not just a hunt for big carpfish – it is also one of the very best weapons for coming into contact with predatory fish such as pike, pikeperch, perch and sheatfish. Among these, the pike is the most popular species, and many of the techniques have been developed for this type of fishing in particular.

Tackle

A carp rod of 11–12 feet (3.5 m) is ideal for pike angling. It facilitates casting out the small, clumsy tackles, keeping good line control, and taking up slack line before hooking. And the rod has the power that is needed to drive the hook into a pike's bony jaw and to steer the fish while playing it.

Leader

The leader should not be of nylon. This material suits small pike but the leader can break when a dream fish shows up.
A leader at least 40 cm (1 ft) long is needed. Best make your own, which is simpler than it sounds. There are several good wire materials on sale, such as Drennan's Sevenstrand or Pikewire. The instructions are on the package.

Up-trace

Preferably one should have an 'up-trace', which is an extra leader above the hook leader. This prevents the pike from reaching and cutting the line over the leader. An example is when the tackle is fished a little above the bottom, as in angling for pelagic pike. Then the bite often comes from below, and the pike can easily catch the line in its jaw during the attack. When fishing in flowing waters, the sinker is frequently set only a few centimeters over the bottom, and baitfish swim at that level or higher up in the water. The risk of the line coming into contact with pike teeth is thus great. The same is true if baitfish have wound the leader around the main line.

With a length of about a meter on the up-trace, there is almost no danger of having the main line cut. Since the sinkers should sit just over the hook leader, you can make several up-traces with different weights, adapted to floats with different bearing weights – or use sinkers of 'Catherine' type, which can be attached according to the weight required.

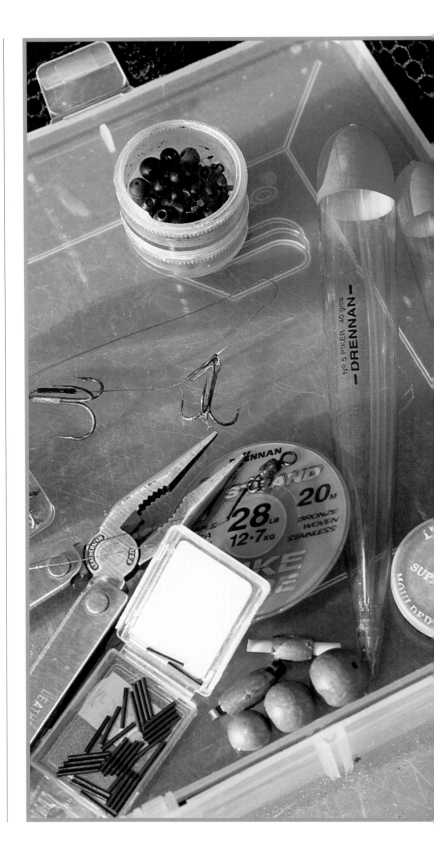

Left: *All that is needed to rig for pike angling. Wire, sleeve, hook and pliers for leaders, floats, sinkers, and plastic beads to mount between sinker and leader, as well as between stop-knot and float.*

Right: *Ready for pike angling. An adaptable float, leader, and plastic bead between stop-knot and float, so that the knot does not slip through the float – and one beyond the sinker, tied to the swivel that holds the leader, so that the knot is protected. The roach is rigged with one hook in its back before the dorsal fin, and one at the breast fin.*

Hook

I prefer a pair of treble hooks. The strike can then be applied immediately, minimizing the risk of hooking a pike in the throat. Forget ideas such as delaying the strike for ten minutes – or as I read somewhere in my youth: lighting a cigarette, smoking it up, and finally hooking – to make sure that the pike has the hooks in its mouth. This is absurd. It makes smoking harmful not only to the fisherman, but also to the fish.

Size 6 is adequate for the biggest pike. Models with small barbs, or with barbs squeezed in towards the shaft with pliers, are easy to loosen.

Tackling on

The baitfish's size determines the distance between the treble hooks on a leader; it should be between 10 and 15 cm (4.5 in). The baitfish is tackled differently depending on whether the fishing is done in lakes or flowing waters. In lake fishing – where the baitfish should swim around the boat, or the place on land where you stand – the upper hook is fastened at the fish's dorsal fin, and the lower hook in its mouth or at a breast fin.

In flowing waters, the upper hook should sit in the mouth, and the lower hook either at the dorsal fin or between the breast fin and anal fin. The fish then adopts a natural movement in the water, and is not dragged crosswise through the water when it is reeled in.

Floats

A sliding float that is stopped with a stop-knot on the line makes depth adjustments simple. A plastic bead between the knot and float decreases the danger of the knot getting stuck in the float or sliding through. I use as light a float as possible, so as to hold up the tackle and baitfish. Use a cigar-shaped float of around 20 g (0.7oz), made of lead, so that it sticks up one or two centimeters.

Top left: With a small aquarium net, baitfish are easy to lift from a bucket.
Bottom left: A quick strike usually puts the hooks in the corner of the fish's mouth – where they sit securely and are easy to loosen.

Line control

Line control is the A and Z. When a pike bites, the line should not be slack. Otherwise the fish may spit out the bait before you are ready to hook, or may have time to swallow the hooks deeply while you reel in. With a fairly taut line, the strike is simple. Point the rod tip toward the fish, reel until you feel resistance, and then strike hard. With a braided line on the reel, the hook will sit tight.

Play it calmly

Take it easy with a hooked fish, if you are not in a spot where it can get stuck. With moderate pressure, you have all the cards in your hand. Preferably, a pike should not be taken so hard that it flies up and shakes its head. This stresses the hooking and tackle so much that it may shake itself loose. A net is an obvious necessity, and ought to be a large one. During pike fishing, a dream fish can take the bait at any time. Keep cool when the fish is ready for the net. Hold the net in the water with its front edge under the surface, lead the fish over it, and lift.

Place

Places for pike angling in flowing waters have been mentioned. In lakes and along coasts, the pike may hold at edges of vegetation, at submerged cliffs – to be fished from the upper to the lower edge – and at reefs or outlets. An echo sounder makes it easy to find bottom structures and schools of baitfish. Where they are, the pike are. Bait just over the bottom is a good beginning, but fishing in free water can be needed to attract pelagic fish such as herring, vendace or smelt.

When the baitfish are hard to locate, or are spread out so that it is difficult to prefer any special place, an advantage lies in turning to mobile pike angling – float trolling.

Float trolling

Rowing with one or two baitfish after the boat – float trolling – is not only as good as the more traditional stationary pike angling, but often far more effective. Basically it is a simple method that has been developed into a fine weapon for hunting large pike.

One of my fishing companions, who has caught (and returned) thousands of angled pike, summed up float trolling like this: "Go with a braided line, fish at depths between two and six meters, and keep the bait at the bottom – you'll catch fish." A good description of the method, but there is certainly more to its effectiveness.

Echo sounder

Bait at the bottom is a fundamental rule with no exceptions. In waters where the pike hunt pelagically, or during the autumn when the baitfish may be holding anywhere in the water volume after autumn mixes it, the quarry may need to be fished at other depths. An echo sounder is thus almost indispensable for successful float trolling. It keeps track of the water depth, cliff edges, shallows and so forth, as well as finding baitfish. Finding schools of baitfish with the help of an echo sounder is often more profitable than aimlessly fishing across a lake in the hope of eventually hitting the target.

Tackle

Rod, reel, line

You can use an ordinary spinning or baitcasting rod, but a carp rod of 11–12 feet (3.5 m) is also preferable for float trolling. Besides having enough spine to drive in the hook, it has a length that enables the tackle to be guided far to the sides for broad fishing. With a baitrunner function on the reel, the risk is avoided of losing your whole bait set-up to a fast bite. As in ordinary pike angling, an inflexible braided line is superior.

Choose an ample net.

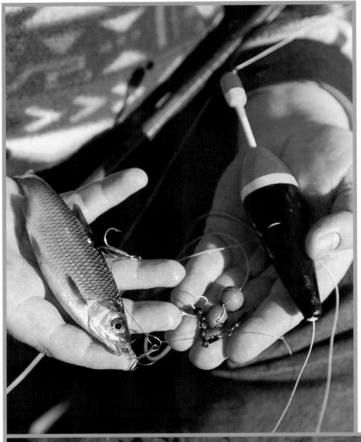

Floats

There are special floats for float trolling, but they are not really needed. An ordinary gliding pike float threaded on the line works perfectly. The special floats are designed not to slide down on the line with the boat's motion, but normally one does not row so fast that this happens with an ordinary float. If it should turn out that the fish on a given day want a faster bait, or if you fish while rowing against the current in flowing waters, the float can be secured with a loosely tied stop-knot below it. This should sit so loosely that the float can easily be pressed down along the line, in cases where you fish deeper than three-fourths of a rod length, since it may then be necessary to reel in more line when a fish is to be netted.

Slow pace

Often the key to success is slow motion. If the float slides down the line, it usually means you are moving too fast. Take a pull on the oars, rest till the boat almost stops, take another and let the boat stop completely, and so on. The reason

Top left: In float trolling, as when angling in flowing waters, the roach should be tackled with the upper hook in its mouth and the rear hook at a breast fin.

Below: Float trolling comes into its own during the colder seasons.

Smaller pike can be held by gripping the upper neck when the hook is removed.

why slow rowing seems to be the winning tune is presumably that float trolling is practiced mainly during the period from autumn until spring. But obviously your speed may need to be varied, and on certain days a much quicker pace may be required to attract bites. The rowing itself gives a varied speed that makes baitfish rise and fall in the water with the strokes. This is one explanation for the fact that float trolling is sometimes much more effective than plain stationary angling.

Leader and 'up-trace'

The same leaders are used as in ordinary pike angling – and especially when going after pelagic fish, an up-trace is essential.

Rigging

The lowermost hook is fastened either in the baitfish's back at the dorsal fin, or at one lateral fin, and the other hook in the mouth. Then the baitfish swims, or is pulled, through the water headfirst. A hook at the breast fin also works as a kind of keep and holds the baitfish upright in the water.

Tactics

The success of float trolling is largely a result of the fisherman's effective coverage of much greater areas than in ordinary pike angling. With an echo sounder, submerged cliffs are found that can be followed with a tackle fished in the upper

In late autumn, winter and early spring, most fish are caught by slow back trolling with pike-angling tackle.

edge and another, deeper tackle farther out. The next rowing tour can be done farther out on the cliff side, or closer to land or the shallows. When seeking pelagic fish, the baits are set at different depths in relation to how the schools of baitfish show up on the sounder.

Unless a pattern emerges after a few bites and the tackles can be fished more similarly, different variants must be tested until the fish loosen up.

A trump in the hand of a float-trolling ace is to row over a hot spot not just once, but also backward to get the bait to a pike's assumed holding place, two or three times. In this way the technique becomes a real skill, where the distinction between untouched bait and a diving float may be only meters.

Place

As in ordinary pike angling, the aim is to fish in the areas where fish are holding, and the places are the same as when fishing from an anchored boat or from land. Float trolling, however, is mainly a technique for still waters. Boat fishing in a stream or river works better in a reverse variant – back trolling.

Back trolling
The art form of pike angling

This special form of pike angling, or float trolling, can be called back trolling since the name rather well describes what it is about. In flowing water, the fisherman slowly releases the boat downstream with one or two pike tackles drifting before it. The technique is ideally suited for long areas with reed-edged stream or river stretches, or along cliffs toward the deep furrow.

When done by an old hand, it looks simple, but it takes time to learn. There is nothing easy about holding a boat against the current so that the tackle works downstream with the right speed and depth.

Depth adjustment

Since the fisherman is holding the boat back, the current presses on the line, and this must be kept in mind when the depth is set. Some over-depth, or extra distance between the float and sinker than the water depth, is needed so that the

How smart is it to fish with anything but a steel leader for these pike?

tackle with baitfish will not rise too high in the water when the boat is kept still or is slowly braked downstream.

'Overleading'

In truly strong current, the sinker weight may have to exceed what the float would tolerate if fishing in still waters. As the fisherman holds back, the current lifts the tackle and the float climbs a bit, so that it stands at a moderate depth without being pulled under.

Extra stop-knot

Tying an extra stop-knot below the float may be necessary, to prevent the current from pressing it down on the line. The knot should be fairly loose, so that the float can be forced down on the line when the playing is finished with the netting.

Equipment
Rod

The rods are the same as in ordinary pike angling: carp rods 11–12 feet long (3.5 m). Some float trollers manage to fish with two rods, but others prefer a single one. The reason is that, as already noted, it is hard to handle the boat with the current at the right speed, so that the tackle drifts properly in relation to the water depth.

Reel

So as not to risk losing the rod at the bite, or in case the boat rushes away downstream when the fisherman is busy with one or two rods, it is best to fish with a spinning reel that has a baitrunner function.

Tackle and rigging

The leader and up-trace are the same as float trolling and ordinary pike angling. The baitfish is rigged just as when angling in flowing waters. The leader's lower treble hook is placed at the fish's dorsal fin or one abdominal fin, and the other hook in its mouth. Then the fish will always be oriented against the current, as if it were swimming freely.

The bite

A bite is felt when the float is clearly drawn under the surface, tips to the side, or slowly sinks as if the tackle has snagged on the bottom. Then you should strike, preferably without the boat drifting away downstream.

Ice along the river edges did not stop this huge pike from plucking up the tackled smelt.

Reed stop or emergency anchoring

A means of preventing the boat from drifting away is to open your bail when the fish bites, so that line can be pulled easily off the reel. Next, row a few strokes toward land, if possible into reeds if they grow along the edge, where the boat will lie more still. Then reel in line until you feel resistance, and make your strike. With the boat in the reeds, you have a good position to play and net the fish without problems. The alternative is to keep the anchor in the prow, tied to the boat with adequate line length for the fishing depth, and ready to be thrown in at a second's notice.

Bottom Angling
Free line and sliding tackle

Particularly in England, it is also common to bottom-angle for pike, sometimes while prebaiting with pieces of fish. The simplest technique is with a free line or an ordinary sliding bottom tackle. By threading a swivel with a snap onto the line, the sinker weight can be changed quickly for adaptation to the casting length or the current.

Bait

The most usual bait is a piece of, or even an entire, dead baitfish. It may be either a species natural to the water – roach, rudd, smelt, eel or the like – or a bit of some other fish: mackerel, herring or sardine. Fatty fish, such as the last five mentioned, are notably attractive when their scent spreads in the water.

Leader and rigging

The leader is determined by the baitfish's size, but normally a leader with two treble hooks is used. Given a whole baitfish, the lower hook is set above its breast fins, and the other hook farther up toward the tail. Then the tackle casts best. Half a fish is attached with the broader end at the lower hook, and the other a little way up. To prevent them from flying off in the cast, large baits are secured with a piece of PVA tied round the bait and the leader slightly up from the hooks, or with a rubber band in the same position.

Floating paternoster

One can use live baitfish on a sliding tackle, but there are better solutions. Most common is a variant of the paternoster tackle, where a float is somewhat up the line and lifts the bait-fish in the water. The leader sits in a three-way swivel 1–1.5 meters (5 ft) up from the sinker. Between the leader and main line is an up-trace, as described above.

Depth adjustment

The float is placed so that the distance between it and the sinker exceeds the water depth. Then the tackle can be 'tightened up' against the sinker for rapid registering of bites.

Rod holder

Usually one fishes with several rods in holders including bite indicators.

Place

Since bottom angling is a stationary technique, it becomes most effective during the cold months of the year. Good places in rivers and streams are the backwaters and current edges – or in lakes, the level bottom below cliffs, the vicinity of vegetation belts, at inlets and outlets.

With equipment on a sledge, and an ice-pick in hand to test where the ice seems unsafe, the fisherman crosses it quickly and securely to the fishing spot.

Ice-angling
A symbiosis of methods

For many years, ice fishing for pike led an obscure life. But since the end of the 1990s, this sport has mushroomed. Ice angling combines the best of old 'tip-up' ice-fishing with modern angling technique. Using three or four rods per person, a couple of fishermen can quickly and effectively fish out hot spots, along cliffs and reed edges, or over shallows and vegetated areas with baitfish.

Equipment
Rod

The perfect rod for ice angling is hard to find in shops. Therefore, devotees make their own from the shortest, softest models of boat rods. The blade is cut just below the ferrule and inserted in the handle. This gives a relatively soft two-part rod of around one meter. It needs to be short, so that the fish can be reached in the landing phase. It should also be tough, to tolerate a fishing day's many movements or to be thrown on the ice at the height of the fight. Glass-fiber blades are thus better than carbon fiber. A soft blade is essential to avoid risking line breakage, when the fish makes strong rushes only a few meters from a fisherman standing stiffly on the ice.

Reel

Both multiplier reels and spinning reels are used. A multi-reel is set to release line as easily as possible, with no risk of backlash. A tangle on the spool when the rod is lying on the ice and the fisherman is fifty meters away does not help matters. Many a fisherman has seen the equipment pulled away over the ice and disappear into the hole with a splash. For spinning, a baitrunner reel is preferable, since it can be free-coupled with a closed bail to avoid the risk of tangle.

Line

The line should be at least 0.45 mm (0.02 in) thick, and of nylon, to withstand wear against the ice edge while playing, and to reduce the risk of line breakage.

Rod holder and bite indicator "Feather"

An angling-gear feather holds the baitfish at the right depth and serves as a bite indicator. It is attached to the angling gear that sits on the ice as usual, and some small improvements can make it perfect. Near the top sits a flat red plastic plate, or a red-painted cork, as a visual indicator. If this is replaced with a red-painted ping-pong ball, it is easy to see from all directions. A piece of silicon tube threaded over the outermost tip, where the line is clamped on, decreases the risk of damage to the line. An eel-bell near the top is a fine acoustic indicator, easy to hear across the ice when a fish bites or the baitfish swims around as a big pike eyes it in the depths.

End tackle

The end tackle is simple. On the line above the leader is threaded a lead shot of 10–15 g (0.5 oz), enough to keep the baitfish at the proper depth, but not so heavy as to prevent it from swimming around attractively. The leader may be the same as for angling in open water: multi-strand wire material such as Drennan Sevenstrand, at least 40 cm (1,2 ft) long, with one or two thin treble hooks of size 6–8. The ideal is a 'semi-barbless' hook model, which can be replaced with ordinary models where the barb is squeezed in toward the shaft with pliers.

Right: Drill a series of holes, pull the equipment sledge along them, and rig rod after rod until you are done.
Far right: An echo sounder shows both the water depth and the locations of baitfish.

Far left: Ready to lower the baitfish.

Middle: The baitfish is sent down and the line is wound a few turns on a ring at the signal flag.

Above: Ready for bites. With one or two eel-bells on the signal flag, the bite can be seen and heard far across the ice.

Bait
Live

Roach is the classic bait, partly since it is easier to obtain, but also because it is a good bait. If correctly attached – with a treble hook in the back, or else one in the back and one in a breast fin – it will stay alive long and swim temptingly down below. Other baits also work, of course. Perch is superb in some waters, but worse in others. Live herring are excellent. A small aquarium net is fine for catching the fish in a bucket, and a sizable ice scoop will keep the hole free from ice.

Dead

Dead baitfish can be used, but are worse. At a guess, fat fish with a strong scent – such as herring and mackerel – should be better than, for example, roach.

Fishing depth

As a little boy, I followed my father in winter for ice fishing, and learned from the experts that roach should hang at the bottom, between half a meter and one meter up. Today's ice-anglers do not obey the old rule. Certainly, fish are also taken at the bottom, but often it is better to fish just under the ice. Especially towards evening, pike rise higher in the water to hunt.

Manual sounding

Sounding out the right depth is achieved by lowering the tackle until the line slackens. Then it is raised by the leader length plus the distance from the bottom that the bait will fish. If the bait is to hang under the ice, the tackle is let down so that the lead shot is just below the ice edge.

Echo sounder

An echo sounder increases the chances of finding fish. It is used both for fast and effective sounding, and to look for schools of baitfish.

Technique

Once the bait roach is lowered, the rod can be laid on the angling gear's spool or on the ice. If there is no snow, the rod should lie 5–6 m (15 ft) from the hole, as a fisherman who approaches the hole after a bite may frighten the pike.

The strike

The strike is made immediately if the fish pulls line. Otherwise, the line can be held carefully between your fingers to feel for movements. If any occur, strike fast.

Playing

After the strike, stay cool and give the fish time to tire out. Americans have a long tradition of ice fishing for big ones, and keep the drag brake set loosely to minimize risks. Instead, they brake with a finger on the spool when the fish rushes or line is to be pumped in.

Time

Ice angling is best under the first snow-free ice when the hunting light is good, and during the spring when the fish gather near spawning sites.

Left:
By gripping it under the gill arch toward the jaw, a pike is pulled up through the hole.

Right: With long forceps, the hook is easily removed even if it sits some way inside the mouth. If the fish is to be released, it may best be left hanging in the hole while the hook is loosened.

Perch and pikeperch
Float angling for perch

In lakes

Float angling with small baitfish is a classic summer pleasure. The tackle is the same as for ordinary pike angling, except that it must be more flexible and without a steel leader. A gliding float that allows rapid depth adjustment and can carry 5–10 g (0.2-0.4 oz) is adequate. Use nylon instead of steel for the leader, around 0.25 mm (0.01 in) thick, or a leader of Kevlar where the risk of a pike biting is great.

Reward for perch angling with roach – a perch weighing over a kilogram.

Hook, bait and rod

A broad-gap single hook, size 2–6, is best. Attach a roach, minnow, bleak or the like, 6–12 cm (2-5 in) long, by its upper lip or in front of the tail fin. If really big perch are the quarry, exchange the single hook for a thin-wire treble hook of size 6–8 for quick strikes, and use a baitfish around 15 cm (6 in) long. The best rods have soft action so that the baitfish is not pulled loose in the cast. Length should be 9–10 feet (3 m) for boat fishing and 12–13 feet (3.5–4 m) if fishing from land.

***Opposite top:** All that is needed for summer perch angling with small baitfish. A gliding float for still waters, an Avon float for waterways with strong current, single hooks with a broad gap in sizes 4–6, and sinkers.*
***Opposite bottom:** The pikeperch angler's accessory box: sliding floats that take 10–20 g (0.35-0.7 oz), sinkers of various weights for both float angling and bottom angling, swivels and snaps, single hooks for small bottom-angled baits, treble hooks of sizes 6–8, and leader material.*

Tactics

Perch are mobile. If they do not bite within 20–30 minutes, try the next spot. Normally the bait is fished just over the bottom, but sometimes the perch are hunting and the baitfish struggle at the surface. Then the tackle should be raised to a meter below the surface. The bites are distinct and the float often disappears with a plop.

Flowing waters

In a waterway the tackle must drift with the current, keeping the baitfish just over the bottom. Brake its drift now and then. In late autumn and early winter, a better bait is often an earthworm or caterpillar under an Avon float (see the section on float angling). A large worm goes on a single hook of size 2–4, or some caterpillars on size 4–6.

Bottom angling for perch
Tackle

From autumn through spring, bottom angling is usually most effective. The simplest tackle is a paternoster, with a hook leader of 0.5–1 m (1,5-3 ft) and a sinker leader of 15–40 cm (6-15 in). The rod should be a quivertip of 11–12 feet (3–3.5 m).

Bait

Good baits are worms or baitfish up to 10–12 cm (4 in) long, rigged as above.

Tactics

Active fish are best. The hot area is fished by casting the bait and letting it lie for between half a minute and a few minutes, before pulling it in 0.5–1 m (1,5-3 ft).

Place
Lakes

In lakes there are perch over free bottoms, along submerged cliffs, near sunken trees, and at inlets or outlets. Bundles of brushwood are classic places for perch angling – artificial fishing spots created by sinking bushes in a place with an adequate depth of 3–6 m (10-20 ft). Small fish collect there and attract perch.

In summer, the right spots are where the wind blows best. It, too, draws small fish that attract perch. In spring, the fishing is hot at the spawning areas of perch. They may lie at a stream mouth, a pile of brushwood, or other spots where branches and rubbish are on the bottom, in which the fish can fasten their roe. During early spring, autumn and winter, perch can also be found over flat clay bottoms, often at depths over 6 m (20 ft).

An echo sounder makes it easier to find places with the right bottom structure and baitfish.

Streams

In flowing waters, perch occur within and near backwaters, behind sunken trees, in patches of vegetation and the like. The harder the current, the denser the perch hold in backwaters. Where no clear backwater exists, they hold in the weakest part of the current, at the inside of a curve or where the stream widens.

Streams and rivers that empty into the sea are especially good. They provide overwintering places for brackish-water perch. The fish run up the streams in late autumn and stay until spawning is finished, whereupon they migrate out to eat themselves fat.

Time

In summer, the best times are dawn and the last hours of daylight, but perch fishing offers several periods of biting during the day. Afternoon becomes ever better, the colder the water is. During winter, the only such period may come in the middle of the day.

Pikeperch

Both live and dead bait are taken by pikeperch. Besides the method for live bait, bottom-angling techniques with dead baitfish are therefore also useful. They range from free-line fishing, where the tackle is only a leader and the bait provides casting weight, to sliding tackle and other bottom-angling techniques for pike.

Leader

Pikeperch are wary of thick leaders, so it is better to use 0.40 mm nylon or modern super-flexible steel material – such as Drennan soft strand wire, or Kevlar if there is much risk of pike biting.

Top: *A missed bite by a perch leaves its mark: the baitfish has only lost scales, without the characteristic wounds from pike teeth. With baits of this size, a treble hook of size 6–8 is better for fast, secure strikes.*

Bottom: *Pikeperch are sensitive to stiff leader materials. As they have gripping teeth, a leader can be of nylon or modern flexible 'clad' steel wire.*

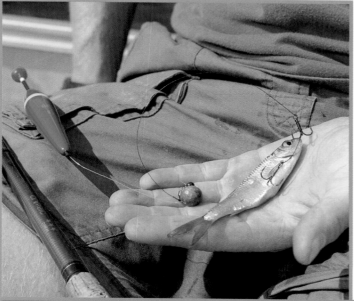

Place

In connection with spring spawning, pikeperch are found near spawning sites on free-lying stony ground, at cliffs with hard bottoms, or below migration obstacles in waterways that the fish run up in. During summer the fish are harder to locate, but usually hold near some kind of change in depth.

Time

Pikeperch are active at night, and then often swim near the surface. But in both early summer and autumn, the daytime fishing can match the angling by dark.

Handling

Fish that are returned to the water must always be handled carefully, and this is especially important with the sensitive pikeperch. Preferably, loosen the hooks with the fish still in the water, when lying in the net, for example. If the fish has to be lifted into the boat or up on land, do so briefly – otherwise the creature will not recover.

Eel

Eels are surrounded by mystery, tension and power. The eel that lies before you in a dark, dripping net may have begun its life fifteen years ago in the Sargasso Sea amid the Atlantic. Like a little transparent monster, perhaps it drifted with the current to a continental coast and, transformed into a thin miniature of your dream eel, took a waterway up to a fishing paradise.

Equipment and tackle
Rod

An eel is incredibly strong and can instantly set itself immovably on the bottom. Without hard and determined strikes, followed by a hefty left, the fight can be lost there. So the rod needs strength and length to lift the fish directly at the strike. A carp rod of 12 feet (3.5 m) is perfect.

Reel and bite indicator

A spinning reel is best, ideally with a monkey-climber as a bite indicator, and an open bail so that the fish can take line freely. Eels are often so sensitive to resistance that you cannot use a baitrunner, as they would let go of the bait.

A simple bite-indicating alternative is to hang a big tin can below the reel, and lay some coins on the spool after opening the bail.

Tackle

Sliding bottom angling is usually most effective. Use a sinker of 20–40 g (0.7-1,5 oz) on a swivel with snap, so that the weight can be altered according to the conditions – as well as a plastic bead before the leader's swivel to protect the knot.

Leader

One of the greatest eel-fishing experts of all time, the late John Sidley from England, believed that a steel leader is essential. In my experience, it happens very seldom that an eel damages a 0.35 mm (0.01 in) nylon leader seriously. But when fishing in waters where every fish is a giant, it may be smartest to use a steel leader anyway. Imagine if a dream fish should disappear into the depths because of a 'sawed-off' leader after many fishless nights.

Prepare your leaders by daylight. It is easier to tie on a new

With a quick strike, the hook often sits in the corner of the eel's mouth.

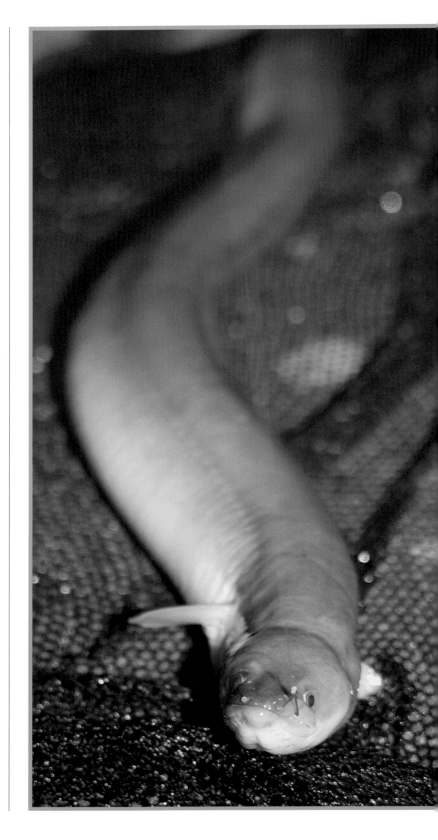

Baitfish for eel is tackled on most simply by drawing the leader through the fish with a bait needle. Be careful that the bait does not hide the hook – the tip should be free for optimum penetration.

leader in the dark than to put one together with a torch between your teeth.

Hook

A hook with a broad gap is best. For earthworms, size 2–4 is adequate, the smaller for one worm and the bigger for several. The same sizes suit baitfish and shrimp. With shrimp, an eel is best caught if the hook sits in the middle of the bait, at a ninety-degree angle.

Bait
Worms

Earthworms are my first choice, but I often fish on a rod with fish or pieces of fish as a test, and to have a bait that is undis-

turbed by small fish. I pinch off a bit of the earthworm to release a little extra aromatic juice.

Baitfish

Besides roach, bleak and small perch, smelt is a good bait as it has a strong, pickle-like smell.

Baitfish are normally best when very fresh. Preferably you should bring small live roaches and bleak in a bucket, and knock them on the head a second before putting them on the hook.

Shrimp

In marine or brackish waters, shrimp tend to be best. When the fishing is done in a harbor, shrimp remains and other rubbish are thrown into the water to attract eels.

Tactics

Eels have the fishing world's sharpest sense of smell. So change the bait often, at least once per half hour. New bait smells stronger, attracts better and catches more fish.

Pull in the bait by half a meter to one meter after the cast, where the bottom allows it, so as to create a smelly trail. With longer 'hot bottoms' the bait is best fished by pulling it in at intervals of five to ten minutes. Often the bite comes just after a pull.

Place
Stationary fishing

Harbors are good because of the natural prebaiting that their rubbish provides. In marine waters, the criteria are different. The biggest eels can be found in waters with sparse stocks – far up in a system of waterways, or in lakes with migration obstacles that make it hard for eels to get there. In dense stocks of eel, few specimens become large. The strongest ones wander far from their relatives, to grow big without a hard fight for food.

Migrating eels

Things are different when fishing for migrating eel. In spring and late summer, the large females start the journey back to their birthplace. Then the fishing is best at strategic places where they have to pass by – at promontories, or near outlets in the lower parts of extensive waterway systems.

Time

Eel fishing is best by dark, in the hours after dusk and until midnight. The best time of year is usually September, but eels can be caught throughout the summer half-year.

Last words

The dilemma for an eel-fishing lover is that eels are becoming ever more rare. Enjoy your eel fishing and the darkness, the excitement, the fish's raw strength – but release the big ones. There are not many left, and the fewer they get, the more our future stocks and eel fishing depend on some of them returning to the water and spawning. A single two-kilogram eel can produce 20 million eggs, which gives a perspective on what one released fish may mean for the future.

Above:
Even small ponds with no clear inlet or outlet can contain big eels.

Left:
Shrimp should be tackled on with the hook through the middle of the bend. A hook at ninety degrees will penetrate best.

Burbot

Fishing by dark is a feature common to burbot and eel angling. But there are important differences, such as the fish's behavior when it takes the bait, and the fact that burbot fishing belongs to the cold part of the year.

Equipment and tackle
Rod and reel

A rod at least 10 feet (3 m) long, for casting weights from 35–40 g (1.5 oz), and a spinning reel, preferably with a baitrunner, using 0.30–0.40 mm (0.01 in) line, make a good basis.

Tackle and sinker

Burbot often gobble the bait fast. Fishing with sliding tackle can therefore yield deeply hooked fish, since the bite is not registered quickly enough. Frequently it is better to fish with a fixed sinker, or bolt tackle. To ensure that the fish does not swallow without the bite being noticed, the leader must be short, 20–30 cm (1 ft). The sinker needs to be at least 50 g (2 oz) if the bolt effect is to work.

Hook

In order to expose the hook tip for penetration when the fish takes the bait in its mouth, a large hook is required. A single hook of size 2–4/0, depending on the bait's size, will do. Circle hooks are best, as they usually hook the fish in the corner of the jaw. For a small piece of fish, hook size 2–1/0 is used, and 1/0 – 4/0 for a whole fish.

Bait

Best is smelt, which outclass other baits in places where they occur naturally. Other good baits are strong-smelling fish such as herring, or shrimp and earthworms. Fish baits and shrimp are preferable, since they attract larger fish compared with earthworms, which can be swallowed by small burbot as well as roach and perch.

Place
Lake

In lakes, burbot are found near deeper areas, 15–20 m (65 ft) being popular. Promontories, shallows, or cliffs with hard bottom, stones, sand or, in some cases, hard clay, are normally best. But when burbot hunt, they come near

Above: One way to increase the tackle's attractiveness is to rig a starlight with a couple of pieces of rigtub near the hook.
Opposite: Burbot fishing is very sensitive to fishing pressure. Whoever wants to enjoy continued good fishing releases the big ones.

land, so it can pay to use short casts of 10–15 m (45 ft)

Flowing waters

In rivers and streams, the most reliable holding places are in backwaters. The stronger the current, the more concentrated the fish are. Along promontories or sharp bends, in deep holes, behind boulder and bridge pillars – these are typical spots.

Power-plant channels can hold plenty of fish. There they are 'chummed' by fish that have been sucked into the turbines. Moreover, some current obstacle is usually there for the fish to linger behind.

Time

Burbot are most active during the winter half-year. From November until the ice forms (where it does so) normally counts as best. If there is open water at the spawning grounds, during the spawning period from January to March, it is even hotter. Spawning occurs on hard bottoms with ample current, at promontories or on free-lying ground.

Burbot are nocturnal. The best times tend to be from dusk onward for a couple of hours.

Sheatfish

Fishing for European sheatfish, which can weigh over 100 kg (200 lb), is the heavyweight challenge of angling. Sheatfish occur naturally in most of the river systems in Eastern Europe, and implantations have established the fish in most of the larger Southern European rivers. When hunting sheatfish, there are chances of catching a specimen bigger than the fisherman.

Drum-fishing

Sheatfish are caught with bottom and float angling by the methods that have been described for pike. But a special kind of angling developed for sheatfish is ever more predominant: 'drum-fishing'.

A drum or jerry can is attached to a stone with a strong line, so that it floats at the surface where the fisherman wants to present the bait. One rows out with the tackle ready – a leader with a baitfish – and ties it to the drum with a 'crack-line' 2–3 m (9 ft) long. Then one rows back and tenses up the line, so that it hangs over the water surface. The rod is placed in a holder pointing upward. Now the baitfish works in the surface and just below it. When a sheatfish bites, the crack-line is torn off, the hook is dug in by the resistance, and the fisherman grabs the rod to dig it in further.

The drilling is usually done from a boat, as this lessens the risk of the fish getting caught in submerged trees, roots or the like.

Equipment
Rod

The rods must be very strong, 9–11 feet (2.5–3.5 m) long, with deep action that allows them to be tensed in an arc against the drum. Glass-fiber rods are better than carbon-fiber ones, since they are more durable and have softer action. This is needed because the fish delivers long blows and may let go if they create slack line.

Reel and line

Multiplier reels that take at least 250–300 m (900 ft), and 0.55 mm (0.02 in) line, are required. The fishing may be done at distances of around and above 100 m (300 ft), and there must be extra line for the fish's long rushes.

The line should be of the 'braided super-line' type in

The sheatfish is secured on a stringer.

strengths of 30–70 kg (60-150 lb), depending on how much rubbish is in the water that the fish can get caught in.

Hook, leader and crack-line

Both broad-gap single and treble hooks are used, in sizes from 1/0 to 14/0, depending on the fish's size. The treble hooks are of sizes 1/0–4/0, and the single hooks of sizes 4/0–14/0. For leaders, the choice is Kevlar of strength 50–100 kg (100-200 lb). The hooks are knotted to the leader so that one can be fastened in the baitfish's back at the dorsal fin, and one in the upper lip or at a breast fin, since the bite comes from below. The leader's length should be 50–100 cm (1.5-3 ft) and it is tied to a strong swivel, rated at about 100 kg (200 lb), to which the crack-line can also be tied.

The crack-line must have the right strength to break when the sheatfish attacks the bait, but not so weak that the hook fails to penetrate. Dacron of 5-7 kg (10–15 lb) is adequate.

Bite indicator

The reel is set with a click or a loose brake. A bite indicator with an alarm that sounds when the rod bends back is used as a complement.

Bait

Live bait is superior to dead bait, and must be as lively as possible. In river fishing, it is important to check often that no rubbish has snagged on the leader and hinders the baitfish's movements.

Carp, bream, crucian carp, large roach, and eel, with weights from half a kilo to two kilos, are good bait.

Place
Flowing waters

The fish hold in deep holes and backwaters, stealing into shallower areas at night to hunt. Good fishing places are at the edges between strong and weak currents, on the insides of curves, outside shallow areas with vegetation, and in clean backwaters.

Lakes

Drum-fishing is most popular in flowing waterways, but also works in lakes. Good spots are near shallow vegetated coves, where deep edges reach up, at belts of plants and the like.

Time

Sheatfishing is best during the summer half-year, but the ideal periods in southern rivers are March–April and September–October.

Fishing is better by night than by day. During sixteen days of fishing on the Ebro in Spain, three fishermen caught 44 sheatfish, only one of them by daylight.

Conditions

The sheatfish relies mainly on other senses than its sight when hunting – among others, its long feelers. A baitfish can be 'fake-attacked' several times before the sheatfish takes it properly. Perhaps this is why the fishing can improve greatly when the water is really murky.

After periods of drought, heavy rain and lightning can get the fish moving. The reason is undoubtedly that the water is stirred up, and because everything edible is washed into the rivers. As usual, however, there are differing opinions; some believe that the fishing is terrible when it rains.

Right: *The rig for livebaiting a large bream on the surface.*
Far right: *Although the sheatfish mouth is big enough it is not always easy to find a hookhold.*

North America

Modern angling has long since conquered Europe. But new challenges arise. The North American continent is a dreamland for anglers. And while American journals such as 'In-Fisherman' have occasionally discussed European techniques, American anglers have only scratched the surface of the possibilities that exist.

Carp

Almost the entire continent offers such fishing as can hardly be imagined by European carp anglers. From southern Canada to the southernmost American states, there are innumerable waters with large stocks of carp. And these are not tiny fish. In rivers, dammed-up reservoirs, and natural lakes, there are plenty of sizable fish – golden, turbocharged mountain carp.

In the USA, carp are widely regarded as vermin. Several states forbid the releasing of carp once they are hooked. In places where angling is unknown, hunting with bows and arrows for carp and other 'rough fish' is a popular amusement.

Exceptions occur, though. One pioneer is Bernie Haines, originally from England but a many-year resident of Houston, Texas. From April to October, he guides European carp-fishing guests on tours along the powerful St. Lawrence River at the border between the USA and Canada.

Alligator gar

Another species of low repute in the USA is the alligator gar. But many European anglers would presumably give an arm or leg to catch one. This is a primitive fish with more than seventy million years behind it, and can weigh over 150 kilograms. Looking like a cross between a crocodile and a monster pike, it leaps during the fight, and has an armored jaw that makes it almost impossible to hook. It is one of the sportfishing world's greatest challenges, living in the southern states' swamps, rivers and reservoirs.

Other species

Many of the southern rivers have Chinese carp weighing over 30 kg (60 lb). Giants, too, are the two 'buffalo' species, of which the 'smallmouth buffalo' is biggest. This carp-like fish can reach weights of around 50 kg (100 lb). Also here are three species of large-grown sheatfish that, apart from their barbels and way of life, are not very reminiscent of European sheatfish.

Above: A small example of the 'bluecat', caught on a bait intended for carp in a southerly lake in Texas. Also in North America are two other large sheatfish species, the 'channelcat' and 'yellowcat'. Both the blue and yellow ones reach weights of around 50 kg (110 lb).

Opposite:
Top: The carp that swim in North American rivers are golden power-packs that have nothing in common with their European cousins except appearance and appetite.
Bottom: This is considered a 'rough fish' by many American fishermen.

F lyfishing is undeniably more a way of life than a mere hobby or an everyday sport. Being a flyfisherman frequently means a special attitude towards the nuances of nature on and under the water surface.

Qualities such as watchfullness, good observational ability, patience, imagination and reaction speed are often ascribed to a clever flyfisherman. To this can be added an almost scientific accuracy in studying what the fish eats, as well as where, when and how it consumes its food.

Flyfishing

The evolution of modern flyfishing

Progress in improving fishing equipment was quite slow. In the mid-1660s, however, hooks began to be made more durable by hardening them. Plagues and fires forced needlemakers, among others, to move out of London. Redditch soon became a center of hook-making, and the old handicraft of smithing was transformed into a large scale operation. Industrialization also brought with it improvements in the quality of hooks: they became thinner and lighter, though still thick and unwieldy compared with those of today.

Even if both Berner and Walton/Cotton showed great interest in the insects taken by fish, it was first in 1747 that the initial book on flytying first appeared, The *Art of Angling* by Richard Bowlker. This is widely regarded as the first handbook on the subject and something of a trendmaker. He not only presented a list of his own flies, indicating some knowledge of entomology, but gave direct instructions for special types of fishing, such as upstream fishing.

The rods which were used during the eighteenth century were primarily for the purpose of taking up the fish's strike. On the whole, flyfishing in those days bore little resemblance to that of today. The line and fly were not cast, but swung out to the presumed holding spot of the fish. Only at the end of the century did small primitive reels began to be manufactured, with room for storing a small amount of line. At about the same time, it had been discovered that the lines could be tapered by twining in more horsehairs at the middle than at the end.

By the outset of the nineteenth century, the rod's length had been considerably shortened from 16-18 to 11-12 feet (around 5 to 3.5 metres). There were frequent experiments with different kinds of rod materials such as greenheart, hickory and bamboo. In the mid-1840s, an American violin-maker managed to construct the first split-cane rod by gluing bamboo ribs together. This was a real breakthrough, as a perfect rod material had now been found along with a superior method of construction in order to build really strong, practical rods.

Greenwell's Glory, one of the classic English wet flies which are still popular among many lfyfishermen.

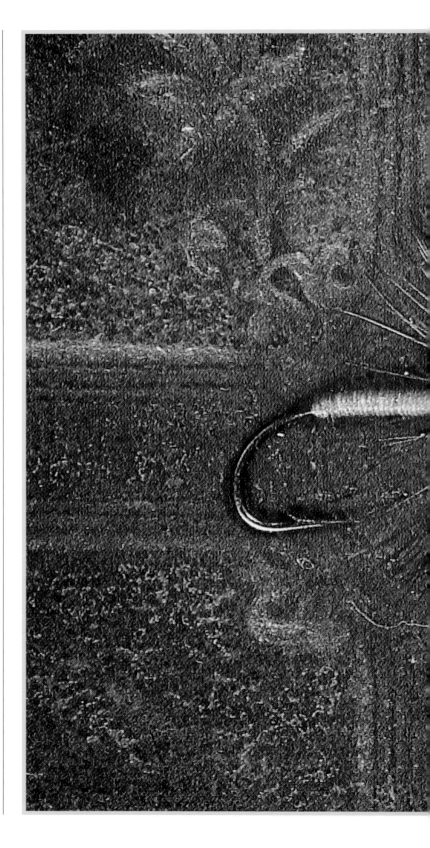

Split-cane rods, compared with earlier types, were light and pliable. In addition, they cast significantly better than their predecessors. However, they were still heavy and hard to handle as casting tools. Despite their overall advantage, it was to be some years before their production could be effectivized to make mass manufacture profitable. Two not entirely unknown names figure in this connection: the Americans Charles Orvis and Hiram Leonard. After about another decade, an Englishman named Hardy began his production of quality rods in the British Isles.

It was not only the development of the fly rod which started things moving in the mid-nineteenth century. Lines were also greatly improved. Thanks to the introduction of oiled silk lines, the casting length could be as much as tripled. More or less simultaneously, the horsehair was replaced by silk gut. Today's modern flyfishing had thus begun to take shape.

Flyfishing as a whole underwent extensive changes during the nineteenth century. The development of equipment, the interest in entomology, the creation of new fly patterns and techniques are all indications of this. A further factor, to be sure, was that flyfishing began to be popular in the true sense of the word. But with the popularization of flyfishing, the distance widened between it and other kinds of sportfishing. It became snobbish, ceremonial, and regarded as a fine art. There were echoes from the days of Berner: such a noble sport should be conducted and perfected by gentlemen.

Flyfishing tended ever more to become a science. Alfred Ronald was the first author to point out the relevance of insect breeding. His book of 1836 was, in fact, the first entomological description of insects in nature and their imaginary equivalents. Ronald's book inevitably increased the interest in insect studies. It suddenly became a matter of great concern to tie exact insect imitations by carefully observing all sorts of flying creatures at the water and recreating these faithfully for the fish.

During the second half of the nineteenth century, a lively debate blossomed about how the fly should be laid out. Upstream casting, downstream casting, and casting more or less across the stream were important questions. It was W. C. Stewart who made himself the champion of the upstream cast in his book *Practical Argling* (1857) which presented the technique and its advantages: by approaching the fish from the rear it is easier to imitate the insects' natural route downstream, and playing can occur without disturbing the fish upstre-

Izaak Walton was no devoted flyfisherman, but he undoubtedly became one of the great founding fathers of sportfishing. In the inset picture below, we see his fishing basket, now kept at the Flyfisher's Club in London.

am (that is, in as yet unfished water). Stewart was also of the opinion that it was more important to show the insect's size, form and appearance than to tie exact imitations.

The reign of the dry fly

Around 1860, dry-fly fishing began to take off in southern England. This new technique gathered ever more enthusiasts, and it did not take many decades before dry flies became ubiquitous, not least in English chalk streams. In the wake of this innovation, there followed a total devaluation of all that wet flies and wet-fly fishing stood for. It was regarded as unsporting and virtually immoral to fish with any kind of wet fly.

It had long been noticed that fish gladly took a wet fly just when it had landed on the water surface or had broken through. The new technique started by trying to get wet flies to fish dry. The fly was dried by means of a number of air casts, then landed on the water and floated until it eventually got soaked and sank under its own weight. Although dry-fly fishing is generally thought to have been "discovered" in England during the mid-nineteenth century, there is proof that the technique was used in Spain already during the seventeenth century, according to the *El Manuscrito de Astorga* (1624).

In any case, the basis of today's dry-fly fishing was developed in the south English chalk streams, for example at Itchen where there were plenty of hungry - although sometimes quite selective - trout and loads of insects. As the fish "learned" to see the difference between real and imitation prey, the wet flies which were dried out by air casting fished less well. The "true and proper" dry fly therefore came as a fresh start, not only because it was a new fashion in itself, but because it fished more effectively.

As to who was actually the first to introduce the dry fly is, as with so much else, a controversial question. Some maintain that it was Pullman in his *Vade Mecum of Fly Fishing for Trout* (1851), while others claim that it was a professional fly tier, James Ogden, who made the innovation. At all events, it was an article in *The Field* during 1857 written by Francis Francis which spread the principles of dry-fly fishing beyond a rather small circle of fishermen.

What then of Frederic M. Halford, widely considered the indisputable father of dry-fly fishing? The fact is that he, according to reliable sources, did not attempt dry-fly fishing until 1868 - that is, several years after the "discovery" of dry

Early attempts were made to tie flies that imitated the natural food of fish. Shown here are some flies from the late seventeenth century, together with their real prototypes.

flies. Yet what Halford did do was to perfect the technique with floating dun hooks.

The last decades of the nineteenth century brought a strong upsurge in flyfishing, not least due to Halford and the group of outwardly passionate flyfishermen who surrounded him. Enormous pains were taken to develop both equipment and techniques. The oiled silk lines were improved, body materials were tested which did not draw in water, and new techniques were sought for tying more durable flies. Halford became a dry-fly fisherman by profession. At the age of 45 he retired in order to devote all his time to the sport. This unbelievable commitment, of course, yielded returns. Together with his fishing friends he developed a standard in regard to rods, lines and flies which maintained its relevance long into our century.

His passionate activity also resulted in a couple of books which are regarded today as established works for flyfishermen. His first and best known, *Floating Flies* and *How to Dress Them* (1886), presented, after years of intensive insect studies in the chalk stream district of Hampshire, nearly 100 duns and spinners. Three years later came his *Dry Fly Fishing in Theory and Practice* (1889): here Halford described in a systematic way all the phases of dry-fly fishing. This is a virtually comprehensive work on fishing with dry flies in the English chalk streams. On certain waters, such as slowflowing streams with selective trout, it is still of great value.

We can say without exaggeration that Halford released an avalanche: interest in dry-fly fishing grew at a raging pace. It became modern to collect insects and make naturally faithful copies with Halford's theories of imitation and his flytying technique as a basis. However, the other side of the coin beca-

me a fanatical attitude that only dry-fly fishing was the correct way to seek contact with the fish. True believers would never have picked up a wet fly with a pair of pincers.

For this tragic development, Halford bears great responsibility, since in his later days he became quite intolerant of divergent opinions. The "father of dry-fly fishing" was unimpressed by wet flies and nymphs. Rather he tried to combat them as if they were a dangerous nuisance in the fly box. Fishing with dry flies for standing fish was the only proper method for him, while downstream fishing with a wet fly was not only ineffective but also a destructive and immoral form of flyfishing.

The challenging nymph

Along with the strong expansion and popularization of flyfishing, equipment was improved as well. Rods became easier to handle and the lines smoother to cast. Not least the Americans contributed much to these developments. When this fishing tackle came to England around 1900, nymph fishing slowly began to arise.

A central figure in nymph fishing was George Edward Mackenzie Skues, the technique's inventor and chief theoretician. Born in 1858, he died in 1949 a full 91 years old and it may be surmised that his success at fishing was one reason for his long life.

Like dry-fly fishing, nymph fishing was developed in the English chalk streams. This is because such streams are fine to experiment in, with their clear water, abundant insect life, and selective fish which have become familiar with hooks due to the active flyfishing.

In the late 1800s, Skues began to experiment. He asked

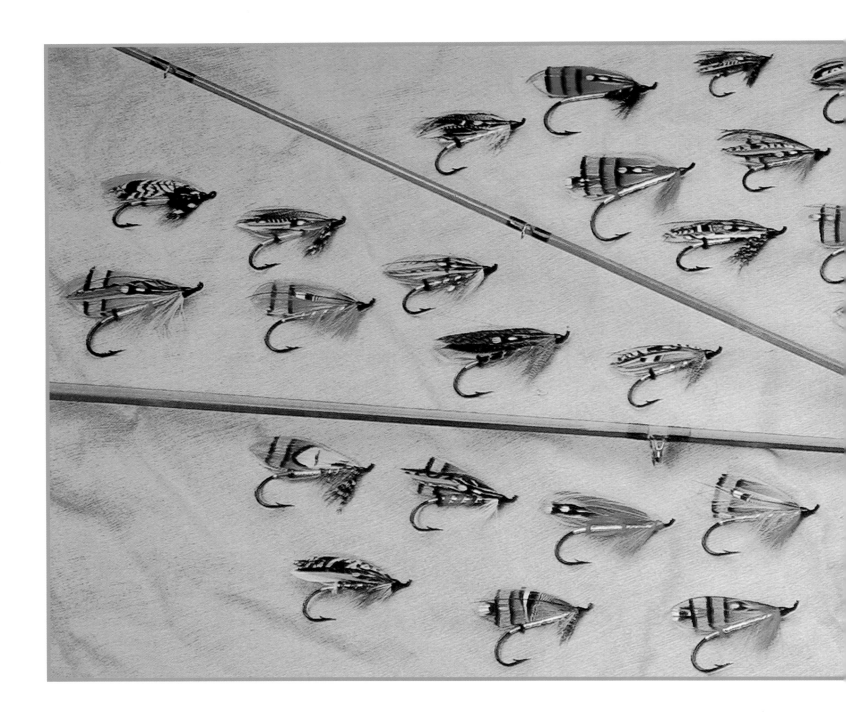

Fully dressed classic salmon flies.

himself: why fish with dry flies when the quarry take food in or just under the water surface?

The idea of fishing with a wet fly when the quarry did not take insects on the water surface was, at the time, heretical to many flybishermen in conservative England. But this did not prevent Skues from pursuing his research: he developed methods and patterns on the theory that fish were occasionally more interested in the hathing insects than in the already hatched ones. Thus soft-hackled, unweighted flies became the alternative to dry flies.

Flyfishing in the United States

The English colonists who reached the North American continent during the eighteenth and nineteenth centuries naturally brought with them a knowledge of, and interest in, flyfishing to their new land. The sport had taken root by the end of the eighteenth century, and it is even thought that special shops then existed for flyfishing materials and equipment.

Serious fishing with a fly began in the United States around 1850. At this time the Wild West was still living up to its name. It was therefore mainly in the eastern parts of the country that people diverted themselves by fishing with

rod, line and hook. In the more civilized Eastern states, people also began to realize that flyfishing was an unusually rewarding form of sportfishing.

In 1887 the book *Fly-Fishing and Fly-Making* by John H. Keene came out. Its main interest is that it shows that people in the USA had come farther in the development of flyfishing than we have tended to believe. The book not only describes how to tie dry flies, for example, but also displays a degree of innovative thinking which was long thought to have been reserved for greater luminaries such as Theodore Gordon.

Despite the country's late entry into flyfishing history in relation to England, the refinement of rods, spools, reels and lines was steadily driven forth. As mentioned previously, it was an American violin maker who, in the mid-1840s, made the first split-cane rods. After about 25 years, they began to be mass-produced and the rods were improved in features like casting ability and weight - so much that the English began to

George M. Kelson.

import them around the turn of the century. English rods at the time were long, heavy and stiff; thus gradually the English took over the American type of rod, which many have seen as a prerequisite for the development of nymph fishing.

The American equivalent of the chalk streams in Hampshire became the Catskill rivers in the state of New York. Rivers such as the Neversink and the Beaverkill are today classic waters in the history of American flyfishing.

In Europe and England, the brown trout was the target for

the hardily casting flyfisherman. This species, however, did not originally exist in the USA. There, people fished instead for brook trout in the eastern states, and for steelhead or cut-throat in the west.

With the growing popularity of fishing, the supply of brook trout in particular decreased drastically. During the 1880s, trout consequently began to be imported from Europe. The first fish were taken from Germany and the species is thus cal-led the "German trout".

As brown trout, and later rainbow trout, were implanted in rivers, the waters became harder to fish. The traditional down-stream wet-fly fishing proved ineffective. These trout were simply not as easy to fool as the brook trout, and flyfishermen were slowly but surely forced to reconsider.

One of those who perhaps came to mean most for the development of American flyfishing was Theodore Gordon. He was something of a loner who, in 1905, settled on the Neversink in order to be able to tie flies and do his fishing in peace and quiet. His literary production was primarily a num-ber of articles in the journals *Forest and Stream* (USA) and *Fishing Gazette* (England). He also corresponded fluently with Halford and Skues. Through this lofty correspondence with two of the great men of flyfishing, he acquired a fine insight into the development of English flyfishing.

At the end of the nineteenth century, Gordon obtained some 50 dry flies from Halford. However, these were tied according to English conditions and were therefore poor imi-tations of the insects which existed in Gordon's home waters. As a fly tier, though, Gordon began to tie his own dry flies with Halford's technique, but modelled on local insects He created many original patterns, the best known being Gordon Quill, and he also developed the so-called "bumble puppies" in the Neversink. These flies were the predecessors of the bucktail patterns, subsequently so much used.

Gordon laid the foundations for the Catskill School, which came to have a huge impact on American flytying. The fanati-cism which marked English dry-fly fishing never reached the USA and there were thus larger possibilities of experimenting. The results were significantly more sparingly dressed flies than the typical dry flies from the vHalford epoch in England.

Another American who has acquired a leading place in the history of flyfishing is George LaBranche. In 1914 his first book came out: *The Dry Fly and Fast Waters*. He is regarded for this and other reasons as the man who made American dry-fly fishing really popular. In the book was presented a technique for effective dry-fly fishing even in relatively rapid waterways. It differed in various respects from Halford's theories, which were primarily suited to the English chalk streams.

LaBranche's fishing technique was distinctive in many ways from the Catskill school, one essential difference being the size and bushy appearance of the flies, which made them float high and remain easily visible to the fish. LaBranche also belongs to those who developed the technique of fishing salmon with dry flies.

In general a different style of flyfishing and flytying arose in the USA as compared with England. An example is the special type of wet flies called bucktails and streamers. They grew up in America during the 1920s and are refinements of the classic wet fly. Observant flyfishermen had discovered that wet flies with silver or gold bodies could be identified as fry by the fish. Gradually there arose a whole lot of different patterns of bucktails (hairwing flies) and of streamers (featherwing flies) which, in one way or another, imitated fish fry in different species and stages.

In addition to those authors already named, Edward R. Hewitt had a great influence on this progress. He was a contemporary of LaBranche, and was one of the great flyfishing authors between the two World Wars. Today he is perhaps best known for his division of flyfishing development into three phases: (1) as many fish as possible, (2) as big fish as possible, (3) as difficult as possible to catch. Hewitt also advanced the view that the presentation of the fly was extremely important: the main thing according to him was not to have as great a range of flies as possible, but to have a smaller number and be able to present them correctly.

Flyfishing is a passion for many people - and for some, a real addiction - which often lasts a lifetime and can seldom be completely cured...

The flies – our deceptive imitations

There are many thousands of fly patterns around the world. Every day new materials and patterns appear. The range is so wide and difficult to survey that a newcomer may well feel confused when he or she is choosing flies for the first time.

However, flies and fly patterns are often two different things. Fly patterns are what you use as a model for tying; flies are what you fish with. All too many flyfishermen and fly tiers overlook this distinction. They place excessive faith in the fly pattern itself, and think more seldom about how the finished fly works and whether it is suitable for fishing.

Among us fly tiers are plenty of "pattern fanatics": fly tiers for whom a fly is acceptable only if tied exactly according to the rulebook, and then only with the correct materials. Thus they become slaves to the pattern, and are unable to tie a particular type of fly if they lack any of the often exotic materials which are prescribed.

It ought not to be that way - at least from the viewpoint of a flyfisherman. The fish are indifferent to tiny details and conceits; they are far more interested in the actual presentation of the fly than in the pattern. What counts for a fish is the total impression, not the absence of a few fibers or a peculiar feather.

Imitations or fantasy flies

If you tie flies for the sake of flytying, you obviously have to stick to the correct patterns and materials. Then it becomes a hobby in itself. But fishing has for many years suffered from the fact that authors are often more inclined to flytying than to fishing. The available literature has therefore given, at least to beginners at flyfishing and flytying, the mistaken impression that fly patterns are something sacred and inviolate.

Fortunately a clear change in this situation has taken place during recent years. New materials and tying methods have arrived, banishing the old classics into oblivion. These materials are easier to work with than the original ones, and are much more durable too.

Plastic tinsel does not break down like the old metal materials, even in the saltiest water. Stainless steel has shown the same advantage in regard to hooks. Polypropylene has revolutionized dry flies, for example, where it is lighter than water

and, moreover, is water-repellent. On the whole, synthetic materials have made life a lot happier for both the fly tier and flyfisherman.

In spite of that, many classics are still in our fly-boxes. They are flies which have been around for longer than most of us can remember flies so simple and ingenious that they still fish as well as on the day when they were first conceived. Often it is not a question of the actual pattern. These eternally young classics are types which be varied according to the conditions and can therefore cover a range of fishing situations. Just think of the "muddler", which can be tied in all conceivable circumstances - from the smallest to the largest - and is fished

A fly pattern can be created from various points of view. It may be a pure fantasy fly, or an exact imitation.

a situation where he or she was forced to get along with the materials at hand. Perhaps quite different materials would have been used if available at the time, and perhaps the finished fly would have been even better. So the fly tier ought to have a relaxed attitude towards the pattern. Flies are primarily intended to be used for fishing and, if one does not happen to have the prescribed material, one replaces it with something similar - maybe even better than the original material - for one's own fishing water!

A fly pattern can be created from various points of view. It may be a pure fantasy fly, or an exact imitation. The fly can be imagined to imitate the fish's natural prey, or it can be designed as a provocation. Thousands of fantasy flies have been conceived through the years, but very few have stood the test of time. England's bright red Cardinal, for example, has survived precisely because of its beautiful appearance and classic name. The same is true of a fly such as Silver Doctor, which is equally popular for brown trout, sea trout and salmon. It is obvious that the pretty colours are what have kept these flies in the fly-box, even more than their ability to catch fish, which is no better or worse than that of many other flies.

Things are different with the imitation flies, many of which have lasted remarkably well. This is especially true of dry flies and nymphs from the age of Halford and Skues. Although first tied around the turn of the century, they have nevertheless managed to retain their status for decades. It was, in fact, first when Swisher and Rickards created the famous "no hackle" dry flies that Halford's original dry flies became obsolete. Among other innovations, that of synthetic polypropylene - then called "phentex" - set the development in motion. Until then, natural materials had enjoyed a monopoly.

Good and bad imitations

On the whole, the classic English dry flies are incredibly poor imitations of real mayflies. Their dense hackle, which was needed to let them float at all, was enough to make them bad imitations. That they still could, and can, defeat shy and selective trout in the southern English chalk streams may tell us more about the fish than about the flies.

We usually say that dry flies float, but they very seldom do so. In order to float, a fly must be lighter than water, and this

both wet and dry. It is a good instance of a true classic: a fly type rather than a fly pattern.

Consequently, a fly pattern should be regarded mainly as a proposal, rather than as a prescription. It ought to be a starting point for individual interpretations. A pattern which has been thought out or developed in order to suit the discerning trout in a quiet English chalk stream cannot necessarily be transferred to other parts of the world. It must be adapted to the fish's size and the water's current speed, depth and clarity, to mention only a few local factors.

Lastly we should consider the way in which a particular fly pattern came into being. Often the fly's inventor has been in

is far from true of ordinary dry flies. A conventionally hackled dry fly is heavier than water and cannot float. It does not sink simply because it is held up by the surface tension. It actually stands on the surface with its many hackle fibers, just as the real insect does with its legs. Both rest on an unbroken water surface and are so shaped that the surface tension supports them. As soon as the surface tension is broken, the fly or insect sinks.

The surface tension of water, however, varies a lot from place to place. The cleaner the water is, the stronger its surface tension, and therefore the greater its ability to support insects and dry flies. When the water is polluted in any way, the surface tension immediately decreases. Then dry flies have difficulty in staying afloat. But what is worse, the same applies to the real insects. Many of them become unable to complete their life cycle, since they are "caught" hanging in the water surface and remain hanging there while they hatch.

Flytiers should take account of this phenomenon. It means that dry flies must be hackled more densely for polluted than for clean water. Actually we may get along well enough without hackle, as the above-mentioned "no hackles" indicate. As their name implies, these flies have no hackle at all, but consist of a tail, a body, and a pair of conspicuous wings. They can still be made to rest superbly on the surface tension, although in an impregnated condition. At the same time, they are silhouetted to the fish, and this is far better than the hackle fibers' imitation of characteristic mayflies. Especially typical of these insects are their upright wings.

Sparsely tied flies are, as a rule, best for selective fish in clear, calm water. They imitate their natural prototypes better than do densely hackled flies, which merely give the fish a confused picture of something that might be edible. Even so, in many situations we are forced to depend on the latter kind of flies - for example in fast waters, where flies with little or no hackle sink instantly.

For such fishing, therefore, special dry flies have been developed, which can stay afloat even in a whirling current. Instances are Wulffs, Kolzer Fireflies, Goofus Bugs and various Irresistibles. These flies are all equipped with strong wings and tail, as well as dense and bushy hackle of the highest quality. This structure enables them to stand high on the water, and keeps them visible to both the fish and fisherman. In the case of Goofus Bugs and Irresistibles, a further step has been taken: they are provided with a sort of "life jacket", an air-fil-

Many flyfishermen think that conventionally hackled dry flies float - in other words, that they are lighter than water. But the truth is that they rest on water's surface tension.

led body of deer hair, which gives them volume and floating force when it really counts.

These ample "floaters" seldom resemble anything in particular, but rather resemble a morsel which the fish are reluctant to pass up. In fast waters, it is nevertheless unnecessary to use the exact imitations which are required in clear, calm water. Fish in a rapid current do not have time to study the fly - they must react fast, or else it is gone again!

But densely hackled flies can also be needed in still waters, for example when fishing with imitations of caddis flies. This often involves large insects that cause commotion when they flutter about, especially during egg laying. Such behavior can be imitated by allowing a dry fly to drag on the surface, a technique which calls for densely hackled flies that do not sink immediately.

Today it has become ever more common to tie certain types of flies with foam rubber such as "polycelon". In this way the finished fly is made to literally float, in contrast to normal dry flies which simply rest on the surface tension. Such an ability is used for flies that have to float on the surface - typical hatching nymphs, or heavy land insects like beetles and grasshoppers. The latter can often be served up to notable advantage with a clear, loud splash that draws the fish's attention to the fly. And this is a technique that demands self-buoyant flies: those with a body of cork or foam rubber, which is easier to work with and also lasts longer. Here is still another proof that synthetic materials have revolutionized flytying and given us completely new opportunities.

Color can trigger strikes

But what is it about our flies that gets fish to strike? An ethologist can provide some insight into this fascinating subject. Ethology is the science of animal behavior, and conducts research on why animals act as they do.

In one of the most classic ethological experiments, it was investigated how the stickleback reacts to different stimuli. As is well known, the male becomes extremely aggressive during the spawning period. He defends his territory and nest against all intruders, especially competing males.

*Dry flies can be tied in numerous ways. Here we see a traditional example (upper left),
a "no hackle" dry fly (lower left), and (at right) the two steps needed to tie a parachute-hackled dry fly.*

During spawning, the males are colored bright red on their bellies, while the females have a large, distended stomach full of eggs. It was studied how the sticklebacks reacted to various decoys. Some of these were exact imitations of males and females, whereas others bore little or no resemblance to them.

The experiment yielded interesting insights into the fish's ways of reacting. Not unexpectedly, close-imitation decoys with bright red colors triggered a violent reaction in the males, which naturally thought that the decoys were competing males. Moreover, decoys with a distended belly attracted great interest as if they were real females.

Yet the truly fascinating result was that perfect imitations did not release stronger reactions than did the less close imitations. It was the color which proved decisive for the males, and the shape for the females. Color and shape were the so-called "key stimuli" which triggered reactions the factors that determined whether there would be any reaction at all. As long as the decoy was red, and preferably bright red, the males showed violent reactions, ignoring all else.

One might think that sticklebacks are more primitive than the salmonoids which we try to catch with flies, but such is not the case. From a purely evolutionary standpoint, salmonoids are more primitive, and the stickleback is among the most advanced fish. The experimental results with sticklebacks can thus very well be applied to salmon and trout.

What can we learn from this as fly tiers and flyfishermen? Quite a lot. It is natural to attempt to imitate, as closely and detailed as possible, the animals which constitute fish food. The more a fly resembles its prototype, the better it fishes - for fish are not stupid, are they?

Well, fish are indeed stupid, at any rate by human standards. They cannot think in the sense of adding two and two. They learn from experience, but do not reason. They have no perspective on their situation and, instead of thinking, react

Opposite: To choose or not to choose the fly is the question.

Streamers may be very effective when the fishing is slow. They are easily visible and are frequently good imitations of small fish. Mickey Finn is undoubtedly a classic streamer that can lure fish to strike even when the water is relatively warm.

MICKEY FINN
Hook: *streamer hook No. 6-12*
Body: *silver tinsel*
Wing: *three sections – yellow, red, and yellow – of hair from polar bear, calf tail, or goat*

to external influences. Whether we like it or not, a fish is a primitive machine, controlled by its environment. The frequent difficulty of catching it is due to various factors which we are seldom able to govern.

This logic serves simply to bring down to reality the controversial "imitation principle". Certainly it may be interesting to tie very exact imitations, but unfortunately the fish rarely set much store by them. From the experiment with sticklebacks, we saw that the color is the decisive key stimulus. If we look at our own flies with the eyes of a fish, things become more complicated.

Fish can see colors - this is a fact. But in regard to dry flies, for example, color is by no means as important as was once thought by fly tiers and flyfishermen. The fish see a fly from below, outlined against the sky in backlight, so they can hardly distinguish between different color tones. In practice, it often turns out that we can do quite well with a small range of dry flies in a few colors.

Down at the water, of course, the fish can study our wet flies. Still, exact colour nuances are seldom decisive. This is because there are large individual differences between natural insects. For instance, nymphs which have to molt their skins are very dark, while those which have just done so are very light. Thus the fish see both dark and light insects at the same time, which means that they are not fastidious about exact colors. After all, they only want something to eat!

Colourful flies can be attractive

When we speak of colors and fish, we must remember that colours above the water surface are not the same thing as colours under the surface. The water absorbs some of the light which enters it. The murkier the water, the less light can get in, and the less significance a fly's colors have. We should also keep in mind that red is the color which fades soonest, and blue is the color that penetrates deepest. The red part of the visible spectrum is least energetic, and blue is most energetic. If you need a visible fly in deep water, it is thus a bad idea to choose a red one, which will look black to the fish and be hard to see. Instead, choose a fly with blue or green colors - ideally with plenty of tinsel, which can reflect the little available light.

Fluorescent colors have always been of great interest to flytiers. For many of us, fluorescent flies have seemed to be something magical, which now and then can save an otherwise fruitless day of fishing. But there is nothing magical about fluorescent colors. Fluorescence is due to energetic ultraviolet light, which is invisible to us. It is the same kind of light that gives a suntan or sunburn. When ultraviolet light, which is especially predominant on gray and cloudy days, hits a fluorescent material, this is activated by the light's energy and shines with unusual strength. Consequently, fluorescent colors are most clear on dark days, although they should not be confused with phosphorescent colors, which can emit light even in darkness. If there is no light, there is no fluorescence either!

In fly patterns for salmon, particularly the so-called "egg flies", fluorescent colours have made notable progress. Here they are quite superior, although of more doubtful value in smaller flies with quieter colours. Fluorescent colours seem to have the greatest effect when they are used in flies that provoke the fish to strike - in other words, flies meant for fish on spawning migrations. But they should not be forgotten if we are fishing in the cold months, when the water contains little food. Then the fish are hungry, and not especially discerning. In such situations, a fluorescent fly can attract great attention and curiosity, yielding surprisingly good results. Later in the year, when food is abundant, fluorescent colors often lose their ability to attract strikes.

A colourful fly like the classic, eternally young "Mickey Finn" is regarded as a natural attractor - that is, a fly which draws the notice of fish with its strong colors. But it is a fly which can also be very effective during the warm months, when there is plenty of food in less bright colors. Strong red-yellow hues are, perhaps, not so impressive after all. Considering the colours of a minnow or stickleback, one can see that almost every color in the spectrum is represented. So who knows? Maybe the fish believe that a fly like "Mickey Finn" is an ordinary small fish.

The fly as a caricature

The experiment with sticklebacks showed clearly that exact imitations are not necessarily the best. Other scientific studies indicate that it can even pay to exaggerate the key stimuli. A good imitation therefore need not be a fly which most resembles the prototype. It may instead be one that overemphasizes typical characteristics of the prototype. We have to think like a caricaturist who instantly hits upon the quirks of his "victim" and exaggerates them. Then there can be no

doubt of whom the picture represents. It might be said that the caricature is more realistic than reality!

If the insect to be imitated is, for instance, a mayfly which has big wings - the fly should have extra large wings. This is actually true of the so-called "no hackle" flies, already mentioned. Usually regarded as exact imitations, they are actually faithful caricatures. Their wings, which are not veiled by any hackle, tell the fish immediately that this is a mayfly.

The classic dry fly is slowly disappearing from our flyboxes and being replaced by new, better and more durable imitations. Not least the parachute flies, whose hackle is wound around the wing root, have become popular. They are easy to tie and rest low on the water, just like the real insects. At the same time, their horizontal hackle adds extraordinary buoyancy. Moreover, the fly lands as light as a feather and always correctly on the water. This is certainly not true of normally hackled dry flies with upright wings, which readily topple over and lie down on their sides.

A mayfly's last winged stage, the spent spinner, is very easy to imitate. This again is due to the modern synthetic materials, which do not absorb water. With them, we can make the flies rest in the surface layer without using hackle. The "poly-wing spinners" are outstanding imitations with a particularly simple structure - a pair of long tail antennae, a polypropylene body, and a horizontal wing of poly yarn. They can hardly be simpler, and the fish love them!

All these imitations rest on the water, while the hook tip and the whole hook bend protrude down under the surface. Ultimately such a fly does not closely resemble its natural prototype. Insects do not break through the surface - they stand on it. Nevertheless, thousands of very selective fish have been tricked by our flies, despite the quite unnatural iron clump which hangs beneath the surface. This could be seen as another proof that exact imitations are not very significant for the fish's view of our flies.

There are fly tiers who make complicated "upside down" flies, with hook points and bends that do not break through the water surface. But these have never been widespread, since they are too hard to tie. As we have seen, even the most selective fish are only seldom able to appreciate our exact imitations, which are primarily for the flyfisherman's own sake!

Fish often let themselves be tricked into taking, even though the fly is really a rather clumsy imitation of natural food.

Function and movement

In the long history of flyfishing there are some examples of amazingly simple flies, so simple that it might be doubted whether they can be used for fishing at all. Frank Sawyer was showered with praise when he created his now classic Pheasant Tail, a fly that consists solely of pheasant cock tail fibers and copper wire. The latter serves partly as binding thread, and partly to weight the fly so that it can sink fast.

Sawyer had noticed that mayfly nymphs of the genus Baetis hold their legs close to the body when swimming. He therefore saw no reason to put hackle on their imitations. With sparse material he was able to contrive the right form and color, while relying on the rod end to give the fly correct movements - an "induced take" which has since become famous.

Oliver Kite, one of Sawyer's disciples, further reduced the Pheasant Tail nymph. He went so far as to use only copper wire on a bare hook, and his Bare Hook Nymph caught plenty of fish. Most of his fishing for fastidious trout took place in the English chalk streams. So much for exact imitations!

Function is a key word when it comes to flies for practical fishing - and regardless of whether they are exact imitations or fantasy flies. The fly just has to work. Dry flies must float, being tied with water-repellent materials; wet flies must sink, absorbing water so as to break through the surface tension. The latter rule is crucial for non-weighted flies: light nymphs, spiders, or wet flies made to be fished high up in the water.

The current speed also influences our choice of material and flytying style. For instance, wet flies for use in still water must be tied with soft material that can look alive and move correctly. Such flies normally fish best when they are sparsely clad. Good illustrations are the classic spiders and soft hackles - their material pulsates at the slightest excuse. Superb in this respect are flies tied with marabou feathers.

The opposite rule holds if wet flies are to be used in fast currents. Here a fly tied with soft material would soon collapse and lose its originally intended shape. One should employ stronger material like cock hackle instead of hen hackle, bucktail rather than marabou, and so on.

If the fly must reach down to fish in fairly deep water, there are two alternatives: using a sinking line to pull the fly. down, or weighting the fly and fishing it with a floating line and a long leader. Both methods have their pros and cons. With a sinking line you do not need to weight the fly, which thus behaves more lively in the water. But when fishing nymphs upstream with a floating line, there is only one solution: weighted flies. Then, of course, you must remember that heavy flies are dead flies with no essential life. In sum, clear limits exist to how much the fly can be weighted without hurting its ability to catch fish. The important thing is always to tie it with soft and vital material.

Recently we have acquired fast-sinking leaders, provided with built-in weights. They allow use of a floating line and non-weighted flies. The leader enables the fly to come down to the fish anyway, while also presenting it with a light and lively fly.

From the casting viewpoint, there are definite limits to how heavy a fly can be. Strong fly lines can carry heavy flies better than light flies, but every line obviously has its limitations. Big, densely hackled dry flies create a lot of air resistance and need relatively strong lines to be laid out against the wind. This is familiar to salmon fishermen who try their luck with big dry flies of the Wulff type. But light flies can also be very heavy. Good examples are the "zonkers" and "puppies" tied with thin strips of rabbit fur. The latter have an amazing ability to absorb water, and a wet rabbit is a very heavy rabbit in terms of casting!

The flyfisherman often needs flies which are really bigger and heavier than his equipment can handle. Such is the case with imitations of many medium-size small fish, and with giant flies for huge game like tarpon and sailfish. If these flies were tied in the conventional way, they would be unduly heavy and impossible to cast.

While tying streamers and bucktails on long-shafted hooks, we usually employ short and light hooks for really large flies. They are provided with a wing which is several times longer than the hook shaft, making a fly that is very large and yet does not weigh much. To prevent the long wing from winding itself round the hook bend, it is frequently tied to the rear of the hook shaft. This is done, for instance, on special "needle-fish" flies - and characteristic tarpon flies, where the long hairwing is simply replaced by saddle hackle.

Nevertheless, it is also possible to tie a tiny fly on a com-

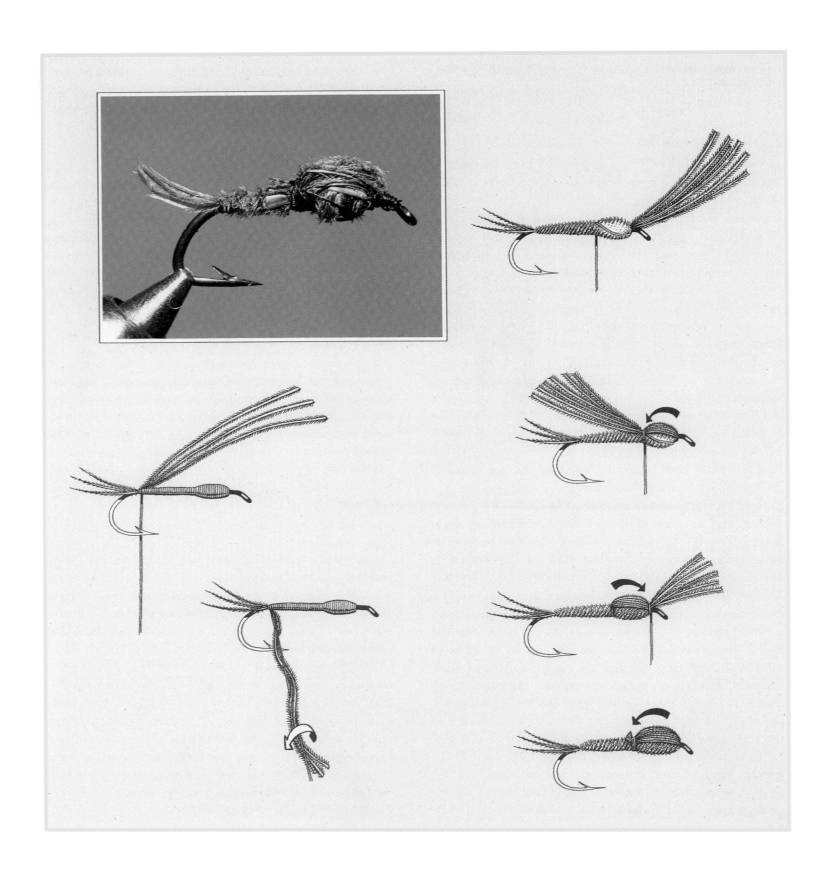

Left: The Pheasant Tail Nymph created by Frank Sawyer is as simple as it is ingenious. Having no hackle, it is tied with only copper wire and pheasant cock tail feathers.

PHEASANT TAIL NYMPH
Hook: No. 12-16
Tail: three fibers from a pheasant cock' tail feather
Body: tied and weighted with red-brorwn copper wire,
            using pheasant cock tail feather fibers are
            wound forward to the head, then bent back and
            forth to make an ample wingcase, and finally
            tied to the head

paratively large hook. Not seldom, we go after big fish that need strong hooks to be played on. But the flies must be small, since they imitate small insects. Such dry flies can be tied "double", with two flies on one hook. This offers a great advantage when the fish take midges of size 18-24. There is ample room for two flies on a hook of size 16, and then you can also use a stronger leader tippet which matches the fish's size better. Imitations of individual fish eggs - "Glo Bugs" - can likewise be made small on rather large hooks, and paradoxically at no cost to their fishing ability. Here is yet another proof that fish see flies with different eyes than we fishermen do.

Adaptation to practical fishing

Flyfishermen and fly tiers are committed, creative people who work continually to keep their hobbies progressing. Originally flyfishing had a very restricted range. The cast was short and the flies could be fished only on or just under the surface. If the fish were not there at that moment, nothing could be done about it. But today's modern, well-equipped flyfishermen want to fish everywhere and under all conditions.

Thanks to developments in gear, we can now reach farther out and deeper down than our predecessors.

When choosing a fly, you should naturally take into account its size, color and dressing, but the presentation is often what determines whether the trout will take.

Equipment

The fly line is what determines the casting weight. So it is essential that the rod be balanced against the line's weight during the cast and presentation of the fly. To obtain this balance, lines and rods are classified by a system called AFTM (American Fishing Tackle Manufacturers' Association). Which class or classes you should choose depends on the water you are fishing in - its current, required casting distance, fish size, and other factors.

Rods

Until the 1950s, nearly all fly rods were made of six glued-together segments of bamboo, with triangular cross-section. This is known as the split-cane technique. The unavoidable disadvantages of such rods were their higher weight (much higher for salmon rods), their greater demands for care and carefulness, their relatively high price and shorter lifetime. The advent of synthetic fibre rods was greeted with joy by many flyfishermen, and these rods soon dominated the market.

Carbon fiber rods began to be produced in the late 1970s. Many of us think—perhaps rightly—that their high-tech construction, low weight, fast action, and superb casting ability have revolutionized flyfishing. But it should be remembered that such rods also have drawbacks. Besides being brittle and delicate, they are fine conductors of electricity, which is a serious danger if they come into contact with high-voltage cables. Tube-built glass-fiber rods, although heavier, are thus still on the market, since these are comparatively cheap and durable, as well as often having excellent casting properties.

For technical developments have made quite good tube-built glass-fiber rods available at a fairly low price. In sum, nothing shows that an expensive rod need be better than a cheaper one.

Apart from the AFTM classification, rods are grouped according to their action—that is, how they work. Normally we distinguish between fast action, medium action, and slow action. A rod with fast action has its elasticity mainly at the top. With slow action, the entire rod works during the cast and playing. Medium action is a popular combination of these types, used in many modern fly rods.

When choosing a rod, you must know what it will be used for. The action, line class, and length are determined by the type of water and the fish's species and presumed size. One-handed fly rods are used for fishing in brooks and streams, small rivers and lakes, ponds and coastal waters Two-handed fly rods are almost exclusively for salmon fishing. Long two-handed rods make it easier to manage a lot of line in the air, but they are heavy and tiring to cast with. A short one-handed rod is convenient when the fishing water is surrounded by bushes and thickets.

The choice of rod depends on further things too. One must check that the handle, reel seat, windings and guides are of good quality and that the rod has enough spine. Generally you can control the line and fly more easily on the water, and achieve a more even casting rhythm, with a longer rod. Rods under 7 ft (2.1 m) cannot be recommended except under very special conditions. For those who need advice when choosing equipment, the following may serve as guidelines.

7.5-9.5 ft (2.2-2.9 m), AFTM class 4-6: fishing in brooks and small streams.

8-10 ft (2.4-3.0 m), AFTM class 6-8: fishing in large streams, lakes, small rivers, and for light coastal flyfishing.

10-13 ft (3.0-4.0 m), AFTM class 9-10: fishing at coasts, large lakes, and for light salmon fishing.

14-18 ft (4.3-5.5 m), AFTM class 10-12: heavy coastal and salmon fishing.

Lines

As the fly line has decisive importance for the cast and presentation of the fly, demands on lines are very high today. They must be supple, light casting, durable, and easy to feed out through the guides.

Functionally, the fly line helps with its weight in carrying out the feather-light fly. Lines are therefore grouped in twelve standard classes, on the basis of the weight of the line's first 30 ft (9 m) measured from the line tip. Higher class means greater line weight.

To make the equipment suitable for different types of fish, we have not only the AFTM system but also variations in the tapering of fly lines. This refers to the line's profile, and two main groups exist. A double-tapered line (DT) is thickest in

In order to cast correctly and present the fly elegantly to the fish, there must be good balance between the rod and line.

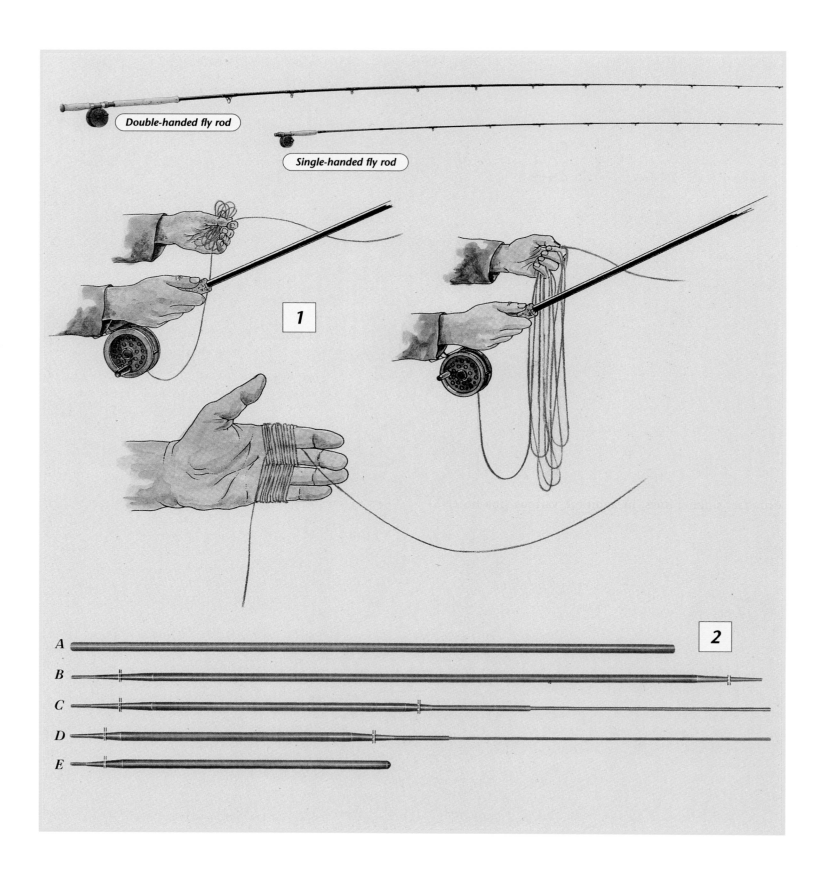

Double-handed fly rod

Single-handed fly rod

1

2

A
B
C
D
E

the middle and becomes gradually thinner toward both ends. A weight-forward line (WF), besides its tip, consists of a "belly" about 26 ft (8 m) long - where the weight is concentrated - and a long casting line.

The DT line is used most, because it allows soft and harmonious casts, which are essential for well-aimed and discreet layout of the fly. Its popularity is naturally increased by the fact that it can be turned round when one end has worn out.

The WF line is suitable primarily for situations that call for a longer cast. Depending on the kind of use, the belly length varies. Most marked and short is the belly on the "saltwater tapered" WF line, which serves especially for long casts with heavy flies in bass and saltwater fishing. The "long-belly" line (WFL) has an extremely long clump that makes it behave like a WF line in long casts, yet like a DT line in short casts. A third type of line is the "shooting taper" (ST), also called "single taper", which consists of a short clump attached in a thin casting line, and operates like a projectile when the fishing needs a really long cast.

There is also a distinction between floating and sinking lines. A floating line (F) is used in dry-fly fishing, and when fishing with nymphs or wet flies on the surface. Sinking lines (S) are required when the fish stay deep. Within these groups are also various classes. We speak mainly of slow-sinking (Intermediate), normal-sinking, fast-sinking, and extra-fast sinking lines. In addition, various sink-tip (F/S) types are on the market, and can be preferable to sinking lines - for they give full control over the floating section, and their sinking end can be adapted to the type of fishing at hand. Rapid currents obviously call for heavier (and thus more slowly sinking) line than do still waters, in reaching down to a given depth.

1. To facilitate the cast and presentation of the fly, it is necessary to control the loose line neatly. At left are shown three common ways of organizing the line as it is taken in. But the most usual method, illustrated at right, is to hold the line in loops with your line hand.

*2. All lines are classified according to their profile. Shown here, respectively from the top, are: **A** Level line (L), **B** Double-taper line (DT), **C** Long-belly line (WFL), **D** Weight-forward line (WF), **E** Single-taper line (ST).*

The line's color is frequently less important than we tend to believe. Fish are hardly frightened by a fly line even if it is very colorful, provided that the leader is long enough. On the other hand, one must keep in mind that light-colored lines are easier to see when the illumination is poor. Sinking lines, of course, do not suffer by being dark.

Fly lines should always be supplemented with a backing line, or reserve, in case a far-rushing fish takes the fly. A backing line also fills up the reel so that the fly line does not wind up in too tight turns. Such lines are made of monofilament nylon or braided Dacron. The latter is usually most expensive, but pays off in the long run since it ages well, is more durable, and tangles less than monofilament line.

Reels

The fly reel is commonly the least emphasized part of our fly-fishing equipment. A functional reel must fulfill two requirements: having enough room for backing and fly lines, as well as being able to play big fish effectively. For salmon fishing in particular, it must tolerate long and powerful runs without breaking down. Playing a hooked fish with a loose line lying on the ground is a cause of concern, with the inevitable tangle and lost fish. At least 100 m (330 ft) of backing line, in addition to the fly line, have to fit on the reel. There must be an adjustable, dependable braking system. The reel should be easy to care for, and soundly constructed with no gap between the spool and housing where the line might get stuck and damaged. Moreover, it should have easily replaceable spools so that you need not carry a reel for each line.

The most usual type of reel is doubtless the traditional one, simply built with no finery. Its handle sits right on the spool, which rotates once each time the handle is turned as the line is wound on - and in the opposite direction as the line is pulled off. When the line is drawn out, the spool is braked by means of an adjustable screw, and you can use your index finger to brake more effectively. This type of reel operates superbly when playing small fish.

Big fighting fish are best chased with a reel whose braking system is more powerful and efficient, such as a slip (clutch) brake or disc brake.

In general one should always choose high-quality reels. Besides making the fishing more enjoyable, they produce less wear on lines and have a more dependable braking system. It is also worth remembering that the reel should not be too

The knots are the weakest link between fly and fisherman, so they must be durable an reliable. **1**. The spool knot
(to tie the backing line on the reel spool). **2**. The nail knot (to tie the leader and backing line on the fly line).
3. The blood knot (for tying together sections of monofil) **4**. The clinch knot (For fastening the fly and leader)

small. It has to hold enough line and backing for the type of fishing you do. And finally, a reel for saltwater use must be corrosion-resistant.

Leaders

The leader's chief duty is to provide an even transition between the relatively thick fly line and the hook eye. A thin leader tip makes it easier to present the fly without alarming the fish, but is too readily broken off by a sizeable fish. Conversely, a thick leader tip can withstand big fish better, yet may be rather clumsy for elegant presentations.

To some extent, the leader's thickness must be adapted to the fly's size. For a thicker leader guides a big fly more accurately than an extremely thin leader tip does.

Leader tips thinner than 0.12 mm (0.005 in) should be totally avoided, and not less than 0.18 mm (0.007 in) ought

to be used for medium-sized fish, while 0.30 mm (0.012 in) is a minimum for salmon and other true fighting fish. Large salmon that need big hooks can even call for up to 0.50 mm (0.02 in) at the tip.

The length and tapering of a leader are also important. A good rule is that it should be a little longer than the rod when fishing with dry flies and nymphs, but that 1.5-2.0 m (4.9-6.5 ft) suffices for wet-fly fishing. A leader is built up from its thicker upper end, via a more or less smoothly narrowing transitional section, to the thin tip. About 60% of its total length should consist of the strong upper part, followed by about 20% narrowing and then about 20% tip. The thickest part of the leader, which is tied or glued onto the fly line, must be around 0.5 m (1.6 ft) long with a diameter of 0.45-0.50 mm (0.02 in).

In addition, the leader has to be flexible, soft and easily cast, non-knotting, and able to keep itself stretched in and on the water. A coiled leader can really spoil your sport, not least when dry-fly fishing.

Even if there are ready-tapered leaders on sale in stores, it is not hard to tie them yourself with pieces of monofilament

Left: A big fish has been hooked amid spectacular scenery. But will the equipment hold against the pressure?

nylon line. The pieces in the leader material should not differ in diameter by more than 0.05 mm (0.002 in), since otherwise the knots are not as dependable.

If you choose to buy leaders ready-made, there is a great range of different types to choose among. Best are ready-tapered knotless monofilament nylon lines – and braided leaders. The latter, flexible and soft, do not curl as easily when they lie rolled up on the reel for a long period, and they give a generally good presentation of the fly.

Flies

We now come to the equipment which not only gave its name to our kind of fishing, but is the very foundation of this sport's existence - the fly. A symbol that unites the hundreds of thousands of flyfishermen all over the world, it is also a source of arguments. Some maintain that a wide choice of flies is necessary, whereas others are content with a few carefully selected flies. Many of us demand exact imitations, but equally often we consider caricatures to be what attracts the fish to strike.

Who is right or wrong in such disputes will not concern us here. Perhaps it is enough to note that our flies and fly patterns are infinitely diverse, and that flies are always a fascinating topic beside the fishing water as well as in the sportfishing stores and magazines.

Internationally, fly patterns are almost uncountable. A lot are pure fantasy flies, while many are precisely tied imitations of particular insects that may live in only one area. There is also a long list of patterns intermediate between imagination and reality. Despite this amazing variety, flies can be divided into main groups: dry flies, wet flies, nymphs, flymphs, streamers, bucktails, lures, salmon flies, and so on.

Naturally a pattern meant to imitate a certain insect has to portray its prototype in all basic respects. Yet this does not require it to be an exact copy in every detail. Only its similar characteristics need be made clear to the fish - in other words, the fly's proportions and the appearance of its body, hackle, wings, and tail must be right.

In any case, flies obviously have to fulfill their elementary functions. A wet fly should sink to the depth where fish are hunting at the time. A dry fly must be able to float high and lightly, in order to be presented as in nature. A flymph ought to remain hanging just in the surface film, or only a few centimeters under it. The purpose of a salmon fly is to somehow provoke the aggressive spawning fish to strike. And so on...!

Accessories

The equipment described until now is an absolute prerequisite for effective flyfishing. But there are quite a lot of items that can make your fishing easier and pleasanter, although not essential to its success.

Clothing should first and foremost be roomy, comfortable and rugged. It ought to give the fisherman proper camouflage, so as not to frighten the fish unnecessarily. Moreover, it should withstand rain and wind, as well as having plenty of pockets to help you organize your fishing adventures.

A fly vest is probably the most common piece of clothing. Its pockets must be practical and accessible. Before investing in a vest, though, you should check that the

fasteners – they must never be allowed to damage the hook point!

Leaders and their materials, too, must be stored so that they are not damaged. If you tie your own leaders, a dispenser is preferable to loose spools, but it must have room for at least five different sizes and the lines should be able to feed without tangling.

Your fly vest or equivalent apparel should also contain a sharp pair of scissors or nail-clippers for purposes such as cutting leader stubs and dressing knots or flies. A sharp knife is necessary for slaughtering and cleaning. Substances that increase the buoyancy of dry flies and floating lines are further examples of essential accessories. A small rotatable lamp which can easily be attached to a jacket or vest is indispensable for flyfishing at night if you want to have a fair chance of switching flies, tying leaders, and other work that needs some light. Scales and a measuring tape, flat-nosed pliers, a hook-sharpener, line grease, and a line basket can be added to complete the picture of a well- equipped flyfisherman.

Those who do not practice "catch and release" fishing, or , land their fish by hand, often need a deep and preferably collapsible landing net, or one with extension handle. And if you fish much from overgrown shores, a variant is a small collapsible landing net that can be carried in a quiver. Short-shafted, wooden framed landing-nets are good when wading, while long-shafted landing nets are more all-round and serve excellently for fishing from low or high shores as well as from boats. The inexperienced salmon fisherman who does not want to risk losing his "dream salmon" when grabbing it by the tail will need a tailer or gaff.

Basic accessories also include some sort of eye-protection. A gust of wind, or a wrong move of the rod, can easily send the fly on a dangerous course and, at worst, into your eye. Ordinary glasses or sunglasses are a cheap guard against permanent eye damage. A clear advantage of Polaroid glasses is that they filter out the sunlight reflected from the water surface, and thus increase your chances of seeing what swims under it.

pockets will really hold fly boxes and are not so shallow that the contents fall out.

Fly boxes ought to float. A box is easily dropped and, if this happens over deep water, a sinking box can be lost forever. Besides, a good fly box should be clearly arranged and must provide maximum protection for the flies and hooks. Dry flies are best kept in boxes with separate compartments that can be opened and sealed simply, or else in spacious boxes where the flies are fastened in foam-rubber bands. Wet flies are less delicate and can thus do well in relatively flat boxes. The same is true of nymphs, streamers and salmon flies, where it is most important that hooks and barbs do not lose their sharpness. We should therefore be very careful with metal clamps and similar

A fishing hat is not only symbolic of fishing success. It also helps to protect the face and eyes from flies that change course during the cast. Besides a broad brim or a screen, the hat should have a deep shape and cover as much as possible of your face, ears and neck.

Sooner or later, one finds that many fine fishing spots cannot be reached without a pair of thigh or body waders. Which of these you choose depends mainly on the water depth. Body waders can take you into relatively deep areas, but they are clumsy to wear in shallow water or on land, and uncomfortable condensation easily forms inside them. Thigh waders are lighter to walk and move in, but limit the depth of water you can enter.

Body waders made of neoprene have many advantages over the "old" rubber type. They are convenient to wade in, provide fine insulation against cold water, and can easily be repaired by the waterside. A drawback is still their expensiveness.

Whether you use thigh or body waders, and whatever the material, certain demands should be placed on their soles. These must primarily be non-slip. The bottoms should be covered with felt or matting, to prevent your slipping on stones and perhaps being taken by the current. Another advantage of silent materials like felt is that they do not scare shy fish as readily when you wade.

As an aid, some kind of wading staff should be used. You can easily make one from any stable length of wood. The important thing is that it does not bend even under heavy force. For this reason, be careful when buying a staff that can be disassembled, as it must be able to support a hard leaning body. A good wading staff should also have an eye or other device where you can attach, for example, a rubber cord to keep the staff from drifting away with the current if you happen to let go of it. Ideally it ought to have a sound muffling "shoe", for instance of rubber, as the fish are then not frightened so easily.

Another helpmate for fishing at some distance from shore is a float-ring (belly-boat). This is used almost exclusively in still or very slow waters. You then have every advantage of a boat, and it is a lot easier to transport and launch. But obviously greater care is needed with sharp objects in a belly-boat. A puncture while far out in a lake can be disastrous. One should therefore always make sure that the belly-boat has a two-chamber system.

Casting with a single-handed rod

As mentioned earlier the casting weight is determined by the fly line. In other words, the fly is transported out to the fish by means of the line. This undoubtedly looks much harder than it is in practice when the art has been learned. For a beginner, getting the fly and line out while avoiding nearby trees and bushes is almost impossible. Yet only a few hours of intensive training are usually required in order to grasp the basics so well that at least ten meters of line can be cast with no real trouble.

To achieve long casts and complete precise presentations, you often have to spend a long time on different fishing waters. But the fact is that fishing can be effective even with

Above: *A fishing hat protects the face and eyes from flies that change course during the cast. Fly box ought to float – a sinking box can be lost forever.*

Right: *Long casts are not necessary for catching fish with a single-handed rod.*

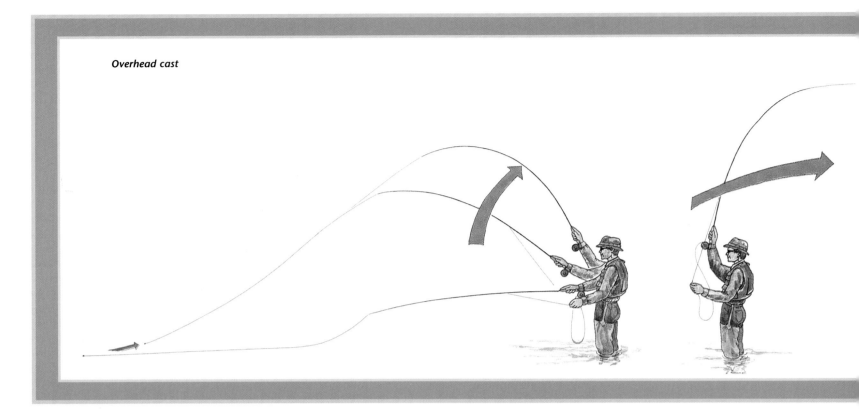

Overhead cast

relatively short casts. Long casts are not at all necessary for catching fish, especially in small waterways. It is, however, quite essential to learn correct presentation of the fly, whether you are casting long or short.

Practice and more practice: this is the recipe for learning how to cast harmoniously. A skilful instructor is certainly worth having, but not a prerequisite - the best teacher of casting is the process of fishing itself.

Basic casting technique

When learning to cast flies, you should start in a place with room for the back cast. Many people begin to practice on a grass lawn, but the best location is a lakeside, since laying the line on the water is an essential part of many casts. For the line's friction against the water - which cannot be obtained on a lawn - helps to build up the action in the rod. Certain casts, such as the roll and switch cast, are just impossible to perform except on water.

It is simplest to begin with a single-handed rod of 8-9 ft (2.4-2.7 m). To protect the tip of the fly line, a piece of leader should always be tied farthest out. Moreover, tie on a fly with its barb nipped off. The fly helps to stretch the leader tip, giving better control over the final phase of the cast.

A good cast is based on harmony between the line, rod, and casting arm. One common beginner's mistake is to force the cast, particularly the forward cast. Many are also afraid that the line will hit the ground, and do not wait until the back cast has really stretched out. As a result, the cast collapses and the line falls in a heap. To avoid this and acquire the right rhythm, you should turn your head during the back cast, watching how the line moves and when it has stretched out completely. Only then does the time come to start the forward cast. Calm, smooth movements are the essence of becoming a good caster.

Here we shall briefly describe the traditional casts and their variants. But the continual progress of developments in equipment makes it likely that opportunities will arise in the future for learning new types of cast - tested and adapted to suit modern rods, reels, lines and leaders.

The overhead cast

This is to be recommended as the basic cast. Before beginning the cast itself, pull 6-8 m (20-26 ft) of line from the reel and lay it out on the water. Hold the rod handle with your casting hand just in front of the reel and your thumb point-

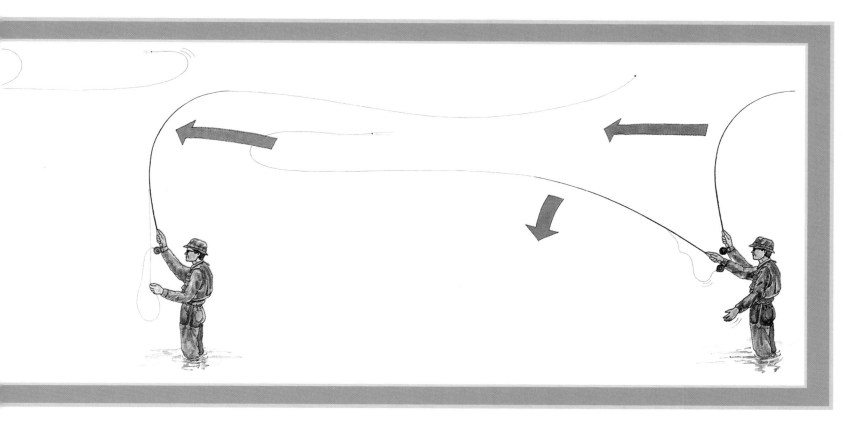

ing toward the rod top. Take the line in your other hand, held at waist height. Stand relaxed with the rod top pointing slightly downward.

Lift the rod upward with a strong but smooth movement. Once it is vertical, stop the back cast. Wait till the line is lifted and stretched out backward. When you feel the outstretched line's weight in the rod top, it is time to start the forward cast by moving the rod forward to a horizontal position - smoothly but sharply. The line now rolls forward over the rod tip and stretches out before you. Make sure that the line hand always follows the rod's movements.

The next step is to try holding the line in the air, without it collapsing on either the backward or forward cast. These air-casts are made by stopping the rod, during the forward cast, in a position pointing obliquely upward. When the line has rolled forward over the rod tip and is nearly stretched out, the rod is moved backward in a new back cast. The line now flies back and stretches out, whereupon you start a new forward cast. Once this can be done without letting the line touch the ground, you have mastered the air-cast as well.

Achieving perfect coordination requires some training and many failed attempts. But when you can keep 8-10 m (26-33 ft) in the air with no trouble, practical fishing can begin. At first, you should choose a shore area with space behind you, so that the back cast meets no obstacles. Despite this precaution, you can expect the fly to get caught occasionally on branches and bushes.

Having learned to cast 8-10 meters at the water, you can increase the amount of line in the air by a few metres each time. Hold the loose line in one hand and, when the accelerating backward-and-forward cast has added more energy, release the reserve line in a forward cast. Now the loose line shoots out through the guides to join the airborne line. This step, too, calls for exact coordination which is acquired only through much expert training. Eventually, you can thus lengthen the cast according to your ability, meter by meter.

Shooting out the line in this way is also useful when presenting the fly - not least in fishing with shoot-lines and certain other types of belly-lines, as well as in dry-fly fishing.

A variant of the overhead cast is the side cast. This horizontal, half-high movement follows the rule that a cast should be stretched out where there is enough space. It comes in handy when, for example, fishing on overgrown waterways with limited free space.

Double haul cast
With a double haul, the cast can be greatly
lengthened, as when wading or in a headwind.

The double haul cast

Although on most waters we can manage with casting lengths of 10-15 m (33-50 ft), longer casts can be necessary in order to increase the chances of a catch, for instance when fishing in lakes. Even while wading, with the line almost nudging the water surface as you cast backward and forward, the technique of a double haul is very useful, since the cast easily collapses if the line touches the water.

A double haul means that you draw the fly line downward with your free line hand during both the backward and forward casts, thus increasing the line's speed and force. Begin with a strong downward haul at the very beginning of the back cast, and then complete it as usual. Just when the forward cast is to begin, make a new haul with the line hand, then release the line when the casting weight is greatest. The loose line will shoot out in the last phase of the cast.

This variant can lengthen the cast by 3-5 m (10-16 ft), but it demands exact coordination between the rod hand and line hand. Since the cast must be calm and harmonious, you should be a relatively good caster before starting to practice it.

Once the double haul is mastered, you can easily feed out a rather long line with some air-casts and finally shoot out the line by 3-5 meters. The double haul's increased line speed can be essential when you are fishing in a powerful headwind and when you need to cast far.

The serpentine cast

This cast is employed primarily in dry-fly fishing when the fly has to drift evenly without drag, even if the current is erratic. Your line hand must hold a certain amount of loose line that can be shot out in the forward cast. At the same time as the fly line shoots out, the rod top is moved rapidly forward and backward, parallel to the water surface. Thus the line lands in big curves on the water. The dry fly will gain a little extra time in order to float freely, before the fly line stretches out in the water and the fly begins to straggle. To lengthen the drift, you can also flick the rod top while releasing a little loose line, which glides out through the rod rings and adds to the line already lying on the water. This way of lengthening a cast can, of course, be used in combination with all casting variants, so that the fly will follow the current freely.

The roll cast

A roll (or switch) cast is used in fishing areas where a back cast is quite impossible to carry out. You can then certainly not cast as far, but with some training a fair length can be laid out.

About 5-6 m (16-20 ft) of line should lie stretched in front of the rod tip. Then the rod is lifted until vertical. Once the line hangs in a curve next to the fisherman, it is cast forward by means of an accelerating whip action upward, forward and

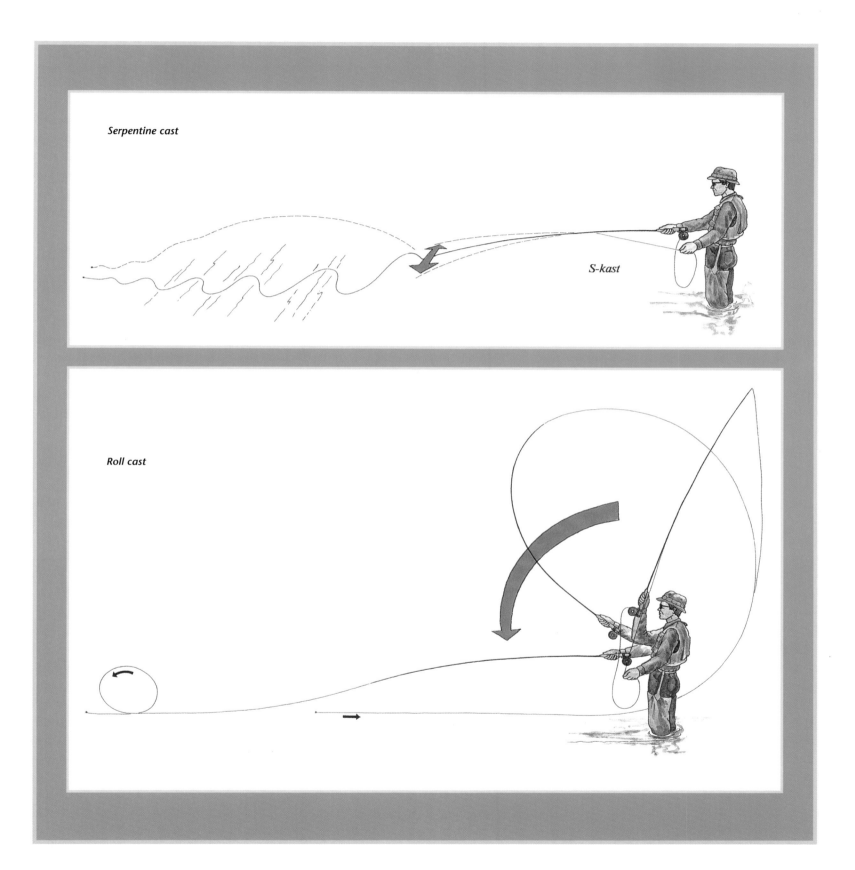

Serpentine cast

S-kast

Roll cast

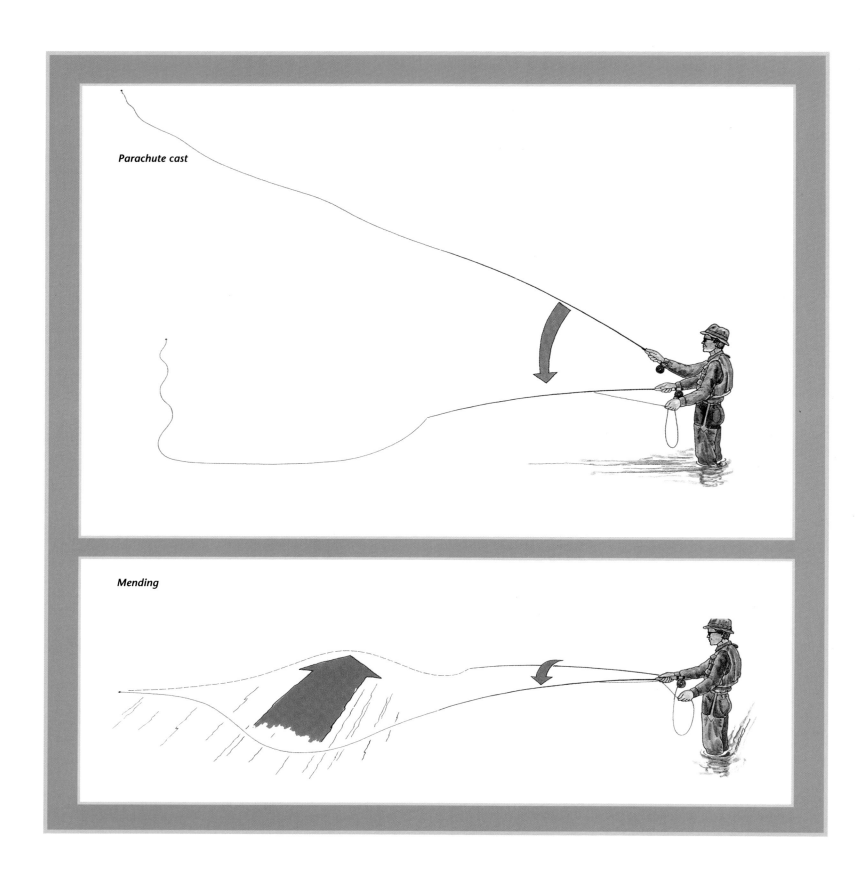

Parachute cast

Mending

then downward. The line rolls out on the water and the fly lands. By pulling out more loose line and repeating the roll cast a few times, the casting length can be increased to more than 10 m (33 ft).

One can also combine the roll cast with other casts, such as the side cast, for effective results in many situations.

The parachute cast

The difference between a serpentine cast and a parachute cast is that, in the latter, you stop the rod top during the forward cast when it is pointing obliquely upward. The line then shoots away in that direction and stretches out at the same height as the rod top. Then you lower the rod, and the fly jerks back a little before landing with the leader in curves. If the cast is done correctly, the fly, leader, and line end will land after the fly line's rear portion. And the fly can drift somewhat farther downstream without dragging.

Mending

The purpose of mending is to prevent flies from dragging or being hindered in their natural drift when the current takes the fly line and drags it along in big curves. You simply float the fly line some distance upstream by mending it, without affecting the leader tip or the fly. Mending is a cast-like movement parallel to the water surface in the current direction. If it is properly performed, the fly line will be laid in a gentle upstream curve. Thus you can considerably lengthen the natural drift-in principle, until the cast is completely fished out and the fly line ends straight downstream parallel to the shore. When fishing for salmon, it is sometimes necessary to mend downstream in order to increase the fly's speed.

Right: Mending the line is a diverse way of controlling the fly and line when they are on the water and fishing in a current. If you cast across or obliquely down the stream, its varying speed affects the line and therefore the fly, whose presentation can thus become worse.

Shown here, the line is mended upstream, by moving the rod tip in a semicircle straight upward and upstream.

Casting with a double-handed rod

Fishing is generally the same with a double-handed rod as with a single-handed rod, but it can be very arduous and energy demanding because a double-handed rod is longer and heavier. Consequently, a couple of variant casts have been developed specially for this kind of fishing. Perhaps the best known is the Spey cast, which works well in nearly all situations if done right. This cast requires relatively little strength, is effective even in a wind, and does not need any space for a back cast. Moreover, it produces no knots on the leader - which are common in, for example, the traditional overhead cast.

The overhead cast

Casting with a double-handed rod differs in several respects from its single-handed counterpart. But the overhead cast is essentially built up in the same way. Obviously it also has the same weaknesses: you need a lot of space for the back cast, the leader can easily become knotted, and you often have to do an excessive number of blind casts which can be tiresome with a heavy double-handed rod. The aim should be to do only one back cast and then lay out the fly.

The underhand cast

The hard work of fishing with long double-handed rods is made much more comfortable by modern, light rods of carbon fiber and/or boron. However, it is still important to learn energy-saving methods of casting.

An underhand cast is not only elegant, but also offers the opportunity of fishing for a long interval without getting tired. In addition, this restful cast is quite effective. Using a back cast, the line is brought under the rod in front of you. When the rod is pointing obliquely backward, the movement stops and the forward cast begins. At this moment the line should not be fully outstretched backward. It must be given the most energy when the rod tip is pointing obliquely forward. With a single air-cast, the line can be laid out nicely in this way.

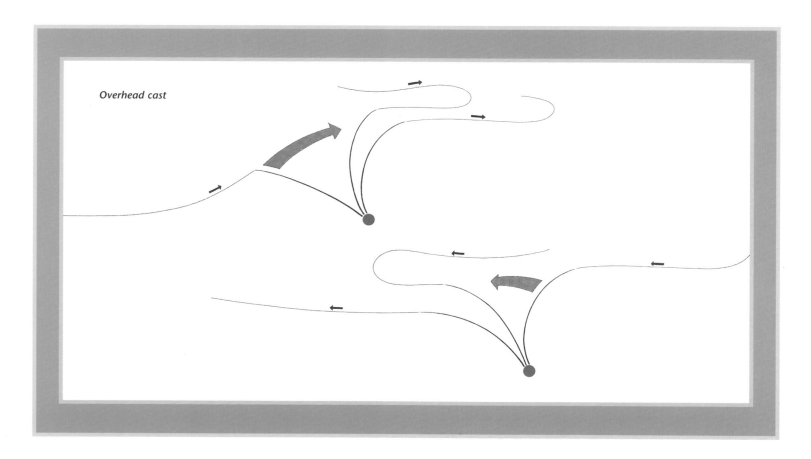

Overhead cast

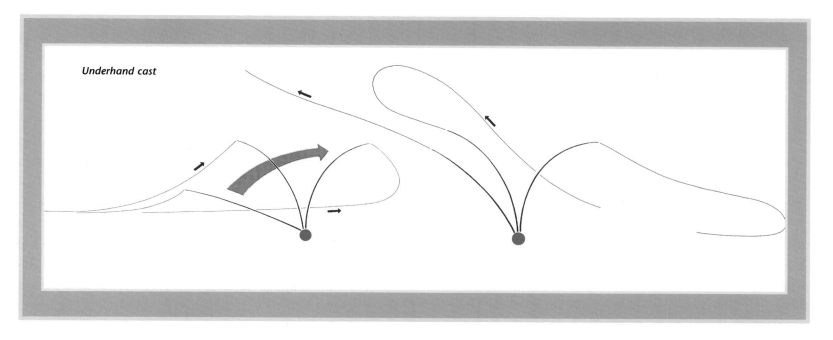

Underhand cast

The switch cast

As its name implies, the switch (roll) cast means that the fly line is rolled out onto the water. This cast comes into use mainly on shores with limited space for back casting. It must also be mastered if you want to learn the effective Spey cast properly.

Your rod should have a good spine. During the back cast, it is brought calmly to a position pointing obliquely backward. Now the line must hang in a soft curve alongside you. In the forward cast, the rod is strongly accelerated forward and downward until it is parallel to the water surface. The line then rolls out across the water in a beautiful bow.

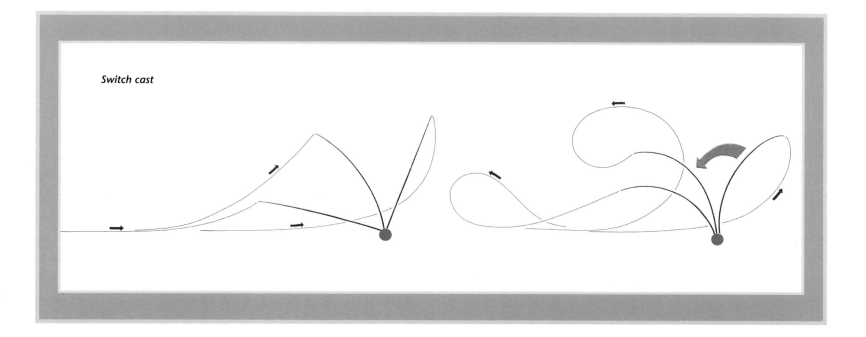

Switch cast

The Spey cast

Like the roll cast, this cast is used on shores where vegetation restricts the possibility of casting backward. It also resembles the roll cast in other essential respects. The important thing is that the fly should be placed in the right position before the forward cast, so that the hook does not catch on the line when the casting direction is changed by 45°. Hence, the fly is often allowed to float straight downstream with the current. A "double" Spey cast exists, too, but here we shall concentrate on the single Spey cast, as it also provides the basis for the double one.

Just as with the roll cast, you lift the line from the water by moving the rod to a position pointing obliquely backward. With an accelerating underhand cast, the line is brought backward and upstream on your outer side. But not so much that the fly line's tip soars into the air- it should nudge the water surface, thus adding force to the forward cast. The greatest transfer of energy should occur when the rod is pointing obliquely forward. However, the rod's own action does most of the work. This cast, as well, must be performed gently and harmoniously in a single sweep. It is easiest to carry out with a floating DT line.

The Spey cast has several advantages. It permits a long cast even where the back cast is difficult because of dense shore vegetation; it is not affected much by strong wind; and it demands relatively little muscle power during the actual cast.

Spey cast

Flyfishing in still waters

Rapidly expanding numbers of flyfishermen are well on the way to charting all the earth's flowing waters. While crowding increases on the "classic" streams - of which the sport's pioneers spoke so enthusiastically in books that remain highly readable - the destinations of flyfishermen are becoming distant and exotic.

Unknown territory in the flyfishing world is thus getting scarce and, if Glasnost applies to us too, we may soon learn whether it is true that giant trout exist in the Soviet rivers running north to the Arctic, where fish of 30-40 kg (66-88 lb) are rumored.

But for those who stay around home, fish have thinned out in the currents of many countries, despite improved management of their habitats. Flyfishing continues to grow anyway, and its practitioners demand the opportunity to fish at a reasonable cost, which also means at a reasonable distance from their origins.

Until now, they have often been satisfied, although most flyfishermen live in urban industrial regions. However, things would be far more difficult if we insisted on pursuing the sport in its "classic" form, along streams with natural stocks of salmonoid fish. The prerequisite has been, and is, that we take advantage of a vast reservoir of fish in our lakes.

Lakes offer virtually unlimited possibilities for flyfishing, apart from the insistence by a majority of us that our fish should have adipose fins. In Scandinavia alone, for example, there are thousands of lakes with more or less intact stocks of salmonoids, and further thousands whose water quality makes stocking especially of rainbow trout a meaningful, and indeed profitable, enterprise.

This is a revival of lake flyfishing in the sense that our pioneers, at least in Great Britain, sometimes fished for both sea trout and ordinary brown trout. At any rate, it is the best explanation for the fast growth of flyfishing. In Great Britain, where many reservoirs have been built to collect fresh water for urban needs, a kind of revolution is in the air: reservoirs are stocked with fish and provide recreation for tens of thousands of new and old flyfishermen.

Put-and-take fakes have enabled flyfishing to go on developing in several parts of Europe. Most of the numerous young people who try flyfishing as a hobby gain their first experience on these still waters. And they are right to do so, since one ought to get through the commonest beginner's mistakes before making an attempt on wild waterways, where the fishing is usually much harder.

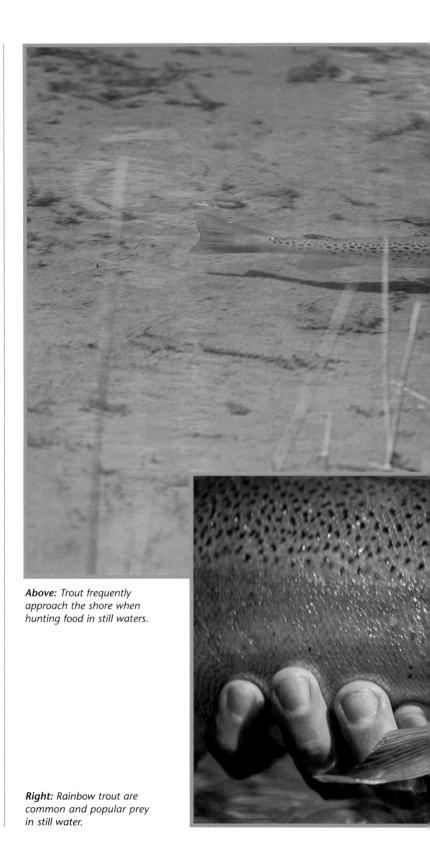

Above: Trout frequently approach the shore when hunting food in still waters.

Right: Rainbow trout are common and popular prey in still water.

You cannot learn to flyfish by reading a book about it. But a good book can provide facts and suggest experiments that pay off. Unfortunately books about lake flyfishing are rare, at least in comparison to those about fish in flowing waters. Once you do manage to learn the correct tactics and strategy for flyfishing, though, you can often catch a lot of fish - and big fish at that.

Reading the waters

People who grow up in districts with abundant waterways soon learn to "read" them as fish do. The fish are where the food is, and the most, as well as largest, fish can be found where the underwater menu is marvelous. Here they stand in the current, or scour a small area, since they need not waste energy on hunting. The current brings them all they can eat, like an endless conveyor belt in a free restaurant.

As a result, some places in a river or stream are better than others - especially where several waterways run together, or where backwaters form that concentrate the food. Adult grayling and whitefish, for instance, assemble there, at times in great schools; and it is there that the flyfisherman encounters the biggest fish. Such trout are usually solitary, because trout defend their territory with zeal and they seldom allow smaller competitors to eat at the same table.

These optimum feeding spots amount to only a fraction of the water surface's total area. Certainly much of a productive waterway can provide food during several months of the year, but not enough of it to support big fish, let alone entire schools of adult fish. However, this is sufficient for small fish until they reach a size adequate to compete for the better feeding places.

Thus, a flyfisherman must be able to "read" a waterway for the movements and color changes that show where its special fish-food resources lie. At times when plenty of insects are hatching, the fish themselves reveal these places by rising greedily. If they do not rise, it can be worth the trouble to watch such places discreetly, as any fish there will give themselves away sooner or later.

Another means of detection is to test a place with a "tempter", one of the favorite dry flies or nymphs that usually yield results even when fish are not rising. Most flyfishermen have, or eventually acquire, a little hoard of such helpmates, which can provoke a fish to strike even if it is temporarily selective - that is, bent on eating a special kind of insect in a particular stage of life.

An experienced flyfisherman has learned his "reading" and soon finds where the fish are feeding, whether or not he is on familiar waters. This is not difficult, at least on small streams. Although it may happen that only small fish take the fly, this does not mean that the water has been read wrongly. Sometimes food is scarce even in the right place - and then the big fish, especially when they are fully grown trout, go back to their hideouts in deep holes under the main current or the root systems of shore trees.

The large fish in streams are almost perfect economic machines. Hunting has to pay off, in other words to yield more food energy than the hunting consumes. When not enough food exists at their favorite feeding places, the fish do not eat at all, preferring to wait. But when the menu improves, they show up instantly to chase away smaller fish and feast on the goodies brought by the current.

This behavior is notably typical of large trout, which - during intense insect hatchings - can be seen "swinging" at the surface as they eat: first a part of the head appears, then the back, and finally the upper tail fin, a sequence repeated three or four times in a row. Having risen to the surface when insects are dense, they take an insect at every "swing". After eating as many as five insects, they glide back to the bottom and soon rise again. For a big trout, it is not economical to rise for a single insect: several must be eaten each time to restore the energy that is spent.

Moreover, this behavior gives the flyfisherman his chance of catching a "dream fish". Such a trout rises so regularly that its return to the surface can often be predicted exactly. A "swinging" trout is also virtually blind, as the movement restricts its field of vision, allowing the fisher man to wade within easy casting distance.

Yet the "reading" of water, and the fishing tactics used at clearly identifiable feeding places, are peculiar to waterways where we can find fish at the same places year after year - and can even catch the same individual fish more than once, at least in the case of trout. For trout are able to spend their whole lives in one limited section of a stream, as long as it contains plenty of food.

In the still waters of lakes, meres and ponds, the same fish species have other habits. Here they seldom meet currents that transport food to particular feeding places. Certain areas do frequently produce abundant fish food, but the fish have to locate those areas at the moments when the supply is greatest.

Even for a seasoned flyfisherman, it is sometimes very hard to tell where the fish are. But just as in running waters, there are special places where, for various reasons, fish can be found: for example, at stony banks and underwater beds, vegetated shores, lee edges, deep edges, coves, islets, channels, promontories, inlets and outlets.

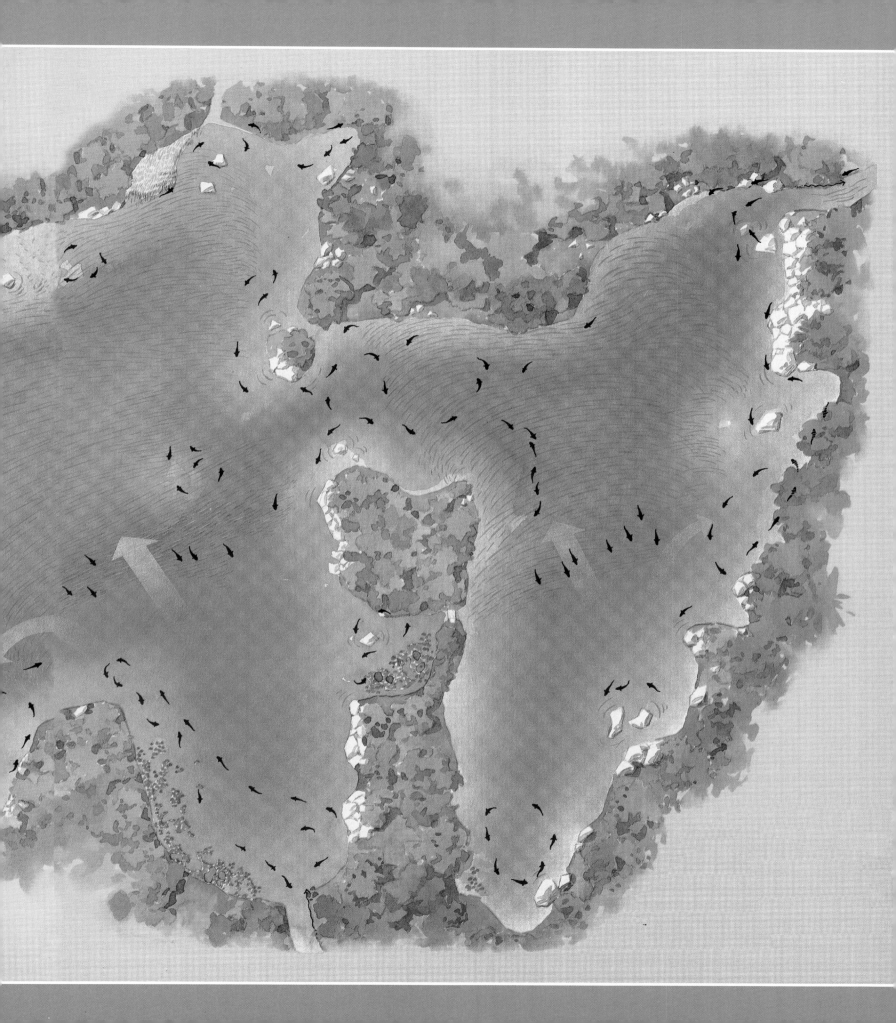

Still-water fly fishing equipment

Something like ninety percent of all the fish caught on flies in streams are taken at a distance of 8-12 m (25-40 ft). Farther away than that, it is much harder to see what the fish is doing with the fly, and more difficult to hook the fish. At over 20 m (65 ft), we seldom succeed.

When fishing in still water, it is much more important to be able to cast far, especially with nymphs and streamers. These depend on the fly being kept in motion all the time, which means that the line is straight.

There is also something that makes longer casts profitable when fishing in still waters: the mere fact that the water is still, and occasionally quite smooth. It is then difficult to get near the fish without frightening them. Currents make it easier for the flyfisherman to hide - he can sneak or wade very close, even to large shy fish, by exploiting the disturbed water's camouflage and the "dead angle" of the fish's field of vision.

Water troubled by waves and gusts of wind can also be used to advantage when fishing in still water, but the "dead angle" seldom can be. For the fish are moving and it is rarely possible to sneak up on them from behind.

Still-water fishing therefore imposes certain demands on the flyfisherman's casting ability, and consequently on the equipment. A long rod of 9.5-10 ft (around 3 m) is adequate, able to cast a light line such as a WF 5 when the wind permits, as it often does when fishing in still water. With a long rod and a light WF line, you can cast farther than 20 m (66 ft) if necessary, yet fish discreetly - which is much more important on calm lake water than in the rough waters of streams.

Another reason for choosing a long rod is that many lakes, not least in the Scandinavian mountains, are relatively shallow and call for wading. But wading at any depth makes it hard to cast with a short rod - the fly tends to hit the water during the back cast, so that the forward cast scarcely resembles what you intended.

Body waders should reach up to the armpits. Thigh waders, which reach only to the crotch, are used less often and only in calm stream waters. Otherwise you might miss many fine fishing opportunities by being unable to wade far enough out to reach underwater precipices which fish usually prefer, notably the tricky and very easily frightened Arctic char.

When fishing in lakes, a long rod and light line are preferable. With this combination, you cast long and also present the fly discreetly, as is often necessary in order to induce the fish to take. A landing net, of course, makes it easier to land the fish calmly and securely when the fight is ending

In regard to other details of equipment, besides flies for still-water fishing, you should be warned against the advice in many fishing books about the length of the backing line More than 50 m (165 ft) may be needed at times, and to lose your first four-pound trout because the backing line is too short would be infuriating, to say the least. A proper length is 100 m (330 ft), though there are times when even that can be too short.

Fishing at the right depth

Sinking lines are used more often in still waters than in currents, except for salmon and sea-trout fishing in deep, cold rivers. There are many situations, and many lakes, where the fly must be fished deep in order to make any contact with the fish. This is especially true in the early part of the season, when the water is cold and the fish seek food on the bottom. But frequently also during the season's warm periods, the fish become hard to reach, fleeing from the warm surface water to the cool bottom-layer. Then, too, a sinking line can come in handy.

However, even if the fly must descend to, say, 10 m (33 ft), it is wise to avoid fast-sinking lines. They maximize the risk of a very troublesome bottom-snag. A better method is to join a floating level-line of class 3 or 4 with a heavy "belly" of only 7-8 m (23-26 ft) made from a sinking line in the middle class range.

Such a line arrangement means that the sinking-line belly's tip will go deepest. The floating shooting line lifts the belly's other end, so that the belly cannot get snagged except, perhaps, at the tip. But nine times out of ten, only the fly gets caught and, if it does not pull loose, you can quickly tie a new one on the leader tip - which, if made properly, has broken nearest to the fly.

For deep fishing, a sinking belly in the middle class range is a good choice. It descends fast enough - that is, it stays at the same depth if you take home the line at the most suitable rate for fishing with nymphs or with small streamers. A fast-sinking belly (or the type called super-fast sinking) has to be pulled home too quickly to avoid a bottom snag, and then the fly will attract fewer fish.

But for moderate depths, say 2-3 m (6-10 ft), a sink-tip line is recommended. It has a sinking tip 3-5 m (10-16 ft) long, while the rest floats. Such a line is often a bit tricky to cast with - the heavier tip "slings" in the cast - and an alternative is a floating line with sinking leader. Nowadays there are braided leaders, from floating to very fast-sinking, and the sinking ones yield the same results as the sink-tip line's tip. They are rather expensive, but many flyfishermen prefer them anyway.

The float ring has created new opportunities for stillwater flyfishermen to cover their waters effectively. Aided by flippers, you can move silently and calmly without scaring the fish.

One does not, after all, need to change the reel or line, but simply changes the leader to fish deep.

Even a floating line with a sinking leader can get caught during the cast. This effect seems very hard to avoid, if you want a line arrangement that protects against too many difficult bottom snags. An old trick is to put a few cloven lead shot balls on the leader to the floating line. This works well, though the shot balls sometimes fly off in their own direction during the cast!

According to an ancient sportfishing rule, the fish is usually caught either at the surface or on the bottom. The same largely applies to stillwater flyfishing, where experience tells us that 95% of the fish are caught with flies on, in, or just under the water surface - and the rest are caught by fishing as close as possible to the bottom.

Certainly there are exceptions. The most important thing, of course, is to fish so that your quarry can see the fly. A fish feeding in the bottom gravel may well rise to a fly that passes 1-2 m (3-6 ft) over its head, if only it glimpses the goodie - and so may a fish swimming at a depth of 1 m (3 ft) if it discovers an attractive dry fly. But the general rule, at the surface or on the bottom, remains a good fishing tactic.

Several other tricks make it easier for the fish to find the . fly, even if you do not hit the center of the rise-ring exactly when the fish creates it. One trick, when the fly - either wet or dry - has landed, is to wait a couple of seconds and then resolutely pull in the line by 30-40 cm (12-16 in), before taking a new pause of two or three seconds. If the fish saw the fly when it fell on or into the water, and wants to take it, the strike will usually come instantly. Otherwise the fly may have fallen in the "dead angle" behind the fish. But the fish will sense the first distinct pull, and as a rule it will turn round and take the fly like lightning.

In a word, letting the fly make noise can be profitable. A good recipe is to supplement reliable wet-fly patterns with a little Muddler head, so that the fly stays hanging in the underside of the water surface. When you carefully retrieve the fly, every little tug will form a ripple around its head – and these "bow waves" seem to attract fish, or at least enable them to detect the fly more easily.

We thus return to the subject of still-water flies. The fly is the most important piece in a flyfisherman's equipment - the only item in the collection that the fish are allowed to see, if the fisherman is handling his gear in the right way.

Flies for still water

Every rule does have an exception, and there are quite a few instances in the rule book of flyfishing. Yet on the whole, two clear differences exist between still-water flies and the flies that have been proven most effective in flowing water.

On the one hand, still-water flies are all bigger by two or four hook numbers. On the other, dry flies are predominant in flowing water, but play a secondary role in still water, where wet flies hold sway and, indeed, "lures" and streamers earn a much larger share of the credit - as reckoned in number and size of fish caught.

This contrast is hardly surprising. Most dry flies imitate mayflies, whose family has far fewer species in lakes, meres and ponds than in flowing water. Caddis flies are equally plentiful in all of these, although their species, too, are definitely fewer in still waters.

However, still waters frequently offer abundant fish food of another kind: the damselfly nymphs, water boatmen and other beetles, leeches, snails and molluses, a rich assortment of land insects such as ants, sloebugs, wasps and crane flies, as well as billions of midges in various stages of life. Not to mention, of course, a lot more fish fry - the kind of food that is often essential if trout, in particular, are to grow really big.

Stoneflies are a family which tends to be strongly represented in waterways that are clean enough, and which sometimes enables us to fish with dry flies as soon as the ice melts. In Southeast European waters like the Austrian and Yugoslav chalk streams, stoneflies may dominate the insect life during much of the season, but they do not occur at all in still waters.

These differences - and there are many more - lead rather inevitably to a choice of fly patterns only some of which are usable in both still and flowing waters, and are then also tied on hooks bigger by two to four numbers if used in still waters.

Occasionally I have tried with American models to compose a "deadly dozen" flies for fishing in streams. Eight or nine of them have been dry flies in sizes from No. 10 down to 18 or 20, while a dozen for still-water fishing have included only 3-4 dry flies. The rest have been wet flies, such as some ample servings of Muddler Minnow, Wooly Bugger, and Bitch Creek Nymph. Nor have still-water dry flies been of negligible

size. The successful Swedish dry fly Streaking Caddis, which imitates a caddis fly and is tied by muddler techniques, has also been included in the dozen for stream fishing, in size No. 8 - besides a wasp No. 10 and a flying ant No. 12.

An exception here is to have a dry midge of size No. 18 or 20 for the golden chances that arise towards the end of autumn, when food is getting scarce in small lakes and the rainbow trout are feverishly hunting what is left - especially midges.

Only two flies have been common to both of these "dozens", apart from the above-mentioned Streaking Caddis. One is Hare's Ear, an imitation of big mayfly nymphs and hatchers as well as big caddis-fly pupae. The other is a Muddler Minnow which sometimes can be an effective lifesaver in either flowing or still waters. But I freely admit that it is difficult to limit the range of favorite flies to just a dozen when fishing in still water. There, the fish are so diverse in diet that I often think every lake deserves its own "deadly dozen".

So a recommendation is that all still-water flyfishermen, when touring several different kinds of waters, take along a field kit in their baggage - namely a reduced set of flytying tools that makes it possible to improvise imitations of those insects and other goodies which the fish prefer at the moment. A collection of ready-made flies that can fully cover all fishing opportunities in all lakes would scarcely be transportable!

Nonetheless, we shall now try to pare down the list of favorites for still water, while also identifying - as far as possible - the insects that they imitate, and which fishing tactic is suitable to them.

Choosing a fly can be difficult – sometimes very difficult indeed. But there are several reliable favorite flies that will tempt the fish in most types of still water.

Large mayflies

The largest mayfly species in Scandinavia's still waters is *Ephemera vulgata*, the "green drake". Its color, from dirty yellow to deep chocolate-brown, is darker than that of the "drake" in flowing waters, *Ephemera danica*. Yet many of the classic mayfly patterns are applicable to it. The kind found most effective by experienced flyfishermen in still waters is tied with burnt feather-wings, parachute hackle and a free rear body, on dry-fly hooks of sizes 10-12.

These imitations are used during early summer in north European waters. It generally takes a couple of days before the hatching starts to excite the fish - but then they often hunt the newly hatched mayflies with a frenzy, splashing almost violently as they rise. One can even see rainbow and brown trout jumping half a meter above the surface in attempts to snap up the flies, and their acrobatics frequently succeed.

During this period the fish are easy enough to catch, if you manage to place your fly on their beat. At the same time, a still-water flyfisherman has fine chances of hooking a real heavyweight - for the feast is shared by all the fish, big and small.

However, as a rule it does not last long. It may occur during several periods of varying intensity, depending on the weather. But the fish soon discover greater rewards in trying to snap up these mayflies before they hatch - particularly when they are just about to hatch, and are floating helplessly in the surface layer.

The mayfly nymph

This nymph can be imitated quite well with a large Gold Ribbed Hare's Ear, whose tail you may want to build with 4-5 fibers from a cock pheasant's tail feather. The result, though, has one drawback: unless greased, it does not float very long if at all.

Therefore, assuming that the same nymph is not to be used also as an imitation of large mayfly pupae (in that case without tail-strands, since the pupae lack such a tail), you can replace the nymph's front section with a more or less equally thick thorax of deer hair, and leave a little bunch of hair tips on each side while dressing it. These bunches imitate the wing rudiments of a hatching "green drake". But the most important thing with this tying method is to obtain an imitation hatcher which floats ungreased - and floats in the underside of the water surface, just like its real prototype.

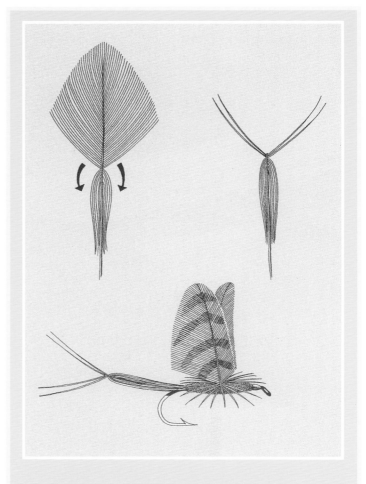

Large mayflies can be tied in numerous ways. This imitation of a "green drake" (dun), tied with parachute hackle, is quite effective – but the pattern must naturally be varied in color and size, depending on which mayflies occur locally.

GREEN DRAKE (DUN)

Hook: *dry-fly hook with downward eye No. 10-12*

Tying thread: *brown*

Tail and reversed hackle: *"wonderwing"-tied badger saddle hackle feather, with four fibers left and bent backward as tail antennae*

Front body: *medium-brown poly dubbing*

Wings: *two burnt pheasant breast feathers, 13-15 mm (0.5-0.6 in) long, tied back to back*

Hackle: *light brown cock, parachute-tied around the wing root*

Head: *black*

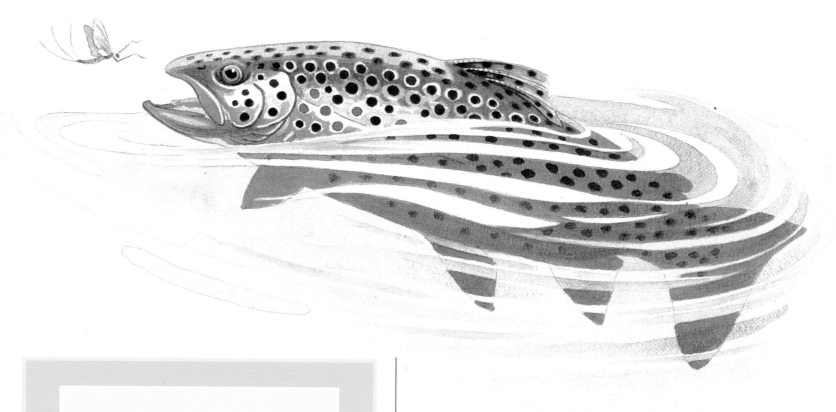

Above: The challenge may be to tempt the trout with an imitation of big mayflies.

This nymph can be fished either weighted or unweighted. If greased, it floats and provides an excellent imitation of large, hatching mayflies and caddis-fly pupae.

GOLD-RIBBED HARE'S EAR (NYMPH)

Hook: *long-shanked wet-fly hook or streamer hook No. 10-14*

Tying thread: *brown*

Tail: *a sparse bunch, 5 mm (0.2 in) long, of pheasant cock tail feather fibers - or, for small hook sizes, a little bunch of brown cock hackle fibres*

Rear body: *dubbed brown, gray, and black fur from a hare's ear, ribbed with round or oval gold tinsel*

Front body: *somewhat darker and thicker dubbing from a hare's ear, with longer hairs "pushed out" to imitate legs and wing cases*

Head: *clear varnish over the tying thread*

One seldom needs other mayfly imitations, or for that matter any special version of the "green drake" such as a spent spinner - the form which falls onto the water with outstretched wings. It does happen that the fish feed wildly on spent spinners, but even then your dun imitations can be applied with great success. A slight trick is enough to make them work wonders: jerk the line to give them a bit of life. Experience shows that the fish, however hungry for dead mayflies, will always prefer them alive if the choice exists.

STREAKING CADDIS

Hook: dry-fly hook with downward eye No. 8-12

Tying thread: black or brown, extra strong

Body: dark-beige or olive-green poly dubbing, amply tied over the rear half of the hook shank and slightly down into the hook bend

Wing and head: muddler-tied with brown or grey-brown deer's hair, clipped so that the fly's underside is flat and the winglhead shape is a pointed triangle

EUROPA 12

Hook: dry-fly hook with downward eye No. 10-16

Tying thread: yellow

Tail: a short bunch of pheasant hen tailfeather fibers

Body (2/3 of the hook shaft): dubbed fur from hare's ear, or medium-grey poly yarn

Ribbing: yellow floss silk

Wings: mallard hen breast feathers, tied in sedge fashion over the body and tail

Hackle: brown cock

Head: clear varnish over the tying thread

Large caddis flies

Imitations of caddis flies, whether the complete winged ones or the larvae and pupae, play an enormous and indeed predominant role when it comes to flyfishing in still waters. This is comparable to the significance of mayfly imitations in flowing waters, although caddis-fly imitations are responsible for much of the catch there as well.

Caddis flies are abundant in virtually all waters. There are several hundred species, ranging from very small flies that require imitations on No. 16-18 hooks to gigantic ones with a body length of 30-35 mm (1.2-1.4 in).

The best-known imitation in Europe is No. 12 in the French Europea series. Tied in various sizes on hook numbers 8-16, it imitates a wide range of caddis-fly species. For some years there has also been a Swedish pattern, now extremely popular in Scandinavia and spreading beyond Europe - the

Streaking Caddis. This is simple but ingenious: a fat banana-shaped body of poly yarn, with a muddler head which is dressed so that the deer-hair tips on the hook's upper side form the fly's wings, creating the characteristic "roof" of a caddis fly at rest.

Streaking Caddis is an unsinkable imitation, and this is important. For the fishing technique that makes it so effective is based upon adept manipulation of the line, which enables the fly to copy the slithering movement on the water surface that is typical of the big, egg-laying caddis flies and is apparently quite provocative to large rainbow and brown trout.

The most successful time for Streaking Caddis is at dusk and night - when the fisherman can no longer see the fly, but will surely hear the noise of the fish striking at it! A Streaking Caddis should then be kept moving with long, distinct pulls of 30-40 cm (1.0-1.3 ft) on the line, at intervals of 5-6

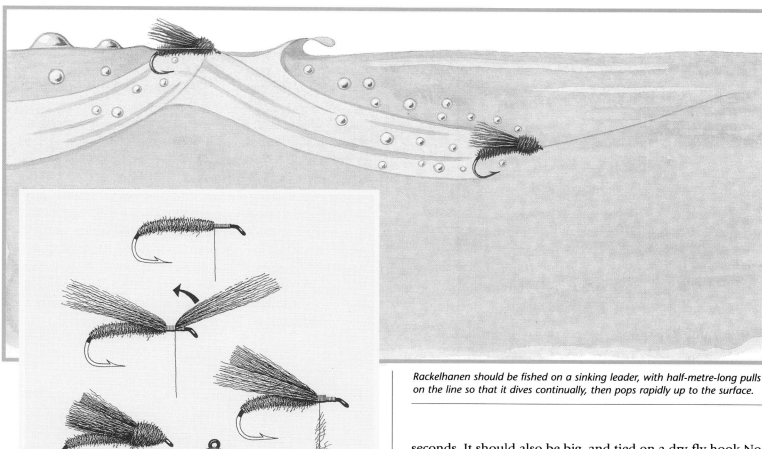

Rackelhanen should be fished on a sinking leader, with half-metre-long pulls on the line so that it dives continually, then pops rapidly up to the surface.

The original version of Rackelhanen has brown wings and body, but many variants have been created. The most popular are one with an olive-green body and beige wings, and another with black body and white wings on hook size No.16.

RACKELHANEN

Hook: *dry-fly hook with downward eye No. 10-16*

Tying thread: *brown*

Rear body: *dark-brown or cinnamon-brown thick poly dubbing, amply tied over the rear 3/4 of the hook shaft*

Wings: *dark-brown or cinnamon-brown poly dubbing, which forms a backward- and upward-pointing V over the rear body*

Head: *a ball of dark-brown or cinnamon-brown, thick poly dubbing*

seconds. It should also be big, and tied on a dry-fly hook No. 8 or 10. Yet this clever fly is equally excellent for fishing in daylight, and it has proved able to tempt even huge grayling that are otherwise unreceptive.

Medium-sized caddis flies

This group of caddis flies was once imitated almost always with Europea No. 12. But that universal fly has recently met growing competition from a new favorite, Rackelhanen. Its Swedish name refers to a hybrid of two large wild wood-hens, the black grouse and capercaillie. The fly thus named is also a kind of hybrid - it imitates both the hatching pupa and the complete winged caddis fly.

The original Rackelhanen fly was invented by the well-known Swedish flyfisherman and rod-maker Kenneth Bostrom. It was made entirely of thick dark-brown poly yarn, apart from the hook and tying thread. This material gives the fly - especially if greased - an outstanding buoyancy which is important for its fishing technique. Rackelhanen must be fished with a "wet", slowly sinking leader, and with pulls of about 15 cm (6 in) on the line, which make the fly dive and then pop up again.

Caddis-fly pupae

There are a lot of imitations of the pupae as well, and the same patterns are used in lakes as in streams. We have already mentioned one of them, Gold-Ribbed Hare's Ear, which seems to work as nicely when imitating pupae as when the fish are hunting mayfly nymphs about to hatch.

Nalle Puh from Finland, too, has a pupa version - tied in sizes from hook No. 10 to 16, with the rear body usually dirty orange or with olive-green dubbing. These imitations have rough, very shaggy bodies which, during the fishing, retain plenty of air in small glittering bubbles, thus adroitly copying the gas-filled coat of a pupa.

In the past two or three years, however, Nalle Puh has competed increasingly often with something called the Super-pupa. This is a series of six or seven patterns, in sizes from hook No. 8 to 16. They have traditional shaggy bodies of rough poly dubbing or natural underfur. The trick is their body hackle, which winds over both the rear and front of the body, and is clipped over and under the hook shaft.

The Superpupa becomes a floating pupa imitation if it is greased - otherwise it sinks slowly. Like other pupa imitations, it can be tied in a great number of color combinations. The best fishing results have been obtained with three versions: No. 16 with dark gray body and dark-blue dun body hackle, nicely imitating small caddis-fly pupae as well as all sorts of other nymphs that are eaten especially by Arctic char; No. 14 with olive rear body and a very darkbrown thorax; and No. 8 with cream-colored rear body, dark-brown thorax and light-brown body hackle. The last of these is fished primarily as a dry fly, either motionless or with short, cautious line jerks. It seldom arouses the fish in streams, but in still waters it has been a terrible killer.

Not only did the Superpupa become a new favorite - it also ushered in a whole new kind of flyfishing. That is, it turned out to be the best fly known until now for catching whitefish, usually a nerve-wracking ordeal. In many waters, whitefish are specialized to eat the drifting insects, largely caddis-fly pupae, which hover some centimeters beneath the surface. An ungreased Superpupa is cast upstream of the whitefish by 3-4 m (10-13 ft) in a stream, while in lakes it is placed 5-6 m (16-20 ft) in front of foraging schools of whitefish so that it can sink to the right depth before they see it. Moreover, it is enjoyed not only by whitefish; you will often get a "bonus" catch of sizeable trout and Arctic char.

All of this pupa fishing has been done with imitations which are presented in, or just under, the water surface. But caddis-fly pupae begin their journey to the surface from the bottom, and throughout the trip they are attacked by greedy fish. Commonly only a few percent of the pupae escape being taken and manage to hatch on the surface in order to reach their fourth and final stage. Yet these few are enough to ensure the insect family's survival.

Imitating a caddis fly that climbs out of the bottom gravel to start its adventurous voyage, though, is hardly easy. Indeed, it may appear hopeless to make a deep-sinking imitation work naturally. This has been done, but mainly in flowing water and by using Frank Sawyer's awfully ingenious Killer Bug. In lakes we should stick to the surface layer, where the fish also certainly come, sooner or later, in their quest for rapidly rising pupae.

Even when fishing in still water, one should act cautiously and try to keep a low profile.

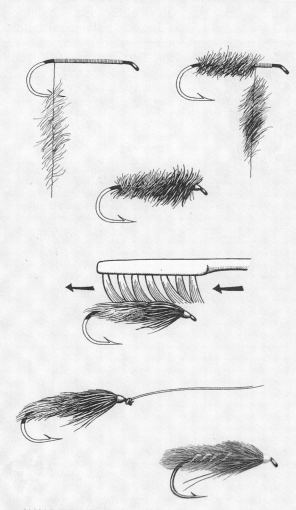

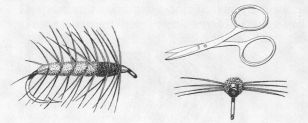

The Superpupa is a terrific pupa imitation which, besides the original (below), also comes in variants: one with an olive-green rear body on hook No. 12-14 and, for Arctic char, one with a dark-grey rear body on hook No. 16.

SUPERPUPA

Hook: *dry-fly hook with downward eye No. 8-16*

Tying thread: *same color as the rear body*

Rear body: *cream-coloured, light or dark olive, or darkgrey poly dubbing, amply tied over 2/3 of the hook shank*

Front body: *dark-brown or black poly dubbing*

Body hackle: *cock hackle over both the front and rear body, light brown (if the rear body is cream-colored) or blue dun, or (if the rear body is dark grey) dark blue dun. The hackle is clipped down over and under the hook shank.*

Head: *clear varnish over the tying thread*

NALLE PUH (PUPA)

Hook: *wet-fly hook No. 10-16*

Tying thread: *beige, brorwn or olive green (according to the rear body color)*

Rear body: *beige, dark orange or olive green, synthetic dubbing of rough, glittering materials. The rear body is tied amply, then "combed " so that it can retain tiny air bubbles (the above illustration shows, too, a variant with a silver-ribbed rear body).*

Front body: *thick, ample dubbing from hare's ear with pushed-out hairs*

Head: *clear varnish over the tying thread*

KILLER BUG

Hook: *wet-fly hook No. 8-14 Tying thread and weighting thin red copper wire*

Body: *three layers of copper wire, under an ample body of red, brown, and grey wool yarn (Chadwick No. 477)*

Head: *three or four turns of copper wire*

Killer Bug was invented by the well known English fly-fisherman Frank Sawyer. This fly sinks fast and can there-fore be made to imitate a caddis-fly pupa climbing from the boffom toward the surface. The copper wire is attached where the hook bend begins, then wound tight-ly forward to just behind the hook eye, and finally wound backward. When it reaches the hook bend, it is used to attach the Chadwickyarn, then wound forward again to just behind the hook eye. Lastly the yarn is wound for-ward and fastened with the copper wire.

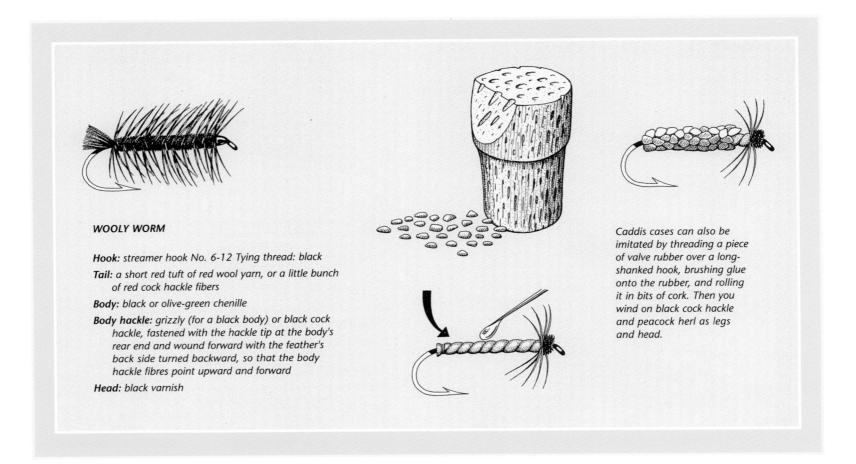

WOOLY WORM

Hook: *streamer hook No. 6-12 Tying thread: black*

Tail: *a short red tuft of red wool yarn, or a little bunch of red cock hackle fibers*

Body: *black or olive-green chenille*

Body hackle: *grizzly (for a black body) or black cock hackle, fastened with the hackle tip at the body's rear end and wound forward with the feather's back side turned backward, so that the body hackle fibres point upward and forward*

Head: *black varnish*

Caddis cases can also be imitated by threading a piece of valve rubber over a long-shanked hook, brushing glue onto the rubber, and rolling it in bits of cork. Then you wind on black cock hackle and peacock herl as legs and head.

Caddis cases

Many caddis flies are at the larval stage of case-builders, which put together a tube-shaped dwelling that covers and protects their rear bodies and part of their front bodies. When they move - slowly and clumsily, since they drag the case with them - you can see their heads and legs projecting from the case's front end.

Some birds strip caddis cases before eating them. Fish cannot do this, but swallow them whole, and this unavoidable "house consumption" explains all the rubbish - pine needles, wood bits, grains of gravel - which is often found in the otherwise empty stomachs of rainbow and brown trout.

Caddis-fly larvae are easy to imitate. The case-building larvae use whatever materials are nearest, and these are often pieces of vegetation, which enable us to imitate the worms with a weighted version of an American favorite, Wooly

Worm. This fly has the right caseworm profile, being made of chenille - the best body material and available in numerous colors (mainly dark olive and black). A weighted Wooly Worm can and should be fished deep, with matchstick-long jerks of the line.

In certain lakes and streams, however, caddis-fly larvae choose a different building material: sand and gravel, which make them harder to copy. An old French method was to thread about 2 cm (0.8 in) of bicycle-tire valve rubber over a long-shafted hook, brush the valve with glue, and roll it in gravel. It is difficult to cast, but its lumpiness can be avoided by imitating the gravel as well - namely with bits of cork, shaved off a wine cork with a rough file! The larva's head and legs on such a valve-rubber fly can be imitated with, for example, a "head" of wound peacock herl, or one or two turns of black cock hackle.

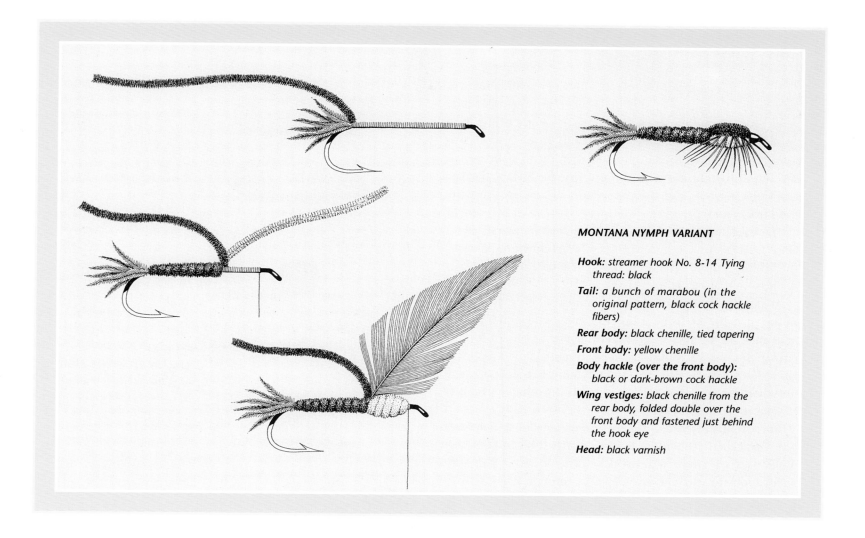

MONTANA NYMPH VARIANT

Hook: *streamer hook No. 8-14 Tying thread: black*

Tail: *a bunch of marabou (in the original pattern, black cock hackle fibers)*

Rear body: *black chenille, tied tapering*

Front body: *yellow chenille*

Body hackle (over the front body): *black or dark-brown cock hackle*

Wing vestiges: *black chenille from the rear body, folded double over the front body and fastened just behind the hook eye*

Head: *black varnish*

Damselflies

This is another interesting family of "flyfishing insects". They play little role in flowing waters, but are extremely important - almost always as nymphs - for fishing in still waters. One should, though, take along one or two good representatives of the few exceptions, meaning imitations of complete winged damselflies.

For it happens that one sees fine rainbow trout which have specialized on, and developed a fine hunting technique for, "dry" damselflies. The fact is that damselflies like to sit on leaves, for example of water-lilies. They sit along the leaf edges with their heads bent out towards open water. Since they can see well and react very fast, the trout have to surprise them, from behind if possible. The fish does so by taking aim, flipping itself over the leaf with its mouth open, and catching the damselfly on the way back into the water on the other side.

But the flyfisherman seldom gets such a chance, as the main role is played by damselfly nymphs. These abound almost everywhere in Scandinavian still waters, except in the mountains - and the fish adore them. While they are not hard to imitate, you will have much more success with patterns that are impressions rather than imitations. The best by far is a Montana Nymph Variant, on which the oarlike gills are copied by a 5-mm long tuss of marabou herl, which makes the nymph wave its tail realistically in the water. This fly is tied in two sizes, on streamer hooks Nos. 10 and 12, both weighted and unweighted. The fly is kept moving with short, distinct jerks or twists of the fly line, because a damselfly nymph moves jerkily.

Ants

Ants, too, play an extensive role in still-water fishing, particularly in the thousands of small lakes in forest regions. Some years ago, a Scandinavian scientist made a study of the food habits of implanted rainbow, brown, and brook trout. It was found that no other food dominated their menu so heavily as did ants during the month of August. This applied to all of the lakes investigated, and the proportion of ants in the fish's food reached 80 percent.

The explanation is that flying ants swarm intensively at close intervals in late summer. They "rain" down on lakes by the billions - up to several hundred per square meter of water surface - and attract all fish to the surface.

At the beginning of an ant swarming, when the ants fall rather sparsely, the fish are easy to catch, being equally eager and unafraid, so that the competition for tit-bits of food is strong. But just a few minutes later, it can be almost impossible to hook a single fish, even though they rise madly. The real ants are then too numerous, and a fish is extremely unlikely to take an imitation ant by mistake.

But towards the end of the swarming, ants fall less densely again and the flyfisherman has his chance. Fish in lakes that are blessed with such swarmings become obsessed with ants, so for a long time - often several weeks - imitation ants remain by far the best flies to use, even on occasions when there are no ants or any other fish food on the surface.

Ant imitations are easy to tie. Two examples may be mentioned. One consists of a couple of "balls" of fine black poly dubbing, separated by a sparse black cock hackle. The wings are not important, but sometimes they are added, made of light-gray cock hackle tips and tied in a V shape between the poly balls.

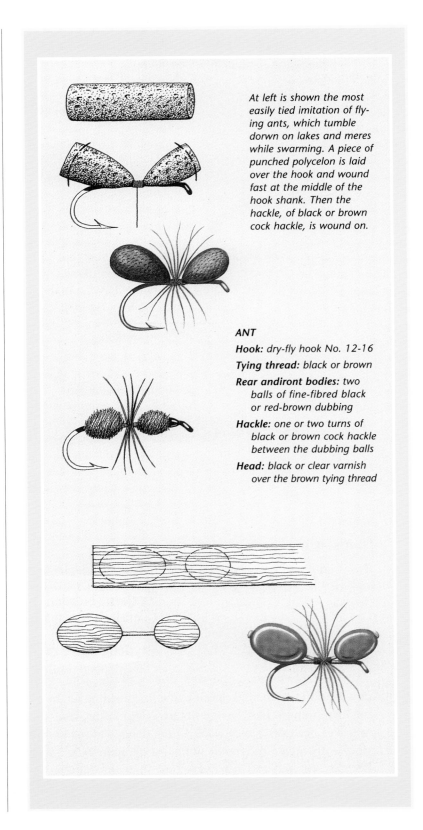

At left is shown the most easily tied imitation of flying ants, which tumble dorwn on lakes and meres while swarming. A piece of punched polycelon is laid over the hook and wound fast at the middle of the hook shank. Then the hackle, of black or brown cock hackle, is wound on.

ANT

Hook: *dry-fly hook No. 12-16*

Tying thread: *black or brown*

Rear andiront bodies: *two balls of fine-fibred black or red-brown dubbing*

Hackle: *one or two turns of black or brown cock hackle between the dubbing balls*

Head: *black or clear varnish over the brown tying thread*

McMurray Ant is another effective imitation of ants. Thefly has superb catching ability, but can be hard to tie – or rather, manufacture – and it seldom lastsfor more than one strike. It is made by sandpapering balsa balls and joining them with a stump of epoxy-glued whole nylon line. The balls are varnished and tied onto the hook shaft. Finally the hackle, of black or brown cock hackle, is wound on and fastened with the tying thread.

A flyfisherman's shadow plays on a cliff alongside a lake. During the evenings and mornings, the fish are often extremely active.

Wasps

Besides flying ants, a great many other land insects become fish food now and then: crane-flies, sloebugs, bumblebees, wasps, peppered moth larvae, grasshoppers, and all sorts of small flies, beetles and so on.

The most important of these are definitely wasps, which may tumble down in such numbers during the summer and early autumn that they make the fish rise eagerly. A wasp rain can result, for example, from a thunderstorm or a frosty night that renders the wasps almost unable to fly.

It is frequently very hard to see whether wasps are the reason why fish are rising. Wasps themselves are quite difficult to see when they have fallen onto the water. Being heavy insects, they lie deep in the surface layer and may well be noticed only if you look straight down at them. But the fish can indicate what is going on by their powerful, gurgling whirls, like the wake of a energetic paddle.

Wasps are imitated in various ways - for instance, similarly to the simple ants made of poly dubbing, but alternating the black poly with dark orange in order to copy the characteristic stripes on a wasp's rear body. Another method resembles the McMurray Ant, using varnished balsa. Or a muddler technique is applicable, ideally with reindeer hair, which is easy to colour black and dark orange.

The popularity of wasps is greatest among rainbow trout. An insect that can evoke the same response is the sloebug, although this smelly creature is by no means as plentiful, and thus not so worth trying to imitate.

Snails

The insects discussed above are basically worldwide - their species may differ from place to place, but the families they represent are found everywhere and the behaviour of fish in regard to eating them is surprisingly universal.

Top right: This wasp imitation can, of course, also be given wings, such as light-grey hackle tips that are tied on between the rear and front bodies. But ant- and wasp-eating fish will take the wingless variety just as readily.

Bottom right: Wasp imitations can also be made in the same way as McMurray Ant – with balsa balls that are sandpapered smooth and varnished in "wasp colours". The hook shank is then glued into a cutout groove. Finally the hackle, of dark-brown or black cock hackle feather, is wound on.

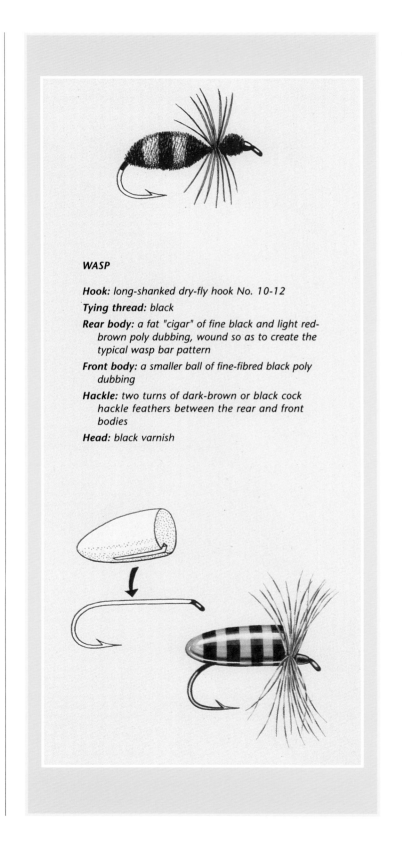

WASP

Hook: *long-shanked dry-fly hook No. 10-12*

Tying thread: *black*

Rear body: *a fat "cigar" of fine black and light red-brown poly dubbing, wound so as to create the typical wasp bar pattern*

Front body: *a smaller ball of fine-fibred black poly dubbing*

Hackle: *two turns of dark-brown or black cock hackle feathers between the rear and front bodies*

Head: *black varnish*

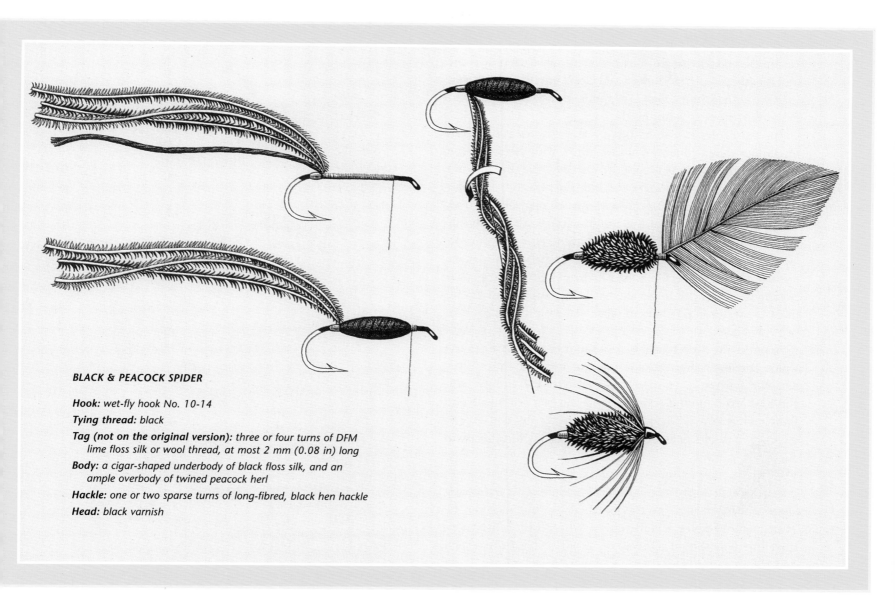

BLACK & PEACOCK SPIDER

Hook: *wet-fly hook No. 10-14*

Tying thread: *black*

Tag (not on the original version): *three or four turns of DFM lime floss silk or wool thread, at most 2 mm (0.08 in) long*

Body: *a cigar-shaped underbody of black floss silk, and an ample overbody of twined peacock herl*

Hackle: *one or two sparse turns of long-fibred, black hen hackle*

Head: *black varnish*

One kind of fish food that was described in a pioneering book, *Still-Water Flyfishing* by Tom Ivens, published thirty years ago, was the relatively unknown group of "pulmonate" (lung-bearing) snails which, during the summer, migrate in great numbers through lakes by drifting with the wind and waves.

It was soon discovered that such snails occur abundantly also outside England - in meres and ponds as well as lakes - and that they are just as appealing to fish there as in the British freshwater reservoirs. In his book, Tom Ivens recom-mends an imitation named Black & Peacock Spider, whose greatest success occurred during August and September.

Ivens' fly does not closely resemble the snail – or slug which it is supposed to imitate, but it is extraordinarily effective if fished very slowly in, or just under, the water surface. That the fish, whether rainbow or brown trout, seem to believe it really is a snail, has been well-proved by the present author. Many of the fish in such catches have turned out to be stuffed with pulmonate snails, and nothing else.

Waterboatmen

Yet another insect that fish in still waters love to gobble is the waterboatman - in Scandinavia and Great Britain alike, as well as in the United States, New Zealand, and several other countries with freshwater salmonoids.

The most common imitation of waterboatmen is British in origin. But success does not always follow with this fly on the leader. For these insects do not occur in all lakes, and only on special occasions do the fish concentrate upon eating that particular family. However, such occasions are memorable indeed, arising mainly when the waterboatmen are swarming. They normally live underwater, but have to come up at regular intervals to renew their air supply, and then they make miniature "wakes" on the surface. When swarming, they fold out the wings hidden under their shoulder-scales, and ascend from the water like Polaris missiles, heading for dry land in order to mate.

After mating, they return in thousands to resume life in the water, and may then form a "rain" of water boatmen. This recalls a hailstorm, as insects fall all over the surface with short, sharp plopping sounds - and the fish react with the same enthusiasm as when ants are swarming. But you have to be lucky to experience it.

Lures

Lures are often large and unlike any known insects. In flowing waters they offer little to the flyfisherman, but they can be exceedingly effective in still waters. When fishing the latter, therefore, you should always take along at least three such odd patterns of different sizes: a Wooly Bugger, a Bitch Creek Nymph - both of them heavily weighted - and a Muddler Minnow, which is the one that can also sometimes give good results in flowing water as well.

Wooly Bugger, which has a fine British counterpart named Dog Nobbler, is tied on a streamer hook No. 8, 10 or 12. The other two patterns call for streamer hook No. 8 and 10. Nobody knows what a Wooly Bugger or Dog Nobbler is supposed to represent, but perhaps the fish take them for leeches. Anyhow they are frequently murderous, especially when fishing for rainbow trout.

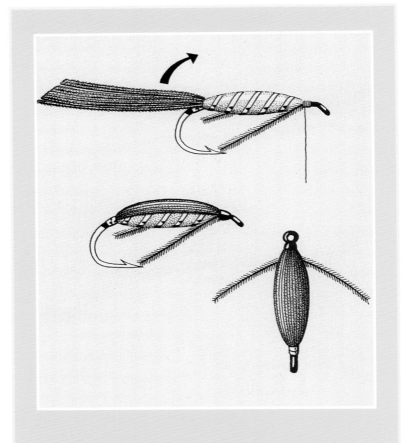

CORIXA

Hook: *wet-fly hook No. 10-14*

Tying thread: *brown*

Body: *amply tied of white floss silk, ribbed with round or oval silver tinsel*

Wing cases: *a bunch of pheasant cock tail feather fibres, tied in at the hook bend, folded forward and fastened at the head*

Legs: *thin peacock herl, one on each side of the body*

Head: *clear varnish over the tying thread*

Right: When fishing in lakes, a long rod and light line are preferable.

Flyfishing in Streams

A waterway's character and geographical location are decisive for the kind of salmonoid fish to be found there. Of course, it has always been difficult for human beings to accept that all fish - especially those in fresh waters - have a limited natural distribution. When we learned the rather simple craft of squeezing eggs from fish and raising trout or salmon fry, we immediately started spreading them into waters where they had not existed. If they were able to spawn and get enough food, they accept ed the new environment.

This is why salmonoids occur at all in the Southern Hemisphere - for instance in New Zealand, Tasmania and Australia as well as in South America, where some of the world's best trout fishing is now found. These places have never possessed natural stocks of salmonoids, which origin ally were confined to our Northern Hemisphere.

The English, in particular, have made a great and laud able effort to implant trout almost everywhere in their former colonies. Residents who had long been away from "good old England" needed at least a few trout to swing their rods at! But the introduction of trout to new waters has not been entirely a positive trend. In many places the new species have prospered enough to completely eradicate the original ones. As a result, several excellent and rare fish species have been lost to posterity. Good examples are the numerous subspecies of the cutthroat trout (*Salmo clarki*), which spread over North America by adapting themselves to the existing water system and its environment.

The massive stocking of salmon and trout from artificial hatcheries has also "diluted" the valuable gene pool of the few surviving wild fish, an inheritance which has taken millennia of adaptation to evolve and which cannot be recreated once it is gone. Often we know nothing about the gene pool of cultured fish, which are commonly degenerated and domesticated after having lived in confinement for generations. Incurable damage has been caused by the uncritical stocking of such unknown material through the years.

The rainbow trout (*Salmo gairdneri)* has thus come to inhabit most of the world, where conditions are suitable for it. But even the European brown trout (*Salmo trutta*) has crossed the seven seas and can now be found in America as well as Australia. The grayling (*Thymallus thymallus*), whose farming is a little more complicated and therefore of smaller commercial value, has not travelled so widely, and exists mainly in the places where nature originally put it.

Holding places

All of the above-mentioned salmonoids live more or less permanently in the same waterways. Some fish may occasionally make visits to a nearby lake, but they are otherwise bound to the stream where they hunt and reproduce. When we fish for them, we must therefore remember that they have a constant need of cover and of food. So we have to look for them where they can fulfill both of these requirements.

This sounds easy in theory, but is harder in practice, due to the great differences between waterways. Each has its own character, and not until we get to know it can we "read" the water and find the fish. Not only that - there are also significant differences between the fish species. Moreover, the fish seldom occur at the same places in summer as in winter. Consequently, locating them in a new and unfamiliar body of water may strike us as a daunting task.

It isn't, though: with a little common sense, as well as some knowledge of fish and their living habits, we can go a long way. To begin with, there is a vast distinction between a slow chalk stream and a rushing river. For example, the current lee is very important to the fish in a river, but not in a chalk stream. Thus it is easier to find the fish in a fast current, where the holding places are clearly visible in its lee. Such places can hardly be noticed in a chalk stream, whose fish occur virtually everywhere - and may hold in the most surprising spots - so that we have to approach the water with extreme caution.

In the Alps of Central Europe, waterways have long been divided into a trout region and a grayling region. In the former, far up in the mountains where the brooks crash down the cliffs, the red-spotted brown trout is the sole ruler of the cold, rushing melt-water. Farther down as the slopes flatten out, we enter the region dominated by grayling - even though trout can sometimes be caught there as well.

This division is not exactly applicable to other parts of the world, but it tells a little about the fish and their demands on the environment. While brown trout can certainly be discovered in the quietest waterways, grayling never occur up in the mountains.

Small flowing waters can offer real surprises and hold much bigger fish than is commonly believed.
Trout exist all over the world and are a classic catch for the flyfisherman in flowing water.

A

The same stretch of flowing water is shown here from above and in cross-section. Illustrated in the inset above are some typical holding places: **(A)** before or alongside stones and boulders, **(B)** just behind or under rich water vegetation that provides shade and protection, **(C)** under the protective hanging parts of trees, shore banks, and large roots. Other common places where fish often hold are, in particular, the necks of rapids and the deep calm water which follows a rapid or a stretch of current.

As was noted earlier, grayling often form small shoals at calm places in a waterway. By contrast, trout are definite loners and do not tolerate other fish in their territory. They also want "a roof over their heads" - being able to hold under a precipice, bank hollow, or overhanging tree. Thus, they are closely tied to shores or at least to fixed structures; yet grayling prefer to stay near the bottom in deep water. Further, whereas grayling are mainly active by day, trout tend to be nocturnal, and big ones are notably shy during the daytime, when they stay well hidden in their holding places. At night they may hunt in amazingly shallow water, where they are also easy to frighten!

An intermediate case is the rainbow trout: seldom clearly nocturnal, but not a shoal fish either. The rarer brook trout prefers a solitary life in deep water, but is normally the greediest of all trout species - a characteristic which it shares with the cutthroat trout, mentioned above, so that both of them are vulnerable to overfishing. In other words, they cannot take the same fishing pressure as does the brown trout, which is shy and soon learns to avoid the fisherman's bait.

These are, to be sure, generalizations that must be adjusted to suit the given fishing waters. But all fish have in common the fact that their holding places differ between summer and winter. In summer, when the water is warm, they gladly move to a stream whose water contains more oxygen. In winter the opposite is true, since their metabolism is slower in the cold water. Then they leave the fast streams and gather in calm places, where they can stand in the current lee to save energy.

It is impossible to specify all the types of holding places in a small waterway, so only the real "classics" will be described here. Among them is the calm water in a pool, below a rapid or a stretch of current. The fish stay in the pool's deep, quiet water and benefit from the food that is brought continually by the current. Usually the fish can be found at the deep upstream end during the hours of light. As darkness falls, the fish often retreat to feed in the shallow water at the pool's lower end, where the current is stronger.

The necks of rapids, with deep and relatively calm water just above a waterfall or rapid, are further good holding places. So is the area where water from a fall pours down into a pool, or even simply a pocket of deep water. Frequently the fish stand all the way into the spray! And large stones or cliffs in the main stream are invariably potential holding places, worth being fished carefully. The fish seldom stand behind stones - where the water tends to be too rough - but generally stay in front or along the sides. There and at the front, a current lee provides the fish with a good vantage point to watch for food brought by the current.

In calm waters, the fish are more bound to the deep channels, especially at the bends where the current has dug into the banks and often hollowed them out. Brown trout are notable lovers of such dug-out banks. Fish also like to linger near the channels that are formed by areas of vegetation. Here the current collects drifting insects and crustaceans, which thus become easy prey.

Trees that have fallen into a stream offer the fish both cover and current lee. A lot of fish may also be found in large pools with quiet backwaters. Except during the cold season, however, fish seldom hold in the backwater itself, but frequently stay just where the current enters or leaves the pool. The backwater exhibits instead, for example, pike and perch. Unlike the salmonoids, these fish do not really belong there - they merely look for places where the current is weakest.

As a whole, the fish are more shy and cautious in small waterways than in big ones. The more water runs over and around the fish, the more secure they feel. In a small stream, therefore, we must be very careful when getting close to the water and the fish. It is best to keep a low profile, moving slowly and wearing clothes that merge into the surroundings as much as possible.

Then the point of readiness has come to start fishing, which can be quite exciting in brooks and streams. Everything happens at close range, making it essential to have full control over both flies and fish. At the same time, small waterways are good schools for the inexperienced flyfisherman, who can learn many things about the fish there and can later apply the lessons to larger, more limitless waterways.

Fish are frequently difficult to see in flowing water, but they may be detectable if you approach the water very carefully.

Types of rise

One very important thing a flyfisherman should be able to do is read different "rise forms". When the fish takes an insect at or near the water surface, it leaves rings or ripples on the surface. These serve to show the fisherman what sort of insect, and in which stage, the fish takes. On this basis the fly is chosen to catch the fish with.

The rise form is the visible sign of the fish's activity, and it can have quite diverse appearances - depending on the insect species, the fish's size and the water movement. In any case, the rise itself is the essence of flyfishing: it means direct eye contact with a hunting fish. Hardly any other sight can be so stimulating, or indeed so frustrating if you fail to catch the fish, which either flees in fright or goes on rising nonchalantly.

It has to be emphasized firstly that a flyfisherman should always wear Polaroid glasses. They not only protect the eyes from a wildly moving fly, but also filter out many of the irritating reflections that prevent you from seeing into the water. Hence they are at least as important as the rod, reel, line and fly - in fact more important, as they provide the best possibility of watching the fish under the surface even if no activity appears on the surface.

If we look farthest down into the water, a glimpse of the fish's side as it turns in the current is often all we see of it. Yet this captivating "wink under water", in the words of Skues, indicates that a fish is making a quick detour in its hunt for nymphs or other prey - a fish, therefore, which can be caught.

"Tailing": the fish eats on the bottom and shows only its tail above the water surface.

Above: "Head and tail" means that the fish takes nymphs and pupae just in or under the surface layer. First you see the head, then the back fin, and finally the tail fin over the water. However, big brown trout and steelheads often display only their backs.

Below: When a fish takes, for example, nymphs just under the surface, the water over the fish moves up and forms "bulges" on the surface. In this form of rise, you very seldom see part of the fish above the surface.

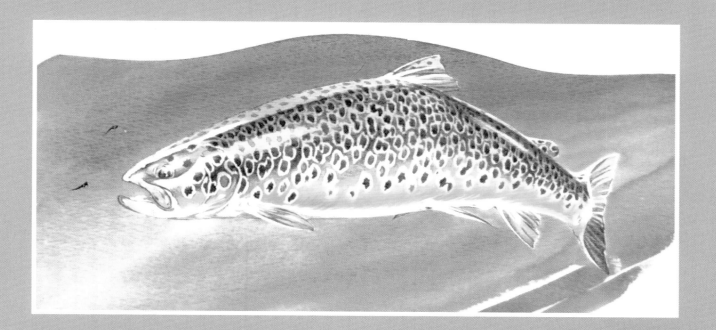

Above: When trout, and other fish in running waters, rise to take an insect that drifts on the surface, they fall back with the current. Thus you see the fish rise downstream of the holding place. To give the fish time to climb to the surface, you must therefore lay out the fly a good way upstream of the assumed holding place. Keep in mind, too, that deep fish need more time to rise than do fish near the surface.

Right: If it is impossible to figure out what the fish presently taking, trial-and-error is often necessary Experienced fishermen know that a lot of flies may have to be tried in a day before finding the "right" one for wary trout

When the water is relatively low, a phenomenon called "tailing" can be observed. In this rise form, the fish almost stands on its head in the vegetation to shake loose insects and crustaceans. It will then stick the tip of its tail out of the water, a characteristic sign. Now and then it moves downstream to pick up the creatures shaken loose, but it rapidly returns.

If the fish is hunting higher up in the water, you can frequently see it flickering in the light or lifting the water. As a result, swells are formed in the surface, leading us to speak of "bulging fish".

Commonly the fish proceeds to take the nymphs and pupae that are hanging motionless in the surface film before hatching. You see the fish "head and tail" - as first the head, then the back, and finally the tail emerge from the water, like a porpoise rolling at the surface. Here we also use the phrase "porpoise rise". When this is witnessed, you know that your leader should still be carrying a nymph, not a dry fly.

A fish takes sizeable prey such as small fish by using its jaws, but it consumes insects and other small animals by sucking them into its mouth, out of the current that flows constantly over its gills. The mouth and gill covers create a pressure drop that sucks the water in; then the mouth closes and the water is pushed back through the gill openings. Any food in the water is sieved out by the gill rakers and is swallowed.

Surface rising

When taking an insect at the surface, a fish usually sucks in some air as well. The air subsequently forms small bubbles on the surface, giving a sure sign that the fish took a winged insect at the surface - in other words, not a nymph or pupa just under it. If so, there can be no doubt that the time has come for a dry fly!

Exactly what happens on the water can be seen much more easily with a pair of binoculars. Moreover, it is always worth carefully studying what the current brings along. By combining the two sources of information, you are as wellprepared as possible, and can really pick out your fish.

We say that a fish "rises" when it takes insects on the surface. The resultant ripples, which spread downstream with the current, were once named "tell-tale rings" by an Englishman. But such rings can look very differently: they may be big or little, violent or controlled. At the violent end of the spectrum, we have fish that are in a hurry to take insects. These may be newly hatched duns, which can lift from the water at any moment and thus evade the fish. Or they may be egg-laying caddis flies that flutter over the surface, or large grasshoppers that are eager to reach dry land. All of them stimulate energetic rises, with big rings and loud splashing.

The same can happen when a fish takes small insects in a strong current, where it must act fast. It may also be a little fish that has difficulty in sucking up insects. Sometimes you then find it jumping out of the water to take the insects on the way down, so that you have to wait a bit for the counterstrike! Conversely, we often encounter very big fish which make no noise, but only leave tiny ripples on the surface, leading us to speak of "sipping" fish or a "sip rise". This latter phenomenon is typical when many small insects are hatching simultaneously on a calm surface. There is plenty of food even for a big fish, which otherwise might not be interested in small prey. It hovers just under the surface to suck in the insects at a leisurely and rather cautious pace. Such hatchings occur among

A sip rise is the commonest form of rise, producing only rings on the water surface. The rings are deceptive as their size gives no clue to the fish's weight.

the Caenis mayflies, and among the small reed knots that cover the surface at times like a carpet - or what the English call a "blanket hatch".

On very quiet stretches of current, you may meet "cruiser" fish that methodically patrol their territories to find insects on the surface. Identical behaviour is common in lakes - and there, too, it is necessary to foresee the spot at which the fish will rise the next time. Then you lay out your dry fly and wait with mounting excitement. Normally, though, a fish rises at a particular place in the waterway, giving you a natural target. Otherwise the dry fly cannot be positioned properly - that is, far enough in front of the fish, which must have time to rise to it.

A fish rises to the surface by angling its breast fins so that the current presses it upward. After taking an insect, it turns the fins downward and swims back to the bottom, assisted by a stroke of its tail. Thus, while climbing to the surface, it drops back with the current. So you see it rise a ways down stream from its holding place. And this means you should lay out your dry fly a good distance farther upstream than you per-

haps thought necessary at first, or else the fish simply won't have time to rise for it!

As a rule the fish rises from the bottom, but it may let itself come up with the current to just under the surface if there are enough insects, and if the current is not too strong. Trout do so often, whereas grayling always stay on the bottom.

In this connection you should remember that, the deeper a fish is holding, the longer time it needs to rise to the surface. Consequently the fly must be served farther upstream of the rise rings. Moreover, the fish will only rise to the insects within a narrow region, the "feeding lane", which is directly above it. Insects and flies that drift towards it out side this region are ignored. The fish does have a wide "window" and can easily see them approaching from the side, yet it will not touch them. Too much energy would be required to move sideways in a strong current, and the fish may also find it difficult to judge the distance and speed to such food. It therefore keeps its breast fins still, and takes only what passes right over its head.

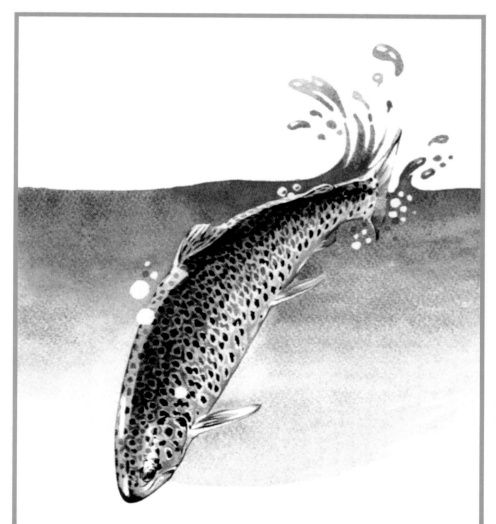

A splash rise occurs when the fish rapidly chase insects that are lifting from the surface or fluttering just above it. A spray rise may occur even when the fish hunts under the surface, if it suddenly swerves at high speed to swim in another direction.

Techniques and methods

Downstream wet-fly fishing

Naturally we begin with the most classic of flyfishing's many methods. The first true flies - long before dry ones appeared - were wet flies, and they were fished downstream. This approach involves simply laying a cast across, or obliquely down, the stream toward the opposite bank. As the current takes the line, the fly follows a curve in towards your own bank. You then take a step or two downstream and repeat the procedure. Thus you work your way down through the most promising stretches of water

Here is a perfect method for the beginner. For if the cast is not laid out well, the current immediately stretches the line and leader again. Besides, many fish get hooked of their own accord during downstream wet-fly fishing. So the method can hardly be more elementary - and still it is capable of refinements that make it amazingly effective in the right hands.

When a fly line is laid straight across the current, it will be pulled downstream in a wide curve. If the current is strong, the pull is so violent that the fly travels across the surface. This is not attractive to fish, and you must compensate for the current's effect by mending the line. The technique is to lift the line from the water and to shift it upstream, reducing pressure on the current. You may have to do so several times as the fly swings through the current.

Until now, we have been describing the classic "wet-fly swing", which is as effective for trout and grayling as it is for salmon and for sea trout. The only difference is that, in streams, we try to imitate the fish's food with our flies. Depending on the current speed, the line can be mended either upstream - if a fast current threatens to tear the fly out of the water - or else downstream. The latter applies if the fly happens to drift into calm water, where it will stop and sink rather lifelessly. This is avoided by mending the line downstream so that the current can take the line and fly again. You are then helping the current instead of fighting it.

Thus, when fishing in streams, mending the line is as important as making fine, exact casts. If you can't mend the line, you can't fish effectively either!

Fishing wet flies downstream is the oldest and commonest method. The line is cast across the current, or obliquely downstream, and the fly follows the flow freely until it drifts into a soft bend at your own bank Often the fish takes just as the outward fishing is ending. Also illustrated here is the fly's drift when mending.

BUTCHER

Tying thread: *black*
Tail: *red feather fibres*
Body: *flat silver tinsel*
Ribbing: *oval silver tinsel*
Wings: *blue mallard wing feather*
Hackle: *black hen feather fibres*
Head: *black*

TEAL & RED

Tying thread: *black*
Tail: *golden pheasant tippets*
Body: *bright red wool*
Ribbing: *thin oval silver tinsel*
Wings: *teal flank feather*
Hackle: *brown hen feather fibres*
Head: *black*

MARCH BROWN

Tying thread: *black*
Tail: *brown-speckled partridge
feather fibres*
Body: *grey dubbed hare's fur*
Ribbing: *gold wire*
Wings: *pheasant hen wing feathers*
Hackle: *brown-speckled partridge
feather fibres*
Head: *black*

*This hairwinged wet fly – with dubbed
wool body, hen hackle, squirrel-tail hair
wing and black head – displays no special
pattern but is a type of fly that has become increasingly common recently. The
USA in particular has a tradition of tying
soft-hackled wetflies with hair wings. Even
in many of the classic wet flies, it can help
to replace the feather wings with thin hair
wings, which last longer and make thefly
at least as attractive to the fish.*

Small flies imitate small insects, which obviously lack enough strength to fight a fast current, and will therefore drift away rather lifelessly. But big flies imitate big insects or even fish fry, which can easily travel against the current. Consequently, small flies (size 12-14) should be fished with no rod movement, whereas larger flies (size 8-10) should be given extra life with the rod tip.

Many of the classic wet flies that are fished downstream were originally imitations of drowned or drowning mayflies. Examples are March Brown and Blue Dun, which should thus be fished by "dead drift" - with no rod movement. But it is more sensible to invest in fly patterns that represent fish fry to a greater extent. These are illustrated by Alexandra, Bloody Butcher and Freeman's Fancy, all with bodies of silver or gold tinsel. A downstream wet fly can be made more functional by replacing the original feather-wing with a more mobile and durable hairwing.

This kind of fishing is often regarded with some disdain as a sort of "fishing machine", covering the waterway mechanically and without any real enjoyment. That may at times be so, but never need be. It is up to the fisherman whether the fishing is to be inspired or routine. Those with insight do not fish through the stream inch by inch, but concentrate on the spots or holding places which look most promising - or on fish that reveal themselves in various ways.

If you have noticed a fish or know a good holding place, here is a useful trick. Lay your fly a fair distance upstream of the fish or holding place, with a slack line. This gives the fly time to sink a little, before the current stretches out the line and leader. When the line tightens, the fly moves up in the water and swings out towards midstream. Often the strike comes just then, as though you were pressing a button - so effective is the trick if done right. The best flies to use are wet ones with a silver or gold body and a thin hairwing. The leader must be thin, of 0.18 mm (.007 in), so that the fly can sink and move freely in the current.

When fishing out, you should make sure that the fly always fishes at the proper speed. If it starts to drag in the surface, decrease the force on it by lowering the rod tip; and if necessary, mend the line upstream. But if the fly drifts into calm water, raise the rod tip; and if this is not enough, mend the line downstream. Eventually the fly will arrive at your own bank, or downstream of you. Then you can begin a new cast.

If the water is deep and being fished from a bank, it should be fished thoroughly before taking in the line for a new cast. This can be done by pulling the line in small jerks with your left hand. Sometimes surprising results are achieved by taking in the line a little faster. A fish may rush in to snap up the fly and disappear!

On a taut line with a wet fly downstream, many fish are hooked in the actual strike. They take the fly and travel with the current, but soon realize their error. The fly does not "taste" right and they reject it. Then the strike must be quick - though not violent. It should be a controlled tightening of the line, rather than a literal striking action.

Frequently the fish can be seen taking the fly in a swirl just under the surface, whereupon you must immediately tighten the line. At other times you can only feel, or see, a gentle tug on the line - so you have to react even faster. There is always more time to spare if you see the fish take than if you simply feel it. Keep your eyes open in order to hook the fish solidly!

Upstream wet-fly fishing

Here is another of the classic methods in flyfishing. It has a lasting association with the Scotsman Stewart and his now legendary "spider" flies. Stewart fished along streams in the Scottish highlands, where the insect life was poor but sudden floods, or spates, were frequent after rainstorms. Thus the fish were seldom large and, though always hungry, they were shy and easily frightened in these small waterways.

As a professional fisherman who lived on his catches, Stewart recognized that downstream wet-fly fishing would not do under such conditions. He began to fish with wet flies in the opposite direction, and tied them so that they were specially adapted to this kind of fishing. His spider flies are simple, with a sparse but very soft hackle, whose fibres truly come alive in the current. They were the forerunners of the now well known "soft hackles", which can be said to represent the fish's food rather than actually imitating it.

The fish didn't have time to reject the fly. It was hooked with a lightning-quick strike and landed after a nerve-wracking fight.

Upstream fishing has several clear advantages, but also demands more of the fisherman. This is perceived as soon as you try it. For the current is a real problem here, as it brings the fly right back to you - and frustratingly fast, if you have not yet learned to control the loose line.

Nonetheless, you can then approach the fish from behind, where it is least attentive. And the fly is presented in the same way as the fish is accustomed to seeing food: drifting freely with the current. Even if upstream fishing is more demanding than downstream fishing, it is a far more effective method in trained hands.

The fly is laid with short casts upstream to the presumed holding places or observed fish. As the current brings it back again, you must take in the loose line and raise the rod tip, so that you always have full control over the fly and its journey through the water. With short casts, raising the rod tip while the fly drifts is sufficient - but with longer casts, loose line must be taken in as well. A long, soft rod of 9-10 ft (2.7-3.0 m) in class 5-6 is ideal for this exciting method, since you thus obtain the best possible line control.

The strike is made when you see the fish turn with the fly. Good eyesight is therefore essential. Here you do not have, as in downstream fishing, the chance to feel the fish strike - for the line is not taut. If you don't see the strike, the fish will almost always have time to spit out the fly. But if you are quick enough, the fish gets hooked even more solidly than in downstream fishing, where you cannot avoid occasionally pulling the fly out of the fish's mouth. So this is another advantage of the present method.

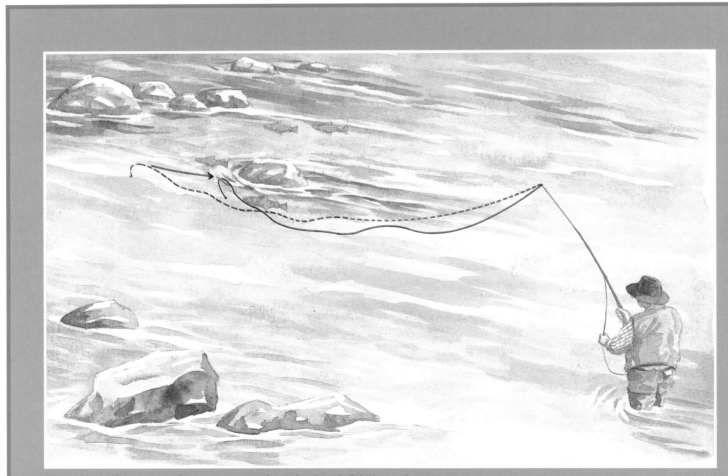

The method offishing a wet fly upstream is used mainly when thefish is very shy. It is also notably effective, since you are behind the fish and cannot frighten it as easily.

This wet fly represents a type that was first tied by James Leisenring. It is thus often called the Leisenring wet fly, and has old traditions in the USA for upstream wet-fly fishing. Its body is of natural hair fibres spun on double silk thread, and the hackle is tied of soft hen feather.

Pete Hidy's flymph is another North American fly. The body is tied like Leisenring's wet fly, but is sometimes ribbed with silk or metal wire (often brass). The hackle is of hen feather and the tail is tied with cock hackle fiber or summer duck.

Stewart's spider flies are as simple as they are ingenious. They have only a floss body and soft, sparsely tied hackle, giving them a very lively movement in the current. These famous spider flies are among the true classics of upstream wet-fly fishing, and were the origin of "soft hackle" flies.

Wet-fly "Fiery Brown".

Upstream dry-fly fishing

Although it was not Halford who "invented" the floating fly, this Englishman's name will forever be associated with the emergence of dry-fly fishing, which he systematized in order to make it an exact science. The purist members of his imitation school thought that dry-fly fishing with exact copies was the only proper form of the sport.

However, as we have already noted, this view soon developed into fanaticism. Imitations were tied of numerous insects - primarily mayflies - which occur on the southern English chalk streams, and these were imitations not only of the species, but also of both sexes and their stages of development in each species! The school went so far in many places as to ban all other kinds of fishing.

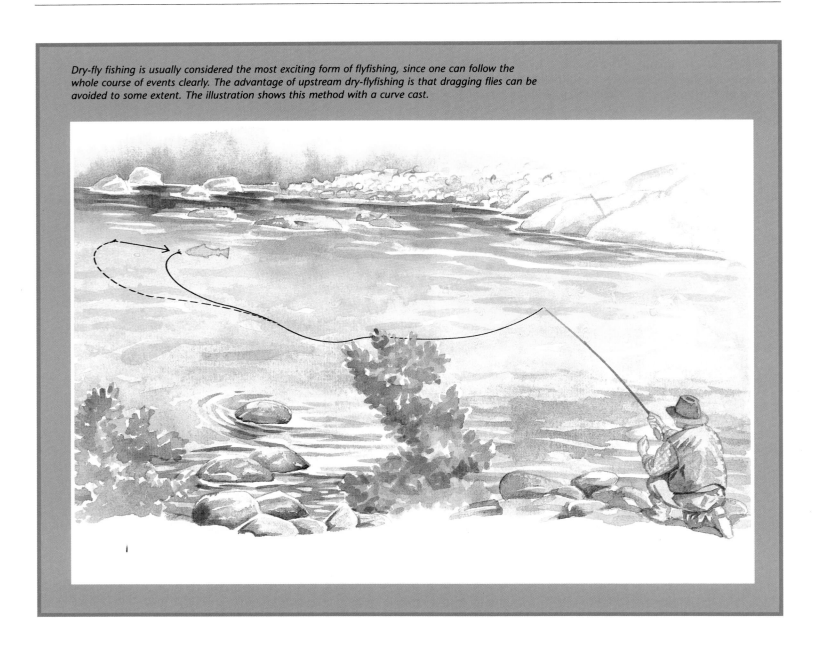

Dry-fly fishing is usually considered the most exciting form of flyfishing, since one can follow the whole course of events clearly. The advantage of upstream dry-flyfishing is that dragging flies can be avoided to some extent. The illustration shows this method with a curve cast.

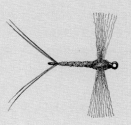

Dry flies of American type have soft wings from the flank feathers of ducks, mainly summer duck. Some well-known examples are the Cahill series, of which Light Cahill is perhaps the most renowned.

"Spent spinners" are mayflies that fall down dead on the water surface with outspread wings after laying eggs. The wings of their imitations can, of course, be tied with feather sections in the time-honoured way, but are increasingly being replaced by synthetic materials, and thus tend to be called "spent polywings". On spent spinners the tail and wing are separated into two equal parts with figure-of-eight tying.

A classic English dry fly. In this type of fly, the wings are made of quill sections. Some good instances are Black Gnat, Coachman, Greenwell's Glory and Blue Dun

Parachute-tied dry flies have the hackle tied in horizontally, wound around the wing root. Here, too, it has recently become ever more common to use synthetic materials in the wings, making "parachute-tied polywings". They can imitate a large number of species, and are thus quite handy and effective on many waters.

Some people regard dry-fly fishing as a simple, easy method. For the whole sequence of events is visible, in contrast to wet-fly fishing where, instead, you need a sort of "sixth sense" to tell you where and how to fish. Yet dry-fly fishing makes clear demands of good casting technique and line control. Whereas a few fish can often be caught by wet flies even with poor technique, dry-fly fishing is uncompromising in its own way. If you cannot present a dry fly lightly, elegantly, and at just the right spot - and if you cannot make sure that it floats freely over the fish without dragging, you won't get any fish. That's just how simple it is!

Dry-fly fishermen soon discovered the advantages of fishing upstream, and this method is still required on most of the classic English chalk streams. One locates a rising fish and sneaks up on it from behind, to within casting distance. The fly is placed far enough upstream so that the fish will have time to notice the fly and, hopefully, rise to it.

The main problem is "dragging" flies. These are dry flies that do not follow the current freely, but make furrows on the water surface. This is because the fly, leader and line do not drift with the same speed. When the fisherman stands on land or in the water, the current pressure on the line and leader will soon be transferred to the fly. It starts to drag immediately, no longer drifting freely like a natural insect, and is therefore usually rejected by the fish.

If you cast a dry fly straight upstream, this problem tends to be minimal. Then the current pressure is normally the same on the line, leader and fly, so they drift with the same speed as the loose line is taken in with your left hand.

Casting straight upstream to a fish that rises, however, will take the line and leader right over its head. This is bound to displease it and, in most cases, it will be frightened and stop rising. To avoid spoiling the opportunity, you should present the fly a little from one side. Lay it at an angle against the current, so that the line and leader do not hit the water over the fish.

As a result, though, the current will push differently on the line, leader and fly. If you leave it at that, the fly will very soon begin to drag, with greater pressure on the line than on the fly. But this can be prevented in various ways, with more or less advanced "trick" casts.

The simplest solution is to cast out a curved line instead of a straight, stretched one. Then the fly undergoes at least a short delay in floating freely downstream before the current has stretched the line, and hopefully the delay will be long enough for the fish to take the fly. Casting a curved line is fairly easy. Most simply, the rod top is shaken from side to side when the line is stretched in the forward cast but is still in the air. This is commonly known as the serpentine cast.

It is much harder to produce so-called "curve casts". We speak of left-hand and right-hand curve casts, or positive and negative ones. The basic idea, of course, is to give the fly extra time to drift freely. Yet curve casts require such fantastic casting ability of the fisherman that most of us give up. They need training and a good understanding of the dynamics of the cast. Here we shall have to pass over these specialized techniques.

Grayling is a very popular quarry for flyfishermen in some parts of the world.
In northern Scandinavia and the Alps, it can be tempted with a dry fly fished upstream.

Downstream dry-fly fishing

Fishing upstream with a dry fly can be justified on many good grounds, as we have seen - when the conditions are right for it. But by no means are they always so. Often a better method is to fish the same fly downstream, quite contrary to the classic and puritanical dry-fly school. Halford would turn in his grave if he could watch such a method being practised on his beloved chalk streams.

The English chalk streams, whose banks were the original cradle of dry-fly fishing, are relatively small and narrow waterways. They provide every reason to fish the fly upstream. Yet when fishing in larger and broader waterways, we frequently meet fish that simply cannot be reached by casting a dry fly upstream. It is then necessary to fish straight across the current, or even downstream, in order to get at the fish.

In large, broad streams, it may be hard to reach the fish if you are fishing a dry fly upstream. Then often your only chance is to fish downstream. A stop cast as illustrated here, or the similar parachute cast, is frequently essential to prevent the fly from dragging as soon it reaches the water.

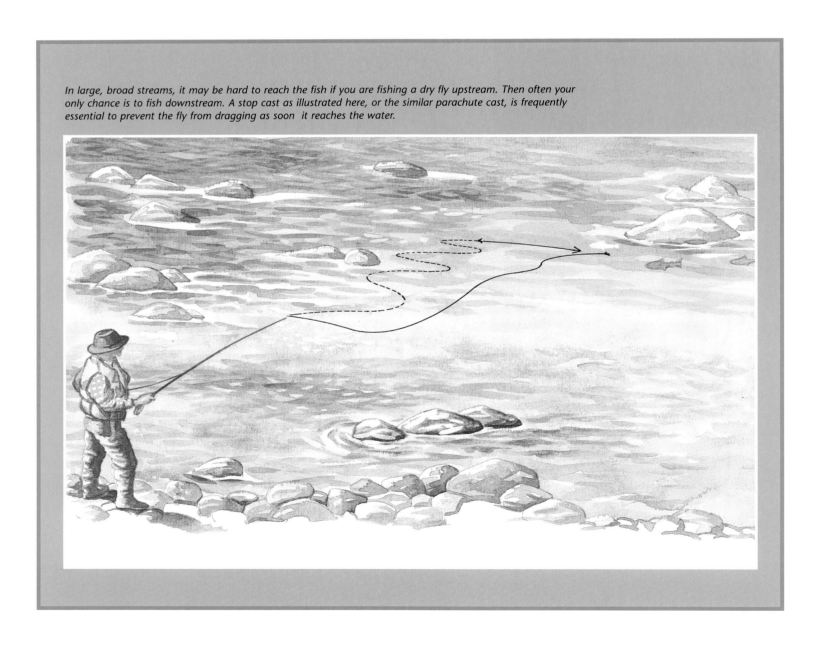

Henry's Fork Hopper is a typical American grasshopper imitation. Its body is tied with deer hair, and the wing with brown-speckled feather fibres. The deer hairs are folded backward at the head and clipped off on the fly's underside. These hollow air-filled hairs give the fly its excellent floating quality.

Here is another grasshopper imitation, loved by trout especially in the USA. This type of fly is characterized by the Muddler head, tied with deer hair and trimmed to the right shape.

Bivisible is an example of a Palmer-hackled dry fly. The hackle is wound over the whole body, from tail to head. This fly can be tied in many colour variants, but all have white hackle closest to the head.

Dry flies with bushy hackle are definitely good all-round imitations, and float very well even in fast currents. They are also easy to tie and to vary in colours. To be really effective, they are often tied with two hackles, wound in sequence.

Humpy is still another high-floating fly for downstream dry-fly fishing It has a big bushy hackle of cock feather, as well as a tail and "body cover" of deer hair. This makes the fly float nicely even in strong current.

Goddard's Caddis was originally tied as an imitation of large caddis flies, but in the USA it is also used on waters where fish eat grasshoppers. It is tied mainly with airfilled deer hairs that make it float high, enabling it to rush across the water surface like a caddisfly or terrestrial insect in a hurry to reach land.

When fishing a dry fly across the stream, you may well have to mend the line upstream at intervals. Still better, though, is to learn the "reach" cast: after the cast has ended, but while the line is still in the air, you hold the rod upstream with an outstretched arm. Thus the dry fly receives a further delay before it begins to drag. Obviously the longer your rod and arms, the longer time the fly will spend drifting freely down towards the fish.

For fishing more directly downstream, the reach cast is not very helpful. Then you should use the parachute cast, whose name tells a lot about how it is done. Quite simply, the forward cast stops too soon, making the line stretch out while high up in the air. Holding the rod tip aloft, you let the fly line fall lightly and elegantly onto the water. The leader, which weighs almost nothing, follows passively along and comes down in a heap. This enables the fly to float freely a while longer, as you calmly lower the rod top and finish with your arms outstretched as usual.

The parachute cast is as indispensable for downstream fishing as the reach cast is for cross-current fishing. In both cases, you can lengthen the fly's free drift by releasing a few metres of loose line through the rod rings. For this to work, the line absolutely must be a weight-forward line, whose thin shooting line is easy to shake out.

As noted previously, fish take only the insects which are on the water surface within a rather narrow region overhead. If the cast is too long, downstream dry-fly fishing allows you to correct it by simply pulling the fly back into place! Once the desired path of drift is attained, you decrease the pressure and release some loose line. This must be done fast, since the line is now taut all the way to the fly.

The same technique can pay off when you need to skate a dry fly across to the fish. Until now, we have tried to make the fly drift as freely and peacefully as possible, and this is certainly the only good rule in most cases. But if, for example, there are big caddis flies, or insects that flutter about on the water surface, then a dragging dry fly is often the only thing that works.

Getting an upstream dry fly to drag realistically is out of the question. Natural insects invariably fight against the current not along with it. The current threatens to push them downstream, which they actively oppose. This behaviour is best imitated by fishing downstream with a dry fly that alternately drags and drifts freely.

The technique can be guided by raising the rod top with a taut line at intervals to release more loose line. But watch out - the strikes become violent when the fly is fished in this way. Here you need a controlled strike as well as a strong leader!

Strikes are relatively complicated, in either upstream or downstream fishing with a dry fly. Indeed they vary from fish to fish, and between different fishing waters. Thus, both fast and slow strikes can be useful in dry-fly fishing. Yet this can be quite frustrating to a beginner: the fly may be torn out of the fish's mouth, or will already have been rejected by it, if the strike is respectively too fast or slow. Luckily, there is a kind of system to follow. Calm fish should be hooked with a calm strike, and quick fish with a quick strike.

For instance, a trout that is holding in a quiet pocket on the edge of a strong current may be in a hurry to take insects on the surface. It shoots up, sucks in the prey and darts back to the depths. Naturally a dry fly will be taken in the same way, but since the fish is accustomed to a fast pace, it is quick to spit out the fly -so the strike must be made instantly.

The opposite is true of a fish that holds in calm water and sucks in spent spinners and other small insects. Knowing that it has plenty of time, it rises slowly to the surface and lingers confidently, sucking in the helpless insects. A dry fly is taken with equal laziness, and a fast strike would be sure to tear the fly out of the fish's mouth. Consequently, the fisherman must control himself – if possible – and delay the strike until the fish is on the way down with the fly. This can be as difficult as it is exciting!

These two general situations are easy to deal with in practice, as we can decide in advance which type of strike should be used. However, one is often forced to make the choice during the strike itself, and that may be even harder.

In calm waters, the fish sometimes makes a side-detour. to take a good morsel which it has seen from a distance. It has to hurry, and its strike is more violent than usual. The same happens if the fish rises at the last moment for a poorly placed dry fly which drifts far to the side. We may have decided in advance that this particular fish requires a calm strike, but now we must make a new decision in a fraction of a second! Similarly, if the fish takes hatching insects that can lift from the water at any time, it may act speedily and require a quick strike.

In general, small fish are fast and big ones are slow. So the rule of thumb is that big fish should be given more time to

In downstream dry-fly fishing, you can easily imitate the insects that fight against the current, by raising and lowering the rod tip. This allows the fly to drag against the current at the surface, or to drift freely a bit downstream. The fish may then take violently when they no longer can stand the temptation.

take the fly and descend with it. This can be difficult to follow in practice - especially if you have been fishing all day for small trout and grayling, which call for quick strikes and may make you unable to change your style. If you then happen to confront the biggest fish of the day, or even of the year, it is worth taking a pause. But once the situation is clear to you, there should be less trouble in adjusting. You can always close your eyes and count to three as the fish takes the dry fly!

Finally keep in mind that, if the fish takes the fly on a long cast, the strike must be made faster than usual. The longer your line is, the longer time it needs to transfer the strike to the fish. Conversely, with a short line you can hook the fish at a more relaxed pace.

Nymph fishing

While puristic dry-fly fanaticism was at its height along the southern English chalk streams, a prominent lawyer strolled by those waters, deep in fresh thought. Professionally he was accustomed to reasons and logical proofs - an ability which he extended to his observations on the fishing waters.

G. E. M. Skues became the next pioneer of flyfishing. He realized that the trout in his chalk streams did not by any means always take the winged insects on the surface even if Halford wished that they did! Quite often, the fish instead took nymphs just under the surface.

These facts led Skues to tie the first true nymph flies. They not only sank like wet flies, but were also imitations as exact as the dry flies of that time. With them, he fished precisely as though they were dry flies; the only difference was that they were presented freely drifting under, or in, the water surface. Such "wet-fly fishing" did not appeal to Halford and his disciples. As a result, Skues had to struggle for years before his method was accepted as a worthy alternative to dry-fly fishing. As luck had it, he succeeded.

The next step towards modern flyfishing was made by Frank Sawyer, a riverkeeper on the River Avon. His job

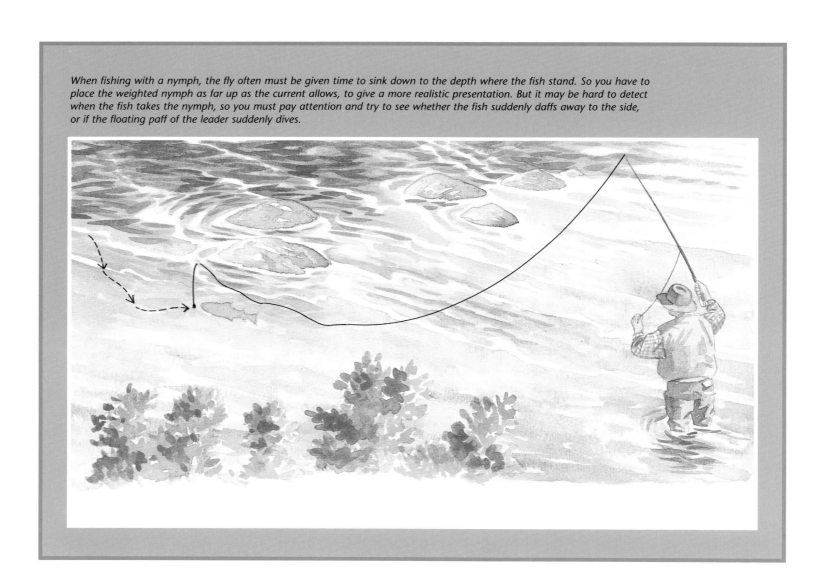

When fishing with a nymph, the fly often must be given time to sink down to the depth where the fish stand. So you have to place the weighted nymph as far up as the current allows, to give a more realistic presentation. But it may be hard to detect when the fish takes the nymph, so you must pay attention and try to see whether the fish suddenly daffs away to the side, or if the floating paff of the leader suddenly dives.

afforded much time to study fish in their natural element Thus he discovered that the trout were often active along the bottom, when no activity was occurring at the surface. Obviously the fish consumed food, so they ought to be catchable.

Just as Skues tied his nymphs as imitations of fully developed mayfly nymphs, Sawyer created the astonishingly simple Pheasant Tail Nymphs, representing smaller nymphs that were not yet fully developed like adults. He had noticed that these always held their legs to the body when swimming. For the same reason, in contrast to Skues, he omitted the hackle from his flies. Instead, he weighted them so that they would sink quickly to the bottom and, therefore, to the fish. Sawyer fished his nymphs upstream towards observed fish, without making any extra movements.

Oliver Kite, also a denizen of the Avon, developed this technique further with his "induced take". If the fish will not take a freely drifting nymph, the cast is repeated and the fly is lifted up in front of the fish's nose - like an escaping insect. And not many fish can resist that!

This is a type of nymph which imitates stonefly nymphs. It comes from the northwestern USA, where it is very popular in fishing for cutthroat trout, rainbow trout and brown trout. The body is often a combination of dubbed material and plastic strips in different colours. The wing cases are of either plastic or tied-down feather sections, the tail and antennae of stiff fibres. Usually it is weighted or tied on a heavy hook.

This Skues nymph is tied with a sneck-bend hook and shows how Skues himself tied it. The nymph has a small dubbed rear body with a conspicuous dubbed breast section, but also soft antennae and a soft hackle. It must not be weighted, as it is usually fished in the upper water or in shallow currents.

Frank Sawyer's classic Pheasant Tail is a very simple but effective fly. It imitates small, not yet developed, nymphs. The fly is weighted with copper wire to sink fast to the bottom, and is thus well suited to upstream nymph fishing, since it must be fished without any extra movements.

Here are two types of caddis-fly with dubbed bodies. These bind microscopic air bubbles to themselves, giving them a silvery appearance like the hatching insect. The imitations can also be provided with "lively" wing cases or hackle, and the body can be ribbed with wire. Such flies may be fished at all levels in the current, depending on how much they are weighted.

In almost every way, nymph fishing is a cross between dry-fly and wet-fly fishing. You can fish upstream or downstream, with a floating or a sinking line. The flies vary from the biggest to the smallest, and are fished underwater like wet flies, but are tied as pure imitations like dry flies. Such a range of variations is enough to confuse even the most zealous beginner at flyfishing.

There is, however, a certain system in the methods and their use. Pure upstream fishing can be done only when the current is not too strong. Under calm conditions, you can fish with a floating line, long leaders and weighted flies. You cast to observed fish or presumed holding places. At all events, the aim is to place the nymph so far upstream of the fish, or holding place, that the fly has time to sink to the right depth.

Once the nymph is at the fish's level, the problem is to detect a strike. This is easy enough if you can see the fish and fly clearly. If only the fish is visible, you must watch for it to make a quick turn aside, when the fly is presumed to be nearby. The white gape of the fish's mouth is a sure sign that it has taken the fly or a natural insect. Whatever happens, you must tighten the line instantly, so that the fish will not have time to spit out the fly. It may hold a very small nymph in its mouth for a long while, and then it is usually hooked well - all the way down in its throat.

If you see neither fish nor fly, you can only rely on the visible signs at the water surface. The line tip or the leader's floating - possibly greased - section may suddenly be drawn under the water. Life is definitely made easier by using a "strike indicator", consisting of a little cork ball, a piece of foam rubber, or a stub of poly yarn. This works like a float and reacts immediately if the fly is taken. Its location along the leader depends on the fishing depth.

Upstream nymph fishing with a floating line and a long leader can be done with any size of nymph. If you choose to fish downstream, you must remember that only relatively large, powerful insects are able to fight against the current. Small mayfly nymphs have no chance, so it is understandable why the flyfishermen on the classic chalk streams always fish their small nymphs of size 14-16 upstream. Anything else would involve an unrealistic presentation of the fly.

Notably active and strong swimmers are the big caddis fly pupae, which like to oppose the current. Therefore, imitations of them can be fished downstream to advantage, meaning nymphs of size 8-12. According to the current, they are fished

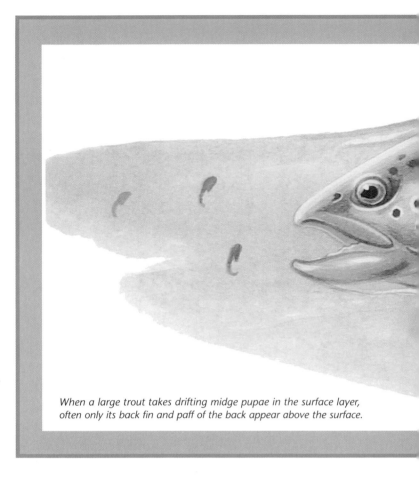

When a large trout takes drifting midge pupae in the surface layer, often only its back fin and paff of the back appear above the surface.

with a floating, sinking, or sink-tip line. Here a sink-tip is preferable to a fully sinking line, since like a floating line - it allows regular mending of the line, which in turn enables the fly to fish correctly. Just as in ordinary downstream wet-fly fishing, the fly should not normally drag.

In really strong currents, nymphs must be fished upstream, using strong equipments, a fast-sinking line, a short leader and large weighted flies. The flies are usually imitation stoneflies of size 2-8. As such fishing is a little violent, its practitioners are not very numerous. The fly is transported upstream with short casts, enabling it to sink before it passes right in front of the fisherman. While the line is sinking, the curent pulls it away, so the point is to hold as much as possible of the line out of the water as the fly sinks. This is best done by holding the rod top high with outstretched arms.

If everything else has been done right, the big nymph will have reached the correct fishing depth when it is just in front of you. Only then does it begin to fish. You must therefore let the nymph drift freely over the bottom as far as possible, by

lowering the rod top at the pace of the fly's drift. Most fish take when your line and arms are stretched downstream, since the fly then starts to climb and swing out of the stream. The strike feels violent in the hard current, but the fish is often poorly hooked. Thus a certain percentage of fish is always lost by this method, but it is still the only one that works well in strong currents.

Finally, a word about the rather unusual form of nymph fishing which occurs each summer in Alaskan rivers. It uses so-called "roe flies" that imitate, in colour and form, individual fish eggs. During the summer, thousands of Pacific salmon migrate up these rivers to spawn and die. On the journey upstream, they are accompanied by grayling, Arctic char, and rainbow trout - which intend to eat the roe left by the spawning salmon. This annual drama is a fascinating sight. Like small grey-black shadows, the roe-eaters flit. among the large salmon at the spawning grounds. When the female salmon releases some roe, they dash forward and partake of it, before the male salmon chases them away.

As the salmon are so plentiful, the roe is a very important supplement to the diets of other fish in the rivers. For the same reason, roe flies are extremely valuable to the flyfishermen who swing their rods in Alaska during these periods. The round, fluorescent flies should not be missing in any fly box!

Roe flies are fished exactly like the nymph fisherman's other imitations, by "dead drift" right over the bottom. Normally you can get by with a floating line and long leader, but in some reaches of water it can be necessary to fish with a sink-tip line. As a rule, the current is strong just over the spawning bottoms.

These flies can be weighted so that they sink quickly to the fish, but then they do not sway freely with the current. So it is better to weight the leader - by fastening lead shot to one of the blood knot's loose ends, or winding lead wire round the leader just above the lowest knot. The fly will thus come down to the bottom and, at the same time, drift freely with the current. This approach can also be used to advantage with any other nymphs.

Streamer fishing

Fishing with streamers and bucktails is both the easiest way of flyfishing, and the method that yields the biggest fish! This may sound paradoxical, but it isn't. There are two reasons: you can do nothing wrong with a big streamer or bucktail, and the fact is that big fish prefer big flies.

Streamers and bucktails represent various small fish, and are tied on long-shanked hooks. In addition, they may be pure fantasy creations. A streamer is tied with soft feather-wings, of saddle hackle or marabou, and it is intended for fishing in relatively small and calm waters. By contrast, bucktails are provided with hairwing - originally hair from a deer's tail, hence the name - and they are consequently suitable for fishing in broad, fast waters. Historically, streamers belong to the American east coast, while bucktails come from the west coast. But apart from that, they are fished in the same way.

The nice thing about small fish compared with tiny insects and crustaceans is that, to a great extent, they can oppose the current. Being strong swimmers, they commonly dare to enter more open and rapid water. As a result, the flyfisherman can fish his flies almost anywhere he likes: up or down or across the stream, either fast or slow. The fly will be equally attractive in all cases, and you need not worry about whether the fly will drag. At the same time, with big flies, we address the largest fish in the water, which of course are notorious fish-eaters. Really large fish have long ago given up eating small insects in favour of more substantial young fish. Otherwise they would never have reached the size that makes them so desirable to us!

Trout are the commonest guests of our fly rods when we fish with streamers and bucktails. Grayling prefer insects and other small creatures, although this does not prevent large grayling from occasionally taking a small streamer. When it comes to trout, one can get the feeling that not even the largest streamer is large enough.

The great majority of small fish in flowing waters are definite bottom-dwellers. This applies not least to the minnows - already mentioned - and the sculpins, which exist in many fast rivers around the world. They not only live on the bottom, but actually spend most of their time resting on it.

All this means that the flyfisherman's long-shanked flies should be fished as deep as possible, with a sink-tip or fully sinking line. Only in the smallest, shallowest waters can you get by with a floating line. On the other hand, you can fish rather daringly with these big flies: fast or slow, upstream or downstream. There are unimagined possibilities of variation, in contrast to the usual fishing with wet flies or nymphs.

It is more than a matter of using your imagination. If the fish does not take a freely drifting streamer, try instead taking home the line very quickly. Now and then you can even "awaken" a lazy trout by letting the fly splash down right on top of its head. One must admit that this is not an elegant manner of flyfishing, but it can be extraordinarily productive.

Normally we fish streamers and bucktails as imitations of the small fish that exist in the given waterway. They are tied, and fished, with maximum realism. However, the usefulness of these long-shafted flies hardly stops there. They are also effective in provoking the waterway's spawning fish to strike.

As noted in Chapter 2, trout are aggressive fish that defend individual territories in the stream. They are aggressive all year round, but this behaviour becomes ever more manifest as the spawning time approaches and they defend their territory with fury against any intruder. The flyfisherman can take advantage of this situation when the fishing season is coming to an end and the trout's spawning time arrives. Then the fish may be hard to attract with ordinary imitation flies since, having feasted all summer, they are fastidious and well-nourished. Besides, they are ever less interested in food and increasingly concerned with spawning.

It is then time to serve a big, colourful streamer or bucktail - a fly whose size and hue can, by themselves, give the fish an impression that some possible rival is encroaching on its territory.

This method of fishing can be pretty exciting. It is important to have a good knowledge of the locality, so that you know exactly where the fish are holding. You have to seek them out with streamers and bucktails of large size, and present the fly right in front of them repeatedly until they react. Often nothing happens on the first cast, so you must continue stubbornly. For the more glimpses the fish gets of the fly, the more irritated it becomes. Finally it cannot endure the temptation and tries to chase away the fly.

Right: Big fish gladly take big flies. Towards the end of the season, when trout are no longer so interested in small insect imitations and try to defend their territory more actively, a streamer or bucktail can be quite effective.

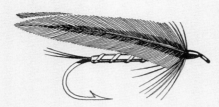

In recent years the word "streamer" has wrongly come to mean all flies tied on long-shanked hooks with long featherwings or hairwings. A traditional streamer, however, has only wings made of long hackle feathers, tied in at the head. The body is often of floss or flat tinsel, ribbed with oval tinsel.

Thunder Creek is an American type of fly meant to imitate small fish fry. Since the food of fish can vary around the world, this fly should be tied in the colours that best resemble small fish in your own water. The wings are tied in three steps: a thin bucktail wing on the hook shank, bent backward; then a dark bunch on the upper side and a light bunch on the underside, both pointing forward; finally the bunches are bent backward and fastened with tying thread.

It is typical of Matuka streamers that the wing feathers are wound along the whole body. The fibres on the undersides of two hackle feathers are removed, and the wing is placed on top of the hook shaft and fastened at the head. Then the ribbing is wound carefully forward through the wing and is attached at the head. Finally a false hackle is tied in.

Bucktails, as the name implies, were originally tied with deer-tail hair. But today they are tied with various types of hair, for example from calf tail, squirrel tail, polar bear or goat. The body is tied, just as in a streamer, off loss and/or tinsel - the wing and hackle being tied in at the head. One may also tie in a tail of coloured or plain feather fibres.

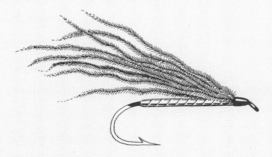

Long-shanked hooks of streamer type, with maraboufeather wings, have become ever more popular. The advantage of this amazingly soft wing material is that it gives a lifelike impression in the water, often attracting fish to take. Such wings create little air resistance, so you can swing out rather large flies even with a relatively light-actioned rod.

The rainbow trout - whose seagoing variant is the steelhead - belongs to those species that gladly take a well-served streamer or bucktail.

At first you frequently feel only a strong blow against the fly, without hooking the fish. The fly has thus only been hit, not taken in the fish's mouth. Yet there is a good chance that one of the following casts will result in a solid strike by what may be the season's largest trout. In any case, such fishing is fascinating once the quarry has been aroused.

In Alaska and British Columbia, every year sees a rather special kind of streamer fishing for large rainbow trout and Arctic char. It takes place when extensive schools of salmon smolt begin their migration downstream toward the Pacific Ocean. They are often smolt from sockeye salmon, which emerge from lakes in the water system - of which the predatory fish are well aware. So the latter gather at the outlets of lakes to feast on the young salmon. If you stumble upon such a smolt migration, you are sure to have exceptional fishing experiences for quite a while. Sparsely dressed streamers and bucktails are the only thing worth putting on your leader.

In several places farther north, trout are regularly caught with mice or lemmings in their stomachs. These small rodents provide the fish with huge chunks of concentrated protein, yielding a colossal spurt in growth. Thus, during good years for mice and lemmings, they are the sole diet of many large trout, and you need to "match the hatch" by serving a delicious deer-hair mouse that floats on the water surface. This mouse is fished dragging, and the fish takes it with a savage strike.

An important point is to fish near the banks, where the fish are accustomed to seeing mice or lemmings tumble in. Big flies are required, so you have to give the fish plenty of time to take the fly before tightening up on the line. Otherwise you will only tear the mouse out of its mouth. Whoever has tried this fishing once is sold on it for a lifetime!

If you fish a deer-hair mouse in quiet parts of a stream, it is often attacked by pike, which offer an entertaining sort of fishing. Pike are not distinctive stream fish, and avoid the fast sections of a waterway, but they can be abundant in sections with deep calm water. Here you may also find small schools of perch that gladly take a little silvery streamer.

Catch and Release

Whatever the method of fishing, stocks of fish in streams are fairly vulnerable. The quantities of food, and therefore also of fish, are strictly limited. In addition, every waterway has only enough holding places for a certain number of fish, especially when they are trout. As a result, we obviously cannot catch more than a small number of fish in small streams, and then only if the streams are in their natural condition.

Today, most waterways are far from being in as good condition as they should be. Damming, regulation and pollution have gone mad among them. In many places, this has meant that no natural reproduction exists any longer. A lot of waters contain only stocked fish. Thus a natural waterway with natural fish stocks is an extremely valuable resource that should be treated with great care.

Rational fish management, in the latter case, is not conducted by harvesting any surplus, but by protecting the fish that are there already. The best approach, of course, is to leave the fish in peace - with no sportfishing. But the next best, and most realistic, is to put back the fish that are caught. This policy is what Americans call "Catch and Release", or "No Kill".

"Catch and Release" is undoubtedly the future basis of fishing management. With a steadily rising pressure on our fishing waters, there is no alternative, unless we degenerate to plain "put and take". Sportfishermen simply cannot afford to continue harvesting the last stocks of wild fish.

"No Kill" is not a form of snobbery, as many Europeans unhappily believe. It is a rational form of fishing management that has been used professionally in the United States for the past 10-15 years, and with good results. There, most fishing is open to whoever has obtained a fishing licence in the given state. Only in a few places is fishing subject to private ownership as in Europe.

This status has made possible a coordinated, more effective fishing management in large water systems, as well as a test of "No Kill" and its effects on a suitably large scale. The American fishing authorities can, whenever they think necessary, impose new and stricter regulations for a particular fishing area. They can immediately raise the minimum size, decrease the allowed number of fish caught, put a waterway under protection - or introduce "No Kill".

The whole process has been gone through in the United States. It began with virgin waters that offered fabulous fish-

ing to the relatively few sportsmen of those times. There were plenty of fish, and big ones. Yet after World War II, the fishing pressure really began to grow, and many such waters were fished out. The authorities set out quantities of new fish, and once again there was a quarry to catch. This was straightforward "put and take" fishing. Next, however, critical voices

Catch & Release is definitely one of the most important aspects of modern fish management. A large trout regains its freedom and – if put back correctly – it can be caught anew.

These stretches soon became popular, since big fish were still to be found there, offering a real challenge to the more demanding sportfishermen. At the same time, many scientific studies showed that the natural fish stocks were growing healthily under this radical form of fishing management. "No Kill" spread subsequently to numerous other waters.

There is no point in introducing "Catch and Release" if flyfishermen do not know how to handle the fish that are caught. All too many will die after being released. But if the fish are handled properly, they will quickly regain strength - and be able to give some other fisherman a lively experience later on. As Lee Wulff once expressed it: "A trout is too valuable to be caught only once!"

The following rules should therefore be followed when releasing fish:

– Use barbless hooks, which make the releasing much easier. They hook the fish better than ordinary hooks do, and are still a lot easier to remove. Press down the barb, file it off, or use true barbless hooks. If a barbed hook sits deep, clip off the leader near the hook and leave it there; the fish will then get rid of it.

– Fight the fish as quickly as possible. This prevents the formation of too much lactic acid in the fish. Never use a leader which is thinner than necessary for this. Super-thin leaders are not "sporting": rather the opposite.

– Let the fish stay in the water as long as possible when the hook is to be removed. Never touch the fish with dry hands, which can injure its protective layer of mucus. Use a landing net of knotless cotton, which is most gentle for the fish. If the fish is to be photographed, hold it with one hand by the tail and the other hand under its front body. Be careful not to squeeze the fish, and never touch its gills!

– Revive the fish before releasing it. Hold its head upstream in flowing water, or move it back and forth in still water, so that fresh water passes over its gills. Not until the gills pump regularly again, and the fish can keep its own balance, is it ready for releasing. The fish should be able to swim out of your hands by itself.

spoke up. People did not want to have fish regardless of the price. They wanted quality fish - born in the wild and raised in natural waters, not in fish farms. It took a long time before the authorities reacted, initially with stronger restrictions on fishing, and later by introducing the first clear "No Kill" stretches on special waterways.

Fishing for salmon and sea trout

I would compare salmon and sea trout to a half-sleeping cat which lies down in the sunshine and pays little attention to its surroundings. Of course, unlike the salmon, a cat will feed when it is hungry, but at times it is provoked to attach something that it has no intention of eating- such as a leaf blowing in the wind. Some reflex action is triggered by the sight of a moving object and induces the cat to chase it. This may have less to do with the object's colour than with its movement, and possibly its resemblance to a small prey.

However, many wild cats survive by being able to run fast, and must be continually on the alert - even practising when they are not feeding. Fish, particularly salmonoids, rely on their speed of interception to get a meal. Possibly on occasions they take a fly when their reflexes have been triggered to attack something that they neither want nor need as food.

Thus, before fishing for salmonoids, it may be very important to learn not only how to cast well, but also how to think and act like a hunter, and to study animals in order to acquire a sense of their behavioural rhythms. One can even make notes of the feeding times of birds, fish and animals such as cattle and sheep. With trout and other fish which feed in fresh water, it is worth observing their feeding times and diet. We cannot directly do so with salmon and sea trout, but we must be aware of the rhythms of wildlife - as well as getting to know the water that we are fishing in.

The future of salmonoid fishing

Another general point to remember is that the future of the wild Atlantic salmon species is severely threatened today. Our fishing should therefore be conducted responsibly, which may mean a limit on catches and the methods of catching. The late British king George V summed it all up by saying: "The wildlife of today is not ours to dispose of as we please. We have it in trust and must account for it to those who come after us."

There is still a great magic in seeking salmon with a fly, and the thrill of the take never pales. Yet unless conservation measures are applied, we may have already lived through the golden years of salmon fishing. Surely mankind will not be so foolish as to let this sport slide into obscurity through wanton neglect!

Throughout most of Europe, the two main species of anadromous fish, Salmo salar and Salmo trutta, are better known by their common names: salmon and sea trout. But the prefix "Atlantic" must be added for salmon, while the European sea trout is perhaps better identified as a sea-run brown trout. This enables us to distinguish them from the five species of Pacific salmon, belonging to the genus Oncorhynchus, and from the sea-run rainbow trout known as the steelhead.

The majority of flyfishermen consider the Atlantic salmon to be the leading sportfish. With experience of many species of salmon and sea trout, however, I am not sure that this accolade is well-deserved. The fresh-run sockeye and coho salmon in Pacific rivers are hard fighters, as is the steelhead. And where else in the world would you find salmon that grow to the size of the chinook or king salmon, nearly 100 pounds (45 kg)?

The techniques of angling for salmon originated largely in Europe. Much of the folklore that has grown up around salmon was created by the British. Not only were they in the vanguard as sportfishermen for salmon, but their influence and expertise contributed a great deal to developing the Scandinavian resources.

Above: *Good casting technique, and long experience on the same river under varying conditions, are typical attributes of a successful salmon fisherman.*

Left: *Atlantic salmon – the ultimate challenge for many flyfishermen.*

Equipment

There are still numerous countries in which many forms of angling are permitted. Nonetheless, many of us feel that flyfishing not only offers a greater challenge, but also represents a better sporting method of catching these lovely fish. It is now several years, for instance, since I have fished for salmon with any other lure than a fly. On many rivers the methods of flyfishing can be very effective, although on a few rivers they are less productive than certain forms of bait-fishing.

It is, then, angling with a fly that will occupy us here. This is a superb way of enjoying sport with worthy fish and once you have mastered some of the basic techniques, it is much easier than might be supposed by beginners.

Much of the tackle used in flyfishing for salmon and sea trout was invented in England. About 150 years ago, backbreaking rods of up to 20 ft (6 m) were fashionable. Leaders were of plaited horsehair and twisted silkworm gut. The most dramatic changes in tackle have taken place since World War II. Today carbon-fibre (graphite) has ousted glass, split cane, greenheart and hickory as rod-building material, while reels have become far lighter and more effective.

Silk lines and twisted flax are virtually things of the past. Modern synthetics give us every required combination in floating and sinking lines. The Association of Fishing Tackle Manufacturers (AFTM) has standardized much of this tackle, so that specific line sizes and weights can be made compatible with rods. Perhaps the greatest benefit that synthetic fibres have brought is in the field of transparent monofilament. Based on nylon, it has eliminated the need for gut or horsehair casts, and some remarkably high breaking strains are produced with minimal diametres.

Traditionally the fly rod was, and still is, double-handed. It may be anything from 12 ft (3.7 m) for fishing a river of modest size, to 17 ft (5.2 m) for a broad river. Much of the flyfishing in Britain and Scandinavia is done with double-handed rods. But North American anglers, who often fish from canoes, have shown a marked preference for the single-handed rod. At least one noted American angler, Lee Wulff, takes great delight in extracting massive salmon on a toothpick-like fly rod of only 6 ft (1.8 m) weighing less than 3 oz (85 g).

Patience, watchfulness and powers of concentration - these are qualities a salmon fisherman needs.

The choice of tackle

In making your initial choice of tackle, however, it is important to decide where you will do most of your fishing, and at what time of year. A lot depends on your location and the size of the river. A Norwegian river in June, for instance, may be nearly at flood level from melting snow - whereas a river of similar size in Scotland or England may already be thinning down to summer level, long after the main snows have melted.

The best choice for spring fishing on Scotland's famous river Spey, and in large Norwegian rivers during summer, is a 15-ft (4.6-m) double-handed carbon-fibre rod. With this I would carry at least two reels: one with a slow-sinking shooting-head line of size 11, and the other with doubletaper fully floating line of similar size. The DT line is almost essential in order to do a proper Spey cast, while the sinking shooting-head line may be cast overhead for long distances. I would also carry a range of flies varying from 2.5-in (63 mm) tubes to size 6 or 8 doubles or trebles, without much concern for pattern.

One can also bring a net, gaff or other implement to extract fish from the river. Many prefer to wade the river with as little encumbrance as possible. For early spring or late autumn in Scotland, and during the summer in Scandinavian rivers, good tackle includes the following items:

- A stout pair of felt-soled breast waders, preferably in neoprene.
- The 15 ft (4.6 m) double-handed fly rod.
- Drum fly reels of 3.75 x 4 in (95 x 102 mm) with adjustable drag.
- A 30 ft (9.1 m) shooting-taper slow-sinking line of size 11, and another of fast-sinking type, attached to oval monofil backing.
- A 30 yd (27 m) double-taper floating line of size 11, spliced to at least 150 yds (137 m) of 25 lb test backing.
- A big box of flies, as outlined here.
- Spools of nylon monofil, between 10 lb and 25 lb test.
- A pair of scissors.

Additional accessories could be a wading stick, net gaff, and so forth. Indeed, if you do not know your river intimately, it makes good sense to have a wading stick. This should have a weighted bottom, so that it is always at hand and does not float on the surface. If floating, it can make trouble and foul up some of the line which you intend to shoot.

As an alternative and back-up outfit, for such fishing in early spring or autumn, I recommend a single-handed rod of about 10 ft (3 m) with a smaller fly reel, and a forward-taper line of size 7 with an 8 lb test leader. This is a much-loved outfit for late spring and summer fishing on the small or shrunken streams of Britain. Moreover, it is fantastic fun to play a salmon on a light, single-handed rod. And there can be little doubt of the tactical value of such an outfit when the rivers have shrunk to their bare bones, with fish that are shy of all but the most slender leader.

When fishing in deep and rapid waters, you should use a short leader, since the pressure of the current lifts up the leader and fly to the surface.

An important aspect of tackle selection and use is your mastery of the best knotting techniques. All knots cause a loss of strength in your leader, and bad knots can be so inefficient that they may reduce the strength by more than half. It is a good idea to learn knots so thoroughly that you can almost tie them blindfolded.

One of the worst knots that may accidentally be induced into your leader is politely known as a "wind knot". Sometimes it may occur in very windy conditions, when the leader gets tangled and a single overhand knot is produced. This makes the leader extremely fragile to sudden loads, and might well break it when a fish is being played. Such knots can be termed "bad casting knots", since they can usually be avoided. All you need to do is open up the loop of the line a little, and lower the rod tip immediately after the power stroke in the forward cast.

Selecting flies

Most discussion of the effectiveness of salmon and sea trout flies is speculative. Since the fish do not feed after returning to fresh water, they may have no interest in whatever we offer them, and no strict logic will tell us what size or pattern of fly will be the best in any given circumstances.

However, salmon can indeed occasionally be caught on a wide variety of fly patterns. Ancient lore suggests that we use big flies in extensive, deep and cold waters - and small flies in limited, shrunken rivers when the water is warmer and the fish are confined to shallower areas. In practice, there is a whole range of techniques which defy the basic rules, although we should never be dogmatic about them.

It is wise to arm yourself with a wide variety of fly patterns, in varying weights and lengths. Sometimes the weight of the fly is more important than its overall size. At other times you may want as small a fly as you can find Generally, there is a lot to gain by having as large a selection as can be carried comfortably.

For fishing in early spring on many of Britain's classic rivers, I use a heavy sinking line and a tube fly, mounted on brass tubing to enable it to sink well down in the water. If the river is full with melting snow or recent rain, it may contain some suspended matter and thus lack the crystal clear quality of a river at normal height. In addition, the water temperature may be a little above freezing, and this could be an occasion for the large fly if fished as slowly and deeply as possible.

Alternatively, the same river in late May or June might need little more than a light floating line, and a singlehooked fly of size 10 or 12 which is lightly dressed and has little weight or drag effect. Still, there are no fixed rules, and I have frequently seen a complete reversal of tactics bring about an unexpected success.

In making your choice of fly pattern and size, it pays off to keep in mind the laws of nature. Nothing in the wild which is preyed upon by other species has a garish appearance. The prey usually has some form of natural camouflage and does not look out of place in its environment. This fact should dictate the choice of fly in very clear water. Do not select a fly which is conspicuous, and it is a good idea to make your flies ever more subdued in colour as they get smaller. In high turbid water, however, you may well need to confront the fish with a more garish lure - and perhaps even intimidate the fish, presenting the lure where it will threaten the fish on an eye-to-eye collision course.

THUNDER & LIGHTNING

Tag: oval gold tinsel
Tip: yellow floss
Tail: golden pheasant crest feather
and Indian Crow
Butt: black ostrich herl
Body: black floss
Ribbing: oval gold tinsel
Body hackle: orange cock hackle
Front hackle: blue guinea hen or blue jay
Wing: brown feather sections from
brown mallard
Topping: golden pheasant crest feather
Sides: jungle cock
Head: black

This is how a classic salmon fly is tied Thunder & Lightning
is a good example of dark flies, which work best by evening
and night or in bad weather (hence the name?) and when
the water is murky.

At right is shown a Silver Doctor. This lightfly is most suitable in fine weather and when the river water is clean and
clear. It belongs to the Doctor series and is also a good
instance of a Mixed Wings fly.

The colour of flies

On the above basis, I find it helpful to use a colour of fly which matches the overall colour of the riverbed. Some rivers are generally brown, like weak coffee without milk, and these call for a dark-brown or black fly. The Spey responds well to this type, and patterns such as the Monro Killer, Thunder & Lightning, and Stoat's Tail are all effective. Other rivers, for example those flowing off bare rock or limestone, are often crystal-clear at times of normal flow, absorbing much ultraviolet light. They may have a blue or green tinge, making flies of the same hue more suitable.

During early spring and late autumn, though, your river will probably be higher than normal, and unusually turbid due to rainwater. I would then recommend slightly brighter or garish flies in yellow or orange for very cold days, and less conspicuous flies for warmer days. Good examples of flies for high, cold water are Yellow Dog, Tadpole, Willie Gunn and Collie Dog.

Nonetheless, the final act of deluding a fish into taking your lure is often unrelated to your choice of fly pattern. It may have something to do with the size of the fly, but usually the decisive factor is how you present the fly. Unfortunately, a fisherman who accepts the advice that he is fishing with the wrong fly might become furious at the suggestion that his casting and presentation are poor. In spite of that, the tactical and technical requirements are most likely to cause failure. And if there is a prerequisite in salmon and sea trout fishing, it is knowledge of the best techniques needed for any given situation.

When choosing a fly, you should naturally take into account its size, colour and dressing, but the presentation is often what determines whether the salmon will take.

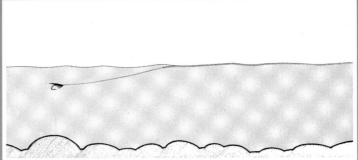

In warm low water, the current is frequently slow. The fish are then eager to rise and take the fly, which can be fished just under the surface with a floating line.

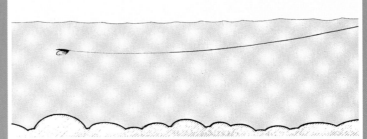

The river level is still low, but the current is faster. Now a sinking line is needed so that the fly will not drag on the surface.

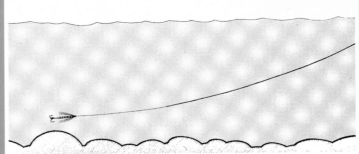

In high cold water, a rapid current is common. The combination of a fast-sinking line with large tube flies is then necessary to get down to the bottom, where the fish lie.

The water's temperature, level and current speed are factors that influence the fish's choice of holding places. A floating line and small flies are useful mainly during the warm months, when the water is low and the current therefore slow. But in the early season, with high and cold water, the current is strong and the fish take the fly at a greater depth. You must then often fish with a fast-sinking line and large flies.

Casting and presentation

Experience shows that this kind of fishing depends mainly on the ability to cast a long line and on intimate acquaintance with the water being fished. The one-week-per-year salmon angler is severely restricted, and his difficulty is compounded if - like so many of us - he likes to try a different river each year. At no time will he ever fish a single stretch of water and get to know it under all its conditions. Yet he will never be able to fish it to full potential until he has tried for several years on the same stretch.

It is not intended here to teach the complexities of casting. A videotape may be more helpful than a book, but the best way to learn is from a professional instructor - not an enthusiastic amateur, however talented - and to spend as long as is needed to master the techniques under his supervision. Anglers often spend surprising sums of money in fishing rents, travel costs and hotel bills, only to prove themselves incompetent at casting when they arrive at the water.

For double-handed fishing, you must be able to cast at least 25-30 metres (80-100 ft). Such distances may not be achieved immediately, but it should not take long to accomplish them comfortably in the overhead mode. It is then very important to master both the single and double Spey casts. These will enable you to fish areas of water that are obstructed by overhanging trees or high banks, and where the overhead cast is impossible.

Letting the rod work

The novice should learn that it is the rod which must do the work - and that style, not brute strength, will make the cast look good and be effective. Ladies and small men often seem to be better stylists, while large and powerful men apparently work hard but do not achieve the right distance or style. But if you have both style and strength, you may well be on the way to becoming an exceptional salmon fisherman!

If you have no experience at all, it will pay to begin with a double-handed rod and a floating line. This gear is more quickly mastered than the single-handed rod or a sinking line, although the techniques are basically the same. The rod must act as a spring when casting, and as a lever when playing the fish. Thus, to get the best from your rod, you must use its springiness - and this is where many problems occur.

Some fishermen simply wave the rod about, using more

Above & opposite: *An experienced salmon fisherman knows that he must let the rod do the work, if he is to fish for a whole day with a long double-handed rod. Every cast has to be as energy-saving as possible.*

muscle than they need. It is the flex of the rod that propels the fly line. No matter how much energy you expend, if you merely wave the rod and do not load it as a spring, you cannot cast far or with great style. Good casting is not an art, but a craft that any able-bodied person can soon learn.

The next difficulty, getting access to good water, has already been mentioned. Direct access to the best waters is not easy, even if you can afford the rent. But it is wise to get the best you can, and to remain a regular tenant over the years until you know the best times of year and the best places for fishing. Such knowledge is not easily won, either - and that is why many of the classic salmon waters have gillies, or guides, to assist the visitor and ensure that he fishes only the most productive areas.

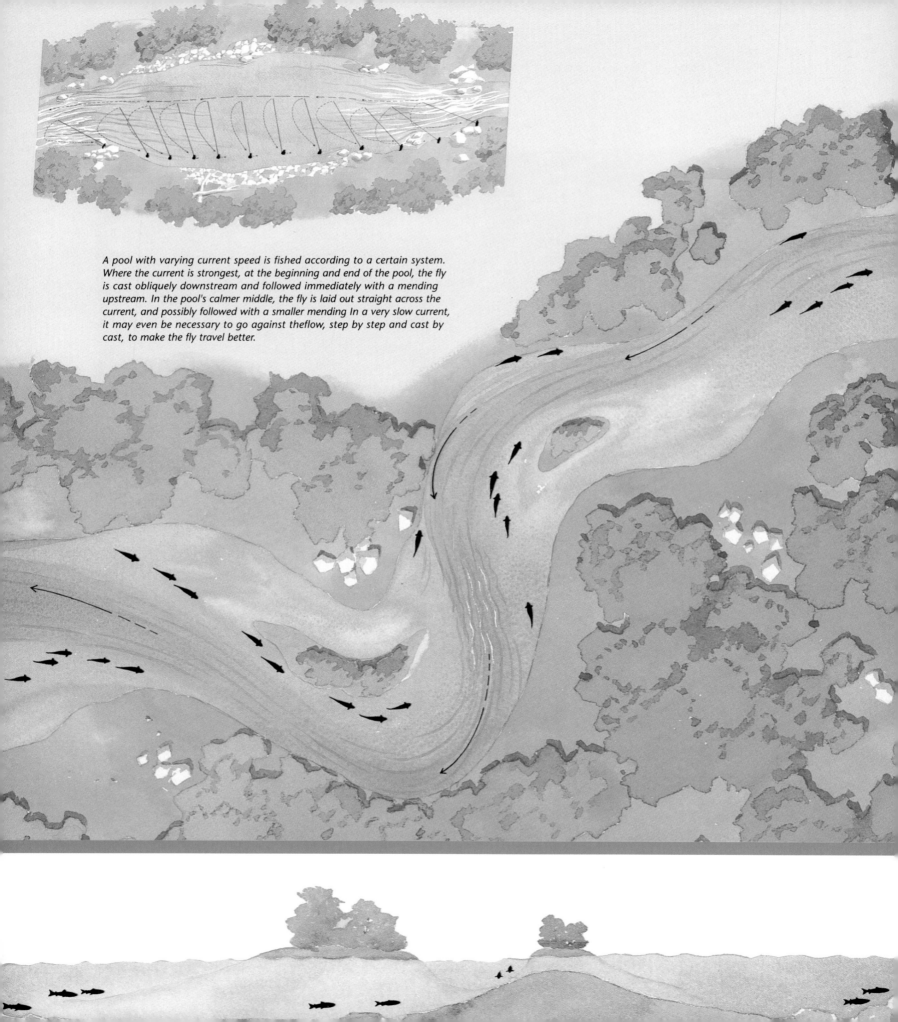

A pool with varying current speed is fished according to a certain system. Where the current is strongest, at the beginning and end of the pool, the fly is cast obliquely downstream and followed immediately with a mending upstream. In the pool's calmer middle, the fly is laid out straight across the current, and possibly followed with a smaller mending In a very slow current, it may even be necessary to go against the flow, step by step and cast by cast, to make the fly travel better.

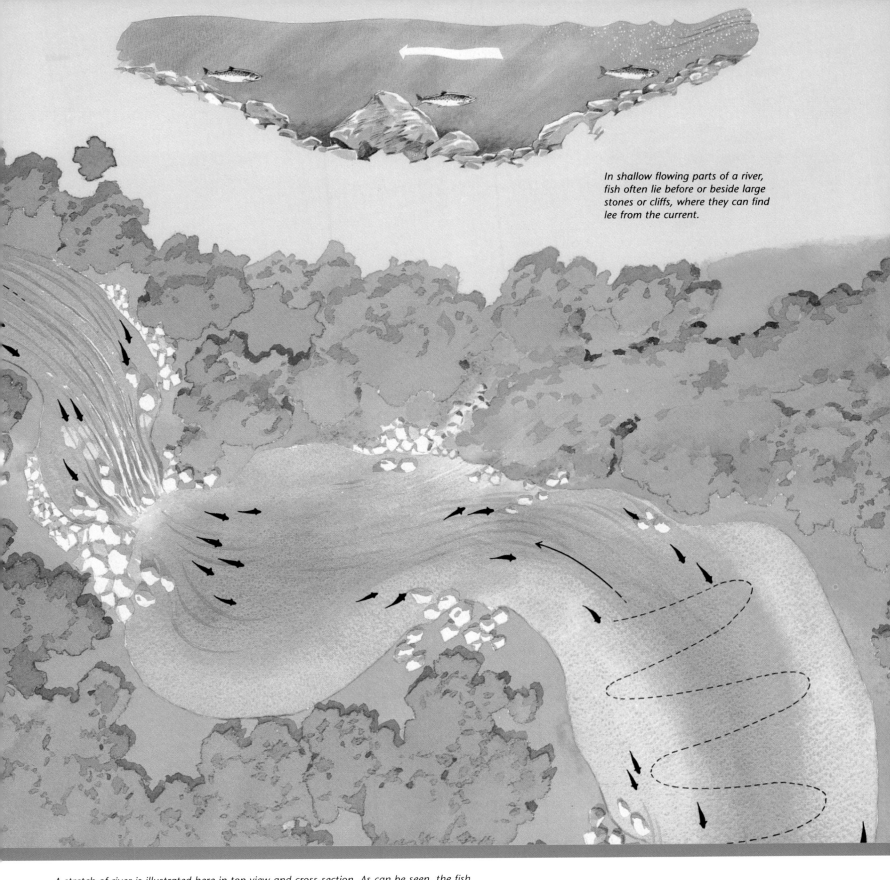

In shallow flowing parts of a river, fish often lie before or beside large stones or cliffs, where they can find lee from the current.

A stretch of river is illustrated here in top view and cross-section. As can be seen, the fish prefer to lie at the inlets of pools - gathering their strength for the next stage of migration - and to rest at the outlets after having overcome previous obstacles. In long wide pools, though, the fish try to lie in the outer edges of the current.

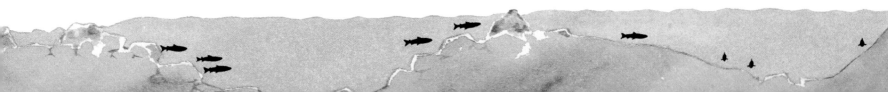

The taking times

At least one British salmon writer has observed that it is impossible to overfish a salmon river. What he meant was that it is not easy to put fish permanently into a non-taking mood, and that they may always - at some time of their own choosing, for some unknown reason - suddenly "come on the take" and grab the first lure they see. In any case, we must evaluate the condition of the fish. A fresh fish entering a new lie for the first time, and taking a brief rest, may be quite likely to snatch at the first thing to antagonize it. Until we know why salmon take our flies, we are naturally only speculating - but experience shows that fresh-run salmon are very vulnerable in this respect, and that many are caught when running without staying long in a lie. Here I feel that it is almost impossible to

overfish the lie or the river. But where the fish have run into holding pools and stayed for some time in a lowering water, it does seem possible to over-intimidate them into a non-taking mood.

There are undoubtedly many instances, in salmon and sea trout fishing, where "familiarity can breed contempt". Moreover, what can we gain by continually flogging a stretch of water when there is a total lack of response? It may make better sense to rest, as well as giving the fish some respite.

The idea of resting a stretch of water, of course, poses hard questions. On many rivers, it is impossible to tell exactly what is happening under the surface. Only by having a fish-counting device at the inlet and outlet of every pool could we determine just what stock it contains from one minute to the next. But since the stock is often a matter of pure speculation, it may be that resting a pool will reduce the chance of familiarity breeding contempt. Indeed, the next time your fly is shown to the fish, some new stock may have moved in, or one of the old residents may have changed its mood.

It is not strictly true that one can never predict the taking times of the fish. Those that settle into lies for several weeks are known to be residents. You may even recognize some of them by the positions in which they show, by their leaping style, and by their size or colouring. However, it is important not to overfish for them - and to fish at times when "all of nature is in tune", as suggested by a knowledge of the behaviour and feeding times of other animals.

Although salmon and sea trout are known to be nonfeeders in fresh water, some memory of their heavy marine feeding may trigger a reflex and make them respond at some times of the day better than at others. One of the most predictable

taking times, throughout the season and in any kind of weather, is the last hour of daylight.

The weather in Scotland may vary greatly during April and May. One day might have air and water temperatures around 5-8° C (41-46° F), while another may have the air at 15° C (59° F) and the water at a magical 10° C (50° F). In any event, when fishing with a fully floating line, it is very important that the air be warmer than the water. Choose a day when the opposite is true, and you may well draw a blank.

As emphasized above, the angler who does best with salmon and sea trout is usually one who lives on, or near, the river he is to fish. He gets to know all its moods and whims, ignoring the temptation to try a new river every year. For this reason, I am now reluctant to try new waters. Age does not leave me enough time to learn them as intimately as I know, for instance, the Castle Grant beat of the Spey, or the Upper Floors beat of the Tweed.

Left: *The salmon has taken the fly, yet many long and dramatic minutes remain before it can be landed.*

Below: *A salmon often rises calmly and slowly towards a fly in the sub-surface. If it decides to take, which is far from certain, it usually does so heavily and decisively rather than violently.*

How to tie a tube fly is shown here. The example is Garry, an all-round pattern that has proved to catch salmon throughout the year, but is perhaps most effective in the early season when the river water is at a high level and low temperature.

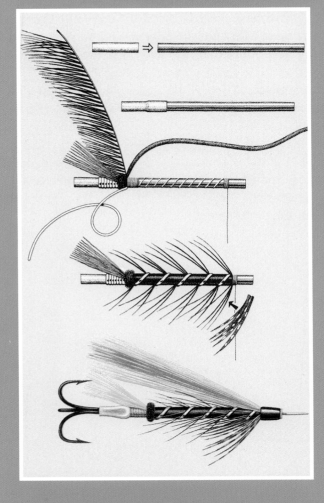

GARRY SPECIAL

Tag: *oval and silver tinsel*
Butt: *black ostrich herl*
Tail: *golden pheasant crest feather*
Body: *black floss*
Ribbing: *oval silver tinsel*
Body hackle: *sparsely tied black cock hackle*
Front hackle: *blue guinea hen*
Wing: *red and yellow bucktail*
Head: *black*

Practical flyfishing

Suppose that you are fishing early in the season, and the river is at nearly perfect height, with a water temperature of around 4° C (39° F) or perhaps a bit warmer as in Scandinavia. You are using a 15 ft (4.6 m) rod, a sinking line, and a garishly coloured 2.5 in (6.3 cm) tube fly. Taking up a position that enables you to cover the lies, you make your first cast.

Initially a few short casts should be made toward the opposite bank, pulling a yard or two of line from the reel at each cast, until you have enough line out. But it should be remembered that a longer cast will allow the fly to get farther down in the water- and that by holding up the rod tip, immediately after the cast, you will keep more line off the water as the fly begins to swing, so that it will sink farther.

Do not be in too much of a hurry to strip back line for the next cast. Let the fly dangle for a few seconds, then casually pull in the first two or three loops of backing. Sometimes during the cold weather of the early or late season, fish will slowly follow the fly and take it only as it is being withdrawn upstream. On occasion, especially in the autumn, my fly has been snatched while hand-lining back at full speed.

These slow tactics offer the best chances in cold weather, but it may be useful to speed them up a little as the water warms. However, salmon - notably the Atlantic salmon react much less quickly than sea trout, which can grab a fly and take you down to the backing in a single rapid movement. Besides, Atlantic salmon differ in behaviour from the same species in North America, which often display real pyrotechnics. All Pacific salmonoids, particularly when fresh-run, are fairly savage on the take, whereas the more ponderous Atlantic salmon of the early spring are rarely willing to snatch and flee like summer sea trout.

In sink-line fishing, you should always try to hold the rod high. As seen in the upper illustration, the fly then has a chance to sink properly toward the bottom. If the rod is held too low, as in the picture below, too much of the line will float on the surface due to friction, keeping the fly "hanging" a little under the surface.

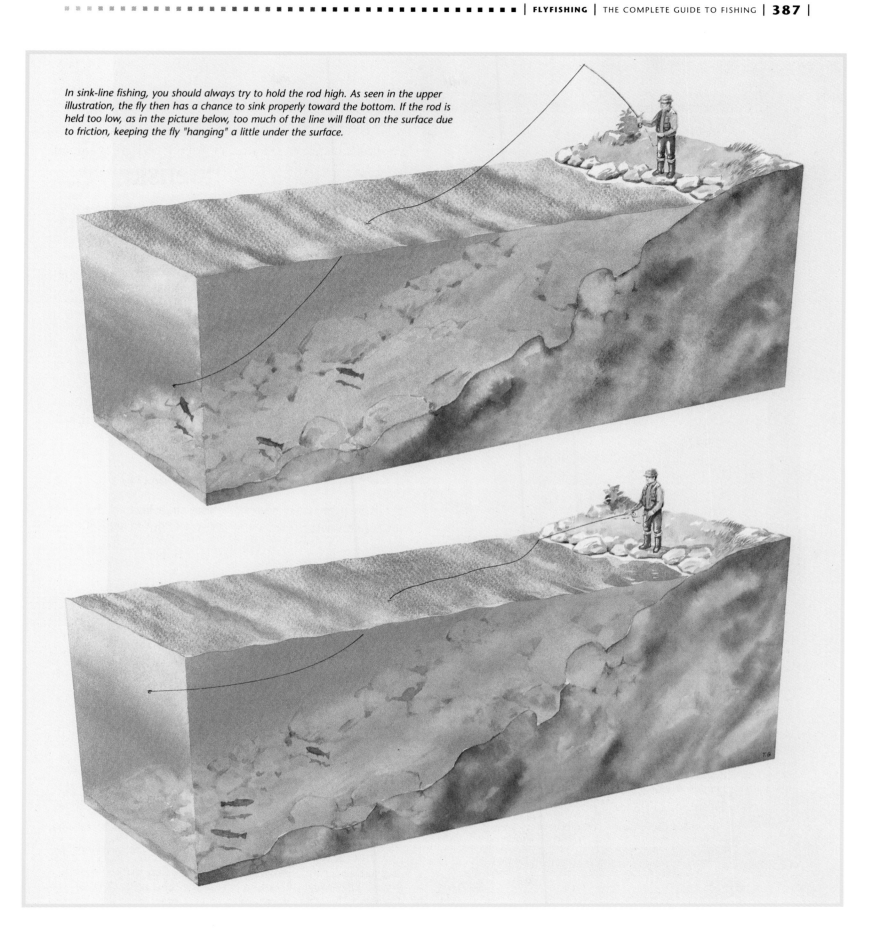

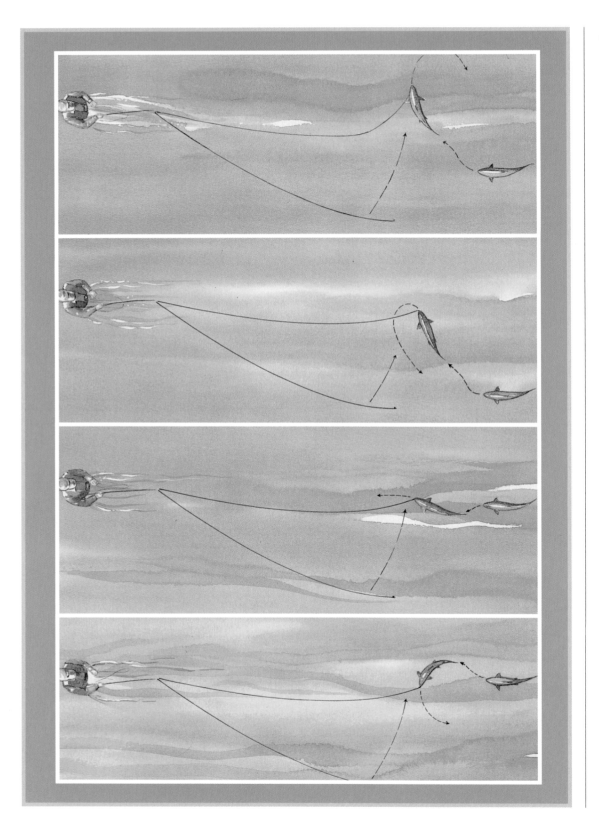

Salmon can take a fly in various ways, and opinions on what to do after the take are almost as numerous as salmon fishermen. Shown here are four common ways for salmon to take. The fish nearly always rises upstream to inspect the fly and possibly take it. Then the fish usually falls back with the current in some direction. Only in the third example does the fish continue upstream after taking the fly.

Though the fish often hooks itself you should always make a clear strike as soon as you feel it on the rod. No matter how it takes the fly and how you hook it, you should let it work against the rod during the whole fight. Give it as little chance as possible to rest, ideally by playing it in the faster part of the current.

Opposite: Will the salmon take the fly - and if so, how?

Hooking and landing

There are several opinions about what to do when a salmon takes the fly. Some anglers, especially those who have read a great deal on the subject, seem to be obsessed with feeding line to the fish at the moment of the take. Others, who may have caught a lot of fish, apparently believe that you should hold hard when you feel the fish and let it hook itself. The present writer prefers the latter view. Possibly a fish in very cold water will get hooked on any slack line fed to it, but I see no reason to do this at any other time. I agree with the idea of holding hard, or even striking, at the instant when the fish is felt pulling on the rod tip.

Exactly what you do after hooking the fish depends to some extent on its mood. It may soon take the initiative and do unexpected things, such as rushing away downstream and threatening to break the line. But usually it stays in the pool where it was hooked, so you need only give line when it pulls strongly, and win back some line when you feel it trying to rest. The fish should be kept active, and preferably in the fas-

ter current. Do not let it get so far downstream that it can lean on your tackle to resist the current.

But neither should you stay opposite the fish simply in order to keep a side-strain on it. This might lead you far downstream from your starting point. Normally I like to play and land a fish from the place where I was standing when I hooked it. Naturally there are times when you have to move, but a good rule is to stand fast.

Before long, in fishing for salmon or sea trout, you will realize that certain conditions must be met if you are to catch fish by design rather than by accident. The angler who has got to know the water in all its moods - and who has learned to cast far - will, in the long run, score heavily over the inexperienced novice. Yet perhaps the main requirement is a "command" of the water. What counts is not merely casting out to the fish, but being able to make your fly move over the fish in such a way that it is more likely to be taken than refused. Achieving effective water command is possible only with expert advice from your gillie, guide or boatsman, unless you have long personal experience of the water you are fishing.

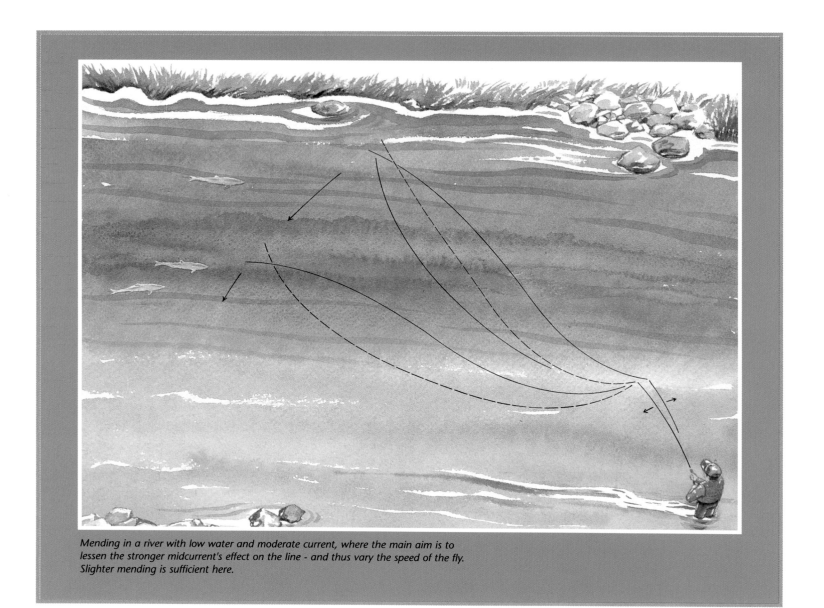

Mending in a river with low water and moderate current, where the main aim is to lessen the stronger midcurrent's effect on the line - and thus vary the speed of the fly. Slighter mending is sufficient here.

Mending the line

One of the first lessons a salmon flyfisherman should learn, particularly if he is to fish mainly with a floating line, is the technique of mending the line. This refers to the movement which you give the line after it is cast and has fallen on the water. Normally a sinking line cannot be mended significantly, so it is important to make a good straight cast that will minimize the central current's influence on the line.

Of course, when fishing a river with a floating line, you are always casting across flowing water where the current's strength varies from one side to the other. Often the central current forms a "belly" in the line, and - as shown by the illu-

strations - this gives the fly an unnatural movement. A very strong central current may cause so much belly that the fly is whipped round in a fast-moving arc, which is frequently quite unattractive to the fish.

But by switching the line upstream, mending its belly formation shortly after it has fallen on the water, you can slow down the fly and enable it to swing round more gradually. Sometimes the current speed varies widely – and the angler who can continually read the situation, mending or modifying the curves in his line, will have greater success than one who merely casts the fly across the flow and leaves it to fend for itself!

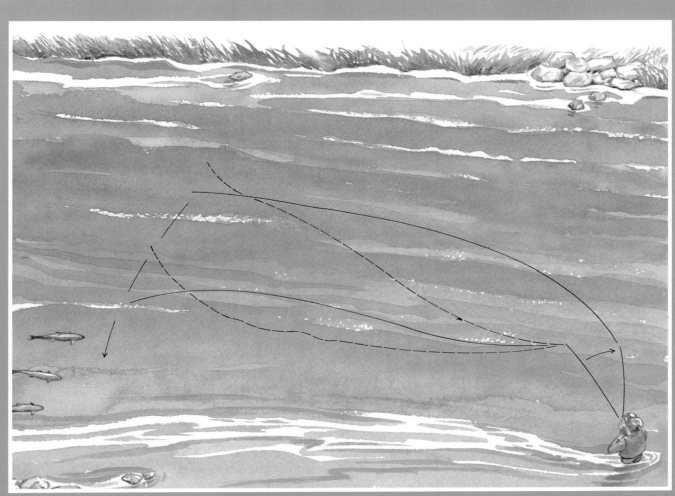

Mending in a river with high water and fast current is often done to decrease the speed of the fly. In waters where the current is irregular and varies in speed, you should keep adjusting the line's curve with bold and slight mendings.

In general, a longer rod improves your chances of creating effective mends. Especially on fast water, an upstream mend is often needed to slow down the fly. But sometimes, in very sluggish water, a downstream mend may be best. This increases the belly in the line, giving the fly more movement and speed to make it attractive.

When fishing with a sinking line, however, there is very little time in which to mend the line. If a sinking line is to be mended at all, this should be done just after the cast, before the fly and line can sink down in the water.

An understanding of the degree of movement which your fly must have in relation to the current, and thus the speed and angle at which it should be fished, will come only with experience. As already noted, a fly that passes too quickly over a lie may not incite the fish to take, while a fly that passes too slowly may be recognized as a trick or may fail to trigger the fish's attack mechanism.

Besides, what triggers a suitable response at one time may not do so at another. There are also variables of air and water temperature and clarity, climate, barometric pressure, oxygen content, and the general mood of the fish at a specific time of day or night. All of these add to the possibilities, and it is still true that no perfect formula can ensure the downfall of fish.

Methods

There are various distinctions between methods of salmonoid fishing. The most common methods on the British, Scandinavian and North American rivers are fishing with a sink-line and with a floating line. The former is most effective when the river is high and cold, whereas the latter is best for a low warm river.

In addition, numerous other approaches are used according to the conditions at hand. For example, on North American rivers it is normal to fish for salmon with a dry fly and a technique called "riffling hitch". In parts of the Scottish highlands, local methods such as "dibbling" are very popular. Large rivers like the Tweed in Scotland, and the Alta in Norway, tend to be fished best from a boat, as when harling.

Fresh-run fish

During the early season, the prime time for salmon fishermen, you can expect to catch some of the freshest fish of the entire season. Some of these may be bearing sea lice the hallmark of fresh-run fish. It is assumed that sea lice can survive in fresh water for only 48 hours, but they have been known to do so for up to seven days under laboratory conditions. Even then, a fish with sea lice must be regarded as excellent, both for sport and on the table. However, you may get a poor fight from a fresh-run fish, especially when the water has warmed a little and when the fish may have run a long way in a short time. Such fish might be already partially exhausted from their swim, needing several days to get back into prize-fighting trim.

Another fish that may be encountered during the early months is called a kelt. This is an Atlantic salmon which entered the river during the previous year and spawned already during that autumn. Not all such fish return quickly to the sea. Many die, as do all the Pacific salmon species and other kelts linger in fresh water, not returning to the estuary until March or April, particularly after a hard winter. Kelts are recognizable by their lean and lanky appearance, ragged fins, and distended vent. One should also look for maggots in gills, and not be fooled by an overall silver appearance - somewhat like that of fresh fish. Such kelts are merely in the process of donning their seagoing coat.

When hooked, a kelt does not normally fight as hard as a fresh salmon. But well-rested kelts may prove to be more

stubborn fighters than is generally appreciated. The law in several countries is that all kelts must be returned to the water, although there are instances in North America where it is permitted to keep them. In any event, they are fairly useless as food.

Late spring salmon

Some Scottish rivers are famous for their early runs of salmon in January, February and March - a period often curiously called "spring" by anglers. Others become better for the sporting angler when spring turns into summer, from April to June. This is the heyday of the flyfisherman who enjoys fishing with a floating line, and when wading is more comfortable, with a general sense of spring in the air. There may still be lots of snow on the mountains, and a strong flow of water in the rivers - but for many of us, this is the peak of the season.

During the past few years, I have almost given up the early season so that I can concentrate on the latter period of better weather. This is a wonderful time to be alive on many of Scotland's classic rivers. Although the spring run on several of them is no longer as prolific as it was thirty years ago, the stocks build up gradually as summer arrives, and the big migrations of fish often do not come until late summer or early autumn.

However, in many other countries with stocks of Atlantic salmon, the season tends to be much shorter. In Norway it is confined to June, July and August, while in Iceland and North America it is more or less the same.

The salmon could not resist the fly, fished with a single-handed rod and a floating line.

Salmon can be caught at any time from early spring to late autumn, but nothing beats an early summer salmon in May.

Summer fishing

One basic difference between Scotland and Scandinavia, as regards fishing, is the size of fly to be used. In Scotland during June, most of the snow has already melted and the rivers are fining down to summer level. A similar river in Norway or Iceland, however, still has a large run-off of meltwater; although the sun is high and air temperatures may be above 20° C (68° F), the water may be little more than 5-8° C (41-46° F). Often, therefore, the Scottish angler who is fishing water around 15° C (59° F) uses flies of smaller sizes (8-12) while the Scandinavian fisherman is still using big tubes and trebles up to 3 in (7.5 cm) long - the type used in Scotland during February and March.

Tactics in Scotland at this time may involve fishing mainly in the early morning and late evening. Certainly little can be achieved by fishing over low water on a hot sunny day when the air temperature soars over 20° C (68° F). Even in Norway, where the fresh fish are then entering the rivers, it might pay to delay your main effort until the sun has sunk behind the lofty mountains - or even, in the region which enjoys the midnight sun, to defer all fishing until evening and continue through the night. Some of the northernmost rivers, such as the famous Alta, are fished only between 6 PM and 6 AM.

Fishing for sea trout

Although salmon and sea trout have been treated above as similar species, they differ subtly in behaviour, and sometimes so much that entirely different tactics are needed when fishing for a specific species. Certain writers even suggest that the two types of fish cannot be related when discussing tactics. However, in reality you will often catch sea trout when fishing for salmon, and vice versa.

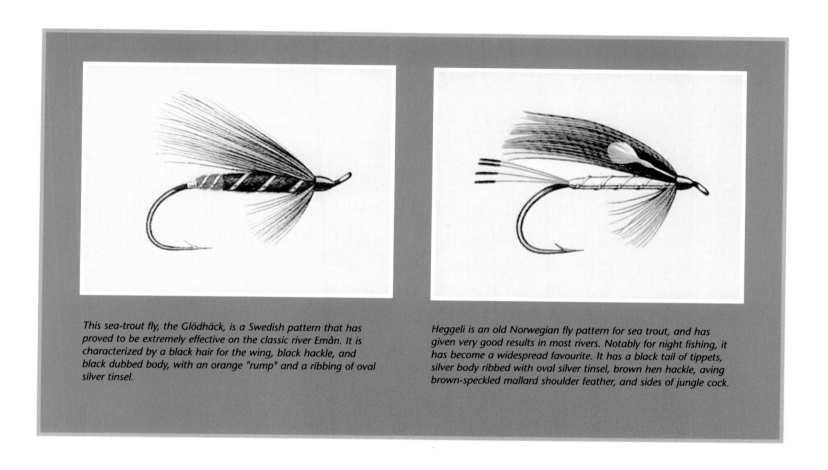

This sea-trout fly, the Glödhäck, is a Swedish pattern that has proved to be extremely effective on the classic river Emån. It is characterized by a black hair for the wing, black hackle, and black dubbed body, with an orange "rump" and a ribbing of oval silver tinsel.

Heggeli is an old Norwegian fly pattern for sea trout, and has given very good results in most rivers. Notably for night fishing, it has become a widespread favourite. It has a black tail of tippets, silver body ribbed with oval silver tinsel, brown hen hackle, aving brown-speckled mallard shoulder feather, and sides of jungle cock.

Below: A sea trout usually takes the fly near or in the surface. The fly should be fairly small, size 6-10. Unlike salmon, sea trout actually feed also after starting their spawing migration, so they tend to take decisively and can seem quick, even violent.

A single-handed rod is the commonest choice for sea-trout fishing, just as for salmon fishing in North America.

Sea trout, particularly those that have been in a river for some time, are very shy. On their first run into fresh water, they may be quite easy to catch - but after only a short interval, it may turn out that they can only be caught at night. In midsummer, on the rivers of northern Europe, this may mean starting as late as 10 PM or so.

On normal waters, you should usually begin with a single-handed rod and a floating line, using flies of sizes 6-10, and fishing in the traditional style - casting across the current and letting the fly swing round. The water's sporting potential will tend to be indicated by the amount of surface activity among the sea trout. Takes are often savage, and the fish present some huge thrills as they charge about, trying to throw your hook. Such sport may last until midnight and complete darkness. But sometimes a dead silence falls, leading you to conclude that the fish have gone down and ended the game for the

night. However, this may be only a "half-time" pause by the fish, so that you can take a brief rest and resume fishing - with a sinking line and a big lure as long as 3 in (7.5 cm). This "second half" may be just the time to catch the larger sea trout, and you may be able to continue fishing until dawn.

Nights with a cold wind, or air colder than the water, should be avoided. Moonlight is not advantageous. The best nights are those with balmy breezes from the south-west, a little moisture in the air, and a myriad of insects dancing in the shadows of late evening. Sometimes, later in the season, the darkest nights offer the best sport of all.

Yet at other times, it is frequently possible to catch sea trout along with salmon. Despite notable differences in tactics, sea trout may respond in much the same manner as do salmon. Indeed, although salmon rarely take after dark, it happens on rivers like the Spey that a fish is caught in late evening and you

Dry flies are often used for salmon fishing in North America, and when fishing for sea trout in a few Norwegian rivers. Among the best known dry flies is the Wulff series, created by Lee Wulff. Here we see Grey Wulff, which floats very well due to its tail and wings of hair, and to its bushy hackle of cock feathers.

GREY WULFF

Tying thread: *black*
Tail: *bucktail*
Body: *dubbed grey wool*
Wings: *bucktail*
Hackle: *grey cock hackle*

do not know what it is until you have netted it. Usually I do not care whether it is a salmon or a sea trout, for both are equally welcome on the table!

Salmon are commonly caught with dry flies in North America, but rarely in Europe. At times a dry fly is very effective for Scandinavian sea trout, even in the middle of the day - yet salmon can seldom be induced to succumb. Only a few times have I caught salmon on a dry fly which was intended for trout, and there have been a few more occasions when I caught sea trout.

Pacific salmon

Of the five principal species of Pacific salmon known in western North America, the most important for sportsmen are the chinook, or king salmon (also called the tyee in parts of Canada), the coho or silver salmon, and the sockeye or red salmon. The others, the pink and the chum salmon, are plentiful but not very interesting for sport, and make only low-grade canned salmon.

My experience of fishing for these species has been confined to Alaska. There I have found that the coho, sockeye, and chinook can provide exceptional flyfishing when they are fresh-run. It is rare to see anyone using a double-handed rod, and only occasionally might one be needed. A light single-handed rod of 9-10 ft (2.7-3.0 m) is usually sufficient. Balance this with a floating line of size 7, sometimes with a sink-tip, and a test leader of 8-10 lbs. Then you can have some super sport, particularly with the coho and sockeye. The chinook does not respond very well to small flies, so it is advisable to use a sinking line and large lures, on extra strong leaders of 20-25 lbs, in case you tangle with a monster weighing over 50 lbs (23 kg).

Much the same techniques as with Atlantic salmon are used for fishing with a floating line. But it pays to go very deep for the chinook, and to fish as slowly as possible. The fight from a chinook is about the same as from big Norwegian salmon, although it lacks the same lustre and cannot be compared on the table. Perhaps the highest gourmet marks are earned by the fresh-run sockeye. Indeed it is this species, when caught at sea, which goes into expensive cans of "prime red salmon". None of the other Pacific species get beyond the "pink salmon" label.

The most popular sea trout on the west coast of the United States is the sea-run rainbow trout called the steelhead. Among the most highly favoured by American flyfishermen, it is reckoned to be the "fightingest" fish on that continent. Many of the biggest specimens are taken with bait-fishing techniques, but a flyfisherman can get good results with large flies on sinking lines.

Saltwater flyfishing

Tackle has improved dramatically. Rods for graphite are available that are light enough even for women to easily cast, making it comfortable to fish with larger and stronger tackle, which is often needed to subdue these powerful fish. Reels developed just for salt water are now so over-designed that they will handle far more than will ever be demanded of them. Fly lines have improved, with special ones developed just for saltwater use. In the world of fly patterns there are now several hundred, where a few years ago anglers only used several dozen basic flies. Even the materials that today's saltwater patterns are made from have changed. Vast improvements have occurred.

For many Europeans shut off from fishing private waters in their countries, and for other fishermen around the world who see their fresh waters deteriorating or disappearing, flyfishermen are looking to other areas where they can enjoy their sport. Salt water offers unlimited opportunities for this. Flyfishermen can effectively catch fish in waters to about 60 ft (20 m) deep with new tackle and flies. In waters less than 10 ft (3 m) deep, fly tackle is often more effective than other types of artificial lures. In very shallow waters (2 feet or less) realistic flies can be presented so quietly that often the flyfisherman can catch fish better than someone using any other tackle, or even bait! This is especially true with wary species such as bonefish which, when feeding, will frequent waters so shallow that their dorsal fins often protrude above the surface. Under these conditions many fish are extremely wary and will flee at the slightest splash of a lure or bait. The silent entry of a fly is often the best way to present to such fish.

Great fighters

Salt water also offers other bonuses. Most fish sought by fly rodders in fresh water do not have many predators. The fish they seek are at the top of the food chain and it is they who are doing the chasing. But in the sea, nearly every fish is being eaten by another that is larger and more fierce. While some bottom-living species, when attacked, can retreat into a cave or under a rock, most saltwater species can only escape by going away. And they must swim faster and farther than the predator or they will be eaten. Such an environment produces fish that are much superior to freshwater fish, as far as speed and endurance are concerned.

All of this is a plus to the flyfisherman. When the hook is set in most saltwater species (other than some bottom-living types), the fish give a far better fight and run off more line than almost any freshwater species. The first time an angler hooks a 5 lb (2.3 kg) bonefish and watches the line melt from his reel as this relatively tiny fish pulls off more 100 yards (91 m) of backing in that first burst of speed, he cannot believe that it is the same fish that took his fly. To battle a tuna, trevally, large mackerel, or any swift open-sea fish is a delight and surprise to the angler who first hooks one of these speedsters. And because of their strength and speed, special tackle is often required to subdue these fish.

There are two basic kinds of flyfishing in the sea: inshore and offshore. Inshore waters are those within about a half mile (1 km) or so of the coast, and usually not more than 12,5 ft (4-5 m) deep. Waters deeper than that are generally regarded as offshore, and usually require different tackle and different fishing techniques.

In colder seas, such as off the coasts of Europe and the northeastern and northwestern United States, flyfishing is not productive for much of the year. Even when it is, generally the numbers of species and times that you can catch them on flies are limited. There are some bottom species in all of these estuaries that will take a fly; mackerel, bluefish and some other species may appear during warmer months. But the most exciting world of saltwater flyfishing is confined to waters where temperatures in the sea rarely drop below 60 degrees and often are 80 degrees or warmer. The closer one gets to the equator, the more opportunities exist for year-round flyfishing. In these warmer seas, food is abundant all through the year and there are many predators that take flies. Many of the species that inhabit these warmer oceans in cold weather will migrate briefly north and then return as the water temperatures drop.

Opposite: Sharks belong to the true big game of the seas, and can be caught with flies in many parts of the world. Offering a long hard battle, they are superb to play on a fly rod.

Flyfishing inshore

When fishing the shallows, two basic approaches are taken. In very shallow, clear waters, such as the flats along the coasts of Africa, Florida, the Bahamas, Yucatan and islands in the south Pacific, many species of fish live in slightly deeper waters, but move into the shallows to feed. Such species include the famous bonefish, permit, tarpon, snook, trevally, threadfin salmon, barramundi, snappers, groupers and channel bass. Much of this is sight fishing, among the most interesting of all kinds of fishing. The angler either wades or else is propelled in a boat (usually with someone poling it) across the flats (shallow saltwater areas are often called flats); it is a combination of hunting and fishing. Both the angler in the bow of the boat, armed with a fly rod, and the person poling the boat are looking for fish. Once the fish is seen, the poler attempts to position the boat so that the angler can make a productive cast. This hunting/fishing offers great appeal to many fishermen, and is a major reason why tarpon, bonefish and permit are among the most publicized and popular of all species sought with a fly rod in salt water.

Noticing the fish

Sight fishing, and knowing how to look for and see fish in the shallows, require some skills. Fortunately, most of them are easy to master. First, the angler needs the proper equipment, so that he can see. A hat is essential, preferably one with a dark under-brim. This cuts down glare reflected from the water and allows the angler to see much better; hats with bright under-brims reflect the glare from the water into the eyes. The other piece of equipment that helps the angler's vision penetrate the surface is a good pair of polarizing glasses. These help to remove most of the glare from the surface. While it is a personal choice, most experienced "flats fishermen" prefer brown or amber-tinted glasses, rather than gray or green-tinted ones. The brown or amber builds contrast and makes it easier to see these fish. It should be remembered that tarpon, bonefish, permit and many other species have silvery sides, which act much like a mirror. When a tarpon, whose back is dark green, swims over light sand it is very easy to see: the back stands out against the light sand. But when the same fish cruises over dark-green turtle grass, it becomes very difficult to see. This is true of all flats fish that are silvery in colour.

Fortunately, there are some skills you can learn that help you to see fish with mirror-like sides. You look for any fish swimming in very shallow water differently than when they are moving in deeper water. A fish swimming in water less than 1 ft (30 cm) deep will create wakes, ripples and small swirls on the surface. Indeed, some fish stand on their heads to root out a bit of food. This means the tail may protrude above the surface, so the angler should look intently at the surface. Anything that moves will instantly be noticeable.

When the fish are in water deeper than that, the angler should look at the bottom. If you look at the surface, you will

Like many other species on the "flats", permit have silvery sides that can make them almost undetectable to us. Being very shy, they are also considered difficult to attract to take.

often miss seeing fish that are cruising below. To understand this, visualize someone looking at a person walking along a road. The viewer does not see the cattle in the field behind the walker. But if the viewer were looking at the cattle and the person walked between him and the cattle, the walker would interrupt his vision and be seen. By looking at the bottom, any movement of fish between the bottom and the viewer is instantly noticed.

The angle of the sun is also important when looking for fish in the shallows. The best angle is to have the sun at your back, or at the back and a little to one side. That is when the

least glare occurs on the water. Sometimes it pays to plan your approach according to existing conditions. If there are white clouds in the sky, it is a good idea to move across the flats so that these clouds are not in the direction of movement. By approaching the clouds, the angler will be looking at the glare on the water, and even polarizing glasses will not penetrate the white reflection. Near islands or tall growth, the fish will be much easier to see if the angler looks in the direction where their dark green is reflected on the surface. This type of background allows the viewer to look clearly at the bottom.

Any unusual disturbance of the surface is also an indicator. If waves are moving in the opposite direction from the wind, something is pushing them. Often bonefish, especially, can be discovered by observing that some waves are moving in a different direction. And nervous waters (any small ripples) are a tip-off that something is creating the disturbance. Many kinds of fish, such as bonefish and sea trout, muddy the water as they root on the bottom. Try fishing where the mud is most dense or bright in colour. That is where the fish are active. By fishing a sinking fly through mud, you can often get terrific fishing. Once in Belize, we found a large mud, and caught bonefish for more than two hours on nearly every cast, using weighted bonefish flies. Casting into the muddiest area of the water, we allowed the fly to fall to the bottom. Then it was moved along in little hopping motions. Rarely did the fly travel more than a few yards before a bonefish found it.

Many fish can be caught near rays, such as stingrays and manarays. Rays often get their food by descending to the bottom, where they pound their heavy wings against it. This frightens shrimp, crabs and other food morsels from the grass and mud, which attempt to flee. The ray then grabs what it can. Rays are slow-moving, but predator species are much swifter and will often hover over the ray. If a shrimp or crab slips out from under the pounding wings, the predator often grabs it before the ray can. This means that the hovering predator is in a feeding mood. The ray creates a long streak of mud that is swept away by the current. By locating the muddiest water, and casting a fly a foot or so uptide from it, the fly can be retrieved over the ray, and into the mouth of a predator.

Planning your catch

Perhaps the main faccor in successfully hooking a saltwater fish, especially in the shallows, is how you approach and make your presentation. A noisy approach or a loud splash of the fly or line near the fish will frighten it. Because these predators are in the shallows and they know they can be seen easily, they are wary and will flee to the depths at the slightest indication of alarm. So the approach to such fish must be silent and carefully planned, and the presentation of the fly must be very correct.

When feeding, most predators working a flat approach it from the downtide side. Therefore, if the tide is flowing from the north to the south, the fish will enter the flat usually from the south, working into the current. The reason is that the tide carries the scent of their prey to them. It is amazing how far fish can smell shrimp, crabs and other food. In fact, some experienced anglers will anchor uptide on a white sand spot. They deposit chum (cut shrimp, conch crab or other fish food) in a sealed pipe drilled with holes to carry the scent to the fish but not allowing them to eat it, or scatter the bait on a white spot on the bottom. Smelling the bait more than 100 yards (91 m) down current, fish will come into the white sand. This makes them easier for the angler to see, so an accurate cast can be made.

It is good to understand that fish feed in the shallows much as a bird-dog hunts. The dog goes into a field downwind, lifts its nose and catches the scent of the birds as it manouvers through the field. Fish do the same thing. Entering a flat from the downtide side, a fish moves into the current, picking up the scent of shrimp crabs and other food. It wends itself back and forth into the current. Armed with this knowledge, an angler has an advantage. By wading or moving in a boat from the uptide side, the angler is in a good position to cast to approaching fish.

Presenting the fly correctly

Of paramount importance in both fresh and salt water is the awareness that, when a fly is offered to a fish, it expects to pursue this baitfish, crab, shrimp or other food source. It does not expect to be attacked by a prey species. Yet we often wrongly give that impression when we present a fly to a fish.

Any fly which is retrieved so that it approaches the fish from the rear, or is brought back directly at the fish, is an unnatural occurrence and the fish will usually not strike. The very best method of retrieving to a fish is in the natural way. If the fish is swimming or facing into the tide, the angler should either wade or move the boat to one side and in front of the fish. Then a cast can be made upcurrent and a few feet to the far side ot the fish. As the fly is retrieved, the current draws it down to the fish. A few feet (1 m) in front of the fish, the fly makes a turn and begins to move upcurrent, back toward the angler. A fish is used to seeing prey species drift toward it on the current and then suddenly, realizing the danger, turn and move away. Such a retrieve is the best of all. Another good method: if a fish approaches you, throw the fly several feet (2-3 m) to one side and in front of the fish - not in a direct line with it. As the fly is brought back, the fish notices it appearing to escape.

Three incorrect or bad retrieves are often made. The angler casts well to the other side of the fish and begins to bring the fly back, but the current sweeps the fly downstream of the fish, and it comes from the side appearing to attack the fish. If a fish is swimming away from you, never throw over its back and retrieve it straight toward the fish. And perhaps the worst retrieve is to throw a fly to a fish lying directly below you, so that the fly lands behind the fish and approaches it from the rear - this almost always results in the fish fleeing.

A typical scene from the tropical and subtropical shallow flats, where fly-fishermen challenge permit and bonefish-among other species. The inset picture shows a tailing bonefish that stands on its nose digging out morsels of food with its tail protruding above the surface.

Flyfishing offshore

Flyfishing in water deeper than 10 feet (3 m), and on the open sea, requires different techniques than fishing in the shallows. In most cases something is used to lure the fish to the angler. Then a fly is presented. One common method is trolling a lure until a fish is hooked and brought near the boat. Many species tend to swim in schools, and others follow the hooked fish to the boat where the angler can make his presentation. Chuggers, sometimes called bloopers, are another way of luring fish within range of the fly caster. A large, floating casting plug devoid of hooks, with a scooped face, is thrown out on the surface. By giving hard jerks on the rod, the lure makes a loud gurgling sound, which many fish find attractive. As they rise to attack the plug, the fly is dropped nearby, usually resulting in a strike. Another method of luring fish is to chum. Ground or chopped pieces of fish, or sometimes even small whole fish, are sent overboard on the tide. Fish are lured to the food source, where the angler can make his cast. This is perhaps the most commonly used method of luring fish within casting range on open water.

Another method is used by billfishermen seeking marlin and sailfish. A hookless bait or artificial lure (called a teaser) is trolled on the ocean to attract a billfish. The angler has a partner who manipulates the teaser. The fish attacks the bait and mauls it, while the teaser is pulled closer. When the enraged fish is lured within a few feet of the boat, the teaser is jerked out of the water and the fly is placed in front of the billfish – which usually attacks it.

The use of lead-core shooting heads, and extremely fast-sinking fly lines that are loaded with lead dust, also allows anglers to fish to depths of 60 feet (20 m) if the tide is not running too strongly. This is often slow fishing, but anglers who are willing to cast the fast-sinking lines and allow them to descend into the depths are catching some very large reef species.

The flyfisherman waits for a fish to show over deep water. Sometimes one can lure the fish up to the surface and closer to the boat so as to cast at them more easily.

Poppers are used mainly in the USA when fishing for cobia, shark and sailfish. These bugs, having a flat or bowl-shaped front part, are often made of plastic, cork or balsa wood. But foam rubber material has become ever more common, since even big bugs are then easy and simple to cast. Popping bugs emit their sound when they scuttle across the surface as you take in the line fast. This sound may be fairly loud and probably makes the fish think some large prey is fleeing. It certainly seems attractive to many saltwater species and often triggers strikes.

Divers are bugs tied with deer hair. For fishing in shallow water, this Dahlberg Diver is superb, although bugs are usually heavy and hard to cast. Most typically, they have a deerhair head that is trimmed to slope backward in a conical shape. Like many other bugs, this one has a hook shield of monofilament nylon line, so as not to snag on underwater plants. It can be fished floating - by taking it in with jerks at the surface, to make a popping sound - and as a streamer, whose slithering movements seem very attractive to fish.

Sliders are a variant of popping bugs, with a conical front body. Due to its streamlined, rocket-like tip, the fly is easy to cast even in windy weather. It also moves more quietly and calmly in the water, which is most useful if you are after shy fish in the shallows. This type offly is meant to imitate small, wounded prey fish at the surface - that is, rather easily caught ones. The colour of a slider has little importance, whereas its size and the way it is fished at the surface often determine whether or not the fish will attack it.

Saltwater flies

Size, colour, shape, and sink rate are all important factors when considering flies to catch saltwater fish. Size is perhaps the most important. Some fish, such as bonefish, have a small mouth; others, such as cobia, snappers and groupers all have large mouths. Offering a 5-in (13 cm) fly to a bonefish is almost certain to result in a refusal. And presenting a very small fly to a big fish with a large mouth will rarely convince the fish to strike. Bonito, for example, roam the world's seas, and they seem to prefer feeding on small 2-3 in (5-8 cm) slim minnows. A streamer fly that imitates these baits will do well. Cobia, sharks, and many other species all want larger flies. Cobia are a good example of where size is often vital to drawing a strike. Even a big 10-in (25 cm) bulky sailfish fly will often be refused by this fish. But a large popping bug that makes considerable noise will often result in a powerful strike. I believe that the popper, though smaller than a streamer, creates so much disturbance that it persuades cobia and other species that here is a much larger prey - and so they strike. Barracudas often scorn streamer flies, but a 0.5-1.0 (2-3 cm)

popping bug that is manipulated quickly across the surface will often cause them to hit. Apparently such a disturbance creates the impression that here is something large and edible that is rapidly getting away.

Frequently size is more important in fly patterns than how the fly is dressed. For some species, however, colour often plays a key role in whether the fish will strike. Striped bass and European bass often like a certain colour better than others. This can vary during the same day, so it pays to experiment with these fish. Sea trout and weakfish will often prefer a chartreuse or bright yellow colour. Fish that live on reefs, where the fly is fished at least 10-30 ft (3-9 m) down, can often be caught sooner on flies that have the dressing made from fluorescent colours, which can be seen in their true tints at greater depths. Snook seem to go for bright yellow combinations. Many offshore species are best caught on streamer flies that have a blue or green back and white belly. Almost all streamer flies fished in open waters are better if their belly is white, the colour of every prey species that predators feed upon.

Surface flies

The most popular surface flies are popping bugs. They were made originally of cork, then of balsa wood, but lately the use of closed-cell foam plastics has increased. These are much lighter and easier to cast, and fairly large bugs can be made that weigh far less than those of the same size in cork or balsa wood. The buoys used by commercial fishermen to mark their traps and pots are an excellent material to fashion popping bugs from. Tough, very light and easy to work with, they make superb popping bugs.

Poppers come in two different designs. The standard bug is one with a flat or cup-forward face. On the retrieve, the line is stripped quickly and the bug moves forward, pushing water and making a popping sound. This is very attractive to many species of saltwater fish. The other type of popping bug is called a slider, shaped more like the cone on a rocket or the front end of a bullet. This pointed bug makes little disturbance on the surface. In situations where fish are wary, or easily alarmed when in shallow water, the slider can be manipulated without a great deal of disturbance, which may frighten the fish. The slider is usually tied to resemble a minnow or baitfish. It represents an injured minnow, struggling on the surface - appearing to be an easy meal for a predator. Many experienced anglers, myself included, feel that the colour of a popping bug is not important. What is important is the size of the bug and how it is manipulated on the surface.

Deer-hair popping bugs are rarely used in salt water, but are a favourite of many freshwater fishermen. The deer-hair bug is bulky, difficult to cast against the ever-present sea breeze; and after being fished for a while, the deer hair soaks up water. This makes it heavier and more difficult to cast, and it doesn't work as well on the surface. However, one deer bug is superb in shallow saltwater situations around the world: the Dahlberg Diver. This has a body and wing of a baitfish, but the head is made from spun deer hair and clipped. The result is a cone-shaped head that slants

back to a large collar. When manipulated on the surface, the bug makes a popping sound. Yet if the retrieve is constant, the bug dives under the water and swims in a wobbling motion. Thus, the lure can be worked as a popper, streamer, or sometimes a combination of the two. It can be popped several times, then made to dive and swim a short distance. The retrieve is stopped and the bug slowly rises to the surface, where the retrieve can be repeated over and over. The bug is almost always dressed with a monofilament weed guard, which allows it to be cast into or near brush, without fear of getting it snagged in the trees.

Below: *Coastal flyfishing along the shallow coasts of northern Europe is sometimes extraordinarily rewarding. Common catches are garfish (see inset), sea trout, mackerel, cod and coalfish.*

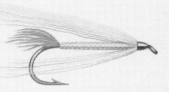

This streamer, of the synthetic material organza, is very common for coastal flyfishing in southern Scandinavia. An organza streamer nicely imitates a little silvery prey fish, and is thus extremely effective in catching, for example, sea trout. Like most streamers, this one is usually tied on straight-eyed hooks 3-5 cm (1.2-2.0 in) long

Ullsocken is a Swedish fly that has long been used in the country's southern salmon and sea-trout rivers. But coastal flyfishermen discovered that it can also be fished as an imitation of a ragworm. Not least the sea trout, which seek shallow coves during the spring in order to feast on these hairy worms, find it hard to resist the fly. Its tail is tied with red wool, the body of peacock herl or floss, and the hackle of brown cock or hen hackle feather.

The above streamer has been given a wing of marabou feathers, and represents an effective type for several species. It can naturally also be tied with hair wings, but its movement in the water is then less lively. The fly can be fished either superficially or deep for sea trout, garfish, mackerel, cod, coalfish and many other species. The wing colours may be varied, yet green, red, yellow, orange and/or blue flies have proved good.

Fly patterns
Tying a wet fly
Fiery Brown

1. Fastening the tail:

Attach the tying thread and cut a V shape of the tail material (for any fly with a tail of hackle feathers). Wind the feather tight with some turns of the thread (Photo 1). Straighten up the feather and pull it toward the hook eye. Clip off the feather stem.

2. Attaching tinsel:

(also floss silk, wool yarn, copper wire etc.): Make an eye of the tinsel around the tying thread (Photo 2). Draw the thread up to breast height and let the tinsel eye slide in toward the hook. Then wind the thread until about 2 mm behind the hook eye (Photo 3).

3. Tying in the body:

Go back with the tying thread to the hook bend, and stop about 2 mm from the tail. Spin the dubbing material around the thread and wind the thread in even turns, first backward and then forth toward the hook eye. Wind the tinsel in even turns until 2-3 mm behind the hook eye (Photo 4).

4. Tying in the hackle:

Cut a V in the hackle feather and stroke the fibres backward, so that only four fibres remain on each side of the stem. Fasten the feather with some turns of the tying thread (Photo 5). Pull the feather in toward the head and clip off. Repeat this process four times, but now place the feather twice somewhat to the right and twice to the left. The fly's hackle is now complete (Photo 6).

5. Tying in the wing:

Clip the wing from two mallard feathers and lay them against each other – front side against back side. Place the feathers directly over the fly body. Form an eye with the tying thread and pull straight upward. Repeat this twice so that the wing is well attached (Photo 7). Cut off excess wing material as near the thread as possible.

6. Tying the head:

Change to black tying thread and wind it tight at the hook eye. Then wind back toward the wing so that the white thread is fastened. Clip off the white thread and form the head with the black thread. Make a whip-finish knot, clip off the black thread, and coat the head with clear varnish (Photo 8). The fly is complete.

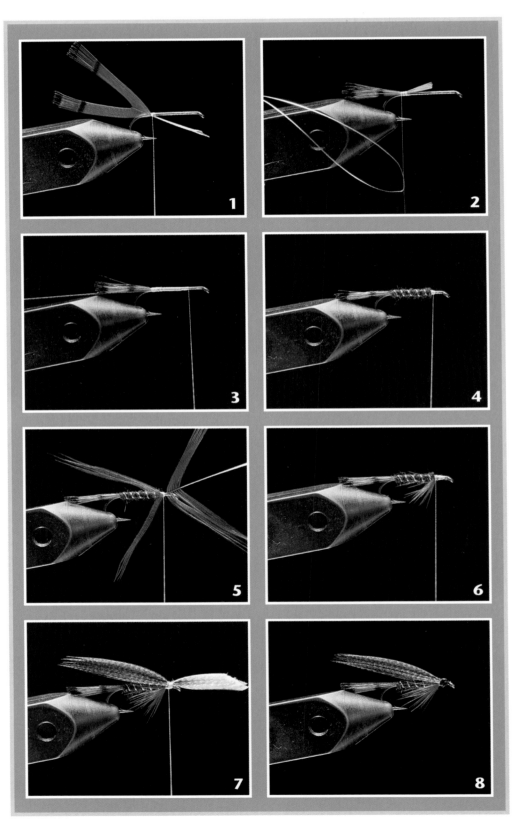

Tying a dry fly
Black Gnat variant

1. Tie in the tail and body:

Fasten the tying thread and tie the tail in the same way as on the wet fly, but repeat twice to give the dry fly better buoyancy. Wind the thread toward the hook eye in even turns. Go back with the thread toward the hook bend, stopping about 2 mm from the tail. Attach the dubbing and wind first backward, then forward so that 2/3 of the hook shaft is covered with dubbing, and possibly trim it (Photo 1).

2. Tie in the wing:

Mix black and natural deer hairs (in equal proportions). Hold the bunch of hair between your thumb and middle finger over the hook – with the hair tips forward – and fasten it with three turns of tying thread. Wind some more turns, and clip off the hairs just in front of the body (Photo 2).

3. Tie in the hackle:

To make a durable hackle, first lay a piece of black tying thread in an eye around the white thread and fasten it. Then lay the hackle over the black thread and fasten with the white thread (Photo 3). Wind the thread about 15 turns forward to the wing and past it, so that it rises (Photo 4). Clip off the hackle stem and the black thread as close as possible to the white thread (Photo 5).

Dub thinly with black dubbing around the black thread. Hold the thread and the hackle together and pinch them tightly with hackle pliers. Twist about 15 turns, and wrap tightly around the hook by going forward and laying each turn just in front of the last. Wind 5-6 turns and fasten with some turns of white thread. Stroke the wing and hackle backward with your fingers and attach securely with the thread (Photo 6).

4. Tie the head (black):

Use black tying thread and wind it in the same way as on the wet fly. Conclude with a whip-finish knot and varnish the head. The dry fly is complete (Photo 7).

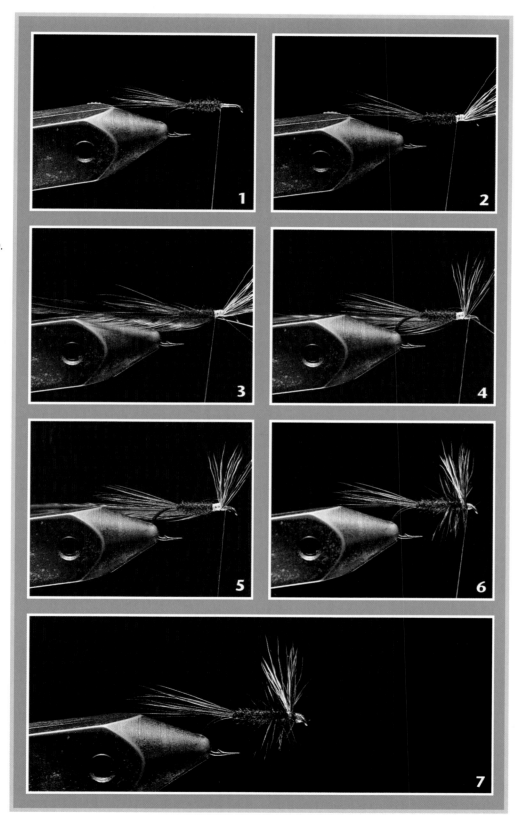

Tying a shrimp fly
Ally's Shrimp

1. Tie in the tail and body:
Wind on the white tying thread and attach the tinsel in the same way as previously. Tie in the tail – as long as the hook – and wind the thread forward to half the body. Clip off the hairs where the head will later begin (Photo 1).

2. Tie in floss and ribbing:
Attach the red floss silk with the tying thread. Wind the silk first backward, then forward, and attach to the body middle. Wind the thread up to the head, attach the black floss, wind backward and then forward, and fasten the floss. Rib with five turns of tinsel (Photo 2).

3. Tie in the wing:
First attach the overwing, then the underwing. Varnish at the fastening to make the wing more durable (Photo 3). Next, choose a centre-tip feather of golden pheasant, ensuring that the feather is as long as the hook. Clip off a bit of the stem, run it into the hook eye, and lay the feather directly over the hook. Hold it between your thumb and middle finger, and wind four loose turns with the tying thread. Hold the hackle stem and pull the feather forward until the squirrel hairs' white tops are visible. Wind two loose turns of thread and pull upward to fasten the feather (Photo 4). Holding the feather between your thumb and middle finger, clip off the stem – first in front of the hook eye, then behind.

4. Tie in the hackle:
Cut a V in one of the hackle feathers. Stroke backward so that only four fibres remain on each side of the stem, and wind it on with a loose turn of tying thread (Photo 5). Clip off the hackle and pull the thread tight. Repeat this process about ten times, but place the feathers somewhat to the right and left, so that the hackle forms a collar round the body.

5. Tie the stripe and head:
Fasten the floss silk with two turns of the tying thread, just before the hackle collar. Wind three turns of floss toward the hook eye to tie the stripe. Attach the floss with one turn of thread, and hold it at about a 45-degree angle to the hook bend (this prevents the floss fibres from sticking up). Repeat and fasten with two turns of thread. Change to red thread and wind it from the front back toward the stripe. Add 1-2 turns around the white thread, clip it off, and form the head with the red thread. Make a whip-finish knot, clip off the tying thread, and varnish the head (Photo 6). The fly is complete.

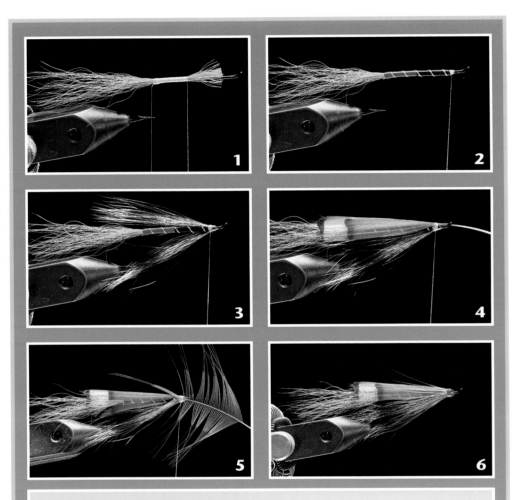

Five tips that simplify flytying:

Use white tying thread.
Thus, when you use light materials in the body or tag, they will be kept even when the fly is in the water. But if black tying thread is used, the fly instead becomes grayish, since the thread then shines through the material.

Use fine cotton gloves when you tie in floss silk.
The floss silk will then not break during the tying, and light colors will keep the same tone throughout the body (hands are almost always a bit dirty, especially after a couple of hours of tying, which often colours the silk).

Thin the flytying varnish with pure acetone in equal proportions.
The varnish then penetrates the thread better, making the fly more durable.

Clip off the material just in front of the head.
This gives an even body, which is very important, particularly when you are to tie a body of flat gold or silver tinsel.

Use your thumb and middle finger when tying wings.
The wing will thus sit quite straight. Using your thumb and forefinger increases the risk of tying the wing in crooked.

Tying a salmon fly
IQ Black Dawn

1. Tie a tag: Attach the tinsel with the tying thread as shown previously. Wind the tinsel with tight, even turns toward the hook bend; stop just over the barb, and wind the thread back to the hook tip. Then wind the tinsel toward the hook tip. Be careful that the turns lie densely and do not overlap each other. Fasten the tinsel with some thread turns and clip it off about 3 mm behind the hook eye. Wind the thread in tight turns to 3 mm behind the hook eye, make a whip-finish knot, and clip off the thread. Varnish the tag 3-4 times for greater durability, letting the tag dry well after each time.

2. Tie in the tail: Cut a V in one of the hackle feathers and stroke the fibres backward, so that three fibres remain on each side of every stem. Tie in the hackle with two turns of thread, just where the fibres divide, and pull the hackle toward the hook eye until the tail is 1 1/2 times as high as the hook gap. Fasten with two turns of thread. Clip off excess material near the thread. Repeat three times.

3. Tie in the butt: Attach floss silk with a turn of tying thread on the hook's underside (see Ally's Shrimp, point 5), as close as possible to the clipped hackle. Wind the floss three turns back toward the hook bend, then three turns forward. Holding the floss stretched downward, run the thread behind and around it. Fasten it with a turn of thread while pulling the floss forward. Wind some more turns, and clip off the floss about 3 mm behind the hook eye. Varnish the butt twice (see Photo 1).

4. Tie in the body and the body hackle: Attach the rib floss and body tinsel to the hook shaft's underside, as near the butt as possible. Wind the thread in tight, even turns forward and stop at the body middle. Clip off the floss and tinsel 2-3 mm behind the hook eye. Fasten the mylar tinsel to the hook shaft's underside, with the gold side toward the shaft. Wind the tinsel backward in tight turns that do not overlap. At the butt, the tinsel is wound forward and fastened with thread. Clip off excess tinsel 2-3 mm behind the hook eye (Photo 2). Take a black cock hackle with fibres as long as the hook gap's height, wet your fingers and stroke the fibres backward. Tie in the hackle feather where the fibres parted, on the hook shaft's underside at the end of the tinsel body. Dub crystal seal on the thread and wind the body up toward the head. Rib the body with five even turns of the tinsel and fasten with the thread. Wind the floss just behind the tinsel and fasten. Then wind the body hackle forward so that each turn lies exactly behind the floss, and finish with two turns in front of the dubbing. Secure with the thread and clip off excess material (Photo 3).

5. Tie in the hackle and wing: Attach the hackle so that the fibres end just behind the hook bend (see Fiery Brown, point 4). Clip off the excess and varnish the fibre ends.
Take two orange hackle feathers, from the nape's left and right sides; lay them together so that the tips lie level. Remove the fluff where they will be wound on. Clip off the stems, but leave 2 mm and tie the feathers with some loose turns of thread. Wind three more turns and fasten by pulling the thread straight up; varnish the winding (Photo 4). Tie in two red flashabou – as long as the hackle feathers – on each side. Trim and varnish. Attach the fox hairs with some turns of thread, clip off the excess, and varnish.

6. Tie in a stripe (see also Ally's Shrimp, point 5): Attach the floss on the hook shaft's underside just in front of the hackle, and wind three turns. Secure with some turns of tying thread. Change to black thread, wind toward the stripe, and form the head as described previously. Conclude with a whip-finish knot and varnish the head 3-4 times with diluted varnish. The salmon fly is complete (Photo 5).

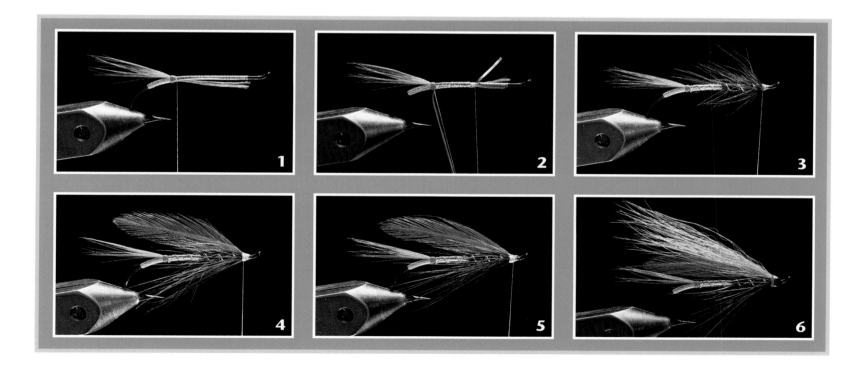

Dry flies

Greenwell's Glory (deer-hair variant)
Tying thread: yellow, waxed 8/0
Body: yellow waxed tying thread
Ribbing: fine oval gold tinsel
Wing: brown and natural deer hair, half of each
Hackle: light furnace cock hackle
Head: yellow tying thread

This classic fly pattern is to imitate yellow-green mayflies, and is fished mainly in trout waters.

Royal Wulff
Tying thread: white 8/0
Tail: white deer hair (or natural deer hair)
Body: peacock herl, back and front, with red floss silk between
Wing: white deer hair (or natural deer hair)
Hackle: two brown cock hackles
Head: black tying thread, possibly with a stripe of fluorescent orange floss silk

This attractor fly is gladly taken by salmon, trout, char, grayling and steelhead in both still and flowing waters.

Coch-Y-Bondhu
Tying thread: white 8/0
Tag: fine oval gold tinsel
Body: peacock herl
Hackle: brown cock hackle
Head: black or white tying thread

This all-round pattern fishes well for trout, grayling and char.

Quill Gordon (deer-hair variant)
Tying thread: white 8/0
Tail: brown deer hair
Body: peeled stem from peacock herl
Wing: brown deer hair
Hackle: dark blue dun cock hackle
Head: black or white tying thread

This fly imitates brown mayflies and is chiefly used for trout, but char and grayling are also fond of it.

Dry flies

Black Gnat
Tying thread: black or white 8/0
Tail: black cock hackle
Body: black crystal seal or crystal hare's ear-dubbing
Wing: black and brown deer hair, half of each
Hackle: black cock, twisted with same material as the body
Head: black or white tying thread

Adams (deer-hair variant)
Tying thread: white 8/0
Tail: grizzly and brown cock
Body: gray dubbing
Wing: brown deer hair
Hackle: grizzly and brown cock hackle
Head: black tying thread

Harkrank (Daddy LongLegs)
Tying thread: white 8/0
Body: natural deer hair
Legs: tail feather from golden pheasant,
  with knee and ankle joints
Wing: brown-coloured grizzly cock hackle
Hackle: grizzly cock saddle hackle
Head: white tying thread

Elk Hair Caddis (deer-hair variant)
Tying thread: white 8/0 • Body: green dubbing
Body hackle: brown cock saddle hackle,
  twisted with same material as the body
Wing: natural-coloured deer hair
Head: white tying thread

This pattern can be made in different colour
variants and sizes to imitate local caddis flies.

Bäckslända (stonefly)
Tying thread: white 8/0
Tail: teal from mallard
Body: yellow dubbing
Body hackle: brown cock saddle hackle,
  twisted with same material as the body
Wing: black jumbo nape
Thorax: brown cock saddle hackle,
  twisted with same material as the body
Antennae: teal from mallard
Head: white tying thread

Sedge Variant
Tying thread: white 8/0
Tail: brown deer hair
Body: hare's ear
Wing: nape feather from ring-necked pheasant
Thorax: brown cock, twisted with body material
Head: white tying thread

The pattern can be made in different colour
variants and sizes to imitate mayflies.

Nymphs and Flymphs

Hare's Ear Larva (weighted)
Tying thread: white 8/0
Body: light hare's ear
Body hackle: brown cock saddle hackle,
   twisted with same material as the body
Thorax: Weight with copper wire and dub with
   dark hare's ear; pick out some hairs to imitate legs
Head: white or black tying thread

Deep Sparkle Pupa
Tying thread: white 8/0
Rear body: green dubbing and yellow antron yarn
Hackle: brown hen hackle
Front body: dark hare's ear
Head: brown tying thread

Gammarus
Tying thread: brown 8/0
Body: dark hare's ear
Ribbing: oval silver tinsel
Hackle: brown hen hackle
Carapace: pearl flashabou
Head: brown tying thread

*A light variant of Gammarus is obtained by using light
hare's ear and light brown hen hackle. In the same way
green Gammarus imitations are made.*

Hare's Ear Flymph
Tying thread: white 8/0
Tail: brown partridge
Body: dark hare's ear
Hackle: light blue dun hen hackle,
   twisted with same material as the body
Head: white tying thread

*For light variants, the light part
of the hare's ear is used.*

Nymphs and Flymphs

Yellow Flymph
Tying thread: white 8/0
Tail: brown partridge
Body: yellow dubbing
Hackle: light brown hen hackle,
   twisted with light hare's ear
Head: white tying thread

Free-living Green Caddis Fly Larva
Tying thread: white 8/0
Body: clear green dubbing
Hackle: brown hen hackle,
   twisted with same material as the body
Head: black tying thread

Green Damselfly Nymph
Tying thread: white 8/0
Tail: green marabou
Body: green marabou
Ribbing: green copper wire
Thorax: green pearl mylar
Eyes: peacock herl
Head: black 8/0

Black Martinez (mylar variant)
Tying thread: black 8/0
Tail: natural guinea hen
Body: black dubbing
Ribbing: copper wire
Thorax: green pearl mylar
Hackle: grizzly hen

MayFly Flymph
Tying thread: white 8/0
Tail: brown partridge
Body: hare's ear
Ribbing: white tying thread
Hackle: brown partridge
Head: white tying thread

Wet flies

Fiery Brown
Tying thread: white 8/0
Tail: orange-coloured tippets from golden pheasant
Body: fiery brown-coloured dubbing
Ribbing: oval silver tinsel
Hackle: orange to fiery brown-coloured cock
Wing: mallard
Head: black tying thread

Black Zulu
Tying thread: black or white 8/0
Tail: red wool yarn
Body: black dubbing
Ribbing: oval silver tinsel
Hackle: black hen hackle
Head: black tying thread

Coachman
Tying thread: white 8/0
Tag: fine oval gold tinsel
Body: peacock herl
Wing: white duck or substitute
Hackle: brown cock hackle
Head: black tying thread

Red Tag
Tying thread: white 8/0
Tail: red wool yarn
Body: peacock herl
Hackle: brown cock hackle
Head: black tying thread

Teal and Silver
Tying thread: white 8/0
Body: flat silver tinsel
Ribbing: oval silver tinsel
Wing: teal feather from mallard
Hackle: blue cock hackle
Head: black tying thread

Streamers

Black Nosed Dose (mylar variant)
Tying thread: white 8/0
Tail: red wool yarn
Body: holographic silver mylar, with
   a band of red tying thread
Wing: white, black and brown hair
   with some strands of peacock angel hair
   between the black and brown
Head: black tying thread

Black and Gold (mylar variant)
Tying thread: white 8/0
Body: holographic gold mylar, witha band of
   white tying thread
Wing: black hair mixed with a little peacock angel hair
Head: black tying thread

Teal and Blue (hairwing)
Tying thread: black or white 8/0 • *Tail:* yellow cock hackle
Body: flat silver tinsel • *Ribbing:* oval silver tinsel
Wing: white squirrel • *Hackle:* peacock-blue cock hackle
Head: black tying thread

Black Satan
Tying thread: white or black 8/0
Tail: red cock hackle
Body: black dubbing or floss
Ribbing: oval silver tinsel
Wing: black hair mixed with a
   few strands of red angel hair
Hackle: black cock hackle
Head: black tying thread

IQ Sculpin
Tying thread: white 8/0
Tail: four brown-coloured grizzly hackle
Body: brown ice chenille
Body hackle: brown-coloured grizzly hackle twisted with ice chenille
Eyes: yellow-black doll eyes • *Head:* small, of white tying thread

*This fly can be tied in several combinations of
colours by replacing the hackle and chenille.*

Sea-trout flies

Ally's Shrimp
Tying thread: *white 8/0*
Tail: *orange bucktail with 2-4 pearl flashabou or crystal flash*
Body: *black and red floss, half of each*
Ribbing: *oval gold tinsel*
Wing: *over- and underwing of white squirrel, with tippet feather from golden pheasant on top*
Hackle: *orange cock*
Head: *red tying thread, possibly with a stripe of fluorescent orange floss*

Hare's Ear Shrimp
Tying thread: *white 8/0*
Tail: *light hair from hare's mask*
Eyes: *0.50-mm nylon*
Body: *light hare's ear*
Back: *10-15 pearl flashabou, varnished*
Head: *white tying thread*

This fly is mainly used for coastal sea-trout fishing.

Ragworm / Leech imitation
Tying thread: *white 8/0*
Rear hook: *Hackle: orange marabou*
Head: *red tying thread, possibly with a stripe of fluorescent orange floss*
Body: *black ice chenille, braided with dycroon 0.22 mm*
Front hook: *Body: black ice chenille*
Head: *white or red tying thread, possibly with a stripe of fluorescent orange floss*

This fly is superb when fishing both in lakes and along the coast, but is also widely thought to fish well for trout, char, pike and bass.

March Brown Silver
Tying thread: *white 8/0*
Tail: *brown partridge*
Body: *flat silver tinsel*
Ribbing: *oval silver tinsel*
Wing: *pheasant hen or substitute*
Hackle: *brown partridge*
Head: *black tying thread, possibly with a stripe of light-brown floss*

This classic fly is also excellent for salmon.

IQ Shrimp
Tying thread: *white 8/0*
Tail: *brown-orange fox with copper angel hair*
Body: *brown-orange crystal seal*
Ribbing: *oval gold tinsel*
Wing: *over- and underwing of brown-orange fox. Above the wing an orange-coloured tippet from golden pheasant is tied in as a back.*
Hackle: *brown-orange cock*
Head: *red tying thread, possibly with a stripe of fluorescent orange floss*

Salmon flies

Blue Charm (hairwing variant)

Tying thread: white 8/0 • *Tag:* oval gold tinsel with yellow floss
Tail: yellow cock hackle • *Butt:* black ostrich
Body: dubbed with black crystal seal
Ribbing: oval silver tinsel • *Hackle:* blue cock
Wing: (1) two blue cock feathers, back to back; (2) two to four pearl
flashabou, one or two on each side of the hackle; (3) brown fox
Head: black tying thread, possibly with a stripe of light-blue floss

Bomber

Tying thread: white 6/0
Tail: white squirrel • *Body:* natural deer hair
Body hackle: Palmer-wound grizzly hackle
Antennae: white squirrel • *Head:* white or black tying thread

*Bomber can be made in many colour variants and sizes.
The fly is an excellent attractor for both salmon and sea trout,
but also works well for other species such as steelhead and pike.*

Sunray Shadow

Tying thread: white 6/0
Body: plastic tube • *Wing:* white squirrel with black goat or fox over.
Peacock angel hair mixed over the wing.
Head: black tying thread, possibly with a stripe of fluorescent
orange floss

This fly is also fine for sea-trout fishing in flowing waters.

IQ Black Dawn

Tying thread: white 8/0 • *Tag:* oval gold tinsel, varnished
Tail: three deep-orange hackle • *Butt:* fluorescent orange floss
Body: rear half of flat gold tinsel, front half of black and gold
crystal seal
Ribbing: oval gold tinsel and fluorescent orange floss
Body hackle: black hackle, but only over the front half
Hackle: black heron or long, soft cock hackle until just behind
the hook bend
Wing: (1) deep-orange hackle pair, back to back; (2) two red
flashabou on each side of the hackle; (3) gold-brown fox,
or raccoon body hair
Head: black tying thread, possibly with a stripe of fluorescent
orange floss

Green Highlander (hairwing variant)

Tying thread: white 8/0
Tag: oval silver tinsel and yellow floss • *Tail:* yellow cock hackle
Butt: black ostrich herl
Body: 1/3 yellow floss, 2/3 green dubbing
Ribbing: oval silver tinsel • *Body hackle:* green cock hackle
Hackle: yellow cock hackle
Wing: (1) two green cock hackle, tied back to back; (2) two pearl
flashabou, one on each side of the hackle; (3) yellow, orange
and brown fox hair, in equal parts, with a strip of
golden-brown fox hair on top
Head: black tying thread, possibly with a stripe of fluorescent
green floss

This classic salmon fly fishes best in clear water and sunshine.

Pike flies

Red Popper (deer hair)
Tying thread: red 6/0
Tail: four red and four grizzly hackle, with around ten red holographic flashabou
Hackle: red and grizzly cock hackle
Body: red deer hair; can also be made of balsa wood
Eyes: yellow-black doll eyes

This fly can be made in many colour variants.

Bullet Frog
Tying thread: white 6/0 • *Body:* yellow and green deer tail
Leg: yellow and green deer tail • *Eyes:* yellow-black doll eyes

Slider (deer hair)
Tying thread: white 6/0
Tail: four orange-coloured grizzly cock hackle and four grizzly cock hackle, with around ten yellow holographic flashabou
Hackle: grizzly and orange-coloured grizzly
Body: white deer hair as belly, and orange deer hair with strips of black deer hair
Eyes: yellow-black doll eyes

This fly can also be tied in green, red, blue or other variants by replacing all the orange with such a colour.

Tarpon Streamer
Tying thread: white or red 6/0
Tail: four white and grizzly cock hackle, with around ten silver holographic flashabou
Hackle: blue cock hackle
Cheeks: around ten silver holographic flashabou on each side
Eyes: silver chain
Body: red tying thread, varnished

This fly can be tied in countless colour variants.

Soft Hackle Fly
Tying thread: white 6/0
Wing: twisted yellow, green and blue marabou
Hackle: teal from mallard
Head: white tying thread, possibly with a stripe of light-blue floss

This fly can also be tied in countless colour variants.

Salt-water flies

Cockroach
Tying thread: *black 6/0*
Tail: *four grizzly hackle*
Hackle: *brown deer hair*
Head: *black tying thread, possibly with a stripe of light-brown floss*

Lefty's Deceiver
Tying thread: *white 6/0*
Tail: *four white cock hackle, with two holographic flashabou fibres*
Hackle: *blue deer tail*
Head: *white tying thread, possibly with a stripe of light-blue floss*

This fly occurs in many colour variants.

Strawberry Blonde
Tying thread: *white 6/0*
Tail: *orange hair with orange angel hair*
Body: *flat silver tinsel*
Wing: *red hair with red angel hair*
Head: *white tying thread, possibly with a stripe of red floss*

The Blonde series exists in several colour variants; see page 218.

Sea Ducer
Tying thread: *white 6/0*
Tail: *six yellow cock hackle, two grizzly hackle, and around ten silver holographic flashabou strands*
Body: *two or three yellow cock hackle*
Hackle: *two red cock hackle*
Head: *black tying thread, possibly with a stripe of fluorescent orange floss*

Hagen Sand's Bonefish Bucktail (variant)
Tying thread: *white 6/0*
Wing: *four yellow cock hackle and four grizzly hackle, tied in back to back as two pairs over each other*
Hackle: *white deer tail*
Head: *ice chenille with yellow-black doll eyes*

The original has a black head of tying thread with painted eyes in yellow and black.

A well-known American reference work defines the word "trolling" as "the method or act of fishing by dragging a hook and line, as behind a boat and near the surface, usually with a spoon bait or the like."

Trolling is a venerable and familiar way of fishing. It has been practiced in fresh, brackish and marine water alike, all over the world, ever since the first hunting and fishing folk climbed into boats.

Among sportfishermen, trolling has always involved the use of a moving boat with sportfishing equipment – in other words with a rod, reel, line, and lure or bait. It is thereby distinguished from methods of dragging for fish which do not directly fight them with a rod and reel.

Certainly trolling is the most international of all sportfishing techniques. It is an approach that can be either simple or advanced, and can be applied to small fish as well as to giants weighing hundreds of pounds. Moreover, it is a method that, with modern accessories, enables one to cover large areas of water and, on a very sporting basis, to make contact with the fish almost regardless of where they occur in a river, lake or sea.

To a growing extent, trolling is concentrated in large water bodies, often with deep and flowing waters, where the majority of fish are not accessible by traditional fishing with a casting rod. It is primarily seaworthy boats and modern navigational aids that have paved the path to fishing waters which, previously, were reserved for nets and other massive-catch equipment.

Contacting fish on the wide open spaces of water is an exciting challenge that involves not only skill at sportfishing, but also good knowledge of fishing biology and navigation. The fish one fights in open waters are almost always in excellent condition – fish that take every chance to show what they are worth in terms of strength, endurance and speed.

In most fishing situations, the external circumstances – such as weather, wind, currents, water level and bottom structure – are more important than the fish itself for the dimensioning of equipment. And it is on this key point that the downrigger has revolutionized modern sportfishing. Downrigger enables you to fish with feather-light baits, and catching fish at very great depths.

Trolling can be done by either an individual or a team. It can be an ideal family diversion, where everybody on board is engaged – irrespective of age, gender, or prior experience. Besides, it is amenable to handicapped persons and does not demand an ability to cast or move for long distances under one's own power. In ice-free waters, it can be done around the clock and all year round, unless the fishing regulations say otherwise.

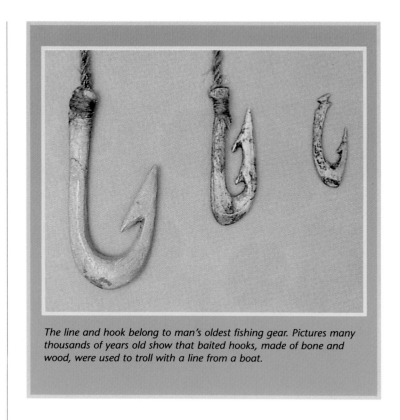

The line and hook belong to man's oldest fishing gear. Pictures many thousands of years old show that baited hooks, made of bone and wood, were used to troll with a line from a boat.

Classic fishing method

Though we have no exact evidence of when the rod made its trolling debut, older fishing literature mentions pioneering trollers in both fresh and salt water, very often where such beautiful, pugnacious, and tasty fish as salmon and tuna live and feed.

A hundred and fifty years ago, the largest lake in Sweden – and in Western Europe – gave rise to what, as far as I know, is the oldest description of lake trolling with a rod. The fishing inspector A. R. Geijer related it as follows:

"When fishing with swivel lures in Vänern, it is best to have four of them out at different depths, in order to determine how deep the salmon are keeping for the day. At the first strike on one or two swivel lures – often two or three are taken at the same time – the rowers should stop the boat instantly, pull in the rear oars, and slowly draw up the swivel lures that have not been striked. But the salmon, or other fish that have striked, can run out with the loose line: usually he runs out quickly for 25-50 meters, and stops. He can then be carefully tired and, finally, boarded with a land-

Waters full of fish in majestic surroundings have attracted many sportfishermen to Scandinavia.
One of the first to thoroughly describe the fishing and its methods was Llewellyn Lloyd, an English enthusiast.
This illustration comes from his book "Scandinavian Adventures" (1853) and represents harling, an effective
and popular way of trolling in the great northern salmon and trout rivers.

ing net or gaff. During the 1850s, this was a highly pleasant and profitable way of fishing, and there were many good days on Vänern when I brought up 12 to 15 beautiful, shining salmon weighing 7-25 pounds (3-10.6 kilograms)."

The traditional Indian fishing waters in the American Northwest became a great center for Pacific salmon trolling early on, with the coastal waters and rivers of British Columbia, Washington and Oregon attracting sportfishermen from near and far. Chinook weighing 83 lbs (38 kg) were taken with rods in these places in the early 1900s.

More than 150 years ago, trolling with a rod, reel and artificial lures, for salmon and trout among other species, was a successful form of leisure fishing in Scandinavian waters. At that time it was often called swivel-lure fishing.

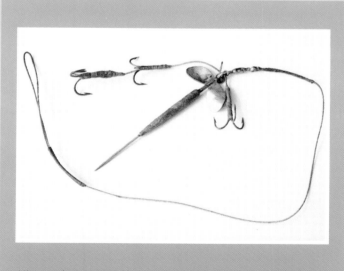

Nineteenth-century tackle for trolling with natural bait. Here, "propeller blades" were used to combine the respective advantages of natural bait and artificial lures for stimulating several of the fish's senses.

Big-game fishing equipment from the first half of our century. The split-cane rod (Salt Water Palakona No.4) as well as the "Fortuna" reel are made by Hardy in England. The line is a 54-strand Cuttyhunk spun from Irish hair. Many big bluefin tuna were vanquished during the 1930s and 1940s in the North Sea and Öresund with this type of gear.

An area as large as the Great Lakes in the northern USA has, of course, attracted many people who can be called pioneering sportfishermen. Still, it is widely accepted that the trolling pioneer George Raff, through his fundamental innovations during the period between the World Wars, was the one who laid the foundations for sportfishing on the Great Lakes. His catches in the deep northeastern part of Lake Michigan, already in the 1920s, revealed colossal concentrations of lake trout and indicated how to get at them with sportfishing equipment.

The big breakthrough for modern trolling techniques, including downrigger fishing, came about in the backwash of environmental conservation efforts in the North American Great Lakes in the 1960s. Twenty years later the wave reached Sweden, which now has the world's best fishing for land-locked Atlantic salmon in Lake Vänern and Lake Vättern. Add to this the fact that in the Baltic Sea, the world's largest brackish sea, trollers take hundreds of Atlantic salmon weighing 45-60 lb (20-27 kg) every year.

The role of big-game fishing

Hunting huge fish in the sea has had tremendous significance for the development of sportfishing, and notably of trolling, around the world. Moreover, it is through big-game fishing that certain places have gained a global reputation and experienced a heyday that would otherwise be impossible.

Tarpon is regarded as the instigator of big-game fishing, and the rivers and coastal waters of Florida were the source of inspiration in the 1880s.

The origins of big-game fishing itself, however, are generally thought to lie at Santa Catalina Island, California. There in 1898, Charles F. Holder, caught a bluefin tuna of 183 lbs (83 kg) and founded the Tuna Club, the world's first big-game fishing club. This organization and its members left a strong mark on the sport during the first decade of our century.

In 1912 and 1913, the trio of William Boschen, Julius vom Hofe and Joe Coxe constructed the first geared reel with a spool that could be disengaged, as well as a drag system that included a reverse catch on the crank. The drag could be externally adjusted via a star wheel. Boschen, a Catalina member, was the brain behind the whole concept, Coxe the source of the idea for the star wheel, and vom Hofe the one who manufactured the prototype reel. To honor Boschen for his pioneering ideas, vom Hofe named the reel B-Ocean.

Fifteen years further on, Oliver C. Grinnell introduced one of the leading lures of all time for trolling: the Japanese feather jig.

West Atlantic and Nova Scotia rod catches came into hot spotlight in 1924, when Zane Grey, the great trolling pioneer of saltwater fishing, brought in a tuna of 758 lbs (345 kg). Zane Grey's distinction as a big-game fisherman had an enormous impact on and world-wide significance for sportfishing during period between the World Wars. Grey made pioneering expeditions with his own boats, on the world's seas.

In Grey's wake , such big-game fisherman as Harlan Major, Michael Lerner, Tommy Gifford, S. Kip Farrington Jr., Jimmy Whittall, Lee Wulff, Van Campen Heilner, Philip Wylie and Ernest Hemingway – another writer, whose work gave the sport a great lift – appeared on the east coast of North America. New fishing arenas, competitions attracting big audiences, and ever heavier fish were the result.

Lerner and Farrington made remarkable catches in Soldiers Rip, Wedgeport, Nova Scotia, which Farrington called "the biggest little fishing hole in the world". The most effective fishing method was no longer angling but trolling at about 4

The downrigger has revolutionized trolling techniques in the last few decades. My first downrigger, made of brass, was built at home during the early 1970s, from a model advertised in an American sportfishing magazine. Equipped with both a line counter and brake, it opened up a whole new world of fishing to me.

The IGFA is an international sportfishing organization, represented in some 75 countries, which registers world records for different line classes and fish species, and supports the worldwide development of sportfishing and fish management.

knots with the hook concealed in mackerel that was dragged about 25 yards (25 m) behind the boat, sometimes with an outrigger pole.

Kip Farrington wrote in *Field & Stream* in 1949 that Öresund – the sound between Sweden and Denmark - was one of the world's best arenas for tuna, that nowhere else on earth was it possible for individual fishermen to take so many tuna on the same day. Swedes and Danes took great numbers of fish over 650 lbs (300 kg), and the record example of 820 lbs (372 kg) rose in 1950 to a Dane, Knud Kyvsgaard. Given the limited resources of the boats in Öresund – most of the fishing was done from cutters – most of the tuna were taken while drifting rather than trolling.

Cairns in northeastern Australia, with the eormous Great Barrier Reef beyond it, is a place that has had enormous significance for the development of saltwater trolling during the second half of the twentieth century. About 60% of all black marlin over 1000 lbs (455 kg) – including a giant of 1442 lbs (635 kg) – have been caught there. The breakthrough came in 1966

when Captain George Bransford, with mate Richard Obach, caught the first 1000-pounder, 1064 lbs (484 kg) to be precise. During high season, there are about 60 highly equipped 50-foot big-game boats operating off "the Marlin Coast".

The pioneering IGFA

It was Michael Lerner of the USA and Clive Firth of Australia who founded the International Game Fish Association (IGFA) in 1939. The organization soon became worldwide, and boasted none other than Ernest Hemingway as vice president from 1940 until his death in 1962. The IGFA began to formulate and print international sportfishing regulations, and to register marine fishing records in accordance with these rules.

The IGFA has been reorganized a couple of times since 1939. At present, one of its main objectives is to promote the best possible protection for species of interest to sportfishermen, and to see that the latter's rights are recognized. A second, and very important, goal is to support programs for tagging sportfish, as well as other scientific efforts to collect data.

Technique and Strategy

A trolling fisherman is like a decathlon athlete. The more fields he masters and combines, the greater his chances of success, whatever the event. Ever more sportfishermen regard trolling as the truly big challenge. This is not only because all-round skill pays off, but, perhaps above all, because trolling in its modern form is one of the most sporting variants of sportfishing activities. Trolling can be done in different a number of different ways from a simple drift boat as well as from an exclusive motor cruiser.

Today's trolling equipment has not only erased traditional concepts and distinctions within trolling. It has also revolutionized the sport in a way that has given boatfishing totally new dimensions. Earlier the "weight" of the gear dictated the depth at which one could fish. Now, thanks to downriggers, leaf-thin lures can be used at a depth of 350 feet (about 100

meters) with a rod and reel weighing no more than ordinary flyfishing equipment. Formerly, too, the line had to be weighted with a sinker in front of the lure, to get it down to a depth of 35 ft (about 10 m). But there are many plugs shaped to easily reach this depth today.

The boat and the equipment aboard, together with biological facts – the whereabouts of the fish and their behavior in different environments – determine, in large measure, the technique and strategy of trolling in the given fishing waters. The technique may involve a choice between surface and depth trolling, or a combination of both. The strategy may consist of how to fish different areas, such as shorelines, deep holes, and skerries. Your decisions often determine how the equipment should be arranged on board the boat, how fast the boat should be driven, and so on. It is through variation that the senses are stimulated, both on and under the surface of the water.

"Systematic" is also a key word for handling the equipment. Place your gear where it is easy to see and reach - and so that it fishes at different depths and distances from the boat without getting tangled.

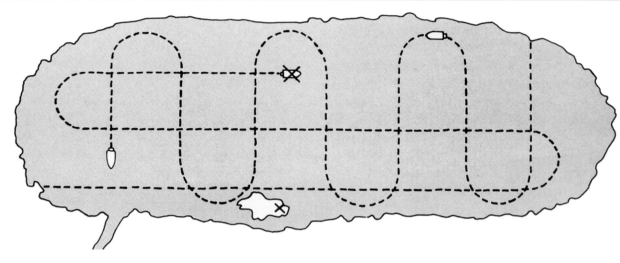

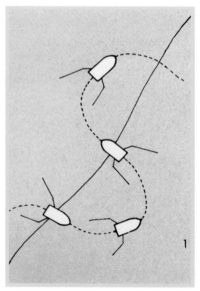

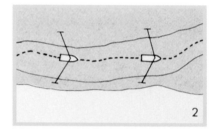

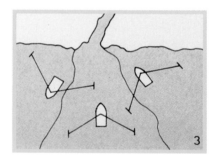

1. Instead of trolling in a straight line, follow a zigzag course over a drop-off or rise. When you turn, the innermost lure slows down and, if it is a sinking type, goes deeper. However, a floating type will temporarily approach the surface.

2. A coastal stretch with varying depth contours and temperature zones can be covered effectively with the help of planer boards and outrigger rods, which bring the lures out sideways from the boat.

3. Junctions are often nutritious and diverse in temperature, so they tend to gather fish. Color contrasts on the surface can reveal how the water flows through a tributary's mouth. Cover the fishing area and its zones by moving across it in different directions.

Above: Trolling enables us to fish over large areas and varying depths, as well as often being successful even in unknown waters. The basic fact under all conditions is that the holding places of fish can change in location - depending on the current, depth, temperature, salinity and bottom configuration. Moreover, both prey and predatory fish concentrate at points, banks, rises, inlets or outlets, and underwater springs. To find their real positions, you must systematically comb the water by trolling in parallel lines: for example, first north-south and then east-west. If you lack modern navigation equipment, landmarks and your own floating markers can guide and assist you in fishing out the water efficiently.

For the initiated sportfisherman, trolling is much more than just aimlessly dragging a lure behind a boat. It is a type of fishing where large areas and varying depths are systematically covered. Guessing can be eliminated by paying attention to the surface features of the water, watching for eddies, temperature spots and birds. With experience, one also learns to understand the language of the water surface under changing conditions, and can quickly analyze questions about the lure or bait, its depth, and the dragging length of the fishing line.

Whether he is surface trolling or depth trolling, and no matter how many rods he is using, it is important for the fisherman to know what effect the maneuvering of the boat has on the lure being trolled. Usually a trolling fisherman zigzags through the water. This makes the lure change speed and run at different depths without the fisherman having to shift gears or speed up the boat. Yawing causes the inside lure to lose speed, going deeper if it is a sinker, or rising if it is a floater. Just as important as knowing how to navigate the boat is knowing which kinds of equipment work well together, and how to present lures and baits in a varied and attractive way in well-thought-out trolling patterns. Using inappropriate equipment can not only lead to problems such as tangles, but also make for inefficient fishing. In other words, the fish may never be attracted to the lure or bait.

Surface trolling

Trolling in surface water is usually done with unweighted line – that is, with only the lure on the end of the line. This can be accomplished with a rod directly from the boat, called flatline fishing, or by guiding the lure away from the boat with the use of an outrigger or a planer board. With the latter, the range of fishing can be broadened and fish can be reached that otherwise might be frightened away by the water turbulence caused by the motion of the boat.

Flatline fishing

Flatline fishing is the oldest and most common variety of trolling. This is what people normally think of as trolling, irrespective of whether it takes place in running water, in a lake, or on the open ocean. The success of flatline fishing usually depends on how far the lure is dragged behind the boat and how it is maneuvered.

For diverse reasons, certain attractive trolling fish congregate periodically over shallow water. If, at that time, there are

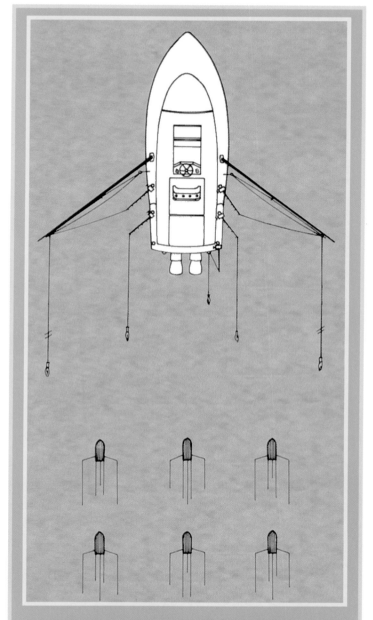

The extreme shyness of some fish species makes it essential to spread your equipment in a systematic way, particularly when surface trolling. This distribution also helps you decide which lures to use and how to manoeuvre the boat. The latter method may go all wrong if you use different types of lines (mono, dacron, wire) in the same trolling pattern, or lures that are too dissimilar.

Normally we describe the trolling pattern as a "W" or "M". The reason is clear from the relationship between the line ends, as illustrated here. To avoid line tangle, the middle line should be either longest or shortest. These standard patterns have been developed through the decades on trolling grounds all over the world.

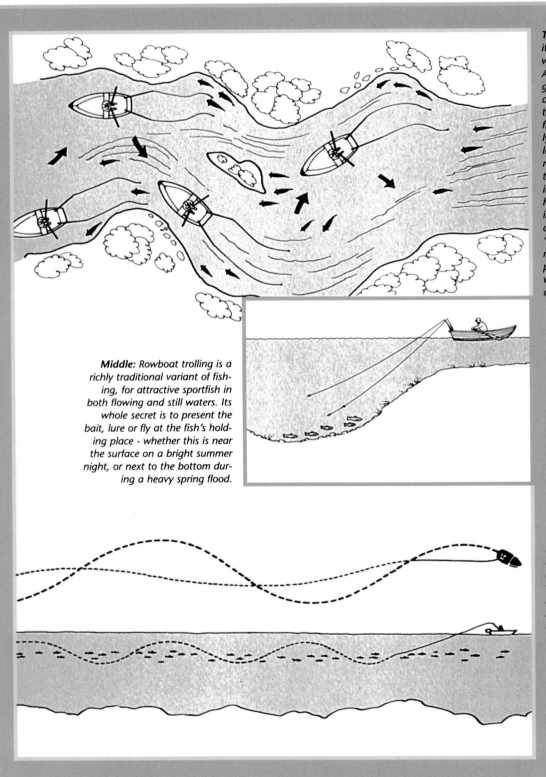

Top: In large, deep salmon rivers it is common to fish by harling, which covers the water effectively. An experienced rower can then give the lure a far more attractive action than what a fisherman on the banks can achieve. The rower/fisherman crosses the river obliquely against the current, while the lures (flies, spoons, wobblers or natural bait) fish downstream over the holding places of fish. By crossing back and forth, he slowly fishes his way downstream. A very important point is that the line and lure, at every turn, should be "stretched out" fully before the next crossing begins. The rowing pace and the setback line length will depend on the river's character and the current strength.

Middle: Rowboat trolling is a richly traditional variant of fishing, for attractive sportfish in both flowing and still waters. Its whole secret is to present the bait, lure or fly at the fish's holding place - whether this is near the surface on a bright summer night, or next to the bottom during a heavy spring flood.

Bottom: A bird's-eye view shows how a lure runs in relation to the boat's zigzag course. The underwater view indicates how the same lure behaves at depth, without increasing the engine turnover or the boat's speed.

several boats at the fishing site, the fish may become especially timid and cautious. If, in addition, the trolling is being done in clear water, the fish can be extremely difficult to entice and the only solution may be to use extra-long fishing lines.

A long line means one that keeps the lure at least 250 ft (75 m) from the boat. This calls for secure hooking, silent lines, and super-sharp hooks. To reduce the wind effect and improve hooking, the flatline may go directly from the tip of the rod to a line release or clip mounted in the boat.

Every year there are, of course, many freshwater, saltwater, and brackwater trollers who claim that they catch lots of fish, such as salmon and salmon trout, almost right up in the foam of the propeller. They maintain that the fish, far from being frightened, are probably attracted by the boat and motor.

In the world of big-game trolling, it is more or less routine to have the lure skip or swim along on the second wave in the wake of the boat. In such cases, a number of different kinds of teasers are normally dragged near the stern.

Simply dragging a long line on a straight course through the water is not very exciting, either for the sportfisherman or for the fish. Variation above and below the surface stimulates the senses. This is where the maneuvering of the boat becomes important. Sometimes an ordinary zigzag is enough to make the lure look like an injured fish.

Ordinarily, however, the zigzag must be complemented by speeding up or slowing down the boat, or else by yawing sharply. When this happens, the zigzag starts to resemble an S-formation. Another good reason for varying the maneuvering of the boat is that fish which escape from the boat, and then quickly return to where they were before, may very well run into the towed lure and strike.

Traditionally, flatline fishing has been classified as surface trolling. Today, however, access to the deep-diving plugs makes this classification seem a bit beside the point. The truth of the matter is that these plugs can go down to depths which, in other circumstances, would be called deep-trolling levels.

Outriggers

The outrigger has its origin in ocean fishing. It was designed to be able to simultaneously position and spread several lures outside the wake of the boat. It therefore projects at a 45-degree angle from the side of the boat. Among big-game fishermen looking for billfish, it is very common to present live bait on an outrigger pole. The bait is presented while skipping on, or swimming just below, the surface. Although the dragging distance from the stern varies, it seldom exceeds 165 ft (50 m).

The number of trolling lures in action behind a boat depends on the size of the craft, the surrounding circumstances – such as waves, wind, currents, and depth of water – and the type of fish one wants to catch. Naturally, even the number of passengers aboard the boat and their competence make a difference.

The size of the boat influences the choice of an outrigger. This determines the size of the lure or bait, which in turn has an effect on the boat speed and line length. An overweighted outrigger offers no attractive lure or bait.

Usually the fisherman employs two outriggers, one to port and one to starboard. Having extra-long outriggers is not as important as how they are used in combination with the navigation of the boat, the fishing tackle and the lure. It is also essential for you to be able to easily and quickly cast an eye at the line release.

The outrigger is equipped with guides or spiders, and usually with a roller guide on top, through which a halyard is passed as on a flagpole. The halyard is provided with a line release, or clip. When the desired amount of fishing line has been rolled from the reel, the line is pinched into the clip. This should be done while the boat is moving slowly. The clipped fishing line is run out toward the tip of the outrigger, where it is placed in position. To prevent it from slipping, the halyard is fastened to the railing with a tensor band. On large and sturdy poles, it is possible to use several halyards and clips at the same time, and thus several lures.

Some fishermen tighten up the fishing line to keep it from getting caught by the wind before the rod and reel are placed in the rod-holder. Others leave a little slack, so that the fish will not feel the resistance right after striking and spit out the lure.

There are also different schools of thought concerning how hard the reel-drag should be set. Some set the drag hard in order to be able to set the hook as soon as the line has been jerked from the clip and stretched. Others use a light drag and let the fish make an initial fast run before the hook is set. However, if the fish jumps, you must strike back immediately.

It often happens that outrigger fish spit out the lure or never get properly hooked. This is because of the slack in the line, called the knockdown, when the line falls as it is jerked from the release by the striking fish. One way to improve on the hooking statistics and catches is to connect a tag-line, sometimes called a stinger-line, to the release or halyard line. The tag-line can be of thick mono (2 millimeters) or dacron (400 lbs) and is usually half a yard (meter) longer than the actual outrigger. It streams aft, typically at a perpendicular angle to the outrigger line when under load. The fishing line will accordingly be dragged farther behind the stern and near the surface than before. When the fish strikes the line is released with less slack and the fish will be better hooked.

Outriggers do not give the same breadth of fishing as one can get when using planer boards. But they are definitely easier to use in combination with downriggers when fishing both widely and deeply. Note that, when using outriggers together with other fishing tackle, the outrigger gear is the first to be deployed and the last to be taken in.

Of course, no rules are without exceptions. The last rule is broken when trolling in Hawaii. There, many boats prefer to use their outrigger poles in a nearly upright position. The pattern used for trolling here is neither to proceed along a broad front, nor to have the lure skip along on the surface. Instead, the idea is to drag the artificial high-speed lures, called kona heads, in a row at 30-130 ft (10-40 m) behind the boat, so that they occasionally break the surface. This causes a trail of bubbles that attracts fish. The technique pays off and results every year in remarkable catches of yellowfin tuna and blue marlin.

Planer boards

The planer board fulfills the same function as the outrigger. It spreads out the lures and makes it possible to fish in water that has not been disturbed by the boat. Fishing with planers is much more common in lakes and coastal waters than on the open ocean. The technique is used primarily during the spring and autumn, when the fish move near the surface or over shallow water. Planers can be used to "serve" lures in water that is too shallow or uncertain for a boat and crew to pass through.

Planer boards come in many models and sizes. When an ordinary planer board is used, the spool or mast must be easy to get at, placed high and as far forward in the boat as possible. This provides a good high line angle between the reel and the planer. It causes the planer to move parallel with, and at approximately the same level as, the boat. The smallest are

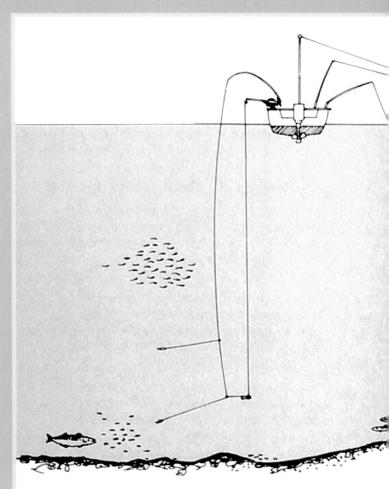

Top: Coastal waters may abound in fish. Some species stay entirely in this zone, though others enter it only periodically. Modern trolling techniques, however, have made it possible to fish these waters even if they are very shallow or sharply plunging.

By using planer boards, you can present lures quite near the shore, for instance where the boat is too deep for the water or where it would frighten the fish. A directional diver will enable you to cover cliff shelves and other formations on a shore slope. A downrigger allows presentation of feather-light lures in, and over, deep edges and holes close inshore.

Bottom: Most fish species migrate between deep and shallow waters. This may happen either seasonally, or several times daily. A point swept by a current, with a deep hole just off it, frequently lies on such a migration route. The illustration shows how to fish a coastal zone and slopes, and finally zigzag around the hole's deep edges.

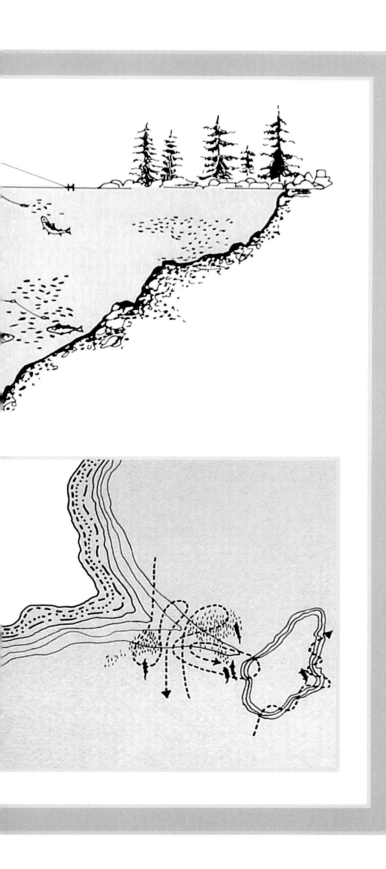

clipped directly to the fishing line. In case of a strike, they are released to slide down the line. They are easy to handle but are also readily disturbed by waves.

How far out the planers are to be placed depends on how many lures or baits you are fishing, how shallow you can go with the boat, and how much space you have in relation to other planer-board fishermen. Some planers allow you to fish up to 250 ft (75 m) from a boat, whereas the smallest have a range of only about 50 ft (15 m).

After the planer board has been put into place, the desired length of fishing line is fed out from the trolling reel. The line is then clipped to a release, which is constructed so as to allow the line to slide along the towline until it reaches the desired position. The rod and reel are placed as far to the stern as possible. When the fish strikes, the line is jerked from the release and the fish is played directly from the rod and reel. The clip slides down toward the plane where it remains hanging, and thus cannot get lost.

Planers may be used to fish surface as well deep-running plugs. The latter demand a little extra resistance from the line release, in order to avoid too many false releases. Do not mix the lures too much, and remember to use lures which work well together – that is to say, which accept the same speed. The length of the dragged fishing line is usually between 15 and 165 ft (5-50 m). Fishing the longest lines nearest the planers reduce the risk for tangled lines.

Depending on the weather, the number of fishermen and their experience, up to half a dozen rods can be deployed from each side of the boat. The disadvantages of planer boards become most apparent during severe weather. They move in a stop-and-go fashion and give false releases. Trying to land a big fighting fish in a heavy head sea causes extra problems because the boat cannot be stopped without risking tangles. If you are alone in the boat when this occurs, there is also a danger that the joy of fishing may become the death of the fisherman.

The tow of the planer is noticeable when steering small boats – especially if only one planer is used, the boat being pulled in its direction. As a matter of principle, when fishing with planers one needs to have plenty of room as one tries to turn the boat. Check to make sure that all planers are moving forward; otherwise the fishing will be inefficient, and you run the risk of tangles or snags.

Deep trolling

A saying that I have heard in many parts of the world is that for every fish you see on the surface, there are ten more in the depths. If so, it is there that you should mainly offer your lures. But how deep is deep, you might ask? No exact answer can be given to this. Over the years, I have learned that what is known as deep trolling in one place may very well be called surface trolling in another.

However, the confusing terminology is not really decisive in trolling. What is important, rather, is that the lures can be presented in a sporting manner at the depths where fish exist, regardless of whether the water is in a shallow flatland lake or a deep ocean trough. And this can now be done – in different ways – much better than in the past.

The line – a crucial factor

How deep a lure can reach on a monoline without extra weight depends upon the diameter and length of the fishing line, the shape of the lure, and the speed of the boat. In a nutshell, one can say that the thinner the line, the more distant the fishing, the better the lure is designed for deep diving, and the slower one trolls, then the deeper the lure will run.

But theory is one thing, and the practice of fishing is another. Here it is not simply a question of getting a lure down to the fish: they also have to be hooked. The longer a monoline, the harder it is to hook the fish. A troller therefore tries to hook the fish with as short a line as possible.

Fast, deep-diving plugs are helpful in this respect. Tests have shown that they can reach to a depth of 33 ft (10 m) using a 12-lb line with a length of 80 ft (25 m). At a speed of

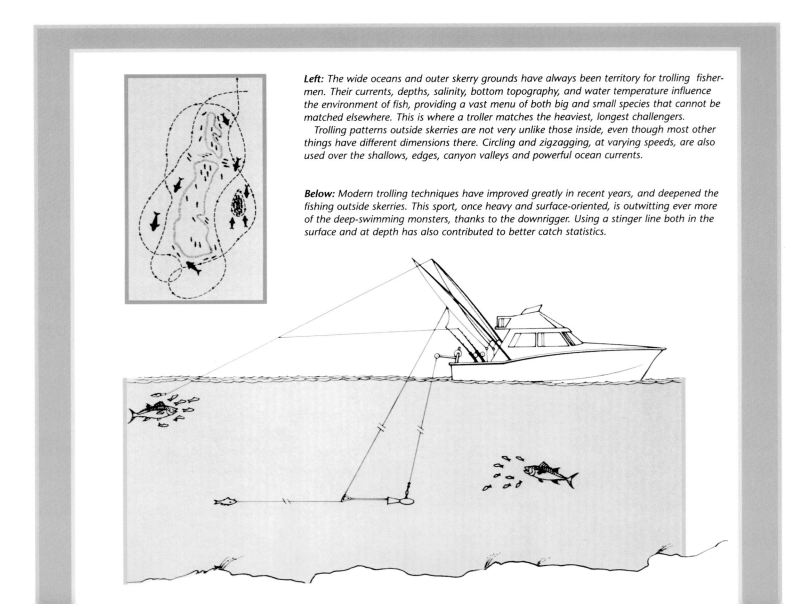

Left: The wide oceans and outer skerry grounds have always been territory for trolling fishermen. Their currents, depths, salinity, bottom topography, and water temperature influence the environment of fish, providing a vast menu of both big and small species that cannot be matched elsewhere. This is where a troller matches the heaviest, longest challengers.

Trolling patterns outside skerries are not very unlike those inside, even though most other things have different dimensions there. Circling and zigzagging, at varying speeds, are also used over the shallows, edges, canyon valleys and powerful ocean currents.

Below: Modern trolling techniques have improved greatly in recent years, and deepened the fishing outside skerries. This sport, once heavy and surface-oriented, is outwitting ever more of the deep-swimming monsters, thanks to the downrigger. Using a stinger line both in the surface and at depth has also contributed to better catch statistics.

1.5 knots, if the lure was released with 165 ft (50 m) of line, the lure descended to a depth of 50 ft (15 m).

An ancient way of reaching thermoclines and bottoms has otherwise been to weigh down the line with some kind of sinker. Today's trollers prefer specially designed sinkers that are shaped so as to give the least possible water resistance and to prevent them from snagging easily. The sinker release type comes in a variety of models, all of which release the sinker when the fish strikes. This revolutionary discovery means that the fish can be played without dragging a heavy weight, thus giving the trolling fisherman a more memorable duel.

Today a troller generally uses mono-, cofilament-, dacron- or superlines – if he or she does not prefer to seek the depths with the help of heavy lines made of lead core or wire. Fishing by these means has a long tradition in many parts of the world, and it has enabled both saltwater and freshwater fishermen to bring up giants from deep currents and bottoms. However, with the arrival of the downrigger in the realm of trolling, the wire line's importance has been diminishing over the past decades.

The advantages are that a feather-light lure can be taken down to great depths with a short line, even in swift currents, and that it is very easy to tell when you have a bite. One needs no special accessories or specially shaped lures to get down to 30 ft (10 m) at 2-3 knots with a line of 100 ft (30 m).

The disadvantages are that the lines often demand special rods and reels, and the fishing must be done with extra care. Nor should they normally be combined with more traditional fishing gear.

The diving planer

Divers have old and global merits in the world of sportfishing. Thanks to various improvements during the 1980s, they are experiencing a well-deserved renaissance, and few trolling fishermen would want them to be missing from the tacklebox. Special high-speed planes are available.

The diving planer is attached to the fishing line above the leader and lure. When the planer hits the water, the resistance of the water causes it to head downward. How deep it goes will depend on its own shape, the lure's shape, the diameter of the fishing line, and the trolling speed. When the fish strikes, the special trip mechanism is released and the fish can be reeled in without much water resistance from the diver.

Some divers can be adjusted so that they move sideways from the boat. These can get down to about 30 ft (10 m) with

Even in a small boat, well-arranged rigging gives good coverage of the water both to the sides and downward.

a 0.45-millimeter line (20 lbs) having a length of 80 ft (25 m). This line diameter is normal for fishing with divers. Even the leader, 3-5 ft (90-150 cm) long, should be at least this thick. All kinds of lures can be fished successfully behind a diver, including dodgers or flashers with squids or flies. The diver itself often seems to function as a lure. The lure is affected by the diver's sensitivity to the movements of the boat, giving it a particularly irrational action.

The diver complements downrigger fishing by widening the parallel pattern of deep trolling. Baits can easily be led over otherwise hard-to-reach shelves on a deep bank. Given a separate line with a special release, it can be used alone as a simple downrigger.

One disadvantage to be reckoned with is that you need a fairly sturdy rod (there are specially designed diving plane rods) when the diver is to be pulled through the water. The pull of the diver on the rod means that the rodholder must also be strong and of high quality. Furthermore – as with other deep-trolling techniques, except that of downrigger fishing – it is difficult to define the depth precisely. The observant fisherman should, however, have no great difficulty navigating through the same trolling patterns as used in surface trolling.

The downrigger

It is said that in the time since sportfisherman started using the outboard motor, no other single piece of equipment has meant so much to fishing as the downrigger. The downrigger has not only deepened fishing but has also widened its horizons.

Generally it can be claimed that, in one way or another, the downrigger plays a role in all sportfishing from a boat, regardless of the type of environment. It provides the fisherman with the ability to determine more precisely how deep or how shallow the lure should run. He is also given the great sporting advantage of being able to adapt his gear to the size of the fish, and not primarily to the surrounding circumstances such as wind, current, and water depth.

A downrigger is a separate piece of equipment that consists of a spool with wire line, and an arm with a guide at the end through which the wire passes. The sinker weight is placed on the end of the wire. The line release is attached to either the sinker or the wire. Most downriggers even come equipped with counters, drag, and rod-holder. The down-

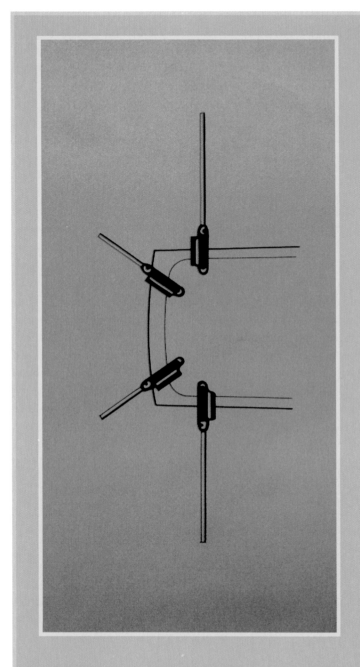

Here the fishing line is mounted in a line release which is coupled to the downrigger's weight. The release can also be placed on the downrigger wire. The line distance between release and lure depends on the fishing depth and the visibility in the water.

The picture shows how you should adapt the number and size of downriggers to the boat's dimensions. It is important to position the rigs so that they will not risk safety on board,

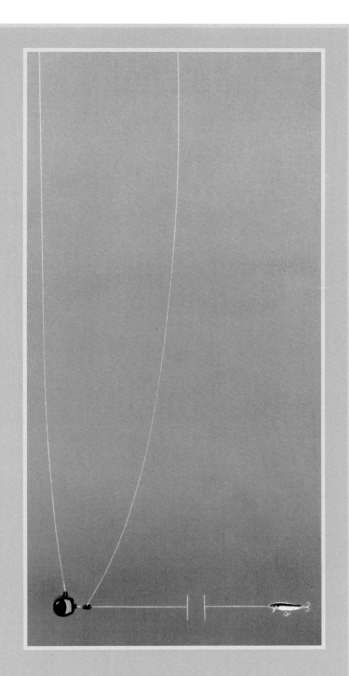

for example by blocking access to a motor. Try also to place them as far astern as possible. But remember that the rod and other items should be easy to reach and keep an eye on.

Long-boomed rigs are best located on the port and starboard decks, and rigs with standard or medium-long booms on the after-deck, since this provides optimum spreading. There are several options for how to mount the rigs in place.

rigger's technical details are described in chapter 3, Trolling Equipment.

The downrigger should be securely mounted, easy to get at, and easy to see. This usually means that it is placed in the stern-most third of the boat. There it can be arranged to point sideways or straight back.

Irrespective of the fishing depth, one should try to keep the sinker as directly vertical under the boat as possible. This is regulated by the sinker's shape and weight. If you can see the sinker in your sonar, then it is in a good position.

The line release is responsible for the first hookup. How hard the release tension should be set depends on type of fish being sought, the trolling speed, and the size of the lure. It is important that the fishing line should not slip in the release. By using several line releases, one can fish several (two or three) lines from the same downrigger cable. This is called " stacking".

The downrigger may be said to function like an outrigger, but in a vertical direction. In some circumstances, it can be used in combinations. Start by pushing the free-spool button on your fishing reel. Use the alarm click and then feed out the desired length of fishing line. This can vary between 3 and 250 ft (1-75 m) depending on the type of fish you are after, how deep they are running, and the depth of visibility. Generally, the deeper you fish, the shorter the line between the release and the lure. A short line allows better hooking, and greater maneuverability of the boat in order to follow irregular bottom contours.

If the fishing reel does not have a line counter, then the dragging length can be estimated, for instance, by eye or by counting the number of hand lengths of line between the reel and the lowest guide on the rod. Place the rod in a rod-holder and the line in the release. Before lowering the sinker weight down to the desired depth, check that the line is not twisted around the tip of the rod.

Remember that the counter indicates how far the sinker is from the point – arm tip or water surface – at which it was set to zero. Therefore, it does not register the level of the sinker and lure with perfect accuracy. Ordinarily a sonar can be used to verify exactly where they are running.

The next step is to reel in the slack and tense the line, so that the specially designed rods assume a J-bend. The line should point as straight down towards the sinker or line release as possible.

A variety of boom lengths on your downriggers will spread out the lures underwater. Models differ as regards the fishing line's attachment and the downrigger's line release, but the line should be fastened so that it cannot slip in the release.

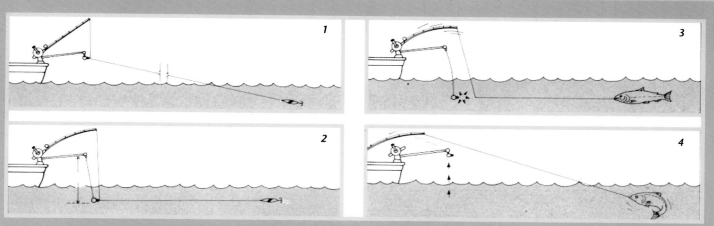

Downrigger fishing involves using light equipment and leaf-thin lures to fish at great depths. The basic technique is shown briefly here.
1. Feed out the line and lure until you reach the desired setback distance. Place the line in the release, which may be on either the sinker or wire.
2. Freespool the reel with your line-out alarm on. Sink the weight and lure to the desired fishing depth, which can be read on the downrigger's counter.

3. When the fish takes, it pulls line free from the release. Usually it is hooked adequately by the release's own resistance at that moment.
4. Grab the rod from the rod-holder, perhaps making an extra strike. Then play the fish directly from the rod. Reel in the downrigger wire and weight as soon as possible.

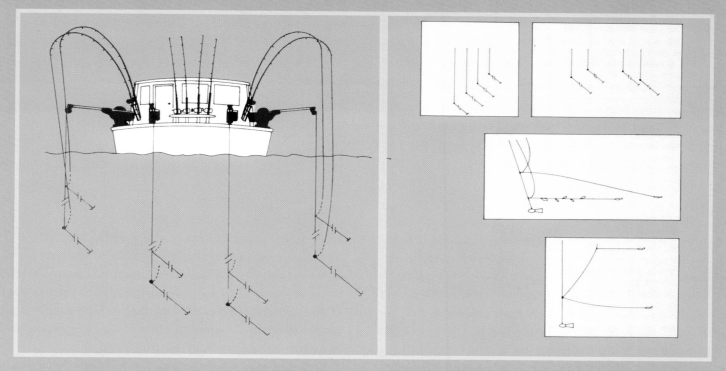

Most downriggers have one or more rod-holders. As shown here, for instance, you can fish with two rods from each downrigger. A reel line is attached in the line release closest to the weight, while a "stacker line" is placed in a release farther up on the wire. It is essential to systematize the rod arrangement on board, so that you can fish well with a minimum risk of line tangle under the surface.

The distance between two line set-ups on the same downrigger wire should be variable, in order to cover a range of depths. Moreover, the setback line distance behind the boat should differ.

Normally the lure is 6-33 ft (2-10 metres) from the weight and line release, but sometimes they are 100-165 ft (30-50 metres) apart. Among other things, the depth of visibility, type of lure, and pattern of currents influence this separation. Generally it is made shorter for fishing deeper.

You can also place several lures close together, to make them look like a school of fish. The same effect is obtainable with diverse models of flashing attractors. By sliding a lure on a short leader along the line, you can give the impression of one fish chasing another. Try to stimulate the fish's aggressivity with your lure arrangement.

Trolling is a fascinating way of fishing. Lining this highroad to the fish are many details for attentive sportsmen to harvest.

Trolling speed

Trolling speed may vary anywhere between a couple of knots and twenty. The range of trolling varieties, however, makes the terminology of speed hard to understand. This is most obvious when, for instance, a marlin troller discusses the subject with a salmon troller. What the former calls slow speed or "no speed at all", the latter takes to be top speed.

The more one trolls, the more one becomes convinced of the great influence the speed of the boat has on the action of the boat as it passes through the water. In the long run, a constant dynamic action has a greater effect than the size, color, and shape of the lure.

There are many factors to consider when the objective is to call forth the lure's most enticing movements. Besides the influence of the boat and the motor, consideration must be given to the current and the presence or absence of wind and waves.

A good estimation of the effectiveness of different kinds of lures under various fishing circumstances is obtained by keeping a fishing log. Remember, though, that if you note a lure as attracting fish "best at 2.5 knots", then this is only valid for the speedometer in your own boat. A speedometer in another boat running parallel to yours may indicate a different figure for the "same" speed. In other words, you cannot easily transfer speed figures from one boat to another.

Each lure has a speed at which it works best. Due to the fact that trollers normally use several lures at the same time, it is important to use lures that are compatible at a given speed. Some lures have a fairly wide range of tolerance with regard to speed. the easiest way to convince yourself of the lure's action is to check it as the lure is let out beside the boat.

As already mentioned, a speed indicator can be a great help. But there may be drastically different temperatures and cur-

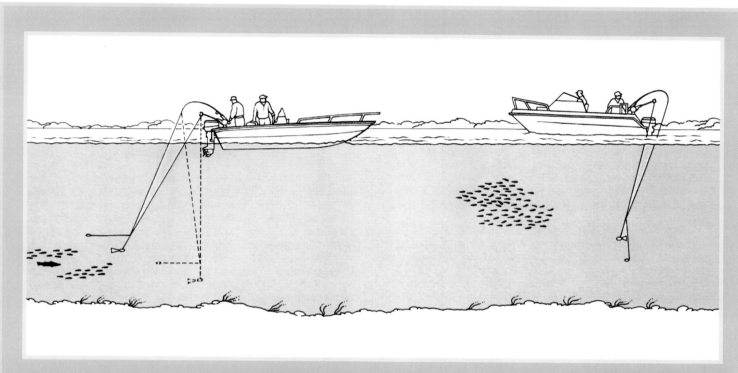

The speed of the boat and lure through the water is decisive for success in fishing. Frequently the conditions at the surface are quite unlike those a few yards below it. For example, currents may be moving in directions opposite to the surface current. The lure will then move very differently from how it did when you tested it at the surface next to the boat.

After a storm, the water mass under a calm surface often flows rapidly in a certain direction. An alert troller can see this from the behavior of his bow waves, from the angles and sounds of his downrigger wires, and possibly from the fact that the fish take only when he is trolling in a particular direction.

Instruments such as a navigator and surface-water speedometer show the speed. If you troll into a current that moves, say, at three knots, the speedometer will show about the same figure. But the navigator, which detects the average speed over the bottom, might reveal that this is only about half a knot.

In this drawing, the boat at left is trolling forward in a strong current. The downrigger wire and lure are pushed upward and do not fish at the intended depth. But the adjacent broken lines indicate what the ideal conditions would be. The weight is at the "correct" depth and the lure's speed is determined by the boat's. The boat at right is going with the current, at about 3 knots according to its speedometer. Here the sinker and lure do not run attractively, as the current is pushing with almost the same speed. For both situations, a good solution may be to troll broadside to the current, and at different angles to it - as well as to use extremely short or long lead lengths, with lures that vary in shape and weight.

rents at a depth of 100-130 ft (30-40 m) than there are on the surface. As a result, the speed you read on the log at the surface does not always match the speed of the lure in the depths.

How can this phenomenon be detected? The surest way is by using an electronic speed and temperature gauge. This instrument sends information about the water temperature and the speed of the currents in the depths by way of telemetry. See Chapter 4.

If you have learned your lessons about the "best speed" for the lures, then all you have to do is speed up or slow down the boat, be watchful and regularly check the action of the rod tips, and the tension and angle of the downrigger wires.

Temperature can also have a great effect on the speed of the boat and the choice of lure. This is because the reaction time of the fish is, in most cases, dictated by the temperature of the surrounding water. In cool water the fish are more likely to be attracted to a slow lure that is vibrating violently, than to one which passes by quickly looking like a fish. In lukewarm water the desired effect might be the exact opposite. It is definitely the sharp-eyed and quick-witted who reap the harvest in the infinitely fascinating worldwide sport of trolling.

Trolling Equipment

Pulling baits and lures through the water from a moving boat can be done either with a simple hand line, with traditional casting gear, or with specially designed trolling equipment. No other group of sportfishermen enjoys as wide a range of options in this respect as the trolling fisherman does – if he or she wants to be ready for everything from the colorful perch in forest lakes to the powerful giants in oceans.

Trolling equipment is not primarily designed for casting. It can be constructed for trolling with a downrigger, for tolerating the wear of wireline fishing, for making strikes with heavy hooks, for pulling up heavy fish from great depths or for having a large line capacity.

In general, this equipment seems to have a well-established form, but its materials are constantly being developed and improved. Today's trolling fishermen are able, largely because of modern design and new materials with less weight as well as more strength, to adapt their equipment to particular fish species in a more sporting and varied way than ever before.

When choosing the equipment, its balance is important. A good reel, line, rod and lure are adapted well to each other. With compatible gear, and proper maintenance, there will be a minimum of problems and a maximum of fishing time.

Classes of equipment

Different pieces of equipment are usually classified in some way when they leave the manufacturer, so that we can match them together correctly. The most common method of classification is a globally accepted line-class system, developed by the International Game Fish Association (IGFA).

Originally this system was introduced for the registering of world records in several line classes. These are 1 kilogram (2 pound), 2 kg (4 lb), 3 kg (6 lb) 4 kg (8 lb), 6 kg (12 lb), 8 kg (16 lb), 10 kg (20 lb), 15 kg (30 lb), 24 kg (50 lb), 37 kg (80 lb) and 60 kg (130 lb). Each figure gives the highest allowed breaking strength of the line when wet, in order to have a record registered in that class. While the IGFA standards are based on the line's strength, they also include rules for the reel's construction and the rod's dimensions.

Another familiar means of dividing up equipment is to classify it on a scale from ultra light to very heavy, in correspondence with the line's breaking strength. This division,

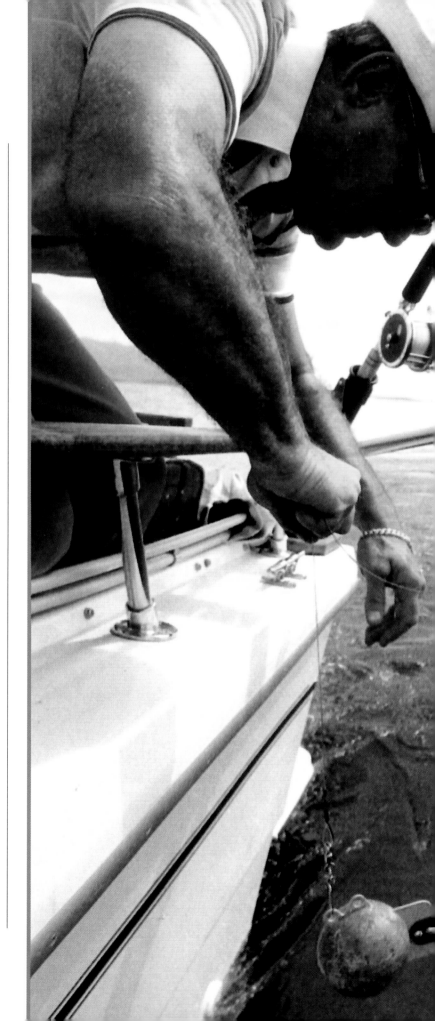

though, is quite flexible. A set-up that proves to be light in a fight with a big tuna will be heavy when it comes to catching ordinary sailfish. Consequently, whether the gear is considered light or heavy depends to a great extent on the fish's size. In any case, the weight classes are: ultralight (1-2 kg), light (4-6 kg), light medium (8-10 kg), medium (15-24 kg), heavy medium (37 kg) and heavy (60 kg). Equipment classified as extra heavy or of "unlimited class" has a line with a breaking strength of more than 60 kg.

There is naturally a vast difference between a set-up in IGFA class 8 kg and one in class 60 kg, as regards strength, weight and appearance. The latter class is built to withstand the real monsters of the world's seas, which sink the scales to at least 500 kg (1,100 lbs) and go by the names of black or blue marlin, bluefin tuna, and the very biggest sharks. By contrast, the former class can be relied upon mainly to tame the leaping salmon of northern latitudes, or the arrow-fast small tuna in southerly waters.

Impacts and rough seas are an aspect of daily life on board, at any rate for the small-boat troller. You should thus insist on a high standard of quality for your equipment from the very beginning, notably for fishing in marine or brackish waters. Of course, you have to do your own part by giving the gear every care and service it requires. This will make your time on board more secure as well as more pleasant. You will also face smaller risks when a dream fish hits the lure, is hooked and jumps up in the air, then bolts away in a long run that almost empties the line from your reel. This is when your relationship with the equipment and with the other members of the crew is revealed.

Regardless of the equipment's line class, it can be used for downrigger fishing. The sinker weight should match the downrigger's size and strength, as well as the type and depth of water.

The rod

Trolling rods differ in their form and materials, depending primarily on how they are used. A deep-trolling rod designed for big salmon and trout in the Baltic Sea has few similarities to a trolling rod for the yellowfin tuna of Hawaii.

The main characteristics of a trolling rod are its length, action and power curve, and the structure and size of its handle, reel seat, and rod rings or rollers. The rod's action shows how it is designed – where the blank flexes, and whether it has fast action, medium action or slow action. In the last case, the rod flexes throughout its length and dampens the fish's movements evenly, whereas tip action means that the rod's upper third is limb and flexes quickly.

The power curve indicates the rod's resistance to deflection. Here the usual division is between light, medium and heavy. With a heavy rod, it is relatively hard to tell how much pres-sure you are putting on the fish. This factor is most important when you fight fish with soft mouths.

Downrigger rods

A downrigger rod's construction makes it far superior to a conventional rod if it is used in combination with a downrigger. The deeper one fishes, the more obvious this becomes. The chief characteristic of a downrigger rod is the J-shaped action curve, which the rod acquires if it stands up tensed in a rod-holder. The rod's extremely fast tip action helps to hook the fish better, while minimizing the line's chance of slipping in the line release. Provided, of course, that the rod is long enough and the downrigger is suitably placed on board.

Downrigger rods come in lengths between 7 and 10 ft (2.1-3.0 m). Most are 8-9 ft (2.4-2.7) long, and divided in two sections. There are models for both multiplier reels and spinning reels. Rods can also have different power curves.

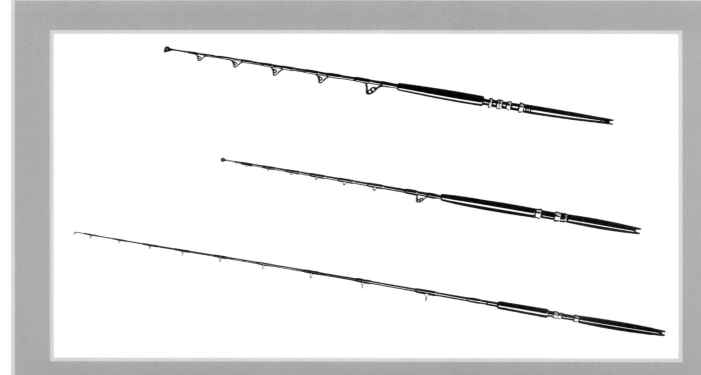

Trolling rods are made for dragging lures or baits, not for casting. Depending on where they are used, they should tolerate standing constantly with strong tension from a downrigger, and being worn by wire lines. They also need enough backbone for powerful strikes with big hooks, and enough capacity to pump up heavy fish from great depths. At top is shown a traditional trolling rod, in the centre a stand-up rod, and at bottom a downrigger rod.

Another striking thing about downrigger rods is their large number of guides, normally from nine to twelve on an 8.5-ft (2.6-m) rod. The guides are closest together at the tip, since they have to lead the line so that it does not lie vibrating against the blank while fishing. This could rapidly ruin even the best line, resulting in lost lures and fish.

The handle should be so long that the rod stands steady in the holder, even on rough seas. A length of 12-14 inches (30-35 cm) will keep the reel and its seat clear of the holder. The foregrip should be at least 5 in (12 cm) long. Both cork and synthetic materials give a good grip, but cork wears down much faster in a rod-holder. The reel seat is another vulnerable part, so the reel seat and its locking ring should be of high quality and keep the reel firmly in place.

The boat's speed, the resistance from the line release when the fish pulls out line, and the rod tip's fast response – all these tend to hook the fish well from the start. A sweeping upward movement when the rod is lifted out of the holder is usually all you need when fishing for salmon. Hard-jawed fish such as pike and walleye demand a stronger counterstrike to get the hook caught.

In recent years, specially designed rods have been introduced for fishing with diving planes. They are normally 9-11 ft (2.7-3.3 m) long, and have a heavy action to be able to pull the plane through the water, 30-50 ft (10-15 m) from the boat. On these rods, too, the guides sit densely in order to control the line.

Stand-up rods

Conventional trolling rods are generally around 7 ft (2.1 m) long, have 5-7 guides including the tip roller, are detachable at the handle, and come with a gimbal butt on the end. The power curve of a classic trolling rod is distributed rather similarly regardless of its class – light, medium or heavy. A weak rod gives fine resistance pressure because of its often evenly distributed action and modest length.

A stand-up rod, in contrast to traditional trolling rods, is primarily built for fighting the fish from a standing position. In European sea fishing, this is the most common fighting position on board. With its action and short length, a stand-up rod is not as ideal for trolling in a rod-holder as the traditional big-game rod, but it is definitely superior for duels along the railing.

The usual length of a stand-up rod is 5-6 ft (1.5-1.8 m). It is not divisible, and the handle is often nearly as long as the blank. Its reel seat sits low, so the reel is easy to balance near your body. The handle's long upper part also enables you to grip it near the center of balance when pulling against the fish. If you play the fish with short, fast pumps, the rod's construction displays all its advantages. To get the most out of these, a fisherman normally uses a very low-hanging rod belt with a gimbal cup, which makes it possible to fight with the hips and legs as well as the arms. A kidney harness can supplement the equipment in the heavier line classes.

Stand-up rods often range over several line classes. For instance, there are rods marked 6-10 kg (12-20 lbs), 15-37 kg (30-80 lbs) and 24-60 kg (50-130 lbs). The short, and frequently tapered, blank may not inspire much confidence, by comparison with traditional big-game fishing rods; but its appearance is deceptive. These rods have a spine which, if properly handled, can lift almost anything up to the surface.

A rod's power curve shows how much it bends under pressure. Its force of resistance is defined as light, medium or heavy. Above is a rod with a stiff blank, and below is one with a soft blank. The action curve, which is often confused with the power curve for a rod, shows where the blank flexes. Here the rod is termed fast, medium or slow.

A downrigger rod under tension. Hallmarks of a trolling rod are its unusual number of guides, and the typical J-bend it assumes when standing tensed in a rod-holder. The many guides are needed to prevent the line from vibrating against the blank, and thus being weakened, while fishing.

The stand-up rod's emergence has enabled contemporary sportsmen all over the world to catch many more fish with three-figure kiloweights from small trolling boats than was possible in the past.

Rod components

A trolling rod consists of the blank, a reel seat, handle and foregrip, ferrules, and guides. The developments in material are very fast, with graphite and mixed materials gaining ground almost everywhere.

The blanks for most contemporary trolling rods are made of composite materials such as graphite and fiberglass, or solely of graphite or tubular fiberglass. In general, graphite rods are more sought-after in the light classes, especially among freshwater fishermen. Carbon-fiber rods feel stiffer than fiberglass rods without loading, but tend to be much more sensitive. A good compromise has been found in the composite rod, which manages to combine the durability of fiberglass with the low weight and sensitivity of carbon fiber.

The handle

Conventional big-game rods are usually detachable at the reel seat, whose main job is to hold the reel steady in a shaky environment. Big-game rods normally have two locking rings that fasten the reel. Reel seats are made of graphite, aluminum, chromed brass, or stainless steel.

The handle may consist of metal, wood, fiberglass, graphite or PVC. A wooden handle can be beautiful, but it requires a lot more maintenance than metal and space-age materials do. Exclusive rods tend to use aluminum, which is lightest but still strong and durable. Some rods in the heavier classes have a curved handle, making it easier to fight from a chair. The rod can be angled more horizontally, with better lever action.

To a growing extent, there is a gimbal nock in the rod's end, even if it is a light one. But you should check that its slot is deep enough, not just decorative. The slot has to make the rod stand more steadily in a holder on the railing, and keep it from turning around during the fight when it is placed in a rod belt,

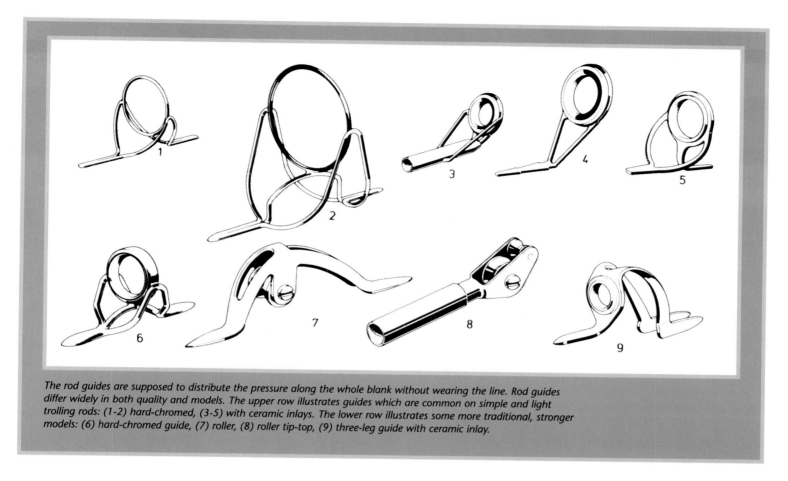

The rod guides are supposed to distribute the pressure along the whole blank without wearing the line. Rod guides differ widely in both quality and models. The upper row illustrates guides which are common on simple and light trolling rods: (1-2) hard-chromed, (3-5) with ceramic inlays. The lower row illustrates some more traditional, stronger models: (6) hard-chromed guide, (7) roller, (8) roller tip-top, (9) three-leg guide with ceramic inlay.

or in a gimbal cup on a fighting chair. The butt should also be made of extra-durable material – metal or graphite – since it is constantly subjected to wear and impact. When a rod is used without a rod belt, the butt should be covered with a rubber cap, to protect both your clothes and your body.

Rod guides

For many sportfishermen, the guides are a rod's hallmark of nobility. It is good advice, then, not to compromise when choosing them.

The task of the rod guides is to hold the line away from the blank, and to distribute the pressure over the whole rod without putting wear on the line. The friction between the line and a guide generates heat, so it is best for big-game fishing to use rollers that rotate as the line runs over them. This, of course, requires them to be kept free from salt deposits and other obstacles, so that they really spin well. On most trolling rods, a tip guide with a roller is a definite advantage.

Roller guides are not preferable, though, when the temperature falls below freezing, since they get plugged up with ice and become more troublesome than useful. Knots can also jam a roller. So always check that sizeable knots, such as a Bimini twist, can pass through the rod's roller and ring guides.

Other high-quality guides to choose among are made of silicon carbide, hardloy and aluminum oxide. Stainless-steel guides are still common on some saltwater rods. As for chromed guides, a line will eventually eat into them because of the salt on it. Tungsten carbide guides, commonly called "Carboloy" guides, are the answer for those who use a wire line. These guides, however, can damage ordinary lines, so a wire-line rod should be used with discretion. As a wire line is not elastic, the rod should be of the slow-action type.

Occasions arise when the trolling fisherman wants to have a rod of 10-15 feet (3-4.5 m) in the boat, for example when fishing with very light lines. A so-called "noodle rod", with rotatable guides, will dampen and compensate for the line's thickness, as well as the fish's leaps and rushes. Similarly, when harling is done from a small boat in a river, it may be desirable to reach out far with the gear – although not, in this case, with extremely light lines or light rods.

Reels

The basic points when selecting a reel for trolling are to be sure that it has enough line capacity for the intended fishing, and that it has a smooth drag which can take the heat of letting out line fast. It must also be able to tolerate a salty environment if used there. Another advantage, which I rank high, is a counter that shows how many yards or meters of line are out. This makes it easier, for instance, to place lures in a relative pattern.

The spinning reel

Trolling for pike, walleye and perch is the main use of a spinning (fixed-spool) reel. The equipment on board then tends to be sparse, as well as easier to supervise and to get at, than when trolling with a downrigger.

Among spinning reels, the Baitrunner or Live liner models are by far the best for trolling. When letting the line out and down, for example, the spool can be disengaged while the slip-drag is still working. In addition, one need not drop the bail in order to feed out the line. The drag is easy to set in advance and to adjust during the fight.

The revolving spool reel

Nine times out of ten, a revolving spool reel is perfect for trolling. A large bait-casting reel serves often as a good trolling reel. The pure trolling reels vary in size, shape and structure according to their purposes. In general, they are strongly built and saltwater resistant, with an ample drag system and a satisfying line capacity. Harness lugs, and an extra safety lock in the form of a clamp around the rod seat, are frequently standard. Reel sizes are numbered from 1/0 to 16/0, or marked with IGFA classes from 12 to 130.

The letter W after a rod's class means that it has an unusually wide spool for its size, and thus holds more line than a normal spool does. Two reels with the same apparent size may also have spools with different geometry and, therefore, line capacity.

You should always check that the spool tolerates the type of line to be put on it, since a tightly wound monoline, for example, may burst the spool gables when it tries to regain its normal length. A good rule is to have a layer of cotton line nearest to the spool axle, and then fill up with the actual line. Spools cast in one piece are strongest. Anodized aluminum and stainless steel are well-tried spool materials, but caution is needed with artificial fibers – even if these make the reel lighter. There should not be any free room between the spool and the reel gable, into which the line can risk sliding.

Line capacity

Inability to exploit all of the reel's line capacity is like going into a fight with a handicap. When the fish strikes, you already have some slack line out, and perhaps a lot if you are trolling with a downrigger. With little line left on your reel, the pressure on the line increases and the fish becomes harder to take home.

Reels have an enormous range of line capacities. And now, with thin, strong superlines, there is room on medium-class reels for a line capacity that a few decades ago was conceivable only on a big-game reel in the heavyweight class. For instance, a 50-class reel can hold about 750 yards of 50-lb monoline, but the same reel can take about 3000 yards of superline in the 50-lb class

Bait-casting reels, and the occasional small trolling reel, have line-spreaders. But no better and more durable level-wind than your own thumb has yet been designed for the heavier reels. Distributing the line with your thumb soon becomes a habit. The handle on a trolling reel should be large and provide a good grip even under very wet conditions. Its shape, though, is mostly a matter of personal taste and opinion.

The reel's gear ratio – how many times the spool rotates for every full turn of the reel handle – is another crucial detail. How much line is laid on the spool with each winding depends on the combination of gear ratio and spool diameter. The more line you have on the spool, the quicker you can take home line. An increasing number of trolling reels are two-speed reels. They come with two gears, mostly shifted with a button. The low gear winds in more powerfully, but it lays up less line on the spool for each turn than does the high gear.

Automatic gearing, which changes from fast to slow winding as the load varies, is used on some trolling reels in the light line classes.

Clicking and braking

A reel with little or no click (line-out alarm) is not a complete trolling reel. This sound is like an alarm clock to tell you that the moment has come at last – something is

Trolling reels vary in size, appearance and construction, depending mainly on the fighting characteristics of the expected prey, and on the conditions at the actual fishing place. The reel shown here is made for big-game fishing. Among other things, it has a lever drag, which is both easier and safer to handle than a star drag.

pulling line off the reel. So the clicking should be clear enough to be heard over the waves' slap and the motor's hum, when the rod is not in your hands. It will also enable you to prevent the spool from backlashing, and thus the line from over-winding if it is being let out when you disengage the spool.

The reel should be easy to take apart and put together – even on board, since you may have to change the spool or give it some other kind of service, possibly on a rolling boat deck. Regular maintenance by disassembling the reel, washing it clean, replacing worn parts and so on, is important in the world of big-game fishing. This is, of course, done most effectively and safely on land or in harbor. Always remember, after fishing, to reduce the drag, regardless of whether it is controlled with a lever or a star wheel. Otherwise, substances like salt may eventually destroy the drag discs, resulting in a jerky and unreliable drag.

Drags regulated by a star wheel have been responsible for catching thousands of world-record fish in all line classes. Nonetheless, they have been increasingly eclipsed by the lever-drag reels. These are easier to handle, brake better and last longer. On them, the spool and drag are coupled in by an arm which, on most reels, sits upon the winder gable.

Setting the drag

Always set the reel's drag for your fishing as soon as the reel is mounted and the line is drawn through the rod guides. And do it on land, not in a bouncing boat. Keep in mind that a drag is better set too loose than too tight. It is also both easier and safer, while playing the fish, to add extra braking with your thumb than to readjust the drag. With a trolling reel, though, there are some golden rules: the drag should be set to 15% of the line's breaking strength in lighter line classes, and to about 25% in heavier classes.

Years of experience give many fishermen an almost intuitive feeling for drag settings. By pulling the line with one hand and thumb-braking the spool with the other, they usually get it right. However, even the most practiced sportfisherman will use a spring-scale to make a more correct adjustment. It is best to let someone else hold the scale, then to knot the line directly in the scale's suspension hook. Next, set the reel's drag lever in the striking position, and keep the rod tip pointing toward the scale. Reverse and adjust the drag setting until it begins to slip at the desired weight figure.

Specific advice for the " perfect" drag setting is difficult to give, as it depends on things like the lure's water resistance, the boat speed, the hook size and, of course, the fish's striking behavior.

Fishing lines

For decades, trolling fishermen have made their choice among monofilament, dacron and wire lines. Roughly speaking, a quarter-century ago the deep troller preferred wire lines, the big-game fisherman dacron lines, and the "everyday troller" monolines for rivers, lakes and skerries. But this division is no longer valid. Increasingly, modern superlines are being used. The downrigger has made it possible to troll with monolines and light equipment at depths which, in the past, could hardly be reached with wire lines. And out on the ocean, modern monolines are now more common than dacron lines, while thin, strong superlines are making rapid advances.

In Europe, lines are usually rated by their diameter (in mm) and strength in kilograms, while in the USA and several other countries it is the line strength in pounds that you buy. Keep in mind that the line absorbs water while fishing; this certainly makes it more flexible, but also reduces its strength by up to 20% after only a few hours of continuous fishing. What also reduces the line strength could be knots.

On the whole, trolling fishermen need thin but strong lines with low visibility, low memory, high abravision resistance and good sensitivity. A non-stretchy line hooks better than a more elastic one. It does not, however, take hard jerks – which are frequent in trolling – as well as a stretchy one does. The stifness and the line diameter may also impede the lure's movement, but can be compensated with a leader of limp line and a loop knot close to the lure.

The line's diameter has an influence on how fast it sinks, how heavy a sinker is needed to reach a certain trolling depth, how much line can be laid on the reel, how clearly the line can be seen, and how easy it is to knot. The line's breaking strength, too, determines what equipment – such as rods – is chosen, how much drag can be set, and how far you can push the equipment during the fight. A thinner line makes a lure go deeper than a thick line does, since it creates less water resistance. For example, a lure goes much deeper if you let out 250 ft (75 m) of line instead of 80 ft (25 m). But it is a lot harder to make a hookup with a long line, because of the line's elasticity.

Hi-Vis or fluorescent lines allow better control over the line spreading. In addition, this type of line is easier to see while playing the fish – an advantage when you are fishing in the dark or want to see quickly which way the fish is rushing. Such lines may, however, yield significantly fewer bites than less visible lines do. One way to avoid this drawback, while keeping the line control, is to taper the line with a neutrally colored leader – such as fluorocarbon, which is virtually invisible under the surface – closest to the lure.

Line twisting can occur when a lure is dragged in the propeller wash – or if you have a poorly rotating swivel, or none at all. The twisting may soon render the line unusable; but if it is discovered in time, a trolling fisherman has a relatively good chance of solving the problem fast. Just take off the lure, swivel and so forth, then feed out the line from the reel into the wake of the moving boat. The line will untwist and regain its original condition automatically.

Before fishing, always check the line's condition for some distance along the spool, not just the outermost turns. You should therefore change, turn or splice the line if you have the slightest doubt about its durability.

Monofilament lines

What we commonly call monofil lines are termed by their makers – according to the manufacturing process – homopolymers, copolymers, tripolymers and cofilament. These words use " homo" for one, " co" for two, " tri" for three, and " polymer" for nylon. Thus, homopolymer is a uniform type of nylon, copolymer is a combination of two types, and tripolymer combines three types. These mixtures were invented to give a line as many good qualities as possible. Copolymer is most popular in trolling circles. It comes in test strengths from 1 lb to 400 lbs, and in several colors.

Big-game fishing brings real excitement. Not only the fisherman but also his equipment must be in perfect trim. The gear has to be well-balanced, with the rod, reel and line adapted to each other. This has led the IGFA to develop an internationally accepted line-class system, which makes it much easier to match the items of equipment. These classes are 2, 4, 8, 12, 16, 20, 30, 50, 80 and 130 lbs (1, 2, 4, 6, 8, 10, 15, 24, 37 and 60 kg). If you buy a trolling rod of IGFA class 10 kg (20 lbs), you should normally match it with a line and reel of the same class. A well-tended and balanced set-up will give the most fishing time and the fewest problems.

Fluorocarbon lines

In appearance, fluorocarbon lines are reminiscent of monoline. They are manufactured not from nylon, however, but from polyvinylidene fluoride, a material that is denser, has a harder surface and does not absorb water in the same way as a monoline. The major advantage with this line is its invisibility under water, a great advantage for trolling in clear water. With less stretch and diameter compared with a monoline in a corresponding class, come the added factors of high sensitivity to bites and hooking ability. Another plus is its durability and good tolerance for ultraviolet light. Such negative factors as stiffness and line memory – which have meant that up to now fluorocarbon lines were used primarily in lighter-weight classes of line and leaders – appear to have been eliminated with the new generation of fluorocarbon lines. There are even hybrid lines on the market, manufactured from nylon and fluorocarbon, in which the advantages of both have been successfully combined.

Dacron lines

A dacron line is spun from dacron fibers. It is hollow, which makes it suitable for splicing. This in turn can mean strong, smooth splices, which easily run over roller guides and through ring guides on a rod. One can also, of course, join dacron lines with knots. In general, the result is less durable than monofilament, and therefore only a few kinds of knots are considered to be reliable, but these provide almost 100% joining strength. However, dacron line is significantly more vulnerable to damage than monoline.

Superlines

Superlines are manufactured from a polyuthlene material that may be either braided or fused. Power Pro is an instance of the former variety, Fireline of the latter. Compared with a monoline, a superline has enormous strength in relation to its diameter, with the glued variant being somewhat thicker than the braided line for the same breaking strength. The fine diameter of the superlines means that they cut through the water with minimal resistance and also give the lure a lively gait. Further, the line's minimal stretch means that a bite is easily registered and the hooking can take place well. For someone unfamiliar with these lines, the minimal elasticity may result initially in a snapped line or the hook's being torn out of the fish's mouth. A monoline or fluorcarbon shocktip leader and a drag set lighter than usual can solve the problem.

Always bed the spool with monoline and then fill it with the desired length of superline, using the UNI knot to join super- and monolines. This and the Palomar Knot are good for connections to swivels, hooks and lures. The Bimini Twist is very useful for doubling the line. The new generation of superlines are streamlined and do not generate the same friction against the guides as older types of lines did.

Metal lines

Lead-core and solid steel lines, thanks to their high specific weight, can sink down to great depths even with very light lures. So they are a good alternative for fishermen who do not use either a downrigger, a diving planer, heavy sinkers, or long-lipped and deep-diving plugs.

Metal lines are stiff and therefore hook well, but they are also much harder to handle than other types of line. Remember that a metal line which has got caught in something, and been stretched, has been weakened as a result. But light rods with slow action, and shock leaders made of monofilament, make it easier to fish with metal lines.

Do not fill the spool with metal line alone; bed it near its axle with a layer of dacron line. Avoid using spools made of plastic – as well as aluminum spools, since in combination with metal lines they corrode very easily in salt water. The metal line that tolerates salt water best is Monel.

Lead-core line is the easiest to handle of all metal lines. However, it rusts in salt water and thus requires special care. As its own name indicates, it has a core of lead wire, around which dacron or nylon is spun. This casing gives it protection and strength, while the core makes it sink fast. Consequently, what increases in the heavier line classes is the size of the casing, not of the core. A heavier lead-core line actually sinks a little slower than a thin one, due to the water resistance. Most lead-core lines change in color every 3 ft (90 cm) or every ninth yard (meter), helping you to see how much line is let out.

Knots and joints

Not even an expensive and excellent line is worth putting between yourself and the fish unless your knots and joints are made with the greatest possible care and thought. Most significant for a trolling fisherman is the ability to join thin lines with thick ones, and to join lines that consist of different materials.

It is also important to be able to double a line in the right way, and then to knot it properly to a swivel. Equally essential is the knack of putting a leader on a hook and fashioning different variants of knots that suit the trolling fisherman's lures. He or she must, in addition, master the craft of the sleeve – both for monofilament and for wire lines – and of joining wire lines by hand, as well as coupling them to the hook and lure.

Some knots should become a part of you. These you must be able to tie with frozen fingers, in the dark, or on a rolling boat deck. It is therefore always best to tackle the equipment on solid land, before the boat leaves the harbor. Practice knots at home, tying them slowly and studying them in detail. Tighten a knot gradually and evenly, never with a jerk.

On most monofilament lines – except those with a very smooth surface finish – the knots become more durable if they are wet before being tightened. A good monoline knot should not slip. Dacron lines, on the other hand, are best joined by splicing or with a few special knots, as mentioned above.

A knot's reliability often depends on how many turns of line are wound into it. Be particularly careful to make the right number of turns, and check that they lie right and tight, so that the knot isn't weakened. A few knots can reach the same strength as an unknotted line and these should naturally be used if the situation permits.

The knots and leader models presented here are old and time-honored. They have been tested under varying conditions on different fish species all over the world, and – when tied right – they are 90% to 100% reliable. My advice is to learn all about the possibilities of the universal knot, which has proved its usefulness particularly in big-game fishing.

It is during the final stage of the fight that your equipment is really put to the test. Line, knots and joints should be among the least likely to break, if the fish is to be safely bagged as shown here.

The UNI knot system

This system has the advantage that, starting from one basic knot, you can vary it so much that the majority of knot problems faced by a trolling fisherman are readily solved. The fundamental UNI knot is one that has long existed in many countries. A corresponding number of names are given to it, but the usual one is its English name – the Grinner knot.

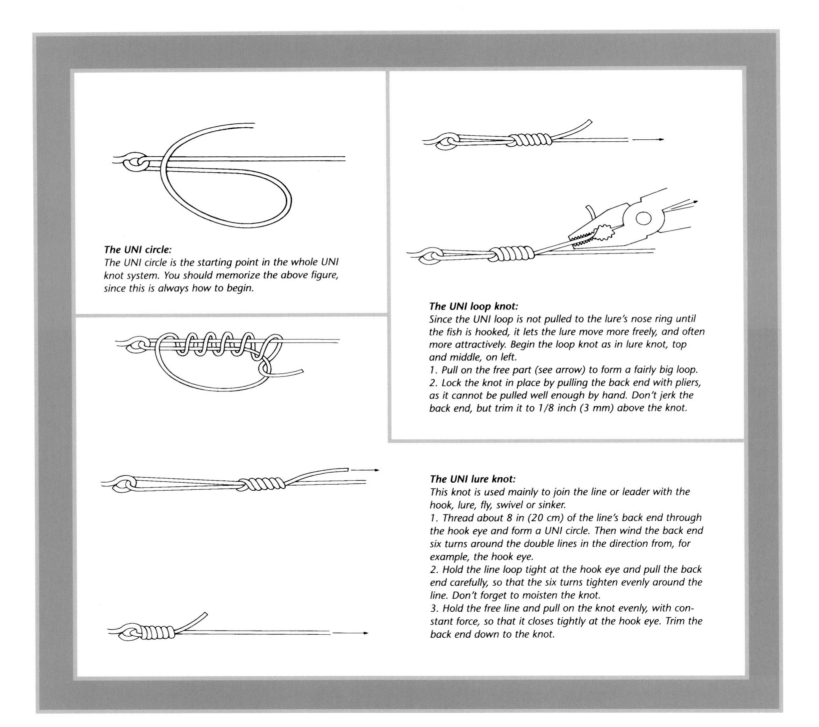

The UNI circle:
The UNI circle is the starting point in the whole UNI knot system. You should memorize the above figure, since this is always how to begin.

The UNI loop knot:
Since the UNI loop is not pulled to the lure's nose ring until the fish is hooked, it lets the lure move more freely, and often more attractively. Begin the loop knot as in lure knot, top and middle, on left.
1. Pull on the free part (see arrow) to form a fairly big loop.
2. Lock the knot in place by pulling the back end with pliers, as it cannot be pulled well enough by hand. Don't jerk the back end, but trim it to 1/8 inch (3 mm) above the knot.

The UNI lure knot:
This knot is used mainly to join the line or leader with the hook, lure, fly, swivel or sinker.
1. Thread about 8 in (20 cm) of the line's back end through the hook eye and form a UNI circle. Then wind the back end six turns around the double lines in the direction from, for example, the hook eye.
2. Hold the line loop tight at the hook eye and pull the back end carefully, so that the six turns tighten evenly around the line. Don't forget to moisten the knot.
3. Hold the free line and pull on the knot evenly, with constant force, so that it closes tightly at the hook eye. Trim the back end down to the knot.

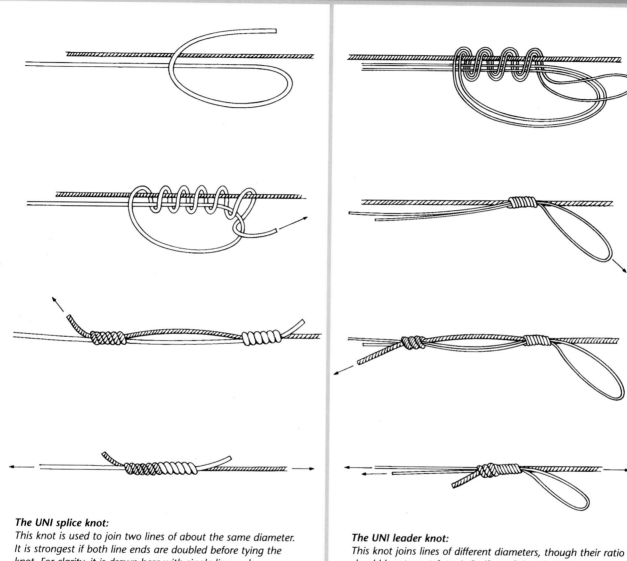

The UNI splice knot:

This knot is used to join two lines of about the same diameter. It is strongest if both line ends are doubled before tying the knot. For clarity, it is drawn here with single line ends.

1. Lay 8-10 in (20-25 cm) of the two lines' back ends parallel to each other. About midway along them, form one end into a UNI circle.

2. Wind the end six turns, as shown. Pull carefully until the turns tighten.

3. Do the same as in 1 and 2 with the other end. Now the knot should look as in drawing. Don't forget to moisten the knot.

4. Pull on both lines' free ends, so that they slide together and lock each other. Pull hard and evenly, then trim the back ends to about 1 mm above the knots.

The UNI leader knot:

This knot joins lines of different diameters, though their ratio should be at most 1 to 4. So if you fish with 0.30-mm line (breaking strength about 10 lbs or 4.5 kg), it should not be joined to a line thicker than 0.65 mm (about 40 lbs or 18 kg).

1. Double 10 in (25 cm) of line (not leader) and make a UNI knot as shown, 6 in (15 cm) from the leader, with four turns.

2. Close the turn by pulling on the double line's loop.

3. Form a UNI circle on the leader and make a 3-turn UNI knot around the leader and main line. Close the turn by pulling the leader's back end.

4. Moisten the lines and pull their back ends hard, so that the two knots slide together. Trim the ends down to the knots.

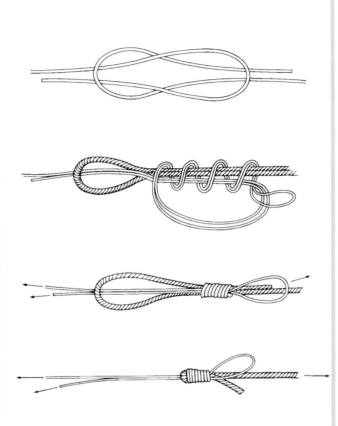

The UNI shock leader knot:

This knot is used when you need to join an extra thick and strong leader with the main line.
1. Double both line ends 10-12 in (20-25 cm). Stick the doubled main line's loop through the leader's loop, far enough to tie a UNI knot.
2. Form the UNI circle and wind the double main line four turns, as shown.
3. Close the turn by pulling on the main line's two ends with one hand, and on the loop with a forefinger.
4. Tighten the knot by pulling on the leader end with one hand, and on the main line's ends with the other hand. Pull slowly and evenly, not jerking. When the knot stops sliding, and the line turns are gripping properly around the leader at the loop, finish the knot by pulling both back ends. Trim well.

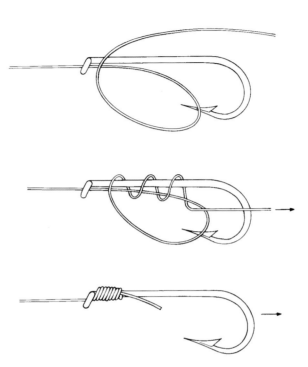

The UNI hook leader knot:

This knot is used to fasten the hook on the leader or main line.
1. Stick the line 8 in (20 cm) through a downturned hook eye. Hold the line against the hook shaft and form a UNI circle.
2. Tie a UNI knot around the hook shaft. Lay at least three turns and close them by pulling the back end.
3. Tighten the knot by pulling the main line and hook bend in different directions. Trim.

The UNI spool axle knot:

This knot is used to attach the line on the reel spool. On fly and spinning reels, the back end is laid around the spool before tying the knot. On fixed-spool reels, make a UNI loop and then tighten it around the spool axle.

The equipment and techniques of modern trolling have enabled ever more fishermen to be in the right place, at the right time, with the right method for hooking whatever they want.

Other types of knots

My complementary knots include the Bimini Twist, Spider Hitch, Albright Knot, Palomar Knot, Bristol Knot, Surgeon Knot and a swivel knot for double lines. You should also be familiar with splicing of different lines, with steel-line and wire sleeves, and with coupling of wires and monolines.

The Bimini Twist

This is a very handy and strong knot with up to 100% reliability. It is used chiefly to join leaders, and when doubling the main line above a terminal tackle. It is fairly easy to tie by yourself if the double line is not longer than 60 in (150 cm), but otherwise two people make the job both easier and safer.

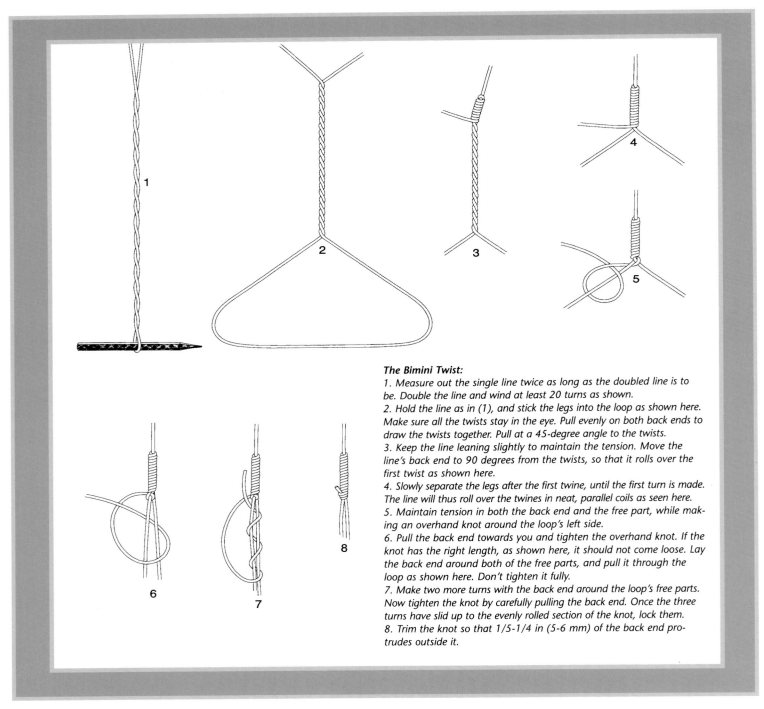

The Bimini Twist:
1. Measure out the single line twice as long as the doubled line is to be. Double the line and wind at least 20 turns as shown.
2. Hold the line as in (1), and stick the legs into the loop as shown here. Make sure all the twists stay in the eye. Pull evenly on both back ends to draw the twists together. Pull at a 45-degree angle to the twists.
3. Keep the line leaning slightly to maintain the tension. Move the line's back end to 90 degrees from the twists, so that it rolls over the first twist as shown here.
4. Slowly separate the legs after the first twine, until the first turn is made. The line will thus roll over the twines in neat, parallel coils as seen here.
5. Maintain tension in both the back end and the free part, while making an overhand knot around the loop's left side.
6. Pull the back end towards you and tighten the overhand knot. If the knot has the right length, as shown here, it should not come loose. Lay the back end around both of the free parts, and pull it through the loop as shown here. Don't tighten it fully.
7. Make two more turns with the back end around the loop's free parts. Now tighten the knot by carefully pulling the back end. Once the three turns have slid up to the evenly rolled section of the knot, lock them.
8. Trim the knot so that 1/5-1/4 in (5-6 mm) of the back end protrudes outside it.

The Spider Hitch

This knot can be tied fast, has high breaking strength, and can often replace the Bimini Twist in light line classes.

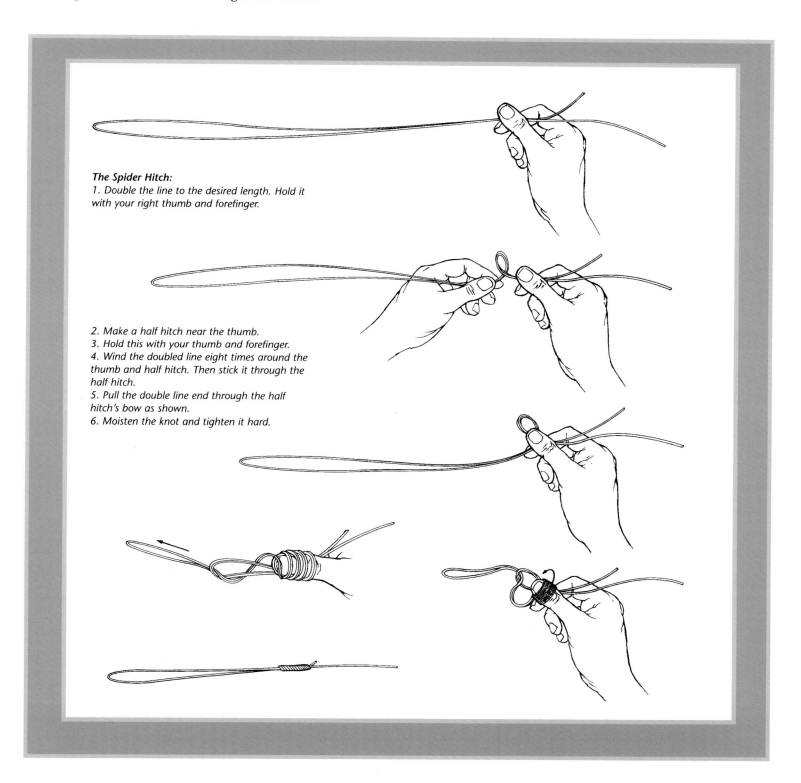

The Spider Hitch:
1. Double the line to the desired length. Hold it with your right thumb and forefinger.

2. Make a half hitch near the thumb.
3. Hold this with your thumb and forefinger.
4. Wind the doubled line eight times around the thumb and half hitch. Then stick it through the half hitch.
5. Pull the double line end through the half hitch's bow as shown.
6. Moisten the knot and tighten it hard.

The Albright Knot

This knot is used to join wire or thick monoline with, for example, thinner monofilament lines. When monolines are joined to solid wire, begin by making a "haywire twist" knot on the wire. Another use is when fishing without a swivel between the line and leader.

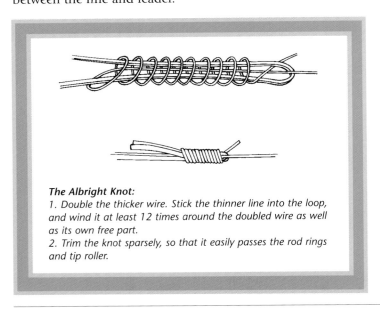

The Albright Knot:
1. Double the thicker wire. Stick the thinner line into the loop, and wind it at least 12 times around the doubled wire as well as its own free part.
2. Trim the knot sparsely, so that it easily passes the rod rings and tip roller.

The Surgeon Knot

This strong knot, easy and quick to tie, is used to unite two lines of the same or different dimensions. It is especially common for putting a leader on the line.

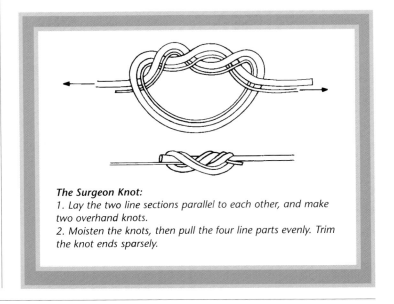

The Surgeon Knot:
1. Lay the two line sections parallel to each other, and make two overhand knots.
2. Moisten the knots, then pull the four line parts evenly. Trim the knot ends sparsely.

The Palomar Knot

A good knot to use with superlines.

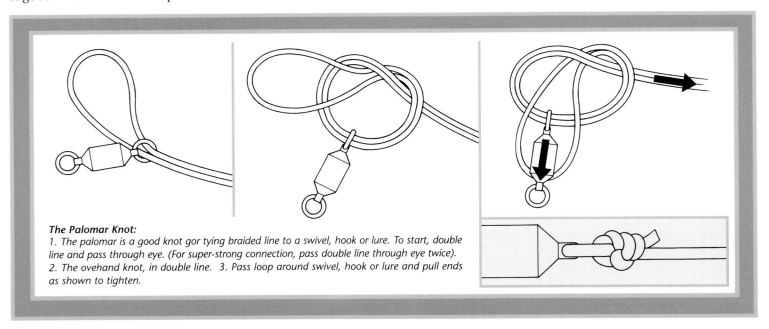

The Palomar Knot:
1. The palomar is a good knot gor tying braided line to a swivel, hook or lure. To start, double line and pass through eye. (For super-strong connection, pass double line through eye twice).
2. The ovehand knot, in double line. 3. Pass loop around swivel, hook or lure and pull ends as shown to tighten.

The Bristol Knot

A supple, strong, net knot for joins between double and single lines.

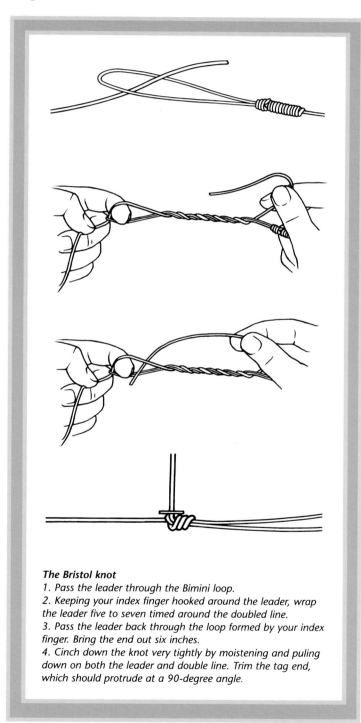

The Bristol knot
1. Pass the leader through the Bimini loop.
2. Keeping your index finger hooked around the leader, wrap the leader five to seven timed around the doubled line.
3. Pass the leader back through the loop formed by your index finger. Bring the end out six inches.
4. Cinch down the knot very tightly by moistening and puling down on both the leader and double line. Trim the tag end, which should protrude at a 90-degree angle.

The Swivel Knot

This knot is used to connect a doubled main line with the swivel.

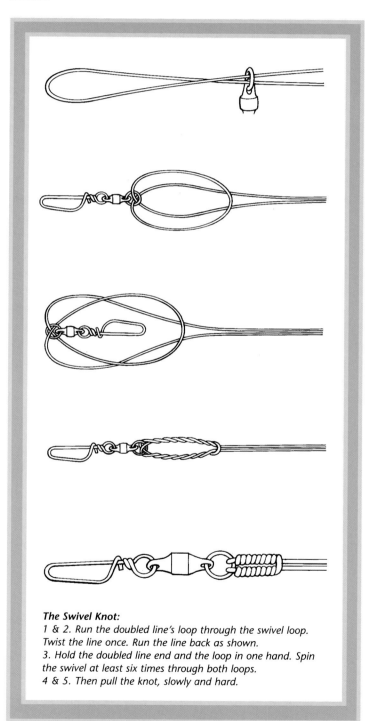

The Swivel Knot:
1 & 2. Run the doubled line's loop through the swivel loop. Twist the line once. Run the line back as shown.
3. Hold the doubled line end and the loop in one hand. Spin the swivel at least six times through both loops.
4 & 5. Then pull the knot, slowly and hard.

The Haywire Twist

This is the internationally name of the standard coupling between a solid wire and a hook, lure or swivel. It is also used when only a loop is made on a single-stranded wire.

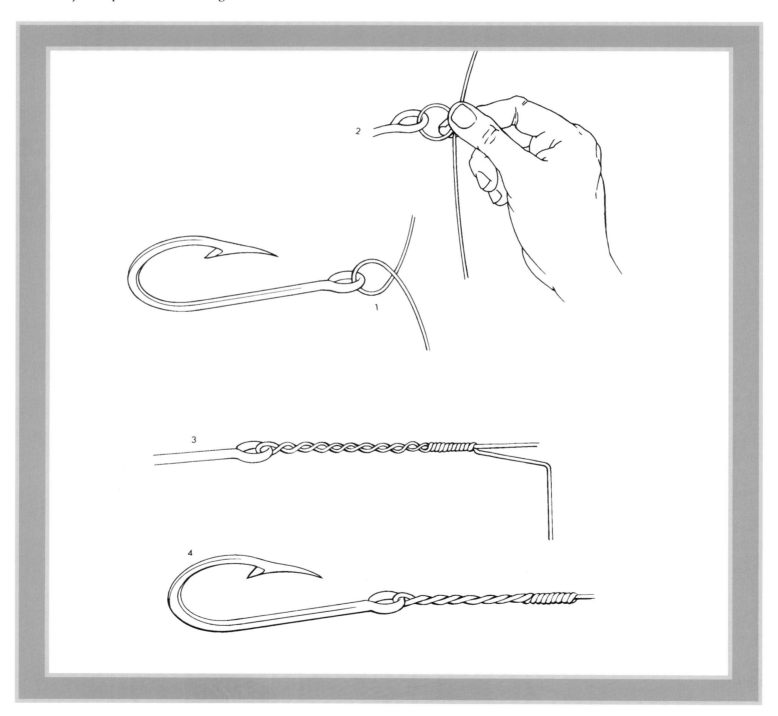

Sleeves

The commonest and easiest way to couple a multistrand wire line or heavy monoline to a hook, lure or swivel is to crimp one or more sleeves over the wire strands or line ends, using a crimping tool.

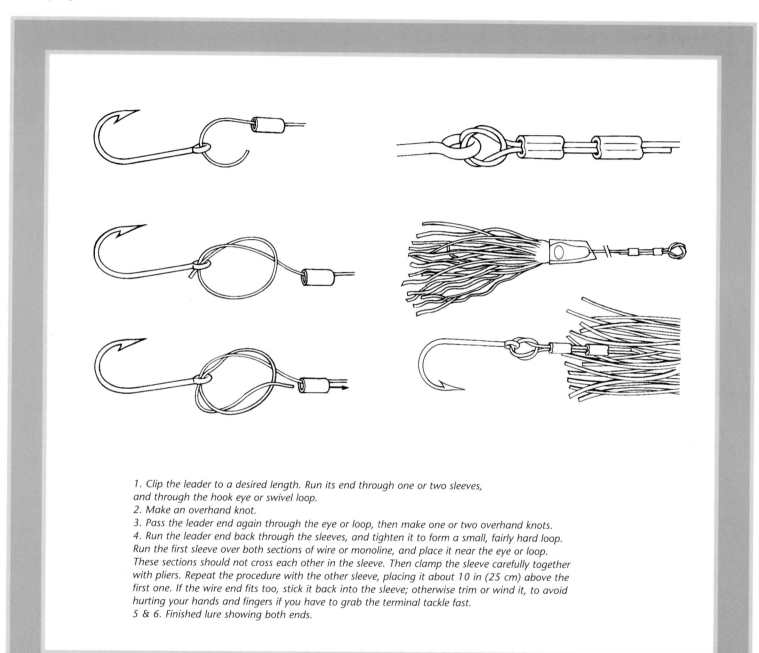

1. Clip the leader to a desired length. Run its end through one or two sleeves, and through the hook eye or swivel loop.
2. Make an overhand knot.
3. Pass the leader end again through the eye or loop, then make one or two overhand knots.
4. Run the leader end back through the sleeves, and tighten it to form a small, fairly hard loop. Run the first sleeve over both sections of wire or monoline, and place it near the eye or loop. These sections should not cross each other in the sleeve. Then clamp the sleeve carefully together with pliers. Repeat the procedure with the other sleeve, placing it about 10 in (25 cm) above the first one. If the wire end fits too, stick it back into the sleeve; otherwise trim or wind it, to avoid hurting your hands and fingers if you have to grab the terminal tackle fast.
5 & 6. Finished lure showing both ends.

Splicing

Dacron can be spliced to either monofilament line or dacron. A spliced line is usually weaker than an unspliced line, but the amount of weakening depends, for example, on how many dacron fibers have broken and how long the splice is. So the splice should be at least 4 in (10 cm) long, or 8-12 in (20-30 cm) for big-game fishing. Its advantage over a knot is that it is smoother and runs easier through loops, with less risk of getting caught at critical moments.

Monofilament to dacron

This simple splicing can make a long, smooth mono leader, which in the long run will tolerate friction and impact better than dacron line alone. Very different line diameters can be spliced.

1. Bend a piece of No. 2-4 fine steel wire, 2 yards (or meters long), into a sharp V-angle. Let us call this handy tool a "splicing needle".
2. Stick the V-bend into the hollow dacron line, about 2 yds (m) from the back end. Pull the dacron over the steel wire until the splicing needle comes out, though not so far that it slips off.
3. Sharpen about 4 in (10 cm) of the monoline's end with a razor blade.
4. Stick the monoline into the splicing needle. Monoline with a breaking strength of 100 lbs (45 kg), or a diameter over 1 mm, will be hard to get double through the dacron line. If so, stick the sharpened monoline into the end of a separate, thinner 30-lb dacron line, and seal the joint with glue.
5. Pull the splicing needle and monoline (with a 30-lb dacron line if needed) through the thicker dacron (reel) line, until the monoline emerges at the starting hole. Then clip off the monoline's sharpened end. Roughen a short part of the new end with sandpaper, drop a little strong glue on the monoline, and stick it into the reel line. Rub the joint smooth.
6. Wrap the "in and out" holes of the monoline with dental floss, for example, and cover the wrappings with strong glue. Then they will run perfectly.

Dacron to dacron

An efficient way to unite lines is with loops. But it is important for the lines to be coupled so that they do not cut each other (see the drawing). So on dacron lines, the loops are usually spliced.

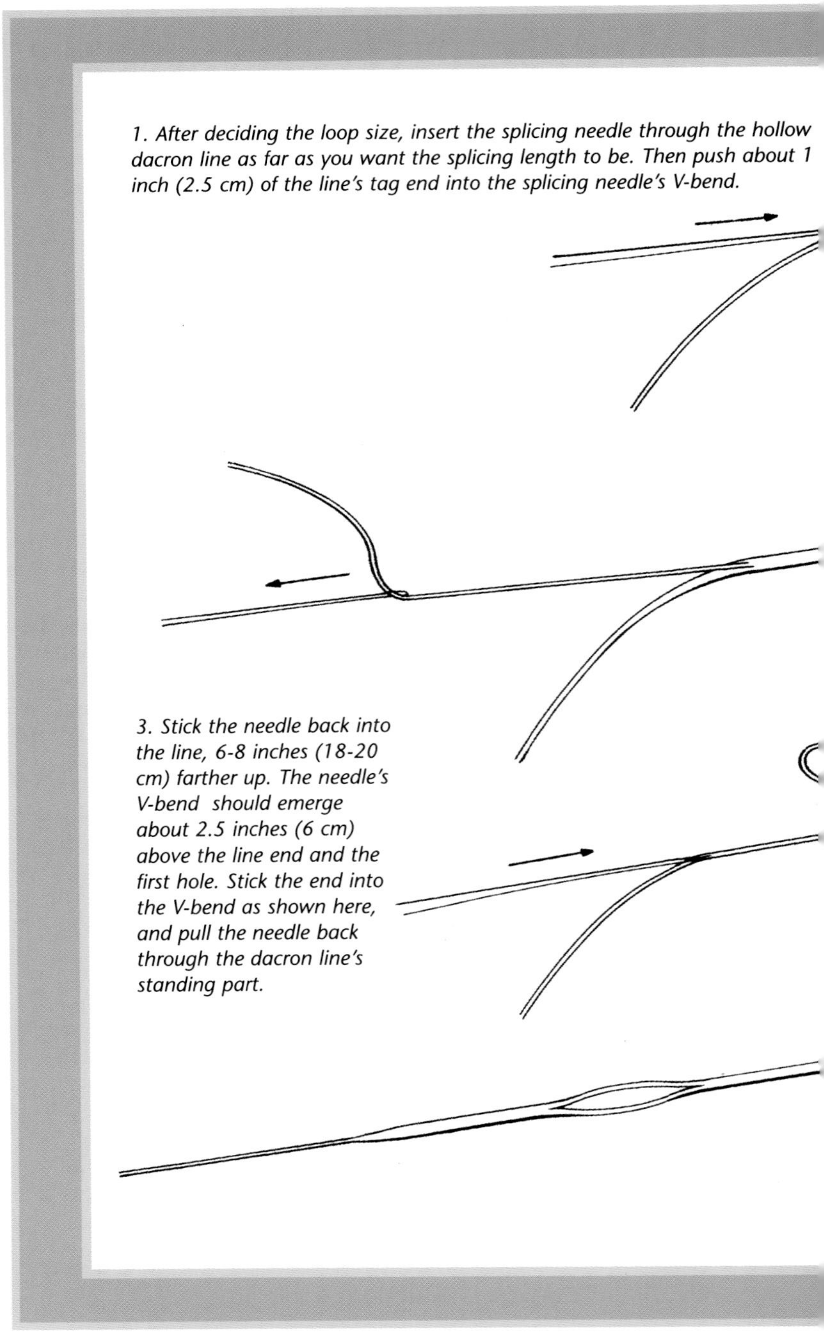

1. After deciding the loop size, insert the splicing needle through the hollow dacron line as far as you want the splicing length to be. Then push about 1 inch (2.5 cm) of the line's tag end into the splicing needle's V-bend.

3. Stick the needle back into the line, 6-8 inches (18-20 cm) farther up. The needle's V-bend should emerge about 2.5 inches (6 cm) above the line end and the first hole. Stick the end into the V-bend as shown here, and pull the needle back through the dacron line's standing part.

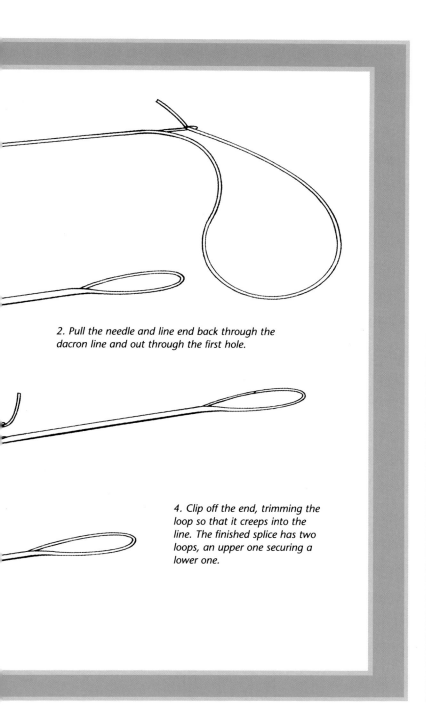

2. Pull the needle and line end back through the dacron line and out through the first hole.

4. Clip off the end, trimming the loop so that it creeps into the line. The finished splice has two loops, an upper one securing a lower one.

To a great extent, trolling involves teamwork. This is seen most clearly in big-game fishing, where the fisherman and crew have to work together in every respect if the catch is to be boarded.

Artificial lures

The trolling fisherman's jewelry casket is his tackle box, full of shiny shapes that seduce the fish and charm the sportsman himself. Some of these well-designed creations are not there to fish with, but simply because they were once effective and can be used to tell good tales about. Others may be so beautiful that one does not want to risk losing them by actually fishing with them.

A troller can normally use the same lures as a casting fisherman does. But he tends to choose specially designed lures, which are dominated less by weight than by their color and form. His starting point, however, is the same: they must be suited to the given equipment, fish species, and fishing environments. Thus he may open his box and pick out a plug, spoon, spinner, hair or plastic lure, a fly or squid imitation, or an offshore lure. Within each group, the lures vary according to shape, color, length, weight and movement.

The equipment on board should remain accessible but be protected and unobtrusive. Here the lures are hung up visibly in vinyl pockets, a tackle-keeper variant which is becoming increasingly popular among boat fishermen.

You shouldn't fall for a lure just because its color and shape please you. Check carefully that the surface finish, hooks, rings and swivels are of good quality, and that they can take the stress of the environment and fishing situations you may encounter. Always sharpen the hooks before these go overboard. Frequently even new lures – and especially big ones – have hooks that need filing or whetting. And don't exchange a single hook for a triple one, or a smaller for a larger one, without thinking: such measures can have a negative effect on the movement of the lure. An unsuitable swivel, or a stiff knot, may also ruin a lure's motion. It is often worth giving the lure room for play with a loop knot.

It is very important for a trolling fisherman to learn how different lures move at various speeds, so that he can match lures properly with each other. Running a high-speed lure alongside a normal, slowly wiggling spoon will mean, at best, that one of the lures is drawn forward at a good pace. Therefore, when letting out a lure, always check first from the boat's side that it has the expected movement in the water. Unequal line thicknesses and lengths can make two identical lures move differently.

The rod tip's rhythm frequently enables a seasoned fisherman to see whether the lure is running right. Some lures – such as stick plugs, jigs and flies – definitely run best if they are constantly influenced by rod movements with the hand. Keep in mind that certain lures are relatively insensitive to speed, and run attractively at both slow and fast speeds. Besides, what a marlin troller calls slow speed may be a maximum speed, or even more, for a salmon fisherman.

In addition, the light's angle and the water's depth have an influence on the visibility of colors underwater. How far down the light can penetrate depends on the season, time of day, and whether it is a sunny or cloudy day. Not for nothing do we speak of "sunshine plugs" and "gray-weather lures". The microorganisms around a lure may also reflect colors from it, making it more visible at times. Fluorescent colors are the most visible, especially fluo chartreuse.

Why a lure works one day and fails the next is an eternal, limitless question. But it can be partly answered if you keep a careful fishing journal. Record when, where, and how the fish strike; give meteorological and hydrological details about individual catches. Then your chances of being in the right place at the right time, with the right equipment, will be considerably enhanced.

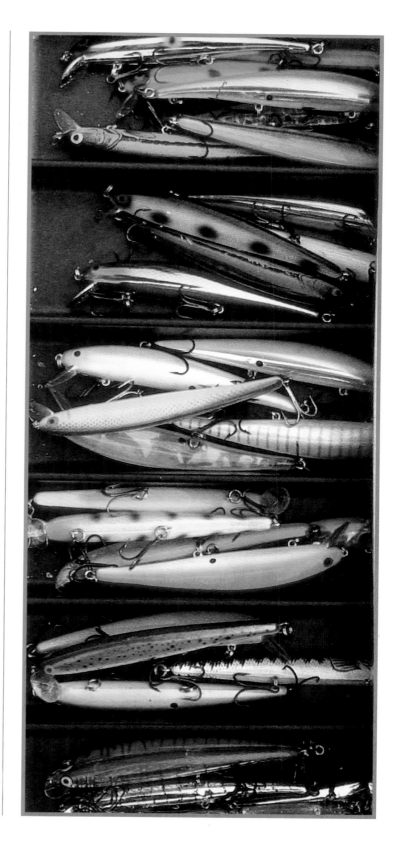

Plugs

A plug is usually designed to look like a bait fish, and classified according to how deep it goes: there are surface, bottom, and deep types. As a rule, though, all of them occur in both floating and sinking versions.

Trolling plugs are comparatively light-weighted, in relation to their sizes of 0.8-14 in (2-35 cm). You can get a good idea of a plug's properties by inspecting the lip, the nose design and the body form. If the nose is angled downward, it tends to dive; if it is cut upward, it tends to rise. Cigar-like plugs do not arouse much attention with their run, but have to be set in motion with the rod tip, or by varying the boat speed. Among other tricks to stimulate the senses of fish are using plugs with two-part bodies, rattling beads in their bodies, or a small propeller at each end.

We generally speak of fast-beating and slow-wiggling plugs, referring to how they make their way through the water. The first type moves with short sidewise throbs that cause rapid vibrations. The second has a more sweeping gait, whose vibrations are also powerful but less busy in tempo.

The hook arrangement varies, of course, between different plugs. Depending on the size, it may be anything from a single hook to three treble hooks. Rapala's 10-in (26 cm) Magnum plug, for instance, has two very strong double hooks. Usually the hooks sit on rings in the body's fixed loops. But on some models, like the J-plug, the hook hangs free on a line that runs at an angle through the plug's body.

Spoons

The spoon is an age-old kind of lure. Tribes around the world have fashioned it from bone and shell for thousands of years. Modern spoons are usually made of metal, but plastic has gained ground even here.

A spoon's range of sizes is about 0.4-12 in (1-30 cm). The really big ones, have brought everything from monstrous Scandinavian pike to the billfish of southern latitudes alongside sportfishing boat sides.

The flashing reflectors of a big spoon can give predatory fish the impression of a fleeing school of prey. Most com-

Shape, color and weight are best varied when you select a set of lures. But don't keep too many lures in the same compartment. Otherwise they hook together and waste your time and temper when changing them on board. Besides, corrosion inside the tackle box may result.

Spoons are most popular among salmon-trolling fishermen. Some of the leading models are illustrated here.

monly, though, the wagging run of a spoon is supposed to imitate the movement of one baitfish. The surface of a spoon may be ball-hammered or bent in a special manner, to create strong reflections. A simple means of giving color to a gold, silver, or bronze-hued lure is to add multicolored stripes on it.

Some spoons are provided with one or more thin steel wires over the hook, which protect the hook from grass and other vegetation to minimize bottom-snagging.

Long thin spoons are more active in their movements than broad ones, which tend to swing wide when being trolled slowly. There are three general types of sheet-metal spoons: thick, medium and thin. A thick model is also commonly used to cast with. Many spoons of this type are excellent for surface trolling, as their own weight takes them down to the desired depth. But a large spoon has the disadvantage that the fish often manages to escape, because of the lure's weight and the abrupt break between the hook and spoon. A solution

here is to use a through-running tackle. The spoon slides up a little way along the line, giving a different load when the fish turns or leaps.

The medium type of spoon has a sheet-metal thickness of 0.02-0.035 in (0.5-0.9 mm). It seldom weighs more than 1/3 ounce (10 grams), so it usually needs help to get down to the chosen depth. This is done most simply by placing a sinker 1-2 yds (m) in front of the spoon.

The thin type, called a flutterspoon, of metal only 0.004-0.016 in (0.1-0.4 mm) thick, is incredibly light. It comes in short wide and long thin versions, according to the baitfish you want to imitate. A flutterspoon is easy to mangle so that, by varying the boat speed, you can make it resemble a wandering little fish that has been injured. Such a feather-light spoon should be fished on a short line of about 2 yds (m) from a diving planer or downrigger, to avoid losing its attractive fluttering movements.

A very important point, when using the lighter spoons, is not to overdimension the hook, swivels and snaps, rings, or the leaders line diameter. It can also be beneficial to exchange a triple hook for a single one.

A spoon is more sensitive to speed than some plugs are, and less tolerant of fast trolling boats. On the other hand, you can often troll slowly with a spoon. The right combination of spoon type and boat speed should be memorized thoroughly.

Spinners

The majority of trolling fishermen keep a set of spinners in their tackle box. Except for those seeking only bass, walleye, perch and char, the less commonly used of all lures are spinners.

This does not mean spinners are bad at catching fish; it shows, rather, that they are customarily thought difficult to troll with. In trolling circles, a spinner is seen as the worst line-twister in the lure box, and its reputation takes time to restore – even among the sportfishermen who, in other respects, are always considered eager to test both new and old techniques.

A spinner does not imitate prey fish, but attracts by virtue of its vibrations, reflections and colors. These are strengthened with hair, rubber, and plastic skirts – or, on some models, with plastic copies of worms and fish. Now and then, the hook is tipped with natural bait.

The blade on a spinner may be short and wide, or long and thin, with a choice of surface finishes. Mother-of-pearl blades are rated highly by many Scandinavian trollers for big char. Short, wide spinner blades can rotate most easily, whereas long thin ones require greater speed in order to spin and be heard.

So-called spinner lures look like a cross between a spinner and a jig. The blade or spoon sits on an arm made of steel wire, and wags forward over the jig head. Other models can carry natural bait such as small fish or worms on the single hook behind its leaden head and spinner blade..

Spin-N-Glo is another admired model, whose ample body with soft plastic wings can also rotate around a wire axle. Like other light spinners, it tends to be most assertive as the last outpost on a cowbell line.

Lures of hair and plastic

Hair lures are among the very oldest artificial lures known to man, while plastic lures are the latest to enter the field. This type of lure is mainly a visual attraction, due to its gait or colors. Some fishermen also heighten the fish's interest by creating smells and sounds. There are lures which need to be continually worked so that their movements do not die out at times.

In fresh water, plastic lures are more popular for casting than for trolling. But in salt water, they are extremely popular with trollers. The largest ones of this kind, such as kona heads, will be discussed under offshore lures.

Hair and feather lures

Either traditional flies, or lures that imitate insects or bait fish, can be made of hair or feathers. So can Japanese feathered jigs. While the first kind need help to reach fishing depths, the last kind sink by their own weight.

The materials of modern hair and feather lures are partly natural and partly synthetic. They may be durable as well as delicate, and can be made either to pulsate heavily or just to glimmer.

In size, material, and other features, these flies and lures are adapted to the water and fish species. A harling fisherman (back troller) should thus have a wide range of them in order to match the shifting conditions, sometimes quite rapid, of river fishing. On the other hand, a marine fisherman's feather lures take more punishment and are chosen in terms of quality rather than quantity.

Plastic lures

The advent of soft plastic introduced " exact" copies of fish, crustaceans, reptiles, mollusks and invertebrates. Certainly the animals most often imitated in these groups are worms. This does not mean they are the commonest in trolling circles, where I would say that squids outnumber all others.

Trolling fishermen, though, have far more enthusiasm about plastic lures in fish form. The fast-vibrating tail of a fish body, on a single hook behind a small jig head, is attractive even to human eyes. Larger plagiarisms of mullet, flying fish and ballyhoo have often been profitable in big-game fishing, when they tempt the appetites of billfish.

Squid copies, as mentioned, are highly praised in all trolling environments. They rate strongly even in waters where the fish have never seen a squid. There are pure copies of octopi, squid and cuttlefish in natural colors – but also very simple, cowl-like models with huge luminous eyes in fantastic colors. Their length varies between 0.8 and 12 inches (2-30 cm).

Colorful, big-eyed plastic lures are conquering ever more expanses of trolling water. This is a diverse collection including, at lower right, some "birdies" - teasers that are dragged in the surface and arouse the curiosity of fish.

These imitations can be draped over natural bait as well as artificial lures, or the hook can be directly tipped with them. Normally, colorful beads or special lead sinkers are placed under the cowl.

Plastic lures are generally inexpensive and need not be used sparsely. They can save a lot of fishing days over difficult bottoms. Since some variants are not very durable, one should check that their dressings can stand being dragged and worn before one tosses them overboard.

Soft plastic can destroy a tackle box unless it is "wormproof", meaning that it tolerates the acid which some plastic lures give off.

Offshore lures

All lures used in the big-game arenas of the oceans can be called offshore lures. They might be Rapala's Magnum plug, Pelagic´s Modulure, ABU-Garcia's giant plastic eels, or big-eyed plastic-skirted lures with hard or soft plastic heads such as the Kona Head, Hooker Softhead and Calcutta.

In this multifaceted realm of constant innovations, the last type is most familiar. It is what we usually mean by offshore lures. Including bibless lures as Modulure and Marauders they also go by the name of high-speed lures, as some of them can take more than 20 knots. On average, they are used at 8-10 knots. But their size, weight and, in

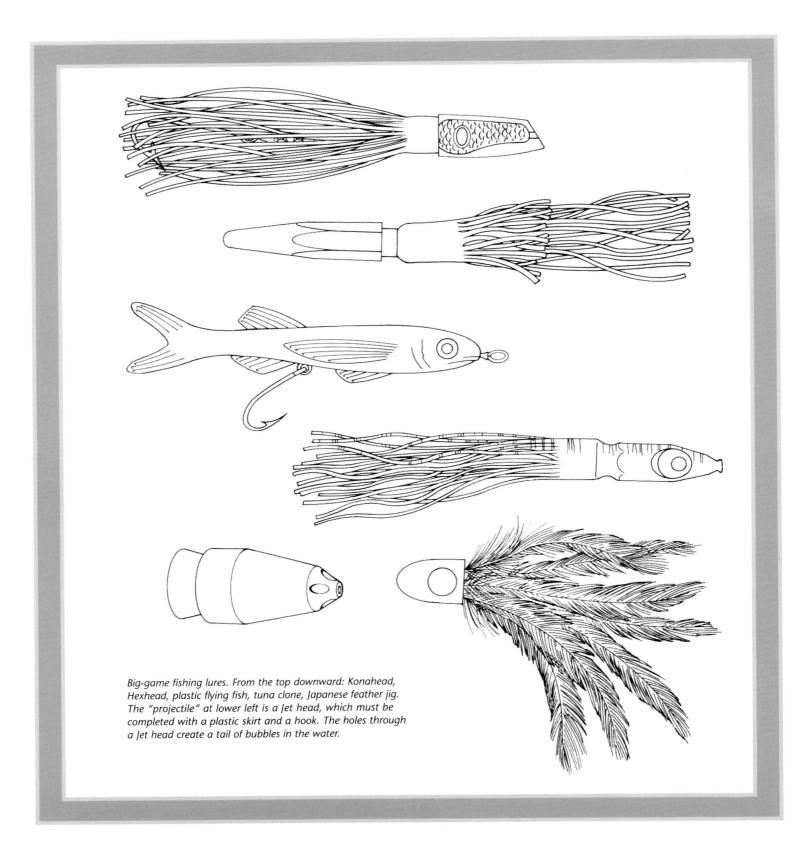

Big-game fishing lures. From the top downward: Konahead, Hexhead, plastic flying fish, tuna clone, Japanese feather jig. The "projectile" at lower left is a Jet head, which must be completed with a plastic skirt and a hook. The holes through a Jet head create a tail of bubbles in the water.

particular, head form are what determine how fast these lures can be trolled, as well as how they move through the water.

Many of them have to go just under the surface and leave a wake of bubbles, or "smoke", after them. They should not break the surface, though the bubble wake can very well raise spray behind them. It is also worth trying to keep the lure on the stern wave's front – the side turned towards the boat. Size, color and model are to be varied within the chosen trolling pattern.

Most fishermen prefer having the liveliest lures closest to the boat, and calm ones farther out. The latter are mainly supposed to attract billfish and tuna, whereas smaller models tend to draw the majority of pelagic sportfish – such as wahoo, yellow mackerel, albacore, bluefish, Pacific and Atlantic salmon.

Offshore lures come in sizes of 4-16 in (10-40 cm). They are sold in diverse colors, both tackled and untackled, with wire or thick monoline, and with single or tandem hook arrangements. The hook is hidden under a fringed plastic skirt, which may be partly made of mylar or pearl bands. The wire or monoline always runs through the head of an offshore lure. As a result, the hole's entrance puts extra wear on the line. With some variants – such as Kona Heads, which are relatively mobile – the wire or line should be checked frequently and carefully.

Normally, offshore lures are big-eyed; some have movable pupils and, in their heads, rattling beads. They are usually identifiable by their head form, classified as flat-faced or scoop-like or torpedo-shaped.

With the exceptionally resistant Modulure plug for sharp-toothed fish, it is possible to change pattern cards in its body, thereby easily testing the day's most marketable color and pattern.

Speed data

As we know already, trolling fishermen have vastly different ideas of what are slow, medium and fast speeds - depending as a rule on the fishing place and species. For instance, salmon trollers consider three knots to be fast, while a tuna troller regards it as slow. The following definitions are due to discussions with sportfishermen around the world:

Designation	Fresh water		Salt water	
Slow speed	0-1.7	knots	0-4	knots
Medium speed	1.8-2.6	knots	4-8	knots
Fast speed	2.7-4.2	knots	8-12	knots
Ultrafast speed	4.3-5.2	knots	12-22	knots

Taking the fresh-water definitions as a basis, some of the most popular artificial lures fall into the groups given below. As can be seen, certain lures are both "strollers" and "sprinters", with a wider speed tolerance than others have. Your own trimming or loading of lures may also make them cross the lines between groups.

Slow speed

Spoons: Sutton, Miller's, Enforcer, Evil Eye, Toby, Utö, Siljan, Apex Hot Spot.
Wobblers: Bomber, Rebel, Rapala, Flatfish, Swim Whizz, Gladsax.
Flashing attractors: mini-cowbells with worms, dodgers with plastic lures and hair flies.
Spinners: Mörrum Spinner, Vättern Mother-of-Pearl, Vibrax Minnow, Mepps Giant Killer, Mepps Aglia, Wally Spin, Buzzer.

Medium speed

Spoons: Toby, Atom, Glimmy, Mörtblänk, Siljan, Professor, Lättke, Storauren, Möresilda, Landa Lukki, Crocodile, Rebel Arrowhead, Loco, Ingö, Apex Hot Spot, Evil Eye, Diamond King, Northern King, Northport Nailer, Southport Slammer, Flutter Chuck (Magnum, Big Ed), Piraten, Finn-Weaver.
Wobblers: ABU Hi-Lo, Cisco Kid, Killer, Rapala, Rebel, Bomber, Bagley Top Gun, Swim Whizz, Nils Master Invincible, J-plug, Jensen, Gladsax.
Flashing attractors: large dodgers, flashers with plastic lures and hair flies.

Fast speed

Spoons: Toby, Landa Lukki Turbo, Evil Eye Monarch, Piraten 66, Northern King (28, Magnum), Flutter Chuck Magnum, Rebel Arrowhead.
Wobblers: J-plug, Bomber Long A., Rebel Fastrac, Rapala (Original, Husky, Magnum, Shad Rap, Sliver), Nils Master Invincible, Cordell Ratt 1 Spot, Bagley Banger, Storm Thunderstick.
Plastic and feather lures: Hooker Softheads, Witch Doctor, Samurai feathers, Tube eels.

Natural baits

In fresh waters, the vast range of fish-like, convenient and effective artificial lures is seemingly gaining ever more ground over natural bait. This is an ominous trend, since natural baits – if used properly – are just as good as in the past. And they're definitely some of the most useful items a hook can be stuck in. Comparisons between salmon catches in the Great Lakes and on the west coast of North America are also clear evidence for the advantages of natural bait.

The salty environment, especially in big-game fishing, is indisputably ruled by natural baits in many places. Bait rigging is still regarded there as an art, and the people who master this work with knife, needle and thread enjoy high status among the world's fishing globetrotters and charter-boat skippers. They harbor no doubt that a well-sewn, well-balanced natural bait is unbeatable when it comes to attracting balky giants.

You can find natural baits in dried, frozen, fresh and living variants. The species are numerous, but a minority of them predominate in fresh, brackish and salt waters alike. Mackerel, ballyhoo, mullet, herring and squids are a strong quintet of baits in the sea. Nightcrawlers, smelt, vendace, and some of those mentioned above are the leaders in fresh and brackish waters.

These baits are not equally suitable for being served in the given form. But normally you obtain the bait stripped or slabbed, or else as a half or whole fish. One basic rule is that the bait should not be too big for the predator to swallow quickly. Another is that the hook(s) should always be as sharp as possible.

Even for a practiced bait-rigger, some time is needed to sew a trolling bait together. An alternative to sewing – as far as small whole fish or filets are concerned – can be to use a bait holder. The bait is usually clamped or pierced into the holder, which is shaped to protect the bait as well as giving it an attractive movement.

Baits are generally prepared before one leaves the harbor, and preserved in a way that keeps them fresh until they are used. A method of preserving fresh – or recently thawed – baits is to lay them in plastic bags, possibly with coarse salt, and then on ice. Avoid freezing a bait that has already been used or frozen.

Remember that live baits cannot be trolled as fast as dead ones. The maximum speed for a live trolling bait is around 4 knots, which saltwater fishermen define as slow. In big-game arenas, though, dead baits are trolled at up to 12 knots.

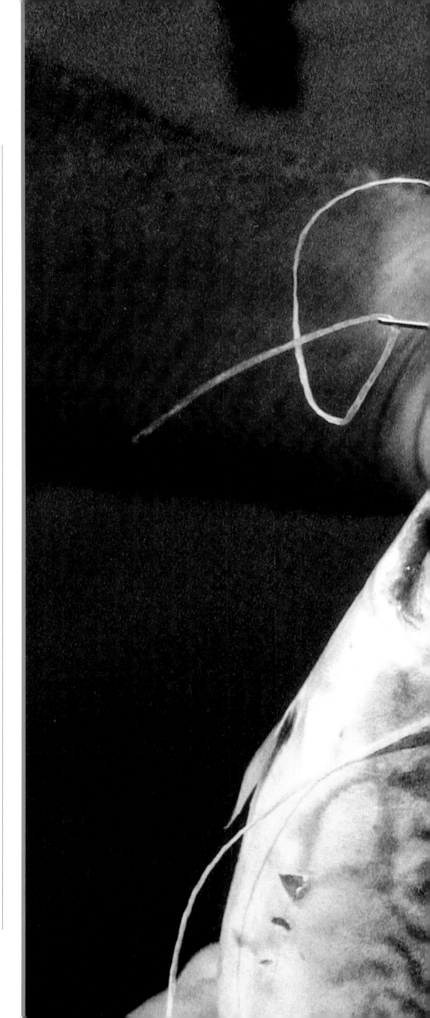

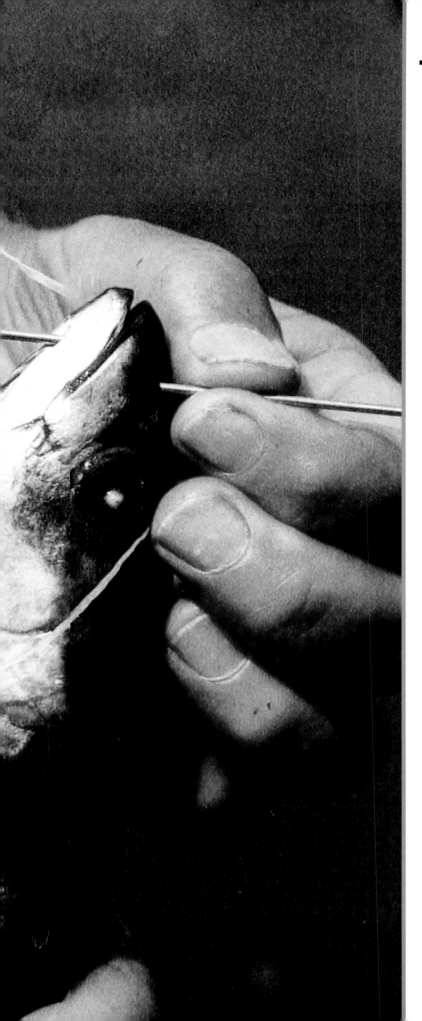

Stripping and slabbing.

A strip bait is undressed down to the bare skin. This is a very ancient kind of bait, easy to cut and preserve, as well as durable in use. It is effective in all trolling environments – whether on the edges of ocean canyons in strips 1 ft (30 cm) long, or on perch shallows in patches 1-2 in (3-5 cm) long. There is no trouble in coloring or dressing it by pulling a very short plastic skirt over it. An additional advantage is that it hooks well, mainly because it is soft and readily swallowed.

The best strip baits come from fish in the mackerel family, which have firm flesh and can be cut easily. Many other strip baits, such as a belly strip from a perch, can be amazingly effective – especially when fishing for their own family. With mackerel fish, too, it is from the belly or side that the 8-12 in (20-30 cm) long, tapering pieces are taken for big-game fishing.

A feather-like shape is best, so that the head end of the bait becomes wider than the tail part. The latter can also be slit. Cut away most of the flesh. Only after these cuts, and the insertion of a well-balanced Kirby hook, does the strip bait acquire its bold, attractive movement. If this does not look right, the reason may be that the hook and leader are not quite centered, or that the bait has slid down over the hook.

Slab baits, on the other hand, are usually wedge-like pieces that have been cut crosswise from a mackerel filet. The hook is pushed through the thick, fleshy part and out through the skin. This bait is fished slashing in the surface, normally without the aid of a sinker.

Left: Bait tackling is a difficult and enviable art to master. Many big-game fishermen and charter-boat captains say that the real difference between a successful fishing day, and a failed one, lies in the ability to handle bait with a knife, needle and thread. The baits are presented in many shapes and sizes. Unless alive, they are normally prepared in advance and kept on ice.

Below: Strip baits - cut from the belly, sides or back of small prey fish related to mackerel - are excellent both as attractors and as natural bait.

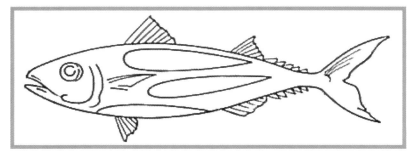

Whole fish

Offered either live or dead, whole fish vary in size according to the predator. In general, though, large trolling baits are more often live than dead. Mackerel, bonito, and bluefish are among the bigger and most popular variants. There are also many ways of rigging whole bait. Its size, firmness, condition and, to some extent, the water depth where it will be presented are the primary factors.

A live bait that is trolled slowly can stay alert for a very long time. The idea is that it should act as naturally as possible, but still send out signals which show that something is wrong. Surface-towed baits last longer than deep-running ones, and pollock tend to survive deep dives better than mackerel.

The rigging itself is important, too. Always use the smallest possible hook(s). The commonest method of rigging up small live baits is to place the hook in the mouth and up through its top jaw. Another is to run the hook through the nose-hole. On larger baits, a piece of dacron line is often threaded through the eye-hole and tied to the bend on a hook, which is secured around the fish's head. This is called a bridle rig and can be done quickly with a little training.

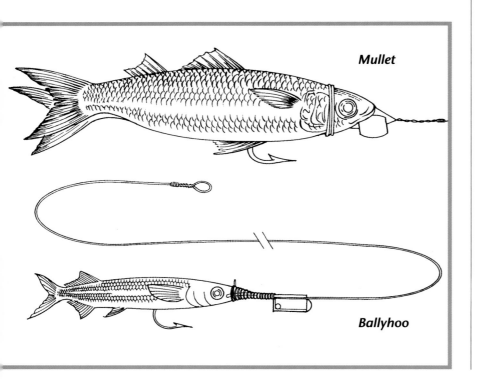

Mullet

Ballyhoo

Big dead baits are ordinarily nose-rigged with a hook and dacron line. Herring and other small baits are frequently hooked through the body and given a double-hook arrangement.

Mullet

Gray mullet is a top-ranked bait. Variants in silver and black, as well as sizes of 2.5-25 oz (75-750 grams), are used in different circumstances. Mullet is called for when the sea is choppy, and silver mullet weighing 3-8 oz (100-250 grams) is especially popular in flatline fishing for the smaller billfish, such as sailfish.

By rigging the bait in diverse ways, you can also vary its behavior. Rigging it without a sinker will skip it on the surface. But to swim just under the surface, it should carry a sinker right below the jaw. A sinker over the nose produces a diving version. The spine is always removed, and this is best done with a deboner.

If the mullet starts to spin, it may be because the hook is sitting too tight or the sinker – if any – is not centered.

Ballyhoo

Many sought-after sportfish eat ballyhoo, which is therefore a much-appreciated bait. It swims in considerable schools near the surface, chiefly in tropical waters. Easily accessible and all-round in use, it is most popular in weights of 3-8 oz (100-250 grams). Ballyhoo serves as a skip bait, and can be frozen and thawed without trouble. A sign that it is fresh, and thus acceptable as bait, is that it still has its dark-blue to black color across the back.

Herring

Herring are pelagic fish and move in enormous schools through the Atlantic, Baltic and Pacific. The extent and spawning times of these stocks vary, as do their migration routes. Bait sizes are commonly 4-12 in (10-30 cm). This is an essential basic food for the mackerel, salmon and cod families. Fat and silvery, it should be as fresh as possible. Herring keeps for a fairly long time on ice, but it has a short "lifetime" when deep-frozen, since – like other oily baits – it softens quickly. So it must be checked and moved often.

Herring bait is served whole (with or without the head), in half-pieces, in bits, or in filet form. The cut variety, divested of its head and breast fins, is a classic salmon bait along the

Herring

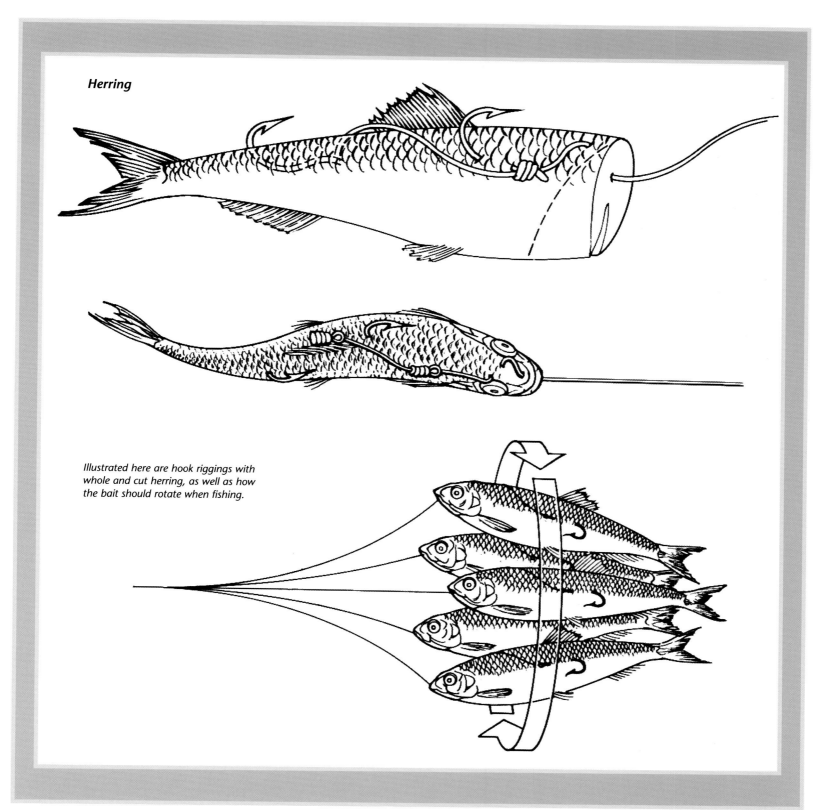

Illustrated here are hook riggings with whole and cut herring, as well as how the bait should rotate when fishing.

western coast of North America. Opinions about how to cut and rig it, however, are numerous. If the cut is straight, the herring will rotate in wider and slower movements than if it is cut at, say, 45 degrees. Most of us prefer a rapid rotation, but it should not be trolled faster than 2.5 knots.

The best hook arrangement is a double one, with the upper hook placed closest to the cut, passing from the inside outward. The other hook is hidden in the tail spool.

Squids

Octopi, squids and cuttlefish occur pelagically in large schools, and make superb bait. These "soft cakes" are gobbled unhesitatingly by fish, and they hold the hook well even with no drop-back.

A squidd is best trolled close to the boat. Rig it carefully so that the bait is balanced: it should not slide on the hook or

divide itself. Time is needed to sew up such a bait, so try to do several at the same time. Squids can be kept frozen for long; if thawed and put in plastic bags, they keep for 3-4 days on ice. But never lay the bag directly on ice; place something like sailcloth in between. This is because a squid loses color and becomes untasty if it comes near fresh water. So it must be thawed in salt water.

Worms

The nightcrawler is probably the world's commonest freshwater bait, an all-rounder that helps the troller mainly to catch walleye, bass, perch and char. The worm is usually put on the hook behind a flashing attractor or artificial lure. Choose the hook size according to the worm's size and the type of predator. If worms are kept dark, cool, and in damp earth, they act much livelier on the hook.

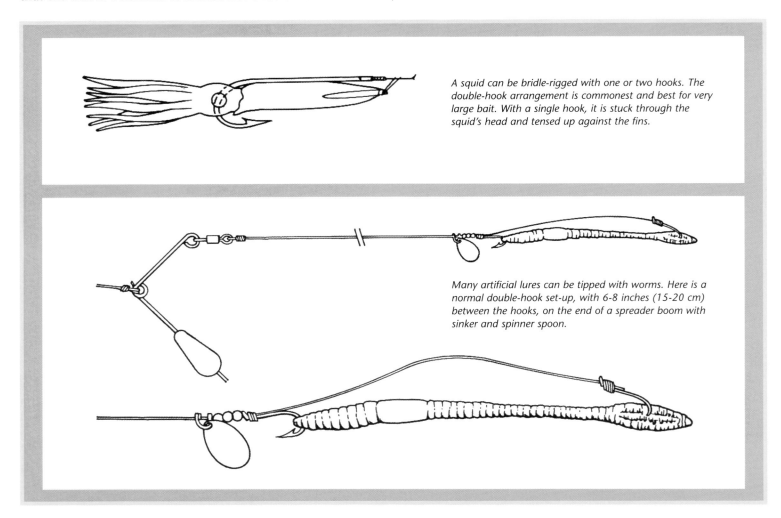

A squid can be bridle-rigged with one or two hooks. The double-hook arrangement is commonest and best for very large bait. With a single hook, it is stuck through the squid's head and tensed up against the fins.

Many artificial lures can be tipped with worms. Here is a normal double-hook set-up, with 6-8 inches (15-20 cm) between the hooks, on the end of a spreader boom with sinker and spinner spoon.

Terminal tackle

For most trollers, the leader is an essential part of the equipment. It is what always takes the worst knocks, and the greatest responsibility in the final stage of the fight. Scraping against the boat keel, railing, and possibly hard-skinned fish bodies, are things it has to tolerate. Then it should be strong and flexible enough to survive hard jerks and fast jumps. A good leader is also easy to grip, and to guide toward the gaff or landing net.

Initially a leader must succeed in presenting the bait attractively, so that it releases the fish's striking instinct. Without a leader, you cannot get very far, no matter how much other gear you have.

Trolling leaders are mostly tapered and divided in several sections, which may be of different materials. Between these, we tend to place a swivel or sinker, shock-absorber or diving planer. Bait moves best on the end of a long limp leader, rather than of a short stiff one. This is especially true when fishing with a metal line, diving planer, or heavy sinker. A limp leader is also better at taking the zest of a big striking fish.

Big-game fishermen generally follow the IGFA rules for composing leaders. The IGFA accepts a leader length of 15 ft (4.57 m) in saltwater line classes up to 20 lbs (10 kg), and a length of 30 ft (9.14 m) above that. In fresh water, though, the leader must not be longer than 6 ft (1.82 m). But the IGFA allows a reel line to be doubled a certain number of times above the leader. The combined length of double line and leader must not, in salt water, exceed 20 ft (6.1 m) in line classes up to 20 lbs (10 kg), or 40 ft (12.19 m) above this. In fresh water, it must not go over 10 ft (3.04 m). Moreover, according to the IGFA, only when the leader reaches the rod tip should anyone grab the leader to guide the fish within reach of a gaff or net.

Ever more leaders are made today with an eye to catch-and-release fishing. The baited hook then sits on a short wire leader, which is coupled by a swivel or spiral link to the rest of the leader. When the fish is brought alongside the boat, judged as to size, and possibly marked, it is set free at the swivel. Sometimes the wire is cut next to the hook.

Leader materials

The fish species and fishing place determine what material the leader should be made of. But there is a trend toward ever more use of monofilament line. Leaders also vary in dimensions, meaning strength and diameter. Besides monoline, they are made of single- or multistrand wire, which may nylon-coated. Monolines and wire come in breaking strengths of over 400 lbs (180 kg). Some are dark-hued to give better camouflage.

In the future, leaders of fluorocarbon and titanium will certainly come to overshadow these older materials. Fluorocarbon is almost invisible in the water, absorbs very little and makes strong knots. Titanium wire comes in single or multiple strands and is rust free. It does not kink, is soft and light, and can be knotted or joined to wire. Final advantages are its negligible stretch and small diameter in relation to its strength.

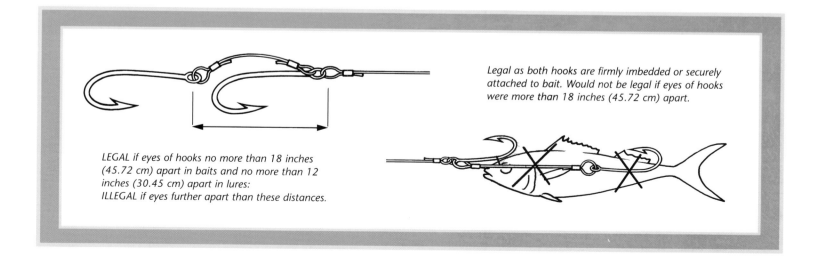

Legal as both hooks are firmly imbedded or securely attached to bait. Would not be legal if eyes of hooks were more than 18 inches (45.72 cm) apart.

LEGAL if eyes of hooks no more than 18 inches (45.72 cm) apart in baits and no more than 12 inches (30.45 cm) apart in lures:
ILLEGAL if eyes further apart than these distances.

Among other components of a leader are the hook, swivel, snap, and sleeve. The wire is coupled with special pliers, or tied by hand. Well-stocked shops sell ready-mounted trolling leaders for different purposes.

On multistrand wire, as well as thick monoline, coupling loops are added all around with the help of sleeves. It is also usually a sleeve that connects the leader and hook. There are various models, sizes and qualities of sleeves – for instance, for wire and/or monoline. Crimping tools exist with cups for sleeves of different size numbers. These are extremely effective, as long as the wire or mono-line has been laid correctly in the sleeve – that is, parallel and not crosswise. Never squeeze the ends of sleeves, and remember that sharp edges may soon ruin the wire.

Hooks

A perfect all-round hook is a fantasy; instead we match the hook size to the dimensions of the bait and the fish, as well as to the rod, reel and line. It is impossible to run a strong hook into a large fish's mouth with light equipment.

The circle hook is receiving increased attention on diverse trolling fronts; particularly solid during the fight for the fisherman, it is merciful for the fish. It comes in different models, and there are even hybrids of the ordinary J-hook and circle-hook. The circle hook almost always catches in the angle of the fish's jaw, holds its grip well, yet is still easy to remove from the fish's mouth.

Big-game fishermen use forged, flattened, short-shanked hooks. They speak of two variants, one with a straight barb, and one whose barb is angled – kirbed or reversed - to the hook shaft. Mustad Southern Tuna is a popular straight model, and Mustad Sea Master is an equally famous angled version. The straight type is common in big-game fishing with both artificial and natural baits, particularly when trolling for long distances with a live bridle-rigged bait.

For salmon bait of the cut kind, hooks like Siwash are the rule. Round-beaten, short-shafted, but long-tipped and angled, they are strong and penetrate well, tending to sit securely even during the wildest fights. Straight Siwash single hooks are popular on the very lightest flutterspoons.

Nickel- and tin-plated hooks easily lose their sting, since they rust. Keep such a hook clean of oxides; always check that it is sharp, and that the hook eye is intact. The latter can otherwise harm the wire or monoline.

Rechargeable, battery-driven hook-sharpeners greatly speed up the job, and can deal with a wide range of hooks, usually giving better results too.

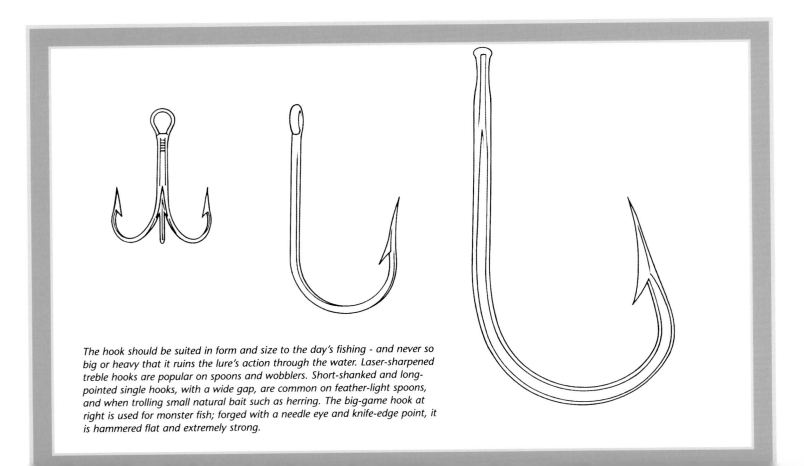

The hook should be suited in form and size to the day's fishing - and never so big or heavy that it ruins the lure's action through the water. Laser-sharpened treble hooks are popular on spoons and wobblers. Short-shanked and long-pointed single hooks, with a wide gap, are common on feather-light spoons, and when trolling small natural bait such as herring. The big-game hook at right is used for monster fish; forged with a needle eye and knife-edge point, it is hammered flat and extremely strong.

Swivels

The chief task of a swivel is to rotate and counteract line twisting. Naturally it should also help the lure to move like a fish as much as possible. Therefore, adapting the swivel's size to the line dimension and other equipment is important. If you have several swivels on a leader, they should be of the same type, material and size. Smaller swivels rotate easier than larger ones.

A leader with a sinker, flashing attractor, and lure requires at least three swivels: one in front of the sinker to eliminate line twisting, and the other two on both sides of the attractor to prevent leader twisting.

Many people use a swivel with a snap as the connecting to the lure. But this is usually needless, if the terminal tackle is effectively attached to the reel line. In ordinary trolling, the lure generally moves better with a snap alone – and best of all with a loop knot.

The swivel's rings often reveal its quality. Sloppily soldered rings, for example, can damage the line and make it break at a knot. Preferable swivels are the ones with stainless-steel, solid rings. A ball-bearing swivel rotates best if the reel line is tied to the ring on the swivel's pin.

Trollers frequently use three-way swivels when the reel line, lure line, and sinker line are attached by three different knots. Tests have shown that the most effective three-way swivel is a self-made one. Place three swivels in a large loop ring; one swivel may be provided with a snap. Since the swivels can run freely in the ring, they center themselves and do not put too much pressure on any single swivel eye.

Snaps and links

Among swivels with snaps, we find several types with different kinds of locking mechanisms. In general, American proprietary snaps, with or without ball-bearing swivels, are preferable. The snap's strength is determined by the wire's thickness and hardness, while its security depends on how well it locks.

In the world's big-game arenas, a double ring Coastlock snap swivel, where the snap is connected to a second ring, rather than the swivel stem, is usually considered unbeatable. The extra ring prevents the snap from rising and locking itself during the outward run. Sampo's McMahon snap, and the corkscrew snap, have many adherents. The latter type is strong, easy to work with, and impossible to open by mistake.

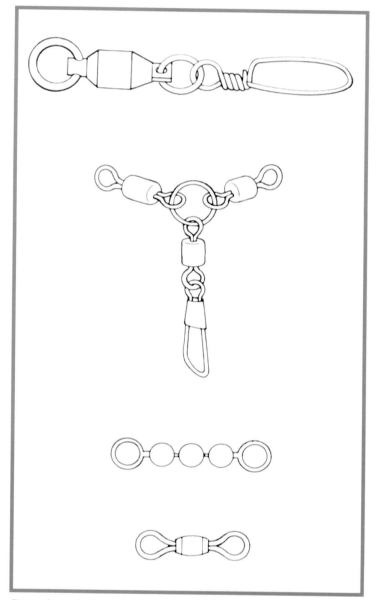

Types of swivels. At top is a big-game ball-bearing swivel, with two solid rings and a coastlock hook. This is the king of them all, and comes in various sizes. The self-centering three-way swivel was built by the author from a ring and three swivels, one of these being a snap swivel. It is worth noting that a solid ring, constructed with no overlaps, is far stronger than a feather ring of the same dimensions.

The bead-chain swivel is a favorite of trollers, due to its supple and flexible form - plus its reliability, which is partly a result of distributing the load on the swivel over many joints.

A barrel swivel of split-head type is better in several respects than one with a single head or twisted eye.

However, I have seen leaders get snarled in the " corkscrew" and snapped by wild salmon leaps. This catch is also conspicuous – for better or worse – because its structure draws a lot of water after it.

Other kinds of links, more or less commonly found in the end tackle, are the duolock snap, the bead.chain swivel, the butterfly link and the glide link. Handy and quickly coupled, they come in different materials, strengths and sizes.

The ring, too, is a type of coupling arrangement, which you should choose with great thought and make special demands upon. The split ring and the solid ring are two versions. Their reliability depends on their strength, resistance to corrosion, and locking arrangement. The solid ring use to be the best. In size, they should be suited to the given lure and hook. With several rings between the lure and hook, one can hook the fish better and ensure that, if it jumps, no break will occur between the lure and hook

Personal equipment

How should a well-dressed trolling fishermen make sure he is protected from head to toe? The answer obviously varies with the latitude, the coast, the season and so on. What can be an advantage on the open sea, such as being easily visible, may prove a great drawback in smaller waters.

Some kind of life-vest, life-jacket or survival suit is obligatory, of course. I never sail south without a Florida cap, Polaroid sunglasses, and antisolar cream. My clothes always include a long-sleeved cotton shirt to shade my arms, and a pair of long light pants with a couple of zippers that can turn them quickly into shorts.

Shoes or boots should be strong, water-repellent and well-sewn, with non-slip soles, so that you can move securely and dry-shod on board. Boots are definitely more protective, but seldom as comfortable.

On your head, according to the climate, there may be a visor, a fishing cap made of Gore-Tex, a knitted cap or a balaclava. In addition there should always be a pair of finger-gloves onboard.

Right: A small boat has many advantages and, with functional equipment, can be turned into an efficient trolling machine.

It is easy to transport between waters, enabling the fisherman to experience a varied sport in diverse surroundings. Often it is shallow-going, whicch permits fishing in waters that are inaccessible to a large, deep-running craft.

Boats and their fittings

For most sportfishermen, a boat is just a way of getting to and from fishing spots. But a boat means a lot more than that to a troller. It is an instrument for fishing, every bit as important to his or her equipment as a rod, line and reel.

A trolling boat may be anything from a small, flat-bottomed car-roof vessel to a big, deep, V-shaped motor cruiser driven by hundreds of horsepower. How the boat looks will depend on when, where and how you fish, and naturally on the size of your pocketbook.

Modern trolling gear has made it possible to fight fish all the time from the ice-melt to the icing-up, and no matter whether they swim deep or shallow. Consequently, the ideal trolling boat should be designed as much for sunny summer days as for chilly winter days. In other words: seaworthy, durable, and

Right: A big boat renders trolling less dependent on the weather and waves. It also off better protection, and room for both fishing and boating equipment. Comfort and spe on board usually mean that you can stay longer at the fishing sp

functionally fitted out. But a perfect trolling boat, suited to all types of water, is and will probably remain a fantasy.

When it comes to trolling boats for private use, most of us select from open center-console boats, walk-around boats and cabin boats in the classes 17-25 feet (5.2-7.6 meters). Here the chances are best of finding an all-round boat that can be transported from one kind of fishing environment to another, while letting you fish shallow inshore waters as well as the deep waters beyond.

The rapid spread of big-game fishing on the world's seas, for top-ranking sportfish such as tuna and marlin, has also led ever more boat manufacturers to make comfortable trolling versions of their flagships in the classes of 30-60 ft (9.1-18.2 m). It is among these flybridge models that we usually encounter the best-known charter boats.

Choosing a trolling boat

When you buy a boat, it is essential to be guided by reality, not personal dreams. A first-time purchaser should analyze his or her requirements very carefully. Try to decide what conditions the fishing will mostly be done under, within the foreseeable future, and base your selection on them. Then you will be most likely to fish both enjoyably and fruitfully.

The foremost rule is that a fishing boat must be as safe as possible. To this end, collect a maximum of facts about the type of boat in question. Many trollers use their boats more during seasons of bad weather than in periods of fine weather, since the fishing is best at the former times. Make sure that the railings or gunwale all round the boat provide support above your knees. The grab-rails should also be strategically placed so that you can move about easily and safely on board.

Check, too, that the scarn deck is wide and strong enough for all the desired equipment to be mounted.

Regardless of what material a boat is made of, it needs maintenance. Some parts are more exposed to wear than others on a trolling boat. The best place to put equipment is not as obvious on a big boat as on a little one. You should see to it that the electronics, for instance, can tolerate salt water and spray. Regularly inspect the steering and engine controls, fittings and hull, stern equipment and the engine itself.

For most sportfishermen, a boat purchase often ends with some sort of compromise. A good first-time buy can be a well-kept boat that has been used by another person who sport-fishes in the same way as you do. Practical and even difficult problems of installation and fitting will then have been solved already.

The boat's size

In a center-console boat, either big or small, you can move freely from the stem to the stern, and from side to side. Thus, fishing and fighting the fish can be done very effectively from this type of boat. In practice, the fishing space may also be more extensive on a small boat than on a much longer and wider one.

Generally speaking, the same advantages – together with significantly better weather protection and stowage space – are found in a walk-around boat. As the name indicates, the cabin is surrounded by a broad sunken passage. Many trolling fishermen in both the New and Old Worlds consider this boat type as close to the ideal as one can come, for fishing on large inland waters and along open coasts.

Small boats tend to allow fishing in shallower water than do the bigger, deep-going types. In addition, fish are not as shy of a small boat. The size and weight are also decisive for whether a boat can be transported by trailer, for easy movement from one body of water to another.

The limits of a little boat are clearest in terms of space for equipment – or if you fish on the open sea. Out there, they provide minimal shelter from wind, rain and breaking waves. Personally, though, I do not think this is such a bother, compared with the mobility of a small boat. But it does become troublesome when trolling equipment cannot be constantly kept in place on the boat. Storage space in a small boat is neither secure nor extensive enough. It is then essential, from the outset, to plan and put away the equipment in the right way,

so that the work of carrying things is minimized and will not diminish your enjoyment or time.

As a rule, in my experience of fishing on small boats, a motor-driven boat should always be driven from a console. Unfortunately, many consoles are far too small for the equipment which a trolling fisherman wants to have available and keep in view.

Larger, decked boats have the great advantage of giving good protection from wind and rain – and, in a wider perspective, of being usable on rough open waters. Their roominess offers not only the opportunity of overnight sleeping, but also easy positioning and handling of trophy catches and equipment, such as a communications radio, echo-sounder, navigation instruments, downriggers, outriggers, fighting chair, lures, tackle, and personal belongings. Besides, their comfort and safety can be much better. These benefits, which enable one to get the most out of the boat, have led many fishermen to invest in a large craft and a permanent place in the harbor.

The helmsman's area

Good elbow room should be the hallmark of the cockpit, no matter whether you wear shorts or a survival suit. The steering gear, engine controls, and other instruments should be well-placed, protected, easily accessible and visible, without blocking your lines of sight.

The range of instruments has naturally influenced the whole center console and the cabin panels. Some modern center consoles can be folded forward, giving easy access to the deck and to any fuel space or equipment underneath them. The console should ideally be protected against wind and rain from three directions by a plexiglas windshield– ample enough to shield both the instruments and the helmsman.

Moreover, a strong rail should run around the steering unit. It may be extended into a T-top or a spray hood, which gives further protection against sun and rain from above.

Rig equipment

The importance and function of a side deck on a trolling boat are often neglected. Most of the praise or blame fall upon the hull design, cabin and engine. Yet the boat's gunwale is what has to take the first, and sometimes worst, knocks when it comes to protecting your boat, your life, and your gear. The top side and rails should be high enough to give support, at least up to the knees, for a medium-tall adult all round the boat.

If the rod-holders and rig equipment are properly positioned, even a small deck space allows you to cover considerable width and depth at the boat's sides and astern.

To a trolling fisherman, the railing – in terms of the scarn deck – also provides an extremely important platform for fishing, both downward and sideways. This is where everything from single rod-holders to complete downriggers and outrigger poles is attached.

The scarn deck on a trolling boat has to be wide and strong, as well as made of a material that is tough, durable, and easy to work. Top-quality wood of correct dimensions is a superb side deck material. If, for example, you add a fiberglass mounting for a downrigger, you will normally need to strengthen it from below with marine plywood.

Rod-holders

For many of us, the first rod-holder is a mobile type that can be attached to a railing. Its steadiness, and ability to point the rod in desired directions, are important Moreover, it must allow you to quickly remove the rod, in order to make a hookup or move to a fishing chair.

A rod-holder's size and strength should be suited for the fishing in question. It would be foolish to put, for example, big-game equipment in simple plastic holders. Such equipment demands robust metal holders with replaceable linings – whether they are flush mounted into side or stern deck, in fighting chairs, or in the rod launcher of a leaning post. Many rod-holders have a cross-pin in the bottom that fits into the gimbal butt of the rod handle, keeping the rod in a definite position. It also prevents the reel from knocking and chafing against the rod-holder's upper edge. In any case, when moving at speed or on rough waters, it can be smart to secure the rod set-up with safety ropes.

Remember to locate the rod-holders on board in a pattern so that they spread the trolling lines as much as possible and avoid tangles. Make sure, too, that they are within reach and can be surveyed from the driver's seat. A rear-view mirror helps the solitary troller to see aft.

Downriggers

A downrigger has the advantage of being able to bring even a leaf-thin lure down to a depth of hundred meter, by means of a sinker weight and line release. When the fish strikes, it pulls line from the release, and can be played directly with the ordinary fishing gear.

Thus, a downrigger is an independent part of the equipment, consisting of an arm with a roller guide and a spool of wire line that runs through the guide. On the wire's end is a heavy sinker weight, in a snap swivel. Also on the wire, or attached to the sinker, is a line release.

Most downriggers have a drag system, depth counter, and rodholder as well. But not all downriggers, or their components, can tolerate salt water – and this is something to watch out for.

The wire's length and strength may vary a little with the rig's size, but around 200 ft 60 m) and 130 lbs (60 kg) test strength are common. The sinker usually weighs 3.5-15 lbs (1.5-7 kg).

Downrigger arms come in short or long sizes of 1-6 ft (30-180 cm), or may be telescoping. The arm length depends on how you want to locate your rigs on board, whether you need to keep the line clear of the propellers and engine mounting, how easy it is to take the sinker weight in and out, and so forth. The sinker is moved either manually or with a small electric motor.

To reduce the stress on the wire, arm and other components, the downrigger should be started and stopped softly. It is also helpful if the rig can be operated with one hand – for letting down, retrieving, and stopping. Adjust the drag so that it slips lightly during the descent, or if the weight gets snagged on the bottom. You should be able to retrieve manually even with an electric rig, in case the current is cut off.

The rig's tip roller should be swiveling and automatically tracks the downrigger weight toward the depths. The pulley itself should be sufficiently deep or protected to prevent the wire from sliding out. Finally, never load the spool with longer or thicker wire than what is specified by the rig manufacturer. Obey the instructions as regards the sinker weight, and always have spare parts on board – such as wire, sleeves, weight snaps, and extra sinkers.

A downrigger strains the side or stern deck hard, no matter what type of mounting is used. There are many versions and models of downrigger mountings, but I personally prefer a swivel base. This makes it possible to tackle lures very near the boat, then swing out and lock the arm in the desired direction.

Another common alternative is to mount downriggers on a "trolling bar disk" at the stern. The bar is fixed, at the desired height, in pedestals which are mounted in the stern deck. There are also mounting board which, like the roof-rack on a car, are mounted across the boat. If the bar has the form of an aluminum rail, the rigs can be positioned easily.

When flush mounted rod-holders are fixed to the side decks, the downriggers can suitably be mounted on an adapter with a tubular foot and guide sloe. Slide the foot into a rod-holder, where a cross-pin in its bottom locks the rig in position. A swivel base on the adapter will further increase the choices for positioning. With the rig in an adapter base, you can also quickly lift it away from the side deck when you need swinging room, or when you want to use the boat for other kinds of fishing.

An accessory that can be very useful on long-armed rigs consists of a pulley on a piece of cord which is attached to the wire. Popularly called a retriever, it helps to pull in the wire when retackling. The cord can then be fixed in a cleat on the downrigger.

On most downriggers of medium or large size, it is now possible to mount one or more rod-holders. Single-rod holders are usually placed on the rig housing, but double-rod holders generally sit farthest down on the arm. You should be able to angle the holders separately, not least in order to spread out the rods.

Makers of downriggers are relying ever more on computers. For instance, the lure and sinker can be raised and lowered at different speeds through the water. This may be important when you have to get the gear up fast after a big fish strikes. The sinker can also be stopped automatically at the water surface, to reduce the load on the arm and wire. The rig's computer can be programmed so that the lure searches certain depths at various time intervals – an advantage when fishing in and around the thermocline. You can even get the bait to continually follow the bottom contours, at a particular distance so that the sinker does not get snagged.

The smallest and simplest downriggers weigh only a few pounds, and have a low profile to occupy minimal space in a fishing bag. They usually hold 80-100 ft (25-30 m) of wire, have a less sophisticated drag than on larger models, and can be loaded with up to some 5 lbs (2 kg) of sinker weight. The arm length is 12-16 in (30-40 cm). These versions come with or without a depth counter, and can be placed in rowlock holes or clamped to the railing. Despite their modest size, they increase the fisherman's range enormously.

In general, it is the boat's size and railings, side and stern deck – as well as the kind of fishing water – that determine the size, number, and positioning of downriggers. But keep in mind the following:

- place downriggers so that they are not a safety risk on board;
- place them in the rear third of the boat;
- place them so that you can get between them to net or gaff the fish;
- if possible, place long-armed rigs at the sides, and short-armed rigs at the stern;
- place rigs and rods within easy reach and view.

Outriggers

As an aid to fishing, the outrigger holder is older than the downrigger. Its main task is to spread the bait lines beyond the boat's wake. Outrigger arms are normally fished at about 45 degrees from the side of the boat. Around Hawaii, however, they are fished in an almost vertical position, at 60-90 degrees, so that the artificial lures will run just under the surface.

Today's arms consist of aluminum, stainless steel or fiber-glass, may be either telescopic or screwed together in sections, and are 15-30 ft (4.5-9 m) long. The shaft requires rigging kits, which usually comprises a halyard line about 100 ft (30 m) long, a shock-cord (with a glass ring in one end and a strong ball bearing snap swivel in the other), a pulley, a line release clip, and an eye strap in the boat.

The shortest outriggers are commonest in center-console boats of up to 20 ft (6 m). They are usually placed in flush hold-ers in the scarn deck. A curved butt section makes them easily portable and collapsible for fishing or transport. Long shafts are found mainly on large motor cruisers, where they may be mounted on the cabin's side and/or on a superstructure, such as a tuna tower. These rods are solidly anchored to the boat with four legs, but are very easy to collapse or raise with a con-trol-knob. Still, they should be secured with a safety rope.

The choice of outrigger depends on the size of the bait, as well as on that of the boat. Most frequently the outriggers are installed about amidships, so that the poles bend aft when in trolling positions. Thus, when a fish strikes, the reel lines do not risk landing in the driver's well and possibly getting caught.

The shafts' bending capacity varies with their construction.

Some are stiffened with several metal spindles. Stiff poles fish well even in rough seas. They may carry double halyards lines, and can spread a number of baited lines at the same time. An all-round outrigger has a stiff lower part and a flexible tip which makes up about 25% of the shaft's total length. Even the shortest version can be a great help. It does become easy to overload in bad weather, which makes the lure jump and splash in the surface – fishing poorly as a result. But this can be corrected by positioning the line and release farther down on a stiffer part of the shaft.

The halyard runs through guides on the shaft, and some-times also through a tip pulley. On this halyard are one or more clips, in which the reel line is clamped. The warping is done either manually or electrically. The halyard is tightened up once the fishing lines and baits have reached the right places and are not in the way.

Planer boards

Another variant of surfacing trolling makes use of a mast and planer boards. The latter, like an outrigger holder, are fished in the open sea to cover waters that are not disturbed by the boat's passage. They are especially handy when a fisherman wants to present baits in shallow water near land, which is unreachable due to the boat's depth.

A planer board may be a traditional otterboard, but is nor-mally designed for its purpose. It can be made of wood, metal,

In fresh and brackish water, most of us widen our fishing with planer boards. These are sent out sideways from a mast with planer lines, to which line releases and rod equipment are coupled.

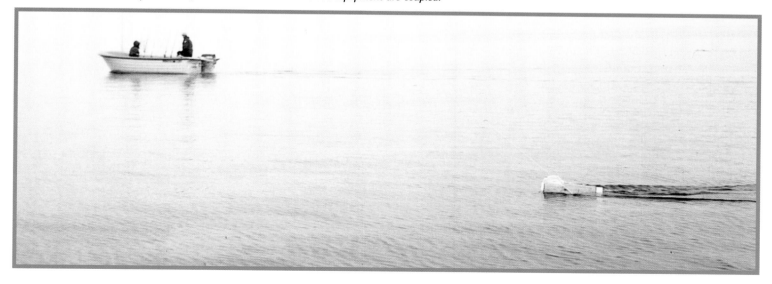

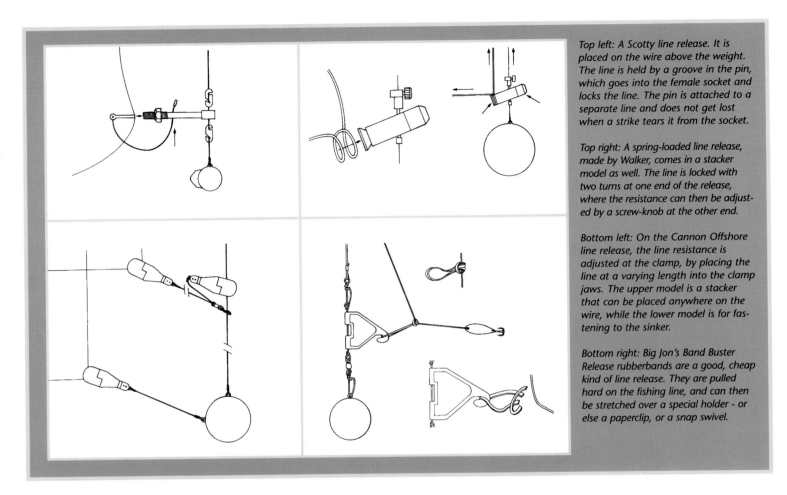

Top left: A Scotty line release. It is placed on the wire above the weight. The line is held by a groove in the pin, which goes into the female socket and locks the line. The pin is attached to a separate line and does not get lost when a strike tears it from the socket.

Top right: A spring-loaded line release, made by Walker, comes in a stacker model as well. The line is locked with two turns at one end of the release, where the resistance can then be adjusted by a screw-knob at the other end.

Bottom left: On the Cannon Offshore line release, the line resistance is adjusted at the clamp, by placing the line at a varying length into the clamp jaws. The upper model is a stacker that can be placed anywhere on the wire, while the lower model is for fastening to the sinker.

Bottom right: Big Jon's Band Buster Release rubberbands are a good, cheap kind of line release. They are pulled hard on the fishing line, and can then be stretched over a special holder - or else a paperclip, or a snap swivel.

styrofoam or glasfiber material. The important point is that it should be simple to use, and ride well on the water. As a rule, the bigger it is, the better it tolerates high speed and rough seas. The yard-long versions are heavy to retrieve, so they put a hard strain on the mast and line spool. To be seen properly, a planer should be painted in some conspicuous color, and carry a pennant or flag.

Between the mast and planer board runs a rope, over a mast pulley that is sometimes spring-loaded. On this line, a release can slide freely. The fishing line is coupled to the release, so that the lure can be presented 80-100 ft (25-30 m) from the boat. If a small diving plane, of the Kuusamo type, is placed between the lure leader and the reel line, you can fish both down and out. When the fish strikes, it pops the line free and can be fought directly from the rod.

The mast, generally 3-6 ft (1-2 m) long, bears one or two line spools that are adjustable in height. It should be made of saltwater-resistant material. Place it as far forward as is practical, and mount it very steadily. Reels with clutch sys-

tem are an advantage. The rope is usually of colorful dacron, about 165 ft (50 m) long, with a test strength of around 130 lbs (60 kg).

Some simple planers, of the Yellow Bird and Rover type, are attached directly on the fishing line and kept in place by a line release. When the fish strikes, the planer slides down the line to a stop, or is just let go. In calm weather, such planers can bring the lure far out to the side, into areas where shy fish may lurk. They take up little room, and are very handy to have in your tackle box.

Line releases

Also called a clip, this device is among the most important in trolling. Its job is to hold the fishing line in place until the fish strikes. Then it has to free the line and, at the same time, give enough resistance to resemble a first counterstrike. An essential requirement is to be able to adjust the resistance that is needed to release the line.

Several models and sizes of line releases exist for fishing

with a planer board, downrigger or outrigger. The sliding type is most common with planer boards, while fixed and movable types are used with the latter rigs. Fixed clips are attached to the weight or on the downrigger wire just above it. But a movable line release, called a "stacker", can be placed at any level on the wire. Thus, two releases on the same wire enable you to "stack", or fish with two rods at different depths from the same downrigger. The main point is that a stacker should be easy to place and release on the wire.

The releasing mechanism varies from one type of clip to another. Some have clamping jaws that simply lock the line. On others, the line has to be wound around a spring device or an arm. Alternatively, the line is locked with a plug. One or two rubberbands can also work well as a link between the sinker/wire and the reel line: the band is torn off when the fish strikes.

On most models, the clip's tension can be adjusted by hand. How hard it should be depends on the given fish species, trolling depth and speed, the sea conditions and the lure's form. But keep in mind that some models which look easy to adjust in a shop may be hard to handle when you are out on a swaying boat deck with wet fingers.

Tension setting is crucial

No matter where the release is placed, you have to watch out that the fishing line does not slip in the release: if it does, a big bow will arise in the line between the rod tip and the release. Then the fish will take slack line just after striking and may be hooked badly. At worst, the lure may slide all the way up to the release, get caught in it, and do no fishing whatever. This is best avoided by using, for instance, specially designed downrigger rods in combination with adjustable clips. The soft tip of such a rod bends attentively into tension, right towards the release, so it causes nothing like the pull on the line and clips that an ordinary spinning rod in the same position creates. The deeper you fish, the more obvious this becomes.

To put things simply, the pressure in the release grows with the fishing depth and the length of fishing line that is out. Couple the heaviest equipment (heaviest line, biggest lure) to the release that is farthest down. In general, fish are hooked best on a short line length, and without too little tension. Excessive tension can make it impossible for a biting fish to jerk the line from the release.

It is particularly difficult, and therefore important, to find the right tension when you are fishing at great depths with live bait

and big-game equipment in your rod-holder. The fish should feel minimal resistance from the bait when striking – otherwise they may instantly spit out the bait. By tensing up with a bit of curve in the line, having a long line out at 30-65 ft (10-20 m), fine-tuning the clip tension, and trolling slowly, you get the desired "dropback" effect.

The tension in the release can be checked in different ways. Most commonly, one tries from the boat to jerk line with the rod from the release when it is at a normal depth or distance. If the line does not loosen, the resistance is usually too hard. A more reliable procedure, especially when fishing at great depths or for big game, is to determine resistance by using a scale. Tie one end of the fishing line to a spring-scale, then place the line correctly in the release, and clamp it with varying strength. On the scale you can read the weight figures that are needed to pull out the line, at each level of tension and length of line.

Fishing at depth

Rubberbands are very popular as line releases. They are cheap, easy to position, and usable either as stackers or fixed releases. In sizes 12-16, they break with a load of 2-9 lbs (1-4 kg), which is enough for ordinary downrigger fishing for salmon, among other things. Size 32 is used by many who fish with equipment in the IGFA classes of 20-30 lbs (10-15 kg). Those who hope to hook a seagoing express train on gear of 50-130 lbs use No. 64 rubberbands. The disadvantage of a rubberband is that its resistance cannot be adjusted, but a solution is to join several of them together. They also have a very short lifetime, being quite sensitive to sunlight. So they should always be stored as cool and dark as possible.

A rubberband release is tightened around the fishing line to prevent it from slipping through, and is coupled to a snap of the Elasti-Clip variety, or to a plain paperclip. This in turn is attached to the sinker or wire. The rubberband is pulled off when the fish strikes. Pieces of it may stay on the line, but usually pass through the rod guides and level-wind. However, get them off as soon as possible.

The "clothespin" model is an easy-to-use version. Its components are tension pads clamp, nylon-covered wire, and a snap swivel that attaches to the sinker. Its tension is adjusted by placing the fishing line more or less far into its jaws. It is available with variable pinching power in the jaws.

Wire and sleeves are parts in the line release that should be carefully checked, because breaks can easily occur here and result in corrosion. Exchange the wire for a terylene line. More-over, rubber pads in the clamping jaws may stick together when a line release stays out of use for long, and this is avoid-able by putting a piece of tinfoil between the jaws. As the pads wear down in time, the clamping strength weakens.

On other release clips, the line release mechanism consists of a powerful C-shaped wire arm. This kind of clip creates very lit-tle wear on the line and is particularly appreciated by those trolling with superlines or in a saltwater milieu. The line goes around the arm in a loop after having first been twisted 5 to 10 turns. The arm's tension is then adjusted with a screw or slide. When the fish strikes, the C-arm open and the line is released.

Fishing at the surface

Planer-board releases should be easy to mount and run on the planer board rope. They generally consist of a metal device, like a ring or paperclip, which has pinch pads. The tension is adjusted by placing the fishing line at different distances into the clips. A fast-wiggling plug needs harder pressure than a light spoon. After the strike, the release slides down along the planer board rope, so you should have a bunch of clips avail-able for continuous fishing.

The range of clips for outriggers is much wider than for planers. Here you can find everything from the simple " clothespin" to the roller-guide version.

Trip-Eze is a spring-loaded version where the line runs over a strong wire arm, which can be loaded with varying resistance. The same is true of Aftco's "Roller-Troller", where the line goes over a roller guide that minimizes the wearing friction. The Roller-Troller can also be obtained as a flatline clip. Its release mecha-nism is mounted in a nylon-covered wire, on whose other end is a strong snap swivel. This construction enables it to be located at many places on board where you want to have a flatline fishing with a line release. Thus your lines will be less snarled or wind-blown, and the lure will run better with improved hooking abil-ity. Flatline clips are easy to make with many different models of line releases. The simplest way is to tighten a rubberband around the fishing line and attach it to the reel handle.

Sinkers

Sinkers can be divided into two categories, downrigger and flatline sinkers. In both groups they vary as regards shape, weight, and sometimes even color. A flatline sinker is used mainly to keep the lure at the desired depth, without twisting the line or hampering the lure's movement. It is usually attached between the fishing line and the leader.

To minimize their resistance in the water, most trolling sinkers have a torpedo-like body. Some are also down-weight-ed or have a keel to stabilize the lure's movement, so that it will be less prone to peculiar twisting or swaying. Moreover, the sinker should have a swivel at each end.

Another type of sinker, often used when trolling with natu-ral bait, resembles a cigar or egg. It is threaded on the leader and placed just in front of the bait, which is thus made to swim like a fish.

Besides the keel sinker, so-called walking type sinkers are used among trollers, especially for fishing slowly along the bottom. This is a Y-shaped construction: one of its arms can

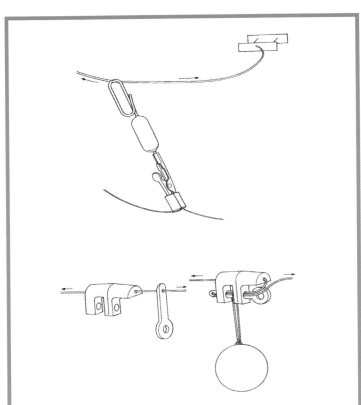

Top: *A Laurwick planer-board release. The fishing line, clamped between alligator jaws, is torn loose when the fish strikes. Then the fish can be played directly off the rod, without any resistance from other equipment.*

Bottom: *A Jettison drop-rig release. This is mounted right on the fish-ing line, usually 30-50 ft (10-15 m) above the lure. The sinker hangs on a short line stump on a line release pin, and "drops off" when the fish strikes.*

take the bumps on the bottom, while the other arm holds the leader and lure away from the bottom.

Downrigger sinkers are in an entirely different weight class, but their size must be suited to the given downrigger. For small rigs that are temporary mount to your boat weights of 3.0-4.5 lbs (1.5-2 kg) are normally used. The very strongest downriggers can take a load of around 16 lbs (7 kg), provided that they are solidly mounted on the boat.

Checking the depth

As long as the sinker is visible in the echo-sounder's conical angle, you can easily keep an eye on exactly what depth it is at. However, the faster and deeper you troll, the larger becomes the difference between the readings on the echo-

sounder and the downrigger. This can be confirmed by eye if you look at the wire's angle to the water surface. What the downrigger's distance counter shows is not how deep you are fishing but how much wire you have out.

There are also tables, produced by the downrigger maker Scotty, which show how deeply different sinker weights run at a speed of 3 knots, with a certain length of line out. These studies used 140-lb test wire and 30-lb (about 0.45 mm) fishing line.

It follows that there are several reasons for having different weights to use at different depths – and, not least, for constantly checking that they are really at the depths where the fish can be found. A normal trolling speed is often 2-4 knots, and it is just in this range, when fishing at depths over 100 ft (30 m), that the changes occur very rapidly.

Illustrated here are a downrigger wire's extension and depth, in feet, for a sinker of 10 lbs (4.5 kg) pulled at a speed of 3 knots, when the line length out is 50, 100 or 200 ft (15, 30 or 60 m). The wire has 140 lbs test strength and a diameter of 0.032 inches (0.81 mm). The faster and deeper you troll, the more weight is needed to keep the sinker in as vertical a position as possible. Try to maintain the wire at an angle of at most 20-30 degrees from the vertical.

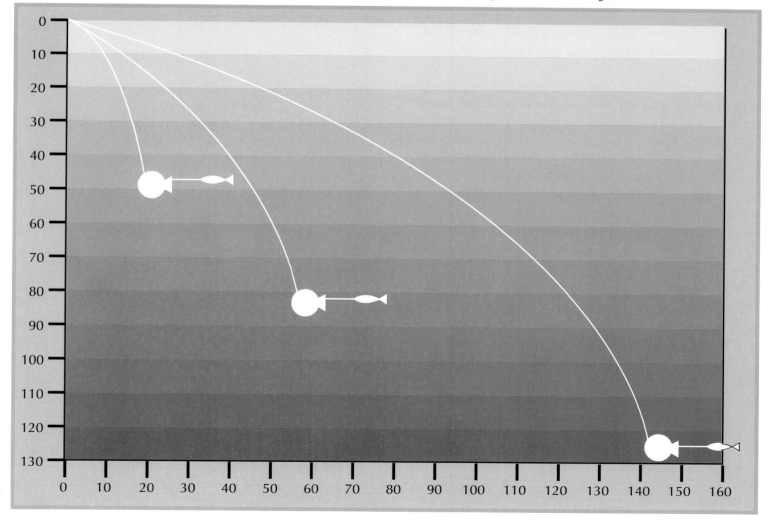

Electronics

Developments in boat electronics have been enormous during the past decade, and to the troller's benefit. All round the world, they are opening up new opportunities. In northern Europe, for instance, the Baltic and many large lakes have become far more accessible than previously. Besides, electronics have made the fishing much safer in both deep and shallow waters. The ability of modern navigation instruments to lead us rapidly and exactly to the fishing places has also reduced fuel costs and increased the actual fishing time. However, high-tech trolling is not what hooks, fights and boards the fish: this calls for a fisherman, not an instrument.

The echo-sounder

An echo-sounder not only gives us an extended "eye" into the world of fish. It is a very important means of rapid and risk-free navigation. Moreover, the information that it supplies about bottom topography, thermoclines, school formations, and individual fish is often stimulating and helps to develop one's fishing.

What we call an echo-sounder is a combination of three units – the monitor, current cable, and transducer. The transducer takes an electrical impulse from the monitor and turns it into a pulse of sound (acoustic pressure) waves. This travels through the water, and is partly reflected back when it hits something – such as the bottom or a fish. Since the speed of sound in water is known (1,460 meters or 4 880 feet per second), the time measured between the outgoing pulse and the incoming echo can be converted into distance. So the echoes from various levels, along with the monitor's image or paper speed, create the picture of the watery world that we see on the screen.

The length of the sound pulses will determine the echo-sounder's resolution: how close together the fish can be and still appear on the screen as individuals. A short pulse resolves, or separates, the members of a school better than a long pulse. But it is also more sensitive to disturbances, and is not as good for depth-sounding. The latter ability depends on other factors too: the water's condition (such as salinity), the bottom structure, the transducer's conical angle of direction and its mounting, and the wave frequency that it uses. The

Trolling fishermen are increasingly building up complete electronic navigation systems in their driving environments.

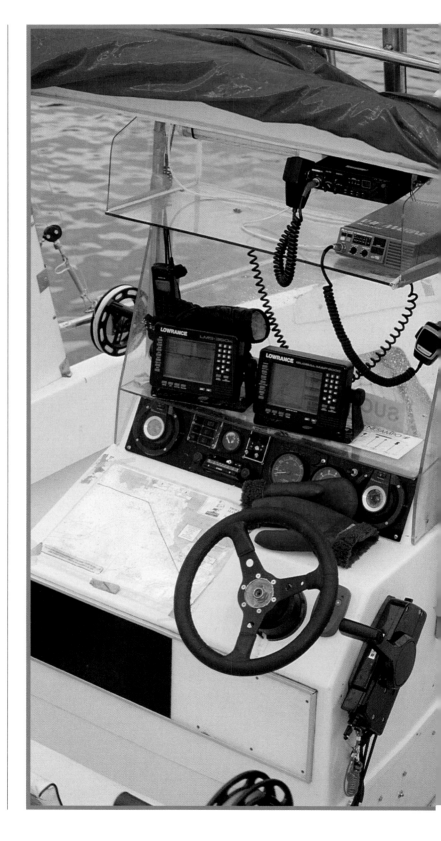

conical angle and the frequency are most important when choosing an echo-sounder for fishing, either inshore or at sea.

Frequency is the number of oscillations per second, commonly measured in kilocycles (kc). A high-frequency echo-sounder is usually said to be one which operates at more than 190 kc, while medium frequency means 75-100 kc and low frequency means 50 kc. Advanced echo-sounders can work with different frequency ranges, which certainly helps to diversify the trolling. For fishing in waters shallower than about 115 ft (35 m), a high-frequency apparatus provides the most information. A low frequency is preferable when fishing at depths of 230 ft (70 m) or more.

The sound waves get weaker as they travel away from the transducer and back again. This loss of strength increases not only with the distance that they travel to an object, but also as their frequency becomes higher. The latter effect is most noticeable in salt water.

Higher frequencies give a clearer echo from small objects, and are less influenced by the motor noise and the hull shape, than lower frequencies. A low-frequency wave, however, is weakened less at long distances. Thus, when it comes to locating fish at great depths, a low frequency is best.

Multidimensional transducers

The transducer sends out sound pulses in a directional pattern that resembles a cone – or more correctly, a lobe. This covers an angle whose size depends on the transducer you use. Such a conical angle might be compared with an adjustable spotlight. The more concentrated the beam is made, the stronger and more revealing is the light inside it. With a wider field of illumination, the beam can expose a bigger area but with a much lower intensity.

There are transducers with conical angles between 5 and 60 degrees. Those with angles up to 15 degrees are regarded as narrow-coned, whereas wide-angle transducers are between 35 and 60 degrees. Normal transducers tend to have a conical angle of 20-30 degrees.

Whatever lies inside the conical angle will reflect sound, and is shown on the monitor as if it were right under the boat – even though, of course, it is not. The wider the angle, the more of the bottom will be exposed. Thus an 8-degree transducer, in the vertical position at a depth of 50 ft (15 m), shows an area of the bottom with a radius of about 6 ft (2 m). This radius will increase in direct proportion to the depth: for example, the same transducer at nearly 200 ft (60 m) exposes a radius of 26 ft (8 m). Yet at the latter depth, a 20-degree

transducer would expose an area some 72 ft (22 m) in radius.

Most trolling fishermen in small boats use 20-degree transducers, which work at high frequencies of 190-200 kc. A wide-angle transducer registers best in shallow water. However, the depth-sounding ability can be improved by working at 50 kc. This combination is preferable if you want to know where the downrigger weights are going.

Multidimensional wide-angle transducers can be pointed in different directions. The monitor can then give us, for instance, a full 60-degree view which covers about 40 meters of the bottom at a depth of 40 meters. Or it might provide three 20-degree pictures, simultaneously visible on separate parts of the screen.

Choosing a fishing sonar

Which type of fishfinder you select depends mainly on when, where and how you fish, as well as on the type of boat. If the fishing water is only in flatland lakes, rivers and coastal zones, with a maximum depth of 165-200 ft (50-60 m), the choice is much easier than if you also fish on deep fjords, vast lakes, or canyon edges out in the ocean. The latter areas call for an echo-sounder of great depth capacity, sensitivity and resolution. To find big fish at enormous depths, a lot of care is necessary with tasks such as installing the transducer and laying the cable.

Among other relevant questions are the following. Should you have a portable echo-sounder or a stationary one? How well-protected should its location be, and how watertight must it be? How much space does it take on the instrument panel? What information about speed, distance of travel, and water temperature does it give? Can it be coupled with a navigator and autopilot? Which echo-sounder is most suited to a given boat and type of fishing?

The LCD sonar

Even though flashers and recorders are still to be seen on instrument panels, it is LCD-sonars that dominate the field these days.

The screen image of an LCD sonar is built up by thousands of liquid crystals, and so the number of "pixels" in the screen is very important for the image's clarity. Often an LCD sonar is easy to handle and can automatically adapt its depth range, picture speed, and sensitivity to the conditions at hand. There are limited possibilities, via replaying, to document what has happened under the water.

Today's LCD sonars provide a clear view of everything from the surface to the bottom. The picture can be in either

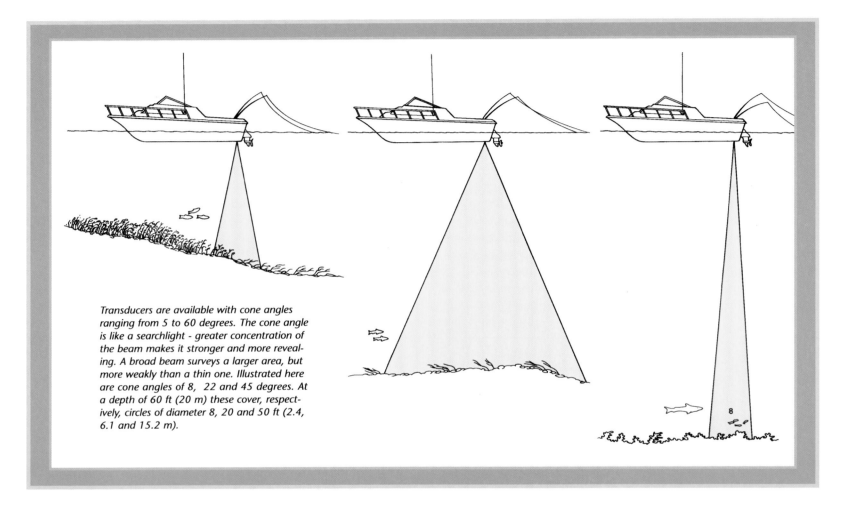

Transducers are available with cone angles ranging from 5 to 60 degrees. The cone angle is like a searchlight - greater concentration of the beam makes it stronger and more revealing. A broad beam surveys a larger area, but more weakly than a thin one. Illustrated here are cone angles of 8, 22 and 45 degrees. At a depth of 60 ft (20 m) these cover, respectively, circles of diameter 8, 20 and 50 ft (2.4, 6.1 and 15.2 m).

black/white or color, or even in three-dimensional form. In the latter case, you get a bottom landscape in perspective – with stones, fish and all the rest.

Many advanced LCD sonars can be bought in small portable models. Their current source is usually a pair of 6-volt batteries. The battery box serves as both a carrier and a steady support in the boat. For those who often use rented boats, a portable sounder is a very handy solution.

Slim, bright and easy to read, LCD sounders with sharp color images of a very high level of image resolution and separation are steadily pushing out the last generation of LCD sounders, which were hard to read in certain light conditions and at certain angles.

The multi-function fishfinder with side-looking sonar is to become ever more common in sportfishing circles. It equips us with an underwater "radar" and reveals the surroundings in a limited vertical or horizontal field under the boat's hull. Its search area can be set to different widths, such as sweeping through a 10-degree field for 330 ft (100 m) in front.

The navigator

For many decades, nautical charts, a compass and an echo-sounder have traditionally been helping most skippers find their fishing spots. The latest, and revolutionary, instrument to guide trolling boats is the navigator. A combined computer and radio receiver, it converts incoming signals to information about position, course and speed, which can be read on a display.

Navigators for sportfishing boats are not fearsome contraptions. What you need, besides the display, are just an antenna unit and electric current. The display can be placed, for example, in a console about half a yard away from the compass and echo-sounder, without risking interference. Being able to

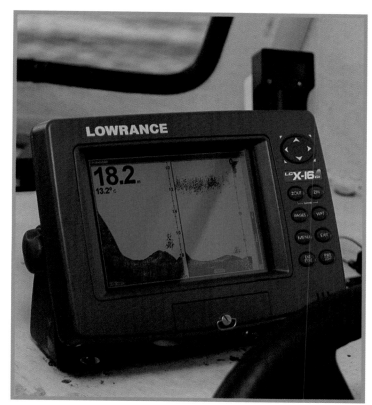

Developments on the electronic side are amazingly rapid. From ever smaller instruments we can extract ever more diverse and useful information, which promotes better and safer fishing. The image screen on this monitor shows information from the speed and temperature sensor, fish finder and navigator. It also plots the boat's course from the starting point until the present position.

mine your position to within less than 3 yards (3 meters).

Navigators are available with different levels of performance and price, so you should approach them with an awareness of your own requirements. In general, a sportfisherman wants to know the boat's position, course and speed. Many of us certainly want a navigator with a brightly lit display, and want it to tolerate tough year-round use in an open boat. Some also want to have the option of coupling other instruments to it, such as an autopilot. The computer's external memory, its ability to be updated and its capacity to store information on waypoints and routes as well as trackplotting are important to investigate when making a purchase.

Even relatively small navigators are convenient and give continuous information on the position, speed and course, as well as data on steering towards various selected "waypoints" on a planned course. They also indicate the strength of radio signals and the battery voltage. Other handy functions are compass correction and "man overboard". The latter means that you need only push a button to record the position, in case of an accident or a place where fish strike.

When the navigator is turned on, it automatically seeks its position without any departure point being programmed in. It gives a signal when this task is done, and it continuously updates the position afterwards, so that you can easily see where you are on a nautical chart – paper or electronic. A plotting function makes navigating significantly easier. Electronic navigational charts exist in a number of advanced versions and packaging (cassettes, CDs) and provide increasingly detailed information of the kind we have expected from traditional charts.

A navigator is very helpful when you want to return to good fishing places – and if you want to feel safe even in darkness, or when the sea-mist closes in fast and cuts off visibility. Like all instruments, though, it can be disturbed or even break down. As long as such things can happen, there are good reasons for preserving your knowledge of traditional navigation techniques.

Radar

In sportfishing waters that are full of islands or boat traffic, radar is becoming ever more common on trolling boats as well. Today's compact radar equipment is absolutely not a luxury, but an extra-safe aid to navigation – not least in darkness and fog.

Radar works like an echo-sounder, but makes use of radio waves instead of sound waves. The waves are reflected when

carry away the navigator when you leave the boat is frequently desired, and there are pocket-sized GPS navigators with plotter functions that can be held in one hand.

For many years, positioning information was provided by the Loran and Decca navigation systems from land-based transmitters with limited range. The reigning system now is GPS (Global Positioning System), which was developed by the United States Defense Department. Employing time-based distance measurements, GPS operates with 21 satellites and three more in reserve. Information is normally taken on board by a 12-channel GPS-receiver.

Systems that improve positional accuracy even more are the American WAAS (Wide Area Augmentation System) and the European EGNOS (European Geostationary Navigation Overlay Service). With a compact antenna that receives DGPS (Differential GPS) and EGNOS/WAAS signals, you can deter-

they hit objects, whose direction and distance are then displayed on a screen. Your own boat is always in the center of the radar image. The boat's position, relative to land and other vessels, is shown continuously. You can also get the radar to produce an alarm if the boat goes on a collision course. Both small and large trolling boats can increase their ability to reflect radio waves by carrying a radar reflector.

Radio and telephone

For today's far-traveling fishermen, it is important to remember that the rules for using communications equipment vary from country to country. What is allowed in your home waters might well be forbidden in neighboring waters. So be sure to check which channels are available for which purposes. In order to be fairly sure of getting radio contact in an emergency situation, you should have a transmitter power of at least 5 watts, and a boat antenna.

The new generation of advanced VHF telephones allows you to make calls anywhere in the world over the telecom network as well as download computer files.

VHF offers coverage everywhere around the clock. This is the system relied upon by most trolling boats of medium to large size. The equipment has become increasingly convenient through the years. Among sportfishermen, the small hand-held versions are popular. A stationary VHF installation, however, generally has a superior range.

A boat with VHF can have its bearings taken and be given radio escort. You can even listen to rescue operations and possibly be able to make a contribution if you are in the vicinity; channel 16 is the international emergency channel. It is also over VHF that coastal radio broadcasts calls, weather forecasts, navigational warnings, and so forth. VHF is without doubt the most secure system, and is now, via DSC (Digital Selective Calling), increasing security even more in emergency situations. Having VHF equipment requires permission.

A good antenna is needed for solid radio contact. In general, the higher the antenna is placed, the longer the range will be. If you have several antennas, make sure that they are spread at different heights, to minimize interference between the instruments on board. Radio equipment also requires excellent "grounding", and the best method is to mount a metal plate on the hull.

A mobile telephone is the most common telecom equipment. By definition portable, it can be used in the boat, in the

The locations of fish are determined largely by the surrounding water temperature. A troller's success depends greatly on his ability to select a boat speed that suits the kind of bait he uses. Information from the depths can be sent up by a torpedo-like transmitter, mounted on the downrigger wire above the weight. Equipped with a blade-wheel and a sensor, it transmits to a monitor where the fisherman can read the data digitally.

car and at home, and it requires no permission. Contact can be made directly or via messages. Its range, however, is limited.

In most places, the traditional CD radio is still the most common communication link between leisure fishing boats. This type of equipment is convenient in size, portable and easy to use. It also has a long range, although it can be sensitive to interference.

Speed and temperature indicators

It is a well-known fact that the water temperature guidelines and sometimes decides where the various fish species occur in lakes, seas, and waterways. To locate the fish, sportfishermen try to check the temperature in different water layers. This can be done most simply by using a glass bottle, a weight, and a removable cork. The most advanced aids are indicators for speed and temperature – together with updated satellite pictures of the fishing area. These are photographs taken with infrared film to reveal the temperature differences in the water, i.e. where warm water meets cooler water.

Some speed and temperature indicators measures both at the surface and at the sinker on the end of a downrigger wire. The current source is the boat's 12-volt battery, and all the information is shown digitally on a little monitor. The other components in the package are a transducer, a cable, and a small torpedo-shaped transmitter. The latter, 9 inches (23 cm) long, has on its bottom a paddle wheel that measures the speed, a sensor, and a wire 12 in (30 cm) long which holds the sinker. This wire has a lower breaking strength than the downrigger wire, which is snapped on the top of the "torpedo". The idea is that, if the sinker gets hung up on the bottom, the light wire will break so that the transmitter can be retrieved.

An indicator is fascinating and instructive to use. Above all, it has proved the profitability of looking for thermal walls, thermoclines, slicks, junctions, inlets. Temperature can change sharply, and surprisingly fast – even in small areas, and in vertical as well as horizontal directions. Speed and temperature indicators are available which measure the light intensity too. With this kind of device, it has been noticed that the light at a depth of 23-26 ft (7-8 m) can become 30% weaker than at the surface when clouds cover the sun, and that 50% of the light can be lost at 50-65 ft (15-20 m).

Temperature charts and thermometers

Temperature charts are divided with a grid system that shows latitude and longitude. Drawn on the map of a lake or coastal area are lots of contour lines, resembling very dense depth curves on a nautical chart. These lines represent temperature variations in the surface water. The areas where many lines run extremely close together are, therefore, hot spots.

As mentioned, there are other and cheaper ways of finding out the water temperature. A common method is to use a hand-held depth thermometer, checking the temperature at different levels from an anchored or drifting boat. In this case the thermometer consists of a cable, 100-200 ft (30-60 m) long, with a sinker and sensor on its end. The cable is run up and down by hand, enabling the temperature to be recorded at various levels, and the depth can be read easily from marks or colors on the cable.

The boat's speed at the surface may not be identical to the lure's speed at a depth of, say, 65 ft (20 m). Down there, quite different conditions can prevail – such as strong currents – which have a negative influence on the lure's motion.

Aids to steering

The autopilot helps you to hold the right course while rigging your fishing lines, as well as to position the boat when the fish is being played, netted or released. In other words, it frees your hands from the wheel. But it does not free your eyes, which have to remain as alert as always.

Autopilots differ in their complexity. Some can be coupled – together with other marine electronics, such as an echo-sounder and navigator – to a central unit, and can provide automatic navigation from one point to another.

An autopilot consists of several units – for basic functions, supply, steering, and remote control. The steering unit may be needed at both the deck and bridge levels. Mount the autopilot on a stable foundation, since great strain can develop in the steering aid between the wheel or tiller and the motor. The autopilot should also be easy to disengage mechanically.

The compass

A compass is essential on a boat. It shows the way to the fishing places, and can save your life in times of need. There are compasses for all kinds of boats, so buy the best available version for your boat model and fishing environment.

With a bearing compass, you can fix the position of a chosen objective on your nautical chart. Cross-bearings enable you also to determine the boat's position. The compass should be installed with a lot of forethought, so that it is easy to read when navigating, and is mounted upon a steady base exactly on the boat's long axis. Place it as far as possible from iron objects, and from sources of disturbance such as the radio, echo-sounder, navigator and log. Keep in mind the potential errors of a compass, due to natural magnetic deviation and to sources of disturbance, when navigating in large areas of unknown water.

Practical fishing

Matching the fish is a manifolded concept. For many people it refers to the actual fight – how one handles the rod, reel, and net or gaff, when playing the fish. Others take it to mean a whole process: all the way from studying the nautical charts in advance, and the biology of the chosen fish species, to the minute when the boat is moored at the pier after a sporting day.

First you have to pick a location that is right for the season, in other words a part of the environment which – depending on factors such as prey fish, water temperature, salinity and spawning – contains the fish of interest. Examples of seasonal places are deep holes, drop offs, slopes, points, reefs,inlets, estuaries and river junctions. Here you must then select the right "hot spot", which depends on the bottom's structure, consistency and vegetation. Account also has to be taken of the water level, current direction, water clarity, temperature walls, weather, and presence of other fish species or human beings.

The next thing to choose is the right level in the water, a depth where fish exist that are willing to strike. You need to decide on the right tackle, namely what is required besides rod and reel in order to reach the fish at this depth – for instance, a downrigger or a planer board – and at what length of line the lure or bait should follow the boat.

A further step is to select the right lure or bait. You have to choose between spoons, wobblers, plastic lures, attractors and natural bait. Within these families, the right size and color must be decided, to resemble the natural diet of the fish in question as closely as possible – although the color may best be determined by the present visibility in the water. After that, it is important to find the right speed for the boat, giving the lure a movement which will attract the fish to strike.

Finally, the fish have to be fought right, in a way that leaves them unhurted and able to regain their freedom. This means getting everything right when you counter-strike, put pressure on the fish, maneuver the boat, net or gaff the fish, and release it with an optimal chance of survival. The last of these stages in the process are what I want to discuss now.

To begin with, if the fight is to be an enjoyable, exciting game of "give and take", it has to be done with properly dimensioned and balanced gear. The equipment should not be so heavy as to quickly kill both the fish and the fight. There ought to be a good match without denying the fish a safe

A fishing fight's most dramatic moments usually occur as it ends. Coordination on board is then crucial. Here, with the help of a stand-up rod, the fish is brought within reach of the gaffer. The handle's long foregrip enables the fisherman, during the fight, to hold it near the centre of balance and pump rapidly, keeping pressure on the fish. A low-hanging rod belt also allows him to use the power of his hips and legs, not only his arms.

return to its watery element – able to grow, reproduce, and eventually offer somebody a new fight.

For me, this is the essence of sportfishing. It is what I strive for, no matter if I am pole fishing, fly fishing, spinning, jigging or trolling. Whether the fight takes place in a river with my waders on, in a lake with a float-tube around my waist, or in a trolling boat is irrelevant. These equipments are just cosmetics surrounding the fight itself. Nor should there be any need to dress oneself with a boat or a float-tube. Freedom of choice, and being able to accept others' way of fishing, are also key elements of the total perspective of sportfishing.

The strike

Often a fish takes the lure so violently that a strike is unnecessary. The boat's momentum, combined with the resistance when the line is jerked from the release, is usually enough to get the hook well caught in the fish's jaw. The fisherman does not have to think about anything except, perhaps, lifting the rod quickly from the rod-holder to adopt a fighting position – either along the rail or in a fishing chair. But if you are holding the rod in your hand when the fish takes, you should answer with a fast strike. Hard-jawed species such as pike and barracuda may even require two successive strikes.

Sometimes the fish is shy and careful, and gives the lure or bait a close inspection before deciding to take it – or else to swim onward. The striking reflex can be released if the lure speeds up or slows down. So an extra pull on the line, or a couple of turns on the reel or downrigger, may be all the stimulation that is needed. At other times, though, a slowly sinking lure can provide the right inducement.

The fisherman should always have a good view over his equipment. With skill, he can often tell whether the lure's movement is attractive by watching the rod tip – that is, if he cannot see the lure itself. Further important points are that the rod has a short reach, that the reel's drag setting is right, and that you have fast reflexes. It is safest to act as if every strike comes from a record fish.

For big game, hooking and boarding the fish are largely

matters of teamwork, where the fisherman, crew members, skipper and boat must be coordinated efficiently. However, the boat is used differently in various parts of the world, especially in connection with the strike. Some skippers slow the boat down to give the fish a chance to swallow the bait. Others speed up as soon as the slashing bill of the fish has struck the bait and the line has fallen on the water after being jerked from the outrigger's release.

Essential, too, and particularly in big-game fishing, is that you get to know the equipment and the routines on board before you start to fish. You must be aware of how much power the rod gives under pressure, and how the reel's braking system works during the strike and playing (see Chapter 4). You should also be aware of how the terminal tackle is constructed. Most losses of big fish, in fact, are due to the fisherman's inadequate mastery of the equipment.

Playing the fish

Usually a fish rushes away immediately after being hooked. As a rule, this is the longest rush of the whole fight. It may either head into the depths or take place just under the surface. In the latter case, the rush normally finishes with a series of jumps or splashes at the surface.

Let the fish rush, but hold up the rod. If you have a conventional type of rod, keep it at least 45 degrees to the water surface, so that the fish feels the pressure from it. Lighten the drag if it is set hard, or if the fish is big and pulls out a lot of line. For as the spool loses line, the pressure on the line will grow in relation to the preset drag level. When only half the line is left on the spool, twice as strong a pull is needed as at the beginning in order to activate the drag. Thus you should never increase the reel's braking power at this stage. Besides, the more line is pulled out by the fish, the more resistance is caused by the line being pulled

Don't stretch out the landing net toward a fish that is not close enough to the boat. Often the fish will react by expending its last strength on a rush that may go toward the keel or propeller, bringing an undesirable end to the fight. Instead, it should be netted quickly and decisively. Lift it fast and try to close the net bag immediately.

through the water. The very weight of the pulled line is usually just what makes the fish slow down.

It is when the fish stops after the first rush that you have to take command. From then on, you and your equipment must keep the fish moving. Remember not to give the fish any chance of resting, since its ability to regain energy with a pause is much greater than yours.

The commonest method of putting pressure on the fish, and thereby regaining lost line onto the reel, is to "pump" it in. But first the drag should be restored with enough force that pumping becomes possible. Pumping technique depends on the type of rod being used, and on whether you fight the fish from a standing or sitting position.

In any case, the basic idea is to raise and lower the rod smoothly until the fish is brought within reach of the boat. While raising the rod, you take in line; when lowering it, you distribute the line quickly and evenly on the reel. If the fish is large and unruly, you may need a rod belt and a suitable harness in order to hold the rod up, as well as to avoid hurting your body and clothes. With a traditional rod, the fish is pumped home while standing, by working the rod at angles between 45 and 80 degrees to the water surface. Your hands, arms and shoulders are what have to provide the power.

With a stand-up rod, you also use your hips and thighs when playing, and thus minimize the strain on your arms and shoulders. The pumping technique with this type of rod involves short, fast rises and falls, allowing 8-12 inches (20-30 cm) of line to be laid up on the spool at each pump. Such a technique is most effective when the fishing is done vertically and the fish is under the boat, since it then has little chance of turning its head downward to dive abruptly.

From a fighting chair, you pump the fish home by sliding back and forth on the chair, while your legs push against a footrest. You slide backward by stretching your legs, just when a standing fisherman would lift the rod. Once your rod is up, you slide forward by bending your knees, and wind line quickly onto the reel as you lower the rod tip.

On a big-game rod, the model of butt may be important. It is easier to play deep-diving fish with a curved rod butt, and surface-going racers with a straight handle. The curvature usually means that the foregrip and reel stay at a proper working distance from your body. This type also gives a low rod-tip angle, which is an advantage when you want to use the rod's leverage.

Always try to keep a constant pressure on the fish: this is what

compels the beast to work against the rod and, in the long run, tire itself out. Never raise the rod so much that you risk creating slack line when the fish rushes toward the boat. Knowing the power bend of your rod will enable you to see, and feel, when it is time to lighten the reel drag. The time has come, at any rate, when the line starts to sing. Never attempt to "break" a fish by putting maximum drag on the reel as you pump in. A soft fish jaw can then easily be ripped apart, and at worst the fish will be lost. The drag should be adjusted so that the fish always has a chance of taking line from the reel if it rushes out unexpectedly.

A fish that jumps with a long line out is seldom able to get free, because of the line pressure. But the risk is much greater when the fish is close to the boat, especially if it has a heavy lure hanging in its mouth. A short, tight, non-stretchy line – combined with the weight and wear of the lure in its mouth – has allowed many a fish to escape near the boat after a long fight.

Try to parry a jump by lowering the rod tip, although not so much that the fish gets slack line. Be sure to lighten the drag when the fish approaches the boat, so that any sudden jerks it makes will not endanger the line. Except in big-game fishing, the line can usually be braked well with your thumb, once the fish is near the boat.

Maneuvering the boat

If you play the fish from a fighting chair, you may need the help of a mate to swing the chair, thus keeping the rod pointed to the place where the line disappears into the water. To assist a tired or inexperienced fisherman in taking home the line, the skipper can back up the boat toward the fish. Another tactic is for the skipper to turn the boat and run parallel with the fish. This enables the fisherman to reduce his drag, and the fish soon tires since it has to pull line in the boat's wake.

In big-game fishing, it is normally necessary to keep the boat and motor going all through the fight. On the other hand, in most cases this is not essential when trolling for salmon. Here you should just try to maintain steering speed until all the tackle is taken in, and then fight the fish from the stationary or drifting boat. But you can operate the motor if you have to move because of the fish, the weather, or other vessels. Thus, stop the motor only when it is time to net the fish – so that the propeller blade will not cut the line and suddenly put an end to the fight. If for any reason you need to keep the boat moving, you will get the most out of the fight by steering around the fish in wide circles.

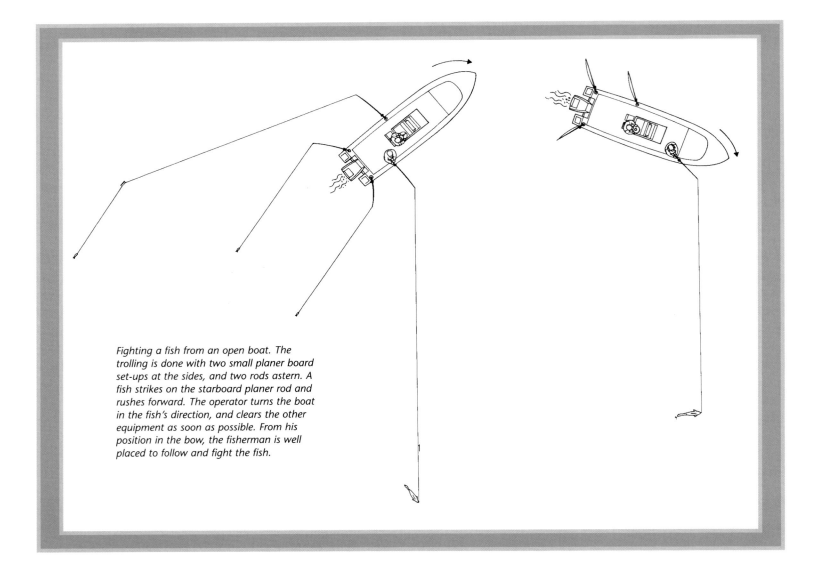

Fighting a fish from an open boat. The trolling is done with two small planer board set-ups at the sides, and two rods astern. A fish strikes on the starboard planer rod and rushes forward. The operator turns the boat in the fish's direction, and clears the other equipment as soon as possible. From his position in the bow, the fisherman is well placed to follow and fight the fish.

One should always be careful not to bring a fish near the boat if it is not yet tired. Its alert jumps, splashes and frightened gyrations are hard to parry, especially if it fights close to the surface. There is then a risk of slack line, and of the fish – with a jump and a hard throw of its head – shaking loose the lure or bait, which may be slung towards the boat. Likewise, there is a good chance of the fish landing on the line and snapping it, or getting tangled in it. Try to keep the fish at a visible distance until the signs of fatigue begin to show: when the rod becomes less strained and the fish's circular movements become ever tighter.

A fish that begins to turn on its side is nearly finished – but not always completely. Often it spends its last strength on a rush just as you extend the landing net or gaff towards it. And with bad luck, it may head straight for the keel or propeller, giving the fight an undesirable conclusion.

Netting and gaffing

Down to the last round in a standing fight, you should maintain a reduced drag, a ready thumb, and a suitable position on board, in order to stick the whole rod into the water if the fish decides to dive under the boat. Do not stretch out the net to try and reach a fish at a doubtful distance from the boat. This will only scare it.

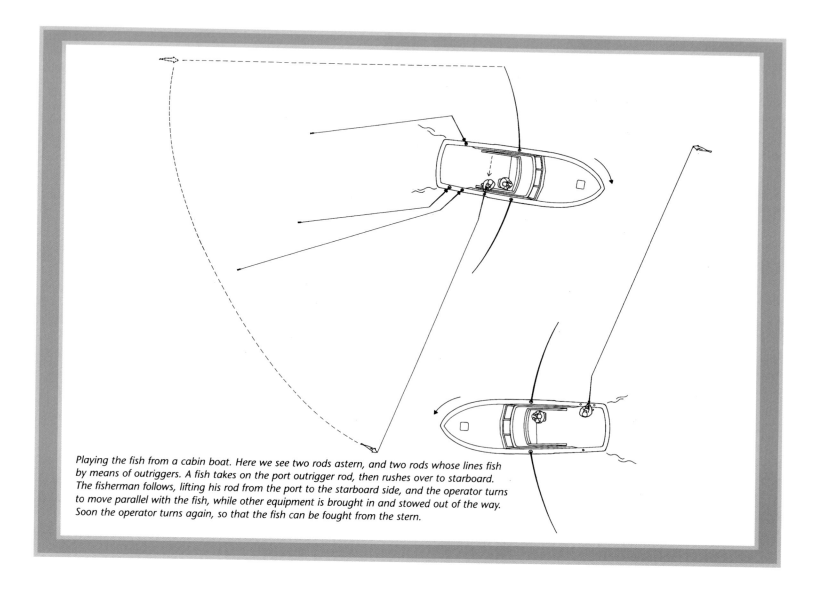

Playing the fish from a cabin boat. Here we see two rods astern, and two rods whose lines fish by means of outriggers. A fish takes on the port outrigger rod, then rushes over to starboard. The fisherman follows, lifting his rod from the port to the starboard side, and the operator turns to move parallel with the fish, while other equipment is brought in and stowed out of the way. Soon the operator turns again, so that the fish can be fought from the stern.

Scoop the fish with speed and determination. The net should be partly under the surface before the fish is pulled in over its frame, head first. Lift the net quickly and try to close it, either by spinning the mesh or by raising it vertically with the shaft along the boat's side. Then shift your hands to the frame and lift it on board. The fish is locked against the side and has little chance of escaping, as long as you have the strength to lift it.

A fish is best gaffed in the head. Ideally the hook can be stuck into the lower jaw, as the fish then stays surprisingly still. It is thus easy to free the fish from the lure with a disgorger and return it unharmed to the water. The hole in its jaw skin is small and will soon heal.

In heavyweight duels from a fighting chair, the last stage is often the most dramatic of all. The skipper must have a good view of everything that happens, so that he can steer the boat quickly. The mate needs room to maneuver the fish alongside the boat. So the fisherman plays a rather passive role during the gaffing, though he has to remain alert. He should stay in the fighting chair with very little drag on the spool, and with the clicker on, so that the fish – if it manages to get loose – will not break the line, or backlashing it on the spool. Any others on board should keep out of the way unless their help is called on.

The climax in big-game fishing approaches when the double line begins to be wound on the spool, and when the ter-

minal tackle's uppermost swivel stays in sight above the water surface. Only when the leader is close enough for a mate's leather-gloved hands should it be grabbed, and the hopefully worn-out fish guided toward the boat side. Do not pull the leader on board: make sure it falls outside, in the water.

If the fish is to be kept, it is first hooked in the head or neck with a flying gaff. Do this while the fish still has its head under the surface – otherwise it may start to roll and thrash uncontrollably in the surface water. Never try to keep a gaffed fish subdued with only your hands; the gaff rope should be quickly lashed on board. Then continue, if necessary, by gaffing in the fish's body before a tail rope is pulled tight at the slender area at the base of the tail. Finally you can knock it for good with a fish billy.

If the fish is to be released, it is sometimes tagged before the leader wire is cut – as close to the hook as possible. Salt water, combined with the fish's stomach acids, will soon dissolve the hook. The fish may need an oxygen supply to its gills before it regains freedom, and is then held with its head down in the water's current direction. Occasionally it is also helped to start off by making slow movements. You can signal to other fishermen that you are marking fish, by raising the IGFA flag with a "T" which stands for tagging.

Salmonoids

The large family of salmonoids is grouped in three subfamilies. One of these includes salmon, trout and char; the other two contain whitefish and grayling.

In the first-mentioned subfamily can be found some of the troller's most pugnacious and desirable opponents. In general, the names of salmon and trout – both seagoing species and those that live entirely in fresh water – are related to the Pacific Ocean when they are Pacific fish, and to corresponding salmonoids from the Atlantic when they are Atlantic fish.

Left: Big game fish are ever more often released, possibly after being tagged. Small billfish are commonly caught up by their jaws, instead of being gaffed, when they are to be tagged or set free.

Atlantic salmon

The species *Salmo salar* is a native of North Atlantic waters, ranging from the eastern Bay of Biscay up to the White Sea and the Baltic. It also occurs around Iceland and along southern Greenland. Previously it was found on the coasts of North America, from the Arctic Circle down to the Hudson River, but nowadays its southern limit is around New England. Moreover, it exists as a freshwater relic in a few areas of northern Europe and northeastern North America. Unfortunately the past 150 years of river exploitation, water pollution, and exhaustive fishing have wiped out very rich salmon stocks in their diverse environments on both sides of the Atlantic.

Trolling is possible for both salmon that are maturing and those that are migrating to spawn. It can be done by back trolling in rivers and trolling in archipelagos or in open waters.

I have matched the Grand Slam trio of Atlantic salmon in their respective surroundings at very different seasons. There have been fascinating encounters during quiet, bright Scandinavian summer nights in narrow river valleys, as well as frostbitten adventures on lakes with snow and rain in northerly winds during periods of fairly constant dusk. Unforgettable, too, has been fishing in a T-shirt on sunny surfaces that recalled the subtropics, even though I was zigzagging on open seas across the 56th parallel.

As a rule, when they emigrate in springtime, the young salmon (smolt) follow the surface currents of lakes and seas. Throughout their time at sea, they continue to hunt in the rich stretches of current, especially over deep water and at convergences of cold and warm water. Rises in the sea or lake floor, jut of land surrounded by currents, bays near deep water, and tributary flow into a bay are, therefore, good places for a salmon troller to cover.

During the spring, salmon run at the surface or close to it, both in the open sea and near land – and the smallest fish are usually highest up. Even during summer, the surface water can attract salmon as long as they find their optimum temperature there. But more commonly, and especially near land, they go and hunt in the thermocline. During the autumn, when the surface water becomes cool and mixed, salmon occur at all levels, occasionally just offshore. In late winter, the very coldest time of year, they head once again for deeper water.

The pre-spawning behavior of salmon is also fairly independent of their environment. They follow certain immigration routes to the spawning river. Usually the heavyweighters

arrive first – in some rivers already during early spring, in others during late autumn. Outside the river, in a fjord or a deep area, they tend to form groups of similar size and wait until the conditions are right for running upriver. Their appetite fades as they approach the river, but they do not entirely stop eating before they start upriver.

Atlantic Sea salmon

Salmon from the North Atlantic's tributaries follow the sea currents toward nutritious northerly waters just south of the Arctic Circle. There they get fat in the Norwegian Sea, around Iceland, and in the Davis Strait between Greenland and Canada. Their main prey are crustaceans, sand eels, stickleback and various species of herring. When returning to spawn, they weigh from 4 to 80 lbs (2-37 kg) depending on their age and genetic qualities.

In general, the troller makes contact with these salmon once they have headed toward their home coasts. They follow the ancient routes of immigration – which can vary with the season – along open coasts, fjord coasts, and skerries. Not seldom, their path is bordered by traps and gillnets, hinting at where a salmon troller should show his lures or baits. The fish may sneak toward the spawning river at some depth, or else approach it in the surface outflow from the river.

With the introduction of modern trolling techniques, rod catches along the Scandinavian west coast have grown steadily.

Pacific salmon

The genus *Oncorhynchus* consists of six species: the chinook (*O. tschawtyscha*), coho (*O. kisutch*), chum (*O. keta*), humpback (*O. gorbuscha*), sockeye (*O. nerka*) and cherry salmon (*O. masou*). However, the last species occurs only around Japan, and is regarded as a transitional form between salmon and trout.

All of these species originate in the Pacific area. but they have been introduced with varying success in different parts of the world. From the viewpoint of sportfishing, the best results with chinook and coho have been achieved in the Great Lakes.

Saltwater fishing

Off the west coast of North America, fishing waters are not stratified during the summer months in the same way as those of the Great Lakes. Instead, the locations of fish are influenced by upwelling water, powerful estuaries, and the tides. One can find maturing chinook hunting in small groups everywhere from the surface down to about 125 yds (m), especially where the temperature is 12-14° C (53-57° F). Here they pursue large schools of anchovy, herring, alewife, smelt, squids and shrimp. They are most active around dawn, and then stay very high up in the water.

Moreover, they may move along bottoms at deep, rocky coasts, feeding on " rockfish" in the clefts. Usually the heaviest salmon of all can be found there. But both the forage fish and the predators could be difficult to detect with an echosounder on rocky bottoms.

The trailer line length is generally 30-65 ft (10-20 m) when the fish run shallow at 10-25 ft (3-8 m) or if the water is quite clear. However, a length of 13-23 ft (4-7m) may well be enough when the fish hunt deeper. It is therefore normal to stack the lures at intervals of 10-13 ft (3-4 m).

Chinook migrating to spawn are not so easily fooled, but they can be located without much trouble since they follow fixed routes – which, on the other hand, may shift with the seasons. Periodically a school pauses in deep holes or along slopes, where the fish prepare their bodies for the coming adaptation to a freshwater environment. As they stay very close to the bottom, your lure must be presented maximum a yard (meter) above it. The most successful West Coast trollers fish at extremely low speeds, sometimes so slowly that the boat barely holds against the tide. The lure – usually natural bait – then rotates lazily and attractively in the current.

Such slow speed provides a fine opportunity to use dodgers in front of the lure or bait. It is thought that the salmon mistake the attractor's sound and shimmer for a competing fish. Often the very biggest salmon are the ones that strike near the bottom during slow trolling. The leader between the attractor and lure or bait is abnormally long – at least a rod length in most cases.

Freshwater fishing

As a rule, the fishing season in Lakes Michigan and Ontario lasts from the end of April to mid-October. The chinook feed mainly on alewife and smelt – but predominantly the latter in Lake Ontario, as shown by analysis of stomach contents.

During the spring, the fish hunt in small schools near the surface over deep waters. When the lakes stratify in summertime, the chinooks head for the thermocline, which is usually about 65 ft (20 m) deep. They occur both in the thermocline and around its upper limit, preferring a temperature of 13° C (55° F). Very seldom do we find freshwater chinooks at the bottom. They also tend to stay half a nautical mile or so from the shores, unless winds push cold water along the shores.

Stocking of Pacific salmon in the Great Lakes has given birth to a huge sportfishing industry. Local tourism generates several billion dollars annually, and has led to charter-boat operations with well-equipped vessels of the size shown here in every harbor. This makes it possible for one and all to try a hand at salmon trolling.

In late summer and autumn, the fish become ever more densely concentrated outside the river mouths. They prepare to run upriver and spawn, which means that they often lose their appetites. Nevertheless, very large chinooks are taken every year at this time.

The troller should know when and where the fish occur under different conditions. He finds these spots with the help of a navigator, always looking for breakpoints over them. These may be where two currents meet, where the temperature shifts for some reason, or where the bottom slopes sharply. To the troller, even dawn and dusk are breakpoints in the life of the fish.

Since the chinook pursue schools of smelt and alewife, they occur around the river mouths in springtime when the latter are spawning, not least in the edge slicks between the outflow river water and the lake water. During the summer, the forage fish are pelagic, according to the temperature and the supply of plankton. These factors can make the fishing quite unpredictable, but it is always challenging. In autumn, river-mouth fishing is emphasized on both Lakes Michigan and Ontario.

To put things briefly, the surface-going spring salmon in Lake Ontario are tempted with fish-imitating plugs, while the salmon that move in the thermocline tend to fall for light Sutton spoons and attractor/squids combinations. The last of these, together with flatnosed plugs, usually work well during the late season, when strong colors with some blue and green are effective. Line lengths and trolling speeds are, once again, adjusted to the fishing depth and visibility, the water conditions and type of lure, as well as the time of year.

In regard to plugs, my impression from chinook fishing on the Great Lakes is that plugs, such as the silver J-plug with blue and green features, are the most common and successful. Small J-plugs or alike (Nos. 2 and 3) are sometimes also used behind dodgers (No. 0 or 1); the separation should be 20-40 inches (50-100 cm) for the lure to acquire the right erratic run. Large J-plugs are run directly from a flatline or on a downrigger, but they can also be profitably pulled on a leader of 48-72 in (120-180 cm) behind a diving planer.

Trout and steelhead

Brown trout (*Salmo trutta*) are native to Europe, and rainbow trout (*Oncorhynchus mykiss*) to North America. They both exist in purely freshwater variants as well as in seagoing ones.

Brown trout occur in many forms, adapted to their particular environments. In European waters they inhabit not only brooks and lakes but also the Baltic and the North Sea. Their inland varieties grow especially large, and specimens of around 44 lbs (20 kg) have been caught.

Lake-run and sea-going trout acquire a silvery gleam as they grow, and they darken when preparing to spawn. But the latter appearance varies, and it can be hard to distinguish large-sized silvery trout from the Atlantic salmon.. One can identify these species most certainly by studying the gill-raker teeth, which are all rod-shaped on the first gill arch in salmon, but are partly knob-shaped in trout.

Sea-going trout

The majority of sea-going trout are not open water fish to the same extent as salmon. Regardless of the season, they stay very close to cliffs and stones, shifting position with the wind and current directions. They enjoy windward shores, and may come right up to land with an onshore wind. But in a constant offshore wind, they move farther out towards more structure bottoms.

All sea trout run up their spawning rivers during the summer and autumn. Most survive their spawning period and return to the ocean. According to taggings, though, they seldom migrate far during their second period at sea, but tend to linger near their spawning rivers.

Trolling fishermen after trophy trout should concentrate on the waters outside well-known rivers of this kind – where herring, sand eels, stickleback, smelt and crustaceans occur. The bottoms may consist of shallow stony ridges, or of sand and gravel interspersed with weed-grown boulders. Here the trout often reside from autumn until spring, especially if there is a warm-water outflow in the vicinity.

Suspended trout usually gorge on schools of herring where the depth is 30-80 ft (10-25 m). As a rule they hunt the herring high up, in the top half of the water. They may also occur in summertime around skerries at such depths, as well as jut of land and islands in strong currents, when the water near land becomes warm.

It is easiest to make contact with sea trout when the temperature is 5-10° C (41-50° F). During the dark months, the fishing is usually best in the middle of the day; but later in the season, the trout are most active at dawn and dusk. Then, and during the night, they go very shallow. In Sweden, the majority of large coastal trout, weighing 22-30 lbs (10-14 kg), are caught over shallow, stony, current-swept bottoms in springtime.

Lake-run trout

Cold, clear lakes are inhabited by large-sized trout that behave much like sea-going trout. They swim near the surface in spring and autumn, often in shallow waters near shore. During the summer months, though, they prefer deep slopes where upwelling cold, nutritious bottom water provides the ideal temperature and attracts prey fish. There, they may hunt very deep in the daytime, but also make occasional shoreward raids at night.

On the other hand, lake-run trout are not as happy as sea-going trout to stay over shallow bottoms during the winter, since the shore waters of lakes are then much colder than sea water. It is only when warm spots arise for various reasons, close to land during the late winter and spring, that lake trout concentrate here. As young the trout live on diverse small animals – but as they grow, their diet turns to fish foods such as smelt, vendace, perch fry and stickleback.

In Ireland and Scotland, lake trolling with flies is popular during the spring. The "loch trout" rarely grows to great size, but its colorfulness is impressive.

A variety of techniques

Trolling for trout is many-folded and usually very instructive. Depending on the environment and time of year, it can be done by simply rowing with a flatline, or by advanced forms of deep trolling.

Planer-board fishing is an efficient technique when it comes to shallow-hunting and shy trout. One can seldom get more lessons or enjoyment from this technique than in springtime, when the trout are hiding close to isolated boulders, or else going so shallow that a boat keel cannot follow them. It is then a real test of precision for both the boat and your equipment.

A downrigger, too, serves well when the lure is to be presented near the surface in salt water – even there is a lot of grass and weeds in the water, since the wire and line collect most of the rubbish in front of the lure. Fishing with a downrigger near the surface, though, usually requires a long line of 100-165 ft (30-50 m), especially if the water is clear, shallow and calm.

Elsewhere, the downrigger and diving planer are unbeatable for showing a lure to suspended trout that hunt herring, or bringing the lure in close to steep shores or cliff shelves. But if the trout are feeding at depths of 30-50 ft (10-15 m), a line length of around 15 ft (5 m) should be enough. Then, too, the thinnest flutterspoons are normally very attractive on short lines behind a downrigger. The best distance between diving planer and lure is about 6 ft (180 cm).

Trout have a diverse diet, so you need a wide range of lures. They tend to prefer lures measuring 2-6 inches (5-15 cm).

Sometimes, however, they are highly selective and just gape at a particular type, size and color of lure. My own trout box is dominated by plugs and spoons, while I prefer silvery lures in the sea and warmer colors in fresh water. A tube fly, squid, or imitation sand eel, behind an attractor presented at depth, may also entice a strike.

The trolling speed must be adjusted to your lure or bait.. Trout are not as fast and mobile at midwinter as, for example, in June; so the speedometer ought to read at most 2 knots in winter. But a lure pulled at 3 knots is no problem for spring trout to inspect long and hard.

A trout troller's equipment should be in the light to medium class. It is really only when fishing with a diving planer that one needs somewhat heavier gear. To spread the lines better and reach shy fish as well, there may be reason to use rods 10-12 feet long at the sides, whereas downrigger rods are usually 8-9 feet long.

Trout can tear the lure from the line release with the same violence as do salmon. Yet they do not rush as far or, therefore, bend the rod into the same steady curve. Instead, they show their strength with brief opposition and short, quick rushes, which make the rod bow often and deeply. Nor are they averse to exposing themselves in leaps, when the water warms up during summer and autumn. In springtime they are more inclined to roll at the surface. My personal judgment is that "small" trout of 10-12 lbs (4-5 kg) are about as pugnacious as a salmon of similar size.

Steelhead

Steelhead is the seagoing variety of *Oncorhynchus mykiss*, the freshwater rainbow trout. Both of these originate in western North America. Rainbow trout are said to be the world's most widespread sportfish.

The steelhead was named for its gray head. In the sea and in large deep lakes, it has a gray-blue back, and is as shiny along the sides as salmon and brown trout. However, it is slimmer in shape than the often chubby rainbow trout. That it, too, can grow very big is shown by the fact that a giant of 42.lb 2 oz (19.1 kg) has been caught by rod in Alaska.

The Skamania steelhead is certainly among the most spectacular salmonoids that can be hooked. Steelhead reputedly prefer water with a temperature of 14.5-16.5° C (58-62° F). Investigations in the Great Lakes have shown that, during the winter, they linger rather passively in deep water around 4° C

(39° F), although when the surface water near land reaches 5.5-6.5° C (42-44° F) they head for it to hunt small prey.

As the temperature rises, they move out into the lake, and are glad to stay where it reaches 7-9° C (45-48° F). They increase in appetite and activity while approaching their summer residence, in the surface layer over deep waters up to 20 nautical miles from land.

Trollers look for steelhead in and around spots of calm water, slicks at open water whirlpools where rubbish collects, and in misty areas. These are usually visible signs of temperature changes in the water.

Fish that regularly cruise in the surface layer tend to be very watchful and shy. The normal recipe for activating the fish is a long line, either hanging from the rod tip or attached to a planer board or downrigger. During the spring, effective lures are slim silvery plugs, 4-6 inches (10-15 cm) long, such as the Cisco Kid, Bomber and Rapala. But in summertime, steelhead – unlike other salmonoids – are often willing to take at midday and swallow a wide range of lures; they seem most partial to red-orange, fish-imittating plugs. Autumn fishing along coasts and river mouths, in dark shore water, is made attractive with fluorescent colors. Slow trolling with Flatfish, Kwikfish and Tadpolly on the line has also paid off.

Many American trollers speak warmly of light-line fishing for steelhead. They fish with soft 12-foot "noodle rods", which are densely ringed and, in some cases, have pliable guides that prevent the line from rubbing against the rod. On the trolling reel is monoline of 2-6 lbs (0.13-0.23 mm) and there may be a small swivel at the line end. Usually a feather-light lure with an extremely sharpened hook is knotted directly to the reel line, with no shock leader in front. Rubberbands are the only line releases used. Every year on this light equipment, the enthusiasts take not only large-sized steelhead.

Rainbow trout, steelhead and other salmonoids are caught during the winter half-year by harling on the faster-flowing stretches of spawning rivers. This is generally done in dory-like "drift boats", light 16-foot aluminum craft that are excellent fishing platforms on water with swift currents and many rapids. The oarsman cover the river from bank to bank, while letting the boat go slowly downstream. An identical technique is used in Scandinavia. The fishing passenger(s) can drag natural bait – such as salmon roe – or spoons, spinners and wobblers, 30-65 feet (10-20 m) behind the boat

Char

The genus *Salvelinus*, which prefers cold water, is wide-spread in the Northern Hemisphere, chiefly in North America. Among its fifteen-odd species, the most popular sportfish are char (*S. alpinus*), lake trout (*S. namaycush*) and brool trout (*S. fontinalis*). Few sportfish can compare with them in beauty. The first two species are of prime interest to trollers.

Char exist on both sides of the Atlantic, in both freshwater and seagoing varieties. The freshwater kind can grow almost as big as the latter, reaching weights of well over 20 lbs (10 kg). Char require clear, cold water with a high pH value, and their optimum temperature is 5-13° C (41-55° F). Big chars usual diet consists of smelt, vendace, stickleback and perch fry.

Sea-going Arctic char live, for example, along the North Atlantic coast of the Scandinavian peninsula and in the Northwest Territory of Canada. Primarily nourished by fish and crustaceans, they have been rod-caught in weights up to 32.5 lbs (14.77 kg).

Large char can be found at all levels in the water during its spring and autumn circulation in northerly lakes. As the water warms up in summertime, the fish move out to deep areas, mostly in the lower limit of the thermocline or beneath it. Consequently, a troller often encounters it over banks swept by bottom currents, or along deep edges at 100-130 ft (30-40 m).

The active hours of char are less restricted to dawn and dusk than in the case of other salmonoids. This is because the light, which can barely penetrate down to the depths where char live, does not determine the urge to hunt as much as it does in higher water layers. The fishing may prove ideal on a sunny afternoon with a rippled surface. It is especially good during longer periods of high pressure, notably before the autumn spawning time.

Lures can be placed at the char's level with a wire line or a diving planer. But the best aid is a downrigger, not least if you have to go deeper than 165 ft (50 m). Attractors seem to draw the char more strongly than other fish. A string of "mini-cow-bells", with a worm on the hook, is the traditional and so far the commonest method. In larger lakes, it is thought most effective to use a mother-of-pearl spinner on the end of a "magnum cowbell". You should troll slowly at 1.5-2 knots.

Lake trout, the giants of the genus, have been introduced in deep lakes in Europé. However, despite their substantial weight, they are not yet near the specimen of 102 lbs (46.3 kg) which has been caught in Canada. Rod caught examples up to 65 lbs (29.48 kg) are known from Great Bear Lake.

Usually lake trout are dark brown-green to light gray, with light patches. They live in deep cold lakes, preferably at temperatures of 7-13° C (44-55° F). So they may appear in shallow water during the spring and autumn – but as a rule they hunt in small groups at deep edges and in holes. Already when 6-8 inches (15-20 cm) long, they turn to fish food, mainly vendace and smelt.

Downriggers are the perfect approach to lake trout. While a number of fishermen still pull down the lure with wire line, most of us definitely call for a downrigger and rods of 8-9 fee with medium to stiff action. At the end of the 0.35-0.40 mm line (20 lb), and 1-5 ft (30-150 cm) in front of the lure – a plug, spoon, or plastic imitation – is usually a chromed attrac tor or cowbell that stimulates the fish with sight and sound Remember that, by keeping a slow , bouncing the bottom with your weight and jigging with the rod tip, you can soon transform the fish's curiosity about the lure into a strike.

Lake trout are heavy fighters. What they tend to offer are not long rushes or abrupt leaps, but strong resistance when you are pumping a 20-lb (10-kg) specimen out of the depths And the very feeling of its power along the downrigger rod's handle, when it stops and shakes its head to get rid of the lure can be just as nerve-wracking as a fish that runs around the boat on the surface. You fight "blind" without knowing how the lure is sitting, unable to follow its course so easily. Thus lake trout are in many ways an extra, peculiar "spice" on the table of trolling in European waters.

Pikeperch/Walleye

Pikeperch belong to the perch family (*Percidae*) and are restrict ed to the Northern Hemisphere (Europe, Asia and North America). Most species of pikeperch live in fresh water, some in brackish water, and only one in salt water. The "European" pikeperch, the zander (Stizostedion lucioperka) is the biggest in this group. It has been rod-caught in weights up to 40.5 lbs (18.37 kg) in Germany. Among the North American species are the walleye (*S. vitreum vitreum*), which is registered up to 24 lbs (11 kg), and the much smaller sauger (*S. canadense*).

Pikeperch have appealed increasingly to sportfishermen during recent decades. They are now caught year-round by various methods in both fresh and brakish waters. Most of the big ones are taken by trolling in the high-pressure periods of summer, when the nocturnal fish hunt very close to the surface. As long as the sun is above the horizon, the pikeperch usually stay deep

The steelhead is the seagoing variety of rainbow trout. Native to western North America, it has been successfully stocked in the Great Lakes. Today it also occurs increasingly in the Baltic Sea. Specimens of over 42 lbs (19 kg) have been rod-caught in Alaska. On the hook, a steelhead is a glistening package of power. Often you see this lightning-fast fish jumping high in the air before the reel-clicker lets you know that something has taken your lure.

in clear lakes. But in murky flatland lakes, with its excellent sight, it may begin to hunt near the surface long before dusk. Small pikeperch hunt in modest groups, and larger ones either alone or in pairs. Spring and autumn, too, may find them in the upper water layers during the early dawn hours and evenings.

Pikeperch hunt not only in the free waters, but also in the shallows along coasts. They like oxygen-rich water with short vegetation, over both soft and hard bottoms. In deep areas they normally stay near the bottom, but during the summer they seldom linger under the thermocline.

At night, pikeperch tend to take for longer and more intensive periods than in the daytime. They seem to rest for an hour or so after sundown, then launch a frantic hunt for bleak, roach, smelt, and small fish of their own kind. They prefer a water temperature of 11-23° C (52-73° F), ideally just under 20° C (68° F).

Slow surface trolling with light, noisy plugs is the traditional and still predominant method of fishing for pikeperch during the summer in Scandinavian countries. But spoons and natural bait (smelt, vendace) also have many advocates there. In North America, it is more common to use "walleye spinners" tipped with nightcrawlers. Pikeperch take carefully, sneaking up to the lure and gladly swimming along with it. You should watch the rod tips closely, use very sharp hooks, and fish with line that is as short and stiff as possible.

Arctic char are among the loveliest fish that can be hooked. Whether you are after land-locked Arctic char or North American lake trout (at right), you should present the lure deep.

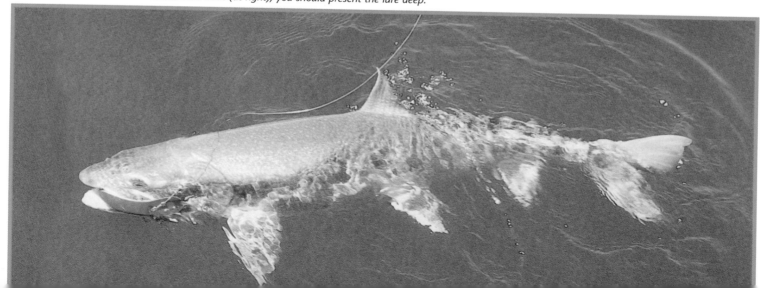

In the United States, year-round fishing for walleye is far more widespread than its counterpart in Scandinavia, no doubt since the sport is more developed. When downrigger fishing for walleye was introduced to Lake Erie, the catches temporarily increased by 15%.

Downrigger fishing is unlike the surface trolling in regard to speed, among other things. The best catches have been made with light flutterspoons, pulled at 2.5-3.5 knots. There should be at least 50 ft (15 m) between the line release and the lure.

The downrigger's effectiveness

Walleye are an almost unbelievably prized sportfish in some parts of North America, especially around Lake Erie in the USA and Ontario in Canada. During the late 1970s, when people began to fish for walleye with downriggers in Lake Erie, the catches grew by an average 15% during late summer and autumn. However, the walleye behaves somewhat differently from Europe's zander. Except in the Great Lakes, it seems to be more bottom-living, although this does not mean it is a deep-water fish.

The spring fishing takes place in shallow waters, but downriggers are used even then. When the depth reaches 5-23 ft (1.5-7 m), the lures (plugs, spoons and natural bait) are released 50-100 ft (15-30 m) behind the boat. In shallow water – where the walleyes are easy to frighten – it is still more common to present the lure with in-line planer boards, or else

directly from a flatline. Only when fish move to deeper water during the summer, at a fishing depth of 30-65 ft (10-20 m), does the downrigger become really effective. Usually the line is 30-50 ft (10-15 m) long at first, but can be shortened while you are fishing. In large lakes, the lures are often stacked to find the right depths for walleye.

Special line releases are generally used for pikeperch fishing, which are a little more sensitive than those for traditional salmon fishing. The trolling speed is dictated by the water temperature: under 10° C (50° F), a typical speed is 1.6-2.1 knots, whereas above 15° C (59° F) the speed should be 2.5-3 knots.

A guide to choosing the lure is that you should fish with dark lures on cloudy days, and bright lures on clear days. Be sure to present the lures at, or just above, the level where the fish hunt – which, as mentioned, is usually the bottom in the USA. Remember, too, that pikeperch / walleye have a strong tendency to hunt from below.

Pike

The pike family (*Esocidae*) comprises five species. Only one of them, the widespread northern pike (*Esox lucius*), also lives in Europe. Another, weighing at most 22 lbs (10 kg), occurs in Eurasia (*E. reicherti*). Those found in eastern North America are the chain pickerel (*E. niger*), the redfin or grass pickerel (*E. americanus*), and the muskellunge (*E. masquinongy*).

Heaviest is the musky, at about 110 lbs (50 kg), but northern pike weigh up to 77 lbs (35 kg). It is said that no more beautiful – or tough – Esox-fish can be hooked than the "tiger musky", a cross between a male northern pike and a female musky. Such hybrids sometimes occur spontaneously in the wild, and they can reach weights of 50 lbs (22.7 kg).

The world's finest stocks of pike are probably those available to trollers in Sweden. This is suggested at least by their catch statistics. The pike in Sweden are spread over almost the whole country.

The eating habits of pike depend on their size. The smaller they are, the more often they take. An old pike can digest food for a week, before stuffing itself again in a few hectic hours.

Pike generally stay close to shores or bottoms, except in large deep lakes and in the Baltic Sea. Here, a salmon or trout troller occasionally comes to grips with big suspended pike that hunt in open waters. Their stomach contents show that they have feasted on schools of vendace or herring. Normally the pike stay beyond the vegetation belt. Among their favorite haunts in springtime are the shallow areas outside estuaries.

In autumn, when coastal waters get cold again, the pike linger at depths of 6-26 ft (2-8 m). But during the coldest season, they reappear far down, where the water is warmest.

Most pike trollers comb the bottoms and deep edges with large, often colorful plugs, 6-12 inches (15-30 cm) long, pulled 65-100 ft (20-30 m) behind the boat.

The trolling set-up may include a couple of rods 6-7 feet long that point straight astern, and a couple 9-11 feet long that stick out from the sides. Be sure that the rods are parallel to the water surface, since this offers minimum wind resistance on your line, as well as maximum chances of hooking the pike when they take. The reel drag is adjusted to the lure's size. Usually the fish are hooked by the boat's speed, so it is important to give them enough line. Still, you should respond with an extra strike.

A pike troller must try to fish with the stiffest (non-stretchy) possible line, separating it from the bait with a leader 12-20 inches (30-50 cm) long, of nylon-covered wire or thick monofilament.

On an increasing number of pike-trolling boats, there is also a downrigger that can place the lure more exactly at the right depth, and can make the hooking more effective. It also enables you to fish with lighter equipment.

Musky

The gigantic musky is a lot more bewitching to North American fishermen than is the northern pike in Europe. Muskies are spring-spawning and once existed only in the northeastern USA, mainly around the Great Lakes, but they have been introduced in many other waters. According to many musky fishermen, the really big ones, exceeding 40 lbs (18 kg), must be taken by trolling.

A musky stays protected, and attacks the lure from its "hide-out"; so you have to present the lure at a holding station, which is its more or less permanent feeding site. Big muskies usually occur at a rocky deep edge, a grassy sandbank at the junction of two tributaries, or a current-swept jut of land that may well be rich in vegetation. Rarely going deeper than 40 ft (12 m), they have an optimum temperature of 10-20° C (50-68° F).

Top: Pike cannot be confused with any other Scandinavian fish. But their body colors and patterns may depend greatly on where they are caught.
Bottom: The musky is the giant of the pike family. Weighing up to around 110 lbs (50 kg), it originated in eastern North America, where few other fish can match it in legendary fame - or in terms of advice about how to troll for it. One agreed fact is that the trolling lures should be large, tough and sharp, like the fish itself.

This bluefin tuna weighing 700 lbs (320 kg) was boarded after a four-hour fight, off Puerto Rico on Grand Canary. At the first irresistible rush toward the continental cliff, it tore 600 metres of line from the reel, which shot up in temperature and sang the highest note of its career.

150 yards of monoline 12-20 lb (0.30-0.40 mm). Classic lures are the Swim Whizz and the "Muskie Bug"; other large, floating, deep-going plugs are also appreciated. The trolling speed depends on the season, but is normally 2.5-3.5 knots. There is no need for very long lines, 10-25 yards being an accepted distance.

Tuna

The 13 species of tuna belong to the large mackerel family. Usually living in flocks or schools, they occur in warm temperate seas around the world. Popular heavies in the family are the bluefin, the yellowfin and the bigeye tuna. They occur together in many places, and I myself have met all three of those species in unforgettable fights in widely separated waters.

Tuna are warm-blooded and have a "heat-exchanger" which can keep their bodies at least 10° C (18° F) warmer than the surrounding water. This enormous tolerance is reflected by the bluefins tunas ability to feed in water with a temperature of only 4.5° C (40° F) in northern latitudes, even though they spawn in tropical waters at 30° C (86° F).

Bluefin tuna

The bluefin tuna (*Thunnus thynnus*) is the largest of all tunafish. Giants of nearly 1,540 lbs (700 kg), 13 yds (4 m) long, have been caught by commercial fishermen, and the rod record is no less than 1,497 lbs (679 kg).

Unfortunately, the bluefin tuna's existence is facing serious threats. The reason is commercial slaughter fishing. The bluefin occurs in subtropical and temperate waters of the North Pacific Ocean, the North Atlantic Ocean and in the Mediterrannean and Black Sea.

There are several varieties of bluefin tuna, named after the Southern, Northern, Western, and Eastern Atlantic regions. They undertake transoceanic migrations, The Northern Atlantic bluefin is certainly the largest.

To match a "jumbo maguro" one do best heading for the east coast of North America. For Europeans, the best choices are the Canaries, Madeira or the Azores – and the Mediterranean offers bluefin tuna of diverse sizes.

When fishing for bluefin tuna, you should use heavy class equipment. The rods will have lever-drag reels and monofilament line in the same IGFA classes. The reel drag should be adjusted to one-third of the line's breaking strength. Also on board should be accessories such as a well-oiled fighting chair, harnesses, flying gaff and tail rope.

A musky is not shy when it comes to eating the forage fish that pass by such places. These include pikeperch/walleye, perch and bass – ideally of good size, so that the musky soon eats its fill.

Autumn is the best time for fishing muskies. It is common to troll with 3-4 rods, 6-7 feet long with a lot of backbone and fast tip. The majority of fishermen use multiplier reels holding around

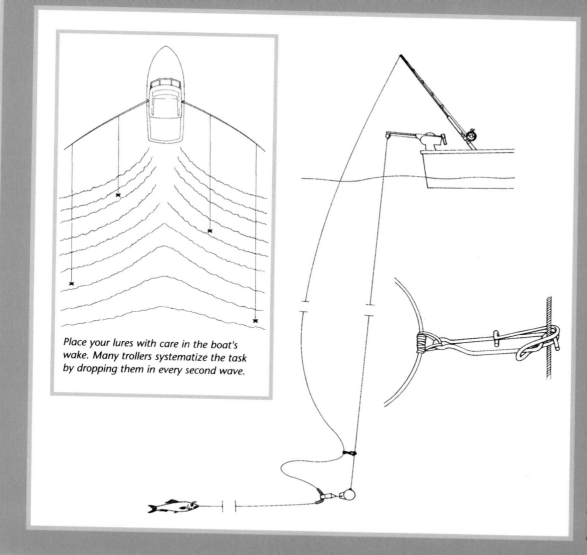

Place your lures with care in the boat's wake. Many trollers systematize the task by dropping them in every second wave.

A fish finds most of its food in the depths. But presenting a live bait down there is much harder than at the surface. Downriggers have thus created new opportunities. To give the fish slack line and time for swallowing, the bait is provided with two line releases. A bridle-rigged mackerel, or a small tuna, swims about 165 ft (50 m) behind the lower release, which sits on the weight. It can be a good idea to wrap the fishing line with wax thread where the line release clamps on, both to protect the line and to keep track of the dragging distance. The dropback loop between the two releases can vary in length, but is normally half as long as the drag distance to the bait. The upper release is a halibut snap, with one end coupled to the downrigger wire, and the other attached to the fishing line by a No.64 rubberband. You should carefully lower the tackle to the desired depth, then tighten the line between the upper release and the reel.

The lure or bait can be presented either with a downrigger or by direct flatline fishing. As long as you use natural bait, the boat should move rather slowly at 3-6 knots. From outriggers, you can also fish with spreader bars or daisy chains, at least 130-165 ft (40-50 m) behind the boat. The third spreader rig should point astern and have a line length of 65-80 ft (20-25 m). Baits – herring, coalfish, mackerel or squid – should run at the surface. With this triple set-up, which might consist of two mackerel rigs and a squid rig, the tuna should get the impression that a school is following the boat. Attractors can be plastic squids or natural bait, the latter being attached to the leader with closed mouths.

When a tuna takes a surface-going lure, the hook can be driven in hard with an extra jab at the throttle, and your rod tip will show the result. Then you have to bring the other lures home, before concentrating on how to maneuver the boat and play the fish. This is often a revealing moment as regards the condition of the fish, fisherman and equipment alike.

Big game on downriggers

Downrigger fishing for tuna becomes increasingly popular nowadays, and logically so, as the fish tend to feed deep. In recent years a number of impressive bluefin tuna have been caught off the northeastern USA, mostly at 50-100 ft (15-30 m).

Once a tuna is on the hook, you need to clean up fast on board. Thus many big-game fishermen prefer rapid electric downriggers, mounted on swivel bases and quick mount adapter for instant mounting in flush rod-holders at the side deck. The downriggers are then easy to stick in and lift out.

Rubberbands are good, cheap line releases in salt water. The following arrangement is suitable for many other big game fish in addition to tuna.

If the fish needs slack line when it takes – which tuna seldom do – you should place two line releases on the line, one above the other. Then feed out the lure to the desired trailer length, which depends for instance on the lure's size and on whether it is alive or dead. Fasten the line in the weight's line release, perhaps rein-

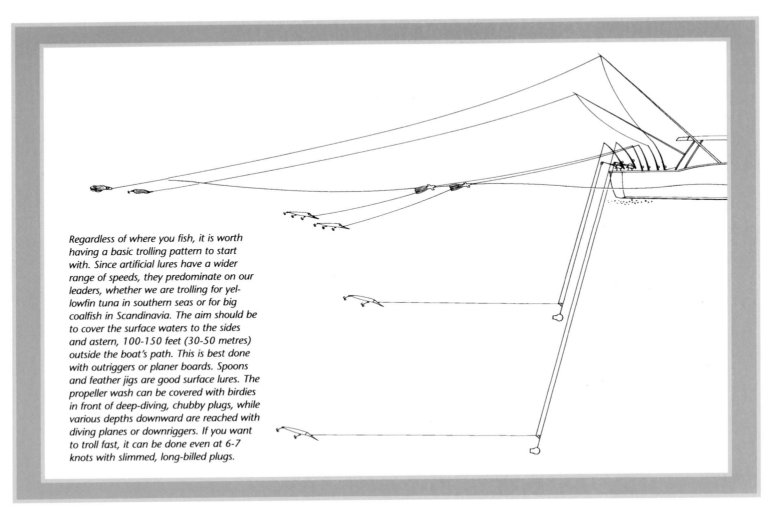

Regardless of where you fish, it is worth having a basic trolling pattern to start with. Since artificial lures have a wider range of speeds, they predominate on our leaders, whether we are trolling for yellowfin tuna in southern seas or for big coalfish in Scandinavia. The aim should be to cover the surface waters to the sides and astern, 100-150 feet (30-50 metres) outside the boat's path. This is best done with outriggers or planer boards. Spoons and feather jigs are good surface lures. The propeller wash can be covered with birdies in front of deep-diving, chubby plugs, while various depths downward are reached with diving planes or downriggers. If you want to troll fast, it can be done even at 6-7 knots with slimmed, long-billed plugs.

forced by an extra rubberband. Sink it 20-40 inches (50-100 cm) under the surface, and feed out the slack line that seems necessary in view of the lure's distance behind the boat. Next, reattach the reel line to the wire with a rubberband – which should be wound several times on the line to prevent slipping. Some skippers use a halibut clamp between the rubberband and the wire.

Lower the lure carefully to the chosen depth. This is especially important when you use live bait. Tighten up the reel line between the rod tip and the upper release, to minimize slack line here. The reel's line-out alarm should be turned on, and the drag set lightly – not a bit harder than in the strike position.

As the fish takes the lure and jerks line from the lower release, it feels almost no resistance because of the slack line, and is thus unlikely to spit out the lure. Only when the slack line has stretched out does the fish encounter resistance, due to the other release and the boat's motion. These forces will hopefully hook the fish before the rubberband breaks and the reel click signals that the first round has begun.

Tuna have flexible diets, but proven baits in both deep and surface waters are the mackerel, bluefish and gray mullet. Live baits will keep longest and move best if they are bridle-rigged. Artificial lures used in salt water for downrigger fishing are usually big plugs, spoons, plastic lures and feather jigs. But make sure that the hooks and their attachments can stand the expected wear.

With artificial lures on the line end, no "drop-back" effect is attempted, but you should clamp the line hard in the single release used. Further, tighten up the reel line as much as possible against the release, and put the reel drag in the strike position.

Yellowfin tuna

A downrigger can also be used to present tuna lures in or near the surface. Artificial lures are usually very effective when fishing for tuna that live in schools, including small bluefin tuna. Where they swim in large schools, their hunting is revealed by the presence of diving gulls and white spray on the surface.

In such situations the yellowfin tuna (*Thunnus albacares*) is among the most impressive fish, whether it is hunting or fighting hooked. Many of us consider the yellowfin, pound for pound, to be the toughest quarry a sportfisherman can match, especially if it is in the 200-lb (100-kg) class. Add to this its amazing beauty, and the fact that it is sometimes nearly impossible to tempt – generally because of its strong concentration on a particular type of food, which may be far smaller than the fish itself, such as baby squids. Thus, even on the open sea, you must "match the hatch" to make the rod tip bend. White feather lures, small or medium-size kona heads, knuckleheads and psychobeads, as well as mackerel, gray mullet and garfish, are undoubtedly reliable here.

Yellowfin tuna occur in the warm temperate oceans, and can reach weights of almost 440 lbs (200 kg. As the name shows, this fish has golden yellow fins.

Fighting the yellowfin tuna is most enjoyable on IGFA class 30-50 equipment, particularly if it can be coaxed to take a surface-going artificial lure. It then tends to begin with a long rush near the surface, followed by a sudden dive against the depth – which may seem bottomless as the fish tears line from the reel.

Bigeye tuna

The bigeye tuna (*Thunnus obesus*) is found in tropical and subtropical seas, except the Mediterranean. It partly recalls the yellowfin tuna, of which it was long regarded as a variant.

Bigeye tuna are pelagic wanderers, and – unlike the bluefin and yellowfin tuna – they prefer deep waters during the day. Their backs are dark blue and their sides silvery. Off Cabo Blanco, Peru, they have been rod-caught in weights up to 435 lbs (197.31 kg). This is probably close to their maximum weight.

Bigeye tuna feed on small mackerel, gray mullet, sardines, squids, shellfish, and certain deep-water species. They are caught from boats by trolling deep with small natural bait – such as squids, gray mullet and mackerel. Artificial lures appeal to them in about the same variety as with yellowfin tuna. However, it is usually only the smaller fish that take such lures near the surface.

An incredibly tough fighter, the bigeye tuna battles intensely and is glad to do so on a long line in the dark layers of the sea. It can quickly regain strength, even after long rushes in cold deep water.

Sharks

Sharks rule a wide realm in the world's seas, and some of their species are prominent trolling fish – mainly the mako and porbeagle, though others can also be caught on trolling lures. The mako shark has a global distribution in tropical and warm temperate oceans. No trolling fish is so greatly respected as the mako. This enormously versatile and aggressive fish can jump around 30 ft (10 m) above the surface when hooked and reach weights of about 1,550 lbs (700 kg).

The mako shark is one of the wildest fish that can take a trolling lure. Many sport- fishermen harbor a kind of hatred for this unpredictable, aggressive racer, which can also leap higher than any other sportfish.

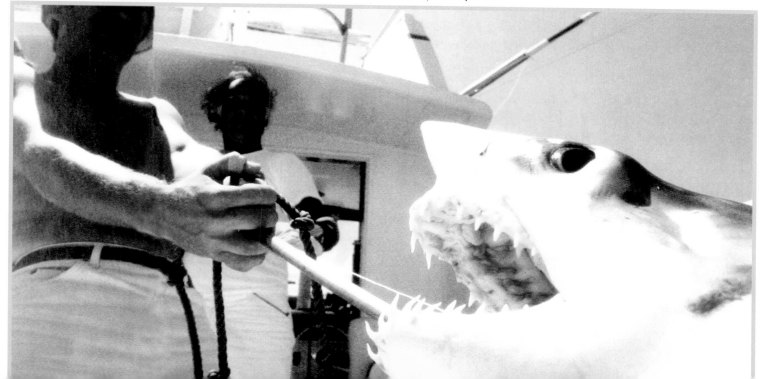

The mako is a fast-swimming, warm-blooded solitary hunter, and eats most kinds of popular trolling fish that cross its path. Makos are caught by either surface or deep trolling; they take artificial as well as natural baits, pulled at 2-5 knots. Capricious in ways of attacking, they sometimes strike without hesitation, but occasionally call for a drop-back effect to be hooked. When they are caught on a down-rigger, the tension in the line release should be set hard, and the distance from it to the lure should be short – about 16 ft (5 m). Usually a couple of extra strikes are needed to drive the hook in strongly.

The porbeagle shark is a close relative of the mako, but can be distinguished by its teeth, fin positions, and darker blue-gray color. Nor does it grow as large: the max weight is about 500 lb (225 kg) This species (*Lamna nasus*) is found in cold to temperate waters of the Pacific and North Atlantic Oceans, and in the Mediterranean. The porbeagle is feeding on herring, mackerel, coalfish and squids at different levels.

Off the rocky coast of Ireland mackerel baits are trolled at about 10 ft (3 m) down and 200 ft (60 m) behind the boat, whose speed is 2-4 knots. A trolled porbeagle fights better than a driftfished one, because the hook sits farther forward in its jaw.

A successful shark tackle, at the end of IGFA class 30-50 lbs (15-24 kg) equipment, may consist of a double-hook arrangement in sizes 8/0 and 9/0, for a mackerel measuring 10-12 inches (25-30 cm). One hook is inserted through the underjaw, then through the upper jaw, while the other is tied to the tail spool with rubber-bands. Between the hook and reel line is a stainless-steel wire, 10-15 feet long, of test strength 300 lbs, and the fishing line is attached to the wire by a roller-bearing snap swivel (200-300 lbs).

Billfish

Billfish – the sailfish, spearfish, swordfish and marlin – occur at southerly latitudes, as in Australia, New Zealand, Africa, the Canaries and Azores, Venezuela, Peru, Costa Rica, Mexico, the USA and Hawaii, Cuba and other islands in the Caribbean. Such "hot spots" are attracting ever more of us to meet these gladiators of the fish world.

Billfish, the gladiators of the fishing world, are a jump-happy and pugnacious family. Their spectacular performances can make the fisherman's shriek as shrill as his reel's.

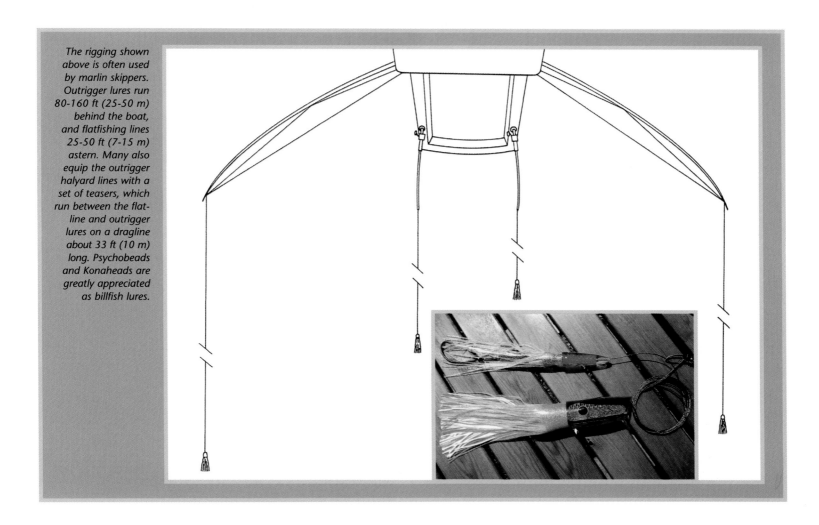

The rigging shown above is often used by marlin skippers. Outrigger lures run 80-160 ft (25-50 m) behind the boat, and flatfishing lines 25-50 ft (7-15 m) astern. Many also equip the outrigger halyard lines with a set of teasers, which run between the flat-line and outrigger lures on a dragline about 33 ft (10 m) long. Psychobeads and Konaheads are greatly appreciated as billfish lures.

Sailfish

The sailfish (*Istiophorus platypterus*) lives in tropical and sub-tropical seas, at temperatures of 22-30° C (71-90° F). Its name is due to the front dorsal fin, which it raises to a height twice that of its own body. Sailfish grow rapidly, the biggest variety occurring in the Pacific, where the record – from Ecuador – is 220 lbs (100.24 kg).

Sailfish are pelagic and often hunt at current edges. Their broad diet includes shrimp, squids, herring, tuna and flying fish. Many methods are used to catch them, but the most common is trolling from an outrigger with filet, whole fish, plastic lures, feather jigs and spoons. When trolling with gray mullet, the speed should be around 5 knots – or fast enough for the bait to smash lightly on the surface. Baits are usually pulled 65-130 ft (20-40 m) behind the boat.

Like other billfish, this species tends to pop up behind or alongside a lure, and inspect it for a while before deciding either to strike or return to the depths. If the sailfish takes, it should be given ten seconds or so, in order to swim away with the bait before you make a strike.

Then the water surface explodes astern, and a silvery-purple monster catapults itself straight into the air. Its entire body shakes, then falls back in a cascade of spray. Usually it comes right up again, and this may go on for a dozen times, but at last it loses steam and the fight becomes more traditional.

A sailfish's dorsal fin is often extremely beautiful in the last stage of the fight. Stretched out, a yard high, it shifts in hue between purple and blue, with clear vertical rows of small black patches. These colors disappear immediately after the fish is dead.

Black marlin

The species *Makaira indica* occurs in tropical waters of the Indian and Pacific Oceans, but catches have also been reported from equatorial Atlantic waters. Among its favorite haunts are reefs and deep edges with nutritious upwelling water. Black marlin give a very powerful impression; they are identifiable, for instance, by their stiff pectoral fins, which cannot be folded in toward the body. They have slate-blue backs, but are silver-white under the lateral line.

Really big marlin are always females, and they can probably weigh over 2,200 lbs (1,000 kg), a metric ton. The record for rod-caught marlin is about 1,560 lbs (707 kg) and comes from Peru.

Black marlin are enormously popular sportfish and have made a big-game El Dorado of, for example, Cairn in Australia. There, as in other places, trolling with equipment in the heavyweight class is a quite common method. The fish takes artificial offshore lures as gladly as large, whole natural baits – bonito, flying fish, mackerel and squids – trolled at 3 to 6 knots. One should keep in mind that a black marlin wants to take some time before swallowing.

Blue marlin

As a rule, the species *Makaira nigricans* occurs between latitudes 45° N and 35° S in the Atlantic, and between 48° N and 48° S in the Pacific. It can also be found in the Indian Ocean.

The blue marlin has a cobalt-blue back, but silver-white sides and abdomen. Along its sides are light-blue vertical stripes, which disappear as soon as it dies. It feeds happily on small members of the mackerel family and on schools of squid. Thus it can normally be tempted with whole large baits such as bonito, gray mullet, mackerel, ballyhoo, runners and squid, although sometimes a small strip bait is enough. Natural baits are used chiefly along the east coast of the USA, while artificial lures predominate in Hawaii's world-famous marlin waters.

Striped marlin

The species *Tetrapturus audax* lives pelagically in the tropical and warm temperate expanses of the Indian and Pacific Oceans. It does not grow as large as the preceding kinds of marlin, but is reputed to be the most active on the hook.

Above: Nowadays it is increasingly common to release a billfish after the fight, thus giving other sportsmen the chance to write new fishing tales. This beautiful black marlin was caught off Pinas Bay (South Pacific, Panama) by Dr. Hans Pfenninger from Switzerland.
Left: Billfish in general are very handsome creatures, with a body shape that reveals their speed at swimming. They wander widely in the oceans, primarily through tropical and subtropical areas. But small swordfish visit Scandinavian waters almost every year.

Striped marlin have been called the "greyhounds" of the sea, due to their speed both under and on the surface. They weigh up to 550 lbs (250 kg) and the rod record, from New Zealand, is 493 lbs (224 kg). These fish are identified mainly by their upward-pointing dorsal fin, steel-blue back, and lavender-colored vertical stripes.

White marlin

Finally we have the species *Tetrapturus albidus* at latitudes 35-45° N in the Atlantic, as well as in the Gulf of Mexico, Caribbean and Mediterranean. It is lighter in color than any of the above marlin species, and the tip of its dorsal fin is rounded. Yet it, too, has beautiful blue vertical stripes along its sides.

White marlin are very popular among trollers with light equipment. They gobble most types of bait in coastal waters. The record rod-catch is 181 lbs (82.5 kg) from Brazil.

A boundless domain

The selection of fish species presented here is only a fraction of all those that exist in the world known as Pisces to scientists. Still, it includes the ones which are most appreciated, both on the fishing line and on the table. Some of them were doubtless what originally set the wave of sportfishing in motion around the Earth. And certainly they have pushed forward another wave with the enormous developments experienced by trolling in the past several years. It is worth remembering, once your rod is in hand or in the holder, not only that every fish species is unique – but also that each individual fish is. One should therefore be careful not to generalize extremely about their striking urges and fighting instincts. Match them on their own terms and discover that the world of fish is full of little giants!

It is truly a wonderful feeling to stroll around during a clear winter day on an ice-covered body of water. The ice drill's sharp cry when it cuts through the surface, the expectant sensation when the bait is lowered toward the bottom, and the first tempting tugs on the line, are all part of it.

Surely the excitement of waiting for a bite was as great for our prehistoric ancestors, when they sank their simple elk-horn hooks through a hole as today's modern ice fisherman does.

Ice fishing

Ice fishing is a way of fishing that goes back far in time. Archaeological finds have shown that prehistoric people also practiced it. Their equipment, however, was made of organic materials. As an attractor, they used a sinker of white bone, and the angling hook was usually of elk horn or a bone from a bird's wing. The tackle employed by early man corresponds to our attractors and hooks, but one thing is certain – it yielded few rewards on days when the perch were sluggish. Our own equipment has been refined and adapted. We now find everything from heavy ice fishing rods to light, sensitive ones that register the most cautious bites, in combination with thin lines and small mormyshka baits to make life tough for even the slyest fish.

Some beginners complain that they never catch anything or are plagued by bad luck when ice fishing. Often, after a few fishless tours, they lose patience and their interest in ice fishing tends to disappear. It is important to be clearly aware that ice fishing is not a chancy, blind approach to fishing, or a matter of monotonously jerking on an attractor that is fished at random below the ice. A sportfisherman who relies solely on his luck without trying to understand the fish's basic behavior, or to learn different techniques for the fishing, will never develop into an adept ice fisherman. On the other hand, one who becomes acquainted with adapting the technique and bait to the prevailing species will discover that the opportunities are wide for rewarding and diverse ice fishing.

Perch are among our most common targets for ice fishing. They exist in lakes, rivers, and some coastal places where the water is not too salty.

Perch – a popular ice fish

The perch's wide distribution and great abundance make it an important sportfish in both summer and winter. It is also high on the list of our most popular prey for ice fishing. Few ice fish attract so much experimenting with jigs and color combinations on the hook as perch do.

Perch enjoy warmth and, during much of the winter, they change from greedy predators into moody and passive fish that must often be persuaded to take the bait. In wintertime a sudden rise of temperature can set the perch moving, and likewise a lowering can make them sluggish and apathetic. Here lies a little of the curiosity that endows perch with such popularity in ice fishing. One of the secrets behind successful ice fishing is to learn how this rapacious hunter functions in the winter and to plan the fishing systematically.

There are many factors an ice fisherman should know which influence the perch's daily activities: wind, current, bottom formations, barometric pressure, and temperature. When fishing in unfamiliar waters, one ought first orient oneself about the water's conditions and the locations of deep holes, steep areas and sunken rocks. Often the land contours of a lake reveal where to look for perch. Heights or cliff walls that plunge into the water are signs of steepness under the surface. An outcrop may indicate that a shallow part of the bottom extends outward. Projecting stones in the middle of the lake are proof of a shoal. Reeds are usually reliable places, where the smaller perch almost always stay parked. You have to watch for snow-

Fishing for perch at the start of spring is a high point early in the year.

free patches on the ice, which let in more light than the ice with a snow cover and can draw fish towards them.

Certain ice fishermen never leave their stations empty-handed. These old hands have learned the tricks of the sport after years of experience. In addition, they have acquired an ability to imagine what is really happening down there at the bottom. They can see the jig's movements and the perch's presence in their mind's eye. As a rule, their character includes a lot of patience and creative know-how: they can adapt their baits to prevailing circumstances. They are flexible and add variety to the fishing. Moreover, their feeling for the fishing is well trained and can sense the slightest jerk on the line.

When the frost and the winter cold descend, the perch begin to wander out toward the deep edges. At this time they are least active in the zero-degree water. After a period of new ice, when they become acclimatized to the change in water temperature, their activity grows again. The larger perch are now found in the vicinity of deep edges – and deep holes. There, the bottom water is always warmest, at a temperature of four degrees.

How long it takes before the perch become ready to bite, especially in shallow lakes and sea fjords, is determined by how long the freeze lasts. If the ice forms after an interval of severe cold, without protracted winds, the bottom water has time to warm up fairly fast, and the fish will be on the move. But if there is a continuing freeze with hard winds, a lake's water layers become mixed and cold throughout. Then a longer time is needed for the earth's warmth to stabilize the bottom water temperature again. Such a cold shock calls for quite a delay before the perch can revive. In January and February the ice is normally covered with snow and the light below it is minimal, so the perch are in very low gear and they feed only briefly. During this dark period only the smaller perch near the shore tend to be active and willing to bite.

As spring approaches and the snow begins to melt from the ice, small fish are tempted up from the bottom to feel the sun's warmth just beneath the ice. Now the bigger perch also regain their interest in hunting. What follows is fine fishing at stream mouths, shallow sea coves, sunken rocks, and other vigorously visited spawning areas.

A perch's swim bladder is closed, and to regulate the pressure it must move into shallower or deeper water when the pressure is high or low. In general, perch head for shallower water at times of high pressure, and are then automatically easier for the ice fisherman to reach. In shallow lakes with no distinct variations of depth, the perch are more strongly influenced by low pressure, since they do not have any opportunity to regulate the air pressure. However, there are exceptions, and one of my best ice fishing experiences took place in a shallow sea fjord before a heavy snowfall. This sort of bite-bonanza may be due to the perch seeking food as a store against long-lasting low pressure.

Baits and equipment

A rough picture of the paraphernalia needed for ice fishing is something to sit on, an ice drill, a suitable rod with a line, and a bait. This, of course, is very simplified, because ice fishing for perch offers many possibilities for diversification with tackle and baits.

To begin with the ice drill, it is a matter of taste whether you choose a drill with a cutter head or with loose bits. The common size is 110–130 mm. An ice scoop is handy for bailing the hole free of slush and snow. With a clean hole in the ice, it is easier to study the line and see how the jig moves in the water, as well as to detect a cautious bite.

The most frequently used natural baits are maggots, but a piece of worm or the eye from a dead perch can serve very nicely.

A seat such as a sleeping-bag chair is essential for making oneself comfortable and concentrating on the fishing all day. There, too, you can store the rod, jigs and other equipment.

The three main types of bait that are employed for perch ice fishing are the vertical jig, the balance jig and the mormyshka.

Vertical jig

When fishing for perch in the winter, vertical jigs are most popular. They differ in terms of weight, color, form and movement. Their length varies from the smallest, at 25 mm (1 in), up to the largest at 80 mm (3 in). Commonest among the colors are brass, copper and silver.

Most jigs certainly do their job well, but the most important thing when obtaining a new jig is to try and learn how it behaves in the water. There is no point in buying a bag full of jigs if one does not know how they work. The jig's size and weight are dictated by the depth you want to fish at. Remember never to send down a large jig in shallow water – it would risk being more destructive than beneficial. One of the vertical jig's tasks is to attract, reflecting the faint light beneath the ice. When the perch has been drawn forth, it should perceive the jig as a small fish that has found some morsel to eat. The colored hook, which is the artificial bait, sits on a three-jointed link or double snapper under the jig, and gives an impression of being edible. This is a

Perch slow down considerably in deep winter, requiring fine-tuned fishing.

little treble hook, provided with colored glue or a piece of yarn.

Sometimes, when the bites at the hole stop abruptly after you have caught a few perch, it is possible to revive the perch's interest by changing the colored hook. The perch can notice differences in hue, and almost always respond positively when a new hook is presented. The usual sizes of colored hooks are 14–18. With the help of a snap you can easily change the hooks when necessary. The colored hook can also be tackled up on a leader, 10–15 cm (6 in) long, which is fastened under the jig, or replaced with a small mormyshka.

Fishing technique

First, lower the jig to the bottom, and knock it on the bottom so that mud and particles are stirred up. Lift the jig slowly by ten to twenty centimeters. Wait a few seconds – the bite comes when the jig stands still. Sometimes an effective method is to make the rod tremble slightly, giving life to the jig. This activity may well yield the first substantial bite. If nothing happens, lower the jig quickly toward the bottom, but make sure that it stops a little way up. Wait a few seconds until the next lift. Vary the motion with an attractive jerk or two.

If you get no takes after several minutes of fishing, it could be worth moving to another hole. Small perch are always the first to arrive, but the bigger fish may need a long time to persuade. Once the initial fish has been hooked, it is important to send the jig down again quickly, so that the school's curiosity has no chance to subside and the perch to swim away.

Equipment for jig fishing

Most devoted ice fishermen for perch take along several rods to be prepared for different sorts of situations. A basic rule is that the jig's size and line thickness should be suited to the prevailing depth for fishing. It is important to keep in mind that a very thin nylon line becomes extremely elastic in deep water, making it more difficult to hook fish. If the fishing occurs in shallow water of 0–4 m (0-12 ft), small vertical jigs are used, enabling you to get by with a line thickness of 0.16–0.18 mm (0.007 in). When moving the fishing out to deeper water of 10–14 m (0.005), a heavier jig is needed, and a line thickness of 0.20–0.22 mm (0.006 in). At great depths of 15–20 m (60 ft), a completely inelastic line is recommended.

A longer ice fishing rod of 35–40 cm (1 ft) is preferable for two reasons. First, you must try to keep as short a distance as possible between the rod and the ice hole, to prevent the wind from disturbing the line so that you cannot notice a fish biting. Second, the fisherman then does not need to sit with his back bent and can relax while fishing. For maximum sensitivity, the rod top or blade should be made of glass-fiber. The blade should not be too soft either, as this impairs its hooking qualities.

Balance jig

Especially on the spring ice, when the snow has melted away, the balance jig is an effective bait, as the hunting light is good and the perch are ready to chase small fish.

Unlike a vertical jig with its slight movements that give curious perch a long time to decide whether to take it, the balance jig has a powerful gait in the water. This stimulates the fish's striking reflex to begin working, and the most sluggish of perch can become excited.

If fished with small, short, intense jerks, the balance jig swims back and forth like a tiny uncertain fish. Another technique is to lift up the jig, about a decimeter each time, and quickly let it drop back toward the bottom, so that it shoots out to the side and then places itself in the middle. The bite usually comes just after the balance jig has stopped.

Sometimes it pays off to bait the treble hook under the balance jig's belly with some maggots. To avoid twining the line below the risk, a two-way swivel can be attached to the line about 40 cm (1 ft) above the balance jig. Thus the jig will not twirl on the line.

The equipment for fishing with a balance jig is the same as with other jig fishing.

Mormyshka

A practical technique is to let a mormyshka fall to the bottom, then lift it slowly until it is 0.5–1.5 m (1.5-5 ft) from the bottom.

Either the mormyshka is kept still during the lift, or you tremble a bit with the rod at the same time as it is lifted. If the water you fish in is shallow, the mormyshka is raised all the way to the ice ceiling. This usually results in the perch following it and biting right beneath the ice edge.

On countless occasions I have begun to fish with a mormyshka just over the bottom and, with each rise and fall, the bites have come higher and higher up in the water layers.

In some waterways there are opportunities to watch the perch while fishing in this manner. Besides being very enjoyable, it is instructive and gives a good idea of how the perch behave under the ice.

A common scenario when watching the fish is that a school of perch slowly glides in with raised dorsal fins. They grow curious and position themselves around the bait. As the mormyshka is gradually lifted from the bottom, the school becomes livelier and one of the fish goes up after it. With stretched out gill-covers, the perch bites when the bait is a decimeter or two above the bottom. This is probably due to fear that the morsel will disappear from view. Once the first fish is hooked, a chain reaction is started with all of them wanting to join the feast.

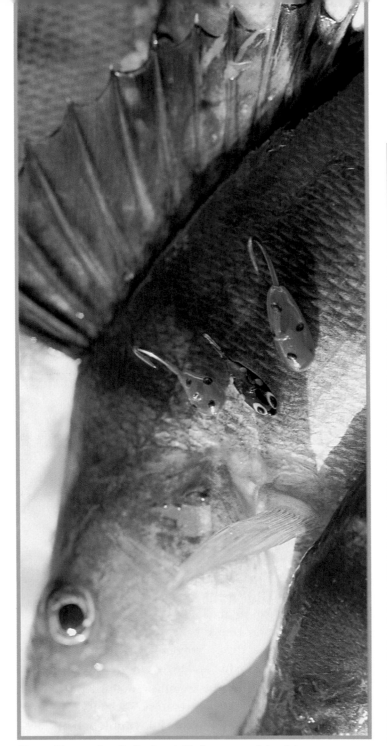

Mormyshkas can be effective 'candy' to liven up perch in winter.

Equipment for mormyshka fishing

There are special mormyshka rods with built-in bite indicators that register the slightest take. These are necessary when the fishing is done at a few meters depth and when the perch are hard to entice.

If it is possible to watch the perch while fishing, you have optical contact and need no bite indicator. Line thickness for mormyshka fishing depends on the size of the mormyshka and the fishing depth, but usually one can do well with lines of 0.15–0.20 mm (0.007 in).

Luring winter perch with bait

Perch angling with live bait gives ice fishing a completely new dimension. With this method the small fish can be sorted out and the fishing directed towards the big perch.

Suitable equipment for such fishing is a short, pliable rod and a spinning or baitcasting reel, loaded with 0.28–0.30 mm (0.01 in) nylon line. The spring-steel rockers that are used as bite indicators in angling for pike can also be excellent for perch. To facilitate the forewarning and detection of bites, you can clamp a little bell on the rocker.

An ice drill of 150 mm (6 in) is sufficient even for large perch. Other accessories that may come in handy are a gaff hook, forceps, scale and camera. During a sunny day between winter and spring, it is hard to imagine a more photogenic subject on the ice than a big black-striped perch.

Tackle

The tackle is easy to manufacture: you thread some bored lead shot onto the main line. Their number and weight are chosen according to the depth and bait. Then tie on a two-way size 8 swivel. Between the sinker and swivel a rubber bead can be threaded on to protect the knot from the lead.

The leader has the same thickness as the main line, and is 30–35 cm (1 ft) long. If perch are abundant at the fishing place, the nylon leader can be exchanged for some pliable wire or Kevlar line.

For perch fishing, one hook on the tackle is enough. Suitable treble hooks must be thin and sharp, in sizes 8–6.

Live baitfish are always better than dead fish. The drawback is that it can be hard and time-consuming to obtain live roach weighing 50–75 g (2 oz).

While fishing, the baitfish are positioned 20–30 cm (1 ft) above the bottom. The main line is set in the rocker's metal clamp and the reel is released. The rocker will stand in an arc and point down toward the hole. When the perch is in good form it swallows the baitfish almost instantly and you can strike fast. But on days when the perch are sluggish, you must not be too quick with the strike – first give them a chance to swallow the tackled-up fish.

The burbot's leopard-hued body makes it a beautiful quarry for ice fishing.

Burbot – the speckled beauty

Burbot belong to the few coldwater species that are very active under the ice when other species are stiff and dull with cold. The burbot is a freshwater fish, but a member of the cod family; its closest relative is the ling. Clear features are its elongated, beautiful yellow-black marbled body, short flat head, and the characteristic barbels that sit under the jaw.

Ever more winter fishermen have discovered the burbot as a potential sportfish and a pleasant complement to the other ice fishing species. Besides, it is a comparatively big specimen. Burbot can reach significant weights of 7–10 kg (20 lb). Alongside the pike and pikeperch, this is one of the heavyweights of winter fishing. The usual weight is from one to three kilograms, and a burbot exceeding four kilos must be considered quite a big fish.

The burbot's spawning is widespread during the winter months from December to March, because of the species' geographical distribution. These months take the fishing to lakes, coastal fjords, and flowing waterways.

The ice fishing starts when the burbot begin their spawning migration. Hot spots are then the known migration routes and spawning grounds, where the fish are often very concentrated in small areas. The typical appearance of a spawning site is stone, gravel, or a hard clay bottom. Usually the burbot are easy to make contact with, but there are exceptions. One friend displayed his stubbornness and patience by waiting on the ice for all of 17 hours in a row to lure up a large burbot. When at last he got his longed-for specimen, which weighed 5.45 kg (10lb), he said: "This speckled beauty was worth many an evening's wait!"

Although burbot are mostly renowned for being dusk and night hunters, they can be found all day and night in certain waters. In lakes where burbot fishing is conducted at depths of 15–30 m (50-100 ft), little light penetrates and the time of day becomes less important.

In some shallow and medium-deep waters of 1–4 m (3-15 ft), dusk has proved to be a good occasion. The burbot have then been inactive during the bright part of the day, and when dark begins to fall their activity resumes. The burbot fishing at such depths is best from sunset until three or four hours later. Periods of severe cold, however, yield poor results. Moreover, one seldom fishes effectively when suffering from the cold.

I have frequently noticed that certain ice holes can be more rewarding than others, despite their being separated by only a meter and a half. Burbot follow definite routes, and there is no use in staying at a particular hole if they do not bite. Change your spots. If some holes produce more fish than others, it may show that these are holding places for the burbot. With the help of an underwater camera, some friends of mine who are burbot fanatics studied a number of ice holes that were drilled in a relatively small area. In the holes that had yielded plenty of fish, the bottom structure was often abnormal – for instance, there might be a jutting log or a large stone that provided the burbot with cover.

Three means of fishing that have worked well, in both still and flowing waters, are the flashing attractor with leader and hook, the sliding bottom tackle, and the jig.

Gliding bottom angling can be combined with one of the other ways. An ice fisherman after burbot who wants to cover a wider area can place several set-ups for bottom angling at the side of the hole he ice fishes in.

The attractor

Fishing with an attractor is the most common and well-known method for burbot. This tackle is used especially in many deep, big lakes where burbot are fished at 15–30 m. The end tackle consists of a large silvery attractor, combined with a leader and a single or treble hook. The size of the attractor depends on the depth of fishing; usually 20–60 g (0.7-2 oz) is sufficient.

The fishing technique is simple. With small, dense movements the attractor is tapped on the bottom, so that sounds and scents spread to the surroundings. Stop the attractor at regular intervals, and carefully tremble with your rod hand, so that only the baited hook moves. Almost invariably, the bite will come as a heavy suck on the line. If you fish with a long leader after the attractor, lift up the attractor now and then to a few decimeters above the bottom. Otherwise there will be a risk that some burbot has taken the bait without any movement, while the fisherman continues unwittingly to tap the attractor on the bottom.

Another variant is to lift the tackle a meter above the bottom, then send it down rapidly and at the same time feed out loose line. The attractor will work its way a meter to the side and lie outside the hole. After that, the rig is hauled home. The baited hook is supposed to slither along the bottom.

If a bite comes without the fish being hooked, just keep trembling the rod slightly. The burbot nearly always come back. But do not wait too long; if nothing has happened for 3–4 minutes, the odds are great that a fish took the bait at the first bite.

The sliding rig in flowing water

In burbot ice fishing the fundamental principle is that the bait should remain in contact with the bottom, since the burbot is a distinctive bottom fish. When fishing in flowing waters at some meters of depth, it can be hard to maintain a satisfying bottom contact with a traditional burbot tackle – that is, an attractor, leader and hook. One of the risks of ice fishing with a large attractor in flowing waters is that the current can lift the attractor off the bottom, so that it hovers and flaps a bit above the intended fishing place. An inexperienced ice fisherman usually reacts by letting out more line than necessary, to regain bottom contact. The current is then likely to form too big a bow in the line between the rod and attractor. At worst, the fisherman will sit and pull on the line bow while the tackle lies still on the bottom. The roe-heavy ladies can be especially cautious when biting, and with an excess of line it may be difficult to detect a bite.

A good tackle in flowing water is a sliding bottom sinker, the model Arsley Bomb, which is stopped with a swivel at 15–20 cm (8 in) from the hook. A suitable hook is a strong single one of size 3/0–4/0. The fishing technique resembles traditional bottom angling, with the only difference that the sinker is knocked on the bottom at regular intervals.

Sometimes the bites from the roe-stuffed burbot come as a careful twitch of the line. The sinker and bait must then lie motionless on the bottom for a few seconds, so that the burbot can calmly suck in the bait.

The jig – a deadly bait

"After the jig hook has been baited with a piece of small herring, the jig skull is activated by the headlamp. With its fluorescent paint, the jig glows like a yellow ball of fire when it is sunk down in the hole. I give the ice fishing rod a rhythmic swaying to make the jig dance on and just above the bottom. Now and then, it hits something solid, presumably a stone or stump. At times, the current takes hold of the thick line, and for a moment the bottom contact is lost. Suddenly the line jerks – something is going on. An instant later, there is a sucking sensation. By reflex, I lift the rod and that wonderful 'log feeling' comes into the line. When I raise the fish from the bottom, the line cuts into my gloves with the burbot's strong jerks. My fishing companion comes to the rescue and helps me get the fish up onto the ice. In the headlamp's light, the burbot's beautiful markings make it an exotic, exciting specimen. It is bigger than any other burbot I have caught. On the way home, I have it weighed on a controlled shop scale. This is a male of 4.86 kg (11 lb)."

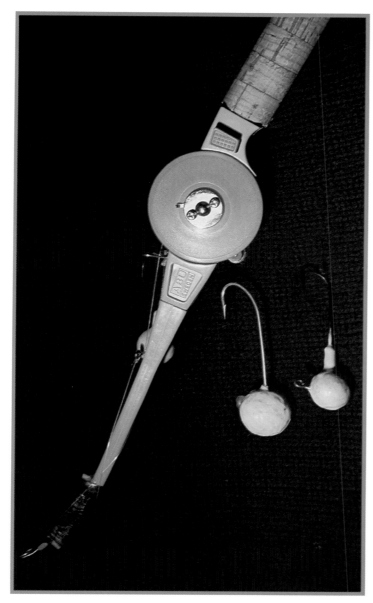

This ice fishing rod's top has been made stiffer to help drive the hook into a burbot's hard jaw.

Many places along a coast can offer good burbot fishing.

The jig has become a popular bait that works in both still and flowing waters. It is most effective in waters no deeper than 5 m (15 ft). The advantages of a jig are that it does not take so much current, and that it also gives a good hooking capacity. A jig's weight is chosen according to the environment in which the fishing will be done.

The jig is baited as follows. A piece of fish is run twice over the hook, and must sit so that the hook tip is visible. It is important, of course, to inspect the jig hook before a fishing tour, and to use a whetstone for maximum sharpness.

The fishing technique is elementary. Once baited, the jig is tapped on the bottom. At regular intervals it is allowed to stand still on or just above the bottom. Sometimes an effective method is to let out a little line while the jig wanders along the bottom, and then to fish it in slowly.

Equipment

Ice fishing for burbot is done with a strong ice fishing rod. Some fishermen shorten their rods a few centimeters so as to make clearer strikes. At depths between zero and 8 m, a nylon line is preferable, of thickness 0.45–0.50 mm (0.02 in). In deeper water, an inelastic line is recommended. Formerly, many burbot fishermen used Dacron line, but one of the drawbacks is that it easily collects ice at temperatures below freezing, which makes it stiff and difficult to handle. The choice of a single or treble hook is a matter of taste; in my own opinion a single hook has worked excellently for bottom angling and fishing with an attractor. Suitable sizes are 1/0–4/0 for a single hook, whereas sizes 2–4 are recommended for treble hooks.

It is wrong to fish for burbot with an ice drill smaller than 150 mm (6 in). For one thing, burbot are substantial fish that can attain great weights. They also have an ability to resist with their tails on the ice roof at the edge of the borehole. If large burbot are the target, do not compromise with the size of the ice drill – invest directly in one of 200 mm (8 in). The easiest way to bring a large burbot out of the ice hole is to stick your hand down and grip it by the gills, but a gaff hook can be good insurance if a huge specimen bites.

A headlamp of the orienteering type is recommended, since it leaves both hands free for changing bait, loosening hooks, and weighing. A knife is needed to cut up pieces of fish or strips of filet. A forceps or hook disgorger is a good tool to have out on the ice if a burbot has swallowed the hook deeply. An irritating problem that may arise at temperatures below freezing is that the baitfish stick together in a clump of ice. To avoid this, the bait can be cut up in suitable strips before the fishing tour. While fishing, the bait is kept in a box in your overalls. Burbot are not particularly fastidious about the choice of bait. The commonest bait is a strip or piece of a fish. Smelt and small herring are excellent bait for burbot.

To find burbot sites, a dash of persistence and patience is required. It pays to be attentive and heed tips. Sometimes, old holding places are of interest to wandering or spawning burbot. Study the chart of your river or lake; it gives valuable information about shallows and deep edges that can be appropriate areas where burbot gather.

Winter whitefish

Whitefish occur in lakes, in the hollows and backwaters of rivers, and along coasts where the salinity is not too high. Ice fishing for whitefish is somewhat tricky, as thin lines and small baits are the keys to success. Among many sportfishermen, going after winter whitefish is enjoyed because one can watch the fish during the process.

When the whitefish are in good form, there can be plenty of 'traffic' at the ice hole, and great triumphs await the adept ice fisherman. Whoever has been able to watch whitefish know how fascinating it is to see one gliding slowly into view. Whitefish are more cautious than the excitable grayling. They usually glide into the hole and take the bait with a suck. You must then keep cool and not strike so soon that the hook is pulled from the fish's mouth.

Considering the whitefish's relatively small and delicate mouth, large baits are unsuitable for it. Common and popular baits for winter whitefish are so-called whitefish-jigs, or small mormyshkas. The whitefish-jig is usually made with a red- or black-painted metal tag, soldered to a small hook of size 10–12. A whitefish-jig is knotted onto the line so that it hangs vertically in the water. Today, the jig has been more or less replaced by the mormyshka as a bait for whitefish.

In some waterways vertical jigs are also employed, with a little mormyshka coupled to a nylon leader 15–20 cm (8 in) long. This tackle is most suited to fishing in deeper waters and flowing waterways.

Whitefish prefer soft bottoms. On coasts, for instance, they are almost always found in elongated coves with muddy bottoms.

After numerous fishing tours, and aided by an underwater camera, my fishing friends made some interesting observations. They noticed that the whitefish followed definite routes. Often the whitefish bite during periods that can be short and intensive, and then disappear as suddenly as they arrived. Previously it was believed that a school of whitefish had vanished from the fishing spot when they stopped biting or showing themselves after a rush to bite. But the camera revealed that the whitefish stayed put and lay low, only reducing their earlier activity to a memory. Every attempt to drill holes near the school resulted in the fish simply moving away.

Fishing technique

In general it can be said that slight tremblings and cautious movements are the best fishing technique for whitefish. Slowly raising and lowering the bait is also effective.

Top right: Whitefish are close relatives of the salmonids, and have a well-developed adipose fin. During the winter they are caught in shallow areas with, for example, a mormyshka or a whitefish jig.
Bottom right: During early spring, when whitefish are gathering in coves before spawning, ide may be encountered. The ide has a fairly high average weight, and is an enjoyable complement to other ice fishing.

A common method is to let the mormyshka down halfway to the bottom and then lift it slowly. At the same time the mormyshka should tremble with a very dense, small movement – as if only the maggots are trembling. Often the strike comes near the ice edge.

On some days, the whitefish are interested in what moves near the bottom. Then the standard method is inverted, that is, the mormyshka fishes from the middle layer downward.

A good trick, when there are few but relatively eager fish, is to have two ready-tackled rods at hand, with a large and a small mormyshka. First the large one is sent down and fished with sweeping movements until a whitefish shows itself. Then the rod with the little bait is used.

If the whitefish passes the bait and seems totally uninterested, you should shift to shallower water in the direction where the whitefish is heading. The shallower the water, the more eager the fish is to bite.

When the ice is thin and shining, patches with old ice or a thicker snow cover are always hot spots. A good way to shut out the light during sunny days is to fill the borehole with ice slush or have a blanket over your head.

Links between bottom color and the mormyshka's appearance

Early in the season, strong colors such as red, and fluorescent red and orange, are effective. Nearer to springtime, smaller and darker mormyshkas should be used. Another basic rule is to use brightly colored baits in dark weather, and dark ones on sunny days.

Many who are accustomed to going after whitefish see a connection between the bottom color and how the mormyshka looks. After years of this fishing, I myself would say the same. In places with a dark, richly vegetated bottom, mormyshkas with red and glaring hues are often successful. On the other hand, black and transparent wine-red mormyshkas, work well everywhere.

Coastal ice fishing

Shallow coastlines, with their isles and shoals, offer very fine ice fishing for whitefish. During certain periods, whitefish occur in great quantities and it can happen that an ice fisherman catches 60–80 fish on a good day. Coastal fishing for whitefish is done with optical contact at depths of 0.3–0.9 m (1-3 ft). It is a wonderful experience to observe fish that glide into the limited field of vision provided by an ice hole and, seconds later, to lift up a struggling whitefish onto the ice.

An important factor in the whitefish's eagerness to bite, during coastal fishing, is how far they have gone into a cove. Fish that have lately come in, or are about to enter from the sea, are not very discriminating and will take anything. At such times, you can tie on a mormyshka that has good visibility and sharp contrast with the surroundings. White color works well if the bottom is dark.

Fish that have been 'in' for a long while are more careful with the choice of color. Then you must strive for colors that agree with the fish's food preference – such as black baits if they eat snails, brown/yellow for shrimp, and transparent wine-red for midge larvae.

Good places to look for winter whitefish are in shallow coves, near shoals out in free water, and around coves. The winds are very important in all sea fishing, and conditions are promising if the same wind has blown for some days, so that the water has had time to stabilize. A southerly wind is best, as the water rises and the fish come closer to land.

Equipment

Fishing with a mormyshka has grown explosively during the past ten years, and this probably owes a good deal to the bait's superiority over the jig, especially when the whitefish are sluggish and difficult to trick.

The mormyshka calls for light, sensitive rods in order to achieve the right trembling of the bait. Avoid line that is too thick, as it dampens the movements for the mormyshka. My own experience has also shown that whitefish are shy of braided or excessive thick lines. Moreover, a braided line is much too stiff for the whitefish's delicate mouth. Suitable line thickness for whitefish ice fishing ranges between 0.16–0.20 mm (0.007).

A large part of fishing for whitefish in wintertime, whether on coasts or lakes, is done with optical contact. Here the ice fisherman can maintain 100 percent observation of what happens on the other end of the line. This makes hooking easier, and no direct strike is needed since the whitefish sucks in the mormyshka, which usually sits well anchored in the upper jaw.

An ice drill of 130 mm will do for most situations. To keep the hole clean, an ice scoop is important. As insulation between your body and the ice, a ground sheet or reindeer skin is needed. During windy days on the ice, the ground sheet tends to be caught up by the wind, resulting in a lot of fast running. This is avoided by tying the ground sheet to something, such as your sleeping-bag chair.

Tiny mormyshkas are powerful medicine.

Maggots are a well-tried bait for winter whitefish. Sometimes sold in different colors, they are normally pre-packed in plastic cans filled with wood chips. The most common and popular colors are red and white. This mixture of hues is very effective for the majority of winter species. It is important that a maggot be baited correctly, to avoid giving the impression of a dead sleeping bag on the hook. To make the fly larva move on the hook in a lively, attractive way, the hook tip is drawn through its thick end, which is marked with two dark spots.

Few species are connected as closely as char with ice fishing.

Char – a wintry beauty

Few species are as strongly associated with ice fishing as the char. It belongs to the salmon family and is one of our commonest coldwater fishes. Typical markings of a char are the white front edges of the breast, abdomen and anal fins; sometimes it also has a bright red abdomen. The char's beautiful looks and its reputation for tastiness make it a highly appreciated species among ice fishermen. For many of them, spring ice fishing for Arctic char is the culmination of winter and must be experienced every year.

To look down in clear water from a well-insulating ground sheet and lure up a fully-grown char is exciting indeed. Under such conditions, one's blood pressure can rise to excess even when used to sportfishing. The char is known for being a fastidious, capricious fish – it may circle for a long time around the bait without biting. Its irritating behavior is what lends fascination to this fishing and demands all sorts of tricks to get it on the hook.

Normally the char has a short period of activity in the morning, after which it becomes very calm for some hours until midday, when it suddenly starts to bite again.

Char are found primarily in high mountain lakes and certain waterways, but also in some large cold lakes. Moreover, their popularity has led to implantation in many waterways where they would not ordinarily exist. The spawning period for char lasts from September to November, and usually takes place at depths of 3–5 m (9-15 ft), although at times down to 20 m (65 ft). A typical spawning site is a shoal or an area with big stones.

The char's habits, appearance and size vary according to where it lives. But compared with trout, it is more pelagic and less territorial, and most often it swims in schools.

Large Arctic char occur mainly in big clear lakes. Those of great size are usually pronounced fish-eaters. A smaller and less shiny variety of Arctic char lives pelagically in some waters, while in others it inhabits the bottoms near the shore. This kind of char seldom becomes a pure fish-eater; its main prey is insect larvae and small crustaceans. Arctic shrimp (Mycis relicta) are frequently the basic diet for deep-water char. In waters where it faces no competition from other fish species, it easily forms abundant dwarf stocks.

Char attractor

The most common tackle for char fishing consists of an attractor and a baited hook. Apart from differences in shape and size, char attractors come in three fundamental colors – brass, copper and silver. In addition, they are wrapped in colored tapes, usually of fluorescent red. Many char ice fishermen use silvery attractors when there is much snow and thick ice. Towards spring, on sunny days, they switch to copper attractors, or darken their silver ones with soot in order to soften the reflections.

The essential procedure is to lower the attractor towards the bottom and wind it up, so that the baited hook hangs some centimeters above the bottom. This is followed with some calm, rhythmical enticements: the attractor is wound smoothly up and down without any jerks. By watching how the line moves in the ice hole, you can get an idea of how the attractor is moving in the water. At intervals, smaller movements and trembling of the rod tip are tried. But no really clear rules exist for how to take the char. A knowledgeable char fisherman knows his bait well. The right movements of the rod, and a feeling for how the attractor is moving in the water, tend to be decisive when it comes to getting a bite.

Char attractors on sale are usually ready-tied with leader and hook. Almost always, however, these are delivered with too short and thick a leader, and the hook is much too thick and provided with barbs on the shaft. This type of hook is difficult to bait with maggots, the result being only that they are torn apart. Therefore, many char fishermen exchange the thick hook for a thinner single hook. Good sizes of single hooks are Nos. 2–4, and many also use small treble hooks under the attractor, a suitable size being No. 10. It is important that the hook be needle-sharp to be able to fasten in the char's hard mouth.

Ice fishing with mormyshka and balance jig

A mormyshka can be either combined with an attractor or used as a bait by itself. When the char are sluggish, a common method is to lay out a motionless rod with a baited mormyshka. This also works well for trout, which are happy to take motionless bait during the winter. Once I watched a char fisherman standing and fishing with an attractor after placing an extra rod with a mormyshka in an adjacent ice hole. Suddenly the rod was dragged fast toward the hole, and he managed to rescue it at the last instant. After a dramatic fight, there emerged a char weighing over three kilograms. The rest of us who were fishing nearby had not felt the slightest suggestion of a bite. This char had certainly been drawn by the attractor's movements, but hesitated to bite until it discovered the mormyshka.

If a char is shy or just swims past the attractor, a little balance jig can be the right medicine. Colors of mormyshkas and balance jigs that work well on char are orange, brown-black and red.

Prebaiting (chumming) for char

Many char ice fishermen have had success at prebaiting the ice hole to bring in the fish. The main idea of prebaiting is to

An attractor with a decimeter-long leader and a maggot-baited hook is the most common tackle for char.

attract the char on the same day or during the following days, and get them to eat the prebait that is dropped down. As always when prebaiting, a strategy is needed since mistakes can easily ruin a fishing place. Be sparing with the prebait, or else it may have the reverse effect – the char become indifferent to the actual bait. Do a little prebaiting each time at regular intervals.

Start on the fishing day by prebaiting the intended ice holes with some fistfuls of food. Special blends for char can now be bought. The mixture is largely composed of cheese curds with a binder of breadcrumbs. Other kinds of prebait that work are maggots, blood powder, boiled rice or coin, and boiled shrimp.

Promenade (two-hole) ice fishing

This approach is used primarily in big lakes that are well known for char. It works best when fishing at great depths for pelagically hunting predatory fish. The principle is to fish with two rods and attractors in a pair of drilled ice holes, while walking

A good rod for char should have a pliable blade that can drive the hook into the fish's hard mouth. Copper and silver attractors are effective colors for char.

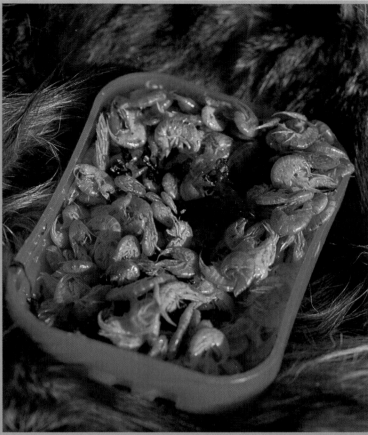

On the Kola Peninsula in Russia, Arctic shrimp like these are popular bait.

back and forth between them. Promenade ice fishing is an effective way of fishing through a particular deep area. If you want the attractor to fish from the bottom to about 12 meters up from the bottom, first let down the attractor to the bottom and lock the reel. Next, pace off 12 (40 ft) meters from the hole, drill another hole and let down the other attractor towards the bottom. Then you need only walk between the holes and fish with a rod in each hand.

For this fishing, one uses strong rods with reels that can be free-coupled. Common baits are vertical jigs, trolling attractors, and light spoons that weigh 20–30 g (1 oz).

Equipment

An ice fishing rod for char is adapted to the type of bait you have chosen to fish with. When fishing with an attractor, the rod should have a rather flexible top, and an ample handle with space for big gloves. The reel must have a stable lock and be able to hold at least 50–60 m (150 ft) of monofilament line 0.25–0.30 mm thick. Thinner lines are needless insofar as you do not fish with small baits. Between the attractor and the hook, you can fasten a leader of some thinner dimension. If the line should happen to break off, you then lose only the hook and keep the attractor.

When fishing with a mormyshka it is necessary to use a thinner line, such as 0.20 mm (0.007 in), for sensitivity. Another alternative is to wind a completely inelastic super-line onto the reel.

For char fishing, an ice drill of 130–135 millimeters (5 in) is a suitable size. If the ice is thick, as in mountain fishing, one can go down to 110 millimeters. Ice fishing for char with optical contact is enjoyable, too, as it enables you to study how the bait and the char behave in the water. This calls for a ground sheet and an ice scoop. It can also be worth putting something over your head, so that the surrounding light or reflections do not come down into the hole.

The grayling – a winter hunter

Grayling belong to the salmonid family, and are desirable sportfish with weights that can reach three kilograms. A grayling of one kilo is a dream fish for most rod-swingers. The species' most evident characteristic is a large dorsal fin, which can be very well developed in the males. Grayling are typical coldwater fish that require oxygen-rich, clear water. They inhabit flowing waterways and the shallow lakes of forests and mountains. Lakes next to the mountains can also hold plenty of fine places for grayling.

Occasionally grayling are found in lakes that also have stocks of pike. Although pike are among the worst enemies of grayling, these antagonists have managed in many places to evolve an ecological interplay. Grayling usually begin to spawn immediately after the ice melts. They spawn mainly in waterways, but may also do so along lake shores, often near the mouth of a brook.

Their aggressive behavior has made grayling a popular and exciting candidate for ice fishing. Frequently when fishing for whitefish with optical contact, I have seen one come rushing through the school of whitefish to take the bait.

The fishing methods during the winter vary, and are governed by the environment at hand. Most commonly, grayling are caught by fishing with optical contact – lying and looking down through an ice hole. The moment when a big grayling exposes itself in the hole is an unforgettable experience. They can hunt in amazingly shallow waters and are often found when only 25–40 cm (1 ft) separates the ice from the bottom. Almost always, they become more eager to bite when in shallower water. An ideal depth when ice fishing for grayling is 30–60 cm (1-2 ft).

On thin ice over shallow water, the grayling may be shy of an ice drill. It is not a bad idea to drill some holes first and let these 'rest' before starting to fish. Be active with the drill crown – a practiced grayling fisherman does not drill at a hole for more than a few minutes. If any grayling are nearby, they usually show their presence with little delay. Once a grayling has come into view, the goal is to entertain it. Some people make the awful mistake of ceasing to move the bait, which can lead the grayling to see through the ice fisherman's evil intent and swim away. One of the tricks of ice fishing for grayling is to get the fish to feel the joy of hunting – it wants to chase after the bait.

Bottom contact is the key to catching grayling. Normally,

Far left: Grayling belong to the salmonid family and are characterized by their large dorsal fin. In wintertime they are exciting sportfish and can be tricked with attractors, balance jigs and mormyshkas.
Left: A grayling of more than two kilos is really a dream fish.

they have a territory and patrol it to find food. This tends to make them interested in anything that moves. Furthermore, grayling have a highly developed sense of sight and are shy of abnormal movements or strong light. By filling the hole with ice slush, or covering it with a blanket, you can minimize the light coming in. When the fishing is done on thin ice, the air should not be too cold, because grayling become sluggish in extreme cold.

The mormyshka

Mormyshkas are a much-liked bait for grayling. Good colors in this case are orange, copper, black, and brown/yellow. Maggots are the commonest bait, and are fastened abundantly over the whole hook.

The technique for a mormyshka is to fish it with strongly swinging movements just over the bottom. Let it also bounce along the bottom, like a little fish fry in wild panic. Such drastic variations in motion can make the laziest grayling see red. If the fish glides slowly and hesitantly toward the bait, do not let it bite, for then it will usually take the bait in a half-hearted yawn that leads to losing the fish. An interested fish can circle for a long time just outside the ice hole's narrow field of vision. Sometimes a glimpse of the fish's fins or a puff of sediment reveals that something is happening. Once the grayling has decided to bite, the attack is lightning-fast as a rule. You need to control your nerves so that the strike does not come too soon. An experienced grayling fisherman told me that, whenever a big one took the bait, he would count '1001–1002' before striking, to make sure that the hook was not torn from the fish's mouth.

Ice fishing by eye in waterways

A popular method of fishing in flowing waters is to use an attractor or a thin jig, of the pike-jig type, with a leader 10–15 cm (6 in) long. A thin, sharp hook of size 4–6 is attached to the leader's end. Just over a decimeter above the attractor or jig, a dropper fly of size 10–14 is tied. Both the fly and hook are baited with maggots while fishing.

The attractor or jig is fished rhythmically a bit over the bottom, so that the whole apparatus stands swaying in the current.

This can be varied by laying the attractor and hook on the bottom, striking it so that particles are stirred up.

In the calmer sections of a waterway a larger mormyshka or a balance jig that is fished near the bottom can be a deadly bait. A really simple tackle that has worked astonishingly well is made by clamping a lead shot above a worm-baited hook. This technique works best in secure places that almost always contain grayling. Here one can also enhance the tackle with a dropper fly, tied a decimeter above the lead shot. The idea is that the lead shot and baited hook should lie on the bottom while the dropper fly sways in the current.

Attractor and fly – a good combination in lakes

In lakes with soft bottoms, for instance of mud and slush, it is very effective to combine an attractor with a fly. Farthest down on the line, a copper or silver attractor is set. During the fishing the attractor hits the bottom and stirs up particles. On the main line, 20–25 cm (9 in) above the attractor, a leader 10–15 cm (5 in) long is tied, with the fly at its end.

Double-hooked flies of sizes 8–6 are suitable for such fishing. Flies that have worked well are Red Tag and Black Zulu. The fly's hooks should be bent outward to facilitate penetration in the grayling's mouth. Their tips should of course be needle-sharp. Maggots or mealworms have proved excellent as bait for this tackle. The bait is threaded onto the fly's hooks.

The fishing technique is to let the attractor continuously work on the bottom while the baited fly sways a little above it. However, an important point is to keep working with the attractor when a grayling approaches. Otherwise the fish will lose interest and swim onward.

The fishing equipment

To make the fishing sensitive, the ice fishing rod's blade should be pliable and have a length of 18–20 cm (7 in). Some practitioners file down the reel lock so that it can easily release line while playing a large grayling.

The line thickness for mormyshka fishing is 0.18–0.22 mm (0.007 in). Fishing with an attractor and fly demands a thicker ice fishing rod. I normally use Abu Pimpel 2 rods, loaded with nylon of thickness 0.25–0.30 mm (0.01 in). These rods have a good handle and a long blade, which make it easy to work with the attractor. A suitable ice drill for grayling is 130 cm (5 in). Since the fishing is almost always done in shallow waters there is a considerable risk of running into the ground, so you should

have a habit of taking along an extra set of bore cutters and tools on a fishing trip.

A ground sheet and an ice scoop are essential items in the ice fisherman's equipment. A gaff hook is useful if a really big fish bites. Small telescopic gaff hooks take up almost no space and fulfill their purpose well. A scale, measuring tape, and camera may be good to have if a trophy specimen shows up.

Rainbow and brook trout
Two North American muscle-fish

Rainbow

The rainbow trout is one of the salmonids, and originally comes from the coastal rivers of the Pacific Ocean. Today it has been implanted over large parts of the world. Its wild temperament and great reputation for being a tough fighter have brought it affection and respect from sportfishermen everywhere.

Rainbow are much appreciated as winter fish, since they are on the take all season and can be caught with a variety of methods and baits. The fishing normally starts in October or November, or right after the ice has spread. On fresh ice, the fishing is almost always superb. Later, during the dark and

Rainbow Trout

snowy period from December to March, the fish live in low gear and take for only brief intervals. Towards spring, when the days grow longer and the sun's warmth begins to melt the snow from the ice, the rainbow becomes more active.

Ordinarily, rainbow swim in deep water at midday and head for shallow areas during the afternoon. They often have hunting routes and patrol these in small schools, for example outside reed edges or stony bottoms. Other fishing spots to find rainbow in are coves, shoals, deep holes, or areas with a good supply of nutrients.

Rainbow keep looking for food all winter and, as a rule, they move through considerable areas and diverse depths. They can be found near the bottom, just under the ice cover, and out in the free water masses. Hence it is important for the ice fisherman to be industrious and purposeful. One day the fish may be in meter-deep water, another at five meters. A portable echo sounder that is adapted to ice fishing can often be very helpful for locating them. Another approach is to fish the bait through the water layers, starting from the bottom and continuing up to the ice edge.

Fishing with an attractor

A traditional char attractor, dropper fly, and baited single hook of size 2–4, make an excellent means of dealing with rainbow trout. The fishing technique for rainbow is as for char. First, let down the attractor to the bottom; then lift the line so that the hook hangs a few decimeters above the bottom. Give some soft jerks on the line to flutter the attractor, and alternate this with keeping it still. Occasionally you can change to a cautious trembling of the rod tip. If no fish are aroused, start jerking again. The rainbow usually bites with explosive force, but sometimes its bites are apprehensive and tentative – for instance, the line may begin to move sideways at an angle beneath the ice. It is then important to make your strike fast. To see more readily when the line moves in the hole, you must keep the hole free of slush from ice and snow.

Fishing with a large mormyshka or balance jig

The rainbow is an active fish-eater and, during the winter, sweeps along in small schools hunting for small fish that are stiff with cold and easy to catch. In shallow water outside reed beds or coves, large orange- and red-colored mormyshkas or balance jigs can be deadly candy for rainbow. In general, the balance jig should be fished with plenty of movement when looking for rainbow. Start the fishing with some slow attractive jerks, and wait for half a minute while trembling the rod; then repeat the jerks. The bite can come at any time. If the rainbow are really on the take it happens when the balance jig is in motion. If they are sluggish, they may prefer a bait that is standing still and shaking.

The fishing technique with a mormyshka is different. Instead of being jerked attractively, the mormyshka should be started near the bottom, and slowly raised for half a meter. Here it can stand and tremble, before being sunk just as slowly to the bottom. Variation is also possible when fishing it from the bottom up to the ice edge. Lift it a foot off the floor, pause and tremble for a few seconds, then lift it another foot and tremble again. Repeat the sequence until the mormyshka has reached the top, whereupon it can be lowered all the way for the same treatment. Be prepared to feel a bite at any point.

Equipment

The ice fishing rod for rainbow trout should be strong and carry a sizable reel, loaded with line of at least 0.25–0.30 mm (0.01 in). Good tackle on the line consists of an ordinary char attractor with a leader some decimeters long, and a single hook of size 2–4. As an extra lure, a dropper fly can be tied above the attractor. The ice bore should not be smaller than 135 mm, since rainbow are fighters and can be big. A cutter of 150 mm (6 in) is ideal and will cope with most locations.

Bringing two or three ice fishing rods on your fishing trip is sensible insurance. Often the attractor summons fish that are shy of an attractor and hesitate to bite. At such times a change to a small balance jig or mormyshka can save the day.

Besides a rod with an attractor, a second rod might be loaded with, say, 0.22–0.25 mm line and given a choice of mormyshkas in orange, red, brown/yellow and black colors. On a third rod, with line of 0.25 mm (0.01 in) , an orange balance jig can be tied. Useful hook baits for rainbow trout are maggots, worms, flavored corn, and power bait. Another fine bait is cooked shrimp. Before the fishing tour, shell and clip the shrimp into odd-sized pieces, for storing in a box while you fish. Also of value are cocktails – combinations of various baits – such as a piece of shrimp and white maggots, or yellow corn and pure red maggots. Here the imaginative ice fisherman has an advantage.

Brook trout

Brook trout, too, belong to the salmonid family, and are among its most beautiful representatives. They originate from western North America, where they live in cold oxygen-rich lakes and flowing waters. The brook trout's hallmarks are a finely marbled green-brown back and a black, contrasting edge alongside the white front edges of the breast, abdomen and anal fins. It is also well decorated with yellow and red spots along the body sides. Unlike the rainbow, which has had difficulty reproducing in European waters, the brook trout has established itself in many waterways and created vital stocks.

Brook trout are distinctly cold-water fish, and enjoy streams that are fed partly from springs with water that stays at a low temperature throughout the summer. Ice fishing for brook trout is a vigorous sport. During the winter these trout are the lake's vagabonds and wander widely beneath the ice. They can be encountered almost everywhere and in the least probable places. Their activity in cold water is what makes them one of the real 'Formula 1' fighters of winter fishing. Their bites are usually violent and explosive.

It is common to find brook trout in shallow waters. There they gladly linger both inside and outside clumps of reeds, or over bottoms with rich vegetation where they patrol back and forth. The brook trout's love of shallow water makes it a rewarding target for ice fishing with optical contact. Occasionally they

appear in places with only a few decimeters deep. When it darts into the field of vision and takes the bait at full speed, like a trimmed torpedo, you're guaranteed to feel a kick of adrenalin!

Fishing equipment and methods

The equipment and methods for brook trout are not very different from those for rainbow. Brook trout are relatively greedy fish and have a rather omnivorous diet. Three excellent baits are the reflector, mormyshka and balance jig – as well as plain traditional vertical jigs that are used to ice fish for perch.

On occasions when the brook trout are busy hunting small fish, it can be worth trying little jigs that are fished through the water layers. The technique involves letting the jig down to the bottom, where it first hops around and stirs up sediment. Then the jig is raised with trembling movements for half a meter at a time. Once it has been fished up toward the ice edge, it is lowered in stages to the bottom.

If the fishing is focused on brook trout, the gear can be pared down to an ordinary ice fishing rod that is suited for perch fishing. But the rod should be of a model with a reel that can be free-coupled quickly and simply. Brook trout seldom grow as big as the rainbow, and a specimen of around a kilogram must be regarded as a fine fish. Nonetheless, since they offer comparatively strong resistance for their size, a line thickness of 0.22–0.30 mm is recommended.

When the snow lies on the ice and you are fishing at some meters of depth, an attractor is preferable. It is more visible and tempting than any other bait. Sometimes brook trout are found even in free waters, so it can pay off to fish through the water layers scrupulously. Begin at the bottom then proceed methodically up to the ice cover. This method applies both to mormyshkas and to balance jigs and attractors.

In shallow water the mormyshka or a small balance jig is usually a more effective weapon. They often bring a bite when the bait is being fished a decimeter or so beneath the ice cover. A suitable size for the ice drill in brook-trout fishing is 130 cm (5 in).

Maggots work well as baits, but smelly baits such as small-scaled shrimp pieces are hard for brook trout to refuse. Just as with the rainbow, it can be worth trying a cocktail on the hook.

Ice angling for rainbow and brook trout

Many ice fishermen have discovered that rainbow and brook trout are wonderful to angle for. These species are full-blown predators and their greed does not differ much from that of numerous other predatory fish.

Sometimes a sensitive, leaded float is used that holds up the bait from the bottom and serves as a bite indicator. One can also fish with a spring-steel rocker, and this method has been described in the section on perch. Keep in mind that fishing with live bait is not allowed in all waters due to the risk of infection. It is important to be prepared and make an early strike – as long as the bait is not too big – since most salmonids are quick to take the bait but can spit it out just as fast if they suspect a 'fly in the ointment'. Suitable sizes for single hooks are 6–4, while size 10 is used for treble hooks.

A guide to equipment

Baits

The equipment determines, to a large extent, how successful and enjoyable your ice fishing will be. Just as during the summer's spinning or flyfishing, it is important in wintertime to adapt your fishing technique and gear in accordance with what you want to catch. A practiced, experienced ice fisherman always selects his or her baits, methods, and techniques on the basis of the water's appearance and the species in mind. The ice fishing rod, line and bait must, in a word, match each other as well as the target.

For the beginner, today's enormous assortment of winter baits – such as jigs, mormyshkas, attractors and vertical jigs – can be like a jungle that one gets lost in. Neither, unfortunately, are there any universal baits that work in all weather. The effective baits vary greatly between different species and fishing waters. A newcomer can save much time by asking the local sportfishing store, or experienced fishermen, about what is best. However, it is not enough to have a complete, shiny set of equipment in order to become a clever ice fisherman. You must get to know your equipment and be aware of how it functions during the fishing. Moreover, every fish species calls for a particular technique and method.

Choosing the ice fishing rod according to the species you fish for

An ice fishing rod's main tasks are to store line, direct the bait, and register the bite. The rod has little importance for playing fished that are hooked. Once the fish is hooked, it is instead the feeling in your fingertips that serves as a drag brake. Today there

A sledge or scooter makes it easier to transport equipment on the ice.

is a wide range of ice fishing rods with diverse lengths and designs to choose from. In spite of this rich assortment, I do not think there is any all-round rod that can cope with all ice fishing. The choice of ice fishing rod depends on your personal requirements, such as its weight, length and sensitivity. It is also important that the rod be balanced and be adapted to the given species, fishing method and water depth. Thus, there is not much point in fishing for burbot at a depth of 10 meters (30 ft) with a rod and line that are suited to perch fishing. Many of us prefer long rods, their advantage being that one can sit in a relaxed manner and nonetheless have the rod tip placed near the ice hole. The rod's length plays a minor role when fishing with optical contact.

An ice fishing rod's handle is made of hard plastic, neoprene or cork. The handle's length and form vary, depending on the

kind of fishing intended. Light and sensitive rods for fishing with small baits are usually provided with short or flat handles. These are best fished by holding them with your forefinger and middle finger opposite your thumb. Larger ice fishing rods, meant to fish reflectors and big vertical jigs, have longer handles and are gripped with the whole hand. Most ice fishing rods have line spools that can wind in, either inset or placed above the handle. By free-coupling the spool, you can smoothly adapt and change the line length for different fishing spots and, when necessary, feed out line to rushing fish. A spool with a large diameter takes up line faster than a small one.

The rod top's thickness and sensitivity vary with the rod's size. For best hooking qualities and feeling, an ice fishing rod should have a glass-fiber top. Too small a top guide will easily ice up, which is very irritating. A well-working top guide must be at least 10 mm ((0.4 in) in diameter.

Below are simplified descriptions of different types of ice fishing rods, divided into three classes of fishing.

Light fishing – Pure mormyshka rods: these sensitive rods are adapted for fishing with thin lines and very small baits. The top is about 24–26 cm (10 in) long, and the short handle gives the best feeling when held with the thumb, forefinger and index finger. Light rods without a fixed mormyshka top: these have a top 28–36 cm (1 ft) long and a short, flat handle. The screw that holds the line spool in place usually also serves as a drag brake. Adapted for fishing with small balance jigs and mormyshkas and, to some extent, light vertical jigs. For perch, whitefish, and small char and grayling.

Medium fishing – The handle fits the whole hand and the adjacent line spool can be free-coupled. Usual length of the rod top is 37–40 cm (1.3 ft). Adapted to fishing with heavier vertical jigs, reflectors, balance jigs and large mormyshkas. For perch, rainbow trout, brook trout, Arctic char, brown trout and grayling.

Heavy fishing – Robust handle, large line spool for free coupling. Strong rod top, usually 45–50 cm (1,5 ft) long. Adapted for fishing with large reflectors and heavy jigs. For burbot, pike, pikeperch, big rainbow and other trout.

Ice fishing line

The choice of line for ice fishing is determined by the bait's weight, the fishing depth, and how big the fish species is. A basic rule: the smaller the bait, the thinner the line. Too thick a line hampers the bait's movements, and loses some of the fine feeling in the rod. But too thin a line in deep water can also reduce sen-

Top left: *Large mormyshkas work well on brook trout, rainbow, grayling, char and brown trout.*

Top right: *A bait box with mormyshkas of various sizes.*

Left: *The balance jig is a good bait for fish of the salmon family, but also for hungry perch.*

sitivity. The thinner a nylon line is, the more elastic it becomes.

A good ice fishing line must be flexible and remain soft and pliable when very cold. Special lines for ice fishing are commonly sold on 25 m (80 ft) spools. Sometimes they are colored for easy visibility against snow and ice. However, it is not necessary to buy any special ice fishing line. Most of the summer lines from well-known equipment manufacturers work equally well in winter.

Ever more ice fishermen have discovered completely inelastic lines that are much stronger than a monofilament line of the same thickness. Such lines convey the bait's movements and give secure hooking in deep water. One of the disadvantages of many inelastic lines is that they absorb water and, in freezing temperatures, become stiff and clumsy to fish with. Moreover, species such as whitefish and grayling can be shy of such lines.

The ice drill

Today, major manufacturers offer a wide range of ice drills. The ice fisherman can find everything from 90 mm (3 in) competition drills to the really big ones of 205 mm. Most ice drills can also be supplemented with an extension if necessary.

When acquiring an ice drill, you should have first decided where the fishing will mainly be done, and whether it will aim at some particular species. For the ice fisherman with all-round interests, a drill of 150 mm (6 in) is preferable. This size covers nearly all fishing except the kind directed toward big pike and burbot.

The ice drill is fitted with either a cutter head or loose blades. The cutter head is the match fisherman's favorite. It wears well and keeps its sharpness for a long time. But it is also more costly and difficult to change when dulled. This type of cutter is best suited to lake fishing, or ice fishing on waters where the risk of grounding is not great.

Loose blades are recommended when the fishing is done over shallow, stony bottoms or in areas where the drill may well run into ground. I always manage to ruin at least one set of drill blades during coastal fishing for grayling. At first I used a cutter head, but after some groundings that made it unusable, I changed to a drill with loose blades. These have the advantage of being easy to change on the drill; besides, an extra set of blades weighs very little and takes up no space in the pack.

For directed pike or burbot fishing, or much drilling in thick ice, a power ice drill can be a sensible alternative. However, it weighs a lot more and is clumsier to transport than an ordinary

Rods adapted for fishing with mormyshkas or light vertical jigs.

ice drill. Also electric drills to be connected, for example, to a scooter battery have begun to make inroads on the market. In the future, electric drills may become more prominent due to the tougher environmental standards.

An ice drill requires few, but important, maintenance measures in order to work well for a long period. After a fishing tour, the drill should always be put in a warm dry place. The cutter is very sensitive to gravel and stones; it will also soon become useless if exposed to knocks and impacts. Make a habit of leaving the edge-shield on the ice drill during transport and storage. If the fishing is done in seawater, be sure to rinse off the cutter after your trip to prevent rusting.

Other equipment

If one is to last a whole day of concentrated fishing, while keeping the feeling in the fishing, one needs to sit comfortably. There are many solutions, but the most convenient is a sleeping-bag chair or similar support, which can also hold your equipment. To follow the fish by eye when ice fishing, an insulating ground sheet or reindeer skin is essential.

An ice scoop is a valuable accessory. It easily removes snow and ice slush from the hole. Keeping the hole clean is especially important for fishing with light baits or when the fish are biting cautiously. Small but useful accessories for the ice fisherman are single and treble hooks of diverse sizes, bait locks, split rings and double snappers. By always having your gear in good order, you will automatically get a better overview of it all. Spare lines, colored hooks, reflectors, dropper flies, and mormyshkas are stored most simply in small boxes or in a special tackle folder.

A little sledge often facilitates transport of equipment on the ice – such as rods, ice drill, and a bucket with baitfish for angling. Many of my friends have chosen to mount fixed tubes on their sledges, where rods for pike and perch angling are stored during transport. Combination pliers, a jaw opener, and forceps are additional items of importance for ice fishing and angling. When fishing in darkness, a torch or headlamp is needed. A small telescopic gaff hook

There are many different echo sounders on the market today. Some are adapted for winter use, but an ordinary echo sounder that serves during the summer months is just as good.

is good to have along in case big fish bite. On spring ice, particularly in the mountains, sunglasses protect against the risk of snow-blindness. When a trophy fish is landed, it can be fun to document the catch with a camera, scales and measuring tape.

Electronic aids

In recent years, electronic aids have gained increasing influence over ice fishing. Special depth indicators and temperature gauges or echo sounders, manufactured for winter use, have become popular additions to equipment. Similarly, GPS navigators (Global Positioning System) are extremely helpful when fishing on large waters. These enable a fisherman to collect interesting waypoints – such as shoals and places with unusual bottom structure – so as to find them again on the next fishing tour.

Some years ago I tested an underwater camera during a variety of fishing occasions. I did not catch any big fish, but the camera frequently yielded invaluable information, which has been very significant on subsequent fishing trips.

Safety on ice

A responsible ice fisherman does not go out onto winter ice without ice-prods. In unknown areas, these should be complemented with an ice-stick, and one should never be alone. The winter fishing starts when the clear ice is at least 10 cm (4 in) thick. Even then, however, a fisherman cannot walk securely everywhere. Keep in mind:

- Snow is insulating and delays the ice formation; even in bitter cold, the ice may melt under the snow if the water is flowing.
- Sea ice is weaker than freshwater ice.
- Spring ice is treacherous; after freezing solid at night, it can thaw at midday into an unstable surface that is perilous to walk on.
- Always have respect for the ice. Never take chances. No fish is worth your life.

Some fishermen believe themselves safe on the ice if they wear buoyant overalls. These will help if you fall through the ice, but they do not help when you have to climb out of the water. Therefore, always wear the ice-prods around your neck.

To catch fish with a rod that one has built by oneself gives both joy and satisfaction. But building a rod also means that it can be adapted to one's special wishes in a way that is impossible with a production line rod.

Building your own Rod

Even the first rod-building attempt of a beginner can and will, result in a better rod than the ones that you can buy in a store. The explanation lies in the fact that the home builder's rod is intended for himself, which enables him to customize it for its user and its intended use in a way that is impossible in a production line rod. The resulting rod often exceeds a mass-produced one in both performance and quality.

To achieve such a result, the rod-builder has to do a little more than just assembling a kit. Building rods from pre-composed kits is not at all recommended - instead one chooses the materials and composes a rod that meets one's own requirements and desires. Thereafter, by independently designing handle and reel seat, and placing them and the line guides on the rod in a way that makes the best use of the blanks properties, one will get a fishing tool with optimal functionality. Finally, by mounting the components with the exactness that is possible only in this type of time-independent handicraft, the rod will become maximally robust and durable.

A bit of terminology

A rod is built on a blank that normally continues straight through the handle, right down to the butt or cap in the bottom of the handle. This is not the case in casting rods, where the handle often is built on a separate frame and the blank is glued into a ferrule in the upper end of the handle frame.

The rod may have one or more ferrules, and in modern rods these are built into the blank to form a unit with the blank sections. The ferrules may be of the "tip-over" type, where the upper section is fitted over the bottom section or the "top-in" type, where the opposite is done. The female ferrule is the hollow part, into which the male ferrule fits.

The top line guide of the rod is also called the "tip-top". It is glued to the blank with melt glue, or nowadays more often with epoxy glue. The line guides have one or two legs and are mounted on the blank by wrapping with rodwinding thread. The wraps are later covered with lacquer. The guide closest to the reel is called the butt guide, or on fly rods the stripping guide.

The transition between the rod handle and the blank is often covered by a hosel or a ring, a winding check, made of metal, plastic or wood. The handle itself is ordinarily made of cork, which is suitably soft and light, warm and pleasant to hold. Also in the handle may be various wooden details for effect. The handle is attached to the rod blank with epoxy glue.

The reel seat may be of metal, plastic or wood. It consists of

The concept of "custom" means individual adaptation and highest possible quality, often combined with a special and costly design.

a partly threaded midsection, the body, with two casings to hold the reel, which are respectively fixed and movable. The fixed casing is called the "housecap", while the movable one is the "sliding cap" or "lock cap". One or two lock nuts press the lock cap against the reel foot, so that this is pressed into the housecap. The reel seat's body, between the threaded part and the housecap, can be replaced by an insert of wood, for example. Some reel seats are pre-designed for this by having had that part of the body cut away: they are termed "skeleton seats", and are usually sold along with a ready-made wooden insert. The bottom part of the rod handle ends in a cap called the "butt", which is normally of rubber or some other material that can tolerate contact with the ground without getting scratched. A reel seat can be either upward- or downward-locking, called uplock or downlock.

Survey of the work process

The first thing to do, when the blank has been acquired, is to wrap the ferrules with rodwinding thread. Next, one notes

Skeleton reel seat with inlay of cork and wood. The inlay, at right, is glued on the blank between the housecap, above in the picture of the reel foot, and the threaded body, below. The whole forms a unit that fits well in the hand and feels good to hold.

which side of the blank is the spine - the rod's stiffest side. This is crucial for correct positioning of handle and line guides. Once it is done, the top guide can be attached with epoxy glue.

Now you start the construction of a complete handle and reel seat assembly, which is thereafter going to be mounted on the blank. The reel seat may have to be cut down to fit the reel foot, the center part of the reel seat body may have to be removed to make a skeleton seat and a wooden insert may have to be made. The actual grip is best made of cork, bought in the form of cork rings, usually with pre-drilled holes: without these, one must drill holes in the rings. Whichever the case, the holes must be adjusted so that each cork ring fits tightly to the blank when the handle is finally mounted.

If the handle is to include wooden details - such as a winding check, butt, or wooden trim rings between the cork grip and the reel seat - these have to be shaped to their final shape before being joined with the cork. Finally, the cork rings and any wooden details are glued together into a single tube, a handle blank, except for the butt which has to be installed later. Ordinary contact glue works well.

The cork wood tube is now shaped into a handle, by hand or by using a lathe. All sections that are to make up the handle assembly are shaped in this way, so that they can be pushed over the blank into place and form a unit, together with the reel seat. The butt is fitted to the handle but will be mounted later. All handle sections have to fit tightly in place. In certain cases you may have to build up the blank's diameter under some of the sections. In this case, do it with masking tape laid on the blank in hard rolls.

The handle assembly is glued into place with epoxy glue of the slow-hardening type. Suitable glue has a curing time of 12-24 hours. The assembly begins with the lowest part of the handle (exception for the butt) and all parts are pushed down over the blank from the top.

When the glue has cured and the handle sits solidly, it is time to try out the positioning of the rod guides. This is done by a combination of test-casting and various static tests. Once the result is satisfying, the guides are mounted on the rod by wrapping with rodwinding thread. The wraps are lacquered, first with a basic lacquer - or color preserver - and then with a protective lacquer, normally of the two-component type. Any wooden details must be lacquered to resist water.

Materials

Many factors determine the choice of blank, and some of these have nothing at all to do with the fishing itself or the rod's function, such as the price. I therefore abstain from giving specific advice on this choice. Rod blanks are produced by numerous manufacturers and have varying characteristics. It is up to each individual to decide what suits him or her best.

Most importantly, of course, one must have a fairly good idea of the quality and properties of the blank one chooses. It pays to look at production line rods of the same brand, and if possible at rods built on the same blank, even if the planned construction is intended to be quite different. Preferably, you should also avoid blanks from the cheapest price class. Building a rod takes a great deal of energy and patience, and a bad blank sets narrow limits for the result.

The reel seat

Reel seats are made of different metals, of graphite-reinforced plastic, and of wood. Aluminum is light, and forms a surface oxide that protects against corrosion in freshwater environments. Unfortunately, it is also rather soft and can easily be deformed under stress. Aluminum reel seats should therefore be made of relatively heavy gauge material.

Nickel silver is an alloy of nickel and iron, which chemically resembles stainless steel but has a silvery shine and is easy to work. Unlike stainless steel, it readily corrodes, which can lead to problems with jammed locking nuts.

Saltwater reel seats may be made of brass. Since brass corrodes rather easily and becomes ugly, such reel seats are chromed. However, chrome on brass has a tendency to loosen.

Titanium has recently become a popular material for reel seats. This metal has the lightness of aluminum, but is not as soft, and provides an ideal reel-seat material.

In addition to chroming, lacquering and anodizing are common methods of surface treatment for metals. Lacquered reel seats are easily scratched, and sometimes the lacquer loosens. Anodization means that the color pigment is bound to the metal surface by an electrochemical process. The color goes deep down into the hard oxide layer - which also becomes extra thick - and both the color and protection become more durable.

Graphite-plastic reel seats are strong, robust, and more comfortable to hold than metal: plastic is an insulator and

A reel seat can be rebuilt in various ways. Shown here is a fly-rod reel seat, modified to form a unit with the handle and so that the reel comes as close as possible to the hand. The housecap is built into the wood and the horn/wood inlay is adapted to the reel foot's length. A fighting butt and other handle features suit the style of the reel seat.

does not lead heat away as easily. Moreover, corrosion is nonexistent in this case. The drawback is the appearance - a gray, drab color is the general rule.

Wood is a material that, unless treated, absorbs water. A wooden reel seat that takes up water will, at best, swell so that the nut gets stuck. At worst, the wood cracks when it dries, or rots if the surface treatment does not allow the moisture to escape. Good wooden reel seats are deeply impregnated with epoxy plastic. The epoxy also binds together the wood fibers, yielding greater hardness and a lower risk of stripped threading.

Threads

In mass manufacture, the threading can be turned or milled, or the piece can be pressed into a thread mould. The reel seat's durability and function depend on the material thickness and the thread profile. Trapezoidal threads (with a rectangular cross-section) are normally turned or milled, and are very durable. Reel seats with turned threads have, as a rule, rela-

Cork rings of different quality. From left to right: Flor cork, "first" or AAA-cork, and A-cork. The quality varies between manufacturers. Flor cork is almost impossible to obtain today.

tively thick material and a high finish. This method is fairly expensive and is used for exclusive reel seats.

Pressed threads usually have a rounded shape. One can see that the thread is pressed because its pattern is also visible on the inside of the reel seat barrel. Press threading is a cheap method of manufacture, but the material must be thin to be formable, and may deform under stress. On threads with a rounded shape, the nut may "slide up" toward the thread spine when tightened, allowing the nut to overlap or lock itself.

Handle cork

Cork comes from the cork oak (Quercus suber). The tree's outer bark is stripped off about every tenth year, and Portugal is the main producing country. The quality of the cork depends on the bark's thickness when it is harvested. The wine industry is a large consumer of cork, and since much of the fine-quality cork goes there, really good cork is unfortunately hard to come by.

Holes and uneven spots in the cork are not only ugly, but make it more difficult to shape the handle, as well as render-

ing it unpleasant to hold and giving the cork a shorter lifetime. Good cork for handles should be clean, even and dense. The highest class of quality is so-called floor cork, followed by the designations AAA, AA and A - then by other letters of the alphabet. Only the best quality fractions are suitable for rod building. One is wise to be careful when buying cork; most of the holes and uneven spots are on the side of the cork that was the outer in the bark, and a cork ring that looks good on one side can be full of holes on the other. For the same reason, one should avoid buying cork details that are glued together from several pieces, such as pre-glued cork tubes or ready-made handles. A faultless surface often hides holes and uneven spots.

Other handle materials

The shortage of cork is bringing forth substitute materials, and one can sometimes find resilient handle materials of the cellular plastic type in the handle. Watch out for soft materials - a handle with too soft a grip becomes uncomfortable and tiring to hold. This type of material is usually elastic and can be shaped in about the same way as cork is shaped.

The effect of rod guides

In order to choose line guides for a rod, you must know how a set of guides will influence the rod's properties. The guides affect the action through their very presence, and this happens in two ways that tend to counteract each other. Depending on the type, size and number of the guides, one way predominates, so the consequences vary. In most cases, it is best if the action is influenced as little as possible, but experienced rod-builders can exploit the guides' placement and the choice of guide type, so as to modify the rod's action.

When you cast with the rod, a certain mass is moved back and forth during the cast. The mass includes the casting weight, bait, lure, sinker, line - but also the mass of the material in the rod itself - its inherent mass. If the rod has a small inherent mass, plenty of power is left to move the casting weight with. The guides' mass is part of the rod's total inherent mass and, if they are too heavy, the blank has to use much of its power for moving itself, leaving less power for the actual cast. The rod feels soft and slow; the upper limit for what it is able to cast becomes lower. This effect often predominates, and therefore one should avoid putting heavy ceramic guides on light rods.

The other effect is caused by the guide feet and frames being less flexible than the blank. Those parts of the blank that are wrapped to a guide foot will thus become more or less rigid. This can result in a generally increased stiffness of the blank, so that the rod in effect becomes faster, or that the rod's action curve is broken so that it loses in performance. Ordinarily this effect is negligible. However, it is discussed among rod-builders and sometimes over-emphasized, which has led to the development of, for example, one-legged snake rings. A basic disadvantage of one-legged snakes is the weakness of the construction, when exposed to stress they bend very easily. Two-legged snake guides are to be preferred - their construction has an in-built stability along the axis of the blank and all the positive qualities of the one-legged ones.

Line speed reduction

If the rod does not cast optimally, the reason is often that line speed is reduced in some way when it passes through the rod guides. Worn and uneven guides both brake and wear the line. Good guides should be made of a material as frictionless and wear-resistant as possible.

To reduce the braking effect, good guides should usually be large. Both spinning and baitcasting reels release line with some kind of sideways movement - the spinning reel in a spiral, the baitcasting reel by throwing out the line in a back-and-forth pattern. On their way through the rod guides, these bows of line are damped or "strangled" successively until the line is straight when it leaves the rod's top. Large bows of line that are pressed through too small guides create the major - and most reducible - part of the braking effect that the guides cause.

Note that this problem has very little to do with friction. What diminishes the power, when the sideways movement is compressed to go through a small guide, is the force that must be exerted to contract the line enough. Let's use the line spiral leaving a spinning reel as an example. The line is "whirling" off the reel - in reality the motion of the line is similar to a three-dimensional sinus wave. This whirling motion causes a centrifugal force that pushes the spiral out from the center. The rod guides squeeze the line together so that it can be pressed through them. The line is forced into a smaller orbit - against the centrifugal force. It then loses kinetic energy and is braked, not primarily due to the friction between the line and guide, but because of this contraction. The line from a baitcasting reel is affected in much the same way, except that its wave is two-dimensional, from side to side, and the effect is not as great. To minimize this braking effect, one should always use guides that are as large as possible.

A fly rod works somewhat differently. The line is being shot from your hand, a line basket or the water surface; the line is stiffer and has a larger surface. The biggest braking occurs at the points where the line's direction changes, and friction plays a more important role. This is generated mainly at the stripping guide, and is minimized by correct guide positioning.

On a fly rod, friction against the blank is very significant - often more so than the friction against the guides. A wet line that drags on the blank can literally cause the line to stick, especially in the back cast when the line lies on top of the backward-directed rod. This braking interferes with the effort to perform an effective double haul and shoot out line. The height of the guides on a fly ring is therefore more important than one might suppose.

Severe braking of the line will naturally occur if it drags against the blank on all types of rod. The guides must always be so high that they keep the line away from the blank. This is true both when casting and when playing a fish - the line may snap if it chafes on the blank under pressure.

Begin the building with a sketch

The blank and other materials have been acquired, the project has been thought through, and you are ready to start building. The first step is to make a plan. Be definite about your desires and demands for the rod, and put them on paper as a sketch. It need not be a formal design, but a clear drawing with all the shapes and measurements will be of enormous help when you create the handle and fit it together with the reel seat. Meanwhile, you also have an opportunity to consider every technical detail, so that you will not stand there later with a couple of glued pieces and suddenly realize that the assembly is not going to work in the way you intended.

Carefully think through all aspects of the rod's use and purpose, and take account of your own characteristics - arms, hands, how you grip a rod, and other personal factors that may influence how you design the rod. A pause in front of the rod display in a fishing tackle shop, with a variety of rods, is well worth the time. Simulate different fishing situations as far as possible, "casting" and "playing" in the way you would actually do.

The important point is your manner of holding the rod and how it feels in different situations. It should be comfortable and natural, without any peculiar sensation. Imagine how your own rod should look and, if you can, avoid being locked into the conventional shapes and dimensions.

Once you are fairly certain about your design, make the sketch and complete it with measurements of thicknesses and lengths. Draw cross-sections of all transitions and joins between parts. Check that every dimension is right and that there is space for the parts.

Rod handles designed with regard to function. The reel seat has been cut so that it just fits into the foot, to minimize the metal surfaces. The wood/cork inlay in the reel seats is swollen out where you hold, to lie well in the hand. The handle's foregrip - in front of the reel, where you never hold - has been minimized. The cork has a larger diameter at the reel seat and farthest down, to provide a good grip, and is thinner in between to minimize needless material.

Wrap the ferrules

All rod ferrules must be wrapped before doing anything else with the blank. Never put together an unwrapped rod ferrule. This cannot be emphasized too strongly, and quite a few rod-builders have been disappointed to see a ferrule crack before they have even begun to build. The material in a graphite rod has almost no resistance to cracking or to compressive forces, since virtually all of the reinforcing graphite fibers run lengthwise.

A female ferrule should be wrapped throughout its length. There is no advantage in limiting, as on certain rods, the wraps to only a bit farthest out and possibly a bit farthest in on the ferrule. When the rod has been put together, the cracking force can arise anywhere. Sometimes the ferrules' shape reveals how far in the male ferrule goes, but sometimes one has to test by very carefully joining the blank parts - without pressing them together - and taking a look. Add 1/16 inches so that the entire ferrule length is definitely wrapped.

On most rods, it is a good idea to double-wrap the ferrule in the outer end. Begin the wrap 1/16 inches inside the point where the male ferrule reaches when assembled, and wrap to the ferrule's outer end. There, turn and wrap back for about 1/4 inches on top of the first layer before terminating the wrap.

Do not use too much thread tension - on thin-walled blanks the pressure of the thread can compress the material so that the blank fits poorly. Exactly how much tension to apply is difficult to prescribe. Some kind of "normal tension" is desirable where the thread lies securely in place without being stretched too much. After this, the winding must be lacquered, at least with a thorough basic layer of color preserver, before the ferrule is put together.

Mark out the spine

Another necessary step before any components can be mounted on the blank is to find its spine. To avoid any misunderstanding in what follows, we should clarify the concept of a spine and what we mean when we speak of the spine side, as well as the opposite "belly" side or however this is designated.

Rod blanks are manufactured by wrapping a graphite cloth, which is drenched in a heat-hardening epoxy binder, around a tapering core of metal. A foil is wound on the outside to hold it all in place, whereupon it hardens in an oven. While heating, the material that will be the blank becomes more or less plastic, and can "wander" around the metal core under the influence of gravity and of the pressure from the outer foil

Wrapping a rod ferrule. It is very important to wrap all the ferrules before assembling the blank, which can otherwise crack.

Walls of varying thickness in the blank give spine-like effects. Here it is clearly seen how the walls of a blank differ in thickness on different sides. Spines exist on rods in all classes of price and quality - the blank shown here comes from one of the most expensive prestige brands.

layer. As a result, the finished blank's walls acquire a varying thickness on different sides, which in turn will become noticeable as small differences in flexibility in different directions.

The spine effect is more or less manifest in different blanks, even within the same production series. In some cases, the blank even turns out to have several "spines" on different sides, because its walls are alternately thicker and thinner. A spine occurs in all types of blanks and is not a problem - if you know has to use the effect properly when building your rod, it can be used to your advantage.

Test to find the spine

Fasten a piece of masking tape around the blank, approximately at its middle, on which to mark the spines that you find.

Then let the blank - this is done with each blank section separately - rest with its top end against a flat support, such as the edge of a table. The blank's lower end rests against your left hand's palm, which you hold fairly high; the blank should lean against the table at about a 45-degree angle. Hold the blank in the middle between your right thumb and forefinger, and press it toward the table so that it bends and tenses strongly. Now roll it back and forth between your thumb and forefinger.

In certain positions during the rolling, the blank will want to lie still: it is softer there and prefers to stay bent in the direction of its bend. In other positions, the opposite is true - it offers more resistance to the given bending. Consequently, it makes a little jump over that position and tries to roll further toward one of the previous states of rest.

Find the direction of bending that creates the most resistance, and mark the side that is upright then (i.e. the side toward which the blank bends when it is giving maximum resistance) with a pencil stroke on the masking tape. Such a side, in whose direction the blank produces more resistance to bending than in other directions, we call a spine side.

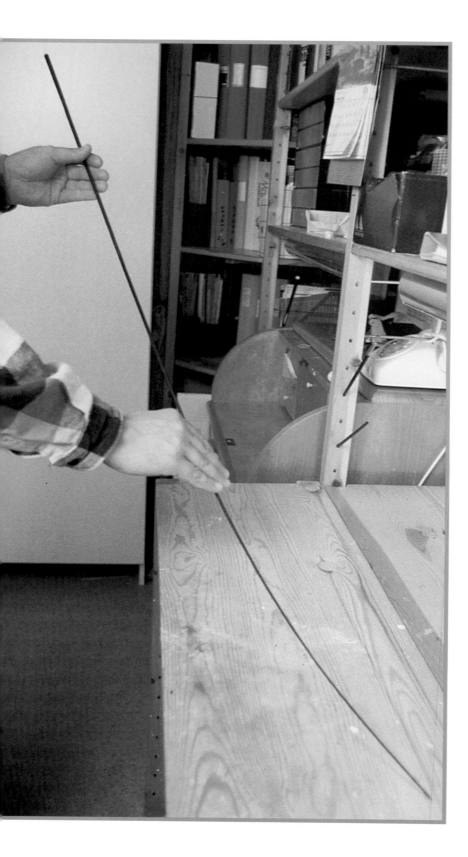

Spine test. The rod top is supported in the left hand, and the blank is pressed with the right hand down toward the table so that it bends. In this position, one rolls it back and forth between the fingers to find soft and hard sides.

The spine's effects and the guides' placement

The orientation of the spine in the rod is significant in several ways for its properties. In particular, the casting distance is affected. When you cast with a spinning or a casting rod, the casting weight that you send away pulls the line out behind it. The initial speed of the casting weight, determined by the power that can be put behind the casting weight's mass, is crucial for the length of the cast. Obviously a number of other factors play a large role, such as the line's braking effect, the bait's aerodynamic properties, and the casting trajectory's angle. Some of these factors - being dependent on the rod's construction, can be influenced when building the rod - and the first of them is the force that the blank can load for sending the casting weight in the outward cast.

A rod works rather like a steel spring or a trampoline in the cast. You tense it with a movement in the opposite direction, a back cast. With a spring or a trampoline, the force it can deliver depends on how strongly it has been compressed or bent down before it is released; it stores energy that is then let go. A rod is tensed in the back cast and delivers energy in the forward cast. The more energy it can deliver, the longer the cast is. If you place the handle, reel seat and rod guides so that the rod's spine side - the side that gives most resistance to being bent - can push the forward cast, it will deliver maximally. Hence, the side that you had on top during the test described previously (the spine side) must face backward when you cast with the rod in your normal manner.

With a fly rod, the mechanics of a long cast are slightly different. The bait itself has no great mass; instead it is the line's mass, and the force behind this, which send out both the bait/fly and the rest of the line. Since the line's mass is stretched out along its whole length, the energy of the outward cast must be made to "travel" along the line, all the way to its outer end. This is done, not primarily with a strong force, but through a distinct "stop" which arrests the forward cast. The force that the blank was charged with in the back cast is thus effectively transferred to the line.

When the rod is stopped in the forward cast, a "fold" or a bow in the line is formed, where the line directed forward

It feels better to hold cork than metal, so a reel seat should be no bigger than necessary. This reel seat is cut to be just long enough that the reel can be removed when it is completely open.

from the rod tip bends back toward the leader and fly that is being pulled forward. This line bow is what must travel forward along the whole line until it straightens out the leader and finally delivers the fly on the water with the leader outstretched. One might say that it is precisely in the line bow that the travelling energy of the line is concentrated. The line bow is braked by air resistance, and the larger the surface it presents for the air to affect, the more the braking. Therefore, a large and wide bow in the line is influenced much more than a small narrow bow.

After the rod has been stopped in the forward cast, it still functions like a trampoline. When a jumper leaves the trampoline, it recoils upward and vibrates for a moment. The rod tip "dips" forward (down) similarly. The depth of the dip is significant for the size of the line fold, small dip, narrow line bow. The oscillations that follow are also damped if the first dip is small. In other words, it is good to place the spine of a fly rod so that it damps the dipping as much as possible. This is done by mounting the handle, reel seat and guides so that the rod has the spine side forward and downward when you cast with it in your normal manner.

Note that all rules for placing the spine are based on the casting direction or casting plane, the "slice of air" that the blank is cutting through back and forth during a casting movement. This does not necessarily mean that the line guides have to be positioned exactly on or opposite the spine side. Many fishermen turn the rod - consciously or not - toward one side or the other when they cast. It is important to have a clear idea of how the rod will be turned in relation to the casting plane. Then you place the handle, reel seat and guides so that the spine will be properly positioned in relation to the casting movement.

Mark plainly on each blank part the side that the reel and rod guides will sit on. Remove old spine marks to avoid misunderstanding later during the building process.

Handle and reel seat

The handle should have a shape suitable to its purpose, adapted to the person who will hold it. Further, it should be no longer than absolutely necessary, since it damps the blank's action to some extent. If it has room for your hand to grip comfortably, this may be enough. The rod's balance must also be taken account of - too short a handle can make the rod feel weighted forward. With a longer handle, you hold the rod higher up and get better balance. If the rod still feels weighted forward, you can always weight it at the bottom end before the butt is glued.

Adapt the reel seat to the reel

A reel seat has only one purpose: to hold the reel securely. Large reel seats that take a lot of handle space often also have a handle function - you hold the reel seat instead of the cork of the handle. This is needless, and frequently impractical; the reel seat does not lie well in the hand, it is cold and unpleasant to hold, and it gives a worse grip than does the cork in a properly produced handle. A way of minimizing the problem is to make the reel seat as small as possible, shortening it down so that it is just big enough for the reel to fit on.

Hole, file, and glue the cork

If the cork has no pre-drilled holes, you can make these with an ordinary wood drill bit. Greatest control is obtained if the drill is fixed in some manner; a drill stand or an upright drill is naturally ideal. The actual drilling is easy, as long as the drill has a high speed, and the cork ring can very well be held with your hand. Make each hole somewhat smaller than, or if possible exactly as large as, the blank's diameter where the cork ring will sit. If you have bought pre-drilled cork rings, it is good if their holes are smaller than the blank diameter, so that you can file them up to the right dimension.

Adjust each cork ring until it can be threaded on and fits tightly at the appointed place on the rod blank. Then number it, so that the rings' order can be kept when you take them off the blank

Next, the cork rings are to be glued together into a tube, a handle blank. This is most easily achieved by using a piece of threaded metal rod - available in any hardware shop - as a core and clamp. By pulling together the threaded-on cork rings with nuts, you can press them together while the glue

Cork can be drilled with an ordinary power drill or, as here, with an upright drill. The cork ring is held with a hand and the drill runs at top speed. Mark on the wooden plate where the cork ring should lie; this makes it easier to get the hole in the middle.

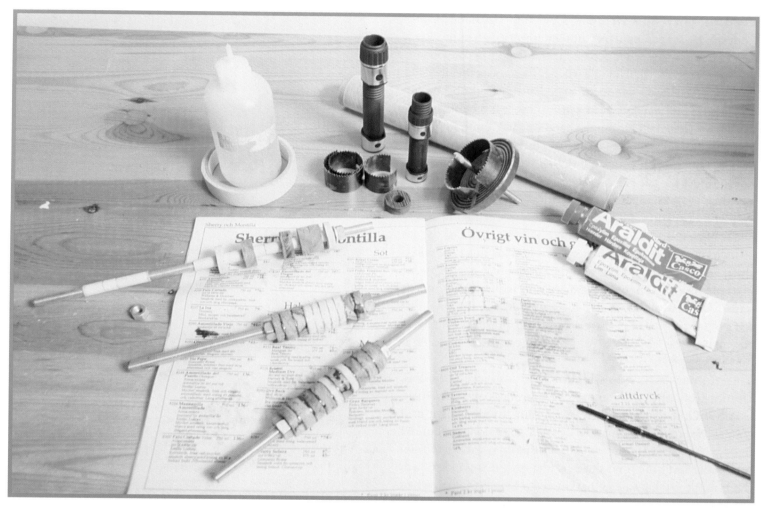

Gluing rings of cork and wood is easiest on a threaded metal rod. Cork is glued with contact glue, and wood with slow hardening epoxy glue. The threaded rod serves as both a guide and a clamp when gluing. The bottle contains methylated spirit for washing off glue. At right of the rod seats is a hole saw, which helps greatly in making wooden blanks for reel-seat and handle inlays.

hardens. The blank can then stay on the threaded rod while you shape the handle.

If the threaded rod is too thin, fill up the gap between it and the cork with masking tape. Wind tape in hard, even rolls so that a continuous cylinder of tape is formed. Set the rolls of tape tightly together along the whole stretch of metal rod where the cork will sit, but make the filling 1/4 inches short, to allow for pressing the cork rings together with nuts during the gluing. Use contact glue, and check afterward that the cork section can be loosened before you proceed to shape the cork.

Wooden trim rings

If the handle is to include decorative rings of wood, these must be turned to their final shape before being glued to the cork. Cork is softer than other woods, and two materials of such different hardness cannot be shaped together. The wooden rings can be turned in the same way as cork and wood is turned into handles and reel seat inserts. The method is described below.

A good way of obtaining raw material for wooden rings is to use a hole saw. The piece you saw out with a hole saw forms a ring and such rings taken from a suitably thick piece of wood are ideal material, which can then be set on a threaded rod and turned. A hole saw is available in any well-stocked hardware store, and the cheapest types cost very little.

Turning cork and wood

Cork can be shaped by hand into an acceptable handle. Use a rasp to create a silhouette as seen from one side, making it a little thicker than the final handle will be. Then rotate the blank 90 degrees and create the silhouette again. This yields the beginning of a handle with a square cross-section. Take off the corners at a 45-degree angle, then file out the handle's final round shape. Go over it with sandpaper, first coarse and then ever finer, until you have the surface that you want. Keep a constant check that the hole through the handle stays in the middle of the blank.

However, it is much easier to "turn" the handle with the help of a rasp and sandpaper, and the result is incomparably better. If you do not have access to a lathe, you can use an ordinary power drill (not battery-powered, as this type is too slow). The drill should be fixed in a horizontal position - for example in a jaw vise, but there are also table fixtures with a screw vise that fits most drills. As support for the threaded rod's other end, you can use a wooden block with a hole in it, clamped to the worktable. For the best result, run the drill at maximum speed.

The turning technique is applicable to both cork and wood. Do not work with a lathe tool as you may have learned in woodworking class - it easily splits thin wooden rings, and cork will go to pieces instantly. Instead, "file" the blank under rapid rotation, first coarsely with a rasp, then with ever-finer sandpaper until the final shape is attained. It is good to turn the rasp the wrong way so that the teeth bite as they do when you pull the rasp toward you during ordinary filing. Cork is so soft that a rasp can otherwise remove too much material before you have time to notice. Support the rasp against the table surface for optimum control.

Change to sandpaper in good time. Work with thin strips and frequently check the handle's thickness. Gradually switch to fine-grained paper and move forward very carefully - too much material can be easily removed at high speed. The secret is the rapid rotation, which produces rounding without unevenness. Sharp edges on the ends, cuttings and terminations are treated with a bit of folded sandpaper that can cut into the cork, or with a hacksaw blank. The latter should also have its teeth turned in the wrong direction to avoid splitting the cork.

If the handle contains decorative rings of wood, the cork is polished down just to the wooden rings' surface. For the last stage, only very fine sandpaper is used.

Wood and cork can be turned easily with a power drill and a screw vice. Support the rasp against the worktable surface and hold it so that it grips with the "rear side" of the teeth. Change to sandpaper strips in good time. Finish with fine-grained abrasive paper.

Adapt the handle to the rod blank

During assembly, all the handle parts are threaded down over the blank from above. If you have been precise with the fitting on the threaded rod, so that all cork rings sat steadily when gluing, the handle should now fit exactly at the intended place on the blank. If the tape has not filled out the rod completely, some of the rings may have moved - if so, the inner hole must be adjusted until it fits. Use a thin round file that reaches through the entire handle; an ideal type of file is the one used to file chainsaw teeth.

If the handle's inner hole is larger than the blank diameter, build on the blank with masking tape. The tape build-up is done with hard, narrow tape rolls at regular intervals. It is spaced so that at most half of the blank's surface is covered with tape - and preferably less since, of course, the handle and reel seat must be glued to the blank, not to a completely covering layer of tape.

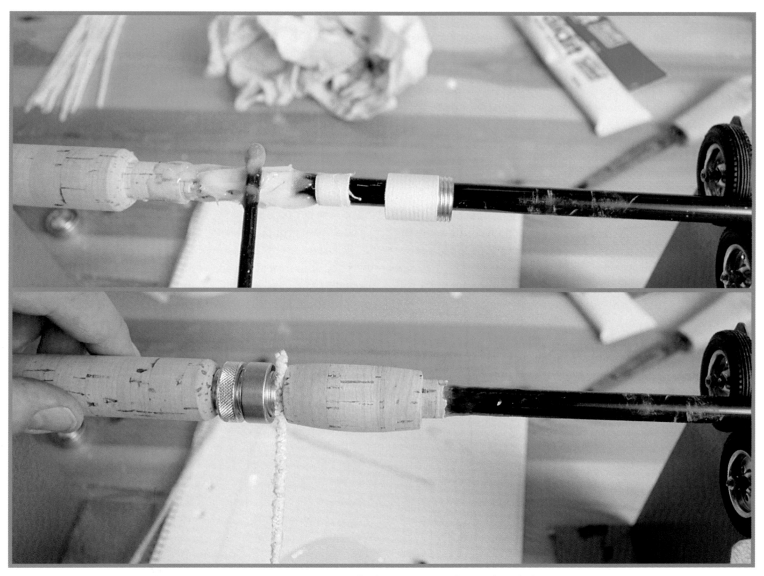

*Top: The reel seat's threaded body is to be glued on the blank next to the handle's lower part. Tape fills out where the base is too thin, with ample interspaces that can be filled with epoxy glue. Plenty of glue ensures that all the spaces under the seat are filled with glue. **Bottom:** The reel seat's middle part of cork has just been mounted, and surplus glue is washed away with the help of a pipe cleaner and methylated spirit before the middle part is slid into place.*

Mounting a handle part

Begin the assembly with the bottom section of the handle, except the butt, which will be left until last. All parts of the handle/reel-seat construction are mounted in the same way. The glue (slowly hardening epoxy) is mixed carefully according to the manufacturer's instructions. The ends of all components in the construction are protected from glue by masking tape, which is wound around both ends of each handle part.

Lay the blank horizontally on a couple of supports. The same kind of support that is used when wrapping will be fine. Put glue on the blank from the intended position of the handle part and a good distance up the blank. When the handle part is pushed down the blank, the idea is that the glue will creep in under it and fill the space between the handle and blank completely. To allow this, there must be glue on the handle well above the part's destination. Finally, press all the parts together and clean off excess glue with alcohol. A pipe cleaner is a good aid for areas difficult to reach.

The rest of the parts

Put new glue on the blank and follow with section after section, as far up as is possible in a single session. Each time, remove the glue bead just before the handle parts slide together, but leave a little glue so that the joint is tight. Clean off with alcohol, but let all protective tape remain until later. When everything is done, the blank and handle are cleaned carefully with alcohol, so that all surplus glue is removed. Take away the protective tape and clean again. Inspect the reel seat's position in relation to the spine/guide placement marks. Also see that the reel seat's housecap has not accidentally become full of glue. Remove any extra glue with a pipe cleaner and alcohol. Let the rod dry.

The glue joints can be put under pressure in many different ways. A perforated plate is threaded over the rod and it is placed on a corresponding plate. These can be drawn together with strings that are twined until tensed, or with threaded rods; alternatively, the upper plate can be loaded with weights. If the parts sit tight on the blank, often no pressure is needed. The butt is mounted when it is clear that there is no need for counterbalancing, and that can not be determined until the guides are mounted.

Guide placement

After the blank, the guides are definitely the most important component of a rod. Good guides have low friction against the line, are high and large, light and flexible. They must, of course, be of the right type and number to function on the rod; and above all, they must be positioned so that the blank's properties can be utilized optimally. Placing the guides properly on the blank is the very key to successful rod building.

Most rod kits and rod blanks are delivered with a guide-placement table. If you follow this, everything is simple - both the number of guides and their positions can be read from the table. But you lose an important dimension in your rod-building hobby if you place the guides according to a table. The main and obvious fact is that, if you grow accustomed to working with such a table, you become helpless when one is lacking, which will happen sooner or later. Less obvious, but more crucial, is that the guide-placement table often does not give the ideal positions for guides on the rod.

The table represents a compromise - an average based on sample tests from the production series. But every blank is individual, and more or less manifest differences always exist.

With luck, the difference between the blank you build on and the "average blank" table you use is rather small, but it can equally be quite large. Placing the guides in a way that takes account of the blank's individual properties and the rod's use, to achieve maximum performance, is central to the success of the rod-building project. It demands extra effort, but learning how to find the correct guide placement really pays off.

Number of guides

Too few guides on a rod will make it hard to position them in a well-functioning manner. The rod is then subjected to needless strain, the blank is unable to cast with its full potential, and a risk of breaking the rod arises. Too many guides, however, have an excessive mass and will slow down the action.

In other words, a trade-off is involved, and good general rules are difficult to give, as each rod has its individuality. The following are therefore only general rules - a given rod may call for slightly more or fewer guides. If you are unsure, it is almost always best to use one guide too many, while keeping in mind the possibility of changing to a lighter type of guide. The risk that the number of guides will be wrong in the end is extremely small. Before the guides are finally positioned, it will become clear from a number of tests whether the right number was chosen at the start.

Fly rods normally need one guide per foot of rod length, perhaps subtracting one guide from the total on a two-handed rod. On a spinning rod, subtract two feet and then use one guide per foot. On a casting rod, subtract only one foot from the length. Some fly rods work better with one guide more than the norm, provided that the blank can bear the whole set. A 9-foot (3 m) spinning rod could thus get by with seven guides, while an equally long casting rod almost always should have eight guides. A fly rod of the same length would need nine or 10 guides. The tiptop is not counted.

Place the guides temporarily

First, glue on the tiptop so that it sits right in relation to the spine markings (depending on the type of rod and casting technique). Use five-minute epoxy, mainly because such a glue joint can easily be loosened. If the top guide ever needs moving or replacing, you need only heat the metal case carefully with a cigarette lighter and the joint will melt. All other gluing on the rod should be done with slow hardening epoxy glue.

Then begin to place all guides provisionally, more or less by

Above: A handle vice is used to press together the handle parts while the glue hardens after mounting on the blank. The vice is made of two wooden plates, one with a hole for the rod blank. The plates are drawn together with the help of two through-going threaded metal bars, washers and nuts.

Below: A well-balanced rod has its balance point in the handle's upper part. If this point is higher up, the rod becomes front-heavy and tiring to cast with. Too low a balance point makes the rod "top-light" and results in less control over the cast. The choice of guides and the handle's placement and length determine the rod's balance. A front-heavy rod can be weighted in the butt - the rod's total weight is much less important than whether it is balanced.

eye. The guides are taped to the blank so that they are easy to shift. The following steps are a careful test of their placement.

Butt guide (closest to the reel, i.e. the stripping guide on a fly rod): its position is determined by the distance from the reel. Set it initially 18-28 inches (46-72 cm) from the center of the reel on a baitcasting rod, depending on the rod's length; on a spinning rod, about 1/3 of the way from the reel foot's center to the rod tip. It should be 28-35. inches (71-91 cm) from the reel on a one-handed fly rod, or a little farther up on a two-handed rod.

Guide #1 (closest to the top guide, we always number the guides from the top down) can not be positioned too far from the tiptop. It supports the thin top section to prevent the tip from breaking. It should sit 4-6 inches (10-15 cm) from the tiptop, depending on the rod's length and not more than 5.75 inches (15 cm) on a one-handed rod. This applies to all types of rod.

Next, attach the other rings provisionally. For the time being, you can place them by eye. They need not be spaced correctly at this stage - we will reposition them on the blank several times before we are done.

Test-casting for the butt guide's position

Please observe that none of the following can be carried out before the ferrule is properly wrapped and lacquered with color preserver.

First and foremost, we must establish the butt guide's final position. This is done by test-casting with the rod. Find a lawn, a football field, or the like, with enough space for you to cast with full force and no worries about the direction or distance. In this step, you must be able to concentrate entirely on how the rod behaves, and to keep your eyes on it instead of where the casting weight lands.

Work in this way with a spinning rod: cast repeatedly and study how the line acts in the area between the reel and butt guide. The line leaves the reel spool's edge in a fairly wide spiral, which is narrowed or choked down to go through the butt guide. If this choking effect is strong, line speed is reduced: if so, the butt guide is too close to the reel, and must be moved up on the rod. Move it up a little, cast again and watch the line at the butt guide. Continue until the line spiral that the reel releases is narrowed by itself and slides into the butt guide more or less unaffected.

If the butt guide is too far from the reel, the line spiral instead begins to widen and whip against the blank in the area between the reel and butt guide. This brakes it even more than the choking described above, and the butt guide must be moved closer to the reel. If you cannot find a well-working position that fulfils these conditions, change to a larger guide or one with a higher frame.

Note the casting distance while you experiment. It will not yet be ideal, as the other guides are probably far from correct in position. But if it increases as you work, this is an effective indication that the butt guide is going in the right direction.

Casting rods

On a casting rod, the problem is more or less the same. The line leaves a multiplier reel with a sideways movement, flapping back and forth in the lateral direction. At the outermost extremes, it is squeezed against the butt guide and braked. Thus, the line contact with the butt guide must be minimized.

Start with a static test. Set the reel on the rod, pull the line through all the guides, and tie it to some fixed object. Let out line and back up for 20-30 yards (18-27 m). Tense the line with the rod pointing in its direction, and wind in while you slowly walk toward the fixed object. When the line spreader is in the outermost positions, the line should no more than barely graze against the butt guide's inner edge. If the line and guide have so much contact that, in the outermost positions, an angle is formed in the line where it passes through the butt guide, you should move the guide upward on the rod. If there is space left in the outermost positions, you can move the guide downward, but you do not have to.

Next, test cast as with a spinning rod. If the line's swing is strangled in the butt guide, move the guide upward. If the line is braked against the blank in the area between the reel and butt guide, move it downward. Make sure that the butt guide is not placed extremely far up on the rod. You don't want line pressing against the blank when the rod is bent, causing line wear and a risk that the line snaps. Much larger guides can be used on a casting rod than those you see on a factory-made rod. Keep a record of the casting distance and move the guide a little up or down until you are sure that you get out the maximum distance.

Fly rods

A fly line, by contrast, is shot from your hand, the ground or the water surface without any actual sideways movement. However, it is thicker and stiffer, and enters the stripping guide at an angle, slightly from one side. It is braked especially by large angles in the line path, and by contact with the blank. An important point is that the line should not be braked in the back cast, if you are to be able to execute an effective double haul.

When test-casting, the line must pass the stripping guide with as small an angle as possible, and without contacting the blank. An angle at the guide arises because your hand is not directly below the rod during the double haul. How you perform the cast is very personal, and your own style is decisive. The angle decreases if you move the stripping guide upward, but simultaneously the risk increases that the line is dragging against the blank somewhere between the handle and stripping guide, especially in the back cast. If you angle the guide a little away from the rod's centerline, toward the side of the hand that is performing the double haul, the line angle will decrease without needing to move the guide up the rod. This effect is larger with a high-frame guide, and the high-frame guide also allows larger distance to the reel, as it holds the line farther away from the blank. Do not move the stripping guide extremely far up the rod.

Once you have found a position for the stripping guide that seems satisfying, cast for a while. Feel the rod, study the line at the stripping guide and in the area between it and the reel, and try to cast as far as possible. As mentioned above, the distance will not be optimal, as the remaining guides are not positioned properly, but try to come as far as you can with the present guide placement. Mark the stripping guide's position and experiment with small deviations upward and downward, until you find the position that enables you to cast farthest and shoot most line.

The other guides

The placement of the other guides is determined by the blank's action curve. In the area between two guides, the load on the blank is greatest in the middle, then decreases to a minimum at the guides, thereafter increasing again toward the middle of the distance between the next pair of guides. To load the rod evenly, the guides' spacing everywhere must be adapted to the blank's capacity for tolerating a load. Where the blank is strongest, fewer guides are needed; where it is weakest, the most guides are needed. Where it bends little if loaded, the guides can be sparsely positioned; where it bends a lot, they should be more densely placed.

If you have managed to position all the guides in accordance with the blank's strength, the strain is equally distributed along the rod, and the rod can be utilized maximally in the cast. If the guides in any area sit more sparsely, relative to the rod's bending curve, than elsewhere along the rod, this area is loaded more than the rest of the blank. The result is inferior casting ability - a chain is no stronger than its weakest link - and a risk of breaking the rod.

When the rod is bent under pressure, the line goes in a straight line from one guide to the next, forming a small angle where it lies against each guide's inner side. These angles should be made as equal as possible in size. In the middle of the area between two guides, the distance between blank and line reaches a maximum (if the guides are placed under the blank as in a fly or spinning rod) or a minimum (if the guides are on top, as in a casting rod). These distances should also, according to scale, be equal along the whole rod, except for the distance added by the guides' height. If these two conditions are fulfilled, the stresses when using the rod will be equally distributed along the blank.

Placing guides on spinning and baitcasting rods

On rods that have guides with a certain height, this can be used when testing for the guides' placement. Set the reel on the rod and attach it in some way, so that the top points obliquely upward at about a 45-degree angle. I use a plastic tube, fastened at the desired angle to some fixed object with tape or string. Then I wrap a piece of cloth around the rod handle to protect the cork, and push it into the tube.

Pull the line through the guides and anchor the line end to, for instance, a chair leg at some distance from the rod top. The line must be able to tense up so that the rod stands in a fairly strong bow, much as when playing a fish. Spinning and baitcasting rods, whose guides have a certain height, are turned to position the guides on top of the blank, as on a spinning rod in use. The line will be held up from the bent blank by the guides, and comes closest to the blank at the guide inter-spaces' midpoints.

In some areas, the guides are spaced so far apart that they cannot hold the line away from the rod when it is bent. The line lies against the rod, forming a "flat point". This means the guides are positioned too sparsely - the line should be kept away from the blank and have no contact with it anywhere, despite the rod's bending.

You now have to relocate the line guides so that all flat points disappear and so that all the line-blank gaps at the middle of each guide interval are equal in size. Begin the repositioning at the top guide and work downward. Note that guide #1 must not be moved down the rod - if it is any farther from the rod tip than the previously mentioned 4-5.75 inches (10-15 cm), there is a serious risk of breaking the tip. But guide #2 can be moved both up and down, until the line and blank are separated as much between guides #1 and 2 as between the top guide and guide #1. When this is done, the separation of guides #2 and 3 will have changed, so you move guide #3 until the line and blank are equally separated there as well.

Thus, you work down the blank in the same way until you reach the butt guide, which must not be moved either - a lot of trouble has already been taken to establish its location. If a flat point occurs between it and the lowest movable guide, one more guide is needed. Then the set is augmented with a guide of the smallest size. After placing it at the top, below guide #1, you work down the rod again.

Be observant in the area between the reel and the butt guide. If the blank's bending there seems disproportionately strong, or if a flat point arises there, the butt guide is too high up. In this case, obtain a larger butt guide and repeat the whole procedure from the start, with test-casting and all, so as to bring the butt guide closer to the reel.

Fly rod guides

Fly-rod guides - especially snake guides - are usually so low that one cannot exploit their height in the way described above. Instead, flex the rod with the rings in the normal position, on the blank's underside and carefully study the line angles at the guides, as well as the distance between the line and blank where it is largest, in the middle of the guide intervals. The line should follow the rod softly and closely, without any strong jerks in the line path. It can be a bit hard to distinguish the critical points at first, but gradually your eye becomes trained and yields reliable judgements.

The guide placement is now completed, and it is time to go out and test-cast again. There is an advantage in having felt your way thoroughly with the rod during the first test-casting. The rod should behave normally on this occasion, and cast distinctly farther than before. Here you receive confirmation that the guides are correctly positioned. If the rod feels feeble or jerky, if it casts worse than expected, or if you get the sensation that it contains a "hinge" somewhere, you should reconsider the ring placement from the beginning once more. But if you have been careful throughout the procedure, this should be needless. When you are satisfied at last, measure and record all the guides' positions - the next step is to remove them, so that the blank and guides can be prepared for the wrapping process.

A workplace for rod wrapping

The rod guides must be wrapped to the blank at the positions that have been found with the tests described above. This is not very difficult, but it calls for precision, being the step that mainly determines the rod's finished state.

Above: Butt wraps are decorative wraps that cover 6-8 inches (15-20 cm) of the blank above the handle. A very American feature, they are often questioned by more conservative rod-builders. In subtle terms, this has to do mainly with taste. An exclusive rod - which a hand-made rod always is - may well have an exclusive appearance. A discreet and tastefully composed butt wrap that agrees with the rod's other colors will accentuate the rod's qualities in a way that should appeal even to the most conservative.

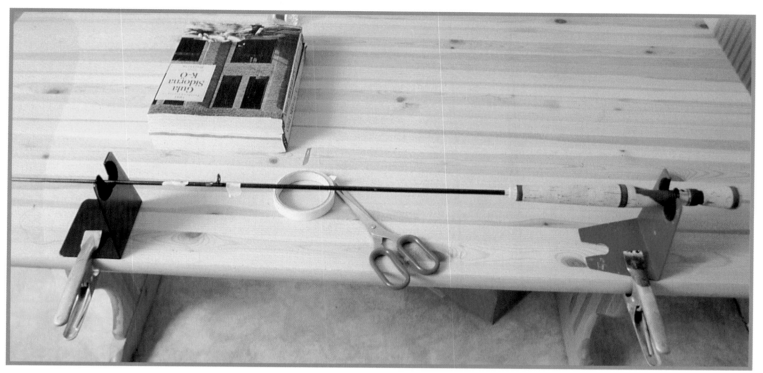

Above: *Workplace for rod wrapping. One works best if the rod lies horizontally in a cradle, such as two modified bookends. The threads lie in a glass and tension is created by passing them through the sides of a phone book. Use more books to increases the thread tension.*

The only practical way to wind efficiently is with the rod lying horizontally in front of you in some kind of "cradle", so that both your hands are free when necessary. A serviceable winding-stand can easily be made from a pair of plastic bookends. Make a rounded, U-shaped cutout in the upper edge of each one, and cushion it with a soft material.

A holder and tension device for the rod-winding thread is also essential. It should stand on the worktable's surface, at the other side of the blank from you. Attach a thread-holder for fly-tying horizontally to a wooden board that is clamped to the worktable's opposite edge, or pull the thread between the sides of a book that lies on the table. The friction through the book gives the thread tension, and it can be regulated by laying more books on top of the first one. The thread spool can be put in a coffee cup beyond the pile of books.

The wrapping is done by turning the blank toward you so that the thread is laid on its upper side. Thus you can always see how the thread lies on the blank and have full control over the results. Besides a winding-stand and a tension device, you need good lighting, a sharp hobby-knife, masking tape, and a tool to adjust and smooth the thread with - a crochet needle works well.

Prepare the guides

The guides must be worked before they can be wrapped onto the rod. The guide foot's outer end is usually rather rough, with a marked edge that has to be filed down. In order for the thread to climb up on it without any problems when you wrap it, the guide foot must taper smoothly and evenly down to the point where its transition over to the blank surface is almost undetectable. Avoid any attempt to even out the transition between the blank and reel foot with tape - this only causes problems. File the guide foot's upper side with a fine-toothed file until it tapers slowly down toward the end, which should be thin without being sharp.

Also file the guide foot's underside. Some guides have an impressed waffle pattern there, so as to "grip" on the blank. It is doubtful whether this has the desired benefit, and primarily it means that the guide foot's outer end cannot be made to lie flush against the blank. So the pattern must be removed, at least on the outer end. Rod guides that lack this pattern, too, often have an underside that is uneven.

Finally, polish away all grades and sharp edges that have been formed by the filing. A knife-sharp edge can dig down into the blank when you are fishing, and make the rod break.

Above: Preparing the line guides' feet before the wrap. The left guide is askew and must be straightened up vertically. One of its feet is on heel, which makes it impossible to wind the thread up on it, while the other is on toe and would be pushed down into the blank material when the wrap is done. The right line guide has been straightened up and its feet are adjusted to lie against the blank. One of this guide's feet is filed down and is ready to be wrapped.

Start the wrap

Each wrap starts on the blank a little way outside the guide foot's end. This first bit before you come up on the foot is called the instep. The instep serves mainly for fastening the thread, and can be kept short. The guide can be temporarily held in place with a narrow strip of tape, which is removed as soon as the thread covers the guide foot enough to hold it tight. The strip of tape must not, of course, cover the guide foot's end - it would then be impossible to remove once the thread has continued up on the foot.

Fasten the thread as follows. First, make a couple of sparse turns with the thread end around the blank, so that the thread from the holder reaches the blank at the point where the instep will begin. The thread turns go over the blank toward you, down and under it, and up its opposite side. They should form a sparse spiral from the instep's starting point in the direction toward the guide, in over the foot and the area that will be wound on. The thread end will now be wound over so that it stays put.

Hold the end against the blank with your thumb, or fix it there with a tiny piece of tape. Start turning the rod towards you to form the wrap. The first turn should cross over the thread end spiral just where the instep is to begin, pressing it against the blank. The second turn is laid next to the first one, crosses over and presses the thread end harder onto the blank.

Continue with 3-4 tight turns next to the first one; then the end is secured and you can release the thumb pressure or remove the tape. Cut the end off so that only a short stump protrudes, and wind turn after turn next to each other so that they cover the cut-off end, passing farther up onto the guide foot.

The potential mistake is that the thread turns are laid too sparsely or too densely, on top of each other. If so, you have only to back up, wind off the misplaced thread, and wind again. The turns should lie next to each other without needing to be packed together. Avoid compressing the turns with hand or tool while you are wrapping, as this only causes further unevenness that makes a smooth wrap harder to achieve. Instead, find the right angle between the thread coming from the tension device and the blank, so that the turns immediately pack themselves together. After a little experimenting, you will find it - nearly, but not quite, at 90-degrees, with the smaller angle directed so that it presses each new turn of thread tightly against the previous. Be especially careful at the slope up onto the guide foot, where the turns want to pack tighter than on the blank, since the thread tension automatically pulls the turns together on the slope. An occasional gap is not disastrous, as it will be smoothed out later, but the winding must not skip wide areas.

When 8-10 turns are left to wrap, it is time to prepare the termination. Stick in a loose thread end, folded double, beneath

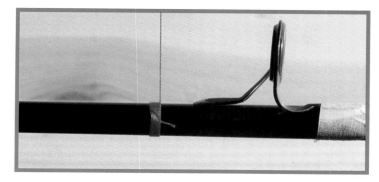

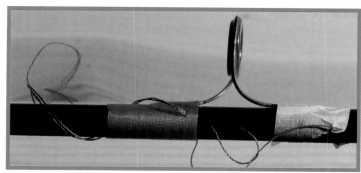

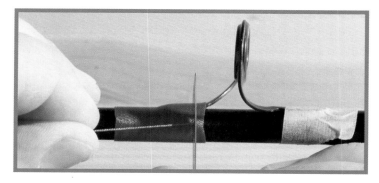

Top: *Start the wrap over the rod thread's end to hold it tight. After 7-8 turns the thread is secure and the end can be cut off. Then wrap over the stump so that it is hidden under the thread.*

Middle *The finishing touch. Set your thumb on the wrap to hold the thread while this is done (not shown in the picture for clarity). A loop is wound in 7-8 turns and the cut-off thread end is inserted into it. With the loop, the thread end is then drawn in under the wrap so that it is secured.*

Bottom: *The moment of cutting off is most critical - a mistake now will loosen the whole wrap. The picture shows how the scalpel blank is pressed vertically down between the thread turns, exactly where the thread end protrudes. Do not saw - rock the knife carefully back and forth, and if its edge is sharp the end comes off easily.*

the last turn to form a loop, pointing in the direction that the thread is wrapped in. Complete the wrap and cut the thread, pressing it tight with your thumb against the blank on the final turn. The severed end is now drawn through the loop and, with its help, can be pulled in under the last turns. These turns will lock it tight with their pressure so that it does not loosen.

Cut off the stump

The thread end that now protrudes from the wrap must be cut off - this is the most critical step of the procedure - so that it is hidden completely beneath the wrap. You must cut right next to the wrap without slicing the turns. Everyone finds a personal method - there must be as many as there are rod-builders. Mine is as follows: hold the thread end tensed with one hand, and follow it down between the wound turns with the knife edge, at the point where the threade end emerges from under the wrap. The knife is held so that it cuts against the rod blank, straight down between the turns. Rock the knife carefully against the blank without sawing, so that the thread end is cut off and nothing else. The knife must be very sharp, and a razor blade is ideal.

Burn off and burnish

There must be no lint or thread fibers at all left on the wrap's surface - this would result in disturbing unevenness in the lacquer. If any thread fringes do stick out, you can burn them off with, for instance, a cigarette lighter or an alcohol lamp. Singe the fibres away by quickly passing the flame over them.

Small gaps in the wrap can be burnished away. The burnishing flattens out the thread and, at the same time, the turns are evened out and shifted slightly. If you burnish in a certain direction, you can shift the thread so that it covers and fills out larger gaps. To do this, use any softly rounded, smoothly polished little metal rod - such as a knitting or crochet needle, the rounded part above the blade of a screwdriver, or the smoothly polished backside of a pair of tweezers. Rub the wrap carefully along the blank, from both ends of the wrap toward its middle, until the thread lies evenly and tightly everywhere.

Alignment

Once all the guides are wrapped to the rod, they must be aligned. Until this stage, you don't have to be very careful about alignment - the precision comes when you make the fine adjustment. Hold the blank vertically at arm's length,

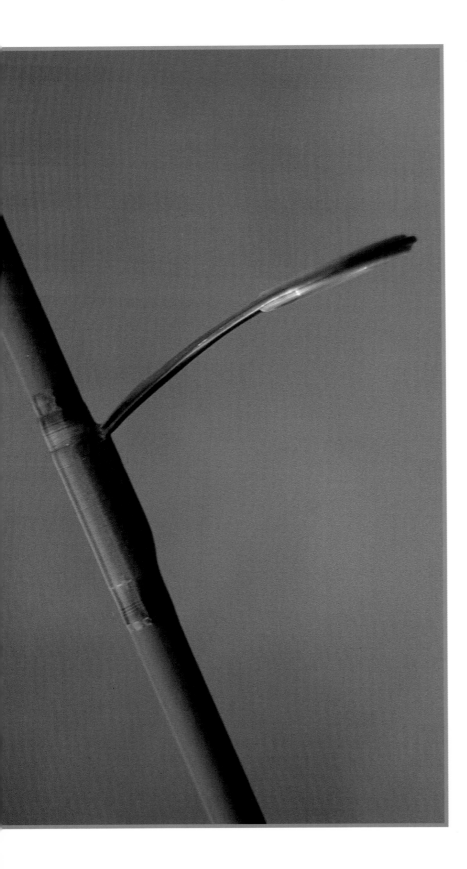

A double-wrapped guide wrap with discreet effects. The underwrap protects the rod and holds the guide foot more securely. The effects are created by making the underwrap of threads in brown, black, violet and blue, with shifts of color that merge together. The uppermost thread is wine-red.

with the guide side turned away from you, and close one eye. Guides that sit askew can be seen easily, and must be moved carefully under the wrap until they are in line. Make the adjustment by pressing sideways on the guide foot with your thumb. Avoid prying at the guide frame, as this can make the guide bend or press its foot down into the blank material. When all the guides are aligned, you can sight through them and check that they form a straight line with the tiptop.

Dust or lint from the thread can be removed with a tack rag, available in paint shops. As soon as the wrap is finished, it must be lacquered with color preserver.

Trim bands and other effects

Trim edges on guide wraps, and other effects give the rod a personal appearance. The color of the wraps can be used to "pick up" the color theme of handle, blank, reel seat and guides, into a color-coordinated rod that looks very professional and attractive.

There are many ways of making trim bands. The simplest is to put two extra "finishing loops" into the end of the wrap where you want a trim edge. When the main wrap is complete and has been fastened, you first use one of the extra loops to fasten the thread for making the edging. Just pull the end of the effect-thread in under the wrap to lock it there. Then wind the effect thread a few turns in the same manner as the main wrap was laid. The other extra loop is for the termination of the edging. With this method, very thin trim rings can be created.

Underwraps

An underwrap is a wrap that is laid on the blank beneath the guide foot. The guide is then mounted on top of the underwrap by means of another wrap, that is laid over the first one. The whole wrap consists of two layers of thread, one that lies between the guide foot and the blank, and one that holds the guide. The underwrap protects the blank so that the guide foot cannot chafe against it, and the guide is held more securely as it is seated on a material with higher friction than the naked blank.

Underwraps, therefore, have more than a cosmetic effect.

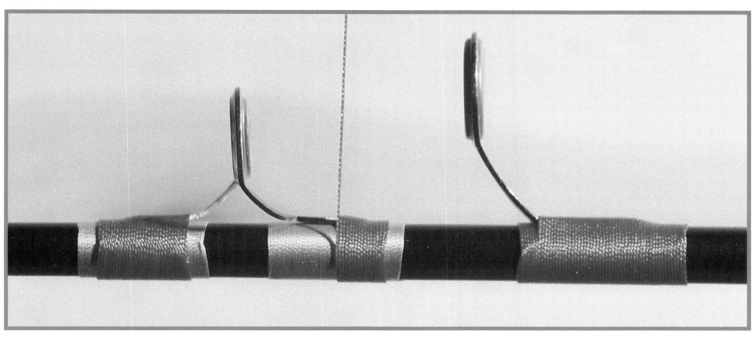

Underwrap. The line guide at left has an underwrap, which protects the blank and holds the guide more securely. The right, one-legged guide has an extra security because the wrap has continued a couple of turns down on the blank, after covering the guide foot. Thus the thread forms a heel in front of the guide foot, which prevents it from sliding out of the wrap.

They also increase the rod's durability in several ways. Underwraps are recommended for all rods except, perhaps, the very lightest.

The difficulty is to make the overwrap even. The thread on top is often inclined to creep down between the turns of the underwrap, which magnifies any unevenness in a manner that is hard to smooth out when the wrap is finished. The trick is to have a very even underwrap, and to make the overwrap with a little less thread tension. If you also make the overwrap in the direction opposite to the underwrap, or with somewhat thicker thread, the bottom layer will not be able to disturb the upper layer's turns.

Lacquering and finish

Your rod is now ready, except for the lacquer that will protect the wraps from wear. After that you just have to bring your work to your favorite fishing water and enjoy the fruit of your efforts. But there is a small detail left. The outcome - a rod built by hand - is a personal combination of technology, art and craft, and like all artists you should naturally sign your work.

The best tool for writing neatly on a rod blank is a block-writing pen of the old-fashioned type that is dipped in an inkwell. It is bought as a nib with a wooden pen shaft, available in a bookshop or a store with art materials. Choose a nib with the thinnest possible point.

Water-based white ink can be bought at the same place. Otherwise, white water-based hobby paint can be diluted with water until it is suitable for writing with. Make a test by writing on a blank surface, letting the result dry and brushing on a little rod lacquer. It is important that the ink does not dissolve when you lacquer the rod.

If the ink does not adhere, you can carefully roughen up the blank's shiny surface with fine steel wool. This should not - and should not need to - be done on blanks with a matted surface. Practice writing on a broken rod or the like, until you can write your name and the date neatly on the rounded surface. Sign the rod and let the ink dry. Do not cover the signature with color preserver, as both ink and hobby paint are water-based and may dissolve in the water-based color preserver.

All wraps must be treated with color preserver, which is necessary to maintain the thread's color to shrink the thread and tighten the wrap and to fill the spaces in the wraps, so that no air bubbles will be formed in the lacquer. Never put rod lacquer directly on a wrap without color preserver, this only leads to cosmetic problems, as the fillings and shiny spots would be visible through the semitransparent wrap that results. Lacquering without a color preserver also causes the rod guides to sit less securely on the rod and make it harder to clear the blank from lacquer if a guide needs to be replaced.

For polymer and epoxy lacquers, a water-based color preserver is used. First, drench the wrap in one treatment, diluted 1-to-1 with water, and allow it to dry. Then lay on two ample treatments at full strength, filling up all air pockets. Let the coatings dry thoroughly between the treatments - color preserver becomes milky if it is laid on a still wet base. Around both sides of each guide foot, a channel is formed in the angle between the foot, thread and blank. It is important to fill this hollow space completely; any air left will form bubbles in the final lacquering.

Two-component polymer or epoxy lacquer gives a shiny, glass-clear surface that never yellows. There are also water-based rod lacquers that provide a good finish but need rather many layers of lacquer, as well as varnish-like rod lacquers. The latter are not to be recommended, as they yellow with time like all varnishes. A rod on which every wrap resembles a little pearl is not only aesthetically disturbing; the rod is also impaired, since the lacquer contributes to the rod's mass, so the layers should be kept as thin as possible.

Mix the base and hardener according to the instructions in a dust-free vessel. I use throwaway muffin forms of paper or aluminum - making sure that they are not pre-treated with cooking fat, as some baking forms are. Stir the mixture well, but slowly, so as to stir in less air. Air bubbles cause unevenness in the finished lacquer, and the bubbles must be removed from the lacquer. Due to viscosity, it takes awhile for all the bubbles to rise, and meanwhile the lacquer begins to harden, which can cause problems when it is to be laid on the last wraps. Therefore, having as few air-bubbles as possible at the start is an advantage, and avoid whipping them into smaller bubbles, as these take longer to rise. Let the lacquer stand for some time in a broad, shallow vessel and, during this interval, dust off the rod with a tack rag. When all the air has risen to the surface, blow lightly on the lacquer in the vessel to burst the bubbles.

Lay on the lacquer

Your brush should be soft and have short bristles, which make it easier to spread the lacquer thinly. Lay the lacquer evenly and distribute it as thinly as possible without leaving any uneven patches. This is a trade-off between too much and too little.

The home builder's rod often exceeds a massproduced one in both performance and quality.

Many of these high-viscosity lacquers are intended to give an even, shiny surface without being penetrated by the thread structure. If they are spread out too thinly, the shiny areas are interspersed with spots where the thread structure goes through. The result is an ugly, uneven surface that needs additional lacquer.

Begin the lacquering at the rod top. As you work, the lacquer will become thicker, and it is easier to brush thinly on the blank's thicker parts, so these should be saved until last. Spread lacquer over all wraps and over your signature.

After the lacquer has been laid on, every wrap should be inspected - repeatedly. Keep an eye out for air bubbles: there may be air under the thread that creeps up only after a rather long spell. During the first hours after lacquering, it is worth going over the rod several times, looking for bubbles. All bubbles that rise to the surface must be removed. Blow carefully on them, or singe them quickly with an alcohol flame. If this does not help, puncture them with a needle.

The rod should rotate in a dust-free place while drying. Otherwise the lacquer will hang on the side that faces downward. Use an electric motor that makes about four turns per minute, fastening the rod's butt end to its axle (wait until after this stage to glue the butt cap on, as its absence makes the rod easier to fasten on the axle), and lay it in the wrapping cradle described earlier above. To prevent chafing, protect the blank's surface with masking tape where it rests against the cut-outs in the cradle.

There are cheap battery-powered grille motors for sale in hardware shops. If a rotation motor is unobtainable, you can lay the rod in the wrapping cradle and turn it at regular intervals until the lacquer has stiffened, which takes around 4 hours.

Some last words on the way

If you follow these directions, the outcome will be a rod that gives you great satisfaction and enjoyment for many hours of fishing. Moreover, it has every chance of being superior to any production line rod that can be bought, even if it is your very first rod.

But the rod will actually make you a more successful fisherman as well. It is a known fact that those who believe in what they are doing can fish better, since they fish more persistently, attentively and creatively. And this belief benefits from an awareness that one's equipment works as it ought to, and that one can utilize it optimally. Whoever has personally built a rod possesses an instrument that is directly adapted to the user and the purpose, with a quality and properties that one has complete control over. No better conditions than this can be desired.

Cooking your catch outdoors over a campfire or at home in the kitchen is without doubt one of the finest endings a fishing adventure can offer.

With its enormous variety of tastes and textures, fish is a fantastic raw material suited to brilliantly simple methods of outdoor cooking and elegant presentations from the kitchen at home. But it is also a sensitive product that demands proper treatment all the way from the water to the frying pan; a fish that is handled correctly gives the person who catches it a degree of gastronomic pleasure equal to the pleasure of the contest itself.

We sportsfishermen devote a great deal of effort to planning our fishing hours, taking care of our tackle, and of course the fishing itself. Most of us probably like to eat fish, too.

But, hand on our hearts, don't we sometimes get a little careless with our catch once the fight is over and the excitement calms down? Aren't we sometimes too eager to bring in one more while they are still biting, instead of taking proper care of the one we just caught? The answer is probably that each of us has at one time or another shown little respect for the fish we caught, once it was landed.

Once a fish is out of water it is very sensitive to bacteria, especially if the air temperature is above 15°C (59°F). This is because fish normally live in an environment with relatively low temperatures. We know that fish move to deeper, cooler water when water temperatures at the surface or near land get too high, and this movement can be regarded as an indication of a fish's temperature preference.

The quick deterioration of fish when exposed to the air is not caused by the introduction of new bacteria, but is a part of a process that can be described as a self-triggered spontaneous combustion. As soon as the fish dies, the enzymes in the flesh set off this process, which causes deterioration by breaking down the cell tissues. The loosening of a fish's bones from the flesh is one of the most obvious signs that this process has gone on too long.

It is therefore very important to handle the catch carefully, partly to delay the internal-combustion process, and partly to protect the fish from bacteria. Fish that are improperly handled are limp and floppy, and have little taste.

Killing and cleaning

If a fish is going to maintain its taste and consistency, there are certain rules that must be followed when killing and storing it.

To begin with, the fish should be killed immediately after it is caught, not only so the fish suffers as little as possible, but also to inhibit the production of lactic acid. The extreme stress of being caught results in the production of large amounts of lactic acid, which considerably reduces the quality of the fish. Allowing a fish to wiggle and flop on land until it dies is the best way to produce a more or less inedible fish.

There are several ways to kill a fish quickly and efficiently. The only equipment needed is a good knife, which is also needed for cleaning the fish. To kill the fish, stick the tip of the knife directly into the brain, which lies a few centimeters

Once the fish is caught, it must be killed and cleaned as soon as possible. The innards are removed carefully so that no bacteria get inside. Then rinse the fish and take out the innermost blood vessels near the spine.

behind the eyes, and do not remove it until the last muscle spasms are over. If you want to drain the fish's blood, however, which is quite common for salmon, push the knife in under the gill cover and cut diagonally to the abdominal cavity, directly behind the gill. In this way, the artery in the throat is cut and the blood is quickly drained.

Another method, mainly for small and medium-sized fish, is to use what is called a priest. A priest is a handle about 12 in (30 cm) long, tipped with lead or brass. The fish is given a sharp knock on the head with the metal ball, just behind the eyes.

Once the fish is dead, the entrails should be removed as quickly as possible, so that the putrefactive bacteria in the intestines and the stomach do not spread to the abdominal cavity and activate a further deterioration of the cell tissue. The best way to clean the fish is to cut the skin on the abdomen, starting at the anal opening and cutting forward. Then remove the entrails care fully, so that no bacteria from the intestines or the gall can spread into the abdominal cavity.

When the fish is cleaned, rinse it in water and remove the clotted blood from the backbone. Using the tip of a knife, cut a hole in the thin membrane at the back of the abdominal cavity, so that the blood there can be scraped with a fingernail or a knife. Rinse the fish once more and the cleaning is finished.

Keeping fish fresh

If you do not intend to prepare the fish right on the beach, you must store it properly so that it does not deteriorate in quality. If you do not plan to eat it for a few days, you should rib the inside of the abdominal cavity with salt or vinegar, allowing no chance for bacteria to grow. Salt is easy to carry with you, but it has the disadvantage of drawing liquid from the fish, leaving it somewhat dry and perhaps even a little tasteless. Vinegar, on the other hand, has a bacteria-killing effect without altering the taste of the fish.

The fish should be kept dry and in the shade. Putting fish in direct sunlight is an invitation to bacteria to start the destructive process. If the fish will be cooked or frozen within a few hours, it can be wrapped in grass or paper, but for a longer time it is best to wrap it in a piece of clean cloth. Woven basket creels, proven by tradition to be good for keeping fish, work so well because they allow air to circulate. One point to remember is that fish should be kept where there is good air circulation, which is also why fish should be stored separately, whether wrapped in grass, paper or cloth.

Unfortunately, many anglers are known to toss their catch into plastic or rubber bags and then let the bag lie out in the sun or in the trunk of a car. This storage method quickly reduces the quality of the fish. This behaviour says two things about the angler. One is that he has little understanding of the effect of bacteria on fish; the other is that he has little regard for the fish once it has been caught.

Preparing fish

There are an amazing number of ways to prepare fish. Some species are best fried, others taste best when boiled, some are perfect for grilling, and there are others that are exquisite when smoked. In general, smaller fish are best when they are fried, and larger fish are best when they are boiled. Fish with a lot of fat, such as salmon and eel, are excellent for grilling and smoking, but the same processes used with lean fish leave the flesh dry and tough.

The first step in preparing a fish is to scale it. It is easiest to scale a fish when it is cleaned because the skin is still soft, but scaling can also be done just before the fish is cooked. First, rinse the fish for half a minute or so, to soften the scales and the mucus. Using a knife or a fish scaler, scrape from the tail to the head until all the scales on one side are gone, then do the same on the other side. Finally, rinse away any scales and mucus that remain.

How to fillet a fish

In preparing a fish, especially if it is to be fried, the fish may need to be filleted. The equipment needed is a flat work surface such as a cutting board, and a sharp knife with a long, narrow blade, called a fillet knife. Scissors are also good to have at hand.

Place the cleaned fish on its side on the work surface and cut carefully around the head and down behind the pectoral fin. Next, make a cut at a slight angle towards the backbone, as close as possible to the head, and continue to cut all the way to the tail, using a smooth, even motion. Cut as close as possible to the backbone to avoid any needless waste. Turn the fish over and cut the other filet in the same way. If the skin is to be removed from the filets, start cutting from the tail forward.

If this is done properly, the result is two beautiful filets. It is not easy to fillet fish, but after two or three practice sessions you should be able to cut a good filet.

How to skin a fish

Sometimes a fish must be skinned. Other equipment needed besides a sharp knife and a flat work surface is a pair of scissors and a pair of tongs. Before laying the fish on the work surface, cut around the fins, about 1/2 in (or 1 cm) deep, and pull them off. Then carefully cut through the skin around the head and down to the abdomen, and along both the abdomen and the backbone all the way to the tail. Make only a surface cut, penetrating the flesh as little as possible. It is now time to put the fish on its side, grasp a piece of skin close to the head with the pliars and firmly pull the skin towards

Left: To fillet the fish, start by cutting around the head. Next, cut off the filet as close as possible to the spine, working from the head towards the tail. If the filet's skin is also to be loosened, cut with the fillet knife from the tail forwards.

Below: The fish is flayed by cutting its skin carefully around the fins and head, and down to the tail on both sides. Then use tongs to grip a flap of skin at the head, and pull off the skin. To get a better hold on the head, it can be nailed onto the working surface.

the tail. Hold the head steady with your other hand. If the fish head is too slippery, you can hold it with a piece of paper or cloth, or you can nail it to the work surface. Turn the fish over and remove the skin from the other side in the same way.

Smaller fish can usually be skinned in one section. Make a gash through the skin around the neck, lay the underside of the fish on the work surface, grasp a piece of loosened skin with the tongs, and steadily pull the skin towards the tail. This method is particularly useful when skinning eels. The last step is to cut off the head.

Grilling

How many times don't you wish you could cook the freshly landed fish right on the beach, without needing to carry half the kitchen with you? The simple solution is to grill the fish over an open fire.

Once the fire is made, carve two sharp points on a forked stick. A small fish can be skewered whole and put directly over the fire. Rotate the stick often, so that it is grilled evenly on both sides.

A fish weighing more than 2 lbs (1 kg) should be opened along the underside so that it has a giant fillet shape, and then put on the roasting stick. The fire should not be allowed to burn too low. A low fire produces less heat, which means that the grilling goes more slowly, and there is a greater risk that the fish close to the bone may not be cooked thoroughly.

The fish is ready to eat when it is brown on both sides and the bones begin to separate from the flesh. Fat fish such as salmon and eel are the best for grilling. Lean fish tend to become dry and hard, sometimes still raw on the inside and tasteless on the outside.

Before cooking a fish over coals, carefully clean and rinse it. Then spice it with, for example, dill or rosemary.

Cooking over coals

This method can be used with both fat and lean fish. In addition, it retains the wonderful aroma of freshly cooked fish. To cook fish over coals, the fire must have died down so that only the glowing coals remain, but the coals must be very hot to cook the fish thoroughly.

Begin by cleaning and rinsing the fish well. Place it on a piece of aluminium foil, and add salt and spices. Dill or rosemary are good choices. If the fish is lean, a little fat rubbed on the foil before the fish is added will make it juicier. Wrap the package securely and place it directly on the hot coals. The fish is ready in about fifteen minutes.

This method is excellent for small fish. Larger fish can also be cooked in this way, but they should be cut into fillets first, so that the fish will be thoroughly cooked. Each fillet should be wrapped in its own package.

Wrap the spiced fish in aluminium foil, and lay the packet directly on the coals. After about 15 minutes it is ready to eat.

Marinating fish

Marinating fish is another ancient preservation method, used today mainly for salmon. Always begin the marinating process by filleting the fish and scraping off the scales. Remember to cut off the fins and to remove as many bones as possible. The materials you will need for marinating are: 1 kg fish, 1/2 dl salt, 1/2 dl sugar, 19 white peppercorns crushed, a liberal amount of dill.

Mix the sugar and salt with the crushed peppercorns, and carefully rub this mixture into the fish filets. Chop the dill finely. Spread a layer of dill in a glass or ceramic dish with low sides that is the same size as the fish. Place the first filet, skin side down, in the dish and cover the flesh side with a layer of dill and spices. Place the flesh side of the second filet on top of the first, with the flesh sides together and the skin sides out. Cover both fish halves with dill and the rest of the spices. Finally, cover the dish with a plate or cutting board, and place a heavy weight such as a stone on top.

If several layers of fish are to be marinated, be extremely careful to arrange the fish in pairs with the skin side always on the outside. The fish should be kept in a cool place for two or three days. It is then ready to be served, but it will keep for several more days in the refrigerator.

Keep in mind that marinating does not kill parasites such as tapeworm which can be found in fish from polluted water. By freezing the fish at a temperature of about—$10\,°C$ ($14\,°F$) for a minimum of 24 hours before marinating, any parasites that might have been living in the fish will be killed.

Smoking fish

Smoking fish demands much more preparation than grilling or cooking over hot coals because you need a smoke oven. Smoking is an ancient method of preserving fish which was used in the past for long-term food preservation. It prevents the internal spontaneous-combustion process at the same time as it slows down the growth of bacteria.

There are two methods of smoking fish: cold smoking, and hot smoking. The latter takes less time and relatively little work.

The principles of hot smoking. With relatively simple equipment, you can build your own hot oven from, say, an old oil barrel.

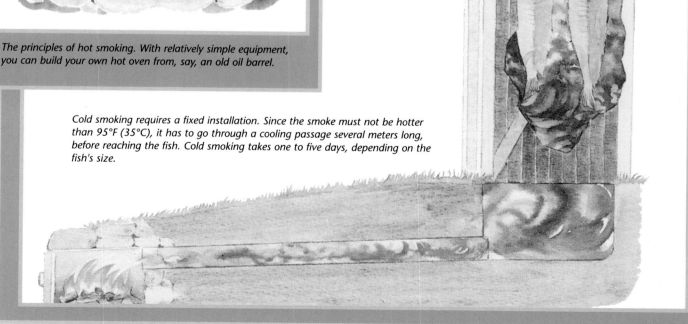

Cold smoking requires a fixed installation. Since the smoke must not be hotter than 95°F (35°C), it has to go through a cooling passage several meters long, before reaching the fish. Cold smoking takes one to five days, depending on the fish's size.

Cold smoking requires a few days, more attention, and a relatively sophisticated apparatus to produce the best results.

Before the fish can be smoked by either method, the fish must be salted and dried. To do this, rub the fish with salt on both sides and in the abdominal cavity, or soak the fish in a solution of salt and spices. The fish is ready in three or four hours. Rinse it in cold water and let it dry several hours in a cool and well ventilated spot. This process creates a membrane that keeps the fish from becoming too dry during the smoking.

Small fish can be hung by their heads while being smoked. If the fish weighs more than 2 lbs (1 kg), the head should be removed and a cut made from the belly up to the backbone, so that the fish can be split into two halves, similar to filets. Remove the backbone and place two sharp sticks crosswise through each fish half.

Hot smoking

Once the fish have dried, they should be smoked as soon as possible. The temperature in the smoke oven should be around 65°C (150°F). Hot smoking can take from two to ten hours, depending on the size of the fish, the heat from the smoke, and how heavily the fish should be smoked. The longer a fish is smoked the longer it will keep, but it also becomes a little drier.

The smoking process begins at a low temperature that increases once the smoking is underway. Coniferous branches or wood chips from hardwood trees are used as fuel. Because different kinds of fuel produce different tastes, some experimentation is recommended to discover the type of wood and the smoking time that produce the taste you prefer.

Hot smoked fish keep well for a week or two if they are kept cold. They can also be frozen and kept even longer.

Cold smoking

As mentioned earlier, cold smoking is a more arduous method than hot smoking because it must continue for at least 24 hours, preferably a few days. In addition, this method requires a permanent and more complicated smoking oven.

In terms of cleaning, salting and drying, the cold smoking process is the same as for hot smoking. Even the fuel is the same. The greatest difference between the two is that the source of heat for hot smoking is approximately one meter underneath the fish, so that the hot smoke rises directly upwards, while the smoke for cold smoking reaches the hang-

ing fish by going through a pipe that is 3-6 ft (1-3 m) long. The cold smoking process is designed so that the smoke temperature will not exceed 95°F (35°C) when it reaches the fish, an ideal temperature being about 82°F (28°C).

Remember that the cover over the smoke oven must be very tight so only a minimum of smoke can escape. Anchor the cover with a stone or another heavy object so that it sits tightly.

Cooking your catch outdoors over a campfire or at home in the kitchen is without doubt one of the finest endings a fishing adventure can offer.

With its enormous variety of tastes and textures, fish is a fantastic raw material suited to brilliantly simple methods of outdoor cooking and elegant presentations from the kitchen at home. But it is also a sensitive product that demands proper treatment all the way from the water to the frying pan; a fish that is handled correctly gives the person who catches it a degree of gastronomic pleasure equal to the pleasure of the contest itself.

Facts about the sportfisherman's catches
What to think about for cooking

Allow 5-7 ounces of boned fish per person. If the whole fish is used, increase the amount to 2/3-1 pound per person.

Preparation time depends on the size of the fish, but if you keep a few simple rules you are guaranteed a good result.

A fish is cooked when its protein coagulates. This takes place at 130-140°F. If the fish gets too hot it becomes dry and dull; the light red flesh of salmon becomes almost white.

Baked skinless fish is done when the color changes from translucent to opaque.

If you are frying or grilling fillets, you should simply cut into them after a little while to see if they are done. Try a few times if you are uncertain.

A fish that is cooked with the bones is done when a knife is just barely able to lift the backbone loose from the flesh.

Fish should be poached, not boiled. This means that the water should maintain a temperature of about 160°F. This enables the protein to solidify evenly throughout the fish. If the temperature is higher, there is a risk that the outer flesh will disintegrate before the inner flesh is done. To preserve the fish's flavor, the cooking water should be adequately salted.

Personally, I think fish tastes best if it is sautéed with the skin on. This goes for filleted fish, too. It is often enough to fry the fillet on the skin side and then let it stand for a couple of minutes before serving.

Salmon

There are two kinds of salmon, Atlantic and Pacific. Atlantic salmon is the superior of the two, but its taste and appearance can differ depending on when and where it is caught. Salmon is best in spring and summer, and the females are regarded as better eating. I prefer salmon weighing 6-1/2 to 9 pounds because the fat content is lower. Finest of all is the cultivated Norwegian salmon, with the best tasting and most tender flesh. The wild Atlantic salmon is longer and narrower; the flesh is redder and not as well marbled.

Baltic salmon belongs to the same species that is caught in the Atlantic. Its flesh is pale because it lives on the fry of Baltic herring and does not ingest carotene from crustaceans. I prefer salmon from other waters because the flesh of Baltic salmon is fattier and looser.

Pacific salmon is not to be compared with Atlantic salmon when it comes to the quality of the flesh. It is drier and the flavor not at all as good.

With salmon, in contrast to many other kinds of fish, there is very little waste. It should be cleaned at once, because the entrails are strongly acidifying and can destroy the flavor of the flesh.

If salmon is bought over the counter, the gills should be pale red and the slime should smell fresh. The blood in the abdomen should be light-colored and dry, and the bones should be firmly attached to the flesh.

Raw Salmon

Raw salmon is a delicacy that requires fresh fish. The best flesh for raw dishes is what is on the backbone when the fish is filleted. It can be scraped off with a spoon and is soft and bland in taste. Otherwise, the flesh from the midsection is used. The texture of the tail section is too hard, and the flesh of the belly is too fatty. Cut the flesh that will be served raw into thin slices, or chop it finely.

Sea trout

Sea trout has a lower fat content than salmon and is thus better suited to raw dishes. It is used in the same dishes as salmon. A fresh sea trout is identified by the same signs as a fresh salmon.

Rainbow trout

Rainbow trout varies greatly in taste depending on where it is farmed and the water it lives in. The flesh is pink, though the color can vary depending on the food the fish gets.

I have encountered broiler-like specimens that were inedible, but if the fish is in good condition and lives free in the ocean, for instance, it is a delicacy. Rainbow trout under 6-1/2 pounds are best for cooking.

Perch

Perch is a fish that is frequently neglected in cooking but very fit for use if it is filleted properly. Perch weighing 2 pounds or less are best for cooking. There is most flesh on a perch in late autumn and in spring. Its quality depends largely on the water where it is caught. A fresh perch is firm in texture, and the eyes are full.

Grayling

Grayling has an exaggerated reputation for deteriorating rapidly after it is caught, but it should be cleaned as soon as it is taken. The gills should be cut away, and the fish rinsed carefully. It should then be salted immediately, stored in as cool and airy a place as possible, and cooked the same day. It is done when the bones come loose.

A fish under 11 pounds should be filleted in such a way that the backbone remains in one of the halves.

If the grayling is going to be frozen, it should be glazed with ice. Rinse the fish and put it in the freezer. After a few minutes, a film of ice will have formed around it. Take it out, dip it in water, and put it back in the freezer. Repeat this procedure four or five times so there is a protective layer of ice shielding the fish from the air. Put each fish in a plastic bag and freeze.

Pike

Pike is best during the cold time of the year. The flesh is firm and lean. The hard scales are best removed. If the fish is to be poached or fried whole, it is fine for the scales to stay on—this helps retain the flavor during cooking. Pike is one of the few fish that tolerate a fairly long cooking time.

Small pike are better to use, because large ones can be tough. Because the flesh holds together well, pike is good for minced-fish dishes. A fresh pike should be stiff, with a fresh layer of slime on the surface. The eyes should be full.

Char

Char is a perishable fish that should be dealt with as soon as possible after it is caught.

It displays itself to best advantage when newly caught and poached, but it can also be prepared the same way as salmon and sea trout.

Cod

Cod is lean and the flesh is relatively loose, so a low cooking temperature is called for. The fish is done, regardless of size, when the temperature is 120°F all the way through. This can be both felt and seen, as the fish is lustrous and glassy at first and then becomes somewhat dull and transparent when the proteins start to coagulate. If the fish gets too hot, the flesh becomes white, dry, and solid. Cooking time depends on the size of the fillet and the temperature of the fish when it goes into the oven. A good way to check on whether it is done is to take the fish out of the oven and cut through a fillet.

A fresh cod should be stiff, with red gills, a fresh smell, and bright, protruding eyes.

Mackerel

Mackerel should smell fresh; after it has been stored for a short time, it smells and tastes stale.

A lot of people think that mackerel is best during spring and autumn, when the fat content is highest. I myself prefer the somewhat leaner summer mackerel. The flesh should be firm and the skin bright and shiny.

Walleye

The walleye is a delicacy, with firm, white, extremely delicious flesh. A walleye of 3-1/2 to 4-1/2 pounds is best in the kitchen, and if it is going to be poached whole, it is best for the scales to stay on. This preserves the flavors in the flesh, and the skin is easy to pull off before serving.

Fresh walleye should be stiff, with slime on the gills, a fresh smell, and full eyes.

Tuna

Fresh tuna is a true delicacy and should be prepared with great care, so that it remains pink inside. Over-cooked tuna is one of the most horribly dry experiences you can have in the way of fish.

In fact, fresh tuna is one of those raw materials that tastes best of all raw. The flesh should smell fresh; if it has stood only a little too long, the flesh acquires a sharp, stale smell.

Equipment for cooking fish on the shore

If you make room for some simple cooking gear in your fishing-bag, your fishing trip can be transformed into a culinary experience by the waterside.

Sharp knife

A good knife is a must, and its importance cannot be emphasized enough.

Seasonings

Old fly boxes with many compartments make good spice jars. They are small, and you will have room for a good collection of seasonings. A few excellent examples would be salt, pepper, dried dill, pink pepper, thyme, and a ready-made fish blend.

Marinade

A marinade heightens and changes the flavor. It consists of seasonings, oil, and an acidic ingredient such as vinegar or wine. The acid together with the seasonings breaks down the cell walls in the flesh, making it more tender.

You can prepare the marinade before the fishing trip and bring it in a bottle. Pour the marinade into a plastic bag. Then put the fish in, press out the air out, and seal the bag.

Your fish will marinate in thirty minutes when you are cooking outdoors. Dry the marinade off with paper towels before you cook the fish.

Aluminum foil

With the help of heavy-duty aluminum foil you can manufacture a tight-fitting pressure cooker in no time at all.

Cooked like this, in its own juice and steam, the fish is succulent and tasty.

The temperature inside the packet is seldom higher than 195°F. The foil lets the radiant heat of the coals in, but keeps the contact heat out.

Baking parchment

Baking parchment can be wrapped around the fish before it is wrapped in foil to be laid on a hot stone or in the coals. Paper towels also work excellently. The paper makes a protective cover that retains the flavors.

Grill

A grill makes it easier to turn the fish on the coals. There are small grills that clip together with brackets.

Small Teflon pan

A small Teflon pan is lightweight and slips easily into your backpack.

Breadcrumb bag

Fill a plastic bag one-third full with fine, dry breadcrumbs and freshly ground pepper, leaving room to shake the fish in the bag.

Burying bag

Mix 2 Tbsp. salt, 3 Tbsp. sugar, and 1-1/2 tsp. white pepper in a plastic bag.

Bury the fish in a double layer of plastic bags and keep it as cool as possible. The best thing to do, if possible, is dig an earth-cooled "pantry" on the shore. A salmon weighing about 2 pounds will be ready in 24 hours.

Flashlight

A flashlight will help you keep track of your food on late summer evenings.

Smoking bag

A heavy-duty aluminum bag filled with alder sawdust and sugar makes an ingeniously simple way to smoke fish. The ingredients are put into the bag, which is then sealed and put on the fire or in the oven. This works best for smaller fish. The bags can be bought at well-equipped fishing stores.

Recipes

These recipes should be regarded as gastronomic guidance. Use them to inspire your imagination and spark your inclination to experiment. As you gain practice and courage, you might find yourself altering some of the ingredients. You will notice that in certain ways, cooking can be like sportfishing: the possibilities are inexhaustible and there are no set rules. Eventually, you may create a completely new dish of your own.

The recipes are calculated for four people.

Sandwich

This recipe makes 20 beautifully marbled sandwiches. A sandwich will keep for a week if stored in its wrap in the refrigerator. Excellent for taking along on day trips.

Ingredients:
1 loaf of unsliced white bread, several days old
1 loaf of unsliced dark rye bread

Herb butter:
1 cluster of parsley
1/2 clove garlic
small piece of leek
1/2 lb. salted butter
1/4 lb. cucumber
2 tsp. salt
1 Tbsp. Dijon mustard
7 oz. thinly-sliced cold-smoked salmon

Preparation:
1. Cut off the top and bottom crusts of the bread. Slice each loaf lengthwise into 4 to 6 slices.
2. In a blender, mix the parsley, garlic and leek. Add the butter and mix again.
3. Slice the cucumber thinly and sprinkle with salt. Let stand for 15 minutes. Then place the slices on a towel and carefully wring out all moisture.
4. Spread the herb butter on a slice of white bread and cover with cucumber slices. Spread the mustard on a dark slice and put slices of salmon on it. Turn these surfaces toward each other. Now put the appropriate filling on the surface of the top slice. Alternating types of bread, continue in the same way until you have a construction consisting of eight (or more) slices of bread. Wrap in sandwich paper, tie it up with string, and wrap the whole package in a damp towel.
6. Place this packet on a cutting board (so the layers are horizontal) and put another cutting board on top to press the sandwich. Put everything in the refrigerator and let it stand for several hours.

To serve: Open the packet and trim the edges of all four sides. Slice and serve.

Fish in paper with a foil jacket

A recipe that suits most sportfishermen. The good flavors of the fish and seasonings stay inside the paper, giving off a glorious fragrance when the package is opened.

Ingredients:
2 lbs. whole gutted fish
salt
pepper
3 Tbsp. butter
1 cluster flat-leaf parsley
1 handful cherry leaves
sandwich paper
aluminum foil

Preparation:
1. Rinse the fish thoroughly and salt and pepper it. Stuff the abdomen with butter, parsley and cherry leaves.
2. Wrap the fish in a couple of layers of sandwich paper. Then wrap in aluminum foil and seal carefully.
3. Lay the fish on the coals. Turn often so the juices will run through the fish and baste it.
4. Open the package after about 45 minutes. Check to see that the flesh comes loose from the backbone.

To serve: Eat directly out of the wrapping or serve on a platter.

Baked fillet of salmon

with Jerusalem artichoke sauce, mushrooms and potatoes

Ingredients:
1-1/3 lbs. filleted salmon with skin
some grains of coarse salt

Sauce:
1 lb. Jerusalem artichokes
2-1/2 cups chicken bullion
1-2/3 cups heavy cream
salt
pepper

Vegetables:
7 oz. fresh mushrooms, one or more of any kind
6 shallots
4 potatoes
2 oz. flat-leaf parsley
salt

Preparation:
1. Peel the Jerusalem artichokes and boil in the chicken bullion until soft. Add the heavy cream. Blend in a blender and strain through a sieve. Add salt and pepper.
2. Divide the salmon fillet into four parts and sprinkle with a few grains of coarse salt. Bake in a 350°F oven for about 10 minutes.
3. Clean and slice the mushrooms. Peel and slice the shallots and potatoes. Chop the parsley. Sauté the potatoes and shallots in butter. Add the mushrooms and continue frying until they are golden brown. Add the chopped parsley.

To serve: Place the fish on a bed of vegetables. Heat the sauce and pour over.

Poached pike with horseradish sauce, carrots and pike roe

Pike has a remarkable flavor and is among the fish valued most highly by the French, who often use it for small pike quenelles. In Scandinavia it is often served poached with grated horseradish and melted butter.

Ingredients:
1 roe-filled pike of about 4-1/2 lbs.
4 carrots
a piece of horseradish
2-3 bay leaves
6-8 whole allspice
7/8 cup heavy cream
flour
butter
salt
pepper
1/2 tsp. 12% vinegar

Preparation:

1. Start by skinning the pike carefully. Then gut it, taking particular care that the egg sacs remain whole. Fillet the pike and cut into beautiful pieces.

2. Clean the roe, salt lightly and refrigerate for several hours. Peel the carrots and cut into long thin slices. Boil them in lightly salted water until tender but still crisp. Grate the horseradish finely.

3. Bring about a pint of water to a boil with salt, pepper, bay leaves and allspice. Let the fillets simmer in the water for about 10 minutes. Remove the pieces of fish and keep them warm.

4. Heat 1-2 Tbsp. butter with 1/2 tsp. flour, adding the cream and a little of the fish broth. Let the mixture cook down into a smooth sauce and season with salt, pepper, 1/2 tsp. vinegar and about 2 Tbsp. grated horseradish.

To serve: Accompany the pike with hot carrots in butter, horseradish sauce, pike roe, some more finely-grated horseradish, and boiled potatoes. A couple of tablespoons of melted butter will further heighten the flavor.

Perch hash

This dish is equally good hot or cold. To go with the perch, feel free to use whatever vegetables are available.

Ingredients:
1-1/3 lbs. filleted perch
1 red bell pepper
1 yellow onion
1 yellow pepper
1 medium zucchini or other squash
1 red onion
4 cloves garlic
olive oil
salt
pepper

Preparation:
1. Cut out the row of bones in the middle of the fillets. Then cut the flesh into small cubes.
2. Peel the peppers with a potato peeler and cut out the core of seeds in the squash and peppers. Cut all the vegetables into small cubes.
3. Pour a generous amount of olive oil into a skillet and carefully sauté the vegetables until they are tender but still crisp.
4. Add the pieces of perch and shake the skillet. Sauté for about one minute more. Season with salt and pepper.

Le Big Mac

A little ordinary respectable tomato ketchup goes well with this fish variation on the world-famous hamburger.

Ingredients:
1-1/3 lbs. fish fillet
2 baking potatoes
1/4 cup olive oil
3-4 Tbsp. butter
3 tomatoes
1/4 lb. fresh spinach
4 sprigs rosemary
4 cocktail sticks, for skewers

Pepper salsa:
1/2 yellow pepper
1/2 red bell pepper
1 tomato
1/2 papaya
chili sauce
salt
pepper

Preparation:
The salsa:
1. Blanch and skin the tomato and peppers. Remove the seeds and cut the flesh into cubes. Cube the papaya.
2. Let the cubes soften in a hot skillet with a little oil. Season with chili sauce, pepper, and salt. Set aside.
3. Set the oven at 390°F. Scrub the potatoes. Leaving the skin on, cut each into four slices of equal thickness. Lay them on a cookie sheet covered with baking paper and paint with equal parts olive oil and melted butter. Salt the potatoes and roast in the oven until they are soft.
4. Cut the fish into eight pieces of equal size. Sauté in butter until golden brown, then sprinkle with salt. Blanch the three tomatoes and cut each into four slices. Clean the spinach and sauté lightly in a little butter.
5. Take four plates and put a roasted potato slice on each one. Cover the potato with a slice of fish and a little spinach. Add another layer of potato, fish and spinach. Top each burger with three slices of tomato flesh.
To serve: Skewer the whole burger with a cocktail stick and garnish with rosemary. Spoon the pepper salsa around it.

Baked fish with asparagus and herbs

This dish generally suits any catch.

Ingredients:
4 skinless fish fillets of about 6 oz. apiece
1 lb. trimmed green asparagus
1-2/3 – 2-1/2 cup chopped mixed herbs, such as parsley, basil and chives
7/8 cup heavy cream
7/8 cup fish bullion
3 Tbsp butter
2 finely chopped shallots
2 egg yolks
salt
freshly ground white pepper

Preparation:
1. Set the oven at 300°F and place the fillets on buttered plates.
2. Cut the asparagus into 1-1/4-inch pieces. Heat the shallots in a little butter without letting them color. Add the heavy cream and fish bullion and cook the mixture down until it has thickened into a light, creamy sauce. Season with salt and pepper.
3. Bake the fish on the plates for about 8-10 minutes. Meanwhile, boil the asparagus in lightly salted water for 2-3 minutes and drain in a colander.
4. Heat the sauce and pour into a blender. Add the egg yolks and blend into a light, fluffy sauce. Pour the sauce back into a saucepan and heat carefully, stirring constantly, without letting it boil, to make a thick, creamy sauce. Fold in the asparagus and chopped herbs.

To serve: Set the fish out on four heated plates and spoon the asparagus and herbs over it. Serve with mashed potatoes.

Lightly grilled tuna

A simple dish, where the tuna harmonizes beautifully with a simple salad.

Ingredients:
1-1/2 lb tuna fillet
3-4 Tbsp olive oil
salt
pepper

Salad:
4-5 tomatoes
1/2 sliced red onion
1/2 peeled cucumber
1 Tbsp. capers
10-15 olives
8 anchovy fillets
mixed salad greens

Red wine vinaigrette:
1/4 cup red wine vinegar
1/2 cup olive or other oil
salt
freshly-ground white pepper

For garnish:
coarsely chopped basil

Preparation:
1. Blanch, peel and seed the tomatoes, then slice. Cut the cucumber into small pieces. Combine cucumber and tomatoes with the other salad ingredients.
2. To make the vinaigrette, first dissolve the salt in the vinegar. Add the remaining ingredients and stir.
3. Cut the tuna into pieces and paint with olive oil. Sprinkle with salt and pepper. Grill the fish very quickly in a hot grill pan.

To serve: Sprinkle the tuna with coarsely chopped basil and serve with the salad.

Dandelion salmon in a pressure cooker

With the help of aluminum foil you can make a "pressure cooker" in which the fish will be steamed in a few minutes.

Ingredients:
4 pieces of salmon (or other fish) of 5-7 oz. each
an armful of tender dandelion leaves
pink pepper
salt
scant 1/2 cup water or wine
4 sheets of aluminum foil

Preparation:
1. Parboil the dandelion leaves in a little salted water. Fold the aluminum foil in half to make a double layer. Place a piece of fish on top of each one and sprinkle with pink pepper and salt. Distribute the dandelion leaves over the salmon.
2. Fold the foil so that it is closed on three sides. Add the water or wine through the open side. Close the packet so that it is completely sealed.
3. Put the "pressure cooker" on hot stone or directly in the fire. The packet will now puff up into a ball.
4. After 4-5 minutes the fish is done.

To serve: Cut a cross in the "ball" and serve at once with soft whipped potatoes or boiled new potatoes.

Fish in chicken wire

Use fresh herbs according to their availability. The chicken wire holds the fish together during grilling.

Ingredients:

1 salmon, walleye, ocean perch or pike
  weighing about 1 lb.
at least 1-1/4 cups coarsely chopped mixed herbs,
  such as lovage, basil and parsley
chives
lemon juice
chicken wire

Preparation:

1. Stuff the fish with the coarsely chopped herbs and chives. Salt the fish inside and out.
2. Skewer the fish on a long stick and then wrap it in chicken wire. Grill over coals for about 25 minutes, turning frequently.
3. Open the chicken wire carefully and take the loose fillet portions from the back.

To serve: Top each fillet with the herb stuffing, sprinkle with cut chives, and squeeze lemon juice over all.